Antitheatricality
and the Body Public

Antitheatricality and the Body Public

Lisa A. Freeman

PENN

UNIVERSITY OF PENNSYLVANIA PRESS

PHILADELPHIA

A volume in the Haney Foundation Series, established in 1961
with the generous support of Dr. John Louis Haney.

Published by
University of Pennsylvania Press
Philadelphia, Pennsylvania 19104-4112
www.upenn.edu/pennpress

Printed in the United States of America on acid-free paper
1 3 5 7 9 10 8 6 4 2

Cataloging-in-Publication Data is available from the Library of Congress.
ISBN 978-0-8122-4873-9

For Heather,
my person

Contents

Antitheatricality
and the Body Public

Introduction

Antitheatricality and the Body Public

At least since Plato, or so we have been taught, the playhouse has been construed as a house under suspicion, a site of endemic moral corruption and existential peril from which we all ought to flee. This antitheatrical posture, composed of a fundamental distrust of representation and an equally strong discomfiture with the bodies that lend themselves to the art of performance, has been eagerly iterated and reiterated for centuries to the point that we have come to take it for a settled truism, an inescapable fact, an inherent aspect of human nature. No less erudite an authority than Jonas Barish has contributed to this mystification by pronouncing in his seminal tome, *The Antitheatrical Prejudice,* that this condition is no mere prepossession but indeed "a kind of ontological malaise, a condition inseparable from our beings, which we can no more discard than we can shed our skins."[1] With just a few exceptions, it is safe to say that this belief, or the presumption of some kind of foundational aversion to the effects of play, has constituted the theoretical and critical point of departure for almost every major discussion of antitheatricality to date. Yet from any number of perspectives, this might seem an odd place to begin. For those who have taken an anthropological approach to performance, for instance, and who have documented the extent to which play and performance serve a fundamental purpose in all human cultures, such an articulation might even seem rather baffling.[2] Indeed, it might be construed as a fundamental misprision that mistakes the effect for the cause. For to posit, as Barish and many others have done, that the persistent denunciation of theater across time and space signifies a "permanent kernel of distrust waiting [only] to be activated by the more superficial irritants" not only glosses over the more consistent human propensity for play but also ignores the more likely possibility that those intermittent irruptions of antitheatrical sentiment are actually the effects of what Barish dismisses, in almost the same breath, as "local considerations."[3]

Antitheatricality and the Body Public is devoted precisely, then, to a careful study of those "local considerations" and "superficial irritants." It holds as a fundamental tenet that theater has ever been located at the center of, and as a site of magnification for, broad cultural movements and conflicts and that antitheatrical incidents, in particular, provide us with occasions to trace major struggles over historical shifts in the nature and balance of discursive power and political authority. This is not to deny the ontological instabilities associated with representation and performance or to minimize the extent to which theatrical performances as such have the capacity to evoke a certain anxiety and discomfort; nor is it to suggest that the propensity for play and the resistance to play are mutually, or even necessarily, exclusive phenomena. But it is to claim that if human beings have a propensity of one kind or another, it is a propensity for theatrical play and that when examined closely, almost all antitheatrical incidents could be said to serve an instrumental purpose as a means to an end rather than as an end only for and to theater per se. By situating antitheatrical incidents as rich and interpretable cultural performances in themselves, I seek to account fully for the significance of these historical conflicts; to delineate when, why, and how anxieties about representation manifest themselves; and to trace the actual politics that govern these ostensibly aesthetic and moral debates.[4]

This principle applies as much to the foundational texts in this tradition—to the works of figures such as Plato, St. Augustine, and Tertullian—as to those successors who would repeatedly borrow from such works to form what the Puritan antitheatricalist William Prynne has fondly termed his "squadrons of authority."[5] Amid the almost innumerable accounts of Plato's pronouncements on the nature of representation, for instance, two of the most neglected aspects of his case against the poets in *The Republic* are, first, that it is articulated in the context of a philosophical rendering of an ideal state or body politic and, second, that the arguments against poetic and theatrical representation serve an instrumental purpose, as much as any abstract philosophical one, as Plato contends for the political authority of the philosophers against the encroaching sway of the poets in this imaginary polis. In a similar vein, it could be argued that Church Fathers such as Augustine and Tertullian perceived the instrumental value of adapting Plato's antitheatrical vision and used it to serve their own political ends of distinguishing Christian from pagan.[6] Perhaps even more significantly, as they contended for power and authority in both the sacred and secular realms, they established a precedent—one that we will see followed again and again by the protagonists who populate this study—that enabled members of a body politic to characterize themselves as belonging to a transcendent heavenly community, a religious and moral commonwealth, whose tenets and strictures could be set against and even surpass the authority of a secular or civil state.

Cited with such great frequency and such great fervor, these "squadrons" could be said to comprise what performance theorists might term the performative repertoire out of which the antitheatrical archive has been built over time.[7] As a cultural scenario that has been enacted repeatedly, each iteration of the antitheatrical prejudice not only mobilizes the ghosts of performances past but also cites those performances as a means both to reify and to legitimate their own truth claims. To construe the antitheatrical prejudice simply as a natural or ontological condition, then, occludes our ability to elucidate the ways in which antitheatrical discourse has been historically leveraged and antitheatrical campaigns often waged for political purposes. Perhaps even more significantly, it obscures the extent to which antitheatrical sentiments are directed not simply toward representational forms but also toward those bodies that act in public as vehicles for those forms.

As many performance historians and theorists have observed, theater has long been distinguished from other representational media, first, by its emphasis on embodied action; and second, by its capacity to conduct a kind of sociological survey as it gathers together in a *public* space, both onstage and in the audience, persons from a cross-section of society to compose, however temporarily, a site of imaginary affiliation, or what I term a contemporaneous body public.[8] I begin my study here, then, with the perhaps obvious yet never articulated observation that in almost every historical instance, the combatants in antitheatrical debates engage one another over the competing notions of the public that they posit both within the theatrical space itself and extending beyond it, discursively, into society at large. In these moments of heightened tension, the public *becomes* the site of contestation, as more often than not the conflict betrays the popular fiction that the body politic encompasses all citizens or subjects and the parties array themselves instead to form multiple and competing bodies public—dynamic amalgams of individuals, organized both physically and discursively around postures of dominion and influence across the public sphere and that operate thus in contradistinction to the rhetorical claims of a transcendent body politic.

A few initial observations here on one of the case studies that will compose this book might help to make these abstract claims a bit more concrete. If we look both at the debates that surrounded the denial of NEA funding to four queer performance artists in 1990 and at the *amicus curiae* and briefs that were filed on both sides in *NEA v. Finley* (1998), the Supreme Court case that ensued, we will quickly discover that a few phrases were persistently batted around: either "the public" full stop, or to be slightly more specific "the American public," or in a cognate version that has its own set of historical and political resonances, "the American people."[9] Seeking to capitalize on what Roman Jakobson might term the horizontal force of metonymies, each side acted as if the mere summoning of these terms could provide some kind of self-evident justification for their case; and each side argued that they represented, protected, and upheld the interests of this supposed "public."[10] Even more intriguing, each side used "the public" in such a way as to imply that it was simply a matter of common sense to apprehend who or what was designated by this abstract phrase. Yet if each side could invoke "the public" as its common cause, it stands to reason that each must have been appealing either to a different public or, at the very least, to a different notion or idea of that public.[11] What lay at the heart of this antitheatrical dispute, then, was a struggle not only over the character of the body politic that governs a nation but also over the bodies public that could be said to represent that nation.

As may be obvious by now, in coining the phrase "body public" as my theoretical term of art, I mean to play upon the more familiar concept of the "body politic" in order both to intimate the ways in which sovereignty itself is a fragile chimera that is always already performed and contested and to signal the ways in which those who inhabit that body politic may just as easily stand apart from it in a posture of critique. I also mean both to borrow and to distinguish my argument from Michael Warner's theorization of publics in his *Publics and Counterpublics*. Warner provides us with a compelling discussion of the historical articulation of publics across time, their variable relationship to civil society and the political state, and the ways in which the idea of a public engages with and operates upon the social imaginary. Most important, he illustrates the ways in which articulations of the "public" also play a significant role in constituting the normative horizons of a given society.[12] All of these ideas find expression in some form or another in my discussions of specific antitheatrical incidents. At the same time, however, I depart from Warner's insistence on construing "publics" and "counterpublics" as strictly discursive formations. For him, publics are "essentially intertextual, frameworks for understanding texts against an organized background of the circulation of other texts."[13] By contrast, I seek to illustrate how "publics" come to be articulated strategically and deliberately as sites of collaboration and resistance not only in the performative, abstract, or subjunctive modes that Warner champions but also in concrete, visible, and embodied forms, beginning in particular with the bodies that inhabit theatricalized space. Whether those are the bodies, as I shall show in Chapter 1, of seventeenth-century lawyers in spectacular procession through the streets of London on their way to perform a masque for Charles I at Whitehall, or, as I demonstrate in Chapter 5, of performance artists who transform their bodies into the very stage and scene of conflict, the fleshy and corporeal presence of these actors is what gives weight and meaning not only to the idea of a body in public but as part of a public body. Hence, while I agree with Warner that the force of "publics" and "public opinion" lies to a great degree in their discursively imagined and indefinite reach, I also argue that their power is dependent upon the extent to which they can be envisioned and palpably felt as a corporeal presence.[14]

Antitheatricality and the Body Public thus examines the particular ways that the theater as both physical space and metaphorical realm has been taken up repeatedly as a site of contestation for positing and projecting publics, and it seeks precisely to delineate those processes by which competing groups strive to define themselves as representatives not simply of "*a* public" but of "*the* public." It contends, moreover, that we cannot fully account for the significance of these cultural conflicts until we examine how combatants of each era engage one another to promote competing notions of the public good and until we identify the extent to which those acts of summoning are either constantive acts that merely designate a "public" that already exists or performative acts that call that very "public" into being. Amid what Richard Meyer in his study of art censorship has termed "public moment[s] of rhetorical excess," it is crucial, then, not only to unpack what motivates these hyperbolic forms of expression but also to interrogate the status and significance of the publics that are posited.[15] How is each "public" represented as a body, by a body, and in what bodies? If both sides claim a public, what "public" or "publics" do they refer to, call upon, or cultivate? And, most significantly, how are those publics leveraged discursively for particular cultural or political ends?

Organized as a set of case studies, each chapter in this book strives to respond to these queries by engaging in a careful excavation of a specific antitheatrical episode in all of its historical particularity. Rather than gloss the surface, I develop a comprehensive description of the contentious discursive environment—political, religious, philosophical, literary, and dramatic—in which each episode unfolds, and I elaborate the character and interests of the various bodies public that contended for dominance and influence in the wider public sphere. By attending to these elements in a select number of the most controversial cases across time, I seek to illustrate a historically consistent pattern rather than a transhistorical phenomenon. In doing so, I aim to demonstrate the historical and political particularity of antitheatrical incidents; and though I restrict myself here—per the limitations of my own expertise—to cases in the Anglo-American archives, I hope to provide a model for further research on the political and cultural significance of antitheatrical attacks in other nations, places, and states. To read an antitheatrical incident on its surface, that is, to accept the moral and aesthetic claims of its protagonists, without investigating either the political interests that drive such controversies or the cultural forces that are mobilized as it runs its course, discounts the prominent role theater has historically played as a touchstone of public life and social consciousness and betrays the many bodies public that have been called into being and have taken their places under and through its auspices.[16]

Chapter 1, "In the 'Publike' Theater of William Prynne's *Histrio-Mastix*," examines documents related to the 1634 Star Chamber trial of William Prynne for the publication of his massive antitheatrical tome. Focusing especially on the conflicting manuscript accounts of Prynne's trial—including one of great significance that I discovered in the course of my archival research—as well as on the rhetorical performances offered both in *Histrio-Mastix* (1633) and in James Shirley's *The Triumph of Peace* (1634), the masque that the lawyers staged to repudiate Prynne, the chapter illustrates how various parties to the conflict sought to use these events to delineate and to publish the rights, privileges, and prerogatives of the bodies public they sought to represent.[17] Drawing on early seventeenth-century political and religious history, the chapter elucidates, moreover, how Prynne's antitheatrical tract provided the occasion for long-simmering disputes over sovereign power and ecclesiastical authority to be acted out as part of a public discourse long before the crisis of civil war brought the formation of parties and factions into high relief. In exploring the performative effects of a procession, a masque, a hulking antitheatrical tome, and the multiple manuscript accounts of a state trial, this first chapter ought to be read as paradigmatic for what follows. It not only underscores the ways in which this study understands performance as a broadly conceived category of analysis, but it also illustrates the variety of ways in which power, authority, and publics may be staged.

Chapter 2, "Political Allegiances and Bodies Public: Jeremy Collier's *A Short View of the Immorality and Profaneness of the English Stage*," moves us forward to the end of the seventeenth century and to an elaboration of that controversy as a screen for parsing and playing out the complex social and political logics that flowed from the settlements of England's Glorious Revolution. Rather than focus on the aesthetic and didactic claims in the case, then, I direct attention to the various political positions advanced both by the plays at which Collier, a stalwart nonjuror, aimed his invective, as well as by his originating tract and the responses and counter-responses that stoked the controversy and raised it to such a feverish pitch. By tracing the various and constituent bodies public—Whig, Tory, Jacobite, nonjuring, and curious amalgams in between—as they waged their contest over a terrain in which political and religious affiliations converged and diverged in response to dynamic and shifting perceptions of common or differing interests, I demonstrate how their competing rhetorical claims for the public good and their recurrent reflections on recent English history were symptomatic of a much larger struggle in post-Revolutionary England over an emergent epistemology of public practice that would be driven not by the hierarchical dictates of religious doctrine and sovereign rule but rather by the more social and secular codes of public commerce and civility.

Chapter 3, "The Political Economy of Bodies Public: Scotland's *Douglas* Controversy," takes on the mid-eighteenth-century contest over John Home's tragedy and reads it as a culminating point in a series of protracted battles over power and authority between the orthodox Presbyterian faction in the Scottish kirk and the secularizing forces of the Scottish Enlightenment. Through an examination of the clashes over clerical patronage and over charges of infidelity against the jurist Lord Kames and the philosopher David Hume that preceded the *Douglas* uproar, I trace how these exchanges reflected major shifts in the political and cultural landscape of eighteenth-century Scotland and demonstrate how this conflict between secular and religious forces had a significant impact not only on the conception of the public sphere per se but also on the distribution of discursive power and authority across multiple bodies public in the sphere of representation. Elaborating on the aesthetics of affect that underwrote the popularity and force of *Douglas* as a theatrical representation, I illustrate how the play became a touchstone for a political and ideological struggle over the substitution of virtue for religion as the guiding force for conduct in public life.

Chapter 4, "Cultivating a Christian Body Public: The Richmond Theater

Fire," extends the discussion of the conflicts between Enlightenment principles and religious discourse by moving across the Atlantic to focus on representations of the deadly 1811 fire in Richmond, Virginia, as an act of divine
judgment. To bridge this transatlantic shift, I trace at the end of Chapter 3 the
influence in publications related to the fire of the Reverend John Witherspoon, a major antitheatrical figure in the *Douglas* affair who subsequently
emigrated to America and ultimately became a signatory to the Declaration of
Independence. Chapter 4 explores both the range of local reaction to the fire
in letters, diaries, newspaper, and pamphlet accounts and the subsequent efforts in moral treatises and pulpits across the nation to take the fire as a dramatic opportunity to call for a renewed turn to religiosity in early
nineteenth-century America. In taking up the sermons preached on the occasion of the Richmond Theater fire, I illustrate how the cultural imaginary
through which the events at Richmond were filtered relied, ironically, upon a
popular vernacular derived from theatrical forms. Even more to the point, I
demonstrate how antitheatrical sentiments were deployed instrumentally, and
the events in Richmond thus opportunely leveraged as part of the Second
Great Awakening, to call Americans together as a body public both to take
account of national crimes and to form themselves into a more perfect Christian nation.

Chapter 5, "Adjudicating Bodies Public in *NEA v. Finley*," takes up the
documents and performances related to the 1998 rulings in this Supreme
Court case. Reading through the prism of the discourse on AIDS that perme-
ates the material, the chapter observes both how the "American public" was
represented as a body subject to contagion as well as how the artists pointedly
cultivated an aesthetic of what I term the "hyper-real real" that forced audiences to confront the disorderly, disturbing, and messy truths of lived bodily
experience. Focusing on the performative significance of Justice Sandra Day
O'Connor's determination that the government acted legitimately in the capacity of "patron rather than as sovereign" when it denied the grants of the
four queer performance artists—Karen Finley, John Fleck, Holly Hughes, and
Tim Miller—I demonstrate that what was ultimately at stake in the case was
not only the authority to legislate which bodies public were sacred and which
profane but also the right to mandate which bodies, as material instantiations
of what I term the "normative real," would exercise power in and over the
body politic of the "American public."

For some, this final leap to the twentieth century may seem rather abrupt,
especially as the NEA case is not tethered as tightly to the genealogy of

antitheatrical precedents—Prynne's "squadrons of authority"—that constitute the performative repertoire in the other cases. It is without question, however, a case driven, as are the others, both by deep concerns about corporeality and the theatrical re-presentation of bodies in public and by the role of the state and religion in the formation and character of public culture. On a slightly more abstract but, I think, even more significant level, the NEA case allows me to draw the arc of history that I have been quietly tracing throughout the study full circle to illustrate the high stakes involved in the Supreme Court's disturbing return in its ruling to the idea of a singular yet dual-natured absolute sovereign—that is, to an "I" that is, in effect, a "We," and a "We" that is, in effect, an "I." Each of the first four cases illustrates some part of the historical dispersion of sovereignty and the devolution of ecclesiastical polity that political theorists have taken not only as the signature of the liberal state but as the sign of political modernity. Whether I am considering the ways in which antitheatrical controversies mediated the beginnings of Puritan agitation, the settlements of the Glorious Revolution, the moderation of religion in Scotland, or the cultivation of a Christian body public in the absence of established religion in America, all of the earlier cases make intelligible some aspect of a cleaving away from the ideal of the absolute sovereign to an articulated conception of popular sovereignty. Paying careful attention to how competing ideas of the public, writ large and variously, are imagined, cultivated, represented, felt, and materialized in each of the earlier antitheatrical incidents is thus critical to our understanding of the ways in which the decision in the NEA case constituted a disturbing recuperation of formerly dispersed powers and makes the fraught implications of that case for the present day that much more palpable and concerning.

All of the chapters thus share a commitment to offering a deep history of the individual incidents that form their subjects, and they are designed as much for experts in each field as they are for curious readers who may have little to no knowledge of the period in question. To this end, they both provide necessary background information and engage field-specific critical controversies. In engaging these events, moreover, I have taken great care to eschew any preconceived notions about what might be said and instead have followed the lead of the archive. This open approach has enabled me not only to discover an important manuscript that changes how we might view the much-written-about Prynne case but also to illuminate how elements that might seem tangential (infidelity charges against the philosopher David Hume in the *Douglas* controversy) or far afield (abortion case law as precedent in the NEA case) prove to be utterly integral to our understanding of the events as they transpired. My goal has been, then, to let these histories, in all of their particularity, speak as much as possible for themselves. I have thus deliberately refrained from an overlong introduction here, allowing instead for the ideas and arguments that power this study to emerge from the period, the archive, and the character of each incident. How well I have done, I leave to the assemblage of bodies public who read this work to judge.

Chapter 1

In the "Publike" Theater
of William Prynne's *Histrio-Mastix*

On Candlemas night, 3 February 1634, a magnificent, torchlit procession filled the streets of London. Extending all the way from Chancery Lane to Whitehall Palace, this dazzling spectacle featured no less than twenty footmen in scarlet livery with silver lace; one hundred Gentlemen of the Inns of Court, mounted on draped horses and sumptuously arrayed in the finest silver and gold lace; hundreds of pages and footmen carrying torches to light the way; a myriad of dancers, musicians, and young boys in brilliant costumes ingeniously designed for the occasion; and finally four elaborately carved and painted Roman-style triumphant chariots, each pulled by six horses and carrying four representative masquers from each of the four Inns of Court. Recalling the extraordinary brilliance of the display and in particular that of the Gentlemen of the Inns of Court who sponsored the event, Bulstrode Whitelocke rhapsodized in his *Memorials of the English Affairs* (1682), "The richness of their Apparel and Furniture glittering by the light of a multitude of torches attending on them, with the motion and stirring of their mettled Horses, and the many and various gay Liveries of their Servants; but especially the personal beauty and gallantry of the handsome young Gentlemen, made the most glorious and splendid shew that ever was beheld in *England*."[1]

Stunning as this spectacle must have been, it was not the only "shew" that the lawyers would produce that evening. Indeed, the procession through the streets of London was merely a prelude to James Shirley's elaborately staged masque *The Triumph of Peace* (1634), which the Gentlemen of the Inns of Court had commissioned for the occasion and would perform upon their arrival at the Banqueting House for the king and queen. Produced for the first time that night, just four days before the commencement of William Prynne's Star Chamber trial for his alleged attack on the king, the queen, and the state in *Histrio-Mastix: The Players Scourge or Actors Tragædie* (1633), the procession and masque were intended by the Inns of Court as a way to distance themselves from Prynne, a member at Lincoln's Inn, and to "present their service to the King and Queen, and testify their affections to them" by manifesting "the difference of their opinion from Mr. *Prynne's* new learning," and by "confut[ing] his *Histrio Mastix* against enterludes."[2]

To all appearances, the procession and masque seem to have fulfilled their particular political purpose. Not only did the king and queen request that the procession take an extra turn around the tiltyard so that they could get a better view of the display, but the queen was so delighted with the masque that she expressed a wish that it might be performed again, a desire that was satisfied expeditiously by the Lord Mayor, when he arranged for the procession and masque to be restaged—this time with the procession following a path from Chancery Lane to Merchant-Taylors Hall, where the masque was again performed before an audience that included the royal pair.

Prynne himself did not fare so well. Accused of "compilinge, printinge, and publishinge of a booke, conteyninge a scurrilous, and scandalous libell, or a volume of Libells against his sacred Ma[jes]tie his Roiall Consort the Queenes Ma[jes]tie The Lords of his Ma[jes]ties Houshoulde, and others, and in generall against the whole State, and his Ma[jes]ties subiects, and people of all sorts," as well as having been a "stirrer vpp of the people to disobedience," Prynne was tried and found guilty.[3] His severe sentence afforded a different kind of spectacle: the loss of both ears in the pillory, as well as degradation at Oxford and disbarment at Lincoln's Inn, a fine of £5,000, the burning of *Histrio-Mastix* by the common hangman, and imprisonment for life without benefit of pen and ink. Three years later, he would be called before Star Chamber again for continuing to write and publish; and in that case, which sealed his status, along with Henry Burton and John Bastwick, as part of the famous triumvirate of Puritan martyrs, he would be condemned not only to have his ears cropped a second time but to be branded on the cheeks with the letters S.L., for seditious libeler (Figure 1).

Weighing in at well over a thousand pages, *Histrio-Mastix* has come to occupy almost monumental status in the history of antitheatrical discourse. Yet, with the obvious exception of the Star Chamber trial itself, the lawyers' extravagant performance and procession constituted the only conspicuous response to Prynne's logorrhaeic text at the time of its publication.[4] Compared

Mr. William Prynne, for writing a booke
againſt Stage players called Hiſtrio-maſtix
was firſt conſured in the Starr-Chamber to looſe both his ears in the pillorie, fined 5000^{li} & per
petuall impriſonment in the Towre of London,
After this, on a meer ſuſpition of writing other
bookes, but nothing at all proved againſt him,
hee was again cenſured in the Starr-chamber to
looſe the ſmall remainder of both his ears in
the pillorie, to be Stigmatized on both his Cheekes
with a firey-iron, was fined again 5000^{li} and ba-
niſhed itito ye Iſle of Ierſey, there to ſuffer perpe-
tuall Croſs-impriſonm^t no freinds being permitted to ſee him, on pain of impriſonment,

Figure 1. William Prynne; line engraving by Wenceslaus Hollar.
Courtesy of the Lewis Walpole Library, Yale University.

with the full-scale pamphlet war touched off at the end of the century by Jeremy Collier's *A Short View of Immorality and Profaneness of the English Stage* (1698), which I will discuss in Chapter 2, the response to Prynne was positively anemic. If anything, as David Kastan has argued, Prynne's tract was "an anachronism at the time of publication and one that had no immediate successors."[5] Indeed, it appears as if Prynne's invective was of almost no account to his theatrical contemporaries, hovering quite literally only on the periphery or margins of their dramatic texts.[6] Despite the fact, moreover, that *Histrio-Mastix* has often been construed in historical accounts of the stage as the "culmination" of a Puritan antitheatrical movement, leading almost directly to the closing of the playhouses in 1642, the actual historical record suggests that it had no significant impact on either theatrical business or playing practices.[7] Contrary to widespread belief, as Martin Butler has noted, "*Histriomastix* did *not* initiate a new wholesale onslaught on the stage."[8]

A number of compelling questions thus arise: Why did the lawyers feel compelled to mount such a spectacular response to Prynne? And what impact beyond that which was officially publicized did they wish it to have? Given the set of circumstances under which the procession and masque were staged, in what ways did this breathtaking display illuminate and comment upon its contemporary cultural and political context? Similarly, with respect to the Star Chamber trial, we might ask how writing against the stage could be construed and prosecuted as a seditious attack on the king, queen, and state? Why did the government take such a drastic line against Prynne for writing and publishing *Histrio-Mastix*? And what rhetorical and political purposes might have been served by staging this elaborate state trial?

In the pages that follow, I will illustrate how the various parties to the conflict used this occasion in the early 1630s to cultivate and address what I have posited in my introduction as bodies public. I will argue that each of these "shews"—the first, a procession and masque, and the second, a government-sponsored trial—constituted a performative spectacle that not only tells us a great deal about the theatrical texture of Caroline London, but also reveals what was at stake beneath the surface of a culture that took visual displays seriously and that understood them as meaningful expressions of political ideologies and interests. Engaging the public in the forms of political theater that gained in force during the extra-Parliamentary era of Personal Rule under Charles I, such spectacles were performative precisely, as I shall demonstrate, because they were taken to be not merely rhetorical forms but rather efficacious rhetorics of power and authority. To the extent, then, that each of these "shews" traced out various topographies of authority, I will argue that they both engaged with, and acted in response to, fundamental concerns in the period over the nature of sovereign power and over the relation sustained between the ideal of the body politic and the pressing reality of ever more restive bodies public.

Where others have devoted attention to how Prynne drew on long-established moral and religious discourses of animosity toward the stage, the aim of this chapter will be to develop a broader understanding of how Prynne mobilized those discourses for political purposes rather than as ends in themselves. My interest in the case of Prynne's *Histrio-Mastix* is thus motivated not so much by an aspiration to trace a Puritan lineage for antitheatricality as by a desire to foreground how Prynne used antitheatrical discourse instrumentally to publicize and promote a Puritan political agenda that questioned the moral probity and political authority of both the ruling sovereign, Charles I, and the religious policies of the Anglican church under the leadership of William Laud, the Bishop of London and soon-to-be Archbishop of Canterbury. On the other side, I seek, similarly, to demonstrate how Prynne's obsessive, citational style made him an ideal defendant for a regime that sought to enforce and to publicize its sovereign authority to determine when speech—whether written or spoken—might be construed as action and hence as actionable.[9] Throughout this chapter, then, I will train my discussion on the particular political issues and interests that motivated Prynne to write, print, and publish his ponderous tome; the lawyers to mount such a spectacle; and the government to prosecute the case with such vehemence and force.

This account is distinguished from others, too, by its commitment to examining in full the extant archive of documents that bear on this case. As much as Prynne's 1634 trial has been written about, the vast majority of critics and historians have relied primarily either on the only version of the proceedings that has been transcribed and published—British Library Additional MSS 11764, as found in Samuel Rawson Gardiner's Camden Society volume—or on the version of the proceedings published in *A Complete Collection of State-Trials* (1730).[10] As a consequence, most scholarly accounts have failed to note that there were a number of different renditions of the 1634 trial that were published and put into circulation in manuscript form.[11] In contrast, my discussion of Prynne's trial will feature a comparative analysis of the multiple and conflicting manuscript versions of the proceedings, including the uniquely comprehensive and only recently rediscovered Houghton Library MS Eng 1359.[12] My concern in this analysis will not be to determine which "edition" of the proceedings represents a more accurate or authentic transcription of the trial—indeed the most popular, or should I say the most widely circulated, version was probably the least reliable representation of those events in Star Chamber—but rather to elucidate how each of these redactions was tailored to address, appeal to, and cultivate different bodies public. Treating these manuscripts as performative texts, that is, as representations designed to act rhetorically to engage, to persuade, and to produce particular audiences, rather than as mere reportage or "truth-telling" historical documents will enable us to trace the ways that competing bodies public were cultivated long before the crisis of civil war appeared on the horizon.

In this respect, this chapter contributes not only to my larger thesis about the political origins and interests of antitheatrical discourse but also to a more specific discussion among historians and literary critics about the emergence of public opinion and an awareness of its role in public culture in early seventeenth-century England.[13] In an era that saw the rise of what Margot Heinemann has characterized as "an informed and articulate public opinion— or opinions," the rudiments of which have caused Christopher Balme to deem the Prynne case as instancing "the first . . . genuine theatrical public sphere," we ought to take seriously every effort made and every strategy used by both Prynne and the government to plead their case to the public.[14] My discussion of both the materials of Prynne's book and the documents in his trial will thus take into consideration not only the politics of religion and morality but also the politics of publication, performance, and public culture.

With these concerns in mind, I want to turn first to the lawyers' procession and performance with which this chapter began. For given the emphasis in this study on situating antitheatrical events in their local circumstances and on providing a strong historical sense of the particular factors—political and religious, philosophical and ideological, social and cultural—that motivated each of these incidents, the lawyers' extravagant repudiation of Prynne provides us with a paradigmatic opportunity to delineate the intensely performative, political culture in which the Prynne case was tried and to illustrate the complex political resonances that could be generated in early seventeenth-century London by something as seemingly innocuous and entertaining as pageantry and play. As spectacles that at one and the same time announced both their theatrical affinities and their belief in the political efficacy of the theatrical, these exhibitions can be read for the ways that the lawyers, acting as a body public, laid claim to an urban topography and, under the guise of submitting to royal authority, demarcated powers and cultivated interests that were distinct from, and even at odds with, those of the sovereign body politic.

Performing the Body Public: The Gentlemen of the Inns of Court and James Shirley's *The Triumph of Peace*

Prynne's *Histrio-Mastix* was published at the end of 1632, less than four years into the Personal Rule of Charles I. During this period there were at least two main sources of political tension and conflict: first, the status of prerogative rule, which is to say questions about the extent and limits of royal power in relation to both statute and common law; and, second, the role of the church and the episcopate, especially under the controversial leadership of William Laud, in the ordering of the religious life of the nation. In each case, what was at stake was whether the ancient rights, customs, and liberties of "the people" had been infringed upon either by the state or by the church and what forms of recourse might be available should that question be determined in the affirmative. While the early Stuarts were forceful advocates for the theory of absolute monarchy, contending that the king could only fulfill his obligation to govern in the interests of the common good by being not only outside but above the law, antiabsolutists contended that the royal prerogative was "subject to legal definition and subordinate to the subject's legal liberties."[15] Similarly, while Laud upheld the position that the Episcopacy was established and empowered *jure divino*, which is to say by divine decree, his opponents argued not only that such claims violated the principle of Royal Supremacy but also that the bishops could only ever exercise their ecclesiastical powers *jure humano*, which is to say by dint of a grant by royal authority.

At the center of the many battles that were fought over these issues stood the common lawyers. Whether they were calling into question the right of the crown to tax the property of its subjects or challenging the jurisdiction of the ecclesiastical Court of High Commission, the lawyers could be found asserting the sovereignty of the common law against both the encroachments of prerogative rule and against the expansion of clerical powers and jurisdictions. They maintained, as Wilfred R. Prest attests, "that the common law was immemorially bound up with the rights and liberties of Englishmen, while the law administered by ecclesiastical and prerogative courts was valid only if sanctioned and received by the common law itself."[16]

In this respect, it might be tempting to surmise that the lawyers entered into common cause with the Puritans. They were united, for instance, by their mutual resistance to the administration in the ecclesiastic Court of High Commission of the oath *ex officio*, whereby subjects were made to swear to answer all interrogatories truthfully before they had even heard what charges were leveled against them.[17] Yet despite areas of common cause, the conventional view that the law societies functioned as "hotbeds of puritanism" is at best, as Prest has demonstrated, a misconception.[18] Even at Lincoln's Inn, whose Puritan affinities were the most pronounced among the four Inns of Court, members were dispersed across the political and religious spectrum. As an utter-barrister at Lincoln's Inn, for instance, William Prynne appeared in Star Chamber as defense counsel for a group who had refused to kneel for the sacrament, a flashpoint in the contentious quarrels between Puritans and Anglicans over the ordering of the church service.[19] At Prynne's own trial, however, the chief prosecutor was William Noy, a fellow member of Lincoln's Inn. As much, then, as the common lawyers might have been involved in contesting the limits of sovereign rule, they were also very much involved in the administration and defense of the policies of Charles I's government.[20] In both aspects, they played a pivotal role in the adjudication of the character and sweep of both sovereign and ecclesiastical power and occupied a position of considerable influence in both the political and cultural spheres. Their deliberate decision to organize themselves into a body for the purposes of theatrical display can thus be read as a calculated move to publish and publicize that power.

A Public Procession

To be sure, the Inns of Court were no strangers to pomp, pageantry, and performance. The societies had long been known for the extravagance and sophistication of their entertainments at yearly feasts, revels, and Christmastime festivities; and, from what we might call a gross public-relations perspective, it must have seemed particularly apropos to respond to Prynne's allegedly seditious, antitheatrical diatribe with a visibly ostentatious display of theatricality. Such a bald explanation is, of course, immediately and intuitively compelling, but it hardly begins to account for the more subtle, strategic advantages and opportunities that the lawyers must have sought to secure for themselves when they decided to take up two of the most heavily symbolic and ritually constrained forms of performance in the period: a masque for a private, court audience and a public procession through the streets of London. Indeed, in choosing theatrical forms that were designed to produce maximum ideological effects as the vehicles for their response to Prynne, the lawyers could not have been unaware either of the historical and cultural weight borne by each of these genres or of the set of generic expectations that would guide their audiences in making meaning out of the events. Since public processions through the streets of London were not a standard part of masque productions, it is safe to assume that the lawyers sought to gain more from their efforts than just the approbation and affection of the court.[21] By attending, then, to the ways in which the entertainments they designed not only conformed to but also diverged from generic expectations, we can develop a much more finely calibrated sense of how the lawyers used the occasion adroitly both to avouch common cause with the government of Charles I and to articulate and to publicize their separate interests as a substantial and independent body public.[22]

Processions through the streets of London had long been the province of royal prerogative and civic pageantry and were typically designed to transform the space of the city into a stage upon which the political hierarchy and social order could be ritually enacted and visibly enunciated.[23] Most notably associated either with royal entries or with the annual Lord Mayor's Show, these processions played a significant part in the formation of civic consciousness during the Caroline period. As James Knowles explains, these "Spectacle[s] of the Realm" sought "to embody reconciliation and inculcate order, not simply in [their] explicit rhetoric, but in [their] very form, especially the processional element, which actually manifested the whole social body and constitution of the City for its citizens."[24] In the case of the royal entry, as Clifford Geertz has observed, the ceremonial form of a progress through the city provided a spectacular vehicle by which kings could stamp the territory "with ritual signs of dominance" and "take symbolic possession of their realm."[25] Characterizing this process as a "civic or communal form of *poesis*," that is, as a way not just of mapping but also of producing the civic community, Steven Mullaney provides us with a way to understand how, in taking up the processional form and in inserting themselves into the specular, political economy of seeing and of being seen, the lawyers sought to fashion a position for themselves as a body public capable of rendering a critique of the body politic.[26]

In 1634, there were at least two particular historical conditions that would have made such an effort on the lawyers' part all the more efficacious. First, as Jean Howard has pointed out, the rapid demographic, economic, and physical expansion of London in the early seventeenth century created conditions that made it possible for "new loci of activity and power" to emerge.[27] The areas both between and beyond the Court of Westminster in the west and the City in the east, including the path through Holborn along which the common lawyers would have proceeded, proved to be fertile ground for the development of an autonomous cultural politics, a space of commerce and habitation cognizant, yet independent of, the usual influences of monarchical authority and civic magistracy. In this context, it certainly helped that the very location of the Inns of Court—in an area of the liberties at a midpoint between the City and the Court—could be construed as a topographical emblem of the common lawyers' emerging status as fulcrums of power and influence in the changing metropolis.

Second, and perhaps more significant from the perspective of performative politics, even as the number of potentially influential sites of authority in London multiplied, the king himself increasingly withdrew both his person and representations of his person from the sight of his subjects. As historian Judith Richards has documented at great length, not only did he take great pains to limit ceremonial occasions for the public witnessing of the royal presence, but he also failed to satisfy the appetite of his subjects for visual displays of royal dominion.[28] Perhaps more to the point here, the king failed to avail himself of the most spectacular instruments of sovereign rule—the royal progress and the royal entry. When Charles I declined to make a royal entry into London for his coronation in 1626, he deprived the public not just of an occasion for magnificent entertainment but also, as David Bergeron has pointed out, for ritual enactments of loyalty to the crown both in the form of allegorical tableaux and in the enthusiastic voicing of acclamation by the crowds.[29]

In short, while Charles may have lavished much attention on the careful cultivation of an aesthetic of monarchical power and authority for his elite audiences at court, he failed to meet wider, public expectations among the citizenry for the theatrical performance of kingship.[30] His prolonged forfeiture of his right to a preeminent place in the public eye and his failure to enter into public practices by which he might instantiate and sustain a broad vision of the body politic created a cultural and political void that others could fill. That the common lawyers decided to stage the very same kind of public procession through the streets of London, in addition to performing a private masque at court, suggests that they recognized the potency of this performative "scenario" for staking their claim to influence and authority in the public space of the body politic.[31]

Accordingly, the lawyers scripted the grand masquers of the four Inns of

Court into this "scene" in the place of honor at the rear of the procession usually reserved for the king, the place, as Bergeron explains, of the "unscheduled
'actor' in the whole panoply of the festivities without whose presence the
meaning of the event would be incomplete."[32] Draped in an "Equipage so full
of State," the lawyers capitalized on the iterative operations of performance
memory to offer themselves publicly as the new surrogates for representing
both the civic and sovereign order.[33] In this manner, they not only embodied
in spectacular form the otherwise abstract prerogative of the common law, but
they also brought to pass a dramaturgical transposition of power to a new
locus of authority in a manner that would have been eminently legible to all
those spectators, all those bodies in public, who had witnessed previous royal
entries. Indeed, as the Master of Revels, Sir Henry Herbert, observed in recognition of what the lawyers had accomplished with this public display, "Their
shew through the streets was glorious, and in the nature of a triumph."[34]

The dramaturgy mobilized by the lawyers in the procession was not, however, simply citational and iterative; it was also a performative vehicle to engage their audience in collaborative acts of political critique.[35] As the lawyers
advanced across the city collecting the applause of the spectators, marked attention was given over at midpoint in the moving pageant to the groups of
antimasquers whose ritual role not only in the contained space of the court
masque but also in the public procession at large was to represent aspects of
discord or misrule in the state. Among those vignettes, one in particular was
designed both to articulate the political interests of the common lawyers and
to censure the unrestrained exercise of prerogative rule: an antimasque filled
with projectors satirizing the monopolies that, as Stephen Orgel and Roy
Strong point out, Charles I "had managed to reintroduce . . . in clear violation of the spirit of the law."[36] While the ritually, symbolic form of the court
masque ensured that the antimasques of misrule would give way over the
course of the represented action to the restoration of order and the exaltation
of right rule, the unscripted and more schematic form of the procession provided for no such scene of resolution or containment. Moreover, where the
meaning of the masque event at court would have been constrained, according to protocol, by the dominating perspective of the king, there was no controlling perspective in the streets of London through which public opinion
might be filtered. As Marvin Carlson has explained, "The great processions
and the dramatic pageants . . . by claiming [an] entire city as their setting, also
made a claim for the involvement of every citizen." By deploying precisely this
performative machinery, one that placed "no barrier between performance

and public space," the lawyers facilitated a diffusion of political power through the citizenry and entered into a provisional alliance with them.[37] The lawyers were thus able to stage the excesses of prerogative rule and to make popular cause along the route of the procession with a dispersed audience that had a reciprocal interest in the power of the common law to curb monarchical overreaching. Indeed, as Whitelocke tells us, "The march was slow, in regard of [the participants'] great number, but more interrupted by the multitude of the Spectators in the streets, besides the windows, and they all seemed loth to part with so glorious a Spectacle."[38] Capitalizing, in sum, on the dramaturgical conventions of the procession, the lawyers managed the spectacle in such a way as to leverage the sovereignty of the common law against the sovereignty of prerogative rule. Through an impressive show of wealth and strength, they inserted themselves into the physical body of the community and engaged the crowds, however fleetingly, in the formation and celebration of an alternative locus of authority—in the production, that is, of a performative body public. Later that evening, in their performance of *The Triumph of Peace*, they would again play upon generic conventions to signal affinities and interests that diverged from those that the occasion at court ostensibly demanded.

A Masque at Court

As a performance genre, the court masque is perhaps the most ritually constrained and aesthetically complex dramatic form of the early modern period. Under the Stuarts, the artistry of the masque was fine-tuned to an exquisite degree, and the tightly structured pattern of action that marked the form under Charles I—moving almost without exception from poetic induction to antimasque, and from antimasque to masque, followed by revels and an epilogue—was transformed into a sturdy yet elastic vehicle both for the symbolic elaboration of the idealizing, neo-Platonic philosophy of the Caroline Court and for the triumphant celebration of Charles I's rule.[39] In scenario after scenario, devisers of these favored entertainments at court would present elements of discord in the state in antimasque vignettes only to dissolve those tensions and facilitate their dramaturgical transcendence in the grandiloquent pronunciations of the subsequent masque and its celebratory apotheoses of the king and his consort into presiding deities such as peace, harmony, and love. The masquers, who were generally represented by courtiers rather than the professional actors who performed in the antimasques, would then initiate the revels by moving from behind the proscenium arch and descending the stage to lead partners from the audience, including, on occasion, the king and queen, in a dance.

For many critics, this last moment constitutes the climax of the evening, as the illusions of the performance are folded into the realities of the court, and the aristocratic performers of the masque are revealed as living embodiments of the very political order they represent on stage.[40] In a paradoxical bait and switch, the disorders of the antimasques, which often alluded topically to genuine political controversies and concerns, are cast behind the proscenium as illusory imaginings, while the idealized conception of an orderly and harmonious state moves across the theatrical divide to actualize itself as the tangible reality of sovereign grace.[41] In this manner, the symbolic narratives presented in these masque performances were treated not as mere rhetorical fictions but rather as efficacious political truths. Within the confines of the court, the masques served as compelling vehicles not only to enforce the sovereign claims of the monarch but also to publicize a resounding image of the king as an adept, benevolent, and divinely ordained governor of the state.

Taking up the masque form in *The Triumph of Peace*, James Shirley designed a spectacle that presented both an overt embrace of and stealthy departure from these conventions and provided the lawyers with a sharp instrument through which they might both celebrate and at the same time level a profound critique of the exercise of prerogative rule under Charles I. Almost all critics agree, as Martin Butler so adroitly puts it, that "the fable of the masque as a whole . . . was a statement about the dependence of Peace and Justice on the institution of Law, and constituted a tactful but firm caution about the necessity of governments acknowledging the constraints of legality."[42] Yet, given the performance conventions and ideological constraints of the masque form, there is considerable disagreement among scholars about the political efficacy of the representation, that is, about whether and how that "tactful but firm caution" would have been received. For Stephen Orgel and Roy Strong, the structural and ideological imperatives of containment that shaped the masque as a dramatic form made it possible for the king to understand "not that royal power must be united with the processes of law, but only that he and his consort were Olympian deities, Jove and Themis guarding over Peace, Law, Justice."[43] More recently, however, scholars have advocated for a more finely calibrated approach to the particular occasions and peculiarities of individual Stuart masques.[44] Advocating for a broader transactional understanding of the masque as a mode of public performance that engages and enlists multiple and competing perspectives, Butler emphasizes that such an approach is even more critical when we take up those "rare occasions on which masques were presented to the court from lobbies outside Whitehall." For those occasions, he admonishes, we ought at least to take seriously how "from the performers' side, the masque would have appeared to be acts of persuasion, in which the occasion was enlisted to give prestige to factions struggling for influence, or to advertise agendas of their own."[45]

Building on Butler's arguments, my discussion of Shirley's *The Triumph of Peace* pays particular attention not only to how the lawyers of the Inns of Court used the occasion to "advertise [an agenda] of their own" both to a public at court and to a more general public at large, but also to how, as with the procession, they did so by both conforming to and differing from significant formal conventions and expectations. Hence, where Butler identifies "four variables"—"an author, a masquer, an audience, and a monarch"—in relation to which the meaning of a masque is produced and situated, I would add a fifth, that of genre.[46] In this case, as I shall demonstrate, the lawyers were able to level a profound political critique of the sovereign claims of kingship under Charles I by offering a metatheatrical performance that belied the performative effects of the masque form's customary move toward ideological consolidation and ritual closure.

With music composed by William Lawes and Simon Ives and elaborate stage designs by Inigo Jones, the action of *The Triumph of Peace* opens in the Piazza of Peace where Opinion and Confidence meet and discuss the arrival at court of Fancy.[47] Soon they are joined by Opinion's wife, Lady Novelty, and daughter, Admiration, and then by Fancy, Jollity, and Laughter. After an exchange of greetings, Fancy inquires about the anticipated masque performance and in particular about plans for the antimasques. To his great dismay, he discovers that no antimasques have been devised, and he expresses fear both for the soundness of the representation and for the safety of the performers should the audience be displeased by this omission. While Fancy's apprehensions alert us immediately to the extent to which generic forms shape audience expectations and guide their responses, his subsequent attempts to satisfy that generic demand by devising an increasingly frenzied series of antimasque vignettes only heightens our awareness of the form's pulse. As scene after scene fails to satisfy Opinion's sense of what might "conduce" to the occasion—the celebration of peace—Fancy remains nonplussed (249). Aiming to prove that he is "not ignorant of proprieties," he insists again and again on his ability to "furnish" an appropriate scene from the inexhaustible and immortal stream from which "Invention flows" (290, 410, 443–45). Thus, in rapid succession, we are treated to no less than twelve delightfully varied anti-masques, featuring a cast of characters ranging from beggars, gamesters, and bawds to projectors, dancing nymphs, and a Don Quixote–like knight. Yet when Opinion and Fancy are rejoined by Confidence, Jollity, Laughter, Novelty, and Admiration, who had been left behind at a tavern, the question of sufficiency still hangs in the balance. A drunken Novelty thus boasts that she "will have / An Anti-masque of [her] own" (470–71), but all further action of this kind is suspended when the characters are frightened off the stage by the heraldic music announcing the grand masquers entrance to the scene.

The main masque quite literally alights upon the stage as Irene (i.e. Peace) descends from the heavens in a golden chariot to chase away the "Profane" and celebrate the "new and brighter" world that is the vision of the king and queen (491, 499). Irene sings for her sister Eunomia (i.e. Law) to join her, and upon her descent from the clouds in a silver chariot, Law joins with Peace in a song that celebrates their mutual intercourse and dependency. Pronouncing the major theme of the masque, they sing together, "The world shall give prerogative to neither; / We cannot flourish but together" (539–40). Drawn from the heavens by her sisters' song, Dice (i.e. Justice) arrives upon a cloud in a white robe and mantle of satin to complete the "perfection of [their] glory" (562). Gazing out across the banqueting hall, the three sisters espy their "parents," Jove and Themis, in the form of the king and queen and address an ode to their glory as they bow to the seat of State. Following their lead, the sixteen grand masquers from the Inns of Court descend, in turn, to offer their own dance tribute to the king and queen. Accompanied by a Genius, who presents them to the King/Jove and Queen/Themis as "the children of your reign, not blood," they are joined by the Hours and Chori, who move toward the State singing a song of exaltation for the "Royal Pair" (632, 659).

All would seem as it ought to be when a sudden noise disrupts this moment of harmony, and confusion ensues as a belligerent Carpenter, along with a Painter, a member of the Black Guard, a Tailor, the Tailor's Wife, an Embroiderer's Wife, a Feather-maker's Wife, and a Property-man's Wife all rush into the scene, protesting their right to be there to witness the spectacle that they all had a hand in producing. "Those stairs were of my painting," exclaims the painter, as each character in his or her turn takes credit for the fabrication of some part of the scene (694). Their demand for spectacle is rebuffed, however, as the masquers stand still and refuse to perform for such an unrefined cohort. Deflated and now sensing the danger they have put themselves in by encroaching so brazenly on the court scene, the Tailor advises, "'Tis our best course to dance a figary ourselves, and then they'll think it a piece of the plot, and we may go off again with the more credit" (705–9). Off they go, leaving the way clear once again for the masquers to advance to their revels with the ladies. The scene closes when a forerunner of morning, Amphiluche, sings of her arrival and other voices call the masquers away to kneel once again before "that bless'd Pair" (776).

In the most schematic sense, *The Triumph of Peace* advocates for an understanding of good governance where the Law supports and is supported by a gracious, sovereign king.[48] To this end, the masque follows the basic outlines of the form, presenting a series of antimasques designed to represent discord in the state that subsequently give way to a masque in which Peace, Law, and Justice descend to the scene to restore order and to pay obeisance to their "parents," Jove and Themis, in the personae of the king and queen. The common lawyers' point is quite clear in this regard; without Law, there can be no Peace: "The world shall give prerogative to neither; / We cannot flourish but together" (539–40).

For many critics, the disruption of the order of action by the artisans results only in a reiteration of the lawyers' overt message of counsel. In Butler's view, for instance, this violation of form "presses the spectators to acknowledge that the apparently effortless magical effects were in fact achieved through an unseen but all-important act of collaboration . . . a clear reminder . . . of the joint enterprise that alone made Charles's rule possible."[49] Taking that viewpoint one step further, Kevin Sharpe writes, "The artisans who rush in . . . remind the courtly audience and the king of the world outside. They are representatives of a people who . . . make Charles a king in reality as well as image: they *are* what they say 'the king's subjects' . . . to deny them is for the monarch to deny his own kingship."[50] For both Butler and Sharpe, then, this metatheatrical breach in the decorum of the masque form signals the intrusion of the world of the real upon the idealized realm of the court, creating a scene in which the illusory truisms of the court masque are shattered by the pressing realities of the commons' demands upon kingship and their constitutive role in maintaining the order and integrity of the body politic.

These observations certainly hold for that discrete moment in the masque, but they fail to recognize this generic rupture as an extension of the more comprehensive dismantling of the form and of its ideological interests that arcs across the entire performance. "Somebody will think this was meant for an Anti-masque" (714–15), the Tailor hopefully exclaims as the rowdy group dances anxiously off the stage, alerting us not only to the perilously uneven power relations negotiated in that moment but also to the ideological interests that the devices of the antimasques were meant to serve. Indeed, I would argue that as the artisans exit the scene, the intrusion is cast quite conspicuously as what we might term, in modern parlance, a Brechtian "*Gestus*," that is, as a moment in the performance "that makes visible the contradictory interactions of text, theatre apparatus, and contemporary social struggle."[51] Performed so egregiously out of order and to such comic effect, this last, gestic antimasque satirizes and brings to the forefront the otherwise conventional role played by these representations of disorder and prompts us to engage in a closer and more skeptical assessment of the earlier antimasques and their dramaturgical effects.

With twelve antimasques in the first part of *The Triumph of Peace*, the masque far exceeds any one of its contemporaries. Indeed, as Clifford Leech observes, "The anti-masque had never been used so freely as here."[52] Little noticed, however, in the critical commentary is the fact that the "free use" of the antimasque is not just a matter of number but also of conception and design. Where other masques draw the action of the antimasques discreetly behind the proscenium, Shirley and the lawyers elect instead to dramatize the very convention, to make visible and to bring forward, as it were, the very artifice of the form. Thus, we watch as Fancy strives over and over again to satisfy Opinion's demand and produce an antimasque that articulates a competing vision of peace in the state. After every failure to meet Opinion's abstract standard of sufficiency and decorum, Fancy simply moves at a more rapid rate to "furnish" yet another scenario that might "happily delight," until the antimasques seem to follow so closely upon one another that they begin to take on an almost parodic aspect. Even at the very end of this series—a series whose excess calls attention to itself—we are still left, as I pointed out earlier, with no resolution as to which antimasque might stand in counterpoise to the grand gestures of the main masque. While each antimasque has been vividly rehearsed, none have been sanctioned or absorbed seamlessly into the ongoing action of the representation. They stand out as potential but not as settled scenarios of action and meaning. Thus, the formal demand is never satisfied, and the structured debate between competing visions of the state that the masque form as a whole was designed to stage is deliberately frustrated and displayed as a device of artifice—"furnishings" akin to Fancy's inexhaustible "immortal stream."

The problem of ideological closure is compounded further by the adamant refusal in the representation to maintain the integrity of theatrical illusion. Indeed, if anything, we are constantly made aware of the fact that we are watching a dramatic entertainment where all is artifice. Thus, not only does

Fancy announce each antimasque as the latest production of his imagination, but we also watch as Fancy and Opinion act as spectators to rather than as characters in the action, commenting upon the relative merits of each anti-masque with respect to the larger entertainment's purpose. The scene of action, which is so crucial to the aesthetic operations and effects of the masque, receives much the same treatment. At one point, for instance, Fancy announces that he will "present" us with "a tavern" (296–97), and all of a sudden the "*Scene is changed into a tavern, with a flaming red lattice, several drinking-rooms, and a back door, but especially a conceited sign and an eminent bush*" (298–99). When Admiration expresses surprise that a tavern had appeared where there was "none within two minutes," Laughter swiftly retorts, "No such wonder, lady, taverns are quickly up. It is but hanging out a bush at a nobleman's door, or an alderman's gate, and 'tis made instantly" (302–5). Calling attention to the contrivances by which the scene is set in the antimasques, Shirley anticipates and then strips away the sense of awe that the later devices of the grand masque were designed to produce. The ironic call for a "conceited" sign and an "eminent" bush satirizes the magnificent effects, or eminent conceits, produced by the machinery of the masque; and we come to see how, with very little effort, a "nobleman's door" could be transformed into a tavern for the commons. As the theatrical apparatus of the masque is laid bare, so too are the distinctions of rank that the structure of the masque was designed to articulate and sustain. Even the elaborate setting of the court could be understood as an effect of stagecraft and artifice.

In this manner, the illusions that usually sustained the entertainments at court were not just repeatedly violated; rather they were unraveled altogether. The unexpected and unruly return to antimasque not only punctuates the metatheatrical refusal of the formal condition and ideological project of the masque performance but also limns a seemingly endless specter of imaginable, antimasque scenarios in which political discontent under the Personal Rule might be embodied and brought beyond the stage's edge. The exalted order of the grand masque is thus belied by the parodic excess of the antimasques and by the Commons' metatheatrical refusal to stay within the frame and be governed by the ideological conceits of the masque form.

This brings us to one final point about how this revision of the masque form should be understood. While the overtly schematic and iterative program of the masque as a whole made it possible for the king and queen to respond enthusiastically to *The Triumph of Peace*, the royal couple was not the only or even perhaps the most important audience for the more subtle, formal critique. At the performance itself, the "Gallery behind the State," as Whitelocke explains, "was reserved for the Gentlemen of the *Inns of Court* . . . that there they might sit together, and none else to be admitted with them into that place."[53] Hovering behind the chair of State occupied by the king, this seating arrangement guaranteed not only that the lawyers would constitute an alternative focal point for the performance but also that they would take up a highly visible position at the entertainment as a substantial body public, that is, as a competing locus of authority, judgment, and interpretation. The presence of such a large body representing the commons at a court entertainment was unusual, and just as the antimasque intrusion of the artisans encroached upon the decorum of the masque and reminded the audience of its artifice, so too did the presence of the common lawyers belie the ceremonial decorum of the court and remind the audience that this was a masque presented *to* the king and not *by* the king. As with the procession, then, the lawyers put their imprimatur upon the performance event and publicly positioned themselves as an alternative locus of creative force and power. Further, their presence as a public body in the gallery acted as a reminder of the constraint of common law on the exercise of monarchical power; and their impressive command of the performative art acted as a portent of their capacity to stage their political interests for a wider public audience.

Additionally, with respect to audience, the lawyers clearly set their sights on cultivating broader public interest beyond the walls of Whitehall Palace not just through the extravagant procession that they staged in the streets of London but also through the medium of print. Lauren Shohet, in her account of how masques moved beyond the narrow pale of the court to reach a wider public, explains, "We have continued to think about masque receivers only in terms of an elite courtly audience, even though a much broader population read masque scripts, discussed accounts of their performances, and participated in non-court events that intertextually evoked courtly scripts."[54] *The Triumph of Peace* is a perfect case in point for her argument, for the lawyers clearly anticipated broad demand for their text and saw to it that three thousand copies of the masque, the text of which included a description of the magnificent procession, were printed ahead of time and made immediately available for sale.[55] The masque became one of the most talked-about spectacles in London, and more copies had to be printed. Most significantly, as Gerald Bentley explains, "The number of issues of the printed text suggests that more people bought copies of it than any other Jacobean or Caroline masque."[56] As much, then, as *The Triumph of Peace* was the "talk of the town,

drown[ing] all other news" before the performance, afterward it was "frequently alluded to and described," becoming a kind of cultural and political
touchstone (Figure 2).[57]

If, as Graham Parry theorizes, the masque entertainments at court were
designed to produce a representation of the body politic in which the "ill hu-
mors" of discontent were purged, then we might say that Shirley and the
lawyers treated the court to an alternative spectacle in which the bodies public
that composed that body politic obtruded into and rankled the scene.[58] Indeed, the text itself takes great care to distinguish these sons of Peace, Law,
and Justice—and hence the grandsons of Jove/Charles and Themis/
Henrietta—as "the children of your reign, not blood," that is, as subjects
bound to the body politic not by the laws of genealogical inheritance but
rather by the merit of the patriarchal head's sovereign rule. By making a show
of their refusal to support the orderly illusions of the masque form, the lawyers rendered a critique not just of the excessive aesthetic and ideological
claims of court entertainments but also of the excesses of royal governance.
Even more significantly, by putting their work so widely and so immediately
into circulation the lawyers ensured the continuation of public discourse
about the masque itself and about the cultural authority and political force
wielded by the Inns of Court in its creation and performance. Thus, even as
the lawyers fulfilled the demand of the king for a show of submission, they
used the theatrical apparatuses of performance, publicity, and print to represent themselves as a substantial and resistant body public.

At the end of his account of the lawyers' procession, Whitelocke inserts a
rather curious note of nostalgic regard for the tale he has just told: "Thus these
Dreams past, and these Pompes vanished. It will be now time to return to the
publick story of the latter part of this year."[59] To those of a more modern cast,
it might seem rather disingenuous that Whitelocke would characterize such
an extravagant display of spectacle through the streets of London as anything
other than "publick." Yet this fleeting remark alerts us to the tenuous status of
that concept in the early seventeenth century, a period of transition when the
term *publick* was beginning to be applied to the communal endeavors of the
broader populous but which still referred in its strictest sense only to those
official actions taken by the state. Facilitated by the expansion of print and
networks for the circulation of news, moreover, the concept of "public opinion" was just beginning to emerge and to be recognized for its political and
rhetorical efficacy.[60]

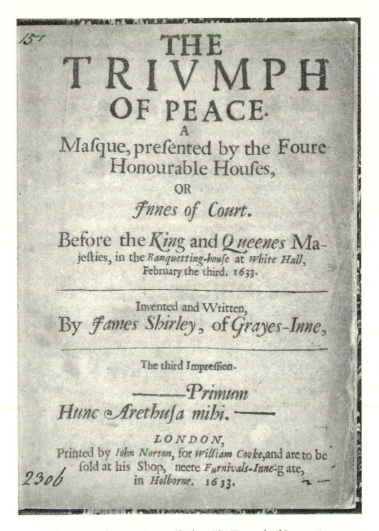

Figure 2. Title page, James Shirley, *The Triumph of Peace*, 1633.
Used by permission of the Folger Shakespeare Library.

This shift in the purview as well as in the technologies and representational calculus of "public" life produced a systemic challenge for the state and
a strategic opportunity for its opponents and critics. Indeed, it was precisely
over these grounds that William Prynne engaged the readers of *Histrio-Mastix*
to contest particular church and state policies for shaping public culture in
the body politic. Embracing print as a performative technology, Prynne
sought to call into being and to publicize an alternative body public—a

constituency of the godly—that could place its own imprint on the public domain. In this respect, as I shall demonstrate below, *Histrio-Mastix* was not simply, or even mainly, an extension of the Puritan antitheatrical tradition, but rather an adept entry in the growing dispute over the contours of public culture and the conduct of secular and religious life in early Stuart England. In the composition of Prynne's *Histrio-Mastix* as well as in the proceedings against him in Star Chamber, then, we can identify both an increasing awareness of, and a heightened interest in developing, a distinction between the body politic and the many potential bodies public. By attending to this aspect of these texts, we will be able trace the development of the political understanding, long before the factions of civil war had solidified, that the cultivation of public opinion constituted a critical element in bridging the gap between those two bodies—public and politic—and that any claim to authority and power was dependent upon the measures taken to do so.

Reading *Histrio-Mastix*

Reading *Histrio-Mastix* is at the very least a vertiginous experience. Running to well over a thousand pages, the text is so heavily glossed, annotated, cross-referenced, and indexed that there is barely any blank space left to spare. Divided into two parts, where the first part is framed and structured as an eight-act tragedy, complete with a prologue and chorus, and the second as a five-act tragedy with a separate, concluding catastrophe, each section or scene in the text presents a syllogistic argument against the theater, bolstered and illustrated by a chain of precedents from the ancients to the moderns, or what Prynne terms his "seven distinct Squadrons" of "Authorities" (545).[61] Amid this dizzying array of proofs, *Histrio-Mastix* presents us with a text that is so repetitive in content and so circular in its reasoning that we might be tempted to concur with those critics who have referred to it variously as the work of an "obsessive mind," a "logorrhaeic nightmare," and an "exercise in sheer lunacy."[62] But if *Histrio-Mastix* was the work of a megalomaniacal madman, then its author, William Prynne, was clearly crazy like a fox, as he was able through this hypergraphic form of expressivity both to attract the publicity he sought and, as Jonas Barish points out, "to turn the terminology of dramatic structure against its usual practitioners" to make it serve his "godly" purpose (Figure 3).[63]

While it would be foolish to think that any reading of *Histrio-Mastix*

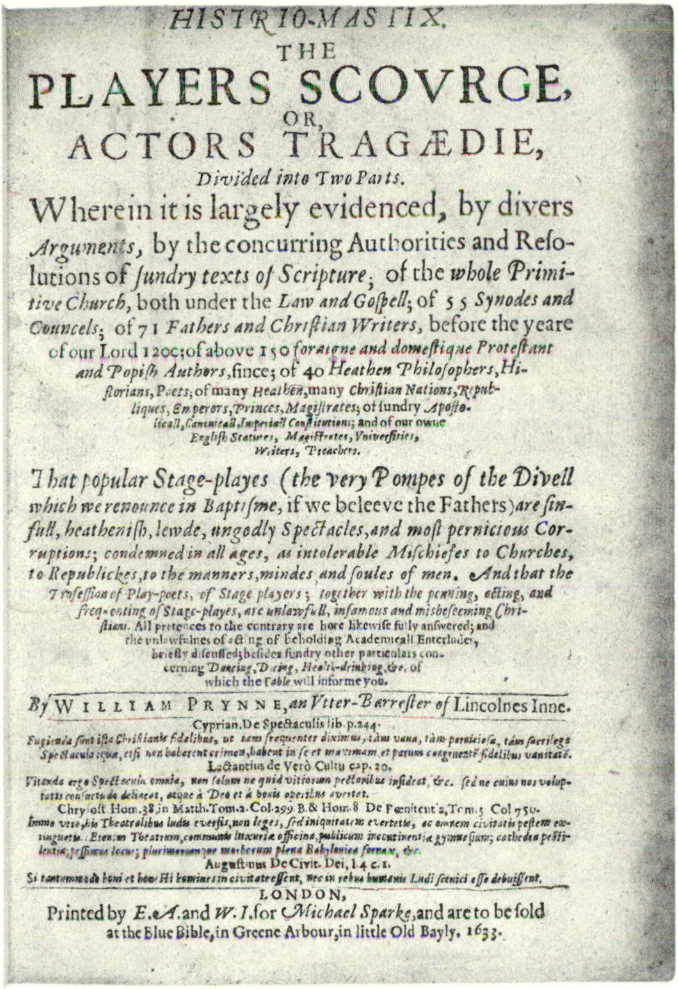

HISTRIO-MASTIX,

THE

PLAYERS SCOVRGE,

OR,

ACTORS TRAGÆDIE,

Divided into Two Parts.

Wherein it is largely evidenced, by divers
Arguments, by the concurring Authorities and Resolutions of *sundry texts of Scripture;* of the *whole Primitive Church,* both under the *Law and Gospell;* of 55 *Synodes and
Councels;* of 71 *Fathers and Christian Writers,* before the yeare
of our Lord 1200; of above 150 *foraigne and domestique Protestant
and Popish Authors,* since; of 40 *Heathen Philosophers, Historians, Poets;* of many *Heathen,* many *Christian Nations, Repub-
liques, Emperors, Princes, Magistrates;* of sundry *Apostoli-
icall, Canonicall, Imperiall Constitutions;* and of our owne
*English Statutes, Magistrates, Vniversities,
Writers, Preachers.*

*That popular Stage-playes (the very Pompes of the Divell
which we renounce in Baptisme,* if we beleeve the Fathers) *are sinfull, heathenish, lewde, ungodly Spectacles, and most pernicious Corruptions;* condemned in all ages, *as intolerable Mischiefes to Churches,
to Republickes, to the manners, mindes and soules of men. And that the
Profession of Play-poets, of Stage players; together with the penning, acting, and
frequenting of Stage-playes, are unlawfull, infamous and misbeseeming Christians. All pretences to the contrary are here likewise fully answered; and
the unlawfulnes of acting, or beholding Academicall Enterludes,
briefly discussed; besides sundry other particulars concerning Dancing, Dicing, Health-drinking, &c. of
which the Table will informe you.*

By WILLIAM PRYNNE, *an Vtter-Barrester of Lincolnes Inne.*

Cyprian, De Spectaculis lib. p.244.

*Fugienda sunt ista Christianis fidelibus, ut tam frequenter diximus, tam vana, tam perniciosa, tam sacrilega
Spectacula ecva, etsi non haberent crimen, habent in se et maximam et parum congruentem fidelibus vanitatem.*

Lactantius de Verò Cultu cap. 20.

*Vitenda ergo Spectacula omnia, non solum ne quid vitiorum pectoribus insidat, &c. sed ne cuius nos volup-
tatis consueto delineat, atque à Deo et à bonis operibus avertat.*

Chrysost. Hom.38.in Matth.Tom.2.Col.259.B.& Hom.8.De Pœnitent.2,Tom.5 Col.750.
*Immo verò, his Theatralibus ludus everisti, non leges, sed iniquitatem exercetis, ac omnem civitatis pestem ex-
tinguitis. Etenim Theatrum, communis luxuriæ officina, publicum incontinentiæ gymnasium; cathedra pesti-
lentiæ; pessimus locus; plurimorumque morborum plena Babylonica fornax, &c.*

Augustinus De Civit. Dei, l.4 c.1.

Si tantummodo boni et honesti homines in civitate essent, nec in rebus humanis Ludi scenici esse debuissent.

LONDON,

Printed by E.A. and W.I. for *Michael Sparke,* and are to be sold
at the Blue Bible, in Greene Arbour, in little Old Bayly. 1633.

Figure 3. Title page, William Prynne, *Histrio-Mastix, The Players Scourge,* 1633.

could be comprehensive, it also seems pointless to expend a great deal of energy explicating its innumerable and reiterative tirades against plays and playhouses, many of which merely recapitulate arguments and citations from earlier antitheatrical tracts, such as Stephen Gosson's *The School of Abuse* (1579) and *Playes Confuted in Five Actions* (1582), Arthur Munday's *A Second and Third Blast of Retrait from Plaies and Theaters* (1580), and Phillip Stubbes's *The Anatomie of Abuses* (1583). Indeed, as I shall demonstrate below, what distinguishes Prynne's text, and hence what we ought to attend to, are not those passages in which he cites antitheatrical precedents—though he certainly takes that pedantic art to a new level of fanatical excess—but rather those moments when he departs from the usual script of antitheatrical vilification both to contest the authority of sovereign, state, and church and to mount a moving defense of Puritan character. In those moments, Prynne engages in what we might term a public-relations war, an effort designed to cultivate and to sway public opinion and to call into being a godly public. Rather than dismiss Prynne's text with the usual global pronouncements, then, I endeavor below both to elucidate its rhetorical project and to offer a sustained analysis of its attacks on those instruments of secular and religious authority that it took to be the most menacing and insidious. Extending Peter Lake and Michael Questier's insight that antitheatrical discourse in the post-Reformation period was "designed . . . to create rather than merely reflect or describe the social and cultural divisions and oppositions," I begin my analysis with a discussion of the context in which Prynne framed his arguments, noting in particular the ways that he articulates social, cultural, and religious differences as potentially political causes.[64] In order to highlight how Prynne engaged his audience and invited them into the theater of his book, I then focus more particularly on the practical concerns and rhetorical effects of the paratexts in *Histrio-Mastix*. Proceeding from there to an elaboration of the main body of the work, I explore how Prynne's rhetorical dramaturgy of call and response was designed to persuade others to join with a diffuse community of like believers in forming a more substantial body public of the godly.

Doctrine, Print, and Public Opinion

By the time Prynne published *Histrio-Mastix* at the end of 1632, he had already assembled an impressive résumé of pamphlet publications that made it clear he was using attacks on seemingly benign social customs as a screen for mounting a more consequential critique of what had come to be known among Puritans

Figure 4. Archbishop of Canterbury, William Laud;
line engraving by Wenceslaus Hollar, after Sir Anthony van Dyck.
© National Portrait Gallery, London.

as the "new conformity," the program of ceremonial and liturgical practices
that had been instituted in the Church of England under the increasingly powerful influence of clerics led by William Laud (Figure 4).[65] Invoking what Lake
and Questier have termed a "chains of sin" logic, whereby venial infractions—
the "quotidian or social sins of the city"—are magnified as precursors to the
inevitable commission of grievous sins, Prynne excoriated contemporary

vanities and fashions as symptoms of both a secular culture and an ecclesiastical regime that were jointly intent on making a sacrifice of "inward efficacie" to
the thralldom of outward forms.[66]

Laud's ecclesiastical movement, variously referred to as anti-Calvinism,
Arminianism, or Laudianism, pitted what Darren Oldridge has described as
two fundamentally different conceptions of the church against one another—
the "visible" church of the clerical elite and crown against the "invisible"
church of evangelical elites.[67] Where the former emphasized greater ceremonialism and conformity in public worship as well as the elevation of both the
church as the house of God and the sacrament as the central focus of the service conducted by the clergy, the latter emphasized the evangelical preaching
of the word both in sermons by ministers and in lectures by laypersons to a
gathered community of believers, as well as the virtues of private prayer and
individual conviction.[68] While many of the practices related to the ceremonies
of the church as well as to the form of prayer arguably fell under the category
of *adiaphora*, or things indifferent and hence open to variations in dispensation, on the theological matter of the doctrine of predestination the Laudians
and the Puritans were sharply and, it would seem, unequivocally divided,
with the Laudians taking the Arminian view of divine grace as "freely available
in the sacraments" and of salvation as "fore-ordained in the light of human
will" and the Puritans adhering to the strict Calvinist view that the decree of
election was God's alone and that no intervention on the part of the human
will could alter who had been chosen by God for salvation.[69]

In pamphlets that attracted both the attention and the ire of Laud,
Prynne rehearsed his Calvinist polemics and took direct aim at what he construed as the ceremonial innovations and Popish tendencies of the Arminian
ascendancy.[70] Prynne was keen, moreover, not only to inveigh against Arminian doctrine and the exalted ceremonialism of the Laudian ecclesiastics but
also to dramatize the plight of the Puritans as persecuted but loyal and patriotic subjects whose writings were being systematically censored and suppressed. Thus, in *Healthes: Sickness*, Prynne campaigns against the pejorative
and stigmatizing application of the term "Puritan," noting that it is most
commonly wielded only by those "who labour to suppresse, and quite abolish
all Temperance, Holinesse, Sobriety, and the very practicall power of Grace,
by prejudicating, censuring, and reuiling them, vnder the names of Puritan-
isme, Singularity, or Preciseness, in a censorious, peremptory, rash, and un-
aduised manner" (80). More significantly, in his *Censvre of Mr. Cozens*, Prynne
declaims against the uneven enforcement of Charles I's "Proclamation for the

establishing of the Peace and Quiet of the Church of England" (14 June 1626), which prohibited "Writing, Preaching, [or] Printing . . . any new inventions, or opinions concerning Religion, then such as are clearly grounded, and warranted by the Doctrine and Discipline of the Church of England, heretofore published, and happily established by authoritie."[71] In particular, he writes against what he construes as an Arminian ascendancy in print, not only charging that while these "*priuate Deuotions*" have been "licensed in a speciall manner for the Presse, euen with an affixed and printed Approbation," the same authorities "doe not onely deny to license, but likewise diligently suppresse and intercept all Answers and Replies vnto them as the intercepting of M[r] *Burton's Answer* at the *Presse,* and the detaining of the *Copie* of this my present *Censure* in the Licensers hands" (¶¶2v–3).

Where historians such as Christopher Hill and F. S. Siebert once embraced Prynne's hue and cry of persecution and press censorship at face value, more finely calibrated studies of press censorship during the Caroline period by such scholars as Anthony Milton, S. Mutchow Towers, and Cyndia Clegg have demonstrated that Prynne's charges were both substantially true and substantially exaggerated.[72] Focusing their attention on the mechanisms of licensing in relation to print output, they have determined that while Calvinist publications were increasingly subjected to prohibition and suppression when it came to the licensing of new books, Calvinist works in the form of both reprinted editions and circulated manuscripts continued to dominate the market in religious books and to reach a large and receptive audience. Thus, Towers concludes, on the one hand, that "by 1637 teaching of unconditional predestination, portrayals of the Pope as Antichrist, and strict sabbatarianism . . . had disappeared from the first editions of the legitimate religious press while at the same time novel ceremonies, practices, and doctrines emerged," but also notes on the other that "reprints and, to some degree clandestine printing as well, reflected pre-Laudian themes."[73] "The great irony," as Clegg notes, "is that the attacks on licensing that characterized how impossible publishing Calvinist writings had become were appended to books extolling Calvinist doctrine."[74]

Still, the aggregate effect of tightening controls on the licensing process was not negligible; and in refuting revisionist claims that the government either lacked the means or the will to enforce strict censorship, all three critics have demonstrated that while the Laudians may not have been able to stem the tide of reprinted Calvinist texts (at least until the Star Chamber Decree of 1637 instituted the requirement that all printed editions be entered in the Stationers' Register), by tightening their stranglehold on the mechanisms of

licensing, Laud and his ecclesiastical cadre of licensers were increasingly able
to restrict the publication of Calvinist works and hence to shift public perception of what constituted church orthodoxy. Thus, as Milton explains, "If we
do not have here simple pervasive censorship, surely we have instead a still
more significant attempt to control what opinion passed for orthodox in the
church, with the aim, not of crushing opposition, but of securing control of
what official, established religion was meant to be."[75] In short, once Charles I
issued his proclamation against the publication of "any new inventions or
opinions concerning Religion," a new battleground opened up in the realm of
print to control what might be deemed the "Doctrine and Discipline of the
Church," a situation eloquently captured by Prynne in *Anti-Arminianisme*
when he wrote in his prefatory appeal to "the High and Honourable Court of
Parliament": "Yea, but how may Parliament infallibly discerne what Tenents
are our Churches genuine Doctrines, when as both sides lay equall claime,
and title to our Church?" (a1v).

Prynne's was not a campaign or a cry, then, against censorship per se, but
rather an acknowledgment of the powers of print to shape public opinion.
Indeed, "no one," as Milton points out, "was campaigning for freedom of the
press as such: the battle was over who would control it most effectively."[76]
Perceiving that they were losing ground in the battle to influence the licensing
process and hence to control public perceptions of church orthodoxy, Prynne
and his confederates adopted the rhetoric of censorship as a new and more
effective tactic in the battle to cultivate public interest and sympathy. Consequently, where the Laudian regime worked both to moderate the works submitted by Calvinist authors and to prohibit those by radical Puritans, Prynne
and his confederates knowingly submitted works for licensing and approval
that they knew to be incendiary in order to publicize claims that the government was engaged in a comprehensive policy of persecution and censorship.
If, as Milton concludes, "there was no effective religious censorship during the
Personal Rule," then Prynne and others still ensured through their tactics that
"there was a widespread *consciousness* of restrictions on the expression of religious views, and a belief that such restrictions were being imposed much more
strictly than they had been in the past."[77] Thus, in a period when the very
ground of officially sanctioned orthodoxy was contested, the propaganda on
each side grew in intensity and ferocity. Both sides in this increasingly acrimonious divide believed themselves not only to be defenders of theological piety
and the true church but also protectors of the state, and both, as Kenneth
Fincham points out, "were most effective when they could mobilise a wider

body of opinion which did not share their ideological perspectives."[78] On both sides there was a keen awareness of the strategic necessity of cultivating public opinion and of gaining and sustaining the allegiance of a substantial body public.

When we read *Histrio-Mastix* in this context, we can begin to recognize Prynne's design for his book, beginning with the dedicatory epistles and building toward a crescendo through the body of the text, as a set of rhetorical strategies designed to engage and to cultivate his audience. As I shall demonstrate below, Prynne mobilizes a dramaturgy of expansive address that culminates in the "Catastrophe" with which he concludes his tome. At every turn and often rather crudely, Prynne strives to draw us into the theatre of *his* book, a tragic narrative of epic proportion in which the religious, cultural, and political stakes are writ large and redemption lies in the embrace of Calvinist proscriptions. What he demands of us and looks to conjure in us is not the passive, emotional response of catharsis but rather the active and resistant rootedness of faith and conviction. In this, his public theater of the book, he thus endeavors to gather together a broad community of bodies public that will throw off the gaudy tragedy of Laudianism in favor of the austere comedy of Puritan reformation.

Playhouses, Play-Books, and the Theatrical Body Public

Prynne's determination both to attack the stage and at the same time to deploy a theatrical metaphor to frame his book suggests the extent to which he understood and sought to engage the playhouses not merely as incubators of immorality but more significantly as rival sites of social and cultural commerce and as historical loci for displays of and contests over power and authority.[79] These, of course, were not new concerns. Theater historians such as William Ringler have long since demonstrated, first, that antitheatrical tracts of the Elizabethan and Jacobean periods were motivated at least as much, if not more, by concerns about social and economic order rather than by moral or theological arguments and, second, that the playhouse occupied a prominent place in the cultural and symbolic topography of the city as a site of jurisdictional conflicts between monarchs and city magistrates.[80] Of particular concern at the time for Prynne, as the dedicatory epistles for *Histrio-Mastix* reveal, was the increase in the number of playhouses in the 1620s and 1630s and the commensurate growth in the market for printed plays. Thus, in the first of his three epistles dedicatory, he plaintively writes that over the course of the seven years he had been collecting and collating "Play-condemning passages," he had been compelled to enlarge his "Discourse" against the stage:

> beyond its intended Bulk, because I saw the number of Players, Play-books, Play-haunters, and Play-houses still increasing, there being above forty thousand Play-books printed within these two yeares . . . they being now more vendible than the choycest Sermons; *two olde Playhouses* being also lately reedified, enlarged, and one *new Theatre* erected, the multitude of our London Play-haunters being so augmented now, that all the ancient Divels Chappels (for so the Fathers stile all Playhouses) being five in number, are not sufficient to containe their troopes, whence we see a sixth now added to them. (*3–*3v)

One of the more enduring ironies of Prynne's *Histrio-Mastix* is that this "player's scourge" provided us with one of the most comprehensive, contemporary accounts of theatrical practices and the material culture of urban playhouses in the Caroline period. In the passage above, Prynne refers both to the rebuilding and enlargement of the open-air Fortune and Red Bull Theatres in 1622 and 1625, respectively, as well as to the erection of the private Salisbury Court Theatre in 1629 in the vicinity of Whitefriars.[81] In citing the expansion of the print market for plays, Prynne was equally accurate. As Heidi Brayman Hackel has observed, assuming an initial run of a thousand for each printed play, "Prynne's figure of 40,000 playbooks would translate to forty editions for these two years, a number identical to W. W. Greg's tally of new and reprinted professional plays in 1631 and 1632."[82]

Prynne's alarm at the number of printed plays was matched only by his disquiet over the size and quality of those printed volumes. Returning with even greater vehemence in his third epistle to the problem of the print marketplace, he writes:

> *Some Play-books since I first undertooke this subject, are growne from Quarto into* Folio; *which yet beare so good a price and sale, that I cannot but with griefe relate it, they are now new-printed in farre better paper than most Octavo or* Quarto Bibles, *which hardly finde such vent as they: And can then one* Quarto *Tractate against Stage-plays be thought too large, when as it must assault such ample Play-house Volumes? Besides, our* Quarto-*Play-bookes since the first sheetes of this my*

Treatise came unto the Presse, have come forth in such abundance, and
found so many customers, that they almost exceede all number, one
studie being scarce able to hold them, and two years time too little to
peruse them all: And this made this Treatise swell the greater, because
these Play-bookes are so multiplied. (**6v)

Here, Prynne frames his massive "Tractate against Stage-Playes" as a response to the burgeoning market for printed plays and construes his entrance into that competitive marketplace as a foray into a battle of the books in which sheer size and paper quality matter. In Prynne's view, Bibles were losing ground in the battle for quality to folio editions of plays by such authors as William Shakespeare and Ben Jonson, even as printed sermons were losing ground to playbooks in the battle for market share.[83] And he was not entirely wrong; indeed, as the statistical analyses of Alan B. Farmer and Zachary Lesser have demonstrated, "The Caroline period was the apex of early modern English printed drama. From 1629 to 1640, the supply of playscripts seems to have rebounded strongly, and play publishers nearly tripled their output compared to the preceding fifteen years, with both first and second–plus editions per year reaching their highest levels for the entire early modern period. . . . As a proportion of the entire trade, moreover, plays were also rising rapidly."[84] In a word, Prynne's perception that the market was being inundated with printed plays while he was completing *Histrio-Mastix* and preparing it for the press was not unfounded, as "publishers brought out more first editions from 1629 to 1631 (21) than they had in the previous ten years combined (19)."[85]

This focus in the epistles dedicatory on the effects of print as much as on the moral errors of playing represents a significant shift in the scope of antitheatricalist ruminations and follows, in part, from the fact that in 1603 James I had prohibited the performance of plays on Sunday, leaving Sabbatarians with no obvious religious pretense for their attacks on the playhouses. Given the correlates between Sunday gatherings in churches to hear sermons and Sunday assemblages at theaters to watch plays, antitheatricalists of the 1580s, as Lake and Questier have pointed out, could articulate a "structurally parallel relationship" between the "godly pulpit and the stage" in a rivalry for the attention of a "culturally and socially mixed, 'popular' metropolitan audience."[86] In his dedicatory epistles, then, Prynne seeks to draw upon and mobilize the legacy of that rivalry even as he relocates the forum for its operations to the marketplace for print. As printed plays gained in market share, attracting more attention and a wider array of purchasers, the market itself, as an abstract formation tied to the manufacture and sale of material objects, came to be perceived by Prynne and many others as an index of public interests and affinities and hence as a significant new battleground in the struggle for influence over social, cultural, and religious life. Indeed, as Alexandra Halasz has demonstrated, "Print permanently altered the discursive field not by bringing books to the marketplace . . . but by enabling the marketplace to develop as a means of producing, disseminating, and mediating discourse independent of the sites and practices associated with and sanctioned by university, Crown, and Church."[87] Prynne's repeated expressions of alarm at the specter of so many printed plays and particularly at the quality of those volumes signals that he was troubled, at least as much if not more, by the notional, discursive space taken up by printed plays as by the delimited physical space in which those plays were performed. In publishing *Histrio-Mastix* and in composing his dedicatory epistles, then, he imagined himself quite literally as fighting a voluminous battle on two fronts—in the unruly round of the playhouse environs and in the marketplace for printed books—to redirect the popular consciousness toward both the religious precepts and the discursive embrace of the godly community.

Not insignificantly, the acuity of Prynne's apprehensions about the dynamic relationship sustained between stage and page has often been curiously misprized. In Halasz's analysis, for instance, the playbook as commodity in early modern England was removed from the public space of overt commerce to the private space of the study, effacing its very relation to what she terms the "eventness of discourse."[88] In her estimation, Prynne simply misrecognized the "commodification of discourse" for the "eventness of discourse," that is, he attacked printed plays where no one else did because he tied them back too closely to the overtly commercial and public experience of the playhouse. What Halasz misses here, however, are the commensurate and reciprocal relations of transmission that obtain between what performance theorist Diana Taylor terms "the archive"—printed playbooks—and "the repertoire"— plays in performance.[89] If, as Taylor theorizes, the printed archive conveys to plays a form of legitimacy and cultural capital, then it is also the case that that legitimacy redounds back to the performed repertoire. Such speculation attains a measure of proof from Andrew Gurr, who writes of plays in repertory at Blackfriars in the 1630s, "The self-conscious function of gentle audiences at the hall playhouses was to 'censure.' For the first time plays had become respectable matter for serious discussion. The king himself made critical notes in the margins of his playbooks and more than once interceded on a matter of critical judgement with the Master of Revels. It became a mode of the town."[90] In short, as it became fashionable for playhouse patrons to train a critical eye on the relationship between playbooks and the plays before them on the boards, archive and repertoire became entwined and entangled with no clear line of delineation between the experience of the one and the other. In lavishing so much attention in his epistle's dedicatory not only on the number of printed plays but also on their quality, it was not, then, as Halasz holds, that Prynne viewed playbooks as objects contaminated by their proximity to performance, but rather that he understood how the elevated commodity of the playbook would reverberate across the event at the playhouse and make playing that much more respectable. As playbooks gained the status of legitimate property, so too would the playhouses achieve a new level of respectability and cultural authority.

This process was already well under way. As Martin Butler and Jean Howard have demonstrated, the public stages and especially the private playhouses were thriving commercial enterprises in the 1630s, attracting fashionable audiences that regarded the theaters as legitimate institutions and increasingly viewed attendance at the playhouse as a respectable leisure activity.[91] Facilitated by representations in which political and ideological conflicts were enacted, the playhouses—elite and popular—cultivated what Margo Heinemann has termed "a growing sense of a new force in politics to be conciliated, manipulated, or silenced."[92]

For Prynne, the growth of a theatrical body public, unmoored from either church or state and in possession of a distinct political consciousness, posed a distinctly new threat. That many of the plays "articulated attitudes which can only be labelled 'opposition' or 'puritan'" would have been less significant to him than the ability of the theaters to draw together the multitudes.[93] As David Kastan explains, "Theaters were places not only where private people came together but where they came together *as a public*. In the theaters people assembled, were provided with a political vocabulary that served to construct and clarify their interests, and were endowed, by the theaters' commercial logic, with an authority over its representation. The audience was thus not merely a public assembly but a public now constituted as a domain of political significance."[94] By attacking an institution that had grown so fashionable and that had captivated such a large audience, Prynne sought to capitalize on the strains of independent thought fostered by theatrical commerce both to call attention to his own interests and to draw that audience away from the playhouses and into the theater of his book—a moral drama of

Puritan resistance and dissent. His diatribe against the stage was not merely an end in itself, then, but rather a bold extension of his customary strategy of using an attack on cultural fashions as the means to articulate a religious and political program. Indeed, as his own entry in the "Index" for *Histrio-Mastix* indicates, for Prynne the "Theatre" was "not alwayes taken for a Play-house, but sometimes for a place of publike meeting where Orations were made, and Malefactors executed" (1,007). The theater in this view was not merely a public place for play performances but also a forum for public gathering and expression, a sociopolitical site where one might make a case in public, to the public, and where judgments as such might be "executed." Capitalizing on this aspect of theater, the "Orations" that make up Prynne's *Histrio-Mastix* seek to cultivate and to mobilize an alternative body public.

Dedicatory Epistles

Prynne's expansive efforts to cultivate a compendious body public are amply on display in the incremental ordering of address in his three epistles dedicatory. He opens the first epistle with an address to the "Masters of the Bench" at his own Society at Lincoln's Inn. Referring to the lawyers' community as a nursery of "Law and Piety," Prynne not only references the site where the work itself was compiled but also marks his affiliation with an institution that, as noted earlier, was associated with the practice of common law as a restraint or check on the exercise of ecclesiastical and monarchical power. In this context, he is particularly keen to represent his condemnation of plays and playhouses as actions taken "out of desire of the publike good" (*3), and he advertises his selfless service to the body public by humbly avowing that he does not care "how it fares abroad, so it may doe good and please at home" (*3v).

   In his second epistle, Prynne deftly performs a somewhat broader address to the "Right Christian, Generovs Yovng Gentlemen-Students of the 4 famous Innes of Court" (*4). As with his first epistle, Prynne is eager to represent himself as acting selflessly not merely by "*pen[ning]*" but also by "*publish[ing]*" a tract dedicated to reclaiming the "*future prop and honour of our English Nation*" from "lewd infernall pastimes not tollerable among Heathens, not sufferable in any well-ordered Christian Republike" (*4, **2). With his reference here to publication, Prynne acknowledges not only that his enterprise is directed toward readers beyond his immediate circle but also that his interest lies in generating the kind of publicity that might be directed toward producing what he construes as the public good. Sensitive as ever to the sovereign proscriptions on print and to the political stakes regarding their observance, Prynne is mindful in this moment, moreover, to offer this enlarged audience an assurance that the contents are "*so farre from any suspicion of* factious Novalty, *or* puritanicall singularity" (**1v). This claim, of course, was specious, and it alerts us to the elaborate rhetorical performance in which Prynne was consciously engaged. Prynne would have known that his writing would be viewed as suspect, yet rather than concede that ground, he uses that anticipated imposition to his advantage, capitalizing on the opportunity afforded by the prefatory address to advertise to his readers the threat of censorship and to alert them to Laudian efforts to control church orthodoxy.

Prynne extends this rhetorical strategy and plays further on audience sympathies by expressing some trepidation about the potentially unpopular task that he has taken upon himself. Given "what estimation Playes and Players have lately purchased in the opinions and hearts of most," he knows that he runs the risk of "reprehend[ing] their vices" (*4v). Nevertheless, he avers, he still holds out hope that the lawyers will consult the lessons of their own learning—"to heare and know, before you sentence: *since Gods Law, & ours too,* doth not judge any man, before it heare him, and know what he doth"— and give his own performance in print a fair hearing (*4v). This is a kind of subtle play, for in pleading here against summary judgment, Prynne not only activates the lawyers' interests but, by inference, also casts aspersion on the practices of ecclesiastical courts such as the Court of High Commission, which was gaining notoriety both for its administration of the oath *ex officio* and for abrogating procedures long associated with the ancient liberties of the subject. Prynne's appeal to the common lawyers thus banks upon their association with and investment in the sovereignty and sway of the common law. In this manner, he positions himself as a defender of ancient English liberties and inserts his polemic not only into the conflict over religious discourse and the control of church doctrine but also into ongoing arguments about sovereignty and good governance.

Having secured his base with the first two addresses, Prynne turns more capaciously in his final epistle "To the Christian Reader." Here, Prynne explicitly figures himself as one entering into "combate in a publike Theatre" against the "Players and Stageplaies" which, in his view, have "growne of late so powerfull, so prevalent in the affections, the opinions of many both in Citie, Court, and Countrey" (**6). Marking his adversarial stance to the popular taste as a necessary public performance, Prynne offers a series of apologia for his volume, submitting, with respect to the "prolixity" of his polemic, for instance, that *"Hee who will cure a large and spreading gangrene, must proportion his plaister to the maladie"* (**6). Drawing on the familiar tropes of disease and cure, infection and purgation that were conventional in antitheatrical discourse, Prynne insists that moral corruption and vice in such great proportions must be met with condemnations and interdictions of *"greatest,"* if not equal, *"virulency"* (**7). On each count, Prynne justifies what others might take to be an outsized response as proportionate to the severity of the crisis and in so doing lays the groundwork for the expansive and wide-ranging cultural, political, and religious project that he will subsequently enact in the body of *Histrio-Mastix*.

Indeed, Prynne enlists his audience of "Christian Readers" to array themselves not just against plays and playhouses but also against all "concomitants of Stage-plays," such as dancing, May-games, Christmas-keeping, Health-drinking, excessive laughter, and amorous pastorals (**8v-***1). While the references to amorous pastorals could be, and were, read as deliberate swipes at Queen Henrietta Maria, who, even as Prynne was readying his book for publication, was involved in preparations and rehearsals for her public performances at Somerset House in Walter Montagu's *Shepherd's Paradise* (1632–33), many of his other comments are directed at recreations and pleasures that had come to be associated with the *Book of Sports*, a royal declaration affirming the right of the people to engage in public sports and lawful recreations after the divine service had concluded on Sundays, first issued by James I in 1618 and later taken up and reissued by Charles I in 1633, arguably as part of a response to the publication of *Histrio-Mastix*.[95]

The original purpose of the *Book of Sports* was at least twofold: first, to bolster the purview and the authority of the state, and second, to inhibit the growth and influence of Puritan Sabbatarianism, a doctrine that held that the whole of Sunday was to be treated as a day of Sabbath worship and that neither labor nor leisure activity were to distract from or interfere with that sacrosanct observance.[96] With respect to the first purpose, the declaration enabled James I, as a matter of political expedience, to insinuate his power and authority into the consciousness of the commonwealth at the most local level both by placing his imprimatur upon, and by encouraging in populist fashion, the ancient customs and pastimes of the people.[97] Reflecting the effort to propound and to attain authority, the *Book of Sports* is striking insofar as it asserts the royal right of power and sovereignty almost at every turn. At the same time, it offers a benevolent and populist rhetoric, as the king condescends to pronounce his pleasure that "after the end of Diuine Seruice, Our good people be not disturbed, letted, or discouraged from any lawfull Recreation; Such as dauncing, either men or women, Archerie for men, leaping, vaulting, or any other such harmelesse Recreation, nor from hauing of May-Games, Whitson Ales, and Morris-dances, and setting vp of Maypoles and other sports therewith vsed."[98]

Where the desire to infiltrate the everyday practices of ordinary people's lives and to reinforce the social order may have formed the primary motives for the promulgation of the *Book of Sports* under James I, its concomitant purpose of enforcing conformity and rebuffing the Sabbatarian campaign of the Puritans came to the fore under Charles I. As Leah Marcus explains, "The fostering of old festival practices became very closely tied to the vexed matter of enforcing religious conformity, and the pastimes were increasingly perceived as extensions of liturgical worship. . . . The old pastimes were a way of taking the Church out into the world and molding the countryside into an image of ecclesiastical order."[99] To this end, Charles I and Archbishop Laud took a more aggressive approach to enforcement than had been customary under the administration of James I, depriving those clergy who refused to read the controversial declaration from the pulpit, barring those who did not attend church service from participation in Sunday games, and preventing Puritan nonconformists from "gadding about" the countryside to attend sermons and lectures in other parishes.[100]

Resistance to these policies of enforcement was commensurate, and as Marcus has demonstrated:

> Political offshoots of the *Book of Sports* controversy could be encountered almost anywhere: in small communities where there were sporadic conflicts between justices of the peace who tried to dampen the sports and holiday celebrants who claimed the "liberty" of pursuing them; in parish churches where ministers were ordered to read out the *Book of Sports* to their congregation (though some refused) and the legality of old pastimes was debated from the pulpit; even in Parliament where the matter surfaced during every session until the beginning of Charles's Personal Rule.[101]

By encroaching upon the concerns of the *Book of Sports*, Prynne deliberately and publicly inserted himself into a popular dispute that encompassed both sovereign authority over public recreations and Laudian jurisdiction over

Anglican orthodoxy and conformity. By expanding both the purview and the address of *Histrio-Mastix* far beyond considerations of the morality or immorality of the stage, Prynne took advantage of the forms of public address afforded both by the dedicatory epistles and, as I shall demonstrate, by the other paratextual apparatuses of the printed text to call into being a body public that might resist the imperial claims upon "Our People" (capital O, capital P), which redound in the *Book of Sports*, and to impose his own claim to order public life, as he later enumerates, upon (small "o") "our Gracious Soveraigne, our Church, our State, our Parliament, our Counsell; yea all our Magistrates, Ministers, People" (500–501).

Prologue

While the epistles dedicatory rehearse the rhetorical and political objectives of *Histrio-Mastix* and initiate Prynne's program for cultivating a godly public, he uses the dramatic apparatus of the Prologue to set the scene for the theatrical course we are about to enter and to shape our perspective on the role he expects us to play. The first lines immediately alert us to the eschatological arc that will guide the dramaturgy of this book: "Svch hath alwayes beene, and yet is, the peruerse, and wretched condition of sinfull man, *the cogitations of whose heart are euill, and onely euill before God, and that continually:* that it is farre more easie to estrange him from his best, and chiefest ioyes; then to diuorce him from his *truest misery, the pleasures of sinne, which are but for a season, yet set in endlesse griefe* " (1). Framing his text as a dramatic excursus into the evil and sinful ways of man, Prynne positions us as active participants and as potential allies in the event. Over the course of the drama to be presented, we will be transformed from mere spectators or witnesses into the subjects of what Prynne construes as a tragic but "reall, and liuely experiment" in which the "prophane, and poysonous STAGE-PLAYES; the common Idole, and preuailing euill of our dissolute and degenerous Age" will be placed before us as a test of our judgment and will (2). The purpose of this "experiment" is not to redeem the many denizens of the playhouse, who, tragically, have already fallen in the trial and given themselves over to these "*ouerspredding abominations,*" but rather to "wrest" those few among us whose enduring affinity for "Christ, Religion, God, or Heaven" might be enlisted in "armes" against this "pestiferous" contagion (4, 3, 6). His book, then, is a kind of theodicy in which the evil of others serves as a fortifying object lesson for those who are better disposed and who, when proffered the "powerfull attractiues" afforded by Prynne's text, may resist temptation and choose Godliness over "Hellish wickednesse" (2, 6).

Having set the scene and articulated the dramaturgical values of his text, Prynne turns next to the project of mobilizing a discourse of sympathy for the Puritans as the maligned protagonists in the ongoing play. Perhaps most perturbing to Prynne is the very denomination of "Puritan" as a pejorative term of opprobrium. In particular, he complains with reference to stage plays, "He that speakes against them, or comes not at them, is forthwith branded for a Scismaticall, or factious *Puritan*" (3–4). Drawing a line of comparison with Tertullian's time in which "*it was the chiefest badge and character of a Christian, to refraine from Stage-Playes*," he elaborates, "Now, (as if Stage-Playes were our *Creed*, our *Gospel*, or the truest embleme of our Christian profession,) those are not worthy of the name of *Christians*; they must be *Puritans*, and *Precisians*; not *Protestants*, who dislike them" (4). Prynne's indignation here derives from his recognition of the discursive force of nominative privilege. He understands that as part of Laud's campaign to shift the center of orthodoxy away from Calvinism and toward Arminianism, this rhetorical sleight of hand constitutes an efficacious strategy for undermining the competing representational claims of the self-denominated "saints."[102] To associate those who would refer to themselves as the "godly" with the tainted name of Puritan is, in effect, to distinguish them from mainstream Protestants.

Rather than exhausting his capital by attempting to recuperate this ignominious term at this point, Prynne instead turns strategically to lay claim to the exalted mantle of godly Christian. Lest we suffer any illusions that assuming that mantle might be easy, Prynne is quick to make clear that such a claim does not come without worldly sacrifice. Dramatizing both the costs and the rewards of his own heroic efforts, Prynne writes, "This being the dissolute, and vnhappy constitution of our depraued times, it put mee at the first to this *Dilemma*; whether to sit mute and silent still . . . or whether *I should lift vp my voyce like a trumpet, and crie against them*, to my power?" (4–5). The condition of godliness emerges in the Prologue as a conscious choice, a call extended by God that contends against the human propensity for apathy and silence. What makes action not only possible but absolutely necessary, Prynne submits, is the recognition that it is also a choice of "Conscience," an "opportunitie" put "into [his] hand" by God, not only to save the self but also to "*rescue*" others in the human community (5). Compelled thus to "doe [his] uttermost, to extirpate, or withstand these dangerous spectacles, or to withdraw such persons from them, as [his] paines, and briefe collections in this subiect might reclaime," he resolves on his auditors behalf "*to endure the crosse, and despise the hate, and shame*, which the publishing of this HISTRIO-MASTIX might procure mee, and to *asswage . . . these inueterate and festred ulcers*, (which may endanger Church, and State at once,), *by applying some speedy corrosives, and emplaisters to them . . .* in these ensuing *Acts*, and *Scoenes*" (5). Styling himself a martyr who, like Christ, sacrifices his earthly well-being for the greater good of all souls, Prynne elicits admiration and sympathy for his plight. In the drama that will be enacted in *Histrio-Mastix*, moreover, the cultural condition of the public playhouse takes on a commensurate symbolic status. It comes to provide a kind of visible correlative for those invisible temptations of the inward soul that are played out in the private theater of divine Providence where all actors, with no guarantee of eternal grace or salvation, are enjoined to act in accordance with the tenets of blind faith. Accordingly, in Prynne's treatise, each man's ability to abandon the spectacular and sensual pleasures of the playhouse becomes an index of his capacity to forsake the concrete rewards of materiality and, like Prynne, to embrace the inscrutable emoluments of godliness.

In his Prologue, then, Prynne crafts an alluring part to be played by his readers. Inspired by his plaintive example, we are primed when Prynne calls upon us in the "ensuing *Acts and Scoenes*" to respond in kind by laying claim to the mantle of true Christians. We are motivated to act heroically, in the face of adversity and in spite of all risk of personal injury to ourselves, to wrest not merely nominative but also doctrinal control away from institutional sites of power and authority. And we are fortified by the "bare, and naked *Trueth*" that while bowing to temporal authority might reap certain rewards in this earthly life, the ultimate cost of such conformity might very well be too high to sustain any expectations in the heavenly realm (6). Subsequently, as Prynne moves from act to act in the main body of the text, the mandates of the Prologue find expression in a strategic preoccupation with the moral and political welfare of the commonwealth, and the "I" of the text slides ever so insistently into an "us" that composes the godly body public of Prynne's imagining.

Mainpiece

While the Prologue limns the dramaturgical and rhetorical thrusts of *Histrio-Mastix*, each of the first six acts in Part 1 turns more particularly to a presentation of Prynne's "Reasons to euince the vnlawfulnesse of Stage-Playes," with the seventh and eighth acts reserved, respectively, for an "enumeration of those

Authorities that concurre together with [him] in condemning Playes and Enterludes" and a refutation of "those miserable Apologies, those vaine pretences ... which their Advocates oppose in their defence" (8, 545, 721). As
various as Prynne's "reasons" might be—they range from accusations about the
devilish origins (Act 1), and the idolatrous ends of theater (Act 2), to the concomitants of theater such as lascivious dancing and gross effeminacy (Act 5)—
each section of Part 1 is geared toward supporting the premise that is first
pronounced in the prefatory "Argument" and then reiterated almost verbatim
at the head of Act 1: "*That all popular, and common Stage-Playes, whether Com-
icall, Tragicall, Satyricall, Mimicall, or mixt of either: (especially, as they are now
compiled, and personated among vs,) are such sinfull, hurtfull, and pernitious Recreations, as are altogether vnseemly and vnlawfull vnto Christians*" (6). Guided by
this axiom and cleaving to a syllogistic mode of argumentation, the scenes
rapidly become repetitive and reiterative, taking on a quality of monotony as
they seek through relentless citation to bolster a Calvinist line of thought.

Against this background of almost mind-numbing recitation, the moments when Prynne moves beyond the narrow confines of his mandate stand
out and gradually attain an aggregate effect. Of particular significance are
those occasions when Prynne uses the camouflage of his treatise against the
theater to impugn the Christian, and more specifically, the Protestant bona
fides of Bishop Laud and Charles I. Littered through the acts, these moments
signal the historical particularity of Prynne's project and bring to light his
specific religious and political program.[103] Thus, for example, in Act 6, Scene
12, which takes issue with the "twelfe effect of Stage-playes" that they "wholy
indispose their Actors and Spectators to all religious duties," we find Prynne
landing blows against Laud for both his suppression of lectures and his diminishment of the role of preaching sermons (521fol., 530–530fol.–532). Similarly,
in Act 6, Scene 5, which takes on the "generall depravation of mindes" effected by stage plays, we find Prynne focusing his argument on the negligence
of kings and magistrates for tolerating such "contaminating pernicious
plagues" as are "not *tolerable* in any Christian well-ordered Common-weale"
(466, 501). Finally, as exemplified in Act 5, Scene 8, which condemns the stage
"co[n]comitants" of "lascivious mixt, effeminate Dancing" (220), Prynne continually assails the postulates of the *Book of Sports*, either on legal grounds—as
a royal declaration promulgated in violation of statute law (241)—or on eccle-
siological grounds—as licensing pagan and idolatrous practices akin to "*our
late crouching and ducking unto new-erected Altars*" (236), a direct dig at Laud's
policies of increased ceremonialism in church services.[104]

Underlying these objections to specific practices is the more consequential project of making a case for the exercise of individual conscience against the hierarchical policies of church and state. Noting, for instance, in the context above, that "men never went as yet by multitudes, much less by Morrice-dancing troopes to Heaven" (244), Prynne reminds his readers that his ongoing experiment is being conducted simultaneously upon at least two stages—in the "publike Theater," which is the province of church and state, and, more significantly, in the private theater of individual conscience, which is the sole dominion of divine providence. Appealing here, as throughout *Histrio-Mastix*, to a higher authority than those represented either by church or by state, Prynne zealously counterpoises what he refers to elsewhere as the "prerogative royall of the King of heaven" against the royal prerogative of the Personal Rule and challenges his auditors to query which master they might better serve (102). In this manner, he introduces a controversial and potentially subversive stricture, which, as noted in the Introduction, authorizes members of a body politic to set themselves apart as belonging to a transcendent heavenly community, a religious and moral commonwealth, whose tenets could be set against and even surpass the sovereign authority of a secular or civil state.

Chorus

Prynne capitalizes on the modes of direct address afforded by the paratextual apparatus of the Chorus to impress these divisions of sovereignty even more urgently upon his audience. Assuming the posture of a voice apart, providing commentary on the ongoing action before us, Prynne draws on the conventional association of the Chorus with the cultivation of community perspectives and, in each of the four Choruses that punctuate the volume, directs that convention toward building public consensus about the right, because righteous, form of government that would obtain in "any Christian well-ordered Common-weale" (501). Thus, for example, in the first Chorus, in a series of passages that would be cited against him in Star Chamber, Prynne impeaches the moral virtue and piety of the king and court for countenancing "those workes of Satan, those Pompes, and Vanities of this wicked world, which euery Christian renounceth in his Baptisme" (42). Having singled out for particular excoriation those theatrical spectacles "such as are acted in priuate houses, and societies," he asks, "Why doe men send for Stage-Playes to their houses; why doe they flocke vnto their Theaters" if it is not out of a "vaineglorious desire of some worldly Pompe, and State?" (47–48). With these reflections, he not only indicts the worldly pastimes of king and court, but he also places in doubt the moral probity and religious authority of those in such positions who would be "so desperately prodigall of their owne Saluation" (61). Appealing, in counterpoint, in the form of an apostrophe to all "good Christian Readers, in the name, and feare of God" (56), he beseeches them to set themselves apart from those who would engage in such "officious compliancy to the course, and fashion of this wicked World" (47) and in an impassioned moment of high drama boldly pronounces, "*You cannot serue two contrary Masters, as the Deuill, or the World, and him [Christ]*" (58). In Prynne's formulation, "all such as are Baptized with the name of Christians" have not only entered into a sacred covenant to obey the laws of Heaven, but they are also thereby warranted to act in good conscience to despise any human law or custom that violates those precepts (61). They can, as it were, serve only one "Master." Putting a fine point on the question, he warns of the consequences they might face in the hereafter for their present neglect of godly strictures: "If you confesse your selues Guiltie now, how can you plead Guiltlesse, *or escape Christs doome, and iudgement then?*" (60). In this manner, Prynne uses the first chorus to convince his readers that the severest "danger of Rebellion, and the highest Periury" lies not in resistance to civil government but rather in abjuring the transcendent sovereignty of the kingdom of heaven (58).

While this first chorus takes the form of an extended argument, in the three subsequent choruses Prynne adheres more closely to the conventional model of direct address, interpretative summary, and community imperative. At the end of Act 6, for instance, Prynne assumes the elevated posture of Chorus, loftily intoning, "You have seene now Christian Readers, the severall bitter fruits, and pernicious effects of Stage-playes, most copiously anatomized in the precedent Act" (568). Continuing in a more measured voice than he is otherwise wont to adopt, he goes on first to summarize the points he has touched upon in the foregoing act and then turns in warm embrace to enjoin, "As therefore *we* t[en]der the honour, love, and worship of our gracious God; the happinesse, the welfare of *our* Church and State, the purity, tranqnility [sic], salvation of *our* owne poore soules, of the soules of *our* brethren, *our* posterity, which succeede us; *Let us* henceforth passe an irrepealable sentence of condemnation against popular Stage-playes, and bid an everlasting farewell to them" (568 fol., emphases mine). My insertion of emphases in the passage above is meant to highlight the pronominal shift that has occurred in Prynne's text, from the lone voice of the "I" of the Prologue to the collective understanding of the "we" and the "us" of the Chorus. Whereas at the outset of the treatise, Prynne styles his audience as a potential ally, by the end of Act 6 he incorporates us into a collective community. As a result of what we have "seene" in the drama before us, we are presumptively constituted, and performatively imagined in the "scene," as part of a godly body public founded upon rational consensus. In light of the compelling, nay overwhelming, evidence presented, it is imagined that we could draw no other conclusions than those that Prynne has already proffered. The companionable "let us" thus performs the assumption of a community ethos, the comprehension of a shared set of values and beliefs, anchored in a genealogy of historical precedent and edified by judicious reason. Following this same pattern of address in the Chorus at the end of Act 7, Prynne appeals to the reader's "wisdom now at last to take the best, the strongest side, not onely in quality, but in number too" (718–19). Summoned to the "scene" of representation, we are to take our place upon the stage and play our role as part of a body public charged with a godly imperative.

Scene the Last

As much as Prynne imagines and cultivates a godly body public, he also works throughout *Histrio-Mastix* to rehabilitate and enhance its public reputation. This project has its culmination in the final scene of Part 1, Act 8, Scene 7, when Prynne takes the occasion to launch a staunch defense and celebration of the character of so-called Puritans. In an act that had been devoted up to this point to a systematic refutation of the "chief Play-propugning Objections" of defenders of plays, Prynne summarily announces, "The grand Objection of our present dissolute times for the justification of these Plays is this; none but a companie of Puritans and Precisians speake against them; all else applaud and eke frequent them; therefore certainly they are very good recreations, since none but Puritans disaffect them" (797). Placing Puritans at center stage in the climactic scene of his tragedy, Prynne devotes the final pages of the act not only to illustrating that it is a "notorious falshood" that "none but Puritans condemne Stage-plaies" but also to demonstrating, as a consequence, that "Puritans are no such Novellers, or new upstart humorists as the world reputes them" (797–98).

It is this latter charge—that "Puritans are no such Novellers"—that alerts us once again to the end game in which Prynne is engaged. Recall that Charles I's Proclamation of 1626 prohibited "Writing, Preaching, [or] Printing . . . any new inventions, or opinions concerning Religion, then such as are clearly grounded, and warranted by the Doctrine and Discipline of the Church of England, heretofore published, and happily established by authoritie."[105] Designed to quiet theological disputation, the proclamation resulted only in further argumentation as Laudians and Puritans each sought to cast the other as "novellers," that is, as introducing "new inventions" into the doctrine and practices of the church. Framed as such, the final scene thus demands that Prynne rehearse yet again the genealogy of precedents that he has iterated time and again throughout *Histrio-Mastix*—a lineage of writings against the stage running from the primitive church through innumerable councils and synods to countless authors, both Protestant and Popish, foreign and domestic—in order to confer the legitimacy and authority of historical continuity upon the Calvinist program. Unmistakably echoing the proclamation, Prynne thus seeks in this final scene to offer unassailable proof that Puritans are "no other, but the true Saints of God, the undoubted successors of the primitive Church and Christians, whose doctrine, discipline, graces, manners they onely practise and maintaine" (798–99). In the theater of Prynne's tragedy, *Histrio-Mastix* ultimately becomes the scaffold or stage upon which the orthodoxy of the Calvinist saints is constructed and rehearsed and the innovations of the Laudian episcopate are indited and decried.

To buttress his claims and to lend a patriotic fervor to his cause in this final scene, Prynne takes on any adverse intimations of state subversion and deflects them onto his Laudian counterparts, whose Catholic affinities were apt to lay them open to suspicion with the wider public. Noting that Puritans are often construed as "seditious, factious, troublesome, rebellious persons both to state and government" (821), he responds not merely by raising the specter of Catholic insurrection but by citing it as historical precedent. "Alas," he asks, "what powder treasons, *what conspiracies* have these poore Play-condemning Puritans and Precisians hatched against King or State? what rebellions have they raised? what publike uprores have they ever caused from the beginning of reformation till this present? what treacheries, what mutinies are they guilty of, that they are thus condemned, as if they were as bad or worse than *Papists, Priests or Iesuites . . . whose very faith is faction, whose doctrine rebellion, and their practise Treason?*" (825–26). Framed as a series of rhetorical questions, this passage in *Histrio-Mastix* conjures historical memories of the traitorous actions of Guy Fawkes and his Catholic co-conspirators in the failed Gunpowder Plot of 1605. Designed to return a Catholic to the throne of England, the plot left in its wake a traumatized body politic, whose latent fears and anxieties about the persistent threat of Catholic malingering and outright insurgency only deepened. Prynne brings those fears to the surface in this climactic scene by evoking the memory of those who would go so far as to sacrifice the safety and welfare of the entire commonwealth to restore Catholic rule. In so doing, he deliberately casts the Laudians as the heirs to a lineage of Catholic sedition and artfully sets them upon the religious and political fringe.

Casting aspersion upon the Laudian faction is not the end of it, however, as Prynne seeks strategically to close the act not only with a thorough vindication of those whom, he bitterly concedes, the world now "stiles Puritans," but also with a stirring encomium to their piety and patriotism (801). Playing his trump card in this game of rhetorical provocation, he avers, "Blessed be to God, we have heard of no Puritan treasons, insurrections or rebellions in our age; and experience (in despite of scandall and all lying rumours) hath manifested, that these Puritans and Precisians are such persons as both *feare God and honour the King*, though they oppugne the corruptions, sinnes, profannesse, and Popish and Pelagian Errors of the times, with all such factious Innovators, who either broach new heresies and superstitions, or revive olde" (826). It is, of course, all too easy for us to look upon these remarks in hindsight as foreshadowing the events of civil war that would take hold less than ten years later; but at the time, the Puritans had not yet formed themselves into an insurrectionary public. There was, as Prynne's appeal to "experience (in despite of scandall and all lying rumours)" makes clear, no concrete action to which the Laudians could point that could be construed as comparable to the Gunpowder Plot. In Prynne's account, then, the world has been led to conceive of the Puritans erroneously as "factionists and mutineers" as a way to distract from the true threat to both king and church that was unequivocally coincident with the Popish tendencies of Arminian doctrine. Wrongfully persecuted for being "the very best and holiest Christians," they have been "ignominiously intituled" with the name of Puritan or Precisian, a tactic that finds its precedent, he submits, in the "ancient scandall which hath beene alwayes laid upon the choycest Saints of God from age to age" (804, 807, 821). Thus situating Puritans in the long line of Christian martyrs, Prynne makes sure to situate the Laudians, by way of contrast, on the wrong side of history, morality, and religion. "Those who are most violently invective, and maliciously despitefull against Puritans and Precisians, both in their words and actions," he avouches, "are such who are unsound or popishly affected in their religion, or prophane and dissolute in their lives" (804).

In sum, if the Prologue and Chorus have prepared us to look to our place in the body public of the transcendent heavenly realm, then this final scene brings the material reality of the Puritans within the Caroline body politic into sharp relief and appeals to our conscience. Embattled and on the defensive against a shifting religious and political center, Prynne seeks to represent the Puritans as a potentially potent body public, faithful to the church and loyal to the state, but in need of a wider community of support. Addressing us, thus, as "Christian Readers" in the final chorus of Part 1, Prynne beseeches us not only as "[we] tender the glorie of Almighty God" but also as we value "the happinesse and safety both of Church and State" to "abominate and utterly abandon Stage-playes" (829). Having "seene now . . . the severall arguments and Authorities against Stage-playes," we understand in this final moment that we are being called upon not only to renounce the stage but also to abjure the political and religious practices with which it has been associated throughout the text (828). Only then, he submits, "shall you then obtaine the intended benefit, and I myselfe enjoy the much-desired end of these my weake Endeavours, which is no other, but Gods owne glory, your temporall and eternall happinesse, and the Republickes welfare" (83[0]). Invoking, as he has before, the "serious covenant [we] have made to God in baptism," we are reminded one last time of our prior obligation to godliness and the laws of Heaven. In serving "Gods owne glory," we will serve not only the interests of our nation on earth but also, and even more important, our own interests in the kingdom of heaven (829).

Catastrophe

This call is echoed and then compounded by the weight of reciprocal obligation in the Catastrophe, which follows hard upon the conclusion of the five acts that make up the second part. Arriving at the Catastrophe after a somewhat more focused disquisition on the "unlawfull" activities of play-poets, stage-players, and spectators, Prynne claims finally to have exhausted his compendious storehouse of erudition and argumentation. Addressing his readers, he writes, "All then I shall desire of you in recompence of my labour, is but this; that as I have acted my part in oppugning, so you would now play your parts in abominating, in abandoning Stage-playes, without which this Play-refuting Treatise, will doe no good, but hurt unto your soules, by turning sinnes of ignorance, into sinnes of knowledge and rebellion" (995). Having vested us with the knowledge we need to recognize sin, we can no longer plead ignorance. Pyrnne has labored mightily on our behalf so that we might choose to join the body public of good Christians and embrace godliness. We owe an obligation not just to him, however, as the tragedy before us has been played out on the wider stage of the kingdom of heaven. Under the obligations imposed by baptism, we are expected, as a matter of individual conscience, to "play [our] parts" in this providential drama and turn our backs not just on stage plays but also on those who countenance them. Insofar as heavenly prerogatives trump the sovereign powers of temporal government, members of the godly public are thus both invited and expected to denounce and to defy any human law or convention that contravenes God's law. To do otherwise, as he emphasizes in the Catastrophe, is to enter knowingly into the "sinnes of . . . rebellion." Prynne's claims for Puritans as the "*chiefest patriots and propugners of Monarchy, of Princes supremacy*" would appear to extend only so far (826).

In this concluding light, it seems no accident, moreover, that in a final fit of citational pique, Prynne inserts a long excerpt in Latin on the iniquity of stage plays from the Spanish Jesuit, Juan de Mariana's *De rege et regis institutione* (1599). Complemented by a spate of marginal directives and glosses on the text, these passages seem to appear at the end of Prynne's long treatise simply as proof that even "loose Iesuits" who take up the question "so severely censure" the playhouse as to leave little doubt about its sinfulness (1,005). Yet Prynne's selection of this particular text is neither an insignificant nor an innocent one, and it is hard to believe that he would have been unaware of its notoriety. Dedicated to Philip III of Spain, Mariana's treatise was designed, much in the manner of Machiavelli's *The Prince*, to offer a young monarch principles by which to rule the state. It immediately came into disrepute, however, for a series of passages in which, as Harald Ernst Braun explains, Mariana not only "appeared to praise Henry III's assassin Jacque Clement as the 'eternal glory of France'" but also "seemed to combine a doctrine of popular sovereignty with a defence of the right of the private individual to kill not only the usurper of the throne but also the *tyrannus ex parte exercitii* (a legitimate ruler) whose exercise of power marked her or him out as a tyrant." Perhaps even more to the point with respect to powers Prynne claims for his godly public, "Mariana . . . repeatedly assures readers that 'there is no doubt that royal power has its source in the *respublica* which may call the king before the law in specific circumstances, and, if necessary, even deprive him of his principate.'"[106] These passages were widely taken to countenance both royal usurpation and regicide, and immediately following its publication, controversy over the text spread rapidly across the Continent. In an address to Parliament in 1616, James I felt compelled to denounce Mariana "for his blatant violation of the theory of the divine right of kings." Though the passages that Prynne reproduces in the Catastrophe are taken from a different section of Mariana's book, the connotation of his selection seems clear. In punctuating his treatise with an excerpt from a text that, as Braun explains, had become "inseparably connected with radical notions of popular sovereignty and the arbitrary murder of kings," Prynne sent a not too subtle message about the political disposition of the state with respect to the godly body public he represented.[107] In his reckoning, the "prerogative royall of the King of heaven" (102) took precedent over the royal prerogative of kings, and the godly body public was not only empowered by its membership in the transcendent heavenly community but compelled by it to challenge any and all authorities that encroached on the exercise and performance of godliness. Kings and magistrates, ministers and bishops, could all be brought before the law of the kingdom of heaven for judgment. That such claims could be construed as seditious when published was the issue that would be adjudicated in the proceedings instituted against Prynne in Star Chamber. That the trial itself became yet another occasion for each side to cultivate a body public can be seen in the competing manuscript versions of the proceedings that were put into circulation.

Histrio-Mastix on Trial

On the flyleaf of the Bodleian Library's Douce MSS 173, a seventeenth-century record of the proceedings in William Prynne's 1634 Star Chamber trial for seditious libel for the publication of *Histrio-Mastix*, there is a handwritten note that reads, "This MS copy contains a great deal of interesting matter yt is not in the printed copies which have been greatly mutilated and abridged, though they contain some things not in this MS."[108] For any scholar engaged in serious archival research, such an annotation would be likely to raise an eyebrow. At the very least, it suggests that a careful collation of the corresponding documents in both print and manuscript ought to ensue before reaching any conclusions about the nature of this historically significant case. Yet while any number of scholars have been keen to situate Prynne's first Star Chamber trial as a discursive turning point in the run up to the English Civil War—most often identifying it as a pivotal step not only toward

construing words as actions but also toward placing words under suspicion for
seditious intent and holding them actionable as such[109]—only one scholar to
date, Cyndia Clegg, has attended to the potential significance of such an uneven and problematic historical record.[110] As a result, scholars have failed to
acknowledge the extent to which the various print and manuscript records
upon which their arguments are based differ dramatically. Those scholars,
moreover, who have bypassed the manuscript records and who have based
their accounts solely on printed versions of the trial that appeared many years
after the fact, have relied problematically, as our mysterious observer might
point out, on texts which contain "some things" that the manuscripts do not,
while "abridging" or "mutilating" other things that appeared in these sources.

     J. G. A. Pocock has engaged the historiographical questions raised by
multiple and conflicting archival accounts and enjoined us to approach such
texts not merely as self-contained expressions of thought but rather as "verbal
performances" that act as "events" in and of themselves, that is, as "happen-
ings" that take up and modify the language, idioms, and rhetorics of a given
moment in order to give shape to the first contours of an interpretive tradition.[111] Following this methodological framework, our task in taking up the
Prynne manuscripts is at least twofold. First, we must set aside the orthodoxies that have grown up around the Prynne case; and second, we must take up
the texts afresh and contextualize them as distinct "verbal performances"
within a culture where, as Harold Love has demonstrated, "scribal publication
served to define communities of the like-minded."[112] In the discussion below,
then, I will draw our attention back to the moment in which the Prynne case
proceedings circulated in manuscript and explore the extent to which both
the gross and subtle variations in these accounts might have provided for quite
different understandings of the trial.

     Although the Court of Star Chamber had not yet achieved the notorious
status accorded to it in modern mythology, the cases before it, often involving
defendants or plaintiffs from the highest echelons of society, consistently attracted great public interest.[113] All of the parties involved in the Prynne case
would have expected it thus to be the subject of accounts not just in personal
letters but also in the manuscript newsletters that carried reports of important
events from London to other parts of the country. These newsletters, as a
number of historians have demonstrated, played a critical role in the years
leading up to the civil war not only in creating significant networks for the
transmission of news but also in giving shape to, and in licensing the formation of, public opinion at every level of society.[114] Every utterance in Prynne's

Star Chamber trial ought to be examined, then, not just for its resonance in the immediate context of the case but also for its potential rhetorical appeal in the context of larger public realms. Hence, rather than privilege any particular account, I will focus my discussion on the ways in which the various manuscript versions were tailored to appeal to the interests and concerns of differing audiences. On this basis, I will argue, as I have throughout this chapter, that Prynne's 1634 Star Chamber trial provided the occasion, a moment of publicity if you will, for competing political interests not only to vie for public authority and attention but also to cultivate and to shape the understanding of those constituencies—those private bodies public—that would prove so critical to the outcome of the English Revolution at the beginning of the next decade.

The Prynne Case and Its Texts

In accordance with Caroline statutes, *Histrio-Mastix* was duly registered at Stationer's Hall on 16 October 1630 and appeared in print at the end of 1632.[115] Convinced that Prynne had produced a text for which he could finally be held accountable for libel, Laud immediately prohibited sales of the tract and took it for examination both to the king and to the attorney general, William Noy, neither of whom were at first convinced that the contents supported prosecution. Not one to be easily thwarted, Laud tasked Peter Heylyn with drawing up a brief identifying all passages in the work that could be construed as libelous.[116] By the end of January 1633, Laud had succeeded in having Prynne examined both by the secretary of the Star Chamber and by Noy, and by February, Prynne had been arrested and committed to the Tower, where he would remain until he stood trial in February 1634.[117]

As Cyndia Clegg explains, there are at least three accounts of Prynne's trial available in print: in John Rushworth's *Historical Collections* (1680), in *State Trials* (1730), and in S. R. Gardiner's *Documents Relating to the Proceedings Against William Prynne* (1877).[118] Together, these published iterations present us with a printed record that is rife with extensive textual inconsistencies, discrepancies in dates, and widely varying selected omissions. Each printed account is thus patently partial in at least two senses of that word. "None of the accounts" as Clegg notes, "appears to be the official witness to the entire proceedings," and Rushworth's account, upon which the editors of *State Trials* drew for their version, is part of a larger collection that was skewed, as he himself informs the reader, to illustrate "'what unusual Powers of

Judicatory were assumed and exercised in the ménage of Government'"
during the era of Personal Rule.[119] Indeed, as Harold Love has observed of the
miscellanies and printed collections that scholars of seventeenth-century history have come to draw so heavily upon, "It does not take much investigation
to discover that the texts of these printed versions are usually corrupt and
heavily sophisticated, and that they were taken from manuscript copies encountered virtually at random."[120] Gardiner's printed edition, which is actually a transcription taken from a miscellany of law papers, British Library
Additional MSS 11764, appears to follow the pattern described by Love, with
the first section of the folio miscellany composed of "Reports of Several Cases
in the Star Chamber in the Reign of King Charles the First" and the remainder of the volume filled with an array of unrelated legal papers and
discourses.

    While a comparison of the printed accounts can tell us a great deal about
the biases that have influenced the historical representation of the Prynne
trial, we can gain even more insight about the interests that shaped initial
understandings of this event by turning to the manuscript records upon which
those printed volumes are based. Clegg reports that there are four manuscript
versions of the trial that "agree with each other": Bodleian Library, Tanner
MSS 229; British Library Stowe MSS 159; Houghton Library MSS Eng 835;
and Huntington Library HM 80.[121] To this list of congruent texts we can add
Bodleian Library Douce MSS 173.[122] The last three are all individually bound
volumes, with both the Houghton and Huntington copies written in a similar, professional secretary hand and presented in gold-tooled, calfskin-leather
bindings with green silk cloth ties. The first two appear in miscellany collections, and one can only speculate that they might have been copied from, or
with, the other volumes. While there are tremendous differences among these
copies in spelling and punctuation, on the whole they exhibit limited, though
at times interesting, textual variants, with the Douce MSS written in at least
two different hands displaying the most variants from the other four copies.[123]
The professional quality and similarities in pagination of the Huntington and
Houghton copies, as Clegg has noted, suggest that they are "scribal copies
from a common source," a product of what Harold Love would classify as
"entrepreneurial publication."[124] Manuscript books of this quality would have
been produced only for cases where there was enough demand to ensure pub-
lisher profitability, a condition that suggests both the high level of public interest in the Prynne case and the class status of those who took an interest in
and desired copies of the proceedings.

Still, as Clegg points out, "None of these manuscript accounts are transcripts of court proceedings," nor is the greatly divergent account found in the British Library's Additional MSS 11764, which, as already noted, Gardiner transcribed and published and on which the vast majority of scholarly histories of these events have subsequently relied. The most exhaustive account of the trial and what appears to come closest to a complete, though not necessarily official, transcript of the proceedings against Prynne can be found in a manuscript miscellany: MSS Eng 1359, Houghton Library, Harvard University. As noted above, this unique manuscript copy has been missing from the historical record and has only recently been written about by historian Mark Kishlansky, who has concluded that the document "does not simply supplement other surviving accounts; it supplants them."[125]

The records related to the case in Eng 1359 fill 278 pages of the miscellany. Not only does the manuscript include the Information, or the initial bill of charges lodged against Prynne, as well as many other important pretrial documents (petitions, answers, depositions, etc.), it also presents us with a much more detailed record of the speeches made, the evidence cited, and the commentaries offered (Figure 5). In comparison, British Library Additional MSS 11764 and Huntington HM 80 offer severely condensed representations of the case at trial.[126] Frequently, they leave out large sections of text that can be found in Eng 1359. Astoundingly, HM 80 omits the presentation of the prosecution's arguments altogether. Line by line and speech for speech, moreover, the two texts share few common phrasings and little common language either with each other or with Eng 1359. The general gist may often be the same, but the particular language and its inflections vary dramatically. Reading all of the texts side by side, it often seems as if they had been assigned to separate court stenographers who recorded completely different performances at trial. With their profound differences in expression so patently on display, the three texts provide us, as I shall demonstrate below, with an unprecedented opportunity both to gather a more comprehensive sense of the trial proceedings and to see more clearly the ways in which these varying scribal publications attempted to shape events, engage audiences, and cultivate public opinion to differing effect.

In its expansiveness, Eng 1359 allows us not only to produce a much more deeply grounded and subtly textured sense of the moment and its concomitant tensions but also to trace the rhetorical strategies employed by each side to make its case not just before the Court of Star Chamber but just as important, if not more so, before a wider public. In particular, it provides us with a

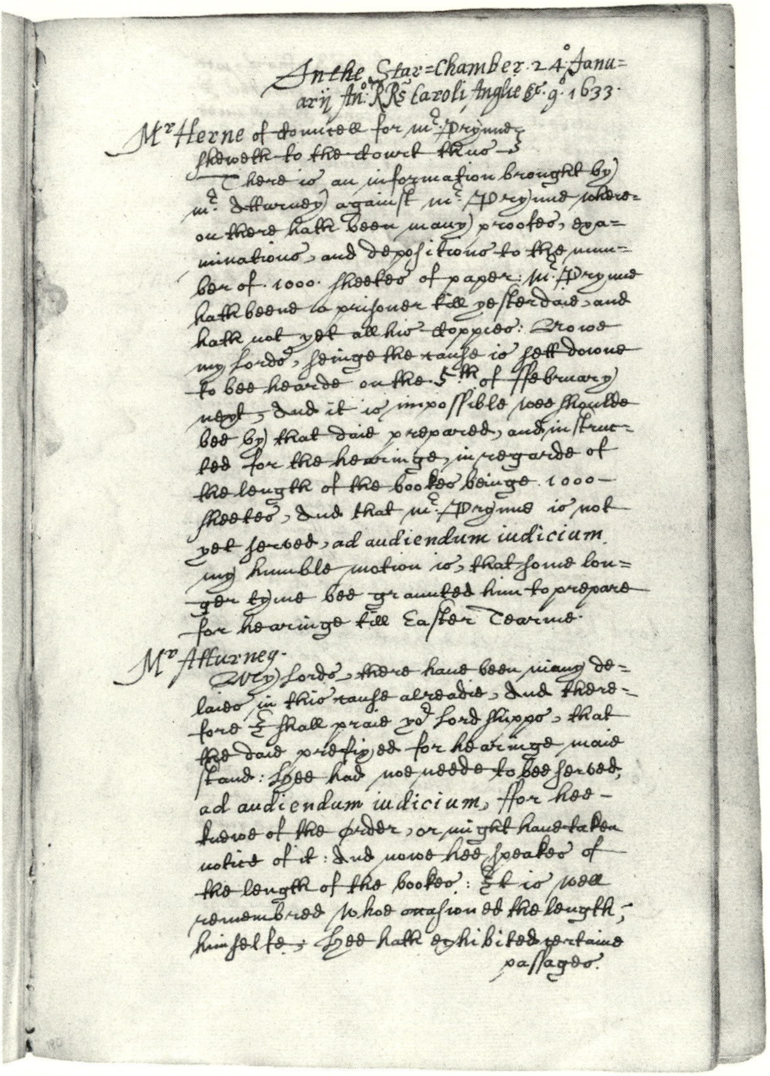

Mr Herne of Councell for mr Prynne
speaketh to the Court thus:—
      There is an information brought by
mr Attorney against mr Prynne wheron
on there hath been many proofes, exa=
minations and depositions to the num=
ber of 1000 sheetes of paper: mr Prynne
hath been a prisoner till yesterday, and
hath not yet all his depposies: Now
my Lords, seeing the cause is sett downe
to bee heard on the 5th of ffebruary
next, and it is impossible wee should
bee by that day prepared, and instruc=
ted for the hearinge, in regarde of
the length of the bookes beinge 1000
sheetes, and that mr Prynne is not
yet forced, ad audiendum iudicium.
my humble mocion is, that some lon=
ger tyme bee granted him to prepare
for hearinge till Easter tearme.

Mr Attorney.
      My Lords, there haue been many de=
laies in this cause alreadie, and there=
fore I shall pray yor Lord shipps, that
the daie prefixed for hearinge maie
stand: Hee had not neede to bee forced,
ad audiendum iudicium, ffor hee—
knewe of the order, or might haue taken
notice of it: And now hee speakes of
the length of the bookes: It is well
remembred who occasion of the length,
himselfe: Hee hath exhibited certaine
passages.

Figure 5. First page, Prynne Star Chamber Trial Proceedings, 1634. MS Eng 1359.
Houghton Library, Harvard University.

much more palpable and finely calibrated sense of the great pains taken by each party in the Prynne case to represent itself as a force of moderation and of the great stress they experienced in working to stage and stage-manage their presentation of interests to a watchful public whose sympathies they sought to cultivate and enlist. By reading each variant text both against this more exhaustive account and against one another, we can demonstrate how, through selective editing, redactions, and paraphrases, as well as omissions of words, lines, entire speeches, and, indeed, of an entire day of proceedings, publishers and copyists not only gave shape to different understandings of the trial in their time but also influenced the historical record today. Thus, where the interest in Eng 1359 lies for Kishlansky in illustrating the "centrality of sedition in the prosecution of Prynne," the interest here will lie instead in elucidating the distinct rhetorical posturings and speech selections of the multiple manuscript versions as redactions of the trial proceedings with differing points of emphasis and appeal for varying and various bodies public.[127]

Preliminaries

That nerves were fraught and tensions riding high, especially over the question of how the trial might be publicized, is immediately on display in Eng 1359 in the breach of decorum that marks the opening moment of the trial on 7 February. Indeed, no sooner has the clerk proclaimed the "Kinges Atturney generall" as "Plaintiff against William Prynne," than Eng 1359, reading almost like a set of stage directions, informs us that the Attorney General, "*here made an interruption*" before all of the defendants, per the protocol, could be announced (201). Sputtering out of turn, Noy warns the members of the court that "Mr. Prynne desireth, that some thinge maie remaine here of Record to shewe, that the Court hath not dealt soe fairelie w[i]th him thus to laie an vniust slaunder vpon the Court" (201). To that end, he informs them, Prynne had sworn out an affidavit just the night before in which he claimed he had not been given enough time to prepare adequately for his defense. Not only does Noy charge Prynne with untruthfulness regarding his claims about the comprehensiveness and timeliness with which the prosecution had disclosed all of the documents it owed to the defense (noting, moreover, that the defense itself and not the prosecution was responsible for the bulk and length of the deposition records), but he also asserts that Prynne had prepared his affidavit in an "undue manner" in order "to laie aspertions vpon the Court" (201v). In light of these considerations, Noy demands that the affidavit "bee taken off the file, and suppressed" (201v). When Prynne's defense counsel counters that Noy had preempted their right to make use of this affidavit as a part of their defense, that Prynne had sworn out this oath on their advice, and that, as such, the affidavit "was not made by Mr. Prynne out of any ill intent" (201v–202), an exasperated Noy only complains once again, "They will haue as much on Record as they can, And other thinges there are which tend to throwe aspersions on the proceedings of the Court" (202).

This exchange, which is missing altogether from HM 80 and sharply reduced to a blunt and not entirely accurate paraphrase in BL 11764, could be said to encapsulate the strategies and parries of prosecution and defense that unfold over the course of the trial. Noy and the government style themselves here as hard pressed but honor bound to respond to every "undue" aspersion, while Prynne and the defense cast themselves as victims of censorship and suppression who intended no "ill intent." Sharply aware of the publicity that would be generated by the trial, each strives to appear as the aggrieved party in the cause: the government, as defender of both the King's Majesty and the Commonwealth; Prynne, as persecuted martyr on behalf of a godly commonwealth. While Noy and the prosecution work at every turn, then, to counter what they frame as Prynne's untruths and half-truths, Prynne, for his part, keeps up his constant prodding, knowing that his constant litany of complaint against the unfair practices of the government and the court, no matter how thinly supported, could only lend an ordure of taint to the proceedings.

That the Attorney General, as representative of the government, appeared to be on the defensive even in the opening moments of the trial suggests both the apprehension felt in certain quarters over the impact of Prynne's combative exhortations and the enormous unease Noy experienced in attempting to constrain himself while managing the government's response in the case. As documented fully only in Eng 1359, moreover, Noy's digressions, outbursts, and asides, provide us with some of our greatest insights into the tensions that suffused the trial and that shaped the government's strategy. Indeed, much like the entry of the artisans who burst upon the scene in Shirley's masque, Noy's inability to constrain himself and to observe the strictures of decorum at the scene of performance acts as a kind of *gestus*, making us aware both of the rhetorical and dramaturgical effects of the carefully crafted prosecutorial strategy and of the ideological interests at stake in this piece of political theater. While the instance above raises the specter of fairness in Prynne's trial— an issue that would be broached again and again by Prynne's team and that has led many historians to question whether Prynne had adequate time to prepare his defense—a second fit of pique, once again recorded only in Eng 1359, alerts us to the strategic configuration of the charges ultimately lodged against Prynne and helps us make better sense of the trajectory of redactions followed in BL 11764.

The fit of pique in question occurs just at the point when the defense counsel, Mr. Holborne, has begun to gather some momentum in calling for passages to be read from *Histrio-Mastix* that might exculpate Prynne of having had any intent of "infus[ing] this dangerous opinion into subiects, That in some Cases there bee lawfull occasions to laie Violent hands vpon Princes" (255). Interrupting Holborne mid-sentence, Noy breaks the decorum of the scene to call out, "It is in *pa* 827, hee hath spent many pages to make men affect the name of puritane: reade it" (257v). Noy's insertion of himself into the scene here is peremptory in almost every sense. Not only does he speak out of turn, but the content of the passage from page 827, duly read out by the clerk and entered into the record supplied by Eng 1359, appears to bear no relation at all to the arguments that were under consideration either here or anywhere else in the trial proceedings. Perhaps even stranger is that rather than pick up where he had been interrupted, Holborne simply whimpers, "My Lords, wee did not call for this to be read," after which another counsel, Mr. Herne, immediately steps in to rest the case for the defense (258). No further arguments are submitted on Prynne's behalf.

While I will have more to say later about the particulars of the defense arguments and their comparative representation in each of the three manuscripts under consideration, we need, first, to apprehend how Noy's outburst betrays the suppressed animus that motivated the proceedings and reveals the careful deliberation with which the government plotted its course against Prynne. The case, as explained above, was initiated by William Laud, whose personal loathing of Prynne had grown out of all proportion. It is not surprising to find, then, that in a brief titled *The Passages Against the King and State in Histrio Mastix*, which bears a remarkable resemblance to that which Peter Heylyn was said to have drawn up at the behest of Laud, the seventh and final heading under which offensive passages from *Histrio-Mastix* are enumerated is designated "Tytles of honour bestowed by Mr. Prynne vpon the Puritans their Innocency Loyaltie & Pietie."[128] Among the passages that were identified and that drew comment under this heading are many that comprise Prynne's defense of Puritan character. Referring, for instance, to Prynne's claims for Puritan loyalty, which I have cited above (*Histrio-Mastix*, pp. 825–26), the cataloger draws the following "Inference": "If there hath beene noe Puritan treasons

Rebellions nor Insurrec[i]ons in theis latter dayes Then haue our Autho[u]rs done them wrong in telling vs of the Rebellion of the Scottish Puriteins against their Queene Mary and the conspiracies of the Gowries father and sonne against K James as alsoe of Hacketts treason here in England."[129] What this passage and the many others found in this section of the document reveal is that in preparing a brief for a case against Prynne, the original compiler was tasked not only with identifying potentially seditious strains in Prynne's tome but also with undermining and rebutting Prynne's strenuous claims for Puritan "Innocency, Loyaltie & Pietie." At a certain point some time later, however, it must have become clear to the government that pursuing this particular line in the case would constitute a strategic misstep; for while all six of the other categories with their correspondent passages, glosses, and inferences can be traced forward fairly consistently from the brief, through the bill of information, and through the passages read out against Prynne in the Court of Star Chamber, the seventh category of allegations disappears from the proceedings. Those categories that remain form the backbone of the prosecution's case and touch only on matters related to the people, the state, and the king's and queen's persons.[130]

The decision to drop the charges related to Puritanism and to pursue only those allegations that bore upon the people and the state, especially as embodied in the persons of the king and queen, suggests that the government was both aware of how resonant Prynne's defense of Puritan character in *Histrio-Mastix* might have been for a wider public audience and wary of the kind of publicity the trial might generate. Rather than play into Prynne's hands by making the interrogation and persecution of Puritans and Puritanism the focal point of its case, the government sought instead, then, to gain a strategic, rhetorical advantage by redirecting attention toward those concerns that might appeal to a wider but apprehensive public: the maintenance of social orderliness and the soundness of established authority. By thus situating itself as a moderating force, the government shifted the discussion away from Prynne's fervent appeal to a godly body public and toward an affecting vision of the sovereign body politic. A comparison of the bill of charges lodged in Eng 1359 and BL 11764 reveals how each manuscript extends this logic of redirection in different ways.

In its pursuit of the charges lodged in the Information against Prynne and his cohorts for "compilinge, printinge, and publishinge of a booke, conteyning a scurrilous, and scandalous libell, or volum of Libells against his sacred Ma[jes]tie, his Roiall Consort the Queenes Ma[jes]tie The Lords of his

Ma[jes]ties Houshoulde, and others, and in generall against the whole State, and his Ma[jes]ties subiects, and people of all sorts," the prosecution in Eng 1359 lays down two separate but complementary lines of argument. With respect, first, to the immediate matter at hand, it casts Prynne as a person of splenetic temper and immoderate judgment, who, as a "longe tyme . . . disturber of the State, a maligner of the government, and a stirrer vpp of the people to disobedience," posed a threat to both the commonweal of the nation and the stability of the state (203). With respect to more abstract concerns, it endeavors, second, to align its interests with those "Subiects" who "haue good cause to blesse God for their happiness" under a magnanimous and gracious monarch who "hath guided his people to all good Conversation as well as by good Lawes, as by his pious example. And yet hath permitted to them their lawfull Recreations and liberties, both in habitt, and otherwise, and this w[i]th moderation . . . to their mutual ioye and Comfort" (202v–203). Simply to press the state case against Prynne appears to be insufficient in Eng 1359 without also providing a rationale for affecting the sovereign government of the king. Under this dispensation, Prynne's principal crimes are that in commending to his readers certain "factious and seditious bookes" by such figures as Leighton and Mariana, he sought to "breed an ill opinion of his Ma[jes]tie and his government in the peoples heartes" and "hath *inferred* that men *maie* . . . laie violent hands vpon Princes" (203–203v, emphases mine).

BL 11764, in comparison, drops all pretense to cultivation and makes no play for the affections of the people. In its condensation of the charges, it presumes a sovereign prerogative over the affections of the people and asserts a governmental jurisdiction under which Prynne is classified as a "malignant man to the State and Government of the Realme, a mover of the people to discontent and sedition" (Gardiner, 1).[131] Prynne does not merely "infer" in BL 11764 that men "may" lay violent hands upon princes; rather he "indeavour[s] to *infuse* an opinnyon into the people that *ytt is lawfull* to laye violent handes vppon Princes" (2, emphases mine). In short, where Eng 1359 exhibits a certain moderating self-consciousness and openness, working not only to press the case against Prynne but also to cultivate public opinion on behalf of the government, BL 11764 proceeds with a blunt emphasis to bring the state charges of sedition ever more closely into focus as foregone conclusions.

It is no surprise to find, then, that historians have often read BL 11764 as a strident document of tyrannical power and subjection. A comparative reading of Eng 1359 forces us, however, to reconsider our perspective on the government's role in the trial. For rather than the assured and strident, we find in

Eng 1359 an ambivalent government that in 1634 still felt compelled both to make a performative pretense to judgment in the balance and to construct a narrative of character in which Prynne's malignity could be weighed on the scales of public opinion against the king's benignity.

The Prosecution

This comparative pattern persists through the prosecution's arguments in Eng 1359 and BL 11764. Following the strategic narrative line of character, Noy's attack on Prynne in Eng 1359 begins with an effort to impeach his integrity and judgment with respect to the publication of *Histrio-Mastix*. Spending a great deal of time at the outset of the trial dissecting Prynne's claims about when he might have composed the volume and how many pages he might have submitted for review and licensing by various authorities, Noy puts on an expert show in the art of examination. He skillfully wields the depositions of other witnesses to catch Prynne out in a variety of contradictions and untruths, and in doing so, he presents Prynne not only as an arrogant and inveterate firebrand, who refused to desist from his efforts to publish *Histrio-Mastix* despite being counseled on a number of occasions to do so, but also as an equivocator who, in his Answers to the Interrogatories, refused on a technicality to acknowledge the book as his own. Making a dramatic show of bringing the actual book physically before the court, Noy artfully directs the testimony of witnesses who could affirm that the book before them was by Prynne and that it was indeed a copy of the text that had been annexed to the Information lodged against him. Confronted by the "physical" evidence of the book, with which Prynne claimed he had been previously denied, the defense counsel could only concede the point, allowing that "Mr. Prynne confesseth, that hee beleeveth the booke annexed to the bill is his, And this hee saith vpon examination since his answeare, w[hi]ch before vpon his oath, hee coulde not saie" (213v).

One might wonder at the selection of this opening point of disputation, but the tactic has at least two significant effects beyond establishing that the book entitled *Histrio-Mastix* was indeed authored by William Prynne. First, it places before the court and the public at large the question of Prynne's integrity, casting him as a disingenuous dissembler and implacable foe, who would take every opportunity to quibble, obstruct, or delay the proceedings. Second, and more significant, it places the book as physical object before our eyes, lending literal and material weight to Noy's defining proposition for the prosecution's case: "The booke is the accuser, The booke is the witnesse, and by the booke hee is to bee đ iudged" (209v).

Thrown down at the outset of the trial, this salvo discursively evokes the spirit of the 1534 statute, 26 Henry VIII, c. 13, which held that all such persons shall be adjudged traitors who "do malicyously whyse will or desyre by wordes or writinge, or by crafte ymagen invent practyse or attempte, any bodely harme to be donne or co[m]mytted to the Kynges moste royall p[er]sonne, the Quenes, or their heires apparaunt . . . or sclaunderously & malyciously publishe & p[ro]nounce, by expresse writinge or wordes, that the Kynge oure Soverayne Lorde shulde be heretyke, scismatike Tiraunt ynfidell or Usurper of the Crowne."[132] Commonly known as the "treason by words" statute, this act, as Rebecca Lemon has explained, "posits the eventfulness of speech, condemning certain types of language as treason out of a fear that they both prompt and constitute violent action."[133] In Noy's rendering, then, the words of *Histrio-Mastix* were to be taken as their own performatives, carrying out actions, transparently, with no supplementary requirement of study or interpretation. The "booke" would be "accuser" and "witnesse," and accordingly, Prynne could be "judged."

Noy effectively deploys the "booke" as "witnesse" to Prynne's crimes in a second sense when he repeatedly construes its physical dimensions as an emblem of Prynne's splenetic excess and immoderation. Amid his review of Prynne's testimony as to the period during which he compiled the materials for *Histrio-Mastix*, Noy snidely observes, for instance, "Soe that, as the man was angrie, soe the bulke grewe" (210v). With this thrust, Noy paints a portrait of a man driven quite literally to great lengths by his own anger. The extravagant "bulke" of Prynne's book becomes an emblem not only of his inability to confine or constrain himself properly but also of the expansive anger that "sufficientlie denotes him" (211). "Take awaie his spleene," Noy sardonically remarks, and you "take awaie his existence" (211).

While spleen accounts in Eng 1359 for the great bulk of *Histrio-Mastix*, it is also what drives Prynne to act without proper regard to rank or station. "My Lords," Noy avers, "Mr. Prynne hath medled w[i]th a businesse not perteyninge to him: There bee two sortes of men, that maie write, or speake against the abuse of Stageplaies, or other abuses: Those that haue a mission, And those that haue a perticuler Commaund, and if such doe exceede the boundes of moderation they maie be regulated, yet are the rather to bee borne with, because they haue either mission, or commaund" (211v–212). The "booke" as "witnesse" thus illustrates Prynne's lack of restraint with respect not only to his social station but also to his proper spheres of professional knowledge and expertise. Characterizing Prynne as among those "laie men" who "interpose, and write of such matters" where they have "noe warrant" and "w[i]thout all moderation" (212), Noy thus lays the groundwork in Eng 1359 for the presentation of a set of charges that will chart, by rank, Prynne's contempt for the structures of order that make the stability of the state possible. Enumerated by degree and rising incrementally from offenses against "people" of "all Rankes & sortes" to magistrates, and from thence to members of the court, the queen's persons, and finally to "his Majesties most sacred person," the charges are organized so that the prosecution appears to be acting on behalf of all members of the body politic who have a stake in an orderly commonweal. In this scheme, Prynne is to be regarded, as the marginal gloss unique to Eng 1359 charges, as one who has "*neither Mission nor Command*" (212).

These kinds of rhetorical thrusts set the tone for the prosecution and shape the narrative presented to both the court and the public in Eng 1359. They are meant to act persuasively, to convince us that Prynne has acted out of order and that insofar as he constitutes a threat to the Commonwealth and the king's person, the state has good reasons to prosecute him for seditious crimes. By comparison, BL 11764 strips the trial account of almost all narrative details related to Prynne's character. The effect of condensation and compression, moreover, is to make Noy's artful examination appear repetitive and disjointed. Before he can build his proofs into an exposition, for instance, it is simply announced in peremptory fashion that Prynne "confesseth" all "to be written by himself without the helpe of any other" (2). This admission of authorship and ownership is repeatedly referenced and serves as an anchor when Noy avouches, in a conspicuously divergent echo of Eng 1359, "The booke is his accuser, and the wittnes agaynste him, beinge the indexe of his minde, and noe doubt but ytt is his booke, and that that booke is his" (2). While BL 11764 retains the first two phrases from Eng 1359 by which the book is construed as "accuser" and "witness," it eliminates all reference to the final act of judgment. Here, the book becomes instead an "indexe" of Prynne's mind, evoking a settled understanding of internalized motive and determined intent and abrogating any necessity for the discerning capacities of juridical deliberation. Though BL 11764 thus preserves the sense of textual transparency that underwrites the prosecution's case, it drops any pretense to the idea of open-ended judgment.

In short, no effort is made in BL 11764 to persuade; judgments are simply pronounced. Though we are told, then, in an echo of Eng 1359, that "ytt appeareth he made the booke as he grewe to be angry, and soe makes ytt swell with anger" (2), the comment is not supported in BL 11764 by a broader narrative of immoderation and indiscretion. Not only does Prynne lack the dimensionality of a character driven by inherent spleen to act against the Commonwealth's interests, there is also no complementary mention of the king's bountiful merits. Without a rationale to support state action, Prynne appears to be the victim of a tyrannical government whose only intent is to assert the magisterial force of its own power, possession, and prerogative. Any trace of the counternarrative of solicitude that might linger in the accusation that Prynne conspires "to withdrawe the people's affection from the Kinge and Governmente" is thus quickly eclipsed in BL 11764 by a move to summary judgment: in making men "beleeve what he saith, the consequences must nedes be soe" (3). What Eng 1359 only circumspectly implies, BL 11764 audaciously declares: "His booke is totally fraught with schisme and sedicion" (3).

As the case turns toward the "proof" stage, during which members of the prosecution team call in turn for the recitation of passages from *Histrio-Mastix* to support the charges lodged in the Information, two distinct images are impressed upon us again and again. Where Eng 1359 offers us a complex portrait of Prynne as a splenetic, immoderate, and pathetic figure, BL 11764 settles on the simple image of a seditious subject. Thus, for example, where BL 11764 launches almost without preamble into a recitation of passages to illustrate the "scandall" rendered by Prynne "agaynst the whole Kingdome in general, the gentry, and the other sorte" (4), Eng 1359 offers us both a preamble and an overview by Mr. Mason in which he expatiates at great length on Prynne's digressions from his ostensible subject—stage plays—to "thinges of a farr different nature" (216v). The "booke," here, with its repeated discussions of frizzled hair, dancing, drinking, and any number of other pastimes, acts once again as "witnesse" to Prynne's inability to confine or to constrain himself. The great size of *Histrio-Mastix*, due in large part to these constant digressions, again becomes an emblem of his excess and immoderation. Indeed, as Mr. Mason "dillegentlie" notes in a side comment that is entirely missing from BL 11764, so driven is Prynne in his maniacal pursuit that he fails to notice that "in this booke, hee hath vouched himselfe above .500. tymes" (219). Only in Eng 1359, then, are Prynne's "vnchristian Censures vpon all men w[i]thout distinction, or difference" (216v) and his absolute "want of Charitie" (218) toward others matched in their extremity by his singular regard for himself.

By omitting Mason's framing argument, BL 11764 eliminates the portrait of narcissistic immoderation that influences our engagement with Prynne in Eng 1359. Instead, BL 11764 concentrates its focus exclusively on illustrating

Prynne's seditious guilt. This difference in emphasis becomes all the more apparent when we turn to Mr. Recorder's section of the prosecution's case. Here, in a striking departure from its usual practice of cutting and compressing, BL 11764 actually includes a number of more extensive passages from and commentaries on *Histrio-Mastix*. For example, where the reading of a passage is cut short in Eng 1359, omitting a critical portion of the text in which Prynne writes that the depravity of stage plays "should cause us all in generall and eache in particular, as we either tender the publicque or our own private well-fare" to cry for "wrathe and vengeance" (6), BL 11764 not only includes those potentially incriminating lines but also offers a censuring comment not found in Eng 1359: "that he maye well meane to instructe the people to arme themselves against the State to effect it" (6). For BL 11764, then, the case against Prynne is open and shut; his expressions on the page constitute a form of seditious rebellion. Thus, at the next juncture in this section, where Eng 1359 only writes, "This is plaine English (my Lords) and setteth forth the Scandall against the governors, and government more fullie" (223), BL 11764 offers, "This needes noe exposicion, for he speaketh with open mouthe against the State" (6).

As the charges mount in rank and BL 11764 continues to pursue a single-minded course, expatiating only, as above, on "those places of this booke, which do traduce the governmente of the kingdom" (5), Eng 1359 continues to pursue a more complex narrative, braiding together a recital of the ill effects of Prynne's splenetic self-regard with an account of the affections that bind a body politic. Eng 1359 moves, then, to indict Prynne not merely for "traducing" the government but more specifically for alienating the affections of the king's subjects, that is, for writing a book which "attempts to detract from Governors, as knowing the people will not heartilie affect the government, and State w[hi]ch they see soe blemished" (222). In this rendering, Prynne's slanders upon the government rise to the level of seditious libel insofar as they "detract" from the affection that the "people" feel for the state. As the prosecutors take that concept forward in Eng 1359, tracing the perilous stakes by rank until the charges "falleth vpon the Kinge," Prynne's words are found repeatedly to have the effect of "draw[ing] men into dislike of his Ma[jes]ties person, and government" (231).

Having built a narrative of affection for the king and queen over the course of the prosecution's presentations, Noy takes care as well in Eng 1359 to associate Prynne over and over again in this final section with the precipitous murders of princes, emperors, and kings. Through the prodigious recitation of passages from *Histrio-Mastix*, many of which have been excised from BL 11764, he seeks both to demonstrate how Prynne's spleen leads him to embrace an arbitrary kind of justice and to illustrate how withdrawals of affection from the king, such as that advocated by Prynne, can lead to a state of anarchy. Finding his most effective line of attack against one so invested in legal procedures as Prynne, Noy opines in his summation:

> What maie bee saide more pernitious, I do not knowe, In this folio
> hee tells you of Nero, and diuers Emperours, and Princes that were
> made awaie, and that by those whoe did it to vindicate their Nobel
> fame, and honnour . . . to teach the people as if there were a iust
> occasion for men to laie their violent hands vpon Princes: If this
> were soe, Then Princes were of all men in most danger. . . . It
> woulde be a strange Kinde of Iustice to beginne w[i]th Execution:
> whereas in the least causes there are legall proceedings, onlie against
> Princes there must bee execution in the first place w[i]th out any
> Iudgment. (236)

In Noy's account, Prynne advocates in *Histrio-Mastix* for a "strange Kinde of Iustice," setting aside the right of due process that he so vociferously demanded for himself in favor of the summary execution of kings. Abrogating the rule of law, he would plunge the commonwealth into a state of anomie "w[i]th out any Iudgment."

While BL 11764 includes a compressed version of the first part of the passage above, it omits this crucial second part as well as Noy's subsequent reflections on the rule of law and the course of judgment: "But in his answeare hee saith, hee meant not any harme, and is sorrie his intentions shoulde bee soe mistaken, and woulde bee his own expositor; Naie, when his words are gone out, the wordes remaine his, and the exposition is anothers: yo[u]r Lordshipps are Iudges nowe of his wordes" (236v). In the representation of the prosecution in Eng 1359, then, Prynne is not simply subjected to the law as he is in BL 11764; rather he is represented as a subject before the law who, if he seeks to presume all of the rights and prerogatives afforded to him, must also assume the responsibilities and obligations required of him. As a matter of both law and right, Noy submits in Eng 1359, Prynne must own his words and leave the "exposition" to others.

In sum, to read BL 11764, a text that cuts away the dual narratives of character and affection that distinguish Eng 1359, is to encounter a document in which the prosecution appears to experience no compunction or self-consciousness in the presentation of its case. No effort is made either to solicit or to engage public opinion; the raw assertion of government powers and sovereign prerogatives is both assumed and performed. To read Eng 1359, on the other hand, is to engage a record in which the solicitude of the prosecution is writ large and in which the burden of presenting a compelling narrative of government forbearance in the face of a splenetic and immoderate foe is anxiously borne. To be clear, I am not suggesting that the "fix" was not in against Prynne from the get-go; indeed, the outcome of the trial was never in question. But what I am arguing is that just as Prynne took care in *Histrio-Mastix* to appeal to and to cultivate a godly body public, so too did the government take care to provide a rationale for its prosecution of Prynne to which a wider public might attach itself. While these efforts are obscured by the partial record of BL 11764 upon which so many historians have relied, they are readily apparent in the lengthier and more comprehensive trial account provided by Eng 1359. The prosecution in Eng 1359 clearly understood that as much as it was appealing for judgment in the Court of Star Chamber, it was also performing before a court of public opinion whose members might require a more persuasive and compelling narrative line. When we turn to an examination of the defense in Prynne's trial, the argument that BL 11764 sharpens the tyrannous edge of the government's case against Prynne becomes all the more persuasive, especially when we juxtapose it with HM 80, which appears to work, in contrast, toward moderating the severity of the case.

The Defense

As in any case at trial, the entrance of the defense onto the scene provides an occasion to redirect the court's attention and scrutiny, to draw an alternative character portrait, and to offer a competing narrative of intent. In Eng 1359, the defense focuses its energies on the question of intent, not only, that is, on Prynne's motives in inscribing *Histrio-Mastix* but also on the government's intentions in construing his words. If Prynne was to be judged "by the book," as prosecution counsel might hold, then the defense sought to draw attention to the standards and procedures that might be applied in the interpretation of those words. Thus, where the prosecution subtly evoked the "treason by words" statute in order to heighten the severity of Prynne's alleged crime, the defense draws attention to the posture that had to be assumed by the sovereign in order to apply that statute. As Rebecca Lemon has pointed out,

"Crises of treason in the early modern period were really crises of sovereignty, not simply because the monarch suffered a violent threat but more frequently because the monarch's response raised questions about the rights and prerogatives of sovereignty itself."[134] Though the defense counsel in Prynne's case does not go so far as to challenge outright the prerogative of the sovereign to construe Prynne's words, it does raise questions about the vindictive spirit with which the government had chosen to do so and about whether, by virtue of its prerogative, the government ought rather to give its subjects the benefit of the doubt. In this respect, Annabel Patterson has elucidated the Prynne case as "paradigmatic" insofar as it raised questions "about how the state functioned as a 'reader' of texts, about the role and status of ambiguity in the reading process."[135] Indeed, as is made even clearer in Eng 1359, the defense tactic was to introduce ambiguity into the reading process where the prosecution had asserted certainty, to concede that while Prynne's words might be subjected to the severest possible construction, the judges had it within their power to apply mercy and choose to read otherwise.

Accordingly, Mr. Holborne opens the defense in Eng 1359 with the strategic submission that "Mr. Prynne humblie casts himselfe at the feete of his Ma[jes]tie and the Court" (242). Conceding, on the one hand, that while Prynne "confesseth . . . that in some things his wordes doe out-reach his intentions by his verie ill expressions: Hee confesseth that his words maie prove an occasion of scandall as hath been charged, And that by an easie interpretation some dangerous opinions maie bee infused into his Ma[jes]ties subiects as hath been noted"; Holborne still maintains, on the other hand, that "when nothinge is charged by the information but inferences out of the whole booke in generall, w[hi]ch must arise out of his intentions, his hearte beinge free of all malevolence, did not giue him notice of these perticulars as they are nowe pressed" (242). In his efforts either to exonerate Prynne or, at the very least, to extenuate his crimes, Holborne strategically casts the government's case under the subjunctive: Prynne's words "maie prove an occasion for scandall" and "dangerous opinions maie be infused into his Ma[jes]ties subiects," but only if the judges uphold the government's superficial or "easie interpretation" to the exclusion of any stronger test of meaning such as a search for the "intentions" that lodge in a man's "hearte." "If it shoulde soe appeare, that his intentions were faire, and honest, though foule and guiltie, in their expressions," Holborne holds that the judges ought to consider his "weake Estate" and so "mittigate the Rigour of that sentence" (243). Under the dispensation mapped by Holborne in these opening remarks and echoed by each member of the defense counsel thereafter, Prynne is neither wholly innocent nor entirely guilty. Admittedly, he has penned the words and published the text in question, but what that text might be taken to mean and what effects it might be said to have are left to the court's discretion.

Placing the authority of the court under even greater scrutiny, Holborne notes not only that "[Prynne] neuer endeavoured to publish this booke but by the approbation of those that had Authoritie in that kinde. . . . Soe that the Ecclesiasticall powers haue iudged of the matter, and manner, And by their license implie, that they finde nothinge in the booke contrarie to Religion and good manners," but also that "hee conceiueth this booke doth differ from all bookes that were euer brought into this Court: ffor there were neuer any brought here, but those that were vnlicensed, and that had some thinge else in them deservinge the Consideration of this Court" (245). If Prynne had harbored ill intentions, Holborne points out, "Hee woulde surelie haue put forth the booke in another waie" (245v), that is, he would either have had the text published overseas or in secret and without license. Indeed, "if his hearte had been guiltie of these foul Crymes laide against him," he certainly would not have placed his name on the title page or distributed it to men of Knowne integritie," including "Mr. Atturney . . . whose dutie it was w[i]th out more perticular commaund to put it in prosecution" (245v).

Though the defense efforts to cast Prynne as a completely open and ingenuous actor ought to be viewed with some skepticism, Holborne's tactics call attention to the aberration of calling in a licensed book for prosecution in Star Chamber and place under suspicion the government's intentions in targeting Prynne for indictment. Despite any animus that any member of the court might harbor toward Prynne, the questions before them were whether the contents of the book "had some thinge else in them deservinge the Consideration of this Court" and why, if there was anything "deservinge the Consideration," Noy had to be prompted by other authorities to move against Prynne and his text. Again and again, then, Holborne focuses attention not just on Prynne's intentions in publishing *Histrio-Mastix* but also on both the government's intentions in prosecuting him and the court's powers in pronouncing sentence upon him. Contending "that all the charges laide on him for foule intentions are but inferences drawne from the booke, and Consequents, many of them, and most of them beinge but probabilities and presumptions" (246), Holborne cuts away at the ground upon which the case stands and implores the court, "w[i]th a mercifull eie reflect vpon him, in giuinge the Sentence" (243).

While Holborne subsequently takes it upon himself to acquit Prynne of the charges of equivocation and perjury, he leaves it to his co-counsel Atkins both to examine the government's methods in interpreting specific passages and to draw a more moderate portrait of Prynne's character. In opening his remarks, Atkins explains that he has been charged not with "any matter of defence, nor matter of iustification" but rather with elucidating "the truth of his reall intentions in some thinges that by the ingenuytie, and eloquence of those Gentlemen on the other side haue receiued that exposition w[hi]ch hee professeth was not part of his intention" (248). Deliberately invoking terms that reference a rhetorical discourse of courtier's tricks, Atkins plays up Prynne's common status and intimates that only those with scheming imaginations could draw the kinds of analogies of which Prynne stood accused. He then works his way methodically through a series of passages that had been recited by the prosecution to illustrate how each one might have been interpreted otherwise either as "relative" and not "positive" expressions or as citations read out of context. If Prynne had truly intended harm to the government and the king, Atkins maintains, it would not have required so much "ingenuytie" or "eloquence" to wrench his words into criminal acts.

In the "conclusion of [his] Apologie for him," Atkins begs that Prynne might lay "fast holde on the Rocke of the Kings favour, and on the mercie, and Compassion of this Court" (249v) and designs an affecting portrait of Prynne to elicit that indulgence:

What his intentions were is onelie knowne to his owne hearte: What his expressions are they haue been laide open, and made knowne to yo[u]r Lordshipps: My Lords, I cannot condemne his hearte, I knowe it not, I cannot search into it, and I will not excuse his penn: Onelie I desire leave to protest thus much, That hauinge knowne him longe in the societie where hee liues, I maie saie in respect of his waies, and actions, exceptinge in the matter of his writinges, That in respect of his Conversation, his wordes, and actions haue not been factious, nor seditious excludinge this matter of publishinge this booke. . . . I maie Compare him in respect of his Contemplation to that Astronomer, whoe gazinge soe much vpon the starrs did not regard his feete, but suffering them to slide hee fell backward into a deepe pitt: Soe the eies of this Gentlemans mindes were soe fixed vpon the seriousnesse of this subiect, that hee forgott to looke downe to his hand that guided his penn, and soe erringe hee is nowe fallen vnder yo[u]r Lordshipps Censure. (249v–250)

Atkins paints a rather poignant portrait of Prynne as a type of socially inept philosopher. Having known him professionally for many years as a member of the Society of Lincoln's Inn, not only can he vouch personally for Prynne's character, but he can also affirm that he has never seen any sign of factiousness in "respect of his waies, and actions." Indeed, he offers Prynne as a kind of parable for error committed innocently. Like the Astronomer who falls into the pit for gazing so intently at the stars, or, as Atkins goes on to suggest, like the "*ovem perditam*" (lost sheep), Prynne is a lost soul, who requires only the light censure of the judges to "bee brought home againe" safely into the fold (250). By this mode of persuasion, Atkins situates the judges as Christ-like saviors, whose merciful judgment could only set a right example and vindicate the wisdom and good intentions of the court.

In this manner, the defense in Eng 1359 provides a powerful counter-weight to the portrait and narrative offered by the prosecution. If Prynne's "intent" is to be placed under suspicion, then so too ought the government's motives to be interrogated. If he is to be judged by his "book," then his words ought to be opened to a variety of interpretations. If his character is to be the subject of scrutiny, then those who know him personally and professionally ought to be able to bear witness to his measured conduct. While all of these arguments may not have affected the outcome of the case in the Court of Star Chamber, they carried the potential both to secure a place of favor in the court of public opinion and to influence the perception of Prynne going forward. The disparities in representation that distinguish BL 11764 and HM 80 not just from Eng 1359 but also from each other reveal even more distinctly the efforts to cultivate competing bodies public.

In the radically reduced versions of the trial offered by both BL 11764 and HM 80, the defense emphasis on "intentions"—with the word repeated over and over again in the opening sections as a kind of echo to conscience—is at first played down. Indeed, the word itself is quite literally written out of both texts by its complete omission from Holborne's initial presentation. Yet where HM 80 picks up on the matter of "intention" in Atkins's examination, BL 11764 still defers, preserving a reference or two only to Prynne's "heart." This might seem insignificant in the general scheme of things, except that where HM 80 not only retains but also embellishes all of those moments in Eng 1359 when Atkins advocates passionately for his client, BL 11764 excises them. Thus, HM 80 not only recites the parable of the astronomer, which is missing in BL 11764; it also supplements that tale by making explicit the implicit analogy in Eng 1359 of the Judges to Christ, imploring on Prynne's behalf, "Soe by ye wonted Charitie bring him to the fold againe; and that as at this tyme you are Assembled to execute Justice Soe that you would in this particular imitate him who hath mercie aswell as Judgment" (HM 80, ff. 6–6v). In a like spirit, while both texts also take up (in reduced form) Holborne's deliverance of Prynne from the charges of equivocation and perjury, only HM 80 concludes this section, in the manner of Eng 1359, with Holborne's fervent wish "that I could in all thinges else cleere his Innocencie as in theis thinges" (HM 80, ff. 3). To be sure, these are small discrepancies; but when compounded with the differential tenor in paraphrase, they intimate the ways in which HM 80 strives to convey the adequacy and passion of Prynne's defense while BL 11764 projects a representation of it as perfunctory and even maladroit. To get a stronger sense of how they each sought to elicit and engage public opinion, we need to turn more particularly to the large portions of the defense that the one includes and the other omits.

There are two major divergences of this kind. The first occurs immediately after Atkins's presentation, when Mr. Herne steps forward as reluctant counsel on Prynne's behalf only in Eng 1359 and BL 11764. The second occurs when Holborne returns to the scene only in Eng 1359 and HM 80 to offer an extensive review and rebuttal of the passages and interpretations put forward by the prosecution. Only Eng 1359 includes both sections of the defense, with Holborne following upon the heels of Herne.

As elaborated fully in Eng 1359, Herne begins his presentation by registering a complaint about the "exceedinge greate advantage" enjoyed by the prosecution in terms of time, material resources, and authority (250v). After beseeching the court "to looke vpon the intentions of Prynne's heart," he goes on in cursory fashion to urge the court to look no further than Prynne's own answer for proof, "(seeinge himself hath sworne it)," that he did not "intend" to offend and begs the court to allow Prynne "to stand before you, rather as negligent of greate dutie soe unadvisedlie to expose to scandall the Kinge, Queene, and State wherein hee liues" (251v–252). Declining to engage in any further dispute over the proofs offered by the prosecution, Herne refers again to Prynne's declarations under oath of "his devotion to the Kinge, Queene, and State" (252), and in an astonishing echo of the slavish encomium upon the queen that had been offered earlier by her Attorney General, Sir John Finch, Herne intones, "As the Queenes Ma[jes]tie is above all other women in the eie of the lawe as a pearle of great price, soe I hope this will excuse him in some thinge: ffor it is a rule that generalls doe not winde in, and include euerie perticular person, much lesse the Queene" (252). After a few more fleeting remarks on the charges laid at Prynne's door, Herne concludes, "I shal saie noe more; ffor as it is o[u]r dutie to speake for o[u]r Clyents, soe it is not o[u]r dutie to forfeit o[u]r discreation for any man" (252v).

If Herne's reluctance to commit himself beyond the most basic sense of professional propriety was not damaging enough to Prynne's case in Eng 1359, BL 11764 preserves only enough of Herne's presentation to make it that much more damning. Indeed, the only sentence reproduced in like spirit in BL 11764 is the final self-serving one: "As hee oweth him servyce as a counsell, hee oweth himself that duetye not to forfeyte his discretion for a clyent" (Gardiner, 15). The remainder of Herne's presentation is reduced to two short points, in both of which he declines to speak for Prynne and directs the court instead to Prynne's answer and examination. All of the references to error and negligence that might constitute some form of a defense have been removed, and the lines of praise for the queen have also disappeared entirely from the text. In sum, if the text of Eng 1359 leaves room to make allowances for Herne's conduct and to construe his remarks as part of a defense tactic, the edited selections in BL 11764 highlight in boldface his utter failure to act as a proper advocate for Prynne.

It could be argued that I am reading too much into this selective editing, but only if we ignore the reversal of textual practice that takes place when we turn to the next section of Eng 1359. Here BL 11764 not only takes care to compound Herne's failures as defense counsel, it also does away altogether with Holborne's dexterous refutation of the prosecution's interpretations of Prynne's words. In sharp contrast, HM 80 cuts Herne's lackluster performance and features Holborne's impassioned defense. Even stranger, HM 80, following its usual pattern of cutting and pasting, takes some of the more arguable points from Herne's presentation and incorporates them where they can be more effective in Holborne's already expansive disputations, a practice that lends great credence to the argument that the editors had access to the full text but that in producing their edition, they excerpted selectively from the sections in order to engage particular interests and elicit certain responses.[136]

As wholly represented only in Eng 1359, Holborne takes care to reintroduce his earlier emphasis on the "intentions" of both Prynne and his judges before proceeding methodically to offer rival interpretations of the passages from *Histrio-Mastix* that had been construed by the prosecution as proof of Prynne's crimes. Citing Prynne's desire "that his intentions maie bee a little cleared" (252v) and appealing to the judges "to accept of the best interpretation of his wordes" (253), Holborne illustrates, sometimes in meticulous detail, how Prynne's words had been taken out of context, misapplied, or twisted altogether to suit the prosecution's interests. Indeed, so passionate is Holborne in his defense here that he commits a fateful misstep by drawing attention to the venue and pointing out that "if Mr. Prynne were guiltie of this, this Court were two mercifull to him to question him" (255). While the judges would ultimately turn Holborne's words to exemplify the great forbearance of the government in charging Prynne with seditious libel in Star Chamber rather than with treason in a common law court, at this point in the proceedings, Holborne's persuasions must have been perceived as quite effective. Indeed, Noy became so discomfited that he was moved, as noted earlier, to disrupt the scene by blurting out references to Prynne's Puritan affiliations.

While HM 80 does not include the full complement of Holborne's remarks, it does retain enough of them to convey an impassioned and compelling defense on Prynne's behalf. Among its omissions, HM 80 deletes Holborne's misstep as well as Noy's outburst and Herne's subsequent interdiction. Holborne appears, instead, to rest the case for the defense without interruption. Thus, where BL 11764 truncates Prynne's defense to such an extent that it appears almost incompetent, HM 80 takes care selectively to retain enough of the text from Eng 1359 to ensure an estimable representation of Prynne's defense counsel.

This divergence in textual representations is punctuated one last time before sentencing when HM 80 retains parts of Noy's rebuttal and BL 11764 excises it altogether. In Eng 1359, Noy's speech is filled not only with attempts to controvert particular defense points—he takes care, for instance, to insist that when he received a copy of Prynne's *Histrio-Mastix*, he moved with all due expediency to bring him in for examination—but also with renewed efforts to discredit Prynne's character and to incriminate his purportedly innocent motives. In an echo of his opening assertion, Noy maintains, in response to Herne, "When the booke is published, and a mans words are out, the interpretation is not his owne: Hee maie not declare his intentions, nor bee witnesse of them, it is soe in other cases of Cryme: The reason is, Hee that hath Committed a boulde cryme, and hath soe little Conscience as to Committ an offence of that qualitie, men beleeuve not what hee saith afterwards, ffor he hath done ill in another Kinde" (265v). Under settled principles of law that, as Noy takes great care to point out, Prynne in his professional capacities as a lawyer should be aware of, he could not serve as witness to his own character in a matter of words any more than he could in a matter of action. In this case, moreover, the words constituted the offense, and Prynne's efforts to clear his intentions were tantamount to disclaiming his own words. Playing on the widely held prejudices associated with that kind of equivocation, Noy impeaches Prynne's efforts to justify the Puritans by closing, "They will not goe in the same waie w[i]th the Iesuites, but whosoeuver will reade both one side, and the other, will finde their princples right ones: They goe in a diverse waie, but to one ende" (267v). For commending "*Mariana* the Iesuite, whoe teacheth more of this doctrine then any man doth," Prynne, despite all disclaimers to the contrary, was to be understood as having published a "doctrine of Rebellion" (267v).

Although HM 80 greatly condenses Noy's speech, it takes great care both to retain those parts of his address that cast Prynne as a perjurer and equivocator and to add a few embellishments that flatter and bolster the state. Remarkably, moreover, and despite the fact that the manuscript had cut Herne's perfunctory appearance from the text, HM 80 preserves Noy's reference to Herne's defense. Not only, then, does Noy still avouch, though in somewhat truncated terms here, "that when a man hath done ill, he is not to bee beleived," but he also presses, in an eerie echo not of the passage from Eng 1359 immediately above but rather of his opening statement in Eng 1359 described much earlier, that "by that Booke w[hi]ch Mr. Prinne gave the Attornie is he nowe to be Iudged by this Courte" (15v–16). Of Prynne's efforts to cast aspersions upon the state for lavishing resources on entertainments during these "late penurious tymes," HM 80 embellishes on Eng 1359 to offer that "there was never State more free or more plentifull then this" (17).

The condensations and embellishments of HM 80 and the extreme economy of BL 11764 bring the contrasts between these two texts into sharp focus. For where BL 11764 cuts away at those elements in Eng 1359 that suggest the competency of Prynne's defense and the judiciousness of his indictment, HM 80 works overtime to enhance those representations. Similarly, where BL 11764 gives us every reason to doubt the probity of the prosecution's case and denies Noy the opportunity to offer his pointed rebuttal, HM 80 refuses even to risk placing the prosecution and its arguable weaknesses on display, relying instead on Noy's succinct rebuttal to convey its strength. Noy's rebuttal thus supplies just enough of the prosecution's case to demonstrate its sufficiency without allowing for it to be juxtaposed with and weighed too closely against the defense arguments. By ceding center stage to the defense, HM 80 is able, moreover, to suggest both that Prynne had enough time to prepare his case and that he received exemplary representation from his counsel. This orientation of the case makes sense when we recall that HM 80 was produced in a fine scribal edition meant to appeal to a consumer of some means, who would add the text to an already considerable library and who would be more likely than not to have a vested interest in the probity and stability of the state. This surmise is borne out all the more convincingly when we turn to sentencing in the trial and engage in the same kind of comparative study. Indeed, as we move toward the completion of our analysis of how the compilers of these texts used selected editing to solicit selective bodies public, it will be worth bearing in mind that HM 80 was clearly the most widely circulated text among the three variants and was surely the only scribal version of the trial that was produced in multiple copies for sale. That HM 80 plays up the interests of the king and queen, retaining and embellishing various encomiums to the royal couple and enhancing each royalist rationale where BL 11764 strips them away, gives us substantial reason to reevaluate how Prynne's 1634 trial might have been perceived in its time by the wider public.

Sentencing

Composed as it was of the members of the King's Privy Council as well as by the chief justices of the King's Bench and Common Pleas Courts, the guilty verdict in Prynne's trial came as no surprise. The severity of the punishment, however, gave some pause, especially since, as Clegg has noted, the censure meted out by the judges in Prynne's case exceeded the bill of charges, moving beyond *Scandalum magnatum* and seditious libel to touch on outright sedition and even treason.[137] Led by Francis Cottington, the Chancellor of Exchequer, the sentencing speeches of the judges were dominated by three emphases. Drawing first on the character portrait offered by the prosecution, the judges took great care to frame Prynne as a person of bad faith, who, having wandered from his profession, made himself into an instrument of the devil. Second, picking up the gauntlet so imprudently thrown down by defense council Holborne, they portrayed their sentence and the court itself as merciful for one whose crimes were tantamount to treason. And third, noting the proliferation and influence of print, they fretted over how their harsh judgments might be received, represented, and publicized in the wider court of public opinion. Following the pattern set in the prosecution and defense, the three manuscripts exhibit only a rough correspondence through the sentencing speeches. Accordingly, as BL 11764 and HM 80 either converge with, or diverge from, both each other and Eng 1359, two distinct perspectives emerge on such issues as sovereignty and the subject, virtue and vice in the body politic, and religious practice and ecclesiastical authority.

The prerogatives of the state and the duties of subjects under the law are laid out most particularly in Eng 1359 by Sir Thomas Richardson, the Lord Chief Justice of His Majesty's Court of King's Bench. Richardson opens his speech by observing, "the greate wise, and necessarie care of this State about writinge and printinge of bookes, to suppresse, and punish mens Enormities," a care he suggests, "had neede especiallie to bee looked too in this age when . . . noe man thinkes himself any bodie vnlesse hee bee in print" (277). Under this dispensation, he declares *Histrio-Mastix* a "*Monstrum, horrendum* . . . a most huge, horrible, mishapen monster," whose author had made himself into the instrument not merely of the devil but also of many other hands and authors. Having followed his peers both in acknowledging the influence of print and in vilifying Prynne and his book, Richardson then distinguishes his sentence by engaging in an exposition of particular points of law and ideology.

Of all the charges laid against Prynne, that of "seditious Libell" appeared to him as the most problematic. "This pointe of sedition is the onlie pointe that troubles mee," he avouched, "For I knowe, and beleeue, And it is a cer-taine truth, That the hearts of the people of the Kings Subiects is the Kings greatest treasure. . . . Nowe for any man Cunningly to insinuate into the heartes of the people, And to bringe the Kinge into an ill opinion w[i]th his subiects; This hath been found, and adiudged Treason in the Kings Bench, And if hee were there Arraigned before mee, I shoulde haue given another Iudgment then heere in this place" (279). Bringing the authority of his posi-tion and experience on the bench to bear on the trial, Richardson leaves no room to doubt that Prynne has committed a crime against the Crown by ef-fecting a division of the king from his people and that only the constraints of venue prevented him from imposing an appropriate sentence of death for this commission of treason.[138] Other members of the court would pick up on this point to cast their sentence in a merciful light, but Richardson's interest at this point lies in articulating the principles of sovereignty at stake and in sham-ing Prynne, as an admitted member to the bar, for his failure both to compre-hend the rule of law and to apprehend the full extent of his own crimes.

Citing passages from *Histrio-Mastix* that depict the assassination of the Emperor Nero, Richardson inveighs, "Why Mr. Prynne, though *Nero* were a wicke [sic] Prince, Is it the dutie of his Subiects by violence to make him awaie? Noe, noe *preces et lacrimae*, this is the Remedie, these are the onlie weapons they must use, not to inspire these worthy Romans to rise vpp against him. . . . It is high treason for any man to stirr vpp the Kings subiects to make him awaie" (279v). Articulating what J. P. Sommerville has termed "the most commonly expressed political principle in early Stuart England," Richardson espouses, "the doctrine that subjects could never justifiably use force against the king."[139] For Richardson, the duty of passive obedience and submission to the sovereign must be upheld by all subjects at all times and under all conditions. Prayers and tears ought to be the remedies of last resort; outright violence was strictly prohibited.

Having laid down a governing principle of absolutist ideology, Richardson turns his attention to the particulars of the rule of law in question and to Prynne's qualifications as an attorney. Citing 25.E.3, in which "it is declared to bee high treason for any man to thinke or imagine the death of the Kinge, or the Queene," Richardson draws the necessary connection by adverting to Prynne's musings on the murder of yet another emperor for his attendance at the playhouse and concludes, "There is noe Defence, or excuse to bee made for this" (280).[140] Probing further into the case mounted by the defense, he expostulates, "His defence is, hee had noe such intention: Mr. Prynne you are a Lawier, And the rule of Lawe is, That when the words, and the intention are equallie patent, then the intention is taken, But heere yo[u]r intention is hidden, and the words are plaine, And there fore they must be taken . . . soe I saie it is a most wicked scandalous, infamous, and most seditious Libell" (280). In Richardson's view, Prynne had committed a double violation; not only had he perpetrated the crimes with which he had been charged, but he had also attempted to controvert the principles governing the application of the relevant statute. In imposing a punishment to suit the crime, Richardson thus condescends to his former colleague, "I am sorrie for you Mr. Prynne, I haue knowne you longe, and haue respected you, But nowe I must forsake you, ffor you haue forsaken God, you haue forsaken yo[u]r Allegiance to the Kinge, yo[u]r respect to the Queene, and yo[u]r charities to the Ladies, and to the people, And you haue forsaken all goodnesse" (280).

In pronouncing sentence in Eng 1359, Richardson follows a mandate that derives from his position of authority as Chief Justice of one of the common law courts. He lays out principles of sovereignty and law and articulates a justification that delineates both the prerogatives of the king and the duties of the subject. The contrasting emphases that emerge in the selective refractions of Richardson's sentence in BL 11764 and HM 80 tell us a great deal not only about the political perspective offered by each manuscript but also about the competing bodies public to whom they may have been addressed.

While both manuscripts compress Richardson's speech, BL 11764 makes the most drastic cuts. Though it retains elements of Richardson's discourse on the sovereign prerogative over the "hartes and good opinyon of a subjecte," it remains circumspect as to the charge of treason, offering only that "to endeavour to defraude the Kinge of this treasure is a most damnable offence, and yf hee were to bee tryed therefore before him, in the places where hee sittes, under the Kinges favour hee would give it another name" (21–22). What that name might be is never articulated in BL 11764, even though Richardson critiques Prynne here for drawing an analogy between Nero and the king and chides him, as in Eng 1359, for having "forsaken God and his alleagiaunce to the Kinge and Queene, and charitye to all the people" (21). In addition to omitting all direct references to treason, BL 11764 also removes Richardson's allusion to the doctrine of passive obedience, *preces et lacrimae*, and excises both his citation of 25.E.3 and his address to Prynne as a "Lawier." The sense that there is much at stake for the commonwealth and the principles of governance that sustain it is thus spirited out of the text, leaving the harsh sentence imposed by the judges to stand on its own without substantial ideological authorization or legal justification.

In contrast, HM 80 not only retains the reference to the doctrine of passive obedience but further embellishes it, offering, "If there bee a good Emperour bless God for him, if a wicked one; wee must fly to ye Weapons of ye Church Preces et Lachrimae, but God be blessed never was England Governed by a more virtuous and religious Kinge" (29). In this manner, HM 80 takes care not only to portray Prynne as one who "striveth to sowe the seede of dissention amongst the people" (28v), but also to praise the king and queen for their exercise of magnanimity, virtue, and grace in safeguarding the public weal. In marked contrast again to BL 11764, HM 80 also retains Richardson's expostulations on the rule of law with respect to the treason statute 25.E.3: "It was adiudged high Treason to have but an ill thought of ye Kinge; but you say, that yo[u]r intentions were good; soe they might if they hadd beene in an equall way, but where you breake into plaine positions, it is not soe" (29–29v). Though this articulation of the statute reads rather cryptically when compared with its full recitation in Eng 1359, it still performs the crucial rhetorical function instituted by its precursor of providing a statutory basis not just for prosecuting Prynne but also for finding him guilty. Where BL 11764 thus leaves the reader with the impression that Prynne's words have been arbitrarily construed, HM 80 provides the legal framework within which those inferences may be classified and exhibited as crimes. This pattern of divergence between

BL 11764 and HM 80 almost invariably repeats itself wherever Eng 1359 expounds on sovereign prerogatives or touches upon the obligations of subjects under the law. Where BL 11764 offers only a blunt assertion of the force of law and judgment, HM 80 provides more judiciously for an articulation of the reciprocal obligations enjoined upon both subject and state within the body politic.

If this contrasting set of selective editing choices in BL 11764 and HM 80 provides for differing articulations of the corporate body politic, other points of divergence illustrate more poignantly their differing treatment of the king's and queen's persons, or the corporeal body natural. The lead in these matters is taken foremost in Eng 1359 by the Lord Chamberlain to the Queen's Majesty, the Earl of Dorsett. To justify his call for an even harsher punishment than that proposed by his fellows—Dorsett thought that the other judges were too lenient in allowing Prynne to have his ears cut off and called instead for his nose to be slit and his forehead branded—he joins a discourse on disease in the body politic to a discursus on the transcendent virtues embodied by the king and queen. Opening first, then, with an address that likens Prynne and his kind to the "swarmes of murmurors" who "are fearefull simtomes of sicke, and deseased tymes," he calls for their purgation in an "expiatorie" or "exemplary sacrifice" (287–287v). For Dorsett, Prynne is no mere man of zeal, as some apologists might have it, but rather an instrument of the devil and a "brittle-Conscienced brother" whose "loathsome" words "shewe [he is] all purple; and Cankered within" (288–288v). Magnifying the struggle against Prynne to biblical proportions, he casts his antagonist not merely as a "Pigmie" who "growes a Gyant" when it comes "to the scandall on o[u]r sacred Soveraigne" (289) but rather as "a Shimei amongst vs that railes against o[u]r David" (289). With the rhetorical pitch thus raised to its highest level, Dorset feels licensed to launch into a lengthy and sustained exhortation: "Doe wee not enioye a Religious, wise, and Noble Kinge, All whose recreations tend to the health of his bodie? . . . When did the State more flourish? When had this Land more peace, what wife feares her chastitie? what women her honnour? . . . When did euerie mans breast tell him hee had such a quiet, and secure Estate?" (289). Having tied the king's health to that of the body politic over which he presides, Dorsett then avouches it an "impietie" to allow those "vile Censures" which have been cast upon the queen to go without response and testifies at great length:

> I that Contemplate her vertues dailie, knowe her excellence to bee
> such. . . . Her heart in her is the Center of Chastitie: Her whole

carriage is mixed w[i]th loue as well as well as [sic] Ma[jes]tie beget-
tinge Reverence. . . . All her actions are guided w[i]th that wise-
dome, and Circumspection, That this woman alone might serve to
iustifie all the sexe. . . . Her life is soe innocent that Casuists might
live by her patterne. . . . Her vertues are such as that in Commemoration of them noe tongue can lie, noe Poet feigne, yet here is a
dogg ^*amonge vs that*^ baies at this Moone. (289–289v)

Dorsett's performance here reaches the very height of its rhetorical appeal to
those who support the royal couple and consider themselves loyal subjects. It
is no surprise to find, then, that where HM 80 preserves and even embellishes
upon this call of praise, BL 11764 strips almost all of it away. This is the case as
well when the Earl of Arundel steps forward to thank God that "wee live in
such an age, That the more his Ma[jes]tie and his Roiall Consort are tried, the
more glorious they are like goulde" (291v). Indeed, not only does HM 80 preserve the main points of Arundel's speech where BL 11764 expunges all but his
concurrence in the sentence, but it also fills out an allusion left incomplete
here in Eng 1359 to liken Prynne more effectively to "ye dogg in ye Fable, that
catched at ye shaddowes and lost the Substance" (HM 80, 40v). In short,
where the full text of Eng 1359 offers up a series of encomiums to the great
glory and virtue of the king and queen, BL 11764 strips them away along with
the compelling narrative of authorization that they confer upon the sovereign.
HM 80, by contrast, preserves that narrative of authorization and makes it
patently clear that Prynne's vituperative reflections upon the persons of the
king and queen constitute no less than an assault upon the body of the entire
commonwealth. Accordingly, HM 80 not only publishes a rationale for the
obedience of the subject, but it also publicizes how the king fulfills his reciprocal obligation to act in the interest of the public good by conducting himself in a virtuous manner.

Dorsett's reference to Prynne as a "brittle-Conscienced brother" tallies
with his reduction of Prynne's crimes to two—"ffirst a Schisme-maker in the
Church; And in the Common wealth a wolfe in sheepes Cloathinge" (290)—
and both utterances touch overtly on the cause that had been so carefully
suppressed by the prosecution: Prynne's Puritanism. Indeed, Eng 1359 clearly
suggests that by and large the members of Star Chamber felt somewhat less
constrained than the prosecution in identifying Prynne's ecclesiastical convictions and in taking him to task for them. This lack of discretion is hard to
detect in either BL 11764 or HM 80, as each manuscript takes great care to

remove many of these passing references. BL 11764 is especially self-conscious about any direct references. Hence, for instance, while it retains Dorsett's satiric portrait of Prynne as one who "wilbe affrighted at a three-cornered capp, sweate att a surplus, sighe to heare musicke, swounde to the signe of the crosse, yett will make noe conscyence to lye, forsweare, and perjure him selfe," it declines to name Prynne overtly as a "brittle-Conscienced brother." Indeed, as if self-conscious about including what would have been eminently readable as a satire not just on Prynne but on Puritans in general, BL 11764 immediately offers one of its few original supplements to the text of Eng 1359, continuing, where it has no textual precedent, that Prynne does all this "for the advantage of the common cause to rayle upon the Kinges estate, and instructe treason" (24). This tactic of redirection, shifting our attention away from matters of religion to matters of state, characterizes much of BL 11764's and HM 80's relationship to Eng 1359. Indeed, in a demonstration of just how provocative the issue of Prynne's Puritanism must have been thought to be, this tactic of discretion is one of the few characteristics that the two manuscripts share in their revisions of Eng 1359. That blunt tactic is no more potently on display in the two manuscripts than in their treatment of Archbishop Laud's sentencing speech.

If we were to peruse only BL 11764 or HM 80, we would conclude that, contrary to all reasonable expectations of character, Laud took no time during his speech to expostulate on matters of religious doctrine or church discipline. Such a conclusion beggars not only reason but also the theatrical imagination, for it was Laud who viewed Prynne as a prime antagonist both to the instauration of Arminian doctrine and ecclesiastical practices and to the enforcement of episcopalian authority. Our faith both in our knowledge of character and our sense of the dramatic moment is thus restored when we turn for comparison to Eng 1359 and discover that both BL 11764 and HM 80 have cut off Laud's oration at precisely the point when, in Eng 1359, he launches into an extended disquisition on matters of doctrine and discipline.

Despite his initial pledge to "contract what I haue to speake," Laud's is the longest of all the sentencing speeches found in the manuscript (296v). As if convinced that the proofs against Prynne's text had been insufficiently learned, Laud spends the first three-quarters of his time discoursing freely on points of law, including the treasonous nature of Prynne's crimes and the weakness of his defense, as well as on more abstract questions such as whether plays are sinful in themselves, *malum per se*, or, as Laud concludes, merely *malum in se*, which is to say, "in themselues, and their owne nature indifferent," but liable to be used in a sinful manner in particular instances to teach lewdness (299v–300). He spends even more time dissecting Prynne's syllogistic method of argument and illustrates how, by its own faulty logic, it might be used to "condemne all things," including Christian religion (300–301v). "Of this sorte are most of his arguments," he opines and boasts, "I coulde take them in this manner, and beare them all to peeces" (301v). Having vindicated the indifferent nature of plays in themselves and invalidated the method of argument by which Prynne went about trying to prove them otherwise, Laud then goes on to repudiate Prynne's genealogical claims by reciting a countervailing lineage of church fathers and reformers who not only "ma[d]e nothinge against plaies in the best acception" but also commended, attended, and even wrote plays of an excellent character (301v). In their usual compressed and redacted forms, the more subtle differences between which I shall discuss in a moment, BL 11764 and HM 80 retain much of this material and basically end Laud's speech there. In Eng 1359, however, Laud continues on at some length, and his speech takes a remarkable turn toward matters of ecclesiastical authority and Arminian doctrine. Taking particular exception to Prynne's writings on the doctrine of predestination, he exhorts:

> My Lords, I saie, that master Prynne doth not vnderstand what
> Arminianisme is: This is positivelie spoken, I woulde
> notw[i]thstandinge doe any thinge that makes shewe of mercie if
> hee woulde but repent of this: but sure hee is farr from it, if hee bee
> of the same minde as his writings shewe him to bee: ffor I thinke,
> that neither himselfe, nor any man will put himselfe to the Austeri-
> tie of penance when hee is sure to goe to heauen w[i]thout Repen-
> tance: My Lords, This is his Tenent, And it is not a small Error, such
> as about the uncoveringe at the name of Iesus, and those smaller
> thinges, but a most dangerous position, it is this, That a Regenerate
> man in the Act of any sinne smitten by the hand of God suddenlie
> w[i]thout repentance actuallie discovered might bee saued.
> (303–303v)

Going so far as to charge Prynne with heresy, he declares, "I knowe Religion, I saie Repentance is necessarie, And if there bee any other waie but hell w[i]thout Repentance, I knowe nothinge in Religion" (303v). With this dramatic peroration on the doctrine of predestination, Laud fulfills our expectations that he would have taken the occasion of a public hearing in Star Chamber to expostulate on both religious precepts and Prynne's impiety. That these expectations are confounded by the texts in BL 11764 and HM 80 only speaks once again to the partiality, in every sense of that word, of these two variants.

Not surprisingly, then, the characteristic slant of each manuscript's partiality is on display in their differential treatment of the materials from Laud's speech that they do retain. First, though both texts engage in their usual course of condensation and compression, for overall content, HM 80 not only maintains a greater fidelity to the text of Eng 1359 than does BL 11764, but it also follows Laud's speech more closely than it does that of any other speaker represented. Thus, where BL 11764 makes cuts, HM 80 preserves both Laud's opening avowal that he holds Prynne "guiltie of high Treason, by a Statute of Edw: ye 3^{d}" (HM 80, f. 48v), and his subsequent endorsement of Dorsett's defense of the queen. Indeed, with respect to the queen's person, HM 80 even supplements Eng 1359, quoting Laud as offering the additional compliment, "If all the malice in ye world were infused into one Eye; yet it could not see anie thinge whereby to disparrage her" (HM 80, f. 49). Second, whatever BL 11764 might give up in expansiveness or inclusiveness, it compensates for with the blunt force of its original additions. Hence, while it does not include the citation of the treason statute, it does insert, without precedent in Eng 1359, what we might infer is its own interpretation of that law: "To wryte any thing that maye have a treasonable exposicion is a most unexcuseable cryme, for hee that wryteth cannott tell of what disposicion his reader wilbee" (27). Third, though in general the sentences represented in both HM 80 and BL 11764 follow the lead of the prosecution in eliminating references to Prynne's Puritan affiliations, HM 80 provides a bit more latitude for occasional references when it comes to Laud's speech. Thus, only HM 80 repeats both Laud's comic anecdote that he has "observed at Court some puritans to be at a play because they would not bee thought puritans; and for better Testimonie that they have been here; have stood vnder ye Candlesticke, and been dropt on by the Candles, and soe have carried away a Remembrance of the place (HM 80, f. 51v–52), and his more somber demurral on the prospect of bringing Prynne before the ecclesiastical Court of High Commission.

In sum, as compared with BL 11764, HM 80 offers us a text that is much more demonstrative and reverent with respect both to the king and queen and to Archbishop Laud. Where BL 11764 performs only the application of law and judgment, HM 80 articulates both the demand of obedience upon the subject as well as the reciprocal obligations of the sovereign. Laud and the king emerge as more sympathetic characters in HM 80 as do the institutions

they embody: the church and the state. In BL 11764, by contrast, Prynne
emerges as the more sympathetic, because more persecuted, figure. Even further, where BL 11764 offers a somewhat raw portrait of a government engaged
in the gross and arbitrary abuse of its power, HM 80 tenders a more palatable,
because modulated and articulated, account of a government pushed to the
limits of tolerance and forced, somewhat reluctantly, to exercise its lawful
powers upon an individual in order to protect the state. Accordingly, where
BL 11764 is most concerned with the judicial outcome, resulting in a representation of the case that emphasizes the stringent application of law and governmental power, HM 80 more clearly invests in illuminating the virtues and
merits of those who exercise those powers. Those who were inclined to vener-
ate loyalty to the state and the Crown would find an apt rendering of magnanimity and forbearance in HM 80. Those who were inclined otherwise would
find in BL 11764 even greater cause for outrage and resistance.

As with the battles that were waged over religious print in which each side
sought strategically to represent itself as a force of moderation and the other
side as introducing innovation and novelty into church doctrine, we find that
each party in Prynne's court trial, as represented in Eng 1359, tried to cast the
other as occupying a position of extremity against which their own posture of
moderation might be measured and affirmed. Where the prosecution painted
Prynne as an unremitting fomenter of sedition and rebellion, Prynne's defenders represented their client as a perplexed victim of government persecution. At the center of this contest, moreover, stood a battle over how words
might be construed, that is, whether words might be construed as actions in
themselves, as the prosecution might have it, or whether words can only be
construed as actions when intent is determined and commensurate, as
Prynne's defenders would have it. The trial thus not only staged a high-stakes
contest between the prerogatives and privileges of the sovereign and the rights
and obligations of the subject, but it also presented differing theories of the
purported crime altogether. To examine the rhetorical strategies enlisted on
each side to cast the other as extreme is hardly to suggest that either occupied
a position of moderation. It is rather to explore the question of how, under
these heightened tensions, each side sought to represent itself *as* moderate. A
full review of the expansive record of Eng 1359 for the rhetorical strategies
enlisted by the prosecution, defense, and judges to stage competing narratives
about Prynne and his book for public consumption has allowed us, moreover,
to see how subsequent redactions, such as BL 11764 and HM 80, altered,

revised, and reshaped those narratives even further to suit differing public tastes and interests. While the general critical bias has been to read Prynne's Star Chamber trial as a gross imposition of tyrannical power and as a harbinger of the conflict to come in which the royal government would find itself on the wrong side of the people, the manuscript version of the trial that was the most widely circulated, HM 80, actually provides for a representation and reading of the proceedings in which Prynne is hardly the victim of arbitrary government that he would make himself out to be and that scholars have been so eager to embrace.

To be sure, I could have focused on any number of other passages, examples, and issues; and certainly now that Eng 1359 has been brought to light, much more will be written both about that Star Chamber manuscript and about its relation to redactions such as BL 11764 and HM 80. As other aspects of the texts are examined, new conclusions will be drawn. Surely, however, no one will contest the fact that selective editing has given shape to very different textual representations of Prynne's first Star Chamber trial. All of this, again, is not to argue that Prynne's sentence was not severe or that the outcome was not overdetermined. It is significant, however, that the rationale for such severity, and hence the extent to which a seventeenth-century reader or prospective member of a body public might be made to believe that the prosecution was not unwarranted, varies according to which manuscript version of the proceedings was read. Driven by the partiality of its selections, each text shaped public opinion and appealed either to a constituency already in place or provided the ideas around which an emergent body public might organize itself. Publishing what was said and by whom in Star Chamber was clearly neither an objective nor a disinterested practice; it was rather a discursive occasion both to publicize a set of concerns and to cultivate the loyalties of what would become an increasingly restive complement of bodies public. As the Lord Treasurer pointed out when the defense complained yet again that it had not had enough time to prepare its case, "This motion is made for noe other end, but *ad faciendum populum*" (240v). To make the people was the end game in the Prynne case. Indeed, as would come increasingly to be recognized across the seventeenth century, only an assembly of bodies public would assure victory in the body politic.

Chapter 2

Political Allegiances and Bodies Public

Jeremy Collier's *A Short View of the Immorality and Profaneness of the English Stage*

By the time Jeremy Collier's *A Short View of the Immorality and Profaneness of the English Stage* (1698) triggered an avalanche of pamphlets both for and against the theater, England had endured a civil war, celebrated the subsequent Restoration of the Stuart monarchy, and weathered the Glorious Revolution, which exiled James II and brought William and Mary to the throne. These epic shifts in power resulted in the destabilization of old notions of authority and legitimacy and, amid the financial and commercial revolutions of the late seventeenth and early eighteenth centuries, reinforced an already growing sense that social hierarchies were both fluid and fungible.[1] While in 1698 the full ramifications of this series of political and religious settlements still had as yet to play themselves out, one thing was utterly clear from the Restoration onward: people across every strata, rank, and social group in later seventeenth-century England were "deeply aware" of an ongoing and yet fundamental transformation in the texture of English political, social, and cultural life.[2] These changes may have been contested, uneven, and fraught with anxiety and, as revisionist historians have been keen to point out, may even have exhibited certain continuities with older modes of political thought and social conduct.[3] Yet, as Steven Pincus and Alan Houston observe, no matter how one might want to spin the debates on continuity and change in this period, there is no way to avoid at least two very basic facts: first, "that a society which underwent two revolutions in less than a century [could not help but undergo] some very profound changes," and, second, "behind all [of the

Figure 6. Jeremy Collier, line engraving by Robert White.
© Victoria and Albert Museum, London.

late seventeenth-century] conversations was a growing acceptance of the legit-imacy of public discussion of affairs of state."[4]

Among those who felt those changes deeply and who suddenly felt li-censed to participate in those public discussions was Jeremy Collier (Figure 6). As a minister in the Church of England before 1689, Collier had committed

himself both to the tenet of passive obedience and to a belief in the indefeasible right of hereditary succession, and on this basis, he had sworn an oath of
allegiance to James II. Refusing to break his oath and roused by his sense of
outrage over the wrongful usurpation of a king, Collier became one of the
most outspoken critics of the accession of William and Mary and a leading
member of the nonjuring church—the alternative communion organized by
those who refused to take the new oaths of allegiance and who were thus deprived of office in the Anglican Church.[5] Though he had published only one
minor sermon before the Revolution, as a nonjuror, Collier published such
well-known tracts as *The Desertion Discussed* (1689), in which he disputed
claims that James II had abandoned the throne and thereby left it vacant; *Ani-
madversions upon the Modern Explanation of . . . a King de facto* (1689), in
which he mounted a relentless indictment of William's claim to the throne;
and *A Perswasive to Consideration Tender'd to the Royalists* (1693), in which he
asserted that subjects had no right to depose a king and enjoined his audience
to shun the "unlawful Assemblies" of what he termed the "Schismatical"
Church.[6] For his actions, he spent several months in Newgate Prison in 1688
and again in 1692. And in 1696, just two years before the publication of *A Short
View* and probably close to the time of its initial composition, Collier increased
his notoriety by accompanying Sir William Perkins to the gallows on the day
of his execution for his role in a plot to assassinate King William. Once there,
Collier, along with two other nonjuring clergymen, added insult to injury by
administering public absolution both to Perkins and to Sir John Friend without requiring their public confession, an action that Collier characteristically
defended in a series of strident pamphlets and for which he was condemned as
an outlaw.[7]

      Given Collier's outsized political commitments and his public notoriety—
he was still technically considered an outlaw when he published *A Short
View*—it ought to come as no surprise that many of his contemporaries considered the publication of this antitheatrical pamphlet as much a political
event as a dramatic or literary one. What is surprising is that literary critics
and scholars have almost uniformly neglected this aspect of *A Short View* and
have instead treated the tract as a text pertaining almost exclusively to the
moral and aesthetic reform of the English stage.[8] In this chapter, I eschew the
usual approaches to the Collier controversy in order to resituate his attack on
the stage, as it was understood in its own time, in the broad context of late
seventeenth- and early eighteenth-century political culture. Treating Collier's
tract as a work that, like Prynne's, used an attack on the theater as a means to

a secure a political end, I explore how Collier sought both to resist the state of political uncertainty and social flux that had been introduced by the Glorious Revolution and to cultivate a body public that would work to reverse its settlements. Such an approach requires not only that I examine Collier's critiques of the stage for their political significance but also that I analyze the plays he attacked and the responses he provoked for the ways in which they too sought to manage some of the more troubling aspects of the post-Revolutionary settlements and to promote particular political positions. In this manner, this chapter continues the general work of this book of illuminating the kinds of historical, social, and political concerns that are mediated by antitheatrical incidents but also looks to delineate the specific bodies public that jockeyed for position in the wider realm of the late seventeenth-century English body politic.

Religious Convictions, Party Politics, and Public Spheres

First published in April 1698, *A Short View* ignited a heated pamphlet war whose ostensible subject, the English stage, impelled any number of the most distinguished writers and critics of the period to weigh in with an opinion on the matter (Figure 7). Over the course of the first year, the number of ripostes multiplied in the form of dramatic prefaces, epistles, essays, and pamphlets; and those responses gave rise to a series of counter-responses and further ripostes, in a cycle that lasted more than ten years and that eventually included not just Collier's *A Defence of the Short View* (1699) but also his *A Second Defence* (1700), *A Dissuasive from the Playhouse* (1703), and *A Farther Vindication of the Short View* (1708).[9] Of all the other antitheatrical pamphlets published during this period, only Collier's attracted this kind of impassioned attention.[10] Most failed to draw even a cursory response, a fact that has been left unexplained by the usual moral and aesthetic approaches to the controversy. This phenomenon can be explained, however, if we begin to take account both of the ways in which Collier's attacks on the theater were immediately understood as of a different kind from the others and of the ways in which the responses he attracted were specific not only to his person but also to the political ideology he espoused and to the larger political conflicts in the period with which, as an outspoken nonjuror, he was so deeply and so publicly engaged.

The Glorious Revolution (1688–89) shattered once and for all many of

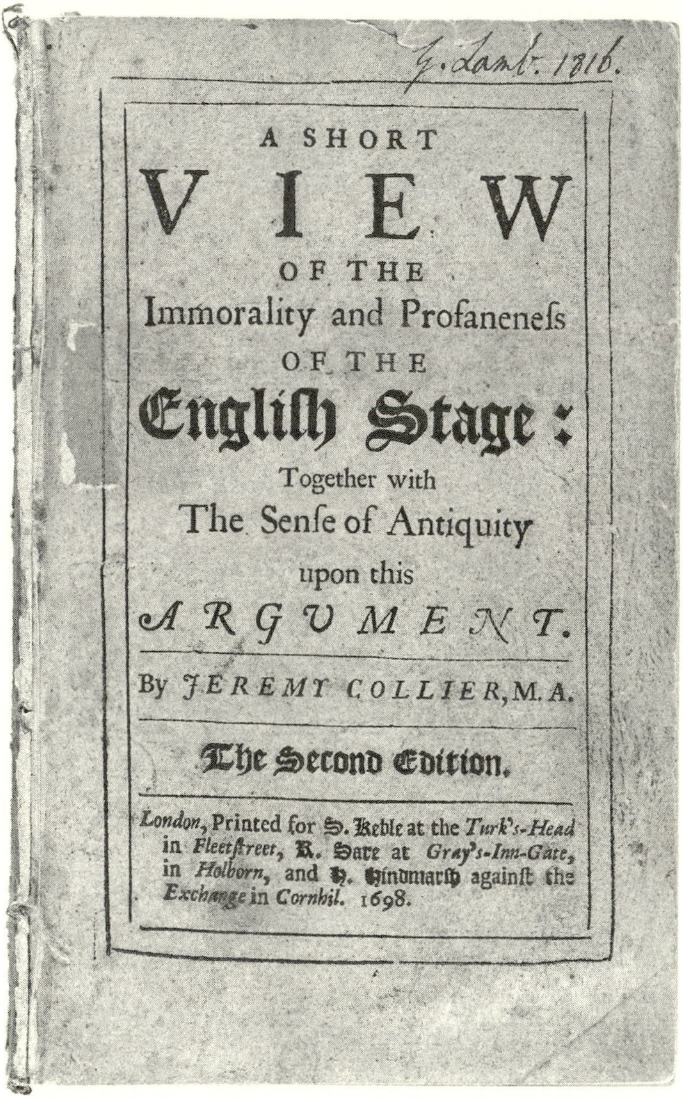

Figure 7. Title page, Jeremy Collier, *A Short View of the Immorality and Profaneness of the English Stage*, 1698.
Used by permission of the Folger Shakespeare Library.

the fundamental premises and truisms of English political, religious, and social life, and no related set of developments had a greater impact on the thrust
and counter-thrusts of the Collier controversy than the growth of support for
the principles of religious toleration and hence the structural reconfiguration
of the status of religion within the state, the consolidation and intensification
of political partisanship, and the emergence of what has come to be known in
critical discourse as the "public sphere." To be sure, each of these developments had already been under way in earlier periods, but the events of the
Glorious Revolution, and the multiple political compromises and religious
settlements that followed in its wake, not only accelerated those transformations but also significantly altered their character.[11] Thus, for instance, while it
could be said that the passage of the Toleration Act only continued the trend
toward what John Spurr has termed "the laicization of religion," that tendency
was propelled forward by new schisms and rifts within the Established
Church, which made the passage of an act of toleration a matter of significant
political necessity.[12] Further, the accession of William and Mary to the throne
and the demand that all clergymen swear an oath of allegiance to these newly
appointed sovereigns not only precipitated the departure of many leading
churchmen to form the parallel Nonjuring Church, but also emboldened dissenters and nonconformists who had supported the Revolution to demand
greater religious freedom and recognition.[13] At the same time, the recent specter of James II's plans for bringing about a Catholic reversion in the nation, as
well as the memory of both the bitter religious conflicts that had characterized
the civil war and the unsuccessful and widely deplored policy of persecution
and religious intolerance that had marked the Restoration under Charles II,
made many in England loath either to engage in theological disputation or to
call for the imposition of doctrinal orthodoxies.[14] Indeed, given the growth
of religious diversity on the ground, the abstract idea of one "true" doctrine
was viewed by many with considerable skepticism. Accordingly, as Blair
Worden observes, the later seventeenth century saw "a growing readiness to
describe as 'opinions' what would earlier have been called 'beliefs' or 'articles
of faith.'"[15]

Under a regime where faith increasingly came to be considered a matter
of individual conscience protected by law rather than a subject of church discipline, the boundaries between church and state were redrawn, and clerical
authority was significantly diminished. In its place, a new rationale for religiosity emerged in the 1690s, one which held, first, that religion "should have
less to say about salvation and more about integrity in our dealings with

ourselves and others" and second, that "if religion were to be saved, moral reformation must take the place of doctrinal conflict."[16] Thus, even as nonjurors like Collier fulminated over the unlawful usurpation of the crown and decried the corruption of clerical authority in the Anglican Church, William III found it politically expedient both to embrace a more comprehensive idea of Protestantism in England and to represent himself as the leader of a godly revolution, that is, as "the providential ruler who had a divine commission to protect the protestant church in England" and who could "return the nation to its pristine faith, piety, and virtue" through a program of moral reform.[17]

As religious doctrine and practice attained a new threshold of politicization in this period, many of the deepest tensions came to express themselves in the ideological claims of political parties and in the intensification of political partisanship. Indeed, party strife became a regular feature of English political and social life, as Whigs and Tories, who had emerged as political parties during the Exclusion Crisis of 1678–81, contended over such issues as the status of the Established Church, the structure of government, and the nature and extent of sovereign prerogative. While, on the one side, Tories lobbied for constraints on dissent, the affirmation of a High Church episcopacy, and the preservation of sovereign prerogative, Whigs, on the other side, advocated for the expansion of toleration to all but Catholics, the diminishment of clerical authority or at least the installation of Low Church or Latitudinarian bishops, and constraints on the exercise of sovereign powers.[18] The tensions generated by these polarized positions were hardly allayed, moreover, by the perturbing presence of the Nonjuring Church and the frequent specter of a Jacobite return. Indeed, as Mark Knights explains, the continual threat of a Jacobite insurrection only ensured that debates over the "extent and legitimacy of royal or popular sovereignty and power" would be recapitulated over and over again and that the public would be forced each time "to decide what or to whom they owed loyalty and allegiance."[19]

From 1688 onward, then, "the rage for party" dominated the political scene and bitter political partisanship gave rise to what historians have variously termed a "fractured" or "divided" society as well as a discursive culture of mutual mistrust.[20] Amid the rancor and strategic distortions of these political contests, "truth," as Knights explains, "became relative to partisan conviction and party institutionalized a system of rival truth-claims."[21] Even more significantly, as each party sought to court and to cultivate public opinion, the public itself "acquired new prominence and importance as a collective fiction with an enlarged role as a legitimizing power and as an umpire."[22] Tories and

Whigs, Jacobites and Nonjurors, Nonconformists and High-Church Anglicans would all make plays for public sympathy and the public affections; and their fervent efforts to publicize and to promote their agendas in essays and pamphlets, histories and periodicals, and sermons and theatrical performances gave rise to the fullest expression yet of both an embodied and a discursive public sphere of exchange and debate.

It ought to be obvious by now that the public sphere to which I am referring here differs considerably in its material manifestations from that theorized by Jürgen Habermas in his influential *The Structural Transformation of the Public Sphere*. For where, as historian John Brewer points out, Habermas's account presents us with an "extremely orderly and tidy" version of the public sphere, one which phantasmatically presupposes "a public of rationally and critically thinking bourgeois intellectuals" who are "capable of acting in a manner that is reasonable, disinterested, and impartial; a public capable, in other words, of transcending partial interests and passions in order to represent and embody a universal public good," what we actually find in the historical record is a public that was anything but rational and orderly.[23] Even the coffeehouses and periodicals upon which Habermas placed so much emphasis as rational sites of criticism have been shown instead to have been well-known venues for the conduct of partisan politics.[24] Indeed, as Gary De Krey has shown, "The press trained the party-conscious London public to perceive politics as a Manichean struggle between parties of political goodness and political madness."[25] The discursive culture of the day was thus one in which even rhetorical claims to civility and politeness could be read rancorously as strategic power plays.[26]

In light of these circumstances, it is more apt to conceive of the public sphere in post-Revolution England not so much as a place for rational debate but rather as a site of contestation over what constituted the rational, the reasonable, and the truthful.[27] Accordingly, we would be well-advised at this point in our study to refer not so much to "*the* public sphere" as to interrogate the contestational formation and play of multiple and competing "bodies public," both literal and figurative, organized and addressed either in physical space or through discursive media, and coalescing around a particular yet mobile set of party opinions and ideologies, social interests, and affiliations. Whether they are referred to as parties or factions—as Tories or Whigs, nonjurors or Jacobites—all claimed to represent the will of the people and the best interests of society and the state, and each sought to model and advance a distinct ethos or mode of practice with which members of the body politic

as a whole might choose to affiliate. To the extent, moreover, that the ideological positions with which each of these parties or factions might be said to
be identified in post-Revolutionary England were themselves not wholly settled or formed, we might better consider them as provisional placeholders or
fluid social assemblages rather than as hardened taxonomical nodes.[28] Cutting as they do across political and religious lines, with the positions adapted
by these groups often neither distinct nor exclusive but rather overlapping
and contradictory, and with individuals associated with one group or another apt to change or shade their loyalties and affiliations, no simplistic set
of binary oppositions could be said wholly to have regulated their conten-
tiously public disputes.[29] The strenuous efforts exerted in the Collier case
should thus be read not so much for the ways that they affirm what we take
to be ostensive definitions for political parties in late seventeenth-century
England but rather for the ways they venture toward performative iterations
of those positions.

Jeremy Collier's Cultural Politics

From this perspective, it makes much more sense to begin an examination of
the Collier controversy not with his didactic introduction, as most have done,
but rather with his polemical preface. For here we find an assertion that alerts
us to the broader context in which Collier meant to situate his attack on the
stage. Setting the terms of engagement, Collier writes, "*To make sure work on't,
there's nothing like* Destroying *of* Principles; Practise *must* follow *of* Course. *For
to have* no good Principles, *is to have* no Reason to be Good."[30] Echoing any
number of his tracts against the accession of William and Mary, Collier maintains that what offends is not simply the representation of lewdness or immorality on the stage but, more consequentially, the kinds of principles those
offenses might emanate from and the influence those principles might exercise over the conduct and consciousness of an audience. Any principle that
does not take its rise from authority, and in particular any principle that is not
articulated and sanctioned by divine authority, is not merely a bad or a false
principle; it is, quite simply, as later passages in *A Short View* make clear, no
principle at all. The "Destroying of Principles" can result, in Collier's view, in
only one outcome—in his own phrase: "a . . . Levelling in Morality" (Preface,
A5r).
    This allusion to "levelling" in the preface is repeated at key moments

throughout *A Short View*, and with it, Collier alerts us both to the political stakes at hand and to the historical consciousness that guides his polemic. By associating the destruction of "principles" with "levelling," he recalls both the radical activities of the Levellers in the 1640s, who advocated for a dramatic expansion of the franchise and the elevation of the House of Commons, as well as the activities of the Whig party, which emerged during the Exclusion Crisis of the late 1670s bearing the colors of the Levellers at its Green Ribbon Club, and which, more recently, had played a crucial role in negotiating the accession of William and Mary.[31] The Glorious Revolution, in Collier's view, had distinguished those who adhered to principle from those who abandoned their principles when it became politically expedient to do so. Those who advocated for the de facto government of William and Mary and those who negotiated the settlements—Whigs and Tories alike—were also those who respected no established forms of order—proof positive, indeed, that they had no principles at all. In this moment, he implied, the Whigs especially, like the Levellers during the previous revolution, had sacrificed a divinely anointed monarch to the supremacy of Parliament and ushered in a period of great uncertainty with respect to order and authority.

From the outset, then, Collier imports an acute sense of the historical and political moment into his antitheatrical polemic, and, as the discussions below demonstrate in greater detail, this was the perspective from which he launched his attacks both on the enterprise of the playhouse in general and on the political workings of the plays he singled out for especial vilification. Like Prynne, Collier recognized the playhouse as a privileged site of social and political intercourse, but he also went much further than Prynne in attending to the ways that the plays themselves encouraged audiences in their capacity as a body public to form their own opinions rather than rely on the judgments of hierarchical authority. Not only did he apprehend how the playwrights of his age fashioned the playhouse into a vibrant site of public engagement; he also recognized how they exploited the theatrical propensities of the stage to explore many of the same political questions that he worried in his polemical works. In examining the works that compose the Collier archive, we ought to attend, then, both to their historiographical import, that is, to how they engaged that historical moment and rendered the various political settlements to which it gave rise, and to their sociocultural implications, that is, to how those political principles were thought to influence the tenor of social intercourse among the bodies that composed the body politic.

Playhouse Publics in the 1690s

Among the numerous discussions and debates about the public sphere and its
various site-ings, few if any political historians mention one of the most obvious and historically notorious spaces for shaping and cultivating public opinion: the theatrical playhouse. Yet as discussed in the previous chapter, theaters
had long been viewed as public sites of unrest and for that reason were not
only treated as a nuisance by public magistrates but were also shut down by
the Puritan regime in 1642 to head off potential disturbances. Upon their re-
opening in 1660, the playhouses resumed their place as an often raucous site
of public gathering and social exchange and, even more important, as Paula
Backscheider has argued, became recognized as a privileged site both for the
"distribution and interpretation of news" and for the modeling and dissemination of competing ideologies.[32]

The political dimensions of the public role played by theaters are made all
the more palpable when we consider that the stage in England had long been
closely associated with the patronage of the Crown. Thus, in the Restoration,
we have the King's Men and the Duke's Men, the two acting companies issued
royal patents and named respectively for Charles II and James, the Duke of
York. As Matthew Kinservik writes, "These names were not merely honorific;
rather, they signified a protective relationship between the nobler patron and
the acting company."[33] Under this dispensation, it is no wonder to find that
the playhouse was construed as an agent or surrogate of the Crown during the
Restoration, and that even after the Revolution it was engaged as a site of
contention in political conflicts over the compass of sovereign power and the
liberties of individuals in the body politic.[34] In this context, moreover, arguments both for and against the stage were often quite explicitly intended and
can easily be read as both enunciations of political allegiances and commentaries on the status of power, authority, and governance in the state and in the
public sphere. Collier's decision to attack the stage thus alerts us to its perceived prominence as a significant site of sociocultural and political influence,
both by virtue of its historical affiliation with the Crown and by virtue of its
immediate engagement and intercourse with a collective of bodies in public.

Indeed, as any number of prologues and epilogues from this period make
clear, the theater was recognized as a privileged space in which a heterogeneous public could be called into being—performatively constituted as it
were—through successive appeals to the pit, the boxes, and the gallery. In this

manner, moreover, it provided a conspicuous experience of affiliation across class, gender, and party lines. If, "for Collier," as J. Hopes explains, "it was not simply the historical events of 1688 that were important, but their pervasive and fundamental influence on post-revolution society," then it makes a great deal of sense that in selecting his target Collier chose a popular, cultural site that often functioned publicly as an ideological instrument of contestation and display and as a locus of competing authority in the public sphere.[35]

In the post-Revolutionary age, the ties between court and playhouse had weakened considerably, and at the beginning of the period, only one acting company remained: the United Company under the direction of Christopher Rich at Dorset Garden and Drury Lane.[36] As court interest fell away, the play-houses worked harder to appeal to a dynamic public at large that was all too attuned to the nuances of political representation. Accordingly, the sudden burst of dramatic works in the 1690s, following what Robert D. Hume has termed the "virtual paralysis of the later 1680s," is distinguishable by its turn away from the heroic and Cavalier energies of the Carolean stage to a preoc-cupation instead with the pressing political questions about power, authority, and legitimacy that, as discussed above, were raised by the Glorious Revolu-tion and the accession of William and Mary to the throne.[37] Indeed, as Derek Hughes points out, "After the Revolution, there [was] an appreciable revival in the demand for new plays" with "forty-six known premières" between No-vember 1688 and the formation of a new theater company at Lincoln's Inn Fields in April 1695 by a cadre of actors who were rebelling against Rich's ty-rannical management practices.[38] Following the breakup of the United Com-pany's thirteen-year monopoly in dramatic entertainments, the number of new plays soared, animated, as I demonstrate below, not just by the novelty of competition between rival acting companies but also by the dramatists' own artistic impulse in this moment of unrest to revive and to explore the unique capacities of dramatic and theatrical forms to question, make sense of, and comment upon the social and cultural implications of the new political settle-ments. Looking beneath the veneer, then, of what scholars such as Hughes and Hume have characterized as a proliferation of low comedy and mediocre drama, I will elaborate the ideological implications of the dramaturgical ex-periments that flourished in these plays. Indeed, insofar as Collier held that "Things *are in a great measure* Govern'd *by* Words," I contend that this burst of creativity was precisely what drew his attention, as it indicated just how polit-icized, contentious, and enlivened public culture, and in particular the body public of theatrical space, had become (Preface, A5–A5r).

Jeremy Collier's Playlist
and the Dramatic Art of Supposition

Over the course of his treatise, Collier takes aim at eighteen plays by six different authors: four by William Congreve, eight by John Dryden, one (extended
over three parts) by Thomas D'Urfey, one by Thomas Otway, and two each by
John Vanbrugh and William Wycherley, a rather slender array of authors and
works given the possibilities. That range of comment is narrowed even further
in chapter 5 of Collier's tract, when he announces that he has singled out four
works for special comment: Dryden's comedy *Amphitryon; or, The Two Sosias*
(1690) and his dramatic opera *King Arthur; or, The British Worthy* (1691);
D'Urfey's three-part *Comical History of Don Quixote* (1694–96); and Vanbrugh's *The Relapse; or, Virtue in Danger* (1696). Declaiming that "since the
Poets here have been prodigal in their Expence, and dress'd themselves with
more Curiosity then ordinary, they deserve a proportionable Regard," he sardonically engages to defend their "Finery" from the "Crowd" and "make
Elbow-Room for their Figure" by allowing them "the Compass of a distinct
Chapter" (177).

Despite this grandiose pronouncement, Collier's selection criteria are
mystifying and idiosyncratic at best. While *Amphitryon*, *King Arthur*, and *Don
Quixote* certainly include a prodigious variety of theatrical spectacle and occasionally require the use of complex theatrical machinery, *The Relapse* remains
a fairly traditional rakish comedy, hardly the occasion of unusual frippery or
expense. All four of the plays he selects, however, were first performed within
a narrow window between 1690 and 1696, and while they might differ substantially in matter, tone, and style, they all share an interest in plots that
meditate not simply upon the unlawful usurpation of power, authority, and
the right to rule but also, I would contend, upon the more foundational problem of framing truth and assigning value in post-Revolutionary Britain. More
abstractly put, all of the works that Collier singles out for critique display a
fascination with what I term the posture of "supposition," that is, with the
potentialities of the ludic conditions that animate and indeed are foundational to theater itself.[39]

This "suppositiousness" in both senses of that word, that is, as counterfeit
or as hypothesis, is what most infuriated Collier about the stage—its capacity
both to generate fictions that reflect, test, and (sometimes too nearly) touch
upon present realities and to imagine or "suppose" alternative possibilities for

the social, moral, and political order. Collier's insistence in his readings of plays on applying such neoclassical principles as the unity of time, place, or action and his strictures against "levelling" of all kinds can thus be understood not simply as a matter of critical judgment but as an effect of both a religious and a political ideology. For Collier, there was only one divinely ordained hierarchical truth and only one way to represent that truth. Dramatists, in contrast, responded to the challenges of this unsettling period with creativity and ingenuity, shaping plots that explored the pressing issues of usurpation and legitimacy, power and authority, conformity and occasional conformity, even as they conducted formal experiments that put into question the very idea of producing reliable knowledge or singular truths. Exploiting the suppositious conditions of the playhouse and capitalizing on the slippery play of language itself, playwrights such as D'Urfey, Dryden, and Vanbrugh avidly illustrated how multiple versions of the truth could be accommodated, rationalized, or even laid alongside one another.[40]

Thomas D'Urfey's The Comical History of Don Quixote

The performative dynamic of juxtaposition is perhaps best represented in the three parts of Thomas D'Urfey's *The Comical History of Don Quixote*. Performed for the first time over the course of two different theatrical seasons and loosely tracking, at least in the first two parts, the plot of Miguel de Cervantes's *Don Quixote*, these plays are often dismissed simply as entertaining romps.[41] As Robert Hume notes, the entire trilogy is "vividly crude, but it teems of life."[42] At first it is difficult not to agree with such assessments; the plays are crass and lacking in linguistic refinement, especially the third part, which devolves into a series of jokes about Mary the Buxom's "bubbies." Yet there is also a tension in these comedies that suggests that D'Urfey might have been up to something more, or at least tried to attempt something more, beneath the unpolished plots and the rough-hewn satire. Derek Hughes hints at this when he writes, "The bawdry of *Don Quixote* suggests that Durfey was hankering for other things, yet nervous about providing them."[43] Hughes ventures no further in his musings on this point, but I would like to pick up on his hint to argue that the politically astute D'Urfey deliberately exploited the picaresque form, almost to the point of absurdity, in order to tender an episodic plot through which he might juxtapose diametrically opposed interpretations of reality and raise timely questions both about the governing vantage point and the shifting sands of various political sympathies.

We first encounter Don Quixote and his loyal, if grumbling, squire Sancho Panca on the third day of their "pursuit of Valorous Adventures."[44] Animated by the belief that he lives in the age of chivalry as represented in romance novels, Don Quixote styles himself a "Knight-Errant, a Tamer of Giants, a Righter of Wrongs, a Defender of Virgins, a Protector of Justice, a Scourge to the Infamous World, and a noble Retriever of the Golden Age" (Part I, I.i.p. 2). In his own description, Quixote thus intimates his awareness that he seeks to live outside of his own time, that is, he consciously seeks to "Retrieve" a lost "Golden Age," a time characterized by different principles and values. Indeed, there are many moments over the course of the three parts when Quixote's uneasiness at having to translate Sancho Panca's perceptions into the language of his own narrative becomes readable as an act of willful or purposeful misprision. Of the windmill, he exclaims to Panca, for example, "They may seem Sails, but to me they are like the hundred Arms of its Brother Giant *Briarcus,* whom I will instantly lop off and destroy" (Part I, I.i, p. 4). The "like" language of simile, a species of what I have been terming supposition, underwrites Don Quixote's actions here, as he tilts away, insisting willfully on construing all events according to his own nostalgic set of values. He recognizes the sails as sails, but what matters is what he wants them to mean "*to [him]*" (italics mine). Indeed, so enamored is Don Quixote of his idiosyncratic ways of viewing the world and of his ability, from time to time, to bend reality to his will, that over the three parts of this "comical history" he consistently, stubbornly, and sometimes ingeniously resists the suppositions of others, that is to say, he refuses to be compelled by the many scenarios and contrivances scripted by others to work a cure for his supposed madness.

Within the confines of the play itself, then, Don Quixote operates as an entertaining butt of satire and derision; he appears foolish to all those who encounter him. Read within the wider context of late seventeenth-century political culture, however, he is an object of laughter not simply because he chooses to believe in the dictates of romance narrative but because as a character, he figures all those in England who refused either to accept or to accommodate themselves to the ideological premises, or, should I say, suppositions of the new social and political settlements under William and Mary. Like Collier, though with a much better sense of play and humor, Don Quixote sets himself up as a "Scourge to the Infamous World," a defender of a mythical time when heavenly, or rather his version of heavenly, justice prevailed.

To be sure, this is a rather loose, associative claim, and I would caution anyone who might look to impose a tight allegorical grid on this even looser series of comedies in which varying points of identification shift so quickly and easily that it becomes rather dizzying. In some respects, that seems to be the very point, that is, the changeability of loyalties, affinities, and points of identification in the wake of revolution and the differing views generated by different perspectives. Indeed, before we get too comfortable with our own laughter at Don Quixote and the antiquated value system he takes such pains to aggrandize, we might do better to ask whether the values touted as alternatives in the plays are any more worthy of our admiration and emulation. To take just one example from the many convoluted subplots that form the bulk of these episodic comedies, we find in Part I a group of lovers whose vows of everlasting devotion to one another are as changeable as a glance. Much like those of James II's subjects, the oaths uttered by these characters are of no enduring value, and their affections are easily transferred. Love and reason are shown to be vulnerable to usurpation, and the characters in the love plots treat one another according to how they come to be construed amid the changing conditions of the moment rather than for any essential or intrinsic characteristics.

Similarly, in a not-so-subtle parallel to what some construed as William III's conquest of England, Sancho Panca in Part II is summarily awarded the governorship of an island by the presiding duke (II.ii., p. 21), whereupon Don Quixote promptly counsels him to set aside any doubts as to his qualifications, for "as to the manner of getting the Government, that piece of self-denial is generally smothered, for if thou has the Conscience to think thou deservest it, 'tis thy own fairly if thou canst get it in Course" (Part II, IV.ii, p. 38).[45] Offering what would easily have been understood as a barbed comment on late seventeenth-century political settlements, Don Quixote perspicaciously remarks that "thou art not the first that has got a Government he was not beholding to his desert for" and goes on to advise Panca that if he wishes to hold on to his new office, he ought to "adorn [himself] with these three vertues or qualifications, which are Morallity [sic], Conscience, and Decency" (Part II, IV.ii, p. 38). Note here that these virtues are characterized not as essential or inherent qualities but rather as "adorn[ments]," the appearance of which can be cultivated to serve the interests of those in office. As Don Quixote so astutely observes, "Morality, is extreamly useful for a Governour, if it were for nothing but to be a Screen, that people might not pry too much into his Religion" (Part II, IV.ii, p. 41). In the supposed "real" world of the drama, then, desert and just deserts are at odds with one another; and conscience, morality, and decency are qualities or "screens" to be put on and off according to interest. Accordingly, Panca follows Quixote's advice, and in an uncomfortable echo of some of the tactics adopted by King William to win broader support, he is no sooner elevated to his higher station then he turns reformer of manners and strict enforcer of the law.[46]

Thomas D'Urfey spent much of his career ingratiating himself to those in power. Once a darling of Charles II, he quickly realigned his oaths and loyalties following the Revolution to court the favor of powerful men in the Williamite regime. In his own life, in other words, he had learned firsthand the fine art of supposition, that is, of accommodating his beliefs and of adapting his actions to suit the times. In his three-part comical history, however, D'Urfey conspicuously takes no position on the various sides. While Don Quixote is surely a figure of mockery for his refusal to accommodate himself to the realities of his world, the values touted by that world are no more worthy than those lauded by the errant would-be knight. They both fail to inspire either faith or confidence. Despite the attempts, moreover, of any number of authority figures across the installments to demonstrate otherwise, we come to understand that there are no singular truths or even a singular framework for the production of truth. There are, rather, only competing party perspectives and truths, each of which entails its own set of abstracted suppositions and practical commitments. What is required, then, as Don Quixote makes all too clear when he beats Panca for not "seeing" properly until he concedes "I do but suppose it, Sir," is that we choose which set of suppositions, under duress or otherwise, we would prefer to embrace (Part I, V.ii., p. 57). To the extent that we sympathize with Don Quixote—and he is indeed the most endearing character amid this rough assortment—we might be tempted to adopt his worldview. But to the extent that we recognize both how his actions are opposed to common sense and how deeply and thoroughly disempowered Don Quixote is, we might choose not to follow "the Knight of the Ill-favoured Face" into battle (Part I, II.i., p. 15). Either way, and much like the puppets that Don Quixote takes for the real in Part III of this comical history, once we do choose, we will be obliged to follow the suppositions that have been scripted for us and duly play our parts.

For Collier, D'Urfey's trilogy was nothing short of profane. With its irreverent and indiscriminate treatment of characters of all stations and political positions of all kinds, it represented nothing less than a profound and thorough-going "levelling" of all persons and principles. "To treat Persons of Condition like the *Mob*, is," Collier wrote, "to degrade their Birth, and affront their Breeding. It levells them with the lowest Education" (305). As this last sentence indicates, Collier was deeply offended by D'Urfey's handling of those among the educated and elite classes and in particular by D'Urfey's satiric treatment of members of the clergy whose claims to authority had long been grounded in their literacy and education. Indeed, Collier devoted a great deal of time and energy both in his discussion of *Don Quixote* and throughout *A Short View* more generally, to cataloging what he perceived as the wide-ranging "Abuse of Clergy" on the stage and to defending the status and privilege of this class of persons.[47] This burning preoccupation is eminently on display in the third chapter of *A Short View*, which is devoted entirely to "The Clergy abused by the Stage," and there, as well as in his discussion of *Don Quixote* and in his 1697 "Essay Upon the Office of a Chaplain," we can read Collier's anxieties over what he and many others—nonjurors and High Church Anglicans alike—took to be the diminished cultural status of the clergy ushered in by the revolutionary settlements.[48] For Collier, satirical figures like D'Urfey's priest Bernardo, who in Part II not only fails to redeem Don Quixote from his idiosyncratic follies but also finds himself bested by this supposedly benighted soul in a debate over the comparative merits of knight errantry and chaplaincy (Part II, II.ii., pp. 16–17), were symptomatic of the larger phenomenon of anticlericalism and heterodoxy run rampant. "The advent of religious pluralism in the 1690s," as Craig Rose observes, meant that clergymen could no longer "rely upon the legal sanction at the disposal of the secular arm to suppress nonconformity and enforce attendance at their churches."[49] This beleaguered sense that authority had been sacrificed and that heterodoxy was leading the nation toward atheism was that much more pointed for nonjurors like Collier, who had refused to foreswear their oath of loyalty and, as a result, had also forfeited the moral and religious sanction of the Established Church.

In his response to Collier, then, D'Urfey pressed hard both on questions about the status of Collier's authority—moral, religious, and otherwise—and on the politics that underwrote Collier's positions. Taking every opportunity in the "Preface" to *The Campaigners* (1698) to remind readers of Collier's compromised status within both the church and the state, D'Urfey casts Collier as an "Angry Malecontent" and as a stubborn holdout against rightful authority.[50] More pointedly, D'Urfey raises the specter of Collier's treasonous performance on the scaffold in the Perkins case by ruminating on the fact that someone who had granted absolution to a wretch who plotted "the Murder of the King, and Subversion of the Protestant Religion and Government" would now have the gall to "set up for a Protestant Example, and a Teacher of Morality" (4). Rechristening Collier as the "Absolver," an epithet that he applies repeatedly throughout the essay, D'Urfey goes on to critique Collier's clerical-ism as of a piece with the same bad-faith politics that he displayed at the gal-lows. Arguing that Collier had provided no occasion to believe that either his "disobedient humour, and turbulent nature," or his interest in "cultivat[ing] his Party with the same Principles as far as he can" had changed, D'Urfey not only remarks that "'tis fault in us in swearing when we should not, and in him for not swearing when he should," but also provides an extended text for an oath of allegiance that he would prescribe for Collier if he wanted his attacks on the stage to be read as anything other than politics by other means (13, 15). "This now," he writes, "with a sincerity proper, and coming to Church to hear our Divine Service, with the *Prayer* for the *King* in't, would give one a little satisfaction as to the Doctors present opinion" (16). In this manner, D'Urfey not only brings Collier's loyalties starkly into question but also makes clear the extent to which he understood the Collier controversy as a contest in which the ideological stakes were quite high and the historical and political consequences considerable.

While *The Comical History of Don Quixote* stops short either of accom-modation or of adaptation, it goes so far as to juxtapose competing ideological systems and leaves the problem of resolution to its audience. Dryden and Vanbrugh would each go one step farther in their post-Revolutionary plays, opting in the former case to present a Jacobite comedy that, on the one hand, unapologetically satirizes the Whig discourse of adaptation and, on the other, engages critically but not entirely unsympathetically with the Tory discourse of accommodation. In contrast, Vanbrugh's comedy, *The Relapse*, not only vindicates the Whiggish discourse of adaptation but also embraces the task of modeling its performative ethos.[51]

John Dryden's Amphitryon; or, The Two Sosias

The tumult of the Revolution was particularly hard on John Dryden. Up until that time, he had enjoyed considerable royal favor, having been elevated under Charles II to the post of poet laureate in 1668 and awarded the office of histo-riographer royal in 1670.[52] Dryden was fervently loyal both to Charles II and to his successor James II, and after a long "process of soul-searching stretching over at least four years," Dryden himself converted to Catholicism in 1685, having attained what his biographer James Winn describes as a "hard-earned personal conviction that Catholicism was the truth."[53] Following the Revolu-tion, Dryden refused to revert to Anglicanism and, despite considerable pressure and numerous attacks on his reputation and person, aligned himself with the Jacobite cause. For his religious and political commitments, Dryden was stripped both of his offices and of the sizable income they brought to him. Forced once again to earn his living in the public marketplace, Dryden returned reluctantly to the stage with two new plays: a tragedy, *Don Sebastian* (1689), and a comedy, *Amphitryon* (1690), both of which would come under attack by Jeremy Collier, with the latter singled out, as noted above, for especial censure and vituperation.[54]

In *Amphitryon; or, the Two Sosias*, the Roman god Jupiter descends from the heavens and assumes the form of the heroic Theban general Amphitryon in order to enjoy a night of pleasure with Amphitryon's wife, the chaste and true Alcmena. In order to prosecute this "Petticoat Affair," he directs his bastard sons Phoebus and Mercury, respectively, to delay the coming of the day and to take the form of Amphitryon's servant Sosia.[55] Much of the comedy in the play revolves around Sosia, who has been sent ahead to announce Amphitryon's latest victory and imminent homecoming. Mercury's task is to keep the real Sosia at bay so as to prevent him from discovering Jupiter's subterfuge and disrupting his amours. In a subplot that conspicuously departs from Dryden's classical and contemporary sources—Plautus's *Amphitruo* and Moliere's *Amphitryon*—Phaedra, who is an attendant upon Alcmena and who negotiates at every opportunity to gain some kind of remunerative advantage, engages in a flirtation with the disguised Mercury, who dangles the promise of a golden goblet before her covetous eyes.[56] At the end of the comedy, Phaedra leaves behind her pretensions to the affections of Gripus—a "mercenary Magistrate" and a "Weather-cock of Government: that when the Wind blows for the Subject, point'st to Priviledge: and when it changes for the Soveraign, veers to Prerogative"—in order to gain a bigger prize, as she negotiates in a witty proviso scene for what are ironically termed marriage "Articles" to be Mercury's "lawfull Concubine" (V.i.11–16, 332–33).

Critics have often seized on the subplot to argue that Dryden deploys it not only to produce a Jacobite satire of the moral depredations and rapacity of Whiggish rule but also to damn the party for its role in negotiating the accession of William and Mary to James's throne. It seems no coincidence, for instance, that Phaedra's bastardized articles are referred to as an "Act of Settlement" (V.i.374–75). Further, insofar as Jupiter has usurped the rightful place of Amphitryon in Alcmena's bed, he is often construed as a tyrannical and capricious stand-in for William who, from the Jacobite perspective, had usurped the rightful place of James on England's throne. James D. Garrison

thus argues not only that the "Jupiter-Alcmena-Amphitryon triangle" highlights the extent to which the "ideals of justice and faith [had] become the
subjects of jest" but also that the subplot in particular signals Dryden's view
that the ascendancy of William and Mary had ushered in an "age of impiety"
in which truth itself had become relative to its price in gold.[57] Although David
Bywaters takes issue with some of Garrison's conclusions, he argues similarly
that in both the plot and subplot, Dryden dramatizes the triumph of power
and interest over truth and piety under a Williamite regime.[58]

In arguing for this Jacobite interpretation, Garrison and Bywaters, like
most other critics, tend to focus most of their attention both on the Phaedra-
Mercury subplot and on what is often referred to as the "amorous rivalry"
between Jupiter and Amphitryon.[59] Alcmena herself is reduced in these readings to a token figure or prize, despite the fact that she plays a much more
significant role in the comedy than the titular Amphitryon.[60] Left unac-
counted for, moreover, is what editors of the text have long noted: that Dryden
took greater care than his predecessors to present Alcmena in a sympathetic
light. Not only did he exaggerate the coarse and worldly qualities of such
characters as Phaedra and Mercury, but he also pushed the dialogue between
Alcmena and Jupiter to heroic heights, generating a strong sense of romance
and erotic tension with what one critic terms some of the "finest blank verse"
he ever wrote.[61] As a result, Alcmena becomes a figure of both audience sympathy and discomfort—sympathetic because of her unwonted and unlooked
for loss of virtue, and discomfiting because she is not entirely without desire
in the case. Only Robert Markley and Jeannie Dalporto have suggested that
something more than the rendering of romantic tension might be at stake in
Dryden's alterations, writing that "her predicament, in some respects, mirrors
the dilemmas that Dryden and many members of his audience faced with
William's arrival."[62] Focusing on Alcmena's troubling place in the comedy, I
expand below on Markley and Dalporto's hint to demonstrate, first, that
Dryden's comedy ought to be read as much more than the blunt-force Jacobite satire that many critics have made it out to be, and second, that Dryden
was much more willing than other political partisans of the age to engage in a
modulated exploration of the political, ideological, and moral quandaries of
individual English subjects and the bodies public with which they chose to
affiliate themselves.

Collier's comments on the comedy are quite instructive in this regard.
Though he never acknowledges the political content of Dryden's satire, he
clearly has political ideologies in mind when he indicts the playwright not just

for "draw[ing]" Jupiter's "Debauch at its full Length, with all the Art, and Heightings, and Foulness of Idea immaginable," but also for not allowing Jupiter to be "contented with his success against *Amphitrion*, unless he brings *Alcmena* into the Confederacy, and makes her a Party *ex post facto*" (178). In Collier's view, the seduction of Alcmena by Jupiter and the "settlement" with which the comedy concludes gratuitously transform Alcmena into a party, after the fact, to the very crime that has been committed against her. Jupiter requires her as his subject to accept his authority, and her reward both for submitting and becoming part of that "Confederacy" will be Hercules, the son she has conceived through her liaison with the god and who is promised to her as one who will redeem an "Impious Age" (V.i.418). For Collier, her mute abjection at the end of the comedy stands as the sign of her coerced acquiescence to this arrangement. Thus construing the comedy through a nonjuring bias, he takes issue with Dryden's treatment of Alcmena and makes clear that any settlement with a usurping monarch constitutes an unacceptable form of compromise and a cause for condemnation.

But what Collier construes as a point of recrimination could be viewed from a different political perspective as an occasion for commiseration and understanding. Indeed, despite the rather heavy-handed Jacobite satire of Whiggish corruption that regulates the subplot, Dryden infuses Alcmena's story with signature elements of what Toni Bowers has described as the paradigmatic new-Tory seduction narrative that was emergent in the wake of the Glorious Revolution—narratives that allowed Tory-oriented subjects to "imagine collusion as, under certain circumstances, a practice of virtue."[63] In her first encounter with Jupiter, Alcmena could be described as the victim of fraud and even, depending on your interpretation of late seventeenth-century statutes, of rape—she has no basis upon which to think that Jupiter is any other than whom he represents himself to be, that is, Amphitryon. However, by the time he returns, for a second encounter to partake again of Alcmena's "fruits of Love" (IV.i.38), she not only has experienced his demand that she reflect on their first night together as the conjunction of lovers rather than the chaste passion of husband and wife—a demand that would be deeply out of character for Amphitryon—but also has endured a painful encounter with the real Amphitryon in which he accuses her of adultery and threatens divorce.[64] Jupiter must work hard to seduce Alcmena in this second scene, but despite having valid reasons for resistance—declaring "I'm odious to my self / For having lov'd thee once" (IV.i.7–8)—she is driven by her own desires to concede, "In saying that I cannot hate, I pardon" (IV.i.80). Astutely underlining the amatory conventions that regulate this scene and that underwrote Tory-oriented fictions, Jupiter, in turn, observes, as Alcmena coyly exits from the stage, "Forbidding me to follow, she invites me" (IV.i.88).

As Bowers has explained, such displays of "collusive resistance" were typical of the new-Tory narratives, for they "offered a way for uneasily collusive subjects to imagine themselves as virtuous, though no longer chaste, political subjects, and a language in which to interrogate a sexual-political culture organized around relations of dominance and subordination."[65] Against her better judgment, Alcmena submits herself to Jupiter's passion; her desire motivates her, and Jupiter's disguise as Amphitryon provides the virtuous alibi for this second tryst. Like so many Tory accommodationists, then, she cannot hate, so she "pardons."

Given Alcmena's opening claim that her love for Amphitryon is so strong that it is as if they are one person (I.ii.1–11), it is difficult not to view her subsequent actions with great suspicion. Consequently, critics have often turned to the trial scene staged in Act 5 both as a crucible moment for the comedy and as one that determines the value that we ought to ascribe to her character. The trial is called when Amphitryon finally manages to force his way into his own home and "breaks in upon [Jupiter's] Love" with Alcmena (V.i.117). Jupiter feigns astonishment and tauntingly challenges Amphitryon to submit to "Impartial Judgment," calling upon Gripus, the corrupt agent of justice, to stand in as "Umpire of the Cause" (V.i. 160, 167). Gripus, of course, is of little to no use. His first and only concern, as he inquires of Mercury is, "On whose side wou'd you please that I shou'd give the Sentence?" (V.i.169–70), and he is confounded when Mercury advises that in this one instance, he "Follow [his] conscience" (V.i.170). Like a great actor, moreover, Jupiter "counterfeits most admirably" (V.i.129–30) in this scene as in every other, answering all of the questions that would require Amphitryon's personal knowledge and displaying the same scars on his body as those that mark the Theban general. Everyone thus remains in a state of bewilderment as to how to distinguish one Amphitryon from the other when Alcmena arrives on the scene.

Alcmena's first concern in this moment is for her loss of "honour and fame," but she quickly checks herself, avouching that her fears are "needless" as her "Heart will guide [her] Eyes / To point, and tremble to its proper choice" (V.i.257–58). And she is not wrong in trusting to her heart's instincts. Indeed, as soon as she lays eyes upon the real Amphitryon, she goes to him, affirming, "There neither was, nor is, but one *Amphitryon*; / And I am only his" (V.i.259–60). For a moment, we begin to think that this comedy might end well, but when Alcmena tries to take Amphitryon's hand, he angrily pushes her away and proclaims her an adultress. Put off by Amphitryon's violent response, Alcmena turns toward Jupiter who cynically beckons her as his "gentle Love: my Treasure and my Joy" and encourages her to "look on thy better Husband, and thy friend" who would "vindicate thy honour from that Wretch / Who wou'd by base aspersions blot thy vertue" (V.i.262–68). Upon hearing these kind words, Alcmena goes to Jupiter, avouching her initial mistake and pronouncing:

> Thy Words, thy Thoughts, thy Soul is all *Amphitryon*.
> Th'Impostour has thy Features, not thy Mind;
> The Face might have deceiv'd me in my choice;
> Thy kindness is a Guide that cannot err." (V.i.269–72)

Critics have often pounced on Alcmena's conduct in this scene to condemn her for being so easily swayed and so changeable in her judgment. Moving quickly past Alcmena's first, instinctive choice, they indict her either for choosing wrong or for choosing her interest. Candy B. K. Schille writes, for instance, that "the lesson of Alcmena's mistake is surely that if one chooses one's lord because one expects to be treated tenderly, one may choose the wrong lord . . . . She has reversed a true judgment for a false one more in her interest."[66] In this reading, Alcmena, for all her goodness, turns out to be just as venal and corruptible as a Phaedra or a Gripus. Yet such condemnation fails to take into consideration the complicated set of circumstances in which Alcmena finds herself ensnared and the extent to which the comedy as a whole, reflecting what it takes to be the political conditions of the day, undermines any capacity to judge persons, identities, or, perhaps more particularly, character. Jupiter's self-regarding machinations, for instance, not only drive Sosia to cede his identity to Mercury but also propel Amphitryon to act out of character, that is, to display behaviors that are not commensurate with the person that Alcmena has formerly embraced as her husband.[67] Perhaps even more significantly, the conventional relationship between identity, agency, and consent has been deranged by Jupiter's confounding claim that no actor takes any actions that he has not already predetermined by design: "Fate," he explains, "is what I / By vertue of Omnipotence have made it: And pow'r Omnipotent can do no wrong" (I.i.102–4).[68] In the case of Alcmena, Jupiter salaciously affirms:

When I made her, I decreed her such
As I shou'd please to love. I wrong not him
Whose Wife she is; for I reserv'd my Right,
To have her while she pleas'd me." (I.i.111)

Under the auspices of an omnipotent god who brooks no dissent and who
blithely and capriciously "transgresses his own laws," there can be no sure
ground either for consent or for judgment. Indeed, as Stuart Sherman has put
it, "Dryden ensures that the extraordinary alternation of the plot will mirror
the ordinary alterations of the world, in which neither heart nor eye prove
adequate to assess human volatilities."[69] Within a culture, then, that had de-
scended to countenance "occasional conformity"—an accommodation that
openly deranged the relationship between principles and practice—questions
of authenticity or inner conviction might seem beside the point. Certainly
there were few if any surfaces from which the truth of things could be assur-
edly read.

     While it is difficult, then, not to view Alcmena's actions with some incre-
dulity, it is equally challenging not to view her with some compassion, as she
woefully intones before falling silent at the end of the comedy: "A simple
Errour, is a real Crime; / And unconsenting Innocence is lost" (V.i.391–2).
How are we to assign value to Alcmena's actions or even to her desires? She is
both virtuous and not so, complicit and not so, much like those Tories who
countenanced the *de facto* rule of William, while still upholding the *de jure*
claims of James.[70] Indeed, in the figure of Alcmena, Dryden renders a rather
heartbreaking portrait of what was required to accept the sovereignty of William and Mary, including the moral compromises of character that were almost prerequisite. And while he was personally unwilling to compromise his
principles, he also concedes in the play's dedication, in what would be construed by some as the consistent application of the doctrine of passive obedience and by others as a Toryesque concession, that he was "no disturber of
the Government" (224). In the sympathetic portrait that he generates of Alcmena, then, Dryden enacts what he esteemed as a "Tenderness . . . which is
Humanity in a Heroical Degree" (223), a quality of principled compassion
that was, perhaps, in too short a supply in those post-Revolutionary days but
that the experienced playwright understood the suppositious space of the
playhouse was capaciously disposed to compass for all parties and all bodies
public.

John Vanbrugh's The Relapse

While Dryden's play vividly dramatizes the anguish entailed either in adhering to the tenets of passive obedience or in entering into a discourse of accommodation, Vanbrugh's comedy, *The Relapse*, displays what might be construed as a more Whiggish temperament, eschewing all such concerns in order to advocate instead for the gravitas to assess and the grace to accept and adapt to fluctuating conditions on the ground. As the waterman in the second scene of the comedy suggests, these were "nimble times" with many "sharpers stirring."[71] Indeed, as noted above, the 1690s marked a period when it was difficult to discern affiliations, loyalties, and status; and hence only those who entered into shrewd calculations, who knew how to distinguish between "weight" and "tale," whether in matters of coin or of character, and who exercised cool judgment in the investment of their resources and capital, could be effective economic, political, and social actors. In a world driven by interest, moreover, where religious convictions had been reduced to competing opinions, Vanbrugh's play suggests that the ability to cultivate a kind of elastic equanimity and to accommodate oneself to that which was de facto rather than brooding over the de jure, was the most effective strategy for achieving social and political comity in the long run.

The comedy, which first appeared on the London stage in November 1696, was envisioned as a corrective sequel to Colley Cibber's *Love's Last Shift; or, The Fool in Fashion*, which had first been performed earlier that same year and which portrayed the sudden and improbable reform of the rakish Loveless, who had abandoned his wife, Amanda, for over eight years and who only renews his vows to her after she seduces him incognito, proving, rather incongruously for some, that a wife could be just as pleasurable as a mistress. In *The Relapse; or, Virtue in Danger, Being the Sequel of The Fool in Fashion*, Vanbrugh removes the reconciled couple from the countryside where they had sought a retired life and returns them to the city, for only there, amid the pleasures, temptations, and variety of that "uneasy theater of noise," can a true trial of self-proclaimed virtue be conducted (I.i.89). Loveless, as the title of the comedy suggests, proves no stoic and quickly succumbs to the attractions of Amanda's widowed cousin Berinthia, who he spots at the playhouse, ironically while watching a play that dramatizes the "relapse" of a supposedly reformed libertine like himself. In the subplot, another favorite of Cibber's sentimental comedy, Sir Novelty Fashion, reprises his role, now as the newly ennobled Lord Foppington, whose prodigal younger brother, Young Fashion, has returned to London from abroad to seek relief from his wealthy, elder sibling. When Foppington refuses to grant Young Fashion any succor, his younger sibling enters into a plot to usurp Foppington's plan to marry Hoyden, a rich, young heiress, who is kept cloistered in the country under the lock and key of her bumpkin father Sir Tunbelly Clumsey.

In considering this comedy in the context of its time, it seems no accident either that Vanbrugh identified Young Fashion as a Jacobite or that this latter plot of usurpation attracted the especial notice and vitriol of Jeremy Collier. Dismissing Amanda and Loveless as "Persons of Inferiour Consideration," the nonjuror protests, "that there is a *Misnommer* in the Title. . . . The *Intrigue* and the *Discovery*, the great Revolution and success, turns upon Young Fashion. He without Competition, is the Principal Person in the *Comedy*. And therefore the *Younger Brother*, or the *Fortunate Cheat*, had been much more a proper Name" (209–10). Collier's peculiar focus on this plot of usurpation and his emphasis on the "great Revolution" that Young Fashion brings about rather than on the adulterous plots or the overtly homosexual character, Coupler, who acts as bawd to facilitate Young Fashion's ruse, provide stark evidence of the extent to which his vision was refracted through the prism of nonjuring ideology.[72] Like the Revolution that brought William and Mary to the throne, the "great Revolution" of *The Relapse* "points," symptomatically in his view, "the wrong way, and puts the *Prize* into the wrong Hand" (210).

Perhaps even more disturbing for Collier, Young Fashion is not only a usurper but a Jacobite usurper, which would seem to be a contradiction in terms. Jacobites were committed to such principles as the indefeasible right of hereditary succession, which would include the rights of primogeniture that relegate Young Fashion to a secondary position and a reduced financial state with respect to his elder brother. For Collier, then, Young Fashion's willingness to set aside his political principles when it comes to pursuing his own economic interests conveys the dismaying moral, "That when a Man is press'd, his business is not to be govern'd by Scruples, or formalize upon Conscience and Honesty" (212). For Vanbrugh, however, who deliberately identifies Young Fashion as a Jacobite, the character's willingness to abandon principle seems to be the very point, as it enables the playwright to point up the hypocrisy of tendering or espousing such affinities in a culture where everyone—Whig, Tory, and Jacobite alike—pursued his or her individual interests—often under the cover of so-called principles. While Young Fashion certainly provides a great deal of distraction and amusement, then, in the rivalry with his brother, Lord Foppington, it is difficult to say who emerges from the comedy either the worse for wear or the better in reputation.

In the contest between Young Fashion and Lord Foppington, critics have generally tended to look more favorably upon Young Fashion. While Foppington adopts a snobbish posture of superiority, Young Fashion plays the attractive trickster of the comedy, whose machinations provide much of the play's entertainment, as he connives and cajoles his way toward marriage and consummation with Hoyden. Of those intrigues, Laura Brown writes, for instance, "The resourceful hero's scheme earns our support as an ingenious and necessary exercise of enlightened self-interest. . . . We do not judge Young Fashion on moral terms, except to the extent that we feel the corruption of his whole society."[73]

There is no doubt that Young Fashion exudes a certain charm and wit that is utterly attractive. Yet, if we take a step back from our attachment to the character, a slightly different and indeed more ambiguous picture emerges. First, just because we want to see Young Fashion succeed in his plot against his older brother does not mean that we or the comedy holds Lord Foppington entirely in contempt. Indeed, as Michael Cordner has noted, "Our sympathies naturally lie with the younger brother; but Foppington is dealt so many superb retorts that it is finally unclear whether the intellectual advantage is really on Fashion's side."[74] Second, Young Fashion only finds himself in an impoverished state because he has not only spent his entire annuity of £200 per year but also mortgaged this asset to cover additional debts. While £200 may seem paltry when compared with Foppington's prodigious income of £5,000 pounds per annum, for the late seventeenth century, it was not an inconsiderable sum. There is no reason to think, moreover, that Young Fashion will be a better husband either to Hoyden or to the substantial fortune—at least £1,500 per annum—that she brings to their marriage. Young Fashion's only strategy seems to be to spend and spend until he has no more. Finally, and perhaps most significantly, the trial of Lord Foppington's virtue that Young Fashion conducts to relieve his own conscience relies on a rather slender application of principle, which is to say, as Collier might, no principle at all. These ambiguities and incongruities suggest that we ought to take a closer look at how Young Fashion's and Lord Foppington's actions are framed and to consider which of these equally flawed characters provides a more apt model for conduct amid the new political economies of the post-Revolutionary public sphere.

We first encounter Young Fashion at the docks upon his arrival from the

Continent, where he has been so profligate in his expenditures that he has no
ready money to pay the waterman for this last leg of his journey. Pretending
that he has only gold but no changeable coins about him, he inveigles the
wary waterman to haul away his almost empty portmanteau as collateral for
the payment he promises to send as soon as he has exchanged his mythical
gold for coin. From the outset, then, we are to understand Young Fashion as a
"sharper" among "sharpers," relying upon, or we might say capitalizing on, his
still genteel appearance to avoid honest payment to a man of lower status.
Those who take him for some kind of class rebel would seem sorely mistaken
in their assessments, for he is most surely no revolutionary man of the
people.

Once the waterman has departed with his illusory recompense, Young
Fashion's servant, Lory, turns to the business of convincing the profligate to
turn to his older brother for financial assistance. When Young Fashion
avouches that he would rather join the army than play the supplicant to his
brother's largess, Lory expresses surprise, as Young Fashion's Jacobite affiliation would seem to preclude taking the required oaths. Mocking Lory's guile-
lessness, Young Fashion pointedly retorts, "Thou mayst as well say I can't take
orders because I'm an atheist" (I.ii.56–57). Indeed, such were the times, as
Young Fashion explains, that the strength of one's "conscience" was not so
much an abstract thing in itself as a malleable substance that "proceeds from
the weakness of the purse" (I.ii.61–62).

This kind of banter would seem to undercut any claims that Young Fashion is a man of integrity, and yet critics have often commended this trickster
as a figure of conscience in the comedy for his momentary qualms about following through on the plot against his brother. Even more, they often seem to
believe that Young Fashion was justified in his "revolutionary" actions. Of the
"trial" of humanity that Young Fashion stages and that Foppington fails, Carlos Gómez writes, for instance, "The trial takes place, but Foppington still
shows no love for his younger brother, providing rebellion with justification."[75] Similarly, Rose Zimbardo holds, "Providence allows Foppington's
own vanity to undo him, and Young Fashion is Providence's instrument, . . .
Young Fashion *will* be helped by Providence because, despite his faults, he has
a conscience; Foppington will be tricked by Providence because he has neither
conscience nor charity."[76] Significantly, in staking these claims, neither Gómez
nor Zimbardo perceive any irony either in offering providential justifications
for this Jacobite's success or in affirming this younger sibling's own celebration
of providential favor (see, for instance, I.iii.278–79). Yet those in Vanbrugh's

late seventeenth-century audience might have found this peculiar mixture of claims to conscience and providence rather incongruous, given that it was the Williamites of the period who worked so hard to articulate and to publicize William and Mary's accession to the throne as the work of Providence.[77] From this perspective, Young Fashion's invocation of Providence marks him not so much as a figure of integrity and conscience as a mercenary willing to turn on his own supposed principles and to make use of any means within his disposal to justify his actions and support his interests. When it comes to his own advancement, the indefeasible right of hereditary succession is no more than a mere obstacle to be overcome, and he is more than happy to invoke Whiggish Providence as his justification. Birth order was no more than the caprice of that "bitch" Fortune, to be railed at for "thrust[ing]" his "coxcomb" brother into the world before himself (I.ii.86–87).

None of this is either to excuse Lord Foppington's callous and at times obnoxious indifference to his brother's need or to defend the class ideologies that privileged the rights of primogeniture. But it is to say that in a comedy that organizes itself around the motif of trials of virtue, the one Young Fashion stages to test his brother's compassion is of a rather more specious kind. When, in the main plot, Loveless falls to the allures of Berinthia's beauty, or Amanda, despite the promptings of her own desire, resists the tempting overtures of Worthy, we understand those moments, in the context of the conflicts and crises of late seventeenth-century political discourse, as having a kind of probative power, as each scenario explores the relative strength of vows formerly avouched and oaths formerly sworn. Pathetically addicted to novelty, Loveless emerges as an emblem of faithlessness, even as Amanda secures her place as a symbol of passive obedience, that is, as a wife/subject who maintains her loyalty to her husband/sovereign even though he abuses his position.[78] Young Fashion can make no such substantial claims.

Where Young Fashion's intrigues are driven by a set of compelling passions and supported by a series of improvisatorial stratagems, Lord Foppington's schemes are guided by a cool calculus and far-sighted perspective. Indeed, despite his foppish behavior, the newly elevated lord is one of the most consistently rational actors in the comedy. Fops, of course, have long provided audiences and critics with much fodder for laughter of a derisive sort. Their extravagant attention to dress, outlandish periwigs, and other fashionable accoutrements; the fuss they make over their personal appearance; and their arguably effeminate affect, all mark them as comic but socially marginal figures— "fools in fashion."[79] Yet, as Susan Staves has pointed out, the manners and

foibles of stage fops also provided a reliable index of shifting tastes in the period and in particular of the emergent forms of masculinity that would ultimately come to dominate social concourse in the next century.[80] As I have
detailed elsewhere, the cultivation of good breeding was increasingly tied over
the course of the eighteenth century "to notions of education and training
and to the quality of a person's skills and manners, in conducting the business
of commercial and social life."[81] There was, in other words, a certain tactical
and material advantage to be gained by cultivating good manners in a public
sphere that was besieged, as Sir Tunbelly Clumsey notes, with "plots and
roguery" (IV.v.12–13).

In Foppington, we find a character who has learned not only to cultivate
what Lincoln Faller has termed an "imperturbable cool"—even when wrongfully confined in Sir Tunbelly's dog kennel—but also a percipient ability to
assess and to manage his material advantages and disadvantages in any given
moment (Figure 8).[82] Even in what appear to be the most inane interactions,
Foppington demonstrates that he knows his interest and follows its dictates.
As he jousts, for instance, with his periwig maker over the style and proportion of that crucial "foretop"—in this case a peruke of such vast proportions
that according to Alexander Pope it was drawn onto the stage in a sedan
chair—he makes clear the distinction between "weight" and "tale" that had
been brought all too vividly into relief during the coinage crisis of the late
1690s.[83] Foppington is not so interested here in how many ounces of hair the
tradesman has used in constructing this essential, even if ridiculous, part of
his wardrobe but rather in the "tale" he expects it to convey to others about his
status and position. While one might be tempted to mock Foppington for
insisting that he will not be "put . . . upon," his point is the not insignificant
one that appearances do indeed tell and that the attention he pays to his outward presentation should be understood as an investment in his future value.
Similarly, where Derek Hughes has characterized Foppington's purchase of his
new title as a foolish extravagance, it might just as easily be construed as an
apt investment, or as the newly minted lord himself puts it, "ten thousand
pawnd well given" (I.iii.16).[84] Indeed, no less sharp an observer of social culture than Berinthia attests, "He has bought a barony in order to marry a great
fortune" (II.142–43). Foppington calculates, in other words, that he will attract a more lucrative match if he has a title to go with his lavish income. By
virtue of this new title, moreover, Foppington not only gains the kind of social cachet that will make him all the more attractive to large fortunes on the
marriage market, but he also gains access to the halls of Parliament, where, by

Figure 8. Colley Cibber as Lord Foppington in John Vanbrugh's *The Relapse*.
© Victoria and Albert Museum, London.

astutely allying himself with the Whigs and making his vote available whenever necessary, he can propel himself into social and political circles that may prove to his advantage over time.

In short, while Foppington is ultimately thwarted by the intrigues of his brother in this particular venture, there is no reason to think that there will not be another fortune looking to marry a title and another opportunity to better his position.[85] Further, while we might mock him and derive a great deal of humor from a society that allows for the purchase of a title, Lord

Foppington nevertheless emerges, as much if not more than his brother, as a shrewd consumer of the new kinds of opportunities afforded by the political and economic culture of the 1690s. One might even go so far as to argue that where Young Fashion engages in an old tactic, masquerading as his brother to gain access to Hoyden, Lord Foppington represents a new and more subtle post-Revolutionary stratagem, hiding in plain sight beneath a cloak of manners and cultivated equanimity to gain access to social and economic opportunity.[86]

Foppington's keen ability to assess his position and to gauge the upside and downside is abundantly apparent in at least two episodes with his younger brother. In the first, Foppington has, unbeknownst to himself, failed the trial of his generosity that Young Fashion stages. Indeed, he proves himself not only impervious to Young Fashion's pleas for assistance but also utterly obnoxious, as he cites his own "extremity" in expenses, having been forced by recent financial straits into the dire position of "retrench[ing] in that one article of sweet pawder . . . dawn to five guineas a manth" (III.i.91–94). Astounded by Foppington's outrageous egotism, Fashion draws his sword and challenges his brother to do the same. Without skipping a beat, Foppington instead offers the following pointed rejoinder: "Look you, Tam, you know I have always taken you for a mighty dull fellow, and here is one of the foolishest plats broke out that I have seen in a long time. Your paverty makes your life so burdensome to you, you would provoke me to quarrel, in hopes either to slip through my lungs into my estate or to get yourself run through the guts to put an end to your pain. But I will disappoint you in both your designs, far with the temper of a philasapher and the discretion of a statesman—I will go to the play with my sword in my scabbard" (III.i.120–29). Foppington reads his brother's challenge as a kind of senselessness, where all the advantages lay on his opponent's side and where he had nothing to gain and all to lose. Adopting what he terms the "temper of a philasapher," his is a kind of complaisance and dispassionate calculation. He demonstrates that just as in matters of love, in matters of the passions, his heart is "à la glace" (III.i.46). Unperturbed and not even a little bit threatened, Foppington leaves Young Fashion shaking with fury and coolly exits the scene, "sword in [his] scabbard," to enjoy the newest offering at the playhouse.

Foppington displays this same uncanny presence of mind even after suffering the greatest of humiliations when Young Fashion, having followed through on his plot to usurp his brother's place, arrives at the scene of Foppington's wedding celebration and announces that Hoyden is already married to him. Though defeated, Foppington again demonstrates his ability to minimize the damage to his person by cultivating a philosophical mind and adopting a diplomatic air of nonchalance. In an extended aside to the audience that begins to turn our sympathies, he pronounces, "Now for my part, I think the wisest thing a man can do with an aching heart is to put on a serene countenance, for a philosophical air is the most becoming thing in the world to the face of a person of quality; I will therefore bear my disgrace like a great man, and let the people see I am above an affront" (V.v.250–55). Having reasoned through his options as to what might be the "most becoming thing," Foppington concedes the ground graciously to Young Fashion. He understands, in other words, that form matters and that the social form here is perhaps more important than any content, as it helps to smooth over and to displace any potential for further violence. He accepts what is *de facto* and, with what he earlier termed the "discretion of a statesman," passes over any arguments that might concern the principles that underpin the *de jure*. Young Fashion, on the other hand, has not learned any lessons in what might be the "most becoming thing." Instead, he gloats over his victory in gaining "this lady and two thousand pound a year" and, in a demonstration of poor form, mocks Foppington for the grimaced expression he adopts (V.v.262–63). Thus, while we have been amused by Young Fashion's ingenuity in gaining ground against his brother, in the end he makes himself unattractive and earns our disdain for his cruel treatment of Foppington in a moment that called for a more decorous and well-mannered response.

If, as Aparna Gollapudi has argued, Colley Cibber sought to stabilize the relationship between surface and depth in *Love's Last Shift* and invest the spectatorial gaze with a kind of moral authority, Vanbrugh's *The Relapse* looks instead to insist upon and to play upon the suppositious and deceptive relationship between appearance and motive.[87] In a "nimble" comedy, driven by the growth and play of metaphor, the slipperiness of referents and the potential for redoubled meaning abound. Plots rely on these kinds of incongruities and the jars and jolts they provide, but ultimately each comedy, including Vanbrugh's, bears the mark of, and is constrained by, the social address of its form.[88] This generic complaisance operates as a kind of parallel to the equanimity cultivated by stage fops like Lord Foppington, whose performative observance of social forms offered an exaggerated model of behavior for a society exhausted by political upheaval and hungry for a stable and clear path to posterity. The culture of sociability that emerged at the very end of the seventeenth century and that dominated social culture in the eighteenth thus offered a new mode for negotiating conflict, regulating conduct, and facilitating exchange in the public sphere. While tricksters like Young Fashion were certainly amusing to watch on the stage, conspiracy and deceit were understood as serious threats off the stage. Young Fashion's stealthy methods could not be regarded, then, as entirely innocuous. Indeed, his unnecessary cruelty signaled a dangerous violence of temperament that compared unfavorably with the philosophical mind cultivated by Foppington. Vanbrugh thus punctuated his comedy with an epilogue, spoken by Foppington, with lines that make the political point of that character entirely clear:

> Far, give me leave t'abserve good clothes are things
> Have ever been of great support to kings.
> All treasons come fram slovens, it is nat
> Within the reach of gentle beaux to plat;
>
> I'm very pasitive you never saw
> A through republican a finished beau
> Nor truly shall you very often see
> A Jacobite much better dressed than he.
> In shart, through all the courts that I have been in,
> Your men of mischief—still are in faul linen. (Epilogue, 11–26)

Where the Jacobite trickster remains mired in the types of deceitful plots that had come to be viewed with suspicion, the conspicuous manners of the Whiggish fop emerge from the comedy as a new kind of reliable currency despite and, ironically, precisely because they constituted a type of socially regulated performance.

It is all too easy to forget that the plays in Collier's repertoire were produced under the specter of conspiracy and rebellion and that Collier himself was viewed as an instigator of violence against the state. Questions about whom or what posed threats to the nation ran rampant, and the political stakes in this culture war were thus quite high. Vanbrugh's advocacy for a kind of cool calculus and complaisant sociability cut against more doctrinaire and radical points of view, and in the pamphlet war sparked by Collier's *A Short View*, the combative nonjuror's "faul linen" would be put on display repeatedly and compared unfavorably with this new mode of presenting bodies in public.

Jeremy Collier's Pamphlet War

While each of the comedies on Collier's "playlist" thus engaged in a kind of supposititious play that illuminated the political, economic, and social issues of the day, they also looked in their own way, as Collier's corrosive comments on the plays protest, to advance a new cultural logic for the bodies public that composed a nation exhausted by tumult and upheaval. What was at stake in both the plays and in the pamphlet war that swept them forward in its wake was whether those bodies public ought to be regulated by traditional forms of religious stricture and political authority—as Collier and his supporters would have it—or whether, given the challenges to authority wrought by the Revolution, they ought to be governed by the more secular and pragmatic forms of stricture and authority favored by his opponents. The pamphlet war accordingly became an occasion for argumentation about the dispersion of sovereignty in the political and social order and the appropriate forms of governance in public life. In this final section, then, I will offer a more expansive account both of Collier's concerns for religious, political, and social authority and of the strong and varied responses his polemics elicited. While I will begin my exploration of the rejoinders in this pamphlet war with central figures such as Congreve, I will end by taking up those entries whose interests lay somewhat further afield but whose partisan engagements in the Collier controversy illuminate the substantial historical stakes and broad cultural reach of this fiercely contested antitheatrical incident.

Collier v. Congreve: On the Abuse of Clergy on Stage

That Collier designed his *Short View* as an extension of his assault both on the legitimacy of the reign of William and Mary and on the Anglican Church for acceding to their reign is best illustrated in his chapter against the abuse of clergy on the stage. Indeed, as I already intimated in my discussion of D'Urfey's *Don Quixote*, this portion of Collier's polemic touches directly on what were for him some of the most irksome aspects of the Revolution settlement and the Anglican Church's role in ensuring that settlement. Collier turns here to what he terms "History and Argument" in order to "shew the Right the *Clergy* have to Regard, and fair usage," and as a first point of justification, he points to "*their Relation to the Deity*" (127). Construing this relationship in terms of an absolute right, Collier asserts, "The Holy *Order* is appropriated to the Divine Worship: And a *Priest* has the peculiar Honour to *Belong* to nothing less then God Almighty" (127). He reiterates this position again and again in the course of his discussion and finally concludes by referring his readers to an earlier essay he had written, titled "The Office of a Chaplain." In that essay, published as part of his *Essays on Moral Subjects* (1697), Collier wrote, "The Church is a distinct Society from the State; and independent upon it: The Constitution of the Church is founded in the Appointment of Christ, in that Commission which he gave the Apostles and their Successors, and consequently does not derive its Authority from any Earthly Power."[89] For Collier, in other words, a clergyman could not, in principle, be compelled by the state to act against conscience, for he neither belonged to nor derived his authority from any human master. Even more to the point, the state could not abrogate the authority of a representative of the church for, as in the case of a monarch's rule, that right belonged only to God.[90]

It would be easy to mistake such pronouncements as a general defense of the Anglican Church and its clergy rather than as an indictment of them. But Collier's status as a leading member of the Nonjuring Church was well-known as were the positions he espoused on its behalf; and his readers, as is patently clear in any number of the responses to him, did not mistake his intent. In Collier's view, the Anglican Church had violated its own principles and, for the sake of political interest and expedience, had acted against conscience to "consecrate the Revolt."[91] Collier's defense of the clergy in *A Short View* would have been understood, then, to bolster only those who had taken up what he termed the "Post of Honour" and refused to subject the spiritual authority of the church to "Secular Power."[92] As he declaimed in his *Perswasive to Consideration*, "To suffer therefore in Defence of Authority and Government, is both a necessary and a noble Instance of Fortitude; so that 'tis no wonder Religion should expect it from us."[93] By abandoning its own principles, the Anglican Church had cheapened its own authority and laid itself open to abuse—the effects of which Collier claims can be seen in the mistreatment of clergy on the stage. His sorrow, anger, and resentment that authority has proven so mutable and that the church and its authority should, by its own actions, be subjected so is nowhere more palpable in *A Short View* than when he bitterly spits, "This is rare Protestant Diversion, and very much for the Credit of the *Reformation!* The Church of *England*, I mean the Men of Her, is the only Communion in the World, that will endure such Insolences as these" (108).

Collier felt compelled to articulate these positions even more emphatically in his *Defence of the Short View* (1699). Published in 1699 and composed primarily as a response to Congreve and Vanbrugh, Collier condemns Congreve's arguments about the representation of clergymen by explicitly equating them with the kinds of equivocations offered to justify the Glorious Revolution, writing, "But Mr. *Congreve* urges, That by improper *Behaviour the Man becomes alienated from the Priest, and so the Folly is exposed, not the Function. . . .* This is much like the old Distinction of *Politick,* and *Personal Capacity,* applied to another Case."[94] This other case, obviously, is that of the deposition of James II, during which many sought to justify their actions by distinguishing between the body politic and the body personal of the king. Collier thus continues:

> Though the Function and the Person are separable in Notion, they are joyn'd in Life and Business. 'Tis true, the Office and the Person are two Things; but yet 'tis the Person which executes the Office: This makes them share a disadvantage in Common; and a Censure frequently slides from the one to the other. . . . Upon this account Persons in Authority, whether Spiritual or Civil, ought to be privileg'd from Abuse. To make the Ministers of *Church* or *State,* the *subject of Laughter and Contempt,* disables their Authority, and renders their Commission insignificant.[95]

On this basis, Collier accuses Congreve of being engaged in a "fit of Levelling" where all forms of distinction and authority are rendered insignificant, a charge that supports an earlier associative leap in the tract whereby the poets of the playhouse came to stand in for a revolutionary Parliament that had exceeded its proper jurisdiction.[96] Commenting on Congreve's assertion that the playhouse has the right to hold the clergy up to ridicule, he writes disdainfully, " 'Tis true, the Article says, They *may be accus'd, and being found guilty, by just Judgment depos'd.* But what of all this? Are the *Poets* their Judges? And is the Stage grown *Doctors Commons,* or *Westminster-Hall?*"[97] This odd piece of rhetoric functions on any number of levels. In the simplest sense, Collier's query challenges the authority of poets to act as judges with respect to clergy, a prerogative, as we have seen, that Collier attributes only to God.[98] In this sense, their judgment is always already insignificant, that is, it does not signify at all. In a more complicated sense, Collier insinuates that "levelling" has penetrated so deeply into the fabric of society that poets now feel free to assume the kinds of prerogatives of judgment already illegitimately seized by

Parliament in pronouncing the desertion of James II and the accession of William and Mary. A descent into anomie had been set in motion, and, if not resisted, the end result, as Collier envisioned, could only be that "societies must break up; and the *Foundations of the Earth be put out of Course.*"[99] Thus, we see, as J. Hopes points out, that "as the possibility of James's returning became more and more distant, Collier's opposition to the revolution took the form of an attack on the false principles which it represented and which it had helped to spread throughout society."[100] In Collier's ongoing effort to bring about a second Restoration, the stage became, in short, just one more front on which to wage the battle. For Collier, in effect, the loss of authority in the body politic—the realm of principle—had given rise to a concomitant loss of authority in the body public—the realm of practice.

Collier's clericalism did not go unopposed, and as the reference to Congreve above indicates, the playwright and others went far beyond simply restoring to "proper and true Signification" the passages of plays that Collier had taken out of context to support his accusations of vice and irreligion.[101] Indeed, almost all of the principal players took great care in their rejoinders and ripostes both to take particular aim at Collier's compromised political position and to attest that Collier, despite his defense of clergy, had done more harm to that office and to the church than any one play could ever do. In his *A Short Vindication of* The Relapse *and* The Provok'd Wife, John Vanbrugh wrote, for instance, "'Tis the Clergy's Invasion into the Temporal Dominion, that has rais'd the Alarm against 'em: It has made their Doctrine suspected, and by consequence, their Persons despis'd."[102] Echoing Vanbrugh's epilogue to *The Relapse*, John Dennis took an even more caustic view of Collier's polemics, arguing that the civil war had been brought on by those "who had an utter aversion to the Stage" and that "he who now discovers so great an aversion to the Stage, has notoriously done all that lay in his little power to plunge us in another Civil War."[103] Calling for "lawful and reasonable pleasures" as a way to keep the peace, he thus maintains, "The Vices which are charg'd upon the friends of the Stage, are for the most part the effects of frailty, and meer human Vices; whereas the faults of its inveterate Enemies, are known to be diabolical crimes, destructive of Society, of Peace, and of human Happiness."[104] With considerable political purchase, Dennis and Vanbrugh thus render strong historical claims against Collier's integrity. For the best use of dramaturgical conventions and effects in this contest, however, we need to look to Congreve's *Amendments of Mr. Collier's False and Imperfect Citations* (Figure 9).[105]

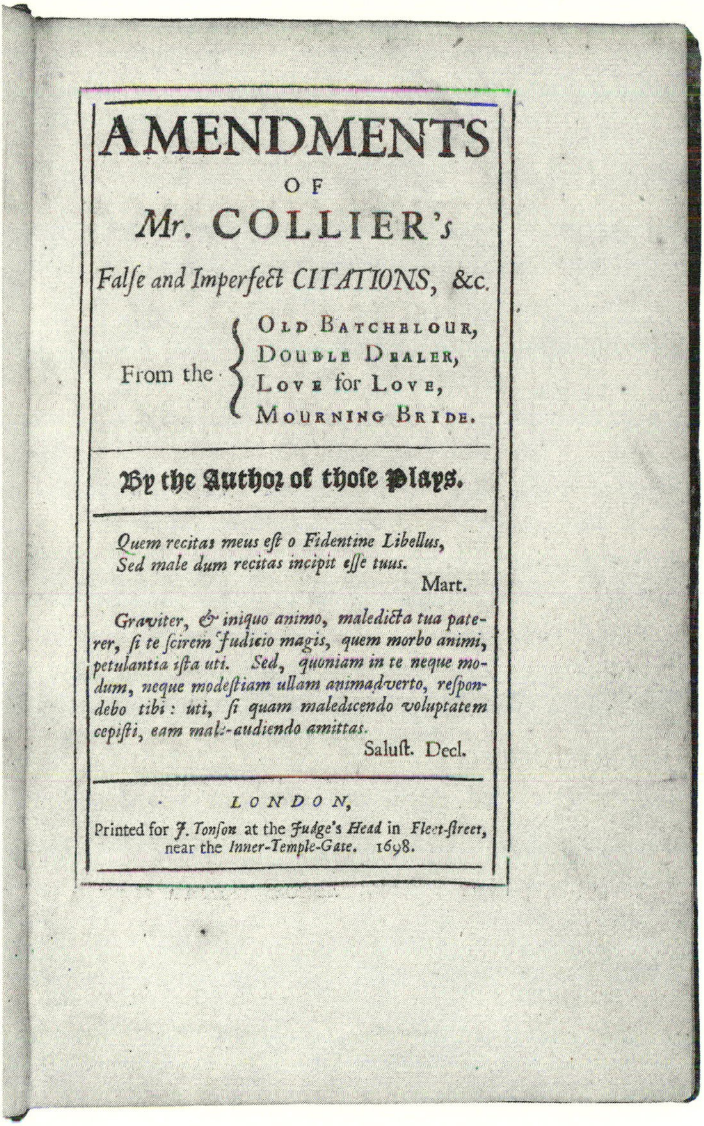

AMENDMENTS

OF

Mr. COLLIER's

False and Imperfect CITATIONS, &c.

From the { OLD BATCHELOUR,
DOUBLE DEALER,
LOVE for LOVE,
MOURNING BRIDE.

By the Author of those Plays.

Quem recitas meus est o Fidentine Libellus,
Sed male dum recitas incipit esse tuus.

Mart.

Graviter, & iniquo animo, maledicta tua pate-
rer, si te scirem Judicio magis, quem morbo animi,
petulantia ista uti. Sed, quoniam in te neque mo-
dum, neque modestiam ullam animadverto, respon-
debo tibi: uti, si quam maledicendo voluptatem
cepisti, eam male-audiendo amittas.

Salust. Decl.

LONDON,

Printed for *J. Tonson* at the *Judge's Head* in *Fleet-street*,
near the *Inner-Temple-Gate*. 1698.

Figure 9. Title page, William Congreve, *Amendments of Mr. Collier's False and Imperfect Citations*, 1698.
Used by permission of the Folger Shakespeare Library.

From beginning to end in his *Amendments*, Congreve situates Collier in association with the iniquitous, the licentious, and the unlawful, and he takes especial care to trace a continuous arc of criminal activity in Collier's *Short View* that runs from "Rape" to "Sedition." Charging Collier first with having committed "a Rape upon [his] Words," Congreve turns the clergyman's attacks into an occasion for the administration of justice by demanding "the Privilege of the *habeas Corpus* Act, that the Prisoners may have Liberty to remove, and to appear before a just Judge in an open and an uncounterfeit light" (4, 10). Congreve's concern here is that Collier took passages from his plays out of context and unfairly distorted their meaning. He thus demands that the entire body of his text be brought forward both as a matter of justice and as a matter of principle. Scholars have noted the extent to which Congreve seems obsessed in his *Amendments* with stripping Collier's pamphlet of what he terms its "Sophistical Varnish" and restoring passages that Collier had ripped out of context, and by and large, they have characterized this performative quirk as an effect of Congreve's defense of the literary, that is, of figuration and figurative uses of language against the blunt literalism of Collier.[106] Yet, for Congreve, I would submit, much more was at stake than simply ensuring that his characters' words would be understood in the context for which they were designed. Rather, his concerns extend to the regulation of social and political culture at a time when the authority of old ontologies had lost their sway and competing epistemologies were being put forward on a daily basis. In a culture where it was now commonly acknowledged that words could be wrangled in the service of almost any cause, what Congreve demanded, then, or at least Whiggishly affected to demand, was a certain kind of "Civility." "I am Civiller to [Collier]," he wrote, "I take his Sense as he would have it understood" (44). Thus charging Collier not only with using language to "Barbarous" ends but also with bending language violently to suit his own interests, Congreve goes on to complete the full rhetorical arc by tying such incivilities, or the willingness to overturn otherwise settled understandings among persons, to the much larger threat of sedition, that is, the willingness to overturn the settlements of 1688 altogether.

Like many other defenders of the stage, then, Congreve was quick to engage Collier's attack on the stage as a form of political subterfuge, and he minced no words when he wrote, "I am not the only one who look on this Pamphlet of his to be a Gun levell'd at the whole Laity, while the shot only glances on the Theatre" (101–2). Taking the position that Collier used his attack on the stage as a cover to condemn the populace at large for its lack of sufficient principle, something Collier could not do outright without risking further legal difficulties, Congreve intimates that the clergyman had even greater objects in mind. Why, he asks, would Collier "ma[k]e such a Bugbear of the Theatre" if it were not to further his interests and scatter his "Seeds of Sedition" by "sowr[ing] the humours of the People of most leisure, that they might be more apt to mis-employ their vacant hours" (106)? Drawing on the popular conceit that the English were a people particularly prone to melancholy and discontent, Congreve indicts Collier for deliberately attempting to drive them from one of the few activities that not only might distract them from their affinities for rebellion but might also prevent such upheavals by providing a space and a technology whereby individuals might be forced to reflect upon their own guilt, innocence, and interests and correct any errant passions.

To illustrate these claims, Congreve alights on the utterly brilliant strategy of examining Collier's conduct as one might that of a character in the playhouse. Initiating one of the more sustained and intriguing sections of his *Amendments*, he announces, "Now let us take a View of Mr. Collier, as he appears upon the Stage" (76–77). Exemplifying what he takes to be the operational mode by which comedy engages in acts of correction and at the same time indicting Collier for his demand that clergymen be exempt from representation on the stage, Congreve insists, "Let Mr. *Collier* be represented as he is, not as he ought to be; that by seeing what he is, Mr. *Collier* may be asham'd of what he is, and endeavour at what he ought to be" (78). In the master stroke that follows, Congreve contrives to put Collier forward as an object of judgment not only for our spectatorial gaze but also for the clergyman's own eyes, and in so doing, he anticipates the growth of a discourse that, as David Marshall has shown us, would come to situate the "figure of theater" and indeed theatricality itself as an instrument for moral inquiry and the modeling of ethical relations.[107] Dividing Collier the priest from Collier the man, Congreve places the priest on the stage so that the "better Part of him" might "take his Place in the Pit, and let the other appear to him like his evil Genius on the Stage" (79). In a refrain that functions as a kind of drumbeat of condemnation, Congreve then goes on to review a host of Collier's behaviors and projects Collier's own reactions to what he might observe in himself. These scenarios range from the fairly benign—"The Player *Collier* shall call the Gentlemen that he converses with, Foot-pads, Buffoons, Slaves, &c. that the Spectator *Collier* may remember they are Christians"—to the rather problematically incendiary—"Mr *Collier* on the Stage shall rack Bawdrey and Obscenity out of modest and innocent Expressions. . . . The Spectator in the Pit shall plainly perceive, that he loves to look on naked Obscenity; and that he only flogs it, as a sinful Paedoguge sometimes lashes a pretty Boy, that looks lovely in his Eyes, for Reasons best known to himself" (80–81).

In this staging of comedy's corrective capacities, that is, of its especial aptitude in a space of supposition for producing vivid spectacles of behaviors that ought to be curbed, each refrain marks yet another point in the exhaustive indictment against Collier's uncivil conduct until Congreve concludes, "No question but if our Author, in the Pit, did behold his Counterpart on the Stage, thus egregiously to play the Fool . . . *the rebuke would strike stronger upon his sense*, and prove more effectual to his Reformation" (87). In this manner, Congreve not only advises Collier to make himself into an object of judgment and look to his own moral reformation, he also effectively situates comedy and the spectacular technologies of the playhouse as the medium through which moral reformation of bodies in public might best be achieved.

Staging History

If Collier was trying to resist and perhaps even reverse the course of history, there were others, both for and against the stage, who had an interest in extending the political settlements of the last ten years. Taking the occasion of an attack on the stage to advance disparate political agendas, many who joined the fray not only offered their own readings of history, but, like Congreve above, they also worked to advance and to cultivate a performative ethos for the deportment of bodies in the public sphere. This pattern becomes even more readily apparent when we venture farther afield from figures like Congreve toward more wide-ranging polemical works, such as *The Stage Condemned* (1698) and *The Stage Acquitted* (1699), and it accords with J. G. A. Pocock's account of "history" and political discourse in the late seventeenth and early eighteenth centuries. In Pocock's view, history as "public time," which is to say "time experienced . . . by individuals who see themselves as public beings" and who "see society as organized into and by a number of frameworks, both institutional and conceptual, in and through which they apprehend things as happening to society and themselves," was deranged in the late seventeenth century by both the failure and the abrogation of traditional forms of authority. As a result, "such orderings and their languages had drawn together to a point where it seems truer to say that time and history were ordered by consciousness of a public realm or political nation, which could itself be ordered and conceptualized in a number of different ways." In this regard, Pocock identifies two basic modes of organization: continuity, where the emphasis is placed on "perpetuating usages and practices, transmitting its different forms of authority and . . . maintaining its legitimacy"; and contingency, where institutionality is diminished and "is now [understood as] a continuous capacity for action rather than a continuous transmission of legitimacy."[108] In some very profound sense, then, the Collier controversy, as we will see below, was finally and fundamentally a dispute both over how the historical events not just of the last decade, but indeed of the last century, were to be understood and over the influence such an understanding ought to wield over social and political relations in the nation.

For Collier, as we have already discussed, the Williamite accession represented a betrayal of the indefeasible right of hereditary succession, a violent break with continuity, and a dangerous movement into a form of public time marked by the contingencies of *de facto* government, where power was negotiated rather than inherited and where, as he put it disdainfully in his essay "Of Power," "Empire consists chiefly in the Submission of other Men's Wills; which is in a manner but reigning by Courtesy."[109] Like Collier, as I shall demonstrate, the authors of *The Stage Condemned* and *The Stage Acquitted*, were aware of themselves as public beings and as part of a public discourse, but given their disparate and often antagonistic political commitments, their relationship to continuity and contingency in the accounts of history they provide is quite different. Indeed, not only does contingency become a source of legitimate action and transformation in their versions of history; rather the moral valences of continuity and of contingency are themselves recalibrated. Though one tract condemned the stage and the other supported it, in both accounts continuity comes to be understood as a form of tyranny even as contingency comes to be construed as a sign of the nation's liberty, an outcome that goes a long way toward illuminating the complexity of the political allegiances that were brought into relief by the controversy.

That the Collier controversy made for strange political bedfellows is no more vividly illustrated than in the troubled coupling of Collier with George Ridpath, the purported author of *The Stage Condemned* (1698), who was just as fierce a Puritan and a Whig as Collier was a High Church Anglican and a Tory.[110] In his epistle dedicatory and introduction, Ridpath makes his motives for entering into the stage controversy clear. Collier, in his opinion, had done a good job up to a point, but ultimately he was hampered by his nonjurancy, which is to say, by his loyalty to the Anglican Church and the Stuart monarchy and to the Catholic tendencies of each institution. In Ridpath's sinister account, the stage was not just a site of immorality or profaneness; it was, more menacingly, one of the insidious vehicles used to "promote the Glorious Design of Debauching the Nation, and to baffle the Evidence of the Popish Plots" and had been, as we saw in the last chapter, since at least the 1630s when Charles I, under the influence of Archbishop Laud, had reintroduced the *Book of Sports* and blasphemed the Sabbath by entertaining at court with Sunday masques.[111] Thus, the martyr in Ridpath's history is not Charles I, as he and James II would be in Collier's account, but rather William Prynne, who, as we have seen, was branded a seditious libeler for assailing the royal prerogatives of the monarch and for challenging the authority of the archbishop. "In those Times," Ridpath tells us:

> None were accounted Enemies to the Play-house but Puritans and Precisians, and in opposition to them it probably was that *Laud* and his Clergy became its Patrons; and it is not unlike that many of the Less-thinking Church-men continue still to favour it on that Account, as being unwilling to condemn that, for which King *Charles* I. and Arch-bishop *Laud* testified so much Passion; but these Gentlemen would do well to remember, *That the Defence of the Stage was never so much the Characteristick of their Church, as was the Doctrine of Passive Obedience; and seeing the Majority of them have relinquished that, they are infinitely the more to blame for still adhering to this.* (9)

Ridpath's commentary cuts in any number of directions, all of which are meant to point up inconsistencies and sophistries in the positions staked out by his political rivals. On the one hand, he praises Collier for coming out against the stage but upbraids him for his Jacobite affinities, that is, for supporting the papist regime that supported and maintained close ties to the playhouse. On the other hand, he mocks those clergymen who seem to have summoned the backbone to overthrow the principle of passive obedience, depose James II, and swear an oath of allegiance to William and Mary, and yet who have not found the wherewithal to root out the agent of Caroline tyranny and Jacobite popery, which is to say, the stage. Thus, he caustically opines, there is "a mighty Neglect somewhere, and the World will hardly be perswaded that our Church of *England* is unanimous in this Matter, *else it were easie for them, who shook King* James *out of his Throne, to overturn the Stage*" (8). In Ridpath's version of history, then, the "Incendiaries and

Fomenters of the Civil War" of 1641 were not the Puritans but rather the "Friends of the Stage, who taught Rebellion against our Constitution, set the King above all Laws, and would have trod Parliaments under foot" (204). Shoring up his political position under the settlements of the Revolution of 1688, he thus avows that those "very Men who were Enemies to the Stage" in "41," which is to say, those who supported the principle of rebellion against tyranny are thus "the firmest Friends this Government [now] has" (204). In this manner, Ridpath aligns himself politically against both the established Anglican Church and the nonjurors and affiliates himself with the hard-line ideology of Puritans in the Societies for the Reformation of Manners movement, who looked to William III in the 1690s to translate the achievements of the political revolution into an equally revolutionary program of moral reformation.[112]

While William III, as Tony Claydon has demonstrated, waged a highly effective rhetorical campaign to position himself as the "patron of the reformation movement," this movement itself did not go unopposed. Indeed, as Claydon concedes, "There is, in fact, considerable evidence from the 1690s that the general run of William's subjects were highly ambivalent about having their manners reformed by statutes, and that many viewed the movement as an excuse for hypocritical interference in private lives. . . . Poets and pamphleteers certainly attacked the movement for . . . reviving the puritan terror of Cromwell's day."[113] It is not surprising to find, then, that a rejoinder to Ridpath, *The Stage Acquitted*, was soon composed and published, presenting an argument on the side of the political base within the Established Church that supported the Glorious Revolution but that sought to constrain the influence and power of the dissenting factions.

The Stage Acquitted presents us with a skeptical dialogue between two figures, Lovetruth and Fairly, who purportedly seek to cut through the reports of the town to get to the truth of the matter over the stage. The strategy of this anonymous pamphlet is to represent Collier and Ridpath as extremists who seek both to suppress individual liberty and conscience and to impose a form of tyranny, either political or moral, upon the nation, while figuring the protagonists, Fairly and Lovetruth, as paragons of rational moderation. Quite cleverly, moreover, the author often pits Collier and Ridpath against one another, not only canceling out the supposed authority of both but also undermining the idea of authority altogether. In this manner, *The Stage Acquitted* prepares the rhetorical way for the new mode of order and governance in the body public that, as we have already seen with Congreve, would be based on reason and experience.[114] Training his sights on Collier first, Lovetruth thus reasons, "It cannot be reasonably doubted but that the *Stage* is of considerable use and advantage to the *Public*; for certainly so eminent a Clergy, as that of the *Episcopal Church of England*, who have the most pure and uncorrupted Doctrine of all the *Christian* world, who are admirable for their *Piety*, and every where valued for their *Learning*, cannot be thought to encourage what would any way tend to the Corruption of the Morals of the *Age*, as Mr *Collier* would seem to affirm."[115] Using Ridpath's account of Charles I's and Laud's affinity for stagecraft against Collier, Lovetruth highlights the internal inconsistency of Collier's position. For if as a nonjuror he venerated the memory of Archbishop Laud and Charles I, then it would seem strange that he would honor that legacy by attacking institutions they so heartily supported; he "could not be ignorant that the *whole body* of the *Clergy* of the *Church of England* in the time of the Martyr, did in an *extraordinary* manner encourage Plays" (17). Mocking Collier's self-righteousness with respect to the abuse of clergy Lovetruth goes on to note that "Mr *Collier* himself has not us'd them very kindly, when he has endeavor'd to deprive them of their hearers, with as much zeal, as he had to rob the Poets of theirs." Fairly replies with all due equanimity that indeed "'tis strange that Mr *Collier* should be angry with the *Stage* for one single *Say-grace*, when he has made so severe a Satire on the *whole body* of the *Clergy* that are for the Government" (17). Referring here to Collier's attacks on the Anglican Church and to his polemic in his *Perswasive to Consideration* against attending church services under the auspices of that clerical regime, Fairly and Lovetruth conclude that the stage could hardly do more damage to the authority of clergy than Collier has already done himself.[116]

Having made their case against Collier, Lovetruth and Fairly then turn to an assessment of Ridpath. Characterizing him variously as a "news-monger," a "scribbler," and a "zany," Lovetruth moves, first, to reconstrue Ridpath's version of antitheatrical history, remonstrating:

> Mr *Prynne* had his tryal, and was cast for acting against *Law*, in broaching ten thousand *false* and *scandalous* Reflections against both *King* and *Church*, as well as the *Stage*; and 'tis a glory to the *latter* to have suffer'd with, and on account of the *former*; and all of this is so far from a Reflection on either *King* or *Church*, as he impudently means it, that 'tis only so on himself; for he has yet shown us no *Evidence* in himself either in *Learning*, or in a Pious and Christian

Spirit, that should make us believe him a *better* Judge of those matters, than the most *Pious* and *Learned Clergy* that ever flourish'd in
our *English* World, and by consequence not inferiour to that of *any*
Age or Nation whatever. (12)

Here Lovetruth casts Ridpath as a dangerous Puritan zealot who defies the
authority and wisdom of an Anglican establishment that favored the stage.
But he leaves it to the usually even-tempered Fairly to express outrage over
Ridpath's skewed version of history, to recall the terrifying specter of the days
of the Commonwealth, and to remind Ridpath of his place in the post-
Revolutionary political order:

How? What were the *Puritans* the only Sticklers for *properties*? Had
not the Church as much to lose? And have they ever been remiss in
the care of the Public Good? Have they betray'd the Trust repos'd in
them by the People? Have they been false to their duty to the Publick Good? If the Church of *England* has been guilty of these Abominable Crimes, let our Author prove it, if not, how came the
Puritans the Guardians of our Liberty? Those who invaded and dis-
obey'd the Laws of their Country, gave not the greatest proof of
their Love to, or Zeal for it; and 'tis evident enough, that even from
the time of Queen *Elizabeth*, when they first appear'd, the wisdom
of the Nation thought they ought to be restrain'd by *Law*, and were
deny'd *Liberty* of *Conscience*, for many years before King *Charles* the
First. 'Tis true, they have now the Liberty they then wanted, but
they should remember to whom they owe that Benefit, *viz.* to a
King of the Church of *England's perswasion*, to the very Bishops
they abuse, to the Lords and Commons, all, or most of the *Church
of England*; and that should teach them more *modestly* towards their
Benefactors. (24–25)

In what appears to be a justified fury, Fairly recalls the violent upheavals of the
1640s and contrasts the radical contingencies of the unlawful usurpation of
government and "Abominable Crimes" of the Puritan regime to the wisdom,
lawfulness, and continuity of the Established Church during the Revolution
of 1688. Although Lovetruth moves to allow that Fairly ought not to hold the
entire body of dissenters responsible for the actions of one man, the pamphlet
makes it clear that the new freedoms enjoyed by dissenters should be

considered a matter not of right but of magnanimity. In this manner, Ridpath's authority is thoroughly undermined, and his ambitious moral and political agenda is exposed as a danger both to "Liberty" and to the "publick good."

As part of its political program, moreover, *The Stage Acquitted* makes every effort to debunk all religious authority and inherited orthodoxies as the crutch of the weak-minded. In this respect, Collier and Ridpath are grouped together, and their appeals to Church Fathers such as Tertullian are exposed as tyrannical impositions of authority that make no rational sense. Perhaps the most damning indictment in this regard comes from Fairly when he observes:

> There is no doubt to be made, but that an industrious man of any moderate share of brains may bring *Fathers* and *Scriptures* too for a thousand *Absurdities* and *Falsities*. This is as evident as daily experience can make it. The Controversies betwixt the Church of *Rome* and *England*, betwixt the Church of *England* and *Dissenters*, betwixt the *Congregational* and *Presbyterian Divines*, betwixt the *Anabaptists* and their *Opposers*; and so on to all the *divisions*, and sub-divisions of opinions, that this Town alone affords us. Which has render'd our Common *Christianity* so obscure, that if we deny our *Reason* to be Judge of the Controversie, and tell us when the *Fathers* speak right, when the *several sides* give the true sense of *Scripture*, we must perpetually wander in the dark, and fall into the unhappy and deplorable state of *Scepticism*. (91–92)

The litany of schisms rehearsed here has an almost absurdist ring to it, yet Fairly's point is demonstrably supported by *The Stage Acquitted*, where we find that Ridpath and Collier, who purportedly support one another in their campaign against the stage, can actually be read to argue against one another. Thus, noting how "in the Controversy betwixt the Protestants and Papists . . . both sides Charge each other with wresting or false quoting the Authorities against them," Lovetruth, like Fairly, condemns the influence of "Faction," "Passion and Interest," and concludes similarly "that the Controversie ought indeed to be reduc'd to the thing itself, without regard to the noisy pretences of Authority" (154–55).

With the truth of any matter so deeply obscured by sectarian interests, the only remedy, as Lovetruth exhorts Fairly early on, is not to give in to cant but rather "like other men, be convinc'd by your own experience; and pay the same for your knowledge that I have done. Read, read, Sir, and see" (4). Extolling scientific discoveries and disparaging the parochial pronouncements of the Fathers, he declares:

> Those *Fathers* that writ against the *Antipodes*, proceeded to actual violence, and built their opinions on several *Texts* of *Scripture*, as the opposers of *Copernicus* will shew in all their trifling Books; and yet *Galliloeus* and *Gassendus* in their defence of that *System* have evidently confuted their opinions; and Experience has evidently prov'd, that the *Scripture* was not to be understood in the same sense the *Fathers* or the Modern *Ptolomists* wou'd have it, there being nothing now more certain, than the Orbicular form of the Earth, and by consequence that there are *Antipodes* . . . which is enough to shew, that we can build no Authority on the *Fathers*, where reason is against them. (92–93)

If Fairly's dissection of religious history, with its emphasis on the endless waves of schism, is meant to convince us of the folly of blindly following church authorities—or, for that matter, of trying to figure out which church authorities to follow—then Lovetruth's dissertation on the historical triumphs of science is surely meant to convince us that the exercise of reason will prove a better foundation for judgment than the "*doctrines of Religion*" ever could be (146). After all, as they point out, "are not all History full of Matter of fact" that heresies and schisms and not the stage are responsible for "more *violent distractions, more Murders, Treasons, Assassinations, and Plots, Conspiracies, Civil Wars, Subversion of States, and the other Innumerable Evils*" (147–48)? Better to apply reason, it would seem, than ever to submit to a doctrine of faith again.

What impels *The Stage Acquitted*, then, is a desire to leave behind the legacy of violence and upheaval that was motivated by religious doctrine and religious faction and an interest in entering into a new era of tolerance, free exchange, and dialogue regulated by reason and sociability—the two qualities exemplified, of course, by the very form chosen for this particular rejoinder. Though not, as Mark Knights points out, "politically neutral," conversation by this time was, nevertheless, well on its way to becoming the very paradigm of politeness, probity, and civility, the privileged mode of interchange in the body public and, for some, the very sign of liberty in the body politic.[117] Thus,

in the public sphere imagined by Lovetruth and Fairly, authority would circu-
late much more promiscuously than it had before, and ideally, though perhaps not in practice, principles would be formed discursively on the basis of
what they characterized as reason. Collier may have sought to use the stage as
a front to turn back time, but, as this chapter has demonstrated, the controversy he provoked provided the occasion instead not only for the reiteration,
looking backward, of the historical settlements in the body politic but also for
the articulation, going forward, of a new mode of governance and engagement in and among the emergent bodies public.

Chapter 3

The Political Economy of Bodies Public

Scotland's *Douglas* Controversy

In February 1755, John Home set out for London on his trusty steed Piercy, a band of merry supporters by his side and a copy of the completed manuscript for his tragedy *Douglas* in his greatcoat pocket in anticipation of a production review by David Garrick.[1] Despite Home's strong letters of introduction and ample connections, Garrick still rejected the play, finding it "unfit for the stage." Not to be discouraged, Home and his supporters arranged for a production of the tragedy to be mounted on the Edinburgh stage, reasoning that "if it succeeded in the Edinburgh theatre, than Garrick could resist no longer." Performed for the first time on 14 December 1756 at the Canongate Theater in Edinburgh and "attended by all the great literati and most of the judges" of the day, the tragedy was an "unbounded success" (Figure 10). The city of Edinburgh was immediately thrown into an "uproar of exultation that a Scotchman had written a tragedy of the first rate, and that its merit was first submitted to their judgment."[2] Indeed, one audience member was so moved by the play and by Scots pride at the origin of this effort that he is reported to have cried out mid-performance, "Whaur's yer Wully Shakespere noo!" thereby inaugurating a nationalist critical tradition that would find its way into all subsequent discussions of the merits of the play.[3]

Based on the old Scottish ballad *Gil Morrice* and written in declamatory blank verse, the play tenders the tale of Lady Randolph and the rediscovery of her long-lost son Young Norval, the secret offspring of her clandestine marriage to a scion of the Douglas clan. The tragedy unravels as Young Norval is murdered by a jealous villain, and the devastated Lady Randolph commits suicide by throwing herself off a cliff. Set in medieval times and played against

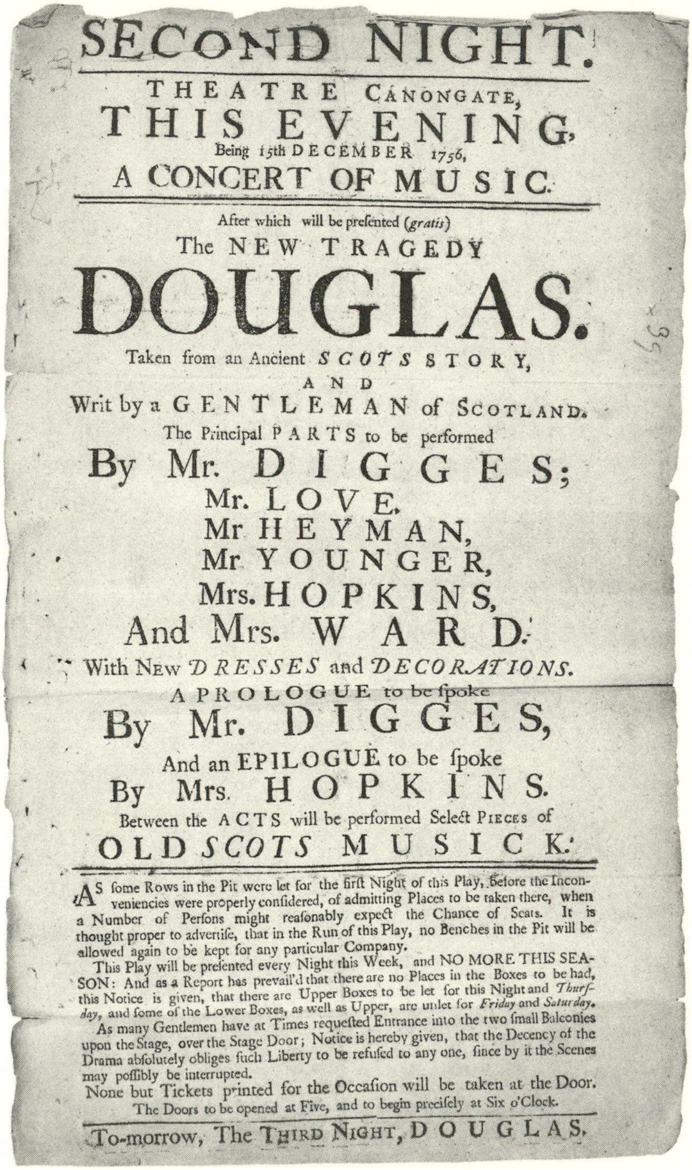

SECOND NIGHT.

THEATRE CANONGATE,

THIS EVENING,

Being 15th DECEMBER 1756,

A CONCERT OF MUSIC.

After which will be presented (*gratis*)

The NEW TRAGEDY

DOUGLAS.

Taken from an Ancient *SCOTS* STORY,

AND

Writ by a GENTLEMAN of SCOTLAND.

The Principal PARTS to be performed

By Mr. DIGGES;

Mr. LOVE,

Mr HEYMAN,

Mr YOUNGER,

Mrs. HOPKINS,

And Mrs. WARD.

With New *DRESSES* and *DECORATIONS.*

A PROLOGUE to be spoke

By Mr. DIGGES,

And an EPILOGUE to be spoke

By Mrs. HOPKINS.

Between the ACTS will be performed Select PIECES of

OLD *SCOTS* MUSICK.

AS some Rows in the Pit were let for the first Night of this Play, before the Inconveniencies were properly considered, of admitting Places to be taken there, when a Number of Persons might reasonably expect the Chance of Seats. It is thought proper to advertise, that in the Run of this Play, no Benches in the Pit will be allowed again to be kept for any particular Company.

This Play will be presented every Night this Week, and NO MORE THIS SEASON: And as a Report has prevail'd that there are no Places in the Boxes to be had, this Notice is given, that there are Upper Boxes to be let for this Night and *Thursday,* and some of the Lower Boxes, as well as Upper, are unlet for *Friday* and *Saturday.*

As many Gentlemen have at Times requested Entrance into the two small Balconies upon the Stage, over the Stage Door; Notice is hereby given, that the Decency of the Drama absolutely obliges such Liberty to be refused to any one, since by it the Scenes may possibly be interrupted.

None but Tickets printed for the Occasion will be taken at the Door.

The Doors to be opened at Five, and to begin precisely at Six o'Clock.

To-morrow, The THIRD NIGHT, DOUGLAS.

Figure 10. Playbill, *Douglas*, Second Night, Edinburgh, 1756.
Reproduced by permission of the National Library of Scotland.

the background of a gloomy and dark landscape, the tragedy, with its scenes of extreme pathos and sudden eruptions of violence, anticipates the kind of gothic melodrama that would become popular in the late eighteenth and early nineteenth centuries. In the more immediate event, Home's triumph in Edinburgh attracted the attention of London, and John Rich took the opportunity forfeited by his rival Garrick to bring the tragedy to Covent Garden in March 1757, where it enjoyed a successful run of nine performances in its first season and became a standard part of the repertory well into the nineteenth century.

For all of the tragedy's eventual success, the "most remarkable circumstance attending its representation," and perhaps the motive for Rich's interest in the transfer of the play to London, was, as Henry Mackenzie comments in his *Account of the Life and Writings of John Home*, "the clerical contest which it excited, and the proceedings of the Church of Scotland with regard to it."[4] John Home was actually the Reverend John Home, a minister in the Presbyterian Church of Scotland with a parish at Athelstaneford (Figure 11). While the "literati" of Edinburgh may have celebrated and cried up Home's tragedy—indeed, as will be discussed, they were probably responsible for much of its success on the stage—an equal uproar was raised both against the play and against theatricality more generally by the orthodox faction in the church. These "High-Flyers," led by Alexander Webster and Patrick Cuming, took exception to the participation in the theater by a member of the clergy, and they instituted proceedings in various presbyteries not only against John Home but also against all of the other ministers who attended the tragedy's performance. In short order, they succeeded in having notices of "admonition and exhortation" against the "illegal and dangerous Entertainments of the Stage" read from all pulpits of the Edinburgh and Glasgow Presbyteries and found at least one minister, a Mr. White, who was willing to be made into an example and submit to a six-week suspension from his pastoral duties for his attendance at the theater.[5] But in the libel against Alexander aka "Jupiter" Carlyle, a great friend of Home's and a leader of the Moderate faction in the kirk, they encountered considerable resistance and were forced to appeal their case from the Dalkeith Presbytery through the Synod to the supreme judicature of the General Assembly. In the end, Carlyle triumphed as the General Assembly upheld the Synod's judgment that the "grounds of proceeding in this affair in the way of a libel, are not sufficiently clear and uncontrovertible," that is, there was no "express law or statute of [the] church which prohibit[ed] her members and ministers to witness theatrical representations."[6] John Home himself avoided prosecution by resigning his ministerial commission and

JOHN HOME ESQ.ᴿ

AUTHOR of the Tragedy of DOUGLAS, &c &c.

Figure 11. John Home; line engraving by Andrew Birrell, after Sir Henry Raeburn.
© National Portrait Gallery, London.

moving to London where, under the patronage and protection of Lord Bute and the Prince of Wales, he went on to produce a number of other plays.[7] In his wake, he left behind an Edinburgh and a Scottish kirk that had been torn apart not just by the prosecutions but also by the heated pamphlet exchanges over the aesthetic and moral merits of *Douglas* in particular and the playhouse in general.

In this chapter, I contend that we ought to view the reaction to Home's tragedy not as an isolated antitheatrical eruption but rather as a point of culmination in a decades-long struggle between orthodox factions of the Scottish kirk and the secular and secularizing forces of the Scottish Enlightenment. To bear this claim out, I explore the clashes over patronage and infidelity that occurred in the years leading up to the *Douglas* affair and demonstrate how the exchanges involved in these controversies reflected major shifts in the political and cultural landscape of eighteenth-century Scotland. Taking a broad approach, moreover, I explain how these changes had a significant impact not only on the conception of the public sphere per se but also on the distribution of discursive authority among various bodies public in the public sphere of representation. Finally, and perhaps even more significantly, I trace how a new and increasingly compelling rhetorical discourse of political economy finds its way into both sides of the debate in the documents related to the *Douglas* controversy. Thus, while the storms over Home's tragedy certainly rained down their fair share of the usual antitheatrical vitriol, in the specific arguments made both for and against the stage, we can identify an increasing investment in a modern discourse of political economy and an acute awareness of the need to address the question of how best to allocate and utilize the resources of the *polis* and regulate the bodies that compose it. While this rhetorical shift might be predicted on the protheatrical side from the Scottish Enlightenment's widespread engagement with and advocacy for economic concerns, the fact that this idiom had also been adopted in antitheatrical materials suggests the extent to which a new cultural politics had already gained hegemonic status in mid-eighteenth-century Scotland. By carefully examining the documents, pamphlets, and accounts preceding and related to the *Douglas* controversy, we can begin to identify this new cultural formation, and, more significantly, we can begin to comprehend how and why a controversy over just one dramatic tragedy could constitute an event so public and so all-consuming as to drive almost all other news related to domestic affairs from the pages of Scottish periodicals.[8] We will also see how one major participant in the *Douglas* controversy, John Witherspoon, would come to influence

American antitheatrical discourse when he emigrated to the colonies to assume the presidency of Princeton University, then known as the College of New Jersey, the preeminent Presbyterian institution in pre- and post-Revolutionary America.

Moderates on the Rise

While *Douglas* may have provided the spark that ignited a full-fledged flame war, the core fuel had long been prepared and stoked. Indeed, though neither an innocent nor a defenseless one, Home was a kind of scapegoat, that is, he provided the occasion for long-seething tensions and conflicts both within the Presbyterian Church itself and between the church and secular forces to erupt. Hence, as Alice Gipson has noted, by the time:

> *Douglas* was written, there were in Scotland two church parties.
> One was the high Calvinistic, headed by men ultra conservative,
> with very extreme ideas as to their clerical obligations, and with
> very little toleration of any degree of social intercourse between the
> clergy and the laity . . . [while] to the other and more liberal
> church-party belonged such men as Adam Ferguson, Alexander
> Carlyle, and John Home, who ordered their lives on the assumption
> that they were none the worse as clergymen for indulging them-
> selves in what they sincerely believed to be innocent social diver-
> sions, and for admitting to their society lay members from whose
> company they might gain both pleasure and profit.[9]

Forming a powerful faction in the Church of Scotland that began its rise as early as the 1720s under William Hamilton and William Wishart and that could trace an intellectual lineage from Shaftesbury to Francis Hutcheson, this latter group, known as the Moderates, celebrated a right of free association; advocated for a more open, liberal, and humane religious attitude; and concerned themselves more with the forms of polite conversation, which we saw emergent in the Collier controversy, than with the contents of church doctrine and theology.[10]

To this end, the Moderates participated as founding members in many of the most eminent clubs and societies of eighteenth-century Edinburgh, including the Select Society, founded in 1754, that numbered among its members not just Home, Carlyle, and Ferguson, but also Adam Smith and David Hume. In what one can only take to be a deliberate citation of Shaftesbury, Carlyle wrote of the Select Society that "it was those meetings in particular that rubbed off all corners, as we call it, by collision, and made the *literati* of Edinburgh less captious and pedantic than they were elsewhere."[11] More especially pertinent to the case before us, Carlyle remarked on the impact of these forums for sociability and conversation on the conduct of church business, observing that while:

> the clergy of Scotland, from the Revolution downwards, had in general been little thought of, and seldom admitted into liberal society, one cause of which was, that in those days a clergyman was thought profane who affected the manners of gentlemen, or was much seen in their company, . . . [by the 1750s], the young clergy began to feel their own importance in debate, and have ever since continued to distinguish themselves, and have swayed the decision of the Assembly so that the supreme ecclesiastical court has long been a school of eloquence for the clergy, as well as a theater for the lawyers to display their talents.[12]

Historians such as Callum Brown have confirmed Carlyle's recollections, writing of the emergence of the Moderates as a dominant force in the kirk: "They discarded much of what they perceived as harsh Calvinism in preaching and church discipline in favour of refinement and elegance, moderation in religious enthusiasm, and philosophizing rather than remonstration in pulpit discourse."[13] In this manner, the nature of discursive practice in the church was transformed, even as the church itself became a site of performance for those who had cultivated eloquence through secular conversation rather than through theological debate.

Such an alteration in the discursive climate and expectations of eighteenth-century Scotland can be traced not only in the church but also in the transformation of the university, the other major Scottish institution that held sway in public life after the Act of Union of 1707. In a series of developments beginning in the 1720s that both paralleled and intersected with those in the kirk, we find a shift away from the scholasticism that had constituted the university as a training ground for clergymen and a move toward a liberal-arts curriculum that would provide the substance and polish for the improvement of gentlemen. With an accompanying shift in the language of instruction from Latin to English, the liberal arts were conceived of in this project not merely as "ornamental accomplishments" but rather, as Peter Jones explains, as "a vital forming-process for the character of citizens in a modern Scottish *res publica*." In short, the university was reimagined and reorganized as an instrument of civility in a nation of liberty, a site for the serious but polite exchange of enlightened ideas, for elegant debates on the new moral philosophy. Like the Moderate members in the church, the new professoriate, as Jones points out, "often found itself at odds with those amongst the orthodox who wished to reclaim the Scottish universities, not for a gentlemanly republican culture with overtones of secularism, but for schools of godliness and good learning."[14]

By the time *Douglas* came along, then, the two major institutions of Scottish cultural life, the Presbyterian Church and the universities, had been infiltrated and transformed by members of the clergy like Home and Carlyle as well as Hugh Blair and Adam Ferguson, who affiliated themselves with and played a significant role in the promulgation of the ideas and voices of the Scottish Enlightenment. Perhaps even more significantly, these clergymen now derived a sense of their own authority not only from their status in the church and the platform of its public pulpits but also from their membership and participation in secular social clubs like the Select Society, whose members' articulated purpose was "to improve themselves in reasoning and eloquence, and by the freedom of debate, to discover the most effectual methods of promoting the good of the country."[15] With accounts of their activities and debates featured prominently in periodicals and newspapers, these private clubs came to exercise an increasingly influential role in shaping the contours of public discourse and, thereby, assured themselves of a significant role in Scottish public life.[16] In this manner, they brought about a fundamental change in the nature and quality of public culture itself. For where the church had once been able to lay claim as a public institution to an authoritative voice in cultural and moral affairs, private individuals now joined together as bodies public to challenge that voice by subjecting long-held orthodoxies and beliefs to the rigors of skeptical reasoning and empirical proof. The fact that many of these new voices belonged to clergymen themselves meant that the church was subjected to the forces of enlightenment and secularization from the inside out. In essence, the Moderates were demanding the creation of a new social and political culture where moral and theological authority was articulated discursively rather than formally.

It is not surprising to find, then, that these societies attracted the early displeasure of orthodox church defenders and were a target for hostile critique. What was heralded in the clubs as the triumph of freedom of thought was cast by conservative clergy and their lay supporters as a cabal-driven promiscuity of thought or freedom to blaspheme. Hence, as early as the 1720s, we find the Reverend Robert Wodrow delivering a dire warning against the "corrupting of the youth," and the long-term effects of such clubs on the ministerial ranks of the Presbyterian Church:

> It's certain that there are many sad tokens of wrath among many that are students of Divinity. When the most practical subjects are given, their discourses are general and desultory, and nothing like anything of seriousness or practical exercise, or anything of the old way of discoursing and preaching. . . . And, considering the burden of Patrons, and the recommendation of Professors, it's the lads of latitude and brightness . . . that are likely to get in to the congregations; and, indeed, the very outward decency and gravity, proper for such as have their eye to Divinity, is not to be seen among them. . . . The Lord appear, and help, God pity this poor Church in time to come!"[17]

In his lament, Wodrow foresees a day when sharp considerations of doctrine, the hallmarks of "outward decency and gravity," will give way to the banalities of "latitude and brightness," a shift in discipline and temperament that he fears will place the very survival of the church in jeopardy. In a particularly prescient moment, moreover, he apprehends not only the link between this new class of ministers and the prerogatives of patronage—the system that determined who would "get in to the congregations"—but also the conflicts to which such a linkage would give rise. Indeed, beginning in the 1730s and continuing over the course of the century, clashes over patronage would become more and more volatile as they became one of the main sites for enacting the struggle for power between moderate and orthodox factions within the Presbyterian Church and the efforts on both sides to publicize their positions.[18] These conflicts not only provide the background and context for the years leading up to the *Douglas* controversy, but also account for the virulence with which that campaign was ultimately mounted and prosecuted.

Patronage

The history of patronage, or the system "whereby an hereditary owner of the right of presentation selected and installed his choice of minister in the parish church," was fraught in Scotland by its frequent implication in complex political negotiations.[19] Associated in the seventeenth century with episcopacy, it was abolished in 1690, following the Glorious Revolution, in favor of the "call," a process whereby the parish itself extended an invitation to a favored candidate in a manner that was thought to accord better with notions of independent governance within the Presbyterian kirk. Yet, as part of a set of wider negotiations related both to the Union of 1707 and to the settlement and defense of the Protestant succession, the right of patronage was restored to the landed classes in 1712 under the government of Queen Anne. The reinstatement of such privileges was meant as a hedge to ensure the loyalties of the aristocracy against Jacobite encroachments. The General Assembly, meanwhile, was assured of its right to overrule patrons in particular cases, and such was the balance of power within the church at the time that this was grudgingly thought to provide for a sufficient remedy.

By the 1730s, however, the Moderates were beginning to emerge in the church as a significant force; and they aligned themselves with patron's rights in order to build their power base and support their cause. As Richard Sher and Alexander Murdoch have noted, "For the Moderates the key issue was the creation and maintenance of a polite, enlightened Scottish clergy leading their nation out of the abyss of seventeenth-century fanaticism. Patronage was therefore esteemed for its partiality to ministers who were moderate in their values as well as Moderate in their ecclesiastical politics. Either way, government and the landed élite were being used by the Moderates to achieve their ends rather than vice versa."[20] Orthodox members of the church who had been mollified by the expectation that the General Assembly would overrule unpopular appointments where there was no local concurrence now found themselves bound to a ruling body that was increasingly likely to support a patron's right against the populist call.

In the 1750s, these disputes reached a particularly acrimonious pitch, with extended conflicts erupting over appointments in Torphichen, Inverkeithing, and Jedburgh. While the last case ran concurrently with and would not be settled until after the *Douglas* affair, with a significant membership seceding from the church, the first two cases preceded the controversy and supply ample evidence of the active role played by John Home and his Moderate brethren in upholding patron's rights and antagonizing the orthodox factions in the church.[21] Moreover, as part of the acceleration of hostilities over the politics of patronage, the cases at Torphichen and Inverkeithing provide a record of the distinct rhetorical and philosophical positions taken on both sides.

The first case was brought forward to the General Assembly in 1751, after the Linlithgow Presbytery had refused to comply with a previous order to admit James Watson as minister to the parish at Torphichen, as appointed by the local patron Lord Torphichen. Pleading a case of "freedom in their conscience," the presbytery protested that "they not only saw a strong opposition in the parish to that settlement; but a flame arisen in the country, which was likely to spread into their own parishes, if they should have an active hand in it: so as to scatter their congregations; and render them, in a great measure, useless as ministers of Christ . . . and useless to the public, in recommending loyalty and good affection to our happy constitution and government."[22] After some deliberations, the assembly rebuffed these claims and voted instead to censure the Linlithgow Presbytery and to command Watson's admittance. Seeing an opportunity to press the case to even further advantage, John Home gained the backing of William Robertson, the leader of the Moderates, and proposed that the disobedient ministers be suspended from the church.[23] That overture was defeated by a great majority, but it indicated the lengths to which the Moderates were willing to go to remove members of rival factions from the church and, given Home's active role in the stratagem, provided ample motive for the vehemence with which he was later attacked when the orthodox factions saw their own opportunity to respond in kind. In the more immediate moment, a group of twenty orthodox ministers and ruling elders filed a dissent, laying down as the first principle that "the censures of the church are never to be inflicted, but upon open transgressors of the laws of Christ himself," and insisting upon an "unalienable right to judge" for every man in such cases as are not "disagreeable to the will of the Lord." This right, they affirmed, as we have seen others do in previous chapters, is "a right which he cannot give up to any man, or society of men; because it is not merely his privilege but his indispensable duty." Hence they asserted that the vote of censure constituted "a stretch of power, derogatory to the rights of conscience."[24]

In the same year, 1751, the assembly granted another patron's petition and ordered the Dunfermline Presbytery to admit Andrew Richardson as minister of Inverkeithing or put themselves in jeopardy of censure. The sentence was not carried out, however, and the case was brought before a commission of the assembly in 1752, which, upon consideration, voted not to censure the presbytery. This action provoked an uproar among the Moderates, including Robertson, Home, Blair, and Matthew Reid, who filed a dissent from the judgment in what became known as "The Manifesto of the Moderates."[25] In a document that formally constituted the Moderates as a formidable body public, they enumerated eight principles in support of their dissent from the judgment of the commission, with their very first reason submitted thus: "Because we conceive this sentence of the commission to be inconsistent with the nature and first principles of society." Conceding that men alone, that is, men in a state outside of society, have "no judge but their own conscience," they go on to assert:

> By joining together in society . . . we consent that regulations for public order shall be established; not by the private fancy of every individual, but by the judgment of the majority, or of those with whom the society has consented to intrust the legislative power. . . . They who maintain that such disobedience deserves no censure, maintain in effect, that there should be no such thing as government and order. They deny those first principles by which men are united in society; and endeavour to establish such maxims, as will justify not only licentiousness in ecclesiastical, but disorder and rebellion in civil government.[26]

Extending this reasoning in the next section, they offer as point of counsel number two: "Because this sentence of the commission, as it is subversive of society in general, so, in our judgments, it is absolutely inconsistent with the nature and preservation of ecclesiastical society in particular." Casting the assertions of "liberty of conscience" as calculated moves "to establish the most extravagant maxims of Independency, and to overthrow from the very foundation that happy ecclesiastical constitution which we glory in being members of," they declare later, under reason three, that if such precedents are allowed to stand, "There is no occasion for this church to meet in its general assemblies any more: our government is at an end; it totters from the very basis; and we are exposed to the contempt and scorn of the world, as a church without union, order, or discipline, destitute of strength to support its own constitution, falling into ruins by the abuse of liberty."[27] With this document as well as an answer to the dissent submitted, the case was brought forward for consideration to the General Assembly, where it was found that the commission had exceeded its powers and "had not done what they were bound to do [which was to] conform to the powers given them by the last assembly."[28] A motion was then passed by a vote of 102 to 56, ordering the Dunfermline Presbytery to admit Richardson.

The case, however, did not end there. Pleading the cause of "conscience," a group of ministers from the presbytery continued to defy the order, and in a last attempt to gain the political advantage, they "humbly" observed in a letter "that ever since the act restoring patronages in the end of Q. Anne's reign, there has been a vehement opposition to all settlements by presentations, where there was but small concurrence; which settlements have already produced a train of the most unhappy consequences, greatly affecting the interest of religion, and, if turned into the stated and fixed rule of procedure, will, in all probability, be attended with every fatal effect."[29] Despite all of these efforts, the order was eventually enforced and Richardson was installed as minister at Inverkeithing. Those ministers who persisted in their disobedience were called to answer, and one of them, the Reverend Gillespie, was deposed and forced to leave the church.

Rehearsed in some detail, the documents in these cases reveal the tremendous gulf that had opened up between orthodox and moderate factions not only on philosophical but also on political grounds as they each sought to mobilize their constituencies and gain the ascendancy. On the orthodox side, we find a rhetoric of strict Calvinism mobilized, emphasizing the rights of individual conscience against the impositions of authority. This right of spiritual independence had been written into the Presbyterian constitution and, under what Robert Wodrow terms the "old way of discoursing," was recognized as the guiding principle of Presbyterian Church governance.[30] The Presbyterian Church may have been made up of a series of hierarchical bodies—the local kirk session, the presbytery, the Synod, and finally the General Assembly—but it was wary of the forms of concentrated clerical power that characterized Episcopal Church governance and provided instead both for a great deal of autonomy for the presbyters at the local level and for an equal voice in church matters between ministers and church elders.[31] In their representations, then, the orthodox faction promoted the interests of the local communities against the impositions of outside authority and pleaded the "case of conscience" and the "unalienable right to judge" against the extension of ecclesiastical power. Hence they argued that the General Assembly had no jurisdiction in the case, for the matter at hand was one of local and internal governance rather than of doctrinal dissent: it did not involve a transgression of the "laws of Christ himself."

In the uneasy balance between the complementary powers of church and state, the orthodox faction thus placed the interests of the church polity ahead of those of civil authority. In their eyes, the Presbyterian Church must give first priority to the imperatives of individual conscience, that is, to individual piety, and any action that either derogates or compromises this imperative may constitute a cause for the "flame" of rebellion, or in this case, secession, to rise. They argued, moreover, that such a violation of church polity would make them "useless" in recommending "loyalty and good affection to our happy constitution and government." In other words, individuals were to be considered first and foremost as members of the church and only secondarily as citizens of the state; ecclesiastical obligations and bonds were to take precedence over, and indeed were to be treated as antecedent to, the claims of temporal life. Under this dispensation, an individual's duty to God was considered absolute and could not be surrendered or submitted to the judgment or legislation either of the state or of society at large. In this manner, the orthodox factions assumed what we might view as a paradoxical posture; their conservative theological stance led them to adopt and maintain a rather radical political position similar to that which we saw expressed in the previous two chapters—the right of the populace to rise up against the impositions of the governing bodies of society.[32]

Reading the "Manifesto of the Moderates" against this political program, a number of critics have thus characterized the treatise as a conservative defense of the hierarchy of the church.[33] Yet there seems to be something even more fundamental at stake in this document, that is, an account of the moral foundations of society and an understanding of the separation and extent of power and authority between the church and the state that necessarily arises from such an account. In other words, while the "Manifesto of the Moderates" may defend the church hierarchy per se, it also intimates and practically calls for the subordination of the church to the more secular concerns of social government. This, of course, follows from the fact that the "Manifesto" initiates its polemic with a stadial account of human society that could just as easily have appeared in any number of the many essays and treatises on the new moral philosophy that littered the Enlightenment landscape. Indeed, one of the major projects of the new moral philosophy and its concomitant genre, natural history, was to provide an account of the origins of human society and to demonstrate how that formation emerges from and is regulated by the principles of human nature. So intense and compelling was this preoccupation that at one time or another almost every moral philosopher, from the most obscure to the most influential, found it incumbent upon himself to offer an account of how man emerged out of the state of nature and entered into the wider realm of society, with all of its attendant moral obligations and duties.

With their opening profession of adherence to "those first principles by which men are united in society," then, the members of the Moderate party announced its departure from an account of human society that took its cue from the theological interests of the church and proclaimed its affinity with the Enlightenment project of the new moral philosophy. Under this rubric, as Peter Jones points out, "The individual was recommended to identify himself as the member of a household, then of a *polis*, and finally of the community of rational beings, rather than as an isolated soul."[34] Consequently, the Moderates gave precedent to civil forms of government over and against the imperatives of the church and the doctrine of individual salvation. Their first concern was not with the moral obligations of what it means to enter into a faith but rather with the moral duties of what it means to enter into the social contract. Following a pronouncedly more secular logic, then, the "Manifesto of the Moderates" does not so much dispute an "unalienable right to judge" as refuse to "admit, that any man's private judgment gives him a right to disturb, with impunity, all public order."[35] In this manner, the Moderates, as a body public, directed Scottish cultural life away from the theological bonds of the church and toward the more tolerant embrace of a civil society.

What the "Manifesto" and the contests over patronage thus illuminate are not merely local struggles over power and authority but rather, on a much more significant and far-reaching scale, the political effects of a fundamental shift in notions of governance from those of an ecclesiastical polity to those of a modern, liberal society in which the separation of church and state was preeminent. While the Moderates may have hedged their bets by casting their position as against the "private fanc[ies]" of individuals only—lest they be accused of blasphemy or infidelity for transgressions against "the laws of Christ himself"—they clearly envisioned a state in which "ecclesiastical society in particular" would take its form from "society in general." For the Moderates, the concerns of the state were to take priority over all others; the church was to be understood as subordinate to the social order as articulated by state and civil law.[36]

In all of these respects, then, the Moderate victories in the patronage battles marked a fundamental shift in the governance of public life in eighteenth-century Scotland. Perhaps most significantly, they indicated the extent to which the Enlightenment project—with its speculations as to the origins of society and its interest in establishing natural law as a fundamental basis for morality—articulated, however ambivalently or ambiguously, a necessary separation of church and state. While these effects and the conflicts over them constitute only an implicit undercurrent in the documents related to the patronage controversies, they came to occupy a more central position in the disputes between the orthodox and moderate factions of the Presbyterian Church in the mid-1750s. At that point, the orthodox factions turned their energies toward pressing charges of infidelity in the General Assembly against Lord Kames and David Hume. Amid the sea of pamphlets, treatises, essays, observations, and analyses produced both to support and to defend against these charges, "liberty of thought" and "the business of the church" became bywords for the heated contests over jurisdiction, or the right both to legislate and to prosecute, that arose as a result of this growing division between church and state. At stake in these exchanges were the governance of society and the role of religion and religious bodies public in modern nation building.

Infidelity

The groundwork for the separation of church and state had been written into law as early as the 1690s, when a proviso in the documents related to the reestablishment of the Presbyterian Church in Scotland held that excommunication from the church could not carry any civil penalties against an individual.[37] With this provision, the profound interconnections between church and state that had governed Scottish public life to that point were recognized, even as the ground was laid for the separation and division of such authority in the future. It is arguably the case, however, that the full effects of this stipulation were not felt until the 1750s, when the work of the new moral philosophers was beginning to gain widespread public acceptance and the social, cultural, and political ramifications of their writings were just beginning to be understood. For orthodox members of the Presbyterian Church, what was most unsettling and indeed threatening about the new moral philosophy was the extent to which it held that moral systems ought to be grounded in human nature, universally defined, rather than in the more particular understandings of religion and religious doctrine. The charges against Hume and Kames sought redress on this point, that is, they sought to restore the authority of the church not only in the determination of moral systems but also in the governance of society in accordance with those moral systems. Hence we find that the abstract philosophical arguments devoted either to proving or to disproving the charges of infidelity against the two are punctuated by sharp expressions of concern over the governance and conduct of individuals and the stability of the state and society. Even more significantly, as the exchanges over Kames's *Essays on the Principles of Morality and Natural Religion* illustrate, they point up the extent to which the struggles between the moderate and orthodox factions revolved around concerns over cultural hegemony in the public sphere.

Charges of infidelity against David Hume and Lord Kames were first brought forward for consideration to a committee of the General Assembly in 1755.[38] This formal process grew out of a two-year pursuit of Kames and Hume in print by the Reverend George Anderson, and it ultimately ended without successful prosecution with his death in 1756.[39] In many ways, Kames was actually an odd target for Anderson and the High-Flyers, especially insofar as he had actually set out to write his *Essays* as a way to distinguish himself from David Hume and, most important, to write against what he viewed as the dangerous tendency toward moral relativism that could be inferred from Hume's skeptical philosophy.[40] As John Price points out, "Home [Kames] intended to demonstrate the falseness of Hume's account or descriptions of causality and to argue for moral laws that are not merely human inventions or conventions and which additionally have authority and sanction from a higher, non-human agency."[41] In the *Essays*, then, Kames sought to provide a stable ground for morality that was anchored in certain immutable qualities of human nature itself. Extending the work of Shaftesbury and Hutcheson, he posited a "moral sense," essentially an instinctive ability to distinguish between right and wrong, as one of the fundamental characteristics of human nature. In Kames's view, the "moral sense" served as the foundation for moral systems and the laws by which conduct ought to be regulated. It not only directed and constrained the appetites and passions; it was the "voice of God within us which commands our strict obedience."[42] Here, then, in opposition to Hume's skepticism and following the benevolent humanism of Shaftesbury and Hutcheson, Kames installs "feeling" at the center of moral systems of obligation and understanding.

Having established the "moral sense" in the second essay, Kames turned
to the issue of causality in what would become the most controversial portion
of his treatise, his essay "Of Liberty and Necessity." As in the earlier parts of
this work, Kames sought in this essay to critique Hume's skepticism and to
repudiate any atheistical tendencies encouraged by his writings. Indeed,
Kames was so intent on articulating a sense of order that he argues in this
section of the *Essays* for final causality and moral necessity, that is, he upholds
the principle that all causes can be traced back to God and hence that all actions can ultimately be understood as compelled by immutable laws. Here is
how he concludes one portion of this essay:

> The sum of what we have discovered concerning contingency in
> events, and liberty in actions is this. Comparing together the moral
> and the natural world, every thing is as much the result of estab-
> lished laws in the one as in the other. There is nothing in the whole
> universe that can properly be called contingent, that may be, or may
> not be; nothing loose and fluctuating in any part of nature; but
> every motion in the natural, and every determination and action in
> the moral world, are directed by immutable laws: so that whilst
> these laws remain in their force, not the smallest link of the univer-
> sal chain of causes and effects can be broken, nor any one thing be
> otherways than it is." (181–82)

For Kames, then, nothing was contingent in the manner that Hume had proposed; all actions and motions, whether moral or physical, were determined.
Yet this supposition led to a new difficulty: the issue of liberty, of how man
might be free to act. In response to this problem, Kames came up with an ingenious formulation, reasoning thus: "Let us fairly own, that the truth of
things is on the side of necessity; but that it was necessary for man to be
formed, with such feelings and notions of contingency, as would fit him for
the part he has to act" (187). In short, man was outfitted with what Kames
termed a "deceitful feeling of liberty," a belief that he was free to act rightly or
wrongly, though in reality he was no more nor less than a necessary agent in
the larger scheme, the subject of immutable laws (207). In his view, the discovery of this artful plan furnished "one of the strongest arguments, for the
existence of the Deity" (216).

The same view, much to Kames's own surprise, was not taken by his critics.[43] Instead, his arguments were construed one by one as proofs of infidelity.

Making a broad argument for including Kames's treatise under the category of the atheistical, George Anderson wrote, for instance:

> All opinions that sap and undermine *religion* are *atheism*; that is, that take away the influence which the belief of a GOD ought to have upon the conduct of men. And this may be done, and is done several ways, without expressly denying the existence of such a being: for instance, to believe that man is not a reasonable and free agent; that he hath no power over his mind and actions, and cannot be a subject of rational and moral government; that he is under a fatal necessity of thinking and acting no otherways than he actually thinks and acts, is atheism. It is also atheism, to think that the moral law is not the law of GOD; and that the regulation of our conduct depends as much upon our own will, as upon his: it is atheism to think that GOD is a false and deceitful being; it is atheism to think that our natural reason cannot lead us to the knowledge of the supreme being; and that there may be more gods than one.[44]

In Anderson's view, Kames had repeatedly violated the sanctity of the deity, first, by proposing "feeling" rather than "reason" as the basis both for morality and for a belief in God, then by suggesting that man was a necessary agent, and finally by intimating that God had deceived men into believing they had the power to act freely when in fact they were "under a fatal necessity of thinking and acting no otherways." Each charge underlines the sense in which Kames's system was perceived to have eliminated any basis for human agency and hence for human accountability—moral or otherwise—and such concerns would be echoed in all subsequent attacks on the *Essays*.[45]

Repeated again and again, these recitations of the allegedly sacrilegious propositions in Kames's work can become mind-numbingly familiar and seem both pedantic and controlling. But if we take a closer look at these extended litanies and trace them back to the root cause of their alarm, we can begin to discern what Anderson and his orthodox followers sought to exert control over, that is, what they thought to be at stake: authority over the system that would govern society. For Anderson, Kames's ideas were dangerous not just because they represented heterodox views per se, but rather because those heterodox conjectures had been systematized: they had been "deliberately digested into a system, and made public" (79). Thus in his view, Kames's "principles" were neither purely abstract nor wholly vain conjurings; their potential to exert a powerful "influence upon practice" was quite concrete and went far beyond what Hugh Blair and others played down as mere "metaphysical disputes, which may perplex the understandings, but never can impair the morals of men" (210).[46] In the most immediate sense, then, each charge in Anderson's catalog can be traced back to a concern over the pragmatic impact or influence that philosophical systems like those of Kames and Hume might have on individual conduct and individual accountability. On a broader scale, Anderson's invective reveals how the formal institutionalization of a system of moral beliefs was understood to represent a means for exerting hegemonic control over a society. Moral systems, whether philosophically or theologically based, were understood to have material interests in the political landscape and public life. Kames's "system," with its focus on moral law as peculiarly adapted to the dispositions of human nature, constituted a threat to the power of a church that relied for its authority on the prescriptions of a remote deity.

As if in counterpoint, then, to the perceived threat of the new moral philosophy, Anderson responds by offering a "natural history" of his own, one in which religion, no less than property or sexual reproduction, plays a fundamental role both in the establishment of human societies and in the maintenance of the cultural and political stability of nations. In a chapter titled "Of the Public Advantages and Disadvantages of Religion," Anderson opens his account by explaining "before any religion, natural or instituted, can be adopted as a support or help to society, it must be digested into a system. . . . And, that such systems may be the more regarded, they are not considered as a collection of philosophical speculations, or moral precepts enacted by human authority; but, so far as I know, they have been delivered as laws bearing the stamp of divine authority" (286–87). He then extends his history by describing the process whereby religion insinuates itself into and thus becomes an integral part of the fabric of civil society:

> WHEN such a religious establishment is once made, every wise magistrate, whether religious or atheistical, may and ought to enforce obedience, with civil sanctions in all that profess the faith and religion settled by national laws. It then becomes part of the civil constitution; and all that join as members of those assemblies, supported at the public charge, must submit to the orders and the directions of such as the government intrust with the administration. Though it is the duty of the civil magistrate, to exclude from those

assemblies as few as possible; yet he ought not to allow every particular member to change, abrogate, or surrogate, the established
forms or systems, at his own discretion. Whatever he may do in another capacity; as a member of a settled religious society, he must
conform to the orders of the society, though of mere human authority and appointment. (287)

In Anderson's vision of how a nation ought to be organized and governed,
civil society takes its form from the imperatives of religion. Furthermore, any
violation of religious doctrine ought to be met with civil sanctions. The civil
and the religious spheres ought to be mutually dependent and coextensive;
indeed, they ought to be inseparable.

From the outset, however, Anderson's account is a troubled one, first and
perhaps most obviously because he adopts precisely the same language he
used to cast Kames's moral system as factitious to describe religion's emergence as a social and political force. That is, despite his intermittent attempts
both to differentiate natural from instituted religion as well as to distinguish
religion from moral philosophy, it appears that religion, just like any other
moral system, must be "digested" and then "delivered" before it can have any
efficacy. Religion, in other words, is always already a fabrication of man. It
may bear the "stamp of divine authority," but that stamp and the impression
it makes are of human manufacture. As a result, Anderson's "natural history"
of religion could be said to account not so much for religion's necessity as for
the process whereby religion might come to dominate the sociopolitical infra-
structure of nations to such an extent that any challenge to an established religion would also constitute a threat to the nation in which it was
established.

Clearly blind to the manner in which he has thus cast religion as contingent rather than as necessary and determined, Anderson tips the hand of his
political interests even further when he adopts an almost Machiavellian logic
by advising every "wise magistrate" regardless of "what he may do in another
capacity," that is, regardless of his actual beliefs, to bring the full force of civil
law to bear on those who refuse to conform to the dictates of a "settled religious society." On such grounds, even an atheist is admonished to conceal his
beliefs in the exercise of public office or risk being looked upon as a "disobedient subject, and a disturber of the civil constitution" (288). In Anderson's
account, the stability of a nation depends once again on the inseparability of
church and state. Yet it is also clear that this arrangement is neither a natural

nor an inevitable or necessarily permanent one; it is subject instead to the vi-
cissitudes of time and place. This explains not only why Anderson focuses so
much attention on the achievement and then the maintenance of a certain
status quo, but also why he ends up describing a political settlement that relies, ironically, on the observation of "established forms or systems," that is, on
precisely the kinds of conventions described and critiqued by one of his main
targets, David Hume. In short, the value of religion in Anderson's own account comes to be situated not so much in the fact that it represents truth per
se, but rather in the convention that it constitutes a truth with time on its
side.

In Anderson's *Estimate of the Profit and Loss of Religion*, then, we find evidence of the extent to which the new moral philosophy and its manner of
accounting for the rise of human societies have come to encroach even on
orthodox thinking. Anderson's main anxiety is not only that time has run out
on the political hegemony of the church in Scotland but also that its historical
prerogative in matters of governance has become visible as arbitrary rather
than absolute. As if exasperated by the failure of his own account to counter
such an impression, he betrays his anxiety when he bursts out, "I, for myself,
and in name of all adherents, request the favour of Mr. *Hume* and his adherents, to let the present established religion alone, until something better, or at
least as good, is ready, by the act of parliament, to be put in place of it" (303).
Undermining any case he might have made otherwise for religion's self-
evident authority, Anderson acknowledges its vulnerability and begs that it be
"let . . . alone." Perhaps even more telling, he does not so much preclude the
possibility of a moral system that could displace religion as argue that such a
system has yet to emerge out of moral philosophy in a form sufficient both to
compensate for the loss of religion and to ensure order and discipline in society. Thus it becomes clear that Anderson's pursuit of Kames and Hume constitutes much more than a defense of religion. Rather, it represents an attempt to
bolster the social and political power of certain factions of the Presbyterian
Church against ideological incursions from other philosophical or theological
formations and the bodies public to which they had given rise. The net result
is that Anderson betrays an instrumental understanding of the role of religion
in public life at precisely the point in his treatise where he most seeks to natu-
ralize it.

As with the patronage battles, then, the vehemence with which the
charges of infidelity were pursued reflects the extent to which the orthodox
faction understood that it had lost the ability to exercise power and authority

not only in the General Assembly, and hence in the church, but also in the organization and governance of the secular realm.[47] A fundamental shift in the discursive landscape had occurred, and the orthodox faction was struggling to regain lost ground. This discursive loss of authority is reflected in and confirmed by the concessions to the new moral philosophy that the orthodox defenders make in their own treatises. Quite simply, in order to enter into debates over jurisdiction and governance, the orthodox faction had to adopt an idiom that construed religion as a sociopolitical institution rather than as a transcendent formation, a discursive state of affairs that is abundantly apparent in the question with which Anderson launches his "natural" history: "*What doth mankind gain, and what do they lose, by* RELIGION?" (210). With this query, Anderson placed the issue of political economy—a major concern for Scottish Enlightenment thought—at center stage in the struggle between the orthodox and moderate factions of the church. By the time those combatants came to blows over John Home's *Douglas*, then, a pragmatic language of political economy, of gain and loss, had already displaced an abstract language of moral accountability as the dominant idiom of the public sphere and the bodies public that sought authority in that sphere.

Political Economies and the *Douglas* Affair

While a discourse of political economy may have lingered on the margins of both the patronage battles and the infidelity attacks, its centrality in the *Douglas* controversy and the extent to which the orthodox factions felt compelled to incorporate it into their arguments against the stage can be seen in the way such concerns frame the first official document to take on Home's tragedy, the "Admonition and Exhortation by the Reverend Presbytery of Edinburgh." Rather than open its offensive against Home with either a firm statement of religious doctrine or a clear proscription against attendance at the theater, the orthodox faction instead decries "the growing luxury and levity of the present age" and avows its "indispensable duty to express . . . deep concern" about the "*unprecedented countenance* given of late to the playhouse" at a time "when the state of the nation, and the circumstances of the poor, make such hurtful entertainments still more pernicious."[48] Expressing alarm over a burgeoning culture of consumer pleasure and interest, the "Admonition" thus opens its assault with an implicit argument that the church can and ought to function as the best guide to the nation not only in spiritual matters but also in economic and fiscal policy. Time, money, and the use of material resources immediately emerge as the critical axes on which the arguments for and against the stage will turn.

This argument of economy is subsequently extended in the "Admonition" to a concern for a well-ordered laboring class. In a rather overdramatic protestation, the address pleads that "to enumerate how many servants, apprentices, and students in different branches of literature, in this city and suburbs, have been seduced from their proper business, by attending the stage, would be a painful, disagreeable task."[49] That the appeal then goes on to take up this burden only supports its claim to act selflessly in the interests of the nation. Citing both the impulse to spend and the loss of labor that attendance at the theater might produce, the "Admonition" thus raises a variety of questions about how best to allocate the resources of the nation so as to build a strong state, one that in a new era of trade and commerce will be productive and generate both profits and prosperity.

In short, as the political economy of the nation moves to the discursive forefront in the "Admonition," concerns about religious convictions and beliefs are muted and even set aside. Any thought that the ministry could be relied upon to act in accordance with religious conviction seems to have been abandoned, as the orthodox faction seems to have recognized and conceded that their arguments might have much more sway if they appealed instead to secular self-interest. Thus they implore, "Is it not a high instance of folly to break down that barrier, and open a door with their own hands for theatrical representations? which are in many respects no less inconsistent with good policy, than unfriendly to religion; and will be found sooner or later, to affect their temporal as well as spiritual interests."[50] In the context, then, of what was supposed to be an "exhortation" to a religious body to condemn participation in theatrical representations, a concern for "temporal" interests and "good policy" emerges. Despite any intentions they may have had to sustain an argument at the level of the sacred, the orthodox faction thus found itself drawn into the growing debate in Scotland not just over how to cultivate, develop, and spend the resources of the nation but also, as a matter of "good policy," over how the labor and leisure of the various classes ought to be regulated and organized.

The form this debate took in the *Douglas* controversy and the extent to which the two sides drew on diametrically opposed views of human nature to shape their arguments can be illustrated best by examining the contrasts between Adam Ferguson's pamphlet *The Morality of Stage-Plays Seriously*

Considered and the anonymous point-by-point response to Ferguson, *The Immorality of Stage-Plays in General and of the Tragedy Called* Douglas, *In Particular.* In mounting his defense of Home's *Douglas*, Ferguson takes great pains not only to defend the stage against any imputation of irreligion or impiety, but also to construe the playhouse, with its public intermingling of people of different classes and sexes, as a critical site for the production of a virtuous, polished, and civic-minded citizenry. This characterization of the theater draws its force from the skeptical, yet optimistic views of man as a sociable animal with an innate moral sense that were advanced by the Scottish moral philosophers. Consequently, Ferguson figures the theater as a "place of public resort," which "under the influence of decency, and in the presence of respectable persons, [could never] be so dangerous, as cabals which are formed in secret, and apart from such influence."[51] Even more significantly, he attributes at least some portion of that creditable status to the attendance at the theater of "people of both sexes, whose rank, whose age and manners, are sufficient to command respect, and to bring decency along with them into any place" (19). For Ferguson, then, the theater is a site of public exchange, where the promise and obligation of sociability necessarily result not merely in a polite but also in a strong civic culture. Thus he situates the playhouse at the center of social and civic discourse and argues that "the Stage ha[d] always made one in every civilized and polished nation" (22).

In stark contrast to Ferguson, the author of *The Immorality of Stage-Plays* incessantly associates the playhouse with the dangers of female sexuality and warns against the commingling of the sexes in public lest it encourage licentiousness amidst a "promiscuous crowd."[52] This detractor draws on a view of the public as unruly and potentially dangerous. For him the playhouse is not a site for the improvement of society, but rather the "rendezvous of the leud [and] the unwary" where, in the absence of any controlling moral authority, the unwary will be led by the lewd to commit unseemly acts (16). Hence, where Ferguson argues that the great can have an improving effect on the lower orders, his detractor finds that they are more likely to fall into temptation than to act as moral exemplars. The inherent weakness of the human soul dictates that man cannot do otherwise, and the anecdotal evidence appears to bear out the case. After all, he offers, "Doth not experience, as well as theology, teach us that our corrupt natures are more liable to be influenced by evil examples than by good ones" (17).

Driven by this pessimistic assessment of human nature, the author takes aim not only at Ferguson's optimistic vision of a public sphere of exchange but also at the political and economic prospects that Ferguson posits as correlative effects of that new social formation. Here, for instance, is what Ferguson, in a rather remarkable because extended polemic, offers on the subject of the right use of wealth and the trickle-down effects of the playhouse economy:

> The very money he lays out for amusement comes at last into the hands of the poor, and is paid as the price of their labour. A part of it we shall suppose is laid out for the amusements of the theatre, and the people who receive it there, are so many hands who distribute that money among the industrious poor. Every Player must be cloathed, maintained and lodged: The money which he receives therefor is paid at last to the spinstress, the weaver, the clothier, and other tradesmen who live by furnishing the ordinary necessaries of life. Whilst from humanity we indulge the poor in their station, we ought from justice to indulge the wealthy in theirs, and to expect that they are to go on agreeable to the habits of living which belong to their station, and which in effect are necessary to the order and good of society and to the maintenance of the poor. (25)

For Ferguson, the playhouse represents a critical cog in the wheel of commerce, a source of economic stimulus where the pleasure of the wealthy trickles down to the poor in the form of a living. Providing the groundwork for Adam Smith's doctrine on the division of labor in the *Wealth of Nations*, Ferguson puts forth a logic which holds that a well-ordered society follows from the division of men into distinct classes with distinct roles and asserts that "it has pleased Providence, for wise purposes, to place men in different stations, and to bestow upon them different degrees of wealth. Without this circumstance there could be no subordination, no government, no order, no industry. Every person does good, and promotes the happiness of society, by living agreeable to the rank in which Providence has placed him" (24). From Ferguson's perspective, a thriving playhouse, with all of its collateral economic effects, should be taken as a sign both of a thriving and well-ordered nation and of an enlivened and polished public sphere.

In contrast, his antagonist construes the popularity of theatrical entertainments as a symptom of national dissipation and immorality. Following the rhetorical pattern we have already seen in the "Admonition," he yokes a scripturally based polemic against the playhouse to contemporary arguments in the luxury debates and points to the fall of both Athens and Rome as woeful precedents that betoken the decline of Scottish society. Writing with a sense of foreboding, the author asserts that the "excessive expences . . . on stage-plays was . . . the very overthrow and destruction of their state . . . that whenever their plays and theatres went up, their manners, virtues, prosperity and commonwealth went down" (15). Thus, where Ferguson finds occasion amid the *Douglas* controversy to delineate the political economy of a new public sphere in which men and women mingle with and influence one another as a body public in positive ways, his counterpart finds occasion only for alarm and apprehension. For this author, Ferguson's new political economy was supported by a dangerously misguided and woefully naive understanding of human nature. In short, where Enlightenment philosophers expressed optimism about human nature, extolling its capacity for improvement and its innate predisposition toward benevolence, the orthodox parties saw a species that wallowed in its own fundamentally fallen condition, inherently corrupt and, if not properly regulated, likely to become enamored of vice and licentiousness.[53] The ideology of material progress that was heralded by Enlightenment thinkers was thus held up by the orthodox factions as a chimera of temptation.

With such fundamental differences in outlook and ideology writ large, the Moderate leadership within the church as well as their secular supporters outside of the church, treated the occasion of the *Douglas* affair as an opportunity not only to assert their dominance over the public sphere but also to articulate the new conception of the public sphere upon which that dominance would be based. It was theirs, in other words, to seize the prerogative in social, cultural, and political matters; and they did so, first, by touting the new social and civic circles of association and influence they had formed and, second, by bestowing the imprimatur of those bodies public upon the *Douglas* debates. For those on the orthodox side, the *Douglas* debates were distinguished by the extent to which they signaled even more insistently than before both the cleaving apart of state or civil discourse from church or ecclesiastical interests and the increasing reliance on a broad discourse of political economy. In these performances of competing cultural interests, the *Douglas* controversy was thus understood in political terms not so much as a sudden or isolated éclat but rather as the opening of yet another battlefront in the ongoing conflict over public influence and authority between orthodox and Moderate factions in the Presbyterian Church. The *Douglas* affair constituted only the belated formal recognition of a redistribution of discursive prerogatives that had, in effect, already occurred.

The Cultural Politics of *Douglas*:
From Scotland to America

In the *Douglas* affair, no one was more cognizant of these profound cultural shifts than the Reverend John Witherspoon, who was, at the time, a leading member of the orthodox faction of the Scottish Presbyterian kirk. Witherspoon played a major role in the attack on *Douglas* and took it upon himself to write against Home's tragedy on at least two occasions. In each instance, he not only focused attention upon the distortions of morality that he believed were concomitant with the theatrical experience but also expatiated at length upon the emerging political powers that were driving what he understood as a cultural transformation of morality and sociability. Of particular interest here, moreover, are the extent to which his antitheatrical arguments in the *Douglas* case would be rehearsed in a completely different context to influence responses to the 1811 Richmond Theater fire, which I write about in the next chapter.

Witherspoon's first riposte in the *Douglas* affair came in the form of a reflection, "On a little name, which has produced three great heroes to support the declining glory of Britain":

An impious j[udge], a wicked sceptic sage,
A stage-playing priest; O glorious NAME and AGE!

What is the glory and honour of any state or church? Is it not politeness in the one, and mildness and moderation in the other? Do not then these gentlemen promote the glory of this church and nation? Is it not our honour to tolerate the two first? Is it not both our honour and happiness to have produced, nourished, and to possess the last?[54]

Witherspoon's sarcastic gloss on the influence of the "three Homes" captures the sense in which this mingling of men from various professions and ranks of society was understood to constitute a threat to more orthodox authorities. Not only was it clear that these affiliations had resulted in a "moderation" of church policy, but they were also perceived to have had an impact on the interests and direction of the civil state and the formation of bodies public within it.

Witherspoon's suspicions were, of course, not without cause. In this instance, for example, it could be argued that he was responding to David Hume's own claims of affiliation in the dedication of his *Four Dissertations* to John Home, complete with a glowing and rather theatrical endorsement of the tragedy. At first Hume had withheld this dedication, as he was reluctant to inflame the situation and imperil his friend's case before the presbytery. But once he learned that Home had decided to leave his parish, Hume took great pleasure in tweaking the ire of the High-Flyers both by going forward with his dedication to Home and by characterizing it as an attempt at "renewing [the] laudable practices of antiquity" in paying due regard to the kind of "liberty of thought, which engaged men of letters, however different in their abstract opinions, to maintain a mutual friendship and regard; and never to quarrel about principles, while they agreed in inclinations and manners."[55] Here, then, Hume celebrates the free exchange of ideas that provided the basis for intellectual camaraderie in the debating clubs, literary societies, and private homes of Edinburgh, Glasgow, and Aberdeen. At such gatherings, a philosopher like Hume could mingle with a member of the bar like Henry Home (Lord Kames), who in turn could converse with a minister, like John Home, who also happened to dabble in theatrical productions.

All of these occasions were distinguished by the principle of free association and the right to speculate on topics moral, literary, political, and religious without fear of censure; and they provided an environment not just for the cultivation of ideas but also for the formation of social and political networks—or bodies public—that could exercise power and influence in the more general spheres of public life. As was the case, then, with Robert Wodrow's attack on the new clubs and societies in the late 1720s, Witherspoon's squib in the 1750s draws attention to these influential circles of sociability. At the center of concern in his attack is what it meant for private men to come together to engage in the exchange of ideas, under conditions that were free from the constraints of institutional or religious authority, and formulate principles and positions that had the potential to shape social, cultural, and political life in the nation at large. To be sure, these clubs and societies would ultimately come to acquire an institutional status of their own, and, as recent scholarship has demonstrated, their idealization of free and equal conversational exchange was just that, an idealization. At the time, however, the aspersions that the orthodox parties cast on these gatherings were motivated by an immediate and not so misguided sense that a profound and potentially irreversible cultural shift was under way and that that shift was taking shape discursively at the level of language, affect, and social convention.

From its inception, *Douglas* fell squarely within the scope of these concerns, first and foremost because it was precisely at such a private gathering that the intellectual luminaries of Edinburgh collaborated to give the tragedy its first rehearsal. Convened at the home of actress Sarah Ward with an audience that included Lords Kames and Milton, and Patrick Murray, Fifth Earl of Elibank, among others, the interested cast featured William Robertson as Lord Randolph, Adam Ferguson as Lady Randolph, David Hume as Glenalvon, Hugh Blair as Anna, Alexander Carlyle as Old Norval, and John Home himself as Douglas.[56]

While the determination of the Edinburgh literati to produce and promote this tragedy could not be more clearly signaled than by the eminence of this gathering, *Douglas* itself, at least on the level of plot, could hardly be said to promulgate either an enlightened worldview or a wholehearted embrace of Scottish nationalism. Indeed, if anything, *Douglas* presents a rather ambivalent rendering of Scottish posterity and a somewhat diffident view of Enlightenment civility. The play itself is plagued by a sense of unrelenting woe as well as by what critics from the outset have termed a remarkable "want of incident."[57] Almost nothing happens. The tragedy as a whole is characterized, then, by an almost unbroken sense of stasis that bears down upon and then compresses what little action there is, a condition captured in the very first scene where, amid a dark and wild landscape of "melancholy gloom," Lady Randolph soliloquizes on the abject state of mourning that she has maintained without abatement for more than eighteen years (I, p. 233).[58] Still stricken with grief over the deaths of her husband and brother and over the loss and presumed death of her son, her marriage to Lord Randolph, despite his solicitousness, is chilly and barren of affection. If, as some critics have recently taught us to do, the unhappy marriage of Lord and Lady Randolph can be read as an allegory for the union of Scotland and England, then the barrenness of their marriage suggests that the political union was one with no futurity.[59] Any hope, moreover, that an independent Scottish future could be restored is no sooner raised by the revelation that the scion of the Douglas family lives in Young Norval than it is dashed by his ignoble death at the hands of the malevolent Glenalvon. Set nostalgically in a heroic past, Scotland appears frozen here, in a state of watchful suspension and despair, waiting for a catalyst of change that will never come. In this respect, the patriotic fervor that was lavished on the tragedy by its supporters seems to stem less from the actual contents of the drama than from the fact that it was written by a Scotsman, set in an independent Scotland of the past, and produced on the Edinburgh stage in defiance of Garrick's unfavorable judgments.

While Home's involvement in the ministry, and the patronage and outspoken support of *Douglas* by leaders of the Moderate faction, provided ample and obvious provocation to the orthodox High-Flyers, the aesthetic ideology embraced by the tragedy provided a more subtle, though perhaps more far-reaching reason for its antagonists to go on the attack. At first, critics of the age had a difficult time deciding what to make of the play and its popularity. Those who took their cues from neoclassical rule books bestowed high praise on Home's adherence to the unities of time, place, and action.[60] But they were deeply disturbed by his failure to observe the dictates of poetic justice. Thus the *Dramatic Censor*, which found in *Douglas* a "piece which has regularity of plot and unity of action to recommend it," also expressed the wish that the ending "had been effected by some other means, or rather that [Douglas] had been saved, as his death is a violent breach of poetical justice, and might have been avoided, even to an amendment of the plot."[61] Not surprisingly, such critics often found common ground with the moralists, who discovered in Lady Randolph's suicide a gross violation of all principles of decency and religion.[62] For those on the side of religiosity, moreover, the greatest danger in the representation was, as the author of *The Immorality of Stage-Plays* makes clear, that Lady Randolph's suicide was "rather calculated to move pity towards the actor, than indignation at the crime."[63]

Indeed, it is precisely the turn in *Douglas* to an aesthetics of affect, where the evocation of an emotional response in the audience, regardless of circumstance, becomes the main dramaturgical end, that worried figures like Witherspoon.[64] For Scottish Enlightenment thinkers, who promulgated the idea of an innate moral sense, however, the aestheticization of affect constituted an efficacious means to bring about the civilizing process and to inculcate virtue. The shift in taste that followed from this ethos over the course of the second half of the eighteenth century can be seen in the contrast between Oliver Goldsmith's immediate expression of distaste at the tragedy's "want of moral" and Elizabeth Inchbald's expressions of high praise for the tragedy fifty years later as a work "written with the minutest attention to morality in fable, incident, and dialogue" where the display of the "passions of grief, joy, fear, and bitter woe . . . found instant access to every heart."[65]

This seems to be precisely how Home wanted the play to operate, as, in

the wake of Young Norval/Douglas's death, Lady Randolph pronounces herself the object lesson of the tragedy, declaiming:

> Grief cannot break a heart so hard as mine.
> My youth was worn in anguish: but youth's strength,
> With hope's assistance, bore the brunt of sorrow;
> And train'd me on to be the object now,
> On which Omnipotence displays itself,
> Making a spectacle, a tale of me,
> To awe its vassal, man. (V, 296)

Despite her ostensibly blasphemous actions, Lady Randolph emerges from
the tragedy as a figure of sympathy rather than of horror or indignation. She
is made into a "spectacle, a tale" of pitiful sorrow, and in this regard, as Home
would have it in his epilogue:

> That pity is the best,
> The noblest passion of the human breast:
> For when its sacred streams the heart o'erflow,
> In gushes pleasure with the tide of woe;
> And when its waves retire, like those of Nile,
> They leave behind them such a golden soil,
> That there the virtues without culture grow. (300)

With what W. B. Worthen has termed its "straightforward address to the spectator's sympathies," *Douglas* "could, and did, generate considerable theatrical
interest."[66] While the meaning of the tragedy thus emerged, as Joseph Donohue has concluded, "only insofar as it relate[d] to the emotions elicited from
the audience," it was precisely the aestheticization of those emotions that was
understood to be the lever for the production of public virtue.[67] The pity en-
gendered for Lady Randolph was designed precisely, in other words, to be the
ground upon which the virtue of spectators would be made to grow. She was
to be, as the anonymous author of *The Tragedy of Douglas Analysed* pronounced, "affliction's standard."[68]

Ranged against those who would "absurdly confine religion to austerity
of features, formality of speech, and abstraction from public amusements,"
defenders of *Douglas* thus saw themselves as engaged in an ideological struggle
over the cultural and political prerogative of shaping public virtue. They

dared, as Inchbald put it, to "encroach on [that] exclusive prerogative of teaching virtue" and celebrated what Francis Gentleman construed as the triumph of a liberal, public spirit over "narrow-minded, illiberal foes."[69] In the wake of *Douglas's* sustained success and to the great dismay of *Douglas's* detractors, they proclaimed, "May ecclesiastical tyranny ever find such a fate, through the sense, spirit and independency of mankind."[70]

Such celebrations only further antagonized those on the orthodox side, who believed that the Moderates were manipulating the occasion both to publicize and to exaggerate their influence and to dress a specious rhetoric of virtue in the cloak of religion. Thus, for instance, John MacLaurin, Lord Dreghorn, wrote in the address to the reader that preceded *The Philosopher's Opera*, his satirical spoof on Hume and Home, "The taste of the country seems to be in a deplorable situation, being abandoned to a club of gentlemen, who are as unable as they are willing to direct it." In his view, the success of *Douglas* was "owing to the influence of party," and accordingly he submitted that it was the "duty of every man who regards the honour of his country, to make a stand against the unhappy barbarism which the cabal I have already mentioned is endeavouring to establish."[71] Here we see evinced a fundamental concern not only over which bodies public—those formed by the literary cabal or those that take their cue from orthodox authority—will lead the Scottish nation but also over the direction they will lead.

Set on the evening of the third night's performance of *Douglas*, *The Philosopher's Opera* presents members of the cabal as the gleefully unwitting instruments of Satan. For some time, he had thought of leaving off his efforts in Edinburgh, as "the opposition [t]here [had] fairly got the better of [him]" and, playing on the name of the most distinguished body public among the literati, only a "small *select society*" had "stuck by him" (I, p. 9, emphasis mine). Recently, however, he had seen a resurgence of adherents, not least of all because of the broad influence of the writings of Mr. Genius, a not-so-subtle stand-in for David Hume. To read Mr. Genius's works, as the philosopher himself boasts, is to be convinced of all of the following: "that there is no God, no devil, no future state;—that there is no connection betwixt cause and effect;—that suicide is a duty we owe to ourselves;—adultery a duty we owe to our neighbour;—that the tragedy of DOUGLAS is the best play ever was written; and that *Shakespear* and *Otway* were a couple of dunces" (II. p. 15). Mr. Genius's utter insouciance in pronouncing the "sum and substance of [his] writings" links the corruption of taste—promoting the tragedy of *Douglas*— with the corruption of morals—the promotion of adultery and suicide. His seduction, moreover, of Sarah Presbytery, the two-hundred-year-old widow of John Calvin and the mother of Jacky, the author of *Douglas* within the satiric ballad opera, makes clear the extent to which MacLaurin sought to portray the influence of the Edinburgh literati as a usurpation of church authority.

While the attack on Hume might be predictable, given his manifest role in promoting *Douglas*, the most disturbing vignette in the ballad opera targets a figure somewhat more remote from the controversy but whose influence is figured as all the more insidious, that of the philosopher Francis Hutcheson, represented here by Mr. Moral Sense, who "pretends to be the most generous disinterested man alive" (II, p. 14). Moral Sense enters the scene touting his willingness to lay down his life for any and all but quickly turns out to be a lascivious drunkard who, appalling even Satan himself, justifies his attempted rape of Moll by pronouncing, "My instinct prompts me to lie with her" (II, p. 15). The ascendant discourse of moral sense is thus cast in MacLaurin's satire as a self-justifying rather than a principled discourse, and its espousal of virtue, in particular, is marked as a chimera of convenience.

In short, as Yoon Sun Lee observes, *Douglas*'s "opponents saw the success of [the tragedy] as the triumph not of a nation but of a small group ambitious for cultural hegemony—a group that preached and practiced virtue in a sense that was merely theatrical, without any tendency to benefit materially the nation or the mass of its citizens."[72] The strategy of those like MacLaurin was thus to represent the Moderates as an arrogant and elitist faction intent on leading the populace into great error. The overabundant tears shed by Miss Weepwell, Miss Sob, Miss Pity, and Miss Blubber as well as by one of Satan's attendants, Sulphureo, on their attendance at the playhouse suggest that the tragedy was not so much the "best play ever was written" as an exemplar of entertainment pandering to the masses and tendering a false because highly aestheticized notion of heroism and virtue (III, p. 18). Indeed, as Miss Sprightly boldly points out, it hardly seems rational to "dub" Douglas a hero merely for killing the "chief robber" in the play (III, p. 19). In their attacks on *Douglas*, then, Home's antagonists directed as much of their venom at the action of the play as at the dangers of a literary cabal deploying an aesthetic of affect to steer Scotland away from its roots in religion toward the false refinements of virtue.

The extent of this apprehension and the way in which the orthodox faction tried to resist its course can be discerned best in Witherspoon's second foray into the *Douglas* affair, *A Serious Inquiry into the Nature and Effects of the Stage* (1757), which stands out amid the more typical fire and brimstone accounts as the most even-tempered and soundly argued piece.[73] Yet what distinguishes this tract from all of the others is not just the logical quality of Witherspoon's arguments but rather their substance—in particular a series of stunning passages in which he articulates the significance of the battle at hand and acknowledges the broad impact that the new moral philosophy had already had on social, moral, and political life in Scotland.

At the outset, Witherspoon marks the occasion of his essay as one of great historical moment. "One thing is certain," he intones. "It hath been, and will be the subject of much thought and conversation among the laity of all ranks, and . . . it must have a very great influence upon the state of religion among us, in this part of the nation" (26). In his view, the rancor over *Douglas* was not merely of passing significance. Rather it represented a decisive struggle over the character of a nation and over the moral and religious values upheld in the conduct of everyday life.[74] In characterizing the rift between the moderate and orthodox factions, he thus conceded, "The truth is, it is our having different views of the nature of religion, that causes different opinions upon this subject . . . there are abundance of advocates for the lawfulness, some for the usefulness, of plays; not that the stage is become more pure, but that Christians are become less so, and have lowered the standard or measure requisite to attain and preserve that character" (31). As Witherspoon understood it, the controversy over *Douglas* was a contest between those who advocated for the secularization of culture and those who wished to maintain an ecclesiastical influence in and over public life. The repercussions of this battle would be felt not just within the Presbyterian Church but also by the nation at large. Hence, while Witherspoon's ostensible purpose in his essay is to "endeavor to shew, that PUBLIC THEATRICAL REPRESENTATIONS, either tragedy or comedy, are, in their general nature or in their best possible state, unlawful, contrary to the purity of our religion; and that writing, acting or attending them, is inconsistent with the character of a Christian," his text also takes up the more diffuse task of surveying and critiquing the ways in which this "different view of the nature of religion" had infiltrated the culture at the levels of both language and social practice (33). What makes his essay stand out among so many others is that he is looking not merely to indulge in blunt harangues against the outrages of the stage and the declining state of morality in the nation but rather to attempt an intervention in what he understood as both a profoundly subtle and yet highly effective cultural process.

In making his case, Witherspoon not only consistently attempts to refute the arguments of political economy that have already been rehearsed, but also, and perhaps more tellingly, offers a series of sophisticated insights into the mechanisms of cultural change. In particular, he squarely takes aim at the ways that the philosophical and moral positions of Scottish Enlightenment thought, and in particular the discourse of virtue, had been translated into linguistic turns with significant and potentially insidious discursive consequences. Taking note of a number of such turns, he expounds, for instance, "So in the moral world, verbal alterations, which are counted as nothing, do often introduce real changes, which are firmly established before their approach is so much as suspected. . . . Should we every where put virtue for holiness, honor, or even moral sense for conscience, improvement of the heart for sanctification, the opposition between such things and theatrical entertainments would not appear half so sensible" (35). Here Witherspoon observes the way that linguistic substitutions alter the connotations of action; they effect "real" semantic change. Almost imperceptibly and even more significantly, they transform the conceptual systems through which knowledge and cultural conventions are formed. Under the cloak of an older system of signification, they announce new and even contradictory meanings. In this case, it was as if "all the friends of the stage [had joined] with David Hume, who hath excluded self-denial, humility and mortification, from the number of virtues, and ranked them among the vices " (86–87). For Witherspoon, these substitutions of virtue for religion represented just a few among the many discursive dislocations produced by the new moral philosophy, and they formed the basis for his critique of an even broader substitution in philosophical discourse: the substitution of aesthetics for morality that could be traced back to the writings of Shaftesbury.

Contesting Shaftesbury's influential notion that an improvement in morals would follow from improvement in the arts, Witherspoon writes:

> There cannot be anything more absurd than to suppose, that the same thing will hold in morals and religion. The dramatic poets in Athens, where the stage was first established, improved upon one another, and refined their own taste, and that of their audience, as to the elegance of composition. . . . But whoever will from this infer, that they improved in their morals in the same proportion, or

by that means, will fall into a very gross mistake. This indeed seems
to be the great error of modern infidels, to suppose that there is no
more in morals than a certain taste and sense of beauty and elegance. Natural talents in the human mind are quite distinct from
moral dispositions, and the excellence of the one is no evidence at
all of the prevalence of the other. On the contrary, the first are many
times found in the highest perfection, where there is a total absence
of the last. (82–83)

Taking full aim at what he casts as a specious mechanism of analogy, Witherspoon marks not only the slippage between conceptual categories of a different kind but also the slippery slope from discursive formation or hypothesis to
cultural convention. To him, this kind of fluidity among categories of aesthetics, sociability, and morality constituted an unacceptable turn.

Thus, in response to Adam Ferguson's claims both for the stage and for
the benefits of sociability it offered, Witherspoon writes:

What a melancholy view then does it give us of the state of religion
among us at present, that when piety towards God has been excluded from many moral systems, and the whole of virtue confined
to the duties of social life, the better half of these also should be cut
off, and all regard to the souls of others forgotten or derided? Nothing indeed is left but a few expressions of compliment, a few insignificant offices of present conveniency; for that which some modern
refiners have dignified with the name of virtue, is nothing but polished luxury, a flattering of each other in their vices, a provocation
of each other to sensual indulgence, and that 'friendship of the
world,' which is 'enmity with God.'" (118–19)

In this manner, Witherspoon takes on the Enlightenment project of sociability and its concomitant interest in the liberalization of the public sphere of
cultural life. That Ferguson "pleads for civilizing the world, and not sanctify-
ing it" is in Witherspoon's view tantamount to "a confession of the weakness
of his cause" (132). That "cause," at least for the moment, however, was in the
ascendancy in Scotland; and the stage, in counterpoint to the church, was
understood as one more platform of address or of potential conversion—one
more place "pernicious and hurtful" in which "an improper method of instruction" could be instituted (94). As Witherspoon's commentary thus makes

clear, the political and cultural stakes in this battle could not be higher, and
his party was rapidly losing ground.

When the invitation to accept the presidency of the College of New Jersey
came along in 1767, it represented an opportunity for Witherspoon, who was
not unambitious, to leave Scotland, where the Moderate party was in ascen-
dance, and take up an influential post in America, where the more conservative and evangelical New Side of the Presbyterian Church was not only on the
rise against the Old Side but had recently staved off a coup by that more liberal faction of American Presbyterianism for control over the college.[75] As
Witherspoon's biographer Varnum Lansing Collier has demonstrated, "the
emphasis" in the letters of invitation was "distinctly laid on the fact that the
eyes of Presbyterian churches in seven provinces looked to Princeton alone to
supply their pulpits; the President would have the power not only to serve the
Church as a whole in the widest and most efficient way by training its ministry, but would also be the revered head of Presbyterian interests in the Middle
Colonies" (Figure 12).[76]

    With this kind of influence in hand, one would think that Witherspoon's
first order of business upon taking up the presidency would have been to reinforce the conservative, evangelical curriculum that had been developed by,
among others, Jonathan Edwards. Instead, as Mark A. Noll has argued, Witherspoon reversed himself and replaced Edwardsian Calvinism with a curriculum infused with the thought and values of the Scottish Enlightenment, a
move that better reflected the secularization of the Scottish universities by the
Moderates rather than the opposition of the orthodox.[77] Perhaps even more
significantly, Witherspoon rejected the practical theology of Edwards and in
his *Lectures on Moral Philosophy* embraced instead the more empirical principles of Francis Hutcheson, whose emphasis on the "natural moral sense" he
had attacked in Scotland. As Noll writes, "Witherspoon, at least in his lectures, set aside an Augustinian distrust of human nature; he denied, in practice, that original sin harmed the ability to cultivate natural virtue; and he
came to speak of achievements of science as triumphs of empirical inquiry
rather than as manifestations of God's glory."[78]

    There are at least two possible ways to account for the "moderation" of
Witherspoon's views. First, the political position of the Presbyterian Church
in America was considerably different from that in Scotland. Where in Scotland, Presbyterianism was the established religion, in America, the Presbyterians were fighting battles on a number of fronts to fend off the establishment

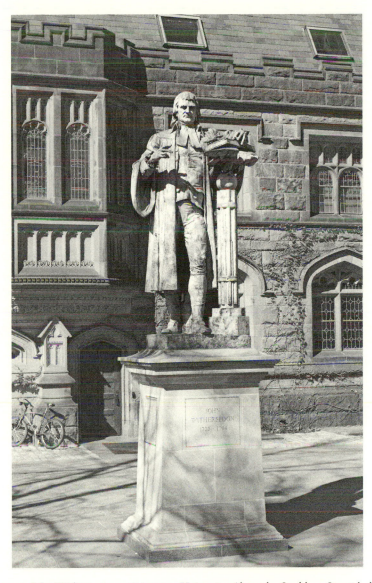

Figure 12. John Witherspoon at Princeton University. Alexander Stoddart, Scottish, born 1959. John Witherspoon (1723–1794), 2001. Cast bronze. Princeton University. PP635.
Image courtesy of Princeton University Art Museum; photo by Bruce M. White.

of an Anglican episcopacy. Second, Witherspoon adapted his views in a revolutionary context as a way to justify the establishment of a republic. In both
cases, the ideas of Scottish Enlightenment thinkers offered certain strategic
advantages. Whatever his motivation may have been, what remains clear is the
extent to which Witherspoon had the power to influence the direction of
early American discourse—providing for the education in his time of no fewer
than "twelve members of the Continental Congress; five delegates to the Constitutional Convention; one U. S. President (James Madison, B.A. 1771); a
U. S. vice president (Aaron Burr, B.A. 1772); forty-nine U. S. representatives;
twenty-eight U. S. senators; three Supreme Court justices; eight U. S. district
judges; one secretary of state; three attorneys general; and two foreign
ministers."[79]

Witherspoon's transformation into a more liberal version of himself was
not, however, without its contradictions or its exceptions, and this was most
particularly the case when it came to his views on the theater. Indeed, no matter how far Witherspoon may have "moderated" his views with respect to
moral philosophy, religion, and politics, his antipathy toward the theater and
his willingness to use his influence to quash the existence of the playhouse
remained a lifelong obsession, so much so that his last dictated letter to his
amanuensis was a "Letter Respecting Play Actors." This 1794 diatribe was
prompted by a letter in the *National Gazette* that offered praise for the improvement of the status of actors on the occasion of the successful opening of
the New Theatre in Philadelphia.[80] Alarmed by such public praise as well as by
the rising fortunes of American theaters—with the opening of the Federal
Street Theatre in Boston coming just two weeks before that in Philadelphia—
Witherspoon's letter was so severe that no newspaper editor would agree to
print it.[81] Once again, and despite the views he expressed otherwise in his
Lectures, Witherspoon reverted to a vision of human nature as essentially corrupt and corruptible. When it was finally published as part of the influential
1802 edition of Witherspoon's *Works*, however, it would play a foundational
role, along with his earlier *Serious Inquiry*, in American antitheatricalism.

Indeed, for proof of Witherspoon's influence, we need look no farther
than the antitheatrical publications that followed the fire on 26 December
1811 at the playhouse in Richmond, Virginia, in which more than seventy
people died. Though many lamented the loss of life and offered sympathy to
the survivors, others, as I shall demonstrate in the next chapter, construed the
event as an act of providence, as proof, that is, of a divine judgment against
the theater and against those who patronized or participated in its

entertainments. In New York, a group of men took it upon themselves to ask the Reverend Samuel Miller of the First Presbyterian Church to preach a sermon on the occasion. Miller had longstanding ties to Witherspoon and to Princeton and at the time of the fire was deeply involved in the formation of the Princeton Theological Seminary, which would function as a complementary offshoot of Princeton College and the Presbyterian establishment in the United States. Whereas Witherspoon offered a mixed, yet powerful legacy of combining Christian Enlightenment with Presbyterian evangelicism, for reasons that I will expound upon at greater length in the next chapter, Miller and his fellows had drifted decidedly toward the more firmly conservative, evangelical camp.[82] Though Miller warned the young men that he would feel compelled to "include a solemn protest against Theatrical entertainments," they "unanimously persisted"; and the sermon was not only composed and delivered, but it was bound as part of a new edition of Witherspoon's *Serious Inquiry* along with his "Letter Respecting Play Actors" and "An Address, By Several Ministers in New-York, To Their Christian Fellow-Citizens, Dissuading them from Attending Theatrical Representations."[83] This latter document was "Designed as an Introduction to Dr. Witherspoon's Inquiry" and not only pointed to the fire at Richmond as an appropriate occasion to inquire into the "moral tendency of the Theatre" but also "embraced the opportunity, offered by the present state of public sensibility, to address [us] on the subject of the Stage, and to direct [our] inquiries into the character of an institution, which is . . . esteemed pernicious to society."[84] It concludes, moreover, with a recommendation that "the introduction of the drama into the schools of literature should be discouraged. It is very unsuitable as a branch of christian education, and has already frequently been the first step to the ruin of youth of promising talents."[85] Riffling through all of these documents is the same sense that we found in Witherspoon of the kinds of social and political influence at stake, the anxiety that these forms of entertainment might get the best of religiosity not only in Scotland but also in America and that "religious taste [might] itself be affected, and under the illusory idea of superior refinement, the enticing words of man's wisdom [would be] apt to be preferred to the demonstrations of the spirit."[86]

Thus, while Witherspoon may have brought with him to America the political refinements of Scottish Enlightenment thought, he also imported a conservative cultural politics. While he looked to the Scottish university and to Scottish texts in his capacity as a leader of the American academy, in his role as a religious leader, he played down any aspect of those texts that might have challenged the cultural hegemony of Christian morality. The overall result of this dual legacy, as Samuel Fleischacker has pointed out, has been a "wider unwillingness—characteristic of America for much of its history—to let intellectuals severely challenge, let alone override, conventional beliefs."[87] In the two chapters that follow, we will trace Witherspoon and this antitheatrical legacy and explore how religious leaders at different but not altogether disparate moments in American history constituted antitheatrical bodies public and brought their political influence to bear respectively in the aftermath of the Richmond Theater fire and in the controversy over the NEA Four.

Chapter 4

Cultivating a Christian Body Public

The Richmond Theater Fire

On December 26, 1811, midway through a performance of the gothic panto-mime *Raymond and Agnes; or, The Bleeding Nun*, a fire broke out at the theater in Richmond, Virginia. The blaze spread quickly, and soon the entire play-house was engulfed in flames. Of the over six hundred people who packed the theater that night, more than seventy died, including the governor of Vir-ginia, George W. Smith; Abraham Venable, the president of the Bank of Vir-ginia and a former U.S. senator; and Benjamin Botts, an attorney who had distinguished himself in the 1807 treason trial of former vice president Aaron Burr. While the loss of these preeminent actors on the public stage of Virginia cast a long shadow over the civic life of the state, the vast majority of those who died that night were women, most of whom either burned, suffocated, or were trampled to death when they tried to escape the theater using the only narrow set of stairs that led from their otherwise enviable perches in the fash-ionable playhouse boxes (Figure 13).[1]

As Richmond went into mourning, so too did much of the nation. Mem-bers of Congress donned crepe bands on their left arms in observance of the catastrophe, and details about what came to be known as the "Awful Calam-ity" at Richmond spread rapidly up and down the Eastern seaboard. Tributes of sympathy poured into the city and were featured in newspapers all over the country. Yet public lamentations for the dead were soon drowned out by equally vociferous calls of recrimination for the multitude of sins committed at the playhouse. Speaking from pulpits as close by as Alexandria and Win-chester, Virginia, and as far-flung as Ipswich, Massachusetts, ministers and

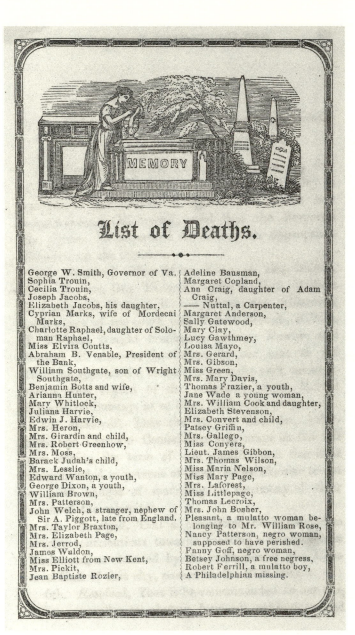

List of Deaths.

George W. Smith, Governor of Va.
Sophia Trouin,
Cecilia Trouin,
Joseph Jacobs,
Elizabeth Jacobs, his daughter,
Cyprian Marks, wife of Mordecai
  Marks,
Charlotte Raphael, daughter of Solo-
  man Raphael,
Miss Elvira Coutts,
Abraham B. Venable, President of
  the Bank,
William Southgate, son of Wright
  Southgate,
Benjamin Botts and wife,
Arianna Hunter,
Mary Whitlock,
Juliana Harvie,
Edwin J. Harvie,
Mrs. Heron,
Mrs. Girardin and child,
Mrs. Robert Greenhow,
Mrs. Moss,
Barack Judah's child,
Mrs. Lesslie,
Edward Wanton, a youth,
George Dixon, a youth,
William Brown,
Mrs. Patterson,
John Welch, a stranger, nephew of
  Sir A. Piggott, late from England.
Mrs. Taylor Braxton,
Mrs. Elizabeth Page,
Mrs. Jerrod,
James Wuldon,
Miss Elliott from New Kent,
Mrs. Pickit,
Jean Baptiste Rozier,

Adeline Bausman,
Margaret Copland,
Ann Craig, daughter of Adam
  Craig,
—— Nuttal, a Carpenter,
Margaret Anderson,
Sally Gatewood,
Mary Clay,
Lucy Gawthmey,
Louisa Mayo,
Mrs. Gerard,
Mrs. Gibson,
Miss Green,
Mrs. Mary Davis,
Thomas Frazier, a youth,
Jane Wade a young woman,
Mrs. William Cook and daughter,
Elizabeth Stevenson,
Mrs. Convert and child,
Patsey Griffin,
Mrs. Gallego,
Miss Conyers,
Lieut. James Gibbon,
Mrs. Thomas Wilson,
Miss Maria Nelson,
Miss Mary Page,
Mrs. Laforest,
Miss Littlepage,
Thomas Lecroix,
Mrs. John Bosher,
Pleasant, a mulatto woman be-
  longing to Mr. William Rose,
Nancy Patterson, negro woman,
  supposed to have perished.
Fanny Goff, negro woman,
Betsey Johnson, a free negress,
Robert Ferrill, a mulatto boy,
A Philadelphian missing.

Figure 13. List of the Dead. From *A Full Account
of the Burning of the Richmond Theatre*. Richmond, 1858.
Courtesy of the Virginia Historical Society, Richmond.

preachers moved quickly in their sermons to frame the fire at the theater as an act of divine providence visited upon a dissipated society.[2]

This chapter explores both the range of reactions to the fire in letters, newspapers, and pamphlet accounts and the subsequent efforts in pulpits to take the occasion of the fire to exemplify the urgent need for a renewed turn to religiosity in early nineteenth-century America. At this point, the new republic was still in the throes of its initial wranglings over who composed "the people" in "We the people" of the U.S. Constitution.[3] Amid the post-Revolutionary push toward greater democratization and in the wake of disestablishment, every effort would be made by competing religious interests to ensure that "the people" of the United States, as long prescribed by the mythical vision of an American covenant with God, would derive its strength and much of its identity from Christian principles and values. In taking up the sermons preached on the occasion of the Richmond Theater fire, then, I illustrate how antitheatrical sentiments were deployed, and the events in Richmond thus opportunely leveraged, as part of the ongoing revivalist movement known as the Second Great Awakening, to call upon Americans to form themselves into a body public that would be dedicated to a reinvigoration of Christian religion in the nation.

Ironically, even as these sermons expostulated against the theater, they also borrowed and adapted the tropes and stylings of the gothic and sentimental dramas that were so popular on the stages of early nineteenth-century American playhouses. The discussion below will be directed not simply toward a description of the events, but toward an examination of how those events were narrativized, that is, of how the conventions of gothic romance and sentimental melodrama were mobilized both in reports of the catastrophic event and in subsequent commentaries and sermons to tell the tale not just of the tragedy at Richmond but of the imperiled social, moral, and religious condition of the nation.[4] As I explore the public discourse that emerged in the aftermath of the Richmond fire, then, I will seek to elaborate how the cultural imaginary through which the events in Richmond were filtered relied upon a popular vernacular derived from the very theatrical forms that were so widely vilified. Seeking to give shape and meaning to the events at Richmond, eyewitnesses at the scene adopted the rhetorical tone and narrative arc of both sentimental melodrama and gothic romance to convey the horrors of the conflagration, even as ministers at a distance from the catastrophe transposed those same conventions to the eschatalogical arc of God's divine drama of sin and salvation. In the first half of this chapter, I explore how the rhetorical and dramatic conventions of gothic romance and sentimental melodrama were first adapted to fashion vignettes that could function as emblems for the tragedy at Richmond. I then turn in the second half of this chapter to the strategic, and somewhat disturbing, use of these same tropes in the antitheatrical sermons that came to define the calamity at Richmond as a tragic, yet providential warning to the American people to heed the call to awakening and repentance and to form themselves into a Christian body public.

A Gothic Melodrama: "I Have a Tale of Horrour to Tell"

Setting the Scene: Thursday, 26 December 1811

Expectations were exceedingly high for an evening at the theater on the night of 26 December 1811.[5] The legislature was in session, and on the day after Christmas, merriment was still very much in the air. The theater was *the* place to be that night, and the playhouse was full to bursting, representing an amalgam of the heterogeneous bodies that composed the city. While the pit was filled by the middle and poorer white classes, and the gallery reserved for free and enslaved blacks, the boxes were occupied by the wealthy and fashionable set, including a substantial population of Jews, who had made their fortunes in Richmond and had achieved a prominent place in its society.[6] Altogether, it was a night to see and be seen to advantage, and large numbers of the most eligible young women, dressed in the latest styles, took pride of place on display in the playhouse boxes. Amid the splendor of the theater that night, no one could have anticipated either the horrors that would be visited upon the audience or the profound repercussions that would ripple out from Richmond across the nation.

Richmond in 1811, like much of the United States during this period, was undergoing an economic boom.[7] Between 1800 and 1810, the population had nearly doubled from 5,730 to 9,735, more than a third of which was composed of either enslaved or free blacks who labored in private homes, industry, and the artisanal trades. Favored by its location along the James River, Richmond was emerging as a center of trade and commerce in the South, with flour, paper, and tobacco among its major export industries. Buoyed by its status as the seat of government, moreover, the small city had grown into an urban metropolis and had gained a reputation as much for its commerce and industry as for its entertainments and diversions. As in much of the South, theater was looked upon with a minimum of disapprobation and, as Patricia Click notes, "enjoyed a general popularity."[8]

Theater had been a mainstay in Richmond since 1784, when Governor Benjamin Harrison pronounced that "a well chosen & well acted play is amongst the first of moral Lessons and tend greatly to inculcate & fix on the mind the most virtuous principles," and granted permission to Dennis Ryan's American Company of Comedians to establish a theater company in the city.[9] Theatrical managers quickly learned that they would experience their greatest financial success if they scheduled the theatrical season to coincide with the legislative sessions. Many of Richmond's most prominent families would come out on those evenings to socialize and to enjoy the night's entertainment, and, as Susanne Sherman explains, "It was this audience which made it possible for an established company of comedians to play a six-weeks' season in the tiny village capital of Virginia."[10] Over the years many of the most prominent touring companies in the country made Richmond one of their major stopping places, and they often imported such stars as Thomas Abthorpe Cooper and John Howard Payne.[11] During the 1811 season, one of the featured actresses was Elizabeth Arnold Hopkins Poe, Edgar Allan Poe's mother, who died on 8 December, just eighteen days before the fire, leaving her two-year-old son an orphan.

The standard repertory at Richmond, like that of most American playhouses in this period, consisted primarily of imports from England, with an increasing emphasis on gothic romances and the sentimental and sensational strains of melodrama.[12] As Martin Staples Shockley reports, "The years from 1806–1812," under the management, first, of Margaret West and then of John William Green and Alexander Placide, "may be considered a golden age of the Richmond theatre."[13] Optimistic about the theatrical future in Richmond, West had opened a new brick theater in 1806 at the same site on Shockoe Hill where the old academy theater once stood. Shoddy construction, including the use of painted canvases rather than plaster to cover the domed ceiling, would contribute to the speed with which the fire would spread on that tragic night in December.

The Fire at the Theater

For the bill on what was to be the last day of a highly successful season and a benefit performance for its manager, Alexander Placide, the Placide Company planned a program consisting of two pieces that were new to the Richmond stage: first, a production of Denis Diderot's sentimental comedy *Le Père de famille* (1758), presented as *The Father: or, Family Feuds*, in a new translation by

Richmond resident Louis Hue Girardin; and second, a spectacle-driven, gothic pantomime titled *Raymond and Agnes: or, The Bleeding Nun* (Figure 14). After the mainpiece and the musical entertainments had been concluded, the actors took the stage for a performance of *The Bleeding Nun*. At the end of act 1, the chandelier, which had provided light for the cottage setting of Baptiste the robber, was raised to a position above the stage, amid the painted canvas scenery, with at least one of its wicks still lit.[14] When the danger was realized, an attempt was made to lower the chandelier to snuff out the taper; but the ropes and pulleys were tangled, and repeated efforts to jerk them free only tilted the chandelier, bringing the burning candle into contact with the canvas scenery and setting it aflame. All attempts to extinguish the fire were unavailing, as the flames spread rapidly from canvas to canvas and then leapt to the domed ceiling, which was covered in yet more canvas material. Panic spread quickly through the house, as burning pieces of scenery began to fall to the stage; and the lead actor in the pantomime, Hopkins Robertson, stepped forward to exclaim, "The house is on fire!" In less than five minutes, flames engulfed the entire theater, racing across the roof above and bursting through the windows. Most of those in the pit were able to make a swift exit through the main door, while those in the gallery, mostly free and enslaved blacks, were able to escape via their separate entrance. For the vast numbers in the two tiers of boxes, however, the situation was much more dire as they were forced to find their way down from the small upper lobby to the main door, shared with the pit, via one very narrow and winding staircase. All too quickly, that way was choked up both by too many people pressing forward through the narrow passage and by those who were either trampled by the crowd or suffocated on the spot by the thick, black smoke that almost immediately blanketed the space. The vast majority of the dead were found, as the appointed Committee reported, either "strewed in heaps at the foot of the narrow staircase which lead from the boxes" or "on the ground immediately *under* the lobby of the boxes above"—the upper lobby having collapsed at some point during the fire to the floor below. In their panicked state, moreover, so many patrons pressed themselves against the front entryway, which opened inward, that even after the upper lobby collapsed, those who had formerly been trapped on the box level still found it almost impossible to force the doors ajar. When the walls of the theater collapsed, those who were still left alive in the building were either burned or crushed to death. Most of those from the boxes who managed to survive the fire, leapt from the windows, sometimes in flames, often injuring themselves terribly in the fall (Figure 15).[15]

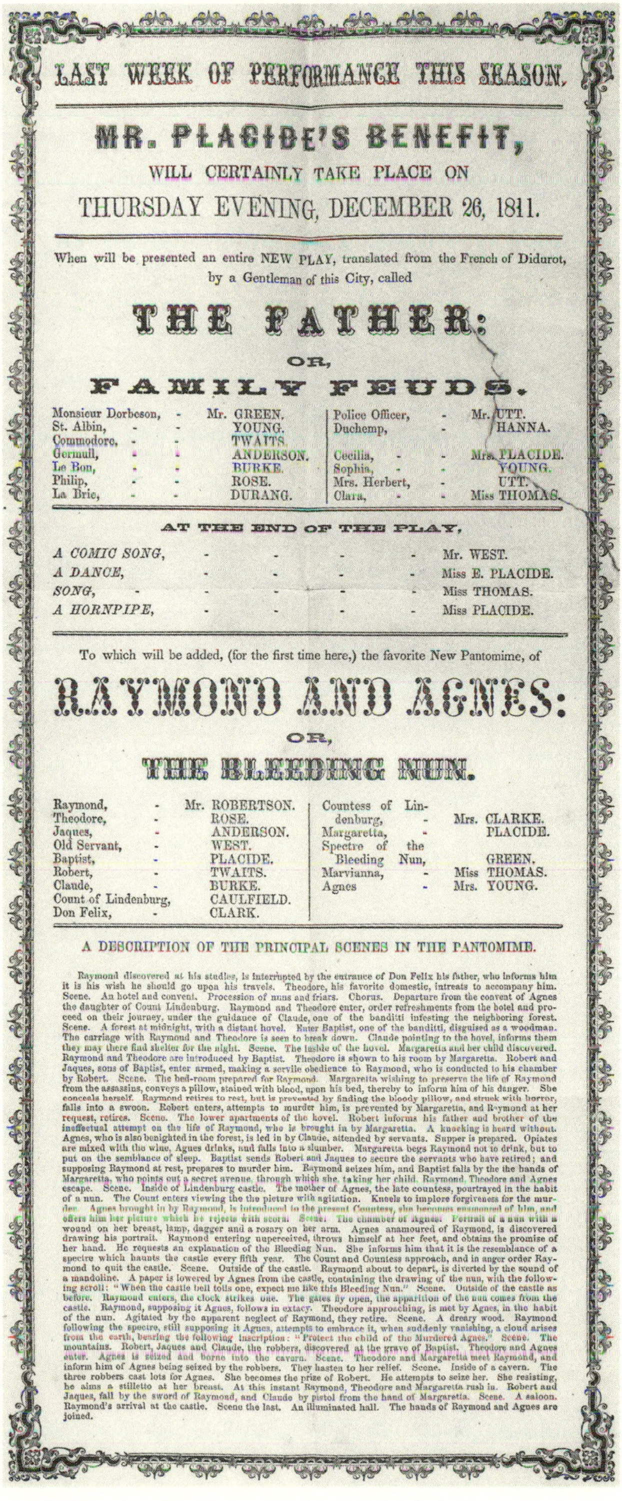

LAST WEEK OF PERFORMANCE THIS SEASON.

MR. PLACIDE'S BENEFIT,

WILL CERTAINLY TAKE PLACE ON

THURSDAY EVENING, DECEMBER 26, 1811.

When will be presented an entire NEW PLAY, translated from the French of Didurot, by a Gentleman of this City, called

THE FATHER:

OR,

FAMILY FEUDS.

Monsieur Dorbeson, -	Mr. GREEN.	Police Officer, -	Mr. UTT.
St. Albin, - -	YOUNG.	Duchemp, -	HANNA.
Commodore, - -	TWAITS.		
Germuil, - -	ANDERSON.	Cecilia, - -	Mrs. PLACIDE.
Le Bon, - -	BURKE.	Sophia, - -	YOUNG.
Philip, - -	ROSE.	Mrs. Herbert, -	UTT.
La Brie, - -	DURANG.	Clara, - -	Miss THOMAS.

AT THE END OF THE PLAY,

A COMIC SONG, - - - -	Mr. WEST.
A DANCE, - - - -	Miss E. PLACIDE.
SONG, - - - - -	Miss THOMAS.
A HORNPIPE, - - - -	Miss PLACIDE.

To which will be added, (for the first time here,) the favorite New Pantomime, of

RAYMOND AND AGNES:

OR,

THE BLEEDING NUN.

Raymond, -	Mr. ROBERTSON.	Countess of Lindenburg, -	Mrs. CLARKE.
Theodore, -	ROSE.	Margaretta, -	PLACIDE.
Jaques, -	ANDERSON.	Spectre of the Bleeding Nun,	GREEN.
Old Servant, -	WEST.	Marvianna, -	Miss THOMAS.
Baptist, -	PLACIDE.	Agnes -	Mrs. YOUNG.
Robert, -	TWAITS.		
Claude, -	BURKE.		
Count of Lindenburg,	CAULFIELD.		
Don Felix, -	CLARK.		

A DESCRIPTION OF THE PRINCIPAL SCENES IN THE PANTOMIME.

Raymond discovered at his studies, is interrupted by the entrance of Don Felix his father, who informs him it is his wish he should go upon his travels. Theodore, his favorite domestic, intreats to accompany him. Scene. An hotel and convent. Procession of nuns and friars. Chorus. Departure from the convent of Agnes the daughter of Count Lindenburg. Raymond and Theodore enter, order refreshments from the hotel and proceed on their journey, under the guidance of Claude, one of the banditti infesting the neighboring forest. Scene. A forest at midnight, with a distant hovel. Enter Baptist, one of the banditti, disguised as a woodman. The carriage with Raymond and Theodore is seen to break down. Claude pointing to the hovel, informs them they may there find shelter for the night. Scene. The inside of the hovel. Margaretta and her child discovered. Raymond and Theodore are introduced by Baptist. Theodore is shown to his room by Margaretta. Robert and Jaques, sons of Baptist, enter armed, making a servile obedience to Raymond, who is conducted to his chamber by Robert. Scene. The bed-room prepared for Raymond. Margaretta wishing to preserve the life of Raymond from the assassins, conveys a pillow, stained with blood, upon his bed, thereby to inform him of his danger. She conceals herself. Raymond retires to rest, but is prevented by finding the bloody pillow, and struck with horror, falls into a swoon. Robert enters, attempts to murder him, is prevented by Margaretta, and Raymond at her request, retires. Scene. The lower apartments of the hovel. Robert informs his father and brother of the ineffectual attempt on the life of Raymond, who is brought in by Margaretta. A knocking is heard without. Agnes, who is also benighted in the forest, is led in by Claude, attended by servants. Supper is prepared. Opiates are mixed with the wine, Agnes drinks, and falls into a slumber. Margaretta begs Raymond not to drink, but to put on the semblance of sleep. Baptist sends Robert and Jaques to secure the servants who have retired; and supposing Raymond at rest, prepares to murder him. Raymond seizes him, and Baptist falls by the the hands of Margaretta, who points out a secret avenue, through which she, taking her child, Raymond, Theodore and Agnes escape. Scene. Inside of Lindenburg castle. The mother of Agnes, the late countess, pourtrayed in the habit of a nun. The Count enters viewing the the picture with agitation. Kneels to implore forgiveness for the murder. Agnes brought in by Raymond, is introduced to the present Countess, she becomes enamoured of him, and offers him her picture which he rejects with scorn. Scene. The chamber of Agnes. Portrait of a nun with a wound on her breast, lamp, dagger and a rosary on her arm. Agnes anamoured of Raymond, is discovered drawing his portrait. Raymond entering unperceived, throws himself at her feet, and obtains the promise of her hand. He requests an explanation of the Bleeding Nun. She informs him that it is the resemblance of a spectre which haunts the castle every fifth year. The Count and Countess approach, and in anger order Raymond to quit the castle. Scene. Outside of the castle. Raymond about to depart, is diverted by the sound of a mandoline. A paper is lowered by Agnes from the castle, containing the drawing of the nun, with the following scroll: "When the castle bell tolls one, expect me like this Bleeding Nun." Scene. Outside of the castle as before. Raymond enters, the clock strikes one. The gates fly open, the apparition of the nun comes from the castle. Raymond, supposing it Agnes, follows in extacy. Theodore approaching, is met by Agnes, in the habit of the nun. Agitated by the apparent neglect of Raymond, they retire. Scene. A dreary wood. Raymond following the spectre, still supposing it Agnes, attempts to embrace it, when suddenly vanishing, a cloud arises from the earth, bearing the following inscription: "Protect the child of the Murdered Agnes." Scene. The mountains. Robert, Jaques and Claude, the robbers, discovered at the grave of Baptist. Theodore and Agnes enter. Agnes is seized and borne into the cavern. Scene. Theodore and Margaretta meet Raymond, and inform him of Agnes being seized by the robbers. They hasten to her relief. Scene. Inside of a cavern. The three robbers cast lots for Agnes. She becomes the prize of Robert. He attempts to seize her. She resisting, he aims a stilletto at her breast. At this instant Raymond, Theodore and Margaretta rush in. Robert and Jaques, fall by the sword of Raymond, and Claude by pistol from the hand of Margaretta. Scene. A saloon. Raymond's arrival at the castle. Scene the last. An illuminated hall. The hands of Raymond and Agnes are joined.

Figure 14. Playbill, Richmond Theater, 26 December 1811. From *A Full Account of the Burning of the Richmond Theatre*. Richmond, 1858. Courtesy of the Virginia Historical Society, Richmond.

The BURNING of the THEATRE in RICHMOND, VIRGINIA, on the Night of the 26.th December 1811,
By which awful Calamity upwards of SEVENTY FIVE of its most valuable Citizens suddenly lost their lives and many others were much injured.

Published Feb.y 10.th 1812 by B. Tanner N.º 79 South 3.d St. Philadelphia

Figure 15. Theater on Fire, Richmond, Virginia.
Courtesy of the Library of Virginia.

The reports of the fire are exceedingly difficult to read. The scene was utterly harrowing, filled both with the agonized screams of those caught in the flames and the sight of their bodies twisting in anguish. In the aftermath, moreover, very little remained by which to identify the victims. Indeed, as Thomas Brown, who later went on to become governor of Florida, recorded in his subsequent *Recollections*, most of the bodies were reduced to mere torsos:

Early the next morning, I went to the place, and saw taken from the smoldering ruins, the bodies—or rather—the blackened trunks, of Seventy two, of the victims which were taken to the Baptist Church nearby. The extremities of all, were burnt off to the knees and elbows, and many higher up, or nearer to the body. Only two had their heads or shoulders remain to the body, the rest were burnt off leaving stumps of the neck. Of Course none Could be known by feature or form. Nor was any thing found about them by which they Could be identified—Except the body of Governor Smith, under which was found his gold watch, with his name on it. . . . And on the Stump of the neck of a very small body, hung a gold chain on which was inscribed, "From my Grand Mother" which was known to be Miss Whitlock, a most lovely girl about fourteen years old.[16]

In a scene worthy of the most disturbing gothic narratives of the period, not only was the dazzle of the Richmond playhouse reduced to a collapsed and ashen heap, but so too were the handsome bodies that adorned the theatrical space transmogrified into grotesque abstracts of their former selves. It is no wonder, then, that as eyewitnesses to the conflagration struggled to frame the events and to make sense of what they beheld, they consistently commandeered the rhetorical and narratological patterns of the gothic romances and sentimental melodramas that had so frequently graced the Richmond stage. In an eerily macabre and distressing turn of events, it is as if those present at the performance that evening had found the perfect occasion to apply the rhetorical techniques and generic conventions of gothic horror, sentiment, and sensibility.

As if modeling the elevated, rhetorical register of gothic protagonists in the throes of fictional terror, for instance, words are repeatedly said to fail when eyewitnesses try to describe the actual scene before them. Thus, Thomas Ritchie, the editor of the Richmond *Enquirer* writes:

> How can we describe the scene! No pen can paint it; no imagination can conceive it. A whole Theatre wrapt in flames—a gay and animated assembly suddenly thrown on the very verge of the grave—many of them, oh! how many! precipitated in a moment into eternity—youth, beauty, and old age, and genius overwhelmed in one promiscuous ruin—shrieks, groans, and human agony in every shape—this is the heart rending scene we are called upon to describe. We sink under the effort. Reader excuse our feelings, for they are the feelings of a whole city.[17]

Like a character in a gothic fiction, Ritchie is struck dumb, appalled by the sensational and sublime horrors to which he has just borne witness—bodies wrapped and roasting in unremitting flames; women set afire, running half-naked from the playhouse; husbands calling out frantically for their wives and wives for their husbands; parents crying out desperately for their children—all compounded in "one promiscuous ruin," a phrase charged with the kinds of passions associated with the erotic violence of gothic narratives and which would be rehearsed to great effect not just in letters, diaries, and newspaper accounts, but also, as we shall see later in this chapter, in the sermons that were preached on the occasion of the fire. Addressing his readers directly, moreover, Ritchie begs their indulgence, even as he blankets them with the inexorable force of his sentiments—"the feelings of a whole city." The frequent exclamation points, the stops and starts in his discourse, and the conspicuous failure of conscious imagination, all project the powerful sentiments associated with gothic discourse and with the irrational sensations of sublime terror.[18] Where conscious thought fails, pure and unadulterated feeling, common, in theory, to all humanity, and communicable by the mechanisms of sympathetic identification, fills the void. Thus punctuating an emotional account of the fire, the editor of *The American Standard* drew on the discourse of sensibility, with all of its problematic distinctions, to assert, that even "the most distant and implacable enemy, and the most savage barbarians will condole our unhappy lot."[19] On a more personal level, Thomas Brown reported that while "the horrible scenes" he had witnessed had at first "shrunk [his] heart into a piece of Callous flesh," he eventually found that his "heart recovered its natural sensibility, And a tear of sympathy moistened my eyelids."[20] "The cries of the dying mother, the screams of the frantic daughter, the phrenzy of the expiring son, and distraction of the husband, were more than enough," wrote another young gentleman to his father in New York, "to draw forth sympathy from an adamantine heart."[21]

In its traumatized state, Richmond sought some kind of solace, most particularly from the horrific realization that most of those who perished in the fire were women and, even more disturbing to the social and psychic configuration of the city, a vast number of young women of marriageable age who were just entering their prime reproductive years. Indeed, more than one commentator observed that while at least fifty women died, somehow all of the members of the state legislature who were in attendance at the theater that evening managed to survive.[22] The absence of male gallantry on the occasion, as indicated by the disproportionate numbers of women lost, was pointedly captured when it was reported that a Miss Couch "without any particular protector, escaped unhurt, one of the last," despite the fact that "being a delicate young lady, she was several times thrown back by inhuman selfish men."[23] While Miss Couch managed to survive the blaze, Mary Clay, Lucy Gwathmey, Maria Nelson, Louisa Mayo, Margaret Copland, and many, many other young women, who in both public and private discourse were consistently and almost conventionally characterized as the "brightest ornaments" of the city, did not.[24] In the face of this trauma, the generic patterns of gothic romance, as exemplified by *The Bleeding Nun*, provided the perfect template for narrativizing the psychic perturbations inflicted by those losses and organizing the emotional life of the surviving public body.[25]

Raymond and Agnes: Or, The Bleeding Nun

Composed by Charles Farley, and including a number of sung musical compositions, *Raymond and Agnes: Or, the Bleeding Nun* had first been performed at Covent Garden on March 16, 1797, and was adapted from the plot of Matthew Lewis's notorious gothic novel *The Monk* (1796).[26] A popular afterpiece for many years, records suggest that it was first performed in the United States in 1804 at theaters in New York and Baltimore, where members of Placide's company were in the cast.[27] While the pantomime was new to Richmond, Lewis's other dramas as well as his gothic novel would have been well-known to audiences there.[28] Indeed, *The Monk* was among the favorites of Richmond readers, along with other gothic novels by such authors as Anne Radcliffe, Charles Robert Maturin, and William Godwin.[29] These reading habits would have provided the Richmond audience with a substantial, popular vernacular for engaging horrific scenes of psychic disturbance.

The Monk traces two intersecting plot lines. In the titular plot, Ambrosio, the outwardly virtuous but secretly vain abbot of a monastery in Madrid, is seduced into a life of sexual depravity by one of the devil's minions in the likeness of a man-woman, Rosario-Matilda. Driven by voracious passion and supplied with supernatural aids by Matilda, he subsequently attempts to seduce the innocent Antonia. When Antonia's mother, Elvira, catches him in the act, he kills her, and later, in the catacombs of the Convent of St. Clare, he brutally rapes and murders Antonia. Only at the end does he learn that Antonia had been his sister and Elvira his mother, from whom he had been separated at a very early age. Once caught and incarcerated by the Inquisition, Ambrosio sells his soul to the devil and suffers an excruciating death. Sexually explicit encounters, rape, incest, matricide, and sororicide are all prominent features of the plot.

In the second plot line, and the one upon which the pantomime is based, Don Raymond de las Cisternas, traveling incognito as Alphonso d'Alvarada, meets and falls in love with Agnes de Medina at the Castle of Lindenbergh, where she has been staying with relatives before being dedicated, against her will, as a nun at the Convent of St. Clare. Raymond had been invited to the castle after having saved himself and Agnes's aunt, the Baronness of Linden-bergh, from a band of men led by Baptiste the Robber. At the castle, Agnes tells Raymond the tale of the Bleeding Nun, the apparition of Beatrice, who, having been forced to take the veil against her will, had escaped the convent to become the concubine of an earlier Baron of Lindenbergh. Extending her life of debauchery, she entered into an affair with the baron's younger brother and on his insistence murdered the baron. To cover up the crime, the younger brother stabbed Beatrice and left her body to rot unburied in a cave outside the castle walls. Every five years, she emerges from her cell, dressed in a religious habit, stained with blood from the wound at her bosom, to inspect her bones. Determined to elope with Raymond and knowing that the castle doors are left open only on the night that the Bleeding Nun appears, Agnes plots to escape by dressing herself in the specter's guise. When she reaches the gates of the castle, however, she finds that Raymond has already left the spot, having unwittingly mistaken the apparition of the Bleeding Nun for the real Agnes. Distraught by Raymond's disappearance and believing that he had abandoned her, Agnes takes the veil at the Convent of St. Clare, where Raymond, after having exorcised the spirit of the Bleeding Nun and laid her bones to rest, finally finds her. In a moment of passion, Agnes gives way to Raymond and soon finds herself pregnant. When their new plan to elope is discovered by Ambrosio, Agnes is imprisoned in the bowels of the convent by the prioress, and it is given out that she is dead. The truth of her whereabouts only comes to light when a mob, enraged by the prioress's abuse of power, sets fire to the convent. Agnes is discovered in the catacombs, on the brink of death and clinging to the putrefied body of her dead child. Nursed back to health, she and Raymond are reunited and finally married.[30]

With its extended scenes of female suffering and its fetishization of female virtue and female sexuality—all not insignificantly confounded in the emblematic figure of the Bleeding Nun—*The Monk* offered a number of uncanny precedents through which to filter the events at Richmond, especially the horrific and torturous deaths of so many young women on the brink of their entrance into sexual adulthood. Perhaps even more eerily, the novel begins with a prolonged meditation on the similarities between performance in the pulpit and performance on stage. As a "celebrated" orator, Ambrosio is construed as a charismatic performer, the likes of which Madrid had never before seen. The crowds that were drawn to hear him speak transform the solemn space of the church into the sociable space of a theater, where "one half of Madrid was brought thither by expecting to meet the other half," and it was "as difficult to obtain a place at Church, as at the first representation of a new comedy."[31] As we shall see later in this chapter, these explicit analogies between church and playhouse and the critique of overt displays of religiosity that they convey offer a kind of insight that cuts rather close, especially as Ambrosio preaches on many of the same themes as the ministers who offered sermons on the occasion of the Richmond fire and leaves in his wake the kind of "enthusiastic silence" that they hoped to inspire.[32]

In the more immediate case, *The Monk* provides descriptions of the fire at the Convent of St. Clare that, with just a few minor changes to the specifics, could have been, and indeed almost seem to have been, adapted to describe the scene at the Richmond Theater:

> The Flames rising from the burning piles caught part of the Build-
> ing, which being old and dry, the conflagration spread with
> rapidity. . . . The Walls were soon shaken by the devouring element:
> The Columns gave way: The Roofs came tumbling down upon the
> Rioters, and crushed many of them beneath their weight. Nothing
> was to be heard but shrieks and groans; The Convent was wrapped
> in flames, and the whole presented a scene of devastation and hor-
> ror. . . . The People now hurried out, as eagerly as they had before
> thronged in; But their numbers clogging up the door-way, and the
> fire gaining upon them rapidly, many of them perished ere they had
> time to effect their escape. . . . Their deliberations were considerably
> interrupted by the sight of volumes of fire rising from amidst the
> Convent's massy walls, by the noise of some heavy Arch tumbling
> down in ruins, or by the mingled shrieks of the Nuns and Rioters,
> either suffocating in the press, perishing in the flames, or crushed
> beneath the weight of the falling Mansion. (*Monk*, 357–58)

From the ironic commentary on the difference between how eagerly the "throngs" rushed in and how frantically they pushed to get out, to the elabo-ration of the causes of death, Lewis's dramatization of the convent fire could just as easily have served as a rendering of the scene inside the Richmond

Theater on the night of 26 December. Indeed, if any further cue were needed to link the two scenes in the minds of eyewitnesses to the events, nothing could have been more vivid than the sight of Mrs. Green, the wife of the company manager, still costumed in her acting attire as the Bleeding Nun, frantically searching through the panicked crowd for her daughter, Nancy, before emerging grief-stricken from the playhouse with arms empty.[33]

The gothic scenes on the pantomimic stage and in Lewis's novel as well as their shared thematic preoccupation with both the threats to female virtue and the allures of female sexuality thus provide the generic frame within which the events of the Richmond fire could be narrativized, romanticized, and even mythicized. Indeed, in the tales that emerged from the fire, there is no shortage of figures for the Bleeding Nun or the breast of virtue stained with blood. Thus, many years later in a magazine devoted to female instruction, we find, for instance, the highly ornamented and eroticized tale of a young man named Lionel, whose object of affection, Ellen Pilton, had rebuffed his advances at the theater earlier that evening with an "averted glance," only to forgive his past transgressions as he grasped her about the waist amid the flames and as the "warm blood" from the gash he had sustained on his cheek "fell on her face and hair, and stained her palpitating bosom."[34] If this vignette was more literal than others in its incorporation of imagery from the Bleeding Nun, other tales that emerged in the aftermath of the fire were just as concerned with, and just as fixated upon, the disposition and fate of the virtuous maidens of Richmond. Indeed, the commemorative tributes, which began to appear in the newspapers in the aftermath, were addressed almost exclusively to young women who had perished in the fire.[35] And among the tales and tributes that emerged in the days, months, and years after the fire, no name appears more often or receives more histrionic treatment than that of Miss Sarah "Sally" Chevallie Conyers (Figure 16), who, along with her supposed consort Lieutenant James Gibbon (Figure 17), emerged as the tragic and tragically romanticized hero and heroine of the Richmond fire.

Tragic Consummation: Miss Sally Conyers and Lieutenant James Gibbon

When it came to the deaths of Miss Sally Conyers and Lieutenant James Gibbon, the fictional machinery of gothic romance and sentimental melodrama was thrown into overdrive. No two accounts are entirely alike in their detail; indeed there are a number of striking disparities, suggesting that admirers

Figure 16. Miss Sally Conyers.
Courtesy of the Library of Virginia.

both near and far took a certain poetic, and sometimes extravagant, license in construing the circumstances of their death. That they were worthy of particular notice was first intimated in a letter composed the day after the fire by an unidentified author: "A case which excites singular sympathy, is that of young Lieutenant Gibbon of the navy.—He had got clear from the house, and saved his mother's life [along] with his own, but finding that Miss Conyers was left behind, he rushed into the blazing building in search of her, and was never seen more: both perished in the flames."[36] Here the focus is on Lieutenant James Gibbon, who had returned to Richmond after being held prisoner in the Tripolitan War (1801–1805) and who, in the aftermath of the fire, would come to be immortalized variously as Sally Conyers's acquaintance, friend, beau, or fiancé. On 2 January, the *Virginia Argus* published a "Narrative"

Figure 17. Lieutenant James Gibbon, by Thomas Sully.
Image courtesy of Frick Art Reference Library Photoarchive.

account of the dead in which the story of Gibbon and Conyers is once again featured, this time with slightly more narrative detail and a great deal more dramatic flourish:

> Lieut. James Gibbon, of the United States Navy, has gone with the rest! Young as he was, he had tasted of the cup of affliction. He was taken captive in the "Philadelphia," and immured in the prisons of Tripoli. On this fatal night, he and Mr. John Lynch were in the same box with Mrs. Gallego, Miss Conyers, Mr. Venable and others. When the alarm was first given, they endeavored to quiet the apprehensions of the ladies; but when the front scene was in flames,

they reached over for Miss Conyers, who had sunk motionless below. They took her over; they held her between them, in a state of insensibility, her head falling over Mr. Lynch's left arm. In this manner they proceeded towards the head of the stairs, when Gibbon said—"Lynch, leave Sally to me; I am strong enough to carry her— she is light, and you can save somebody else." Mr. L. replied—"God bless you, Gibbon, there is the stair," and then turned round to seek some of the other ladies. Poor Gibbon and his lovely and interesting companion, sunk together.[37]

Note the differences, here, between this account and the earlier one. In the first, Gibbon ran back into the theater to rescue Sally Conyers; in the second, he was in the boxes *with* Conyers when the fire broke out and remained with her inside the theater until they died. It would be hard to say which set of actions is more heroic, but the details offered about Gibbon as a young man who had "tasted the cup of affliction" are not insignificant. The surrender of the *Philadelphia* to Tripolitan forces in 1803 and the prolonged captivity and consignment to forced labor of her more than three hundred crewmen was a signal event in the first Barbary war.[38] References to Gibbon's naval service thus allowed authors not only to inject a note of heroic forbearance into the romantic discourse they sought to build around Gibbon and Conyers, but also to illuminate that story with the dark specter of gothic tortures suffered under the "barbaric" conditions of enslavement. That Lieutenant Gibbon had reportedly lost an arm in the war and hence would have had difficulty managing this heroic feat did not seem to matter to the admirers of this doomed couple; indeed, it is never mentioned in these accounts.[39]

The true stakes in these representations come most fully into focus in the extended paean to the "*memory of* Miss Sarah Chevallie Conyers," which appeared in the 12 January edition of the *Virginia Argus*. In this singularly effusive tribute, we are treated to a full review of the many virtues, attainments, and "personal as well as mental charms" of the twenty-year-old Miss Sally Conyers. We learn not only of her many accomplishments—her fondness for "polite literature," her mastery of the romance languages (French, Spanish, and Italian), her pleasing ability at the "Forte Piano," and her deft skills at drawing—but also of her extraordinary beauty and mien—her "most lovely expression of countenance," the "feeling melody of her voice," the "captivating" quality of "her conversation," and the "magnetical attraction" of her "sweet and fascinating" manners. "To these accomplishments," we are told:

Miss Conyers united a temper as mild and gentle as the gale of
spring. It was so placid and benign, that it was said to be lovely even
in its frown. Her bosom was always glowing with generosity, and
she loved to praise the merits of others, whilst she concealed her
own with the sweetest modesty. Her heart was the fountain of affection, and possessed all the finer feelings of the human soul, but her
good sense acted as a salutary curb on her acute sensibility, and
armed her with becoming fortitude. She possessed a *sweet-souled
piety* and *genuine benevolence*, that extended the hand of sympathy
to the afflicted, and of charity to the distressed. *No* soul was ever
more *grateful* to those who were kind to her, and none ever took a
livelier interest in the happiness of her friends. Her disposition,
which was naturally a little pensive, had been rendered still more
serene and plaintive by delicate health. But the loveliest attribute of
her character, was her fondness for *domestic life*, for she preferred
the social circle of her family and friends, to all the pomp and vanity of the world. Her attachments possessed a secret yet sublime enthusiasm, and her friendships every characteristic excellence that
ever distinguished that most amiable of social virtues.[40]

Sounding like the ideal woman in an eighteenth- or early nineteenth-century
novel, Conyers is portrayed here as invested with all of the conventional marks
of a romantic heroine. The only thing missing from this description, although
an allusion to the "lustre" of her countenance comes close, is a rehearsal of the
"dazzling whiteness" of her skin, a standard trait for romantic heroines in novels
of this period, including those in Lewis's *The Monk*, where each of the female
protagonists is graced by this racialized distinction.[41] This glaring omission in
what is otherwise a rather stereotypical description for a heroine in this period
stands out and makes sense only when we understand it as symptomatic of the
trauma experienced by Richmond society at having lost so many "fine" examples of white womanhood. Race was at issue here, as was the class of persons
who perished. Indeed, as Thomas R. Joynes explained in a letter to his brother:

It was supposed when the fire was first discovered, that the house was
intentionally set on fire, and that it was only the precursor of scenes
still more tragical than the one which has happened. It was supposed
by many to have been the signal for *insurrection*, and that those who
escaped the fury of the flames, might have to encounter an enemy

more destructive than fire itself—But there is now no doubt but that those fears were groundless—if there had been any intention of that kind, it would have been carried into effect when the flames were at their height, and all the inhabitants were collected there.[42]

The threat of insurrection by enslaved blacks was ever on the minds of Richmond residents, and racial distinctions were enforced not only in the social and economic spheres but also in the generic conventions of the fictions they consumed.[43] To be a romantic heroine in Anglo-American representations of this period required the possession of "dazzling whiteness." The implicit color of Sally's skin thus grounds not only the eroticization of her person but also drives the interest in her potential fecundity, that is, in the promised reproduction of her whiteness.

For it was not simply that Richmond lost so many white women to the flames but that it lost so many white women on the brink of their marriageable and childbearing years.[44] Conyers's death is not lamented in *The Virginia Argus* solely because society had "been called on to deplore the loss of an individual of fin[e] accomplishments . . . [and] amiable virtues," but more distressingly because "with her [it had] been deprived of one of the fairest flowers of Virginia in the sprightly morning of its youth." It is no accident, then, that Conyers is compared in this tribute to Milton's Eve at the moment in *Paradise Lost* when God bestowed her upon Adam as his wife: "There was grace in her step, heaven in her eye, in all her gestures dignity and love."[45] What Milton terms "nuptial sanctity and marriage rites" (VIII.487) were the prognosticated future for Sally Conyers. The tribute to her thus ends where it began, with a lament both for the loss of her maiden prospects and for the anticipated consummation of all the merits she had cultivated:

> To lose such a being—at such a time—so unexpectedly—in the
> most interesting period of life, when the most anxious sensibilities of
> her bosom were alive for a congenial spirit, who is left to deplore her
> loss, must sharpen the poignancy of regret in every soul of feeling.
> Had she descended less immaturely to the tomb—had her virtues
> and talents been permitted to shoot and expand themselves in administering the morality of the parental board, the keenness of the
> calamity might have been in some small degree alleviated by the reflection that the ordinary period of human life had passed away and
> those expectations realized which had been promised to the world by

the dawn of her youth. But alas! even this feeble consolation has been denied, for it has pleased Divine Providence to call her in the bloom of youth and adolescence to a happier and a better world.[46]

As any reader of eighteenth- and early nineteenth-century novels knows, "the most interesting period" in a young woman's life was that epoch when she had just come of eligible age for marriage and was entertaining the attentions of similarly eligible young men.[47] The recognition of her own desire was, by convention, the cause of the "most anxious sensibilities of her bosom." In this description, moreover, the end of this period is marked not just by marriage to a beloved, but more consequentially by the fruits of motherhood, when all of the virtues enumerated above could be brought to bear in "administering the morality of the parental board."

Perhaps even more significant for our interest in the processes whereby history comes to be narrativized through fictional forms, we ought to note the references above to the "congenial spirit, who is left to deplore her loss" and for whom those "anxious sensibilities" were "alive" in her bosom. These references, as well as an earlier bow to the "sorrows of him to whom she was bound by the ties of a still softer sympathy," strongly suggest that the anonymous author of this paean *rather than* Lieutenant Gibbon was Conyers's favored suitor. The author's emotive lament for the fallen "prospects of [their] intellectual happiness!" certainly suggests that a strong, romantic attachment had been contracted between the two.

Whether Conyers and Gibbon were engaged or enjoyed a romantic liaison of any kind appears, however, to be beside the point.[48] While the two may have been no more than mere acquaintances, it is clear that the public at large had not only a strong interest in setting aside any contradiction but also an investment in generating ever more high-flown accounts of the ill-fated pair. In any number of poetic accounts of the fire, then, we find Conyers and Gibbon at the climactic center. In "Richmond's Lament," for instance, the melodramatic tale of this doomed romantic couple provides the sentimental emblem of the tragedy over whose loss all must weep. Written by no less a figure than the Reverend Dr. Ezra Stiles Ely, a prominent leader in the Presbyterian Church who would go on in 1827 to propose the formation of a Christian political party, the poem begins with a description of the merry scene at the theater that night where:

Hundreds of mothers dress'd with ease
Contented might their daughters please;

And lovers faced the wint'ry breeze,
To gain a healthful ruddiness.

Having set the scene at the theater as a stage for "coquetry" and budding romance, Ely turns his attention to the events of the fire, and especially to the
heroism of Lieutenant Gibbon amid those now "fainting females" enrobed in
"fiercely blazing drapery":

From the high windows, see! they leap,
And timid maidens dare the steep;
While angels would, might angels, weep,
The fragments of humanity.

Lucy and Sally fallen there,
Lo! Marg'ret comes, with Mary fair,
The flames just dying in their hair,
T' expire in sad society!

Out rushes now young Gibbon brave,
While floods of fire his temples lave,
Who risques his life a child to save,
And safe regains his memory.

Impell'd by it, he stems the crowd,
For one to whom his life he'd vow'd,
And calls her with such thunders loud
As brought the roof down speedily.

He dies! a hundred with him die!
But ah! the maid heard not his cry,
For many saw her body lie
Mangled without the theatre.

Her snowy breast unstain'd before,
Some leaping foot most rudely tore;
And deep the print that bosom bore,
Which lately swell'd with sympathy.[49]

In this rendition of events, the two lovers do not die together in one another's arms as they do in other versions of the tale. Instead, Sally's "mangled" body is found outside the theater, her "snowy breast" now stained, in a fashion reminiscent of that of the Bleeding Nun, with the rude impress of another man's boot. Gibbon is equally emblematic. The exclamation that "a hundred with him die" refers not simply to the others who died in the fire, but also to those who either filtered their hopes for posterity through this fated youth or identified with Gibbon through the dynamic of sympathetic spectatorship. Whether literally or figuratively, then, at least a hundred "die[d] with him." In this manner, Gibbon's display of extraordinary courage comes to stand in for the valor of men in general, even as it elides the fact that male gallantry was in very limited supply that evening. Gibbon's outsized heroics fill that disturbing gap, even as Conyers's exemplary character makes her a match worthy of his valor. The tale of Conyers and Gibbon thus lent itself to a cultural imaginary that in the face of immense grief and anguish needed to invent a romantic hero and heroine.

Perhaps the most disturbing poetic account of the romantic couple appears amid an enumeration of the dead in Samuel Gilman's *Monody on the Victims and Sufferers by the Late Conflagration in the City of Richmond, Virginia.*[50] Basing his account on the "Narrative" published in the *Virginia Argus* and appealing to what he termed "the high excitement of the public sensibility," Gilman, who was also the author of Harvard's commencement hymn, "Fair Harvard," and would go on to play an influential role as a Charleston pastor in the promotion of Unitarianism in the South, dramatized the scene at great length as a sensational melodrama of gothic horrors:

> But who is he, that back distracted flies,
> And swells their sorrow with a lover's cries?
> Brave, faithful GIBBONS! my recording verse
> Shall not forget thy story to rehearse.
> Weep, lovers, weep! where shall such faith be found?
> Such dreadful constancy, such courage sound?
> In vain through all the throng he seeks his fair;
> No arms embrace, no voice salutes him there.
> But hark! the hero forms the rash design,
> To perish, or his dearer self to join.
> "And is that angel still amid the fire?
> "I'll bring her out, or in th'attempt expire!"

No raging flames impede his quick return;
His flames within with tenfold fury burn.
With frantic strength he stems th'impetuous throng,
Whole crowds opposing as he bursts along.
But ah! too late for help of human hand,
The fair he sees in flames envelop'd stand.
She, in that agonizing hurry left,
Of hope, and e'en of reason's light bereft,
His well-known voice mid the dire uproar hears:—
That calms her shrieks; that stops her bitter tears.
She meets the rolling frenzy of his eye,
And as the panting youth draws eager nigh,
Round his dear form her stiffen'd arms are flung,
Love's accents fault'ring on her scorching tongue.
Parch'd are those lips that yield a last caress,
And sear'd that bosom his embraces press.
One burning tear from her despairing eyes,
Drops on his hand—the helpless maiden dies!
—He too expires;—but it will ne'er be known
Whether by fire he died, or grief alone.
The lovely maid and youthful hero brave
Sink down together in one fiery grave.
The wrapping flame is their funereal shroud,
Their knell, the shrieks of an expiring crowd.
Weep, lovers, weep! where shall such faith be found,
Such dreadful constancy, such courage sound?[51]

Framing the tragic couple as an emblem of faith, constancy, and courage, Gilman romanticizes their last moments together in high-flown fashion. Conyers is eroticized as an object of desire even as she is "envelop'd" in flames. Her "scorching tongue," "parch'd . . . lips," "sear'd bosom," and "despairing eyes" are enumerated one by one in a perverse echo of the desire summoned through a Petrarchan blazon. Her outstretched arms, "stiffened" by the flames, lock Gibbon in one final and deadly embrace. Whether Gibbon died by the fire or by "grief alone," the couple emerged phoenix-like from their "one fiery grave," ever "lovely" and "youthful" to be immortalized in the poem's refrain as a model for faithful lovers everywhere. Enshrined thus in memory, their melodramatic tale of gothic romance became the distinct vignette that would be recounted over and over again in histories of the Richmond Theater fire to this day.[52]

As the disparities in the various accounts above make clear, we cannot be sure what really happened to either Miss Sally Conyers or to Lieutenant James Gibbon: did they die together or apart, by fire or by grief, inside or outside the theater? What I hope to have illustrated, however, is how and why they came to be immortalized in the aftermath of the fire as the tragic couple who died together for love. Whether the two were or were not engaged was apparently immaterial when weighed against the dominant cultural need for a narrative that could palliate the sense of horror and overwhelming grief to which the fire gave rise. If the scene at the theater was thus framed initially as a tale of gothic horror, in which the victims laid claim to universal tears of sympathy, then the scenario also demanded a specific romantic hero and heroine around whose fate the meaning of the fire could be organized. Framed by both gothic and sentimental tropes, Miss Sally Conyers and Lieutenant James Gibbon emerged for public consumption as the romantic protagonists in a gothic melodrama. That the narrative of the Richmond Fire came to be emblematized in the fate of a romantic couple, rather than, say, in the loss of a child or the destruction of an entire family, tells us a great deal about where the psychic disturbance of the trauma came to be lodged, that is, as I have suggested above, in the loss of so many young women of marriageable age.[53] Thus, the accounts of the Richmond fire reveal that even as gothic romance and sentimental melodrama provided popular vehicles in early nineteenth-century America for the expression of various cultural anxieties and social concerns, they were also deployed historically to encapsulate and to contain the horror and anguish that was experienced over the tragic loss of so many young women and thereby bind together a grieving body public.[54]

If, as I hope I have demonstrated in the first half of this chapter, publics can be bound together by a shared vernacular derived from fictional and dramatic forms, it is also the case that those vernaculars could be deployed to different ends. While the gothic and sentimental were deployed both to make sense of the traumatic event and to channel that trauma into a narrative of a melodramatic romance—an ill-fated couple caught together in an unthinkable end but finding some kind of consummation in their shared deaths—the "monitory lessons" which follow later in Gilman's *Monody* suggest that the same gothic and sentimental vernacular could also be used to elicit a Christian spirit of religiosity and to help build a Christian body public.

Sermons on the Occasion of the Richmond Theater Fire

The Second Great Awakening and the Building of Monumental Church

In the aftermath of the fire, the remains of the dead were so scorched, mangled, and ashen that the Executive Council of Richmond determined they could not "with convenience be removed from the spot on which they were found."[55] An order was thus issued to inter all of the remains together in one common tomb on the spot and to purchase the property of the destroyed playhouse for the purposes of building a suitable memorial. On Sunday, 29 December, a "mournful procession," composed of members from all aspects of Richmond society from the Executive Council to ladies in carriages and grieving citizens on foot and horseback, solemnly moved through the streets of Richmond to the former site of the theater pit. There the Episcopalian minister John Buchanan read the funeral service, and the remains of the dead were laid to rest in a brick tomb measuring thirty feet square and five feet high.[56] Two large mahogany boxes were all that were required to contain the relics of everyone who died on the site in their common grave—Christian and Jew, white and black, male and female (Figure 18).

To honor the dead and provide succor to the living, the following Wednesday, New Year's Day 1812, was set aside for a day of humiliation and prayer.[57] Sermons were preached at locations across the city, including at the synagogue, where Samuel Mordecai spoke, as did many among the clergy of Richmond, of the uncertainties of life and the consolations of religion.[58] Construing the events as an "awful warning" sent by divine providence, the Reverend John D. Blair meditated similarly at a Presbyterian service on how, without disqualifying anyone "for the social duties, or any of the sweet & innocent enjoyments of life," a way might be found to "improve the ever memorable occasion for the benefit of the living."[59]

To the comfort and satisfaction of many, it was decided that the best way to memorialize the dead would be to replace the theater with a church. The site of the theater was thus "consecrated" to the dead "as the sacred deposit[ory] of their bones and ashes," and plans were soon made to build what would come to be known as Monumental Church above that communal resting place.[60] After some wrangling between the Presbyterians and the Episcopalians, led by the chief justice of the Supreme Court, John Marshall, the Episcopalians gained the upper hand; and in 1814, Monumental Church was dedicated as an Episcopal church, in which Chief Justice Marshall and his family would occupy pew number twenty-three (Figure 19).[61]

Figure 18. Brick tomb beneath Monumental Church, Richmond, Virginia.
Commemoration ceremony, December 2011.
Courtesy of the *Richmond Times-Dispatch*. Photo by Mark Gormus.

Up until that point, the two denominations in Richmond had worshipped together in the old governmental Hall of the House of Delegates,
with the ministers, Parson Buchanan for the Episcopalians and Parson Blair
for the Presbyterians, alternating in the pulpit each Sunday. After the fire, the
push for a revival of religion in Richmond intensified, as each denomination
brought in evangelical leaders to preside over new churches in the city, the
Reverend Richard Channing Moore for the Episcopalians, who was named
both rector of Monumental Church and bishop of the Virginia Diocese, and
the Reverend John Holt Rice for the Presbyterians, who would take the pulpit
at the new Presbyterian Church, known as "Rockett's" Church, and would
later come to fill, by contemporary report, an influential "space in public observation, as a preacher, an author, a controvertist, and a theological professor."[62] This turn in Richmond in the aftermath of the fire both to a heightened
religiosity and to an investment in denominational growth and rivalry marked
a sudden conversion for a city that had long been resistant to the proselytizing
addresses of evangelical Christianity associated with what has come to be
known as the Second Great Awakening.[63]
    Construed in its broadest iteration as spanning the decades between the

Figure 19. Monumental Church, Richmond, Virginia, 1812.
Courtesy of the Library of Virginia.

1790s and the 1830s, the Second Great Awakening brought to pass the most wide-reaching revitalization and expansion of Christianity in U.S. history and resulted in a general Christianization not just of Richmond but also of private and public conscience in the young nation. Mass conversions at outdoor camp revival meetings and sermons laced with evangelical fervor in the church pulpits resulted not only in the explosive growth of new denominations and sects but also, as in Richmond, in the restoration and revitalization of such older denominations as Episcopalianism and Presbyterianism.[64]

While it has become commonplace in some circles to cast that development as all but inevitable, in the aftermath of the American Revolution and at the founding of the early republic the road to an evangelical Christian America was not immediately clear. Even as doctrinal diversity had grown with the emergence of new denominations, such as the Methodists and the Baptists, overall church membership before and during the Revolution had declined.[65] The outlook for religion was quite bleak, and "for most American clergymen," as John Boles observes, "the final years of the eighteenth century were freighted with despair."[66] At the Constitutional Convention, moreover, it became readily apparent that, despite fervent religiosity among some of the delegates, any attempt to establish one religious denomination as the national religion would sunder any hopes of national unity.[67] The American people were a religiously plural mass. Different denominations enjoyed majority status in different states, but even those majorities were threatened by growing diversity among the populace. Any move to establish one church on a national level would have been met with stalwart resistance from other denominations. In short, as Gordon Wood explains, "It was not enlightened rationalism that drove these evangelicals but their growing realization that it was better to neutralize the state in matters of religion than run the risk of one of their religious opponents gaining control of the government."[68] The Constitution (1789) and the Bill of Rights (1791) thus held, first, that there would be no religious test for public officeholders and, second, as part of the First Amendment, that "Congress shall make no law respecting an establishment of religion, or prohibiting the free exercise thereof."

None of this, of course, meant that the vision of America as a Christian nation especially graced by God had been relinquished.[69] Evangelicals were quick to frame any falling away in the numbers of church members as a providential challenge to rebuild, revitalize, and expand religiosity in America, and they came to believe that they would have greater success in fulfilling that vision without the burden of government interference.[70] "All were convinced," as Nathan O. Hatch points out, "that the very meaning of America was bound up with the kind of new beginning which their own movement represented. The kingdom of God could yet be built in America if they were true to their own special calling." The end result was the emergence of a "popular religious movement" that "did more to Christianize American society than anything before or since."[71]

Impelled, moreover, by the inclusive and egalitarian impulses unleashed by the Revolution, Americans of all types came to embrace an "inalienable right" not just to choose religion but also to shape the tenets of their faith and to interpret the Bible for themselves.[72] "In religion as in politics," Edwin S. Gaustad explains, "the people moved into a role of greater participation and control. No longer did churches belong to the colonies or to the states; now they belonged to the people. And those denominations that most readily adjusted to this new circumstance prospered most conspicuously in the opening decades of the nineteenth century."[73] Where evangelical denominations were quick to exploit the freedoms that came with an absence of governmental regulation, older denominations with rigid institutional structures of membership and discipline struggled to meet the demands of those Americans who sought liberty in their religious practice.[74] With respect to doctrine, moreover, the orthodox tenets of absolute predestination and limited election were construed as elitist, and a revolt against the strict Calvinism identified most particularly with Presbyterians and Congregationalists ensued.[75] Methodists, on the other hand, who tendered a strain of Arminianism that allowed for the exercise of free will in the work of salvation, succeeded in converting the masses both through the revivalist techniques that they perfected at large camp meetings and through an effective circuit of itinerant preachers that reached into the western frontiers. As they and other new sects that tendered the possibility of universal salvation—the Universalists and the Disciples of Christ, as well as splinter groups like the Shakers, the Millerites, and the Stoneites—gained in popularity, so too did many of the older denominations find themselves adapting their position on the doctrine of election to accommodate the explosion of populist and egalitarian sentiment.[76] As the sovereignty of "the people" came to be translated into the sphere of religion, Americans embraced an ethos of "voluntary association" in spiritual matters that was commensurate with their new sense of individual freedom. The demise of both national and state establishments thus resulted not in the collapse of religiosity in the United States but rather in the creation of a competitive marketplace of religions in which no one denomination enjoyed government favor but in which all were free to work, without government impediment, to expand their numbers and shape belief in the new nation.[77]

All of these efforts were directed, then, not merely toward the individual convert but rather, as Carroll Smith Rosenberg has pointed out, toward "the conversion of the world to evangelical Protestantism and the remaking of the home society into a nation pure and Christian."[78] Individual conversions were construed as the foundation of a politically independent, Christian body public, and those numbers were reinforced through the creation of Bible and religious tract societies, Sunday School and missionary societies, and a dramatic increase in the number of religious newspapers in circulation.[79] Thus constituting a mass social movement that placed evangelical Christianity at the center of popular culture and the public body that consumed it, the Second Great Awakening built upon its address to the individual to instantiate what Frank Lambert has termed a "*Christian* civil religion" in the heart of the American body politic whereby the presumptions of the sacred would come to pervade, subtly and almost imperceptibly, the assumptions of the secular.[80]

The Richmond Theater fire provided the occasion for many in the city to engage the emerging discourse of religious sensibility and evangelical hope that was sweeping the nation, and there is evidence that a number of residents underwent conversion experiences either after escaping the flames or after witnessing the events. In her *Autobiography* recollected many years later, for instance, Caroline Homassel reveals that on the very day of the fire, she received her "first insight into [her] real condition, which was a sinner in the sight of God," when she and a friend had snuck out to hear the Reverend John Holt Rice preach. Homassel reports that "it was the one fear of my own beloved uncle and aunt that I should become a devotee to religion, a fanatic, as they regarded all who spoke of or longed for spiritual religion" and that they had "forbidden" her from attending the service. While her aunt and uncle's predisposition against religion could be said to have been the prevailing bias among the socially prominent citizens of Richmond before the fire, for many like Homassel, the playhouse fire proved a providential turn in pointing up the "gay and dissipated life" that true religion found trivial and wasteful. As she recounts, no one could convince her thereafter to partake of such amusements as card games and assemblies: "The light was shown me, and how could I be happy in darkness."[81]

A similar evangelical fervor inspired the architect of Monumental Church, Robert Mills, who wrote almost a year after the fire, "I wish to produce in the finish of the building all . . . which the peculiar circumstances which have occasioned its erection require, to strike the senses & thro' them the mind of the people of Richmond—with solemnity and devotion." Approving of the spirit of religiosity that had swept through Richmond, he reflected, "Among many here the awful visitation of providence . . . will never be forgotten, and I am led to believe from what I have seen and heard that to many the affliction has been sanctified, . . . God is able out of evil to bring forth good. I humbly pray, that the awful visitation with which he has visited Richmond may redound to his glory in the salvation of all its inhabitants."[82]

Arising out of the ashes of the playhouse, Monumental Church became an important symbol of this impulse toward religious renewal and spiritual awakening both for the city of Richmond and for the nation at large. Thus, in a rousing sermon preached in the Capitol at Washington, D.C., on Sunday, 29 December, the chaplain for the House of Representatives, Reverend

Nicholas Snethen, enthused on the horrific events in "the once gay and thoughtless city of Richmond":

> Above all and in all, we rejoice at that Christian feeling displayed in the purchase, which converts the Playhouse into a Church, and sets up the altar of God in the place where, in our judgment, Satan held his seat, and we would heartily say to magistrates, ministers and people, go on and prosper in the work of reformation and regeneration, until you have the substance of happiness in the room of the shadow—could our fellow creatures who suffered in the burning Theatre speak to us from their graves, how would they entreat us to flee the forbidden paths of vice and impiety.—O! how would they beseech us to prepare to meet our God, to be always ready, because we know not what a day, what a moment, may bring forth.[83]

Framed as a moment of national reckoning in the halls of the nation's Capitol, Snethen's oration celebrates the plans for the erection of Monumental Church even as it displays a number of characteristics that could be said to be typical of the sermons preached on the occasion of the Richmond Theater fire.

First, though it engages in the kind of antitheatrical rhetoric that we have seen before—the playhouse is characterized as the "seat" of Satan, at the altar of which the "gay and thoughtless" people of Richmond blithely worshipped—the emphasis of the address falls less upon the pitfalls of vice than upon the evangelical virtues of "reformation and regeneration." Second, in issuing his call to the assembled audience, Snethen strategically presses into service many of the same gothic tropes and melodramatic flourishes that structured local accounts of the fire. Here, for instance, in a macabre display of suppositional speech that would find even more vivid realization in some of the other sermons, the voices of the dead are ventriloquized, beseeching the living to "prepare" for their own day of judgment. Mobilizing the strategies and tactics of what Jill Stevenson has astutely theorized and termed an "evangelical dramaturgy," Snethen and other ministers, who worked to give meaning to the event and thereby cultivate a Christian body public, borrowed liberally from the popular tropes, motifs, and techniques of sentimental melodrama and gothic romance to produce in their auditors the effects of an "affective piety" that would render belief a visceral, bodily experience.[84]

Third, and perhaps most significantly, Snethen's speech in the nation's capital shares in the understanding that the cultivation and production of a

Christian body public constituted a national imperative. Drawing upon the providential narrative of the United States as God's chosen nation—a discourse of American exceptionalism that reaches at least as far back as John Winthrop's "City on a Hill" address—Snethen's remarks, published soon after the fire, remind Americans that they are to consider themselves "especially" as actors on the stage of a divine drama directed by God and that they should take care, accordingly, to comport themselves in a manner that conforms to the values of Christian piety.[85] "Improvement" was the byword as each minister sought to situate the fire as an ominous, yet providential warning of divine displeasure visited upon a dissipated society and called upon the Christian community to respond with signs of sympathy and repentance. The fire at Richmond was thus to be understood not merely as an occasion for lament. Rather, it was to be embraced as an "opportunity" tendered by "the providence of the Almighty" in order that we might "seek that temper and practice of righteousness which exalteth a nation."[86]

In the discussion below, I will trace these characteristic emphases and focus on the ministerial stagecraft of the sermons preached on the occasion of the Richmond Theater fire in order to elucidate how clergymen caught up in the evangelical throes of the Second Great Awakening availed themselves of the opportunity to call into being and to cultivate a Christian body public. Drawing on well-known passages from the New Testament for their texts, these ministers engaged in complex oratorical performances that leveraged the dilations of sympathy—encapsulated in Romans XII:15: "Rejoice with those who rejoice, weep with those that weep"—against the constrictions of repentance—emblematized in Luke XII:3: "unless you repent you will all likewise perish"—in order, at one and the same time, both to summon and to shape a communal body of godly individuals. In this manner, the Richmond Theater fire supplied ministers and preachers up and down the eastern seaboard with an apt, dramatic occasion not only to attack the theater but also to alert their congregants to the woeful dispensations of providence, to "awake" them to the perils of an unregenerate life, and to guide them toward the more propitious path of conversion, reformation, and regeneration. Thus tracing the rhetorical tactics of those ministers who used their authority in the pulpit to offer their congregations not just the assurances of consolation but also words of admonition, I illustrate, moreover, the ways in which the fire at Richmond was "staged" in these sermons as an emblem of national crimes that could be expiated only through national acts of faith.[87] Bringing a religious discourse to bear on the imperatives of civic duty and drawing on the long tradition of the American Jeremiad, ministers ominously raised the question not just of the futurity of the United States but of its very status as God's chosen nation and cast its source of salvation in the public assemblage of a large body of Christian souls.[88] Played out on the providential stage of American exceptionalism, individual conversions could thus be construed as the necessary condition for the fulfillment of a national covenant with God.

"Become Real Christians"

Perhaps the most histrionic sermon preached on the occasion of the Richmond fire was also the one with the closest ties to the city and its citizens. Archibald Alexander's *A Discourse Occasioned by the Burning of the Theatre in the City of Richmond, Virginia* was delivered at the Third Presbyterian Church in Philadelphia on 8 January 1812 at the request of the more than one hundred Virginia students who were in attendance at the medical school of the University of Pennsylvania.[89] A Virginia native himself, Alexander had deep ties both to the city of Richmond and to the rising evangelical movement in the Presbyterian Church. Before being called to the pulpit in Philadelphia, he had been president of Hampden-Sydney College, an institution near Richmond that was "founded for the purpose of raising up an evangelical ministry."[90] Within months of delivering his address to the young men in Philadelphia, he would be installed as the first professor of didactic and polemic theology at the Princeton Theological Seminary, the Presbyterian academy that was established out of dissatisfaction with the training that prospective ministers were receiving at Princeton College. There, along with Samuel Miller, who, as I mentioned in the previous chapter, drew on the legacy of John Witherspoon to deliver the most comprehensively antitheatrical sermon on the occasion of the Richmond fire, Alexander would preside for more than thirty years over the preparation of a "learned, orthodox, pious, and evangelical Ministry" for the Presbyterian Church.[91]

In his early years as a revivalist pastor in Virginia, Alexander had gained a reputation as one of the "great extempore preachers of his day," and that ability to convey a certain excitation and spontaneity of address is everywhere in evidence in his sermon preached before the young medical students in Philadelphia.[92] While many of the sermons delivered on the occasion of the fire stood at a great distance from the actual events, Alexander found himself in the position of addressing himself to a group of young men who invariably had lost parents, siblings, relatives, or friends in the conflagration. The dramatic potential for the event was staged by the students themselves, as they

marched in solemn procession as a body public through the streets of Philadelphia from the University of Pennsylvania to the Third Presbyterian Church
and were joined along the way by other "young gentlemen of the city" who
"caught the sympathetic flame, and requested to participate in the mournful
procession."[93] As the students made a public spectacle of their grief and cultivated sympathy in the public space of the city, so too would the Reverend
Alexander stage their grief to cultivate a community of Christian sympathy
and repentance within the sanctified space of the Presbyterian Church.

As I indicated was typical for many of the sermons on this occasion, Alexander's oratorical performance traces an arc from the dilations of sympathy
epitomized by the scripture from which he takes his text (Romans XII.15:
"Rejoice with those who rejoice, weep with those who weep") to the constrictions of repentance with which he concludes his address (emblematized by
Luke XII.3: "unless you repent you will all likewise perish"). Drawing, moreover, on the long tradition of using sermons as occasions to draw together the
community and to articulate the tenets by which its members ought to regulate their conduct, Alexander opens his sermon with an extended disquisition
on the "legitimate and proper exercise" of Christian sympathy (9). Contrasting "the system of ethics prescribed by the Stoics" with "that inculcated by
Christianity," Alexander imports into his discourse a popular model of classical republicanism, even as he signals the "perfectibility" of that model in
Christian America (7). How the young men comport themselves on this occasion *as men* had consequences for national posterity.[94] Hence he assures them
of the masculine character of sympathy: "There are occasions when not 'to
weep with them that weep,' would be rebellion against every principle which
ought to govern us" (9). When confronted with the "sad catalogue" of the
names of those who were not just their "countrymen" but their "esteemed
friends and intimate acquaintances . . . beloved relatives; and alas! . . . the distressing sight of the *endeared name of a sister*," "nature," he tells them, "con-
strains you to weep, and Religion approves it. Tears are becoming, even in the
manly countenance, when distresses like these pass in review before our eyes,
and approach so near to our bosoms" (11). The use of italics—"*endeared name
of a sister*"— in the text above alerts us early on to the performed and performative aspects of these printed sermons. As Alexander deploys italics, capital
letters, and rampant punctuation to signify affect, emphasis, and points of
conviction, the effect of reading the text practically morphs into the theatrical
experience of seeing it and hearing it as it was staged, set, and performed in
the exalted *mise en scène* of the church pulpit.[95]

Whether delivered amid the raucous field of a revival meeting or in the more staid but no less earnest setting of a church congregation, the sermon in this era provided a vital instrument for delineating, cultivating, and regulating a Christian body public. Sermons had always occupied a central position both in oral and print form in American culture, so much so that at least one critic has seen fit to deem them "America's First Mass Media" form.[96] Under the Puritan regime in seventeenth-century America, the sermon functioned not simply as a moment of admonition and exhortation to sinners and saints, but also as an occasion to draw together the community of Protestant individuals by articulating a shared set of values and by elaborating the doctrinal tenets by which they were to govern their behavior. As Harry S. Stout explains, sermons "not only interpreted God's plan of redemption and told the people how they must live as a church but also defined and legitimated the meaning of their lives as citizen and magistrate, superior and inferior, soldier, parent, child and laborer."[97] As a performative medium, then, the sermon publicly gave shape to the social body, even as it provided a framework within which individuals could make sense of their lives and contemplate conversion.[98]

Funeral sermons, of which those on the Richmond Theater fire are a kind of variant, provided a particularly apt occasion for elaborating the divine drama of individual salvation and national posterity. While the occasion itself attested to the paradoxical certitude and potential suddenness of human mortality, the description of the departed's life and conduct called attention to the inexorable embrace of God's everlasting judgment. As oratorical performances aimed at a wide audience, not only did they provide a "public forum for the experience of loss," but they also, as Desirée Henderson has shown, "constructed a communal memory of the dead and directed the living in their response to death."[99] In their address to gathered congregations, then, ministers consistently sought as much to console their members as to delineate how, by acting their parts in the sacred drama, death might be "improved" upon by the living so as to incur God's eternal blessing. If handled with appropriate rhetorical and emotional care, no occasion, as Emory Elliot has demonstrated, was believed more conducive to "discover[ing] new saints among the as yet unregenerate."[100]

In the first part of his discourse and at strategic moments thereafter, Alexander performs what Abram van Engen has termed the "logic of sentimentalism," whereby the cultivation of sympathy—"feel[ing] in order to stir feeling"—offers a mode of expanding and delineating a Christian community.[101] Yet while the display of sympathy in these sermons may have been the necessary condition for inclusion in the community of humanity, it was not, in and of itself, accounted the necessary requisite for inclusion in the godly community. That higher bar of belonging, of admittance into the realm of Christian fellowship, could only be satisfied by conversion and repentance. Much more vigorous methods were required to achieve this end, and as Gregory Jackson has shown, revivalist preachers, following new theories of knowledge that privileged emotional sensations as catalysts for perception, thought that conversion and repentance could only be triggered by heightening such emotions as fear, anxiety, and terror through visual rhetoric that could "bypass cognitive processes."[102] Designed to appeal to a more heterogeneous population, their sermons increasingly employed a gothic rhetoric of suffering and redemption, vividly supported by theatrical images and scenarios "calculated to pierce the hearts of the most recalcitrant sinners" and trigger their conversion.[103]

Employing rhetorical techniques that were typical of such revivalist addresses, Alexander moves in his discourse from a logic of sentiment and sympathy to the generation of provocative visual tableaux that are reminiscent of the gothic horrors that were spectacularized on the Richmond stage the very night of the fire. Directly addressing the young men who grieved for lost family members, he, at first, appears to shy away from such practices, avouching that "every fresh recital, every additional circumstance, only serves to increase the horror of the scene, and more deeply to interest our feelings" (9). But this gesture is almost immediately recognizable as a rhetorical feint, as he moves strategically by ever more fierce gradations to ratchet up precisely those very feelings of grief, horror, and anguish that abrogate all rational thought. Lamenting the confounding loss of so many, he first presents his auditors with the spectacle of sudden death: "In the midst of health—in the moment of mirth and exhiliration [sic] in the full flow of earthly joy, perfectly thoughtless of futurity, and unsuspicious of any danger, more than a hundred respectable citizens, are overwhelmed in one promiscuous ruin!" (10). Having raised the curtain just a bit, however, he lowers it again, exclaiming, "O! the dismal scene of horror, of misery, and of death, which here presents itself to our view! . . . to pourtray this shocking scene is neither practicable nor desirable. Permit me, then, *to drop the curtain over the catastrophe of this dismal tragedy!*" (10). Deploying a rather ill-chosen, not to mention dramatically italicized, theatrical metaphor, Alexander continually teases his audience with evocative glimpses of the horrors suffered, playing upon the perverse but irresistible desire to see, before he opens them up to full view. Coyly intimating that his auditors needed "no highly wrought description" to make the impression of the scene any deeper or more indelible on their consciousness, he then goes on to offer just such a series of "highly wrought" images of the pain and suffering visited upon the bodies of the dead. In order to convey the theatricalized tone taken by Alexander, I shall quote from these descriptions at length:

> That view of this mournful catalogue . . . which more especially interests our tender feelings, and awakens all the exquisite sensibilities of our nature, is the large number of respectable females, it contains. . . . But that which should excite our sensibility to the utmost, and wind up all our sympathetic feelings to the highest pitch, is, that the greatest part were young ladies, in the very prime and bloom of life! . . . O! who can think, without exquisite anguish, of so many gay and blooming virgins, decorated with the charms of beauty, and accomplished by the refinements of art, delicate and tender to excess and accustomed only to caresses and endearments, perishing by a death so cruel, and by torments so excruciating! Who can describe the chasm which has been made in numerous respectable families; and the agony which has been, and is still endured! Tell us, ye bereaved mothers . . . the pangs which have rent your breaking hearts, since you beheld the scorched, bruised, and disfigured bodies of your once beautiful daughters. (15)

Placing before his auditors' eyes the lurid image of a host of virgins cut down in the "very prime and bloom of life," "scorched, bruised, and disfigured," Alexander scripts the young women of Richmond as the sacrificial victims, whose grotesquely mangled bodies are meant to strike terror in the hearts of his auditors, leaving them in a state of such heightened sensibility that they will turn to religion to alleviate the pain of their own "exquisite anguish." He strikes even more deeply and intimately into those hearts when he entreats, "And why need I attempt to describe the poignant pangs of the disappointed lover, (the day of whose nuptials might perhaps have been fixed,) when he beholds the beauty which he so much idolized, transformed into a frightful and deformed skeleton!" (16). As Alexander fills the anticipated nuptial bed of the "disappointed lover" with the "frightful and deformed skeleton" of his beloved, he offers up an exemplary instance of a recurrent motif in American reform literature that Karen Halttunen has deemed the "pornography of pain." Identifying this motif as a formation that "took shape in the late eighteenth and early nineteenth centuries," Haltunnen illustrates how, in the service of their mission, reformers strategically deployed representations of "pain as obscenely titillating."[104] Accompanied, as we see in Alexander, by coy justifications, demurrals, and apologies for their sensationalized accounts, the virginal flesh that was so coveted by lovers in life is transformed, ostensibly in the service of moral "improvement," into an eroticized spectacle of putrefying bodies and "exquisite" death.

Still fixating on the fate of young women but shifting from a gothic to a sentimental register, Alexander expands the circle of anguish by placing before his auditors' eyes the vivid tableaux of a grief-stricken mother who had sent her daughter off to the city for the very first time, only to receive the news of her daughter's harrowing death in the flames. "O! fatal visit!" he exclaims, "Methinks, I see the fond mother taking the last leave of her beloved daughter, little suspecting that it was the last!" (17). "Fancy[ing]" that perhaps even in that moment "some unaccountable foreboding seizes the mind . . . as the object of her fond hopes and anxious fears is carried from her sight!" (17), Alexander, like an expert author of sentimental fiction, heightens the fatalistic arc of the tragedy and begins to weave into his narrative an affective ideology of moral feeling.

In the next scene, Alexander turns to that day when "a letter comes 'tis true; but what horror chills the blood, when it is seen not to be inscribed in the well known hand of the dear girl; and is addressed to the father instead of the mother" (17). Turning to the other half of the parental dyad and marking the father as the figure of authority and ownership within the familial domain, Alexander continues with his vision: "Methinks I see his veteran hand tremble, whilst he breaks the ominous seal! And the countenance which had remained unmoved, whilst death was braved at the cannon's mouth, now turns pale as ashes, whilst he reads the few incoherent sentences by which he is made to realize more than ever the gloomiest hour that had painted on his imagination!" (17). By design in Alexander's oration, auditors are repeatedly transformed into spectators; not only are we made to bear witness to the almost unendurable agony of a mother's grief, but we also gain access to the private fears "painted" within the inner precincts of the father's imagination. As we see the father who had braved death on the battlefield brought low by the awful news of his daughter's demise, we are drawn irresistibly into that theater of sympathy, so astutely theorized by Adam Smith, in which many believed the moral sentiments might be formed.[105] Having engaged our sympathies in the action of this sentimental tragedy, Alexander takes the opportunity to exhort, "RELIGION is the only cure for griefs like these" (18).

Shortly thereafter, Alexander raises the dramatic pathos of the occasion to its highest pitch when, from his position in the pulpit, he performs the part of the grief-stricken mother, giving voice to all of the confusion and anguish she might feel in the moment of her greatest despair:

> "O!" says the pious mother, "why did I ever consent to let her go out of my sight; what sin and folly have I been guilty of, to commit her to the gaieties and dissipation of the metropolis! My poor girl is for ever gone; but I am to blame for her permature [sic] death; O could she have been permitted to die a natural death at home; or any kind of death, whilst engaged in serious and pious exercises, I would have been contented! But O! to be burnt alive!—To die in the theatre! To be snatched in a moment from time to eternity! To be hurried instantly from thoughtless gaiety to the bar of GOD! The idea is too dreadful! What soul can endure it! Gracious Heaven! send relief to a heart bursting with grief!" (18)

In tendering this bold performance, Alexander places before our eyes yet again not simply the grieving mother but also the mother's horrific vision of her daughter as she was "burnt alive" in the theater. More significantly, even as he gives vent to those sorrows, he also gives shape to moral sentiments. In his rousing rendition, the mother has especial cause to bewail her daughter's death; for she was swept away to the "bar of GOD" from the "thoughtless gaiety" and "dissipation" of the theater.

Although he had remonstrated earlier in his sermon that "genuine pity, and compassion for objects of real distress have been perverted, and almost extinguished, in a multitude of persons, by the artificial excitement of a set of spurious feelings, produced by the contemplation of scenes of fictitious distress" (8), Alexander has no difficulty indulging in what he himself concedes was "in part, a fancied case" to achieve his larger end of reformation. Yet if we pause too long to ponder the irony and even hypocrisy of such a move, we would miss the rhetorical sleight of hand through which he gains rather than loses authority in this moment. For not only does Alexander confess to his melodramatic flight of fancy, but he also avouches that it was "suggested by the recollection of a modest and amiable young lady, whom I happened to see, when on a visit to Virginia last summer, in company with a pious mother, at a solemn religious meeting, where she appeared to be deeply interested and to enter very devotionally into the exercises of the day" but whose name "alas!" he finds "enrolled" in the list of the dead: "She perished in the flames on the fatal twenty-sixth of December!" (18). This dramatic disclosure of private grief licenses Alexander's words on the occasion and serves as the token for his admission into the community of sympathy. By tendering this personal confession, he conveys authority to his "public TESTIMONY" against the theater and other amusements as, "UNFRIENDLY TO PIETY—UNFRIENDLY TO MORALITY—UNFRIENDLY TO HEALTH—UNFRIENDLY TO TRUE DELICACY AND GENUINE REFINEMENT" (19). In this manner, he directs private feeling and the cultivation of sentiment toward a very public, not to mention capital, end. Thus, where the "experience of sympathetic identification characteristic of the sentimental novel" results, as Glenn Hendler has demonstrated, in the preparation of readers to participate "not only in the reading public, but also in the political public," the deployment of a discourse of sentiment and sympathetic identification in the sermons of Alexander and others equips their auditors and readers to participate in a religious body public.[106]

With the structure of sentiment now firmly in place, Alexander concludes this section of his sermon with a graded series of exhortations. In a general fashion, he proclaims first that those who "do not even suspend their attendance on public amusements, in consequence of the alarming dispensation which has occurred, for a single day, clearly evince a destitution of a tender and amiable sympathy with their suffering fellow citizens; and also discover a state of society, the most alarming to the reflecting mind, which can easily be conceived" (19–20). Having thus stipulated the affective threshold that governs membership not simply in the community of sympathy but also in the commonwealth of "fellow citizens," he then turns to the providential arc of history to delineate the imminent peril of the nation as a whole: "If there be a moral conclusion clearly deducible from the records of history, it is, that such an infatuated devotion to pleasure, in the midst of threatening judgments, and public calamities, is a certain indication of a people being ripe for ruin, and a sure forerunner of it" (20). The fate of the nation hangs in the balance here, as Alexander raises the question of whether America would betray its destiny by ignoring the providential omens conveyed in these "public calamities" and continuing on its dissipated way, or whether as "a people" it would heed those auspicious warnings and commit itself to the work of repentance and reformation. Turning his attention more particularly to those gathered before him, he lays that burden at their feet as a first test, enjoining:

> I hope that you will fully evince your grief, and the depth of the im-
> pression made on your minds by this awful dispensation, by acting
> up fully to the spirit of that ordinance of the common council of the
> capital of your native state, which prohibits all public amusements
> for the space of four months from its date, and that during this pe-
> riod at least, you will religiously abstain from every species of public
> amusement, and more especially from attendance at the theatre.
> While your native state mourns with such bitter anguish, it is no
> time for you to be seen in the scenes of gaiety and dissipation. (20)

As an initial act of faith, the young gentlemen were to perform or "evince" their grief by binding themselves in sympathy with those of their "native state" and by abstaining "religiously" from attendance at public amusements. Membership in the religious community of sentiment thus required, at the very least, a certain diligence in "acting up" to the form of moral conduct.

As if sentiment were not enough to compel his auditors toward an em-brace of religion, Alexander reverts one last time to the shocking register of the gothic and allows his spectators one more prurient look beneath the cur-tain. Speaking of the vanity of human wishes, he urges:

> What a fading flower is beauty, and its attendant graces and accom-
> plishments! And how strikingly is this exemplified in the melan-
> choly scene which we have been this day contemplating! To receive
> the full impression of this truth, you must cast your eyes on that
> long and mournful procession, which slowly ascends the Capitol
> Hill. You must draw near and inspect the contents of those huge
> coffins which contain all the earthly remains of once celebrated
> beauty.—But ah! instead of the brilliant eye, the fair complexion,
> the winning smile, and the indescribable charm of countenance,
> you now behold the ghastly skulls, mangled limbs, bones and ashes,
> indiscriminate; so that neither age, nor sex, nor colour, any longer
> can be recognized." (21–22)

Recalling the "promiscuous ruin" that he had cited earlier, Alexander literally directs his auditors to look inside the coffins on their way to their entombment, to the sight of a macabre and disorienting tableau of mangled bodies, indiscriminately laid out, one upon another, without respect to the usual, hard social distinctions of age, sex, or race. Only then, after having jolted the sensations of his audience to the highest pitch of unrelieved anguish and confusion this final time, does Alexander move to his concluding exhortations and to an articulation of the constrictions of repentance that were typical for the occasion:

> True religion is not a *form*, but a living principle within. . . . Permit me to conclude this discourse, by considering the dispensation which has occasioned our meeting here this day, in the light of a solemn warning. Yes, my hearers, if ever the warning trumpet of a righteous Providence sounded loudly in our ears, it doth this day. . . . *I tell you nay: But except ye repent, ye shall all likewise perish.* . . . Receive the warning, then, and suffer the word of exhortation. The views and impressions produced by this deplorable occurrence, however painful at the present, may be precious in their effects, and should not be suffered to pass off without originating such resolutions and purposes, as shall become the foundation of a new course of life. . . . My last advice, therefore, is, BECOME REAL CHRISTIANS. Make religion a personal concern. . . . And may the God of all grace crown the exercises of this day with his blessing, for Christ's sake. (27–28)

As a counter to theater itself, Alexander offers the assembled gentlemen the opportunity to immerse themselves in an ongoing sacred drama and to accept an invitation to act their part in the divine community of the godly and the saved. In so doing, he elucidates how the burden of contrition lay not just upon the individual consciousness but rather on the Christian body public as a whole. The Richmond fire is thus "staged" in these exhortations as a warning, "the views and impressions" created by it, the catalyst for new resolutions and purposes.

In all of these respects, the Richmond Theater fire provided Alexander with a singular opportunity to trace the contours of the fallen and dissipated world and the immanent expanse of the kingdom of heaven. By transposing sentimental and gothic tropes to this divine drama, moreover, he transmogrified the burning, scorched, and mangled bodies of the young women into the material vanishing point through which the imperative of membership in the abstract Christian body public could be articulated and its triumph assured.[107] Thus, even as the purposeful variations in print typography and the heavy-handed use of punctuation alert us to the performative aspirations of his text, they also help us to see and to hear how, in spectacular fashion, he and others in the pulpit used the occasion of the Richmond Theater fire not only to bring their auditors and readers to the brink of conversion but also to impel them forward to take their place in the body public of a Christian nation.

"This Country, This City, This Congregation, Now Stand Warned"

While Alexander's sermon before a congregation full of young men who had a personal connection to the calamity at Richmond focuses on the conduct of "CHRISTIAN" gentlemen and touches only obliquely on the nation's fate, ministers and preachers who stood at a greater distance from the events in Richmond—such as George Dashiell in Baltimore (from whom the epigraph above is taken), Elijah R. Sabin in Boston, and George Richards across town in Philadelphia—were emboldened to take sharper aim at what they construed as the crisis of religion in the national body.[108] For his sermon "in the presence of the Supreme Executive of Massachusetts," for instance, Sabin found it imperative to point out that "the event is not only recent, but at home, in the midst of our own nation. Not enemies and foreigners were the subjects of it, but our friends, members of our national community, and sharers in our national and individual blessings."[109] Sabin thus takes great care in this space marked by governmental authority to draw a distinct connection between the posterity of the nation and the diligence displayed by his fellow countrymen in doing all that they can to "make [their] calling and election sure" (19).

Known for his close friendship with one of the most charismatic and influential figures of the Second Great Awakening, the itinerant preacher Lorenzo Dow, Sabin was the chaplain for the Massachusetts House of Representatives at the time of his address and the first Methodist ever appointed to that post in a state that for so long had been dominated by the Standing Order.[110] Although he may have lacked Dow's mesmerizing genius, he certainly had no difficulty bringing a considerable set of theatrical skills to bear in shaping his sermon on the Richmond fire into a dramaturgical event. Indeed, as he strove to take full advantage of what he construed as an opportunity "so favorable for a full and powerful display of evangelical truth" (3), he deployed many of the same gothic and sentimental techniques that we saw in

Alexander's discourse. Going one step further in devising his theater of sympathy, he asked his auditors to "imagine" that the very house of worship in which they were currently sitting was "now on fire," and then proceeded to dramatize the scene of horror that would unfold there as if in real time:

> Let us imagine . . . "the gathering element was rolling on its flames and columns of smoke, threatening to devour every human being in the building. That the most heartrending cries were pervading the house, husbands asking for wives, females and children shrieking for help." Some trodden to death, others thrown back from the windows into the devouring flame, from which they were struggling to escape;—every avenue blocked up with the hurrying, affrighted crowd; multitudes "reaching out their imploring hands and crying out, Save me, O sir, save me!" All ages and sexes plunging promiscuously from the windows; some dashed to pieces with the fall, others crowded to death by those who followed them; others escaping with dislocated joints or broken bones; others thrown down headlong, by the pressing crowd, half roasted, or with their flaming cloaths threatening instant death. Fancy, that at last you escaped, to see others still coming to the windows, yea, your own wives, children, and parents, ready to escape from thence,—that you spread your arms to catch them, and every moment expected to clasp the object of your affections—but oh, the disappointment! They fall backwards, you see them no more! . . . And to complete this picture of ruin and distress, the *venerable father* of this commonwealth, should perish in his excess of humanity to save others; while fathers and mothers deplore the loss of their children, husbands lamenting their lost companions, wives bemoaning their burnt husbands, and nothing seen or heard but tokens of unutterable distress and unfeigned anguish;—and tell me, what would be your *own feelings*, after making every effort to escape, if you must give yourselves up at last, to the devouring flame! (9–10)

By transforming a house of worship in Boston into a proxy for the space of the Richmond Theater, Sabin vividly sets his listeners in the places of those who perished in the terrifying conflagration. In doing so, he reminds the members of this assembled body that they too were performers on the divine stage of Providence and no more innocent in God's eyes than the sufferers at

Richmond. As such, and as was due in the case of a tragedy that befell their fellow countrymen, they were to understand that they had a "*deep concern* in the event" (5). Further, while Providence had made an example of those who perished, "half roasted" in the flames at Richmond, the tragedy could just as easily have unfolded in the playhouse at Boston. Thus supplementing his own description of the awful scene with lines taken from published eyewitness accounts, Sabin blends just enough fact and fiction in his macabre performance both to work his auditors up into an alarmed frenzy and to prepare them, each with his or her "*own feelings*," to embrace any and all means by which they might be able to "improve" upon the event (10). In this manner, Sabin brings his auditors both into a relationship of sympathy with those who suffered in Richmond and into a state of difference; for unlike those who perished, they still had the chance to provide evidence of their repentance and embrace a justifying faith—"except we repent" as the invocation of the refrain here indicates, "we shall all likewise perish" (15). The first proof of their contrition could be performed individually "by *totally* forsaking that amusement, which unhappily brought our fellow countrymen to their distressing death" (19). Yet the "debt of sympathy" that was owed on this occasion, "by far the most distressing of any recorded in the history of our nation" (6), could be "fully paid" only, Sabin held, when the "whole nation" as a corporate body was "ONE in sorrow as well as joy" (10). Thus, while conversion might have been considered a matter of individual consciousness, the sins of the nation were construed as a corporate responsibility, that is, the burden of contrition and the way to national salvation lay with the Christian body public as a whole.

In a similar vein, George Dashiell characterizes the fire as "an awful revelation of the Divine Hand held up to the American people" that "no one but an hardened infidel [could] doubt."[111] Notorious across the Baltimore episcopacy for his evangelical tendencies and for his habit of preaching "heartfelt sermons intended to evoke spontaneous conversions," Dashiell pounces on the opportunity occasioned by the Richmond fire to offer his congregation a short history of the young nation as one marked by one of the most "rapid advances in corruption" ever seen in "any country" (8).[112] Maintaining that "some awful display of the Divine Hand was necessary to rouse us from the sleep of death, and bring us back to the good old paths," he brushes brusquely past Alexander's and Sabin's more temperate expressions of sentiment in order baldly to proclaim the belief that those who suffered in the fire at Richmond were "victims immolated for their country's good" (8). According to this view, God in his mercy had made an example of those theatergoing citizens who, unmindful of their role on the divine stage of Providence, had taken their places in "open houses of sin" (8). In offering this address, he could hope only that "God [would] grant, that their *sufferings* may prove a lasting public benefit!" (13). Thus calling for the "abolition" of these "Synagogues of Satan," which had so recently multiplied in "abandoned and reprobate" cities such as Richmond and Baltimore (9), and tendering in support of his call the kind of antitheatrical genealogy that we have seen exhibited over and over again, Dashiell maintains his patriotic belief in the mythical covenant, "that God yet looks with an eye of mercy upon this country. That this shall be the happy land in which he will finally display the riches of his grace, the triumphs of Christianity, and the glory of the kingdom of JESUS" (8). All that is required, as he explains, is that "our country hear, and obey the warning voice!" (9). "Except ye repent," as he exhorts us earlier, and as we have now heard many times before, "ye shall all likewise perish" (7).

While Sabin and Dashiell focused their address more particularly on individual acts of repentance through which the nation might be saved and its faith renewed, George Richards took the occasion to offer a prescription for acts of contrition on a national scale. In his view, the corporate body of America was implicated in a number of sinful enterprises, not limited to but especially embodied by the national crime of slavery. Richards was a Universalist minister, and while he brought to bear in his lengthy address much of the Enlightened rationalism for which his denomination was known, he still embraced the spiritual-minded paradigm of sympathy and repentance that shaped the remarks of so many of his peers.[113] Delivering his lecture on 16 February 1812, more than seven weeks after the fire, Richards had had the opportunity to observe the outpouring of sympathy that the nation had directed toward the citizens of Richmond. Yet, while the "cups of consolation" may have been full to overflowing, he clearly was not convinced that Americans had entered fully into complementary or sufficient acts of contrition and repentance (3). The expansive embrace of sympathy was, to Richards, the easy part; true repentance and the disciplined embrace of evangelical religion required a more deliberate and laborious effort. Over and over again, then, he entreats "the serious, the solemn attention of this respectable, respected, and crowded audience" to heed his warning and recognize the arrogance of thinking themselves any less guilty of sin than those who perished in the fire. Taking his text from Luke XIII and intoning the usual refrain, "except ye repent," at every possible juncture, he seeks to spark "that moral and spiritual improvement, which leads to individual, and terminates in national repentance" (8).

To this end, he opposes "legal" to "evangelical" penitence, ultimately intimating that while American law may allow the enslavement of African peoples, evangelical religion required its subjects to render their obeisance to a higher authority, that is, to God's law under which slavery constituted a sin. For Richards, whose arguments against slavery presaged the conflicts of another era, the events in Richmond as well as the specter of war on the horizon (the imminent War of 1812) were just two "tokens of approaching national judgment" that would befall the "slumbering millions of this new found world" if they failed to perform the necessary acts of humility and contrition and continued to countenance such transgressions (19). Directing his address to Congress, he thus expostulates at great length:

> Representatives of more than seven million people! You have wept with them that wept. A nation has felt for the living: a nation has mourned the dead: America, in you, has assumed, "the garment of heaviness:" the United States have breathed the language of condolence. But suffer me to ask, with reverential respect, when this moment of sympathy was past; a moment evanescent as "the morning cloud;" and transient as "the early dew," were there no sins found among yourselves. . . . A full month has borne witness to sympathetic sorrows. But indulge me to query, if one of these mournful days, has been allotted to humiliation and prayer, at the footstool of the throne of Almighty God? Or have your supplications, intercessions, and cries, ascended in unison to him . . . that it may please the majesty of his grace, to inspire the president, senators, and representatives of 'so great a people.' . . . Are not most of these iniquities in the midst of our tents? Has eternal justice, no claims, in behalf of twelve millions of Africans, who have been annually sacrificed, for almost a century past, to the demon of commercial avarice; the spirit of European luxury; and the genius of American indolence? Has moral retribution, no demands, in favour of the Aboriginals of this country? . . . Are the groans, the tears, the sighs, the mighty wrongs of more than one million, one hundred and ninety thousand slaves, unregistered in the volume of omniscience? Can a doubled, a trebled population of misery, which is the fact in Tennessee, be forgotten before God? No, surely, no! Shall not I visit for these things? saith the Lord: Shall not my soul be avenged on such a nation as this? (21–26)

While I have had greatly to abridge the passage above, the text cited still captures the trajectory of Richards's thought. In his view, the resolution by Congress to wear crepe bands for thirty days in a display of sympathy and mourning, was no more than that—a vain show. Without a commensurate resolution to act upon that sympathy by declaring a national day of fasting, humiliation, and prayer, Congress had not fulfilled its obligations of repentance in accordance with the claims of "eternal justice." Thus he challenges members of that esteemed body to reflect both on whether as individuals they are free from sin and on whether the nation as a whole stands secure in the promise of salvation. For Sabin, slavery and the inhumane treatment of Native Americans constitute two indelible blots in the American record, and the principle of "moral retribution" must be satisfied. National crimes called for national acts of contrition and repentance. Hence, while individuals might come to the bar of God alone, as members of the body public that composed America, they would each also be held responsible for the sins of the nation as a corporate whole.

While Richards may have traveled rather far afield in raising his voice to Congress, he returns at the end of his sermon to the more typical tropes of these orations to instruct and admonish those who stood immediately before him. To the "young men of Virginia!" and the "young men of Philadelphia," he offers praise for the concrete steps they took toward moral and religious "improvement" by processing through the streets of Philadelphia and attending Alexander's service at the Third Presbyterian Church. These "public, devotional act[s]," he decrees, "recognised, your dependence upon God . . . and acknowledged the necessity of religion" (26–27). In exchange, he takes the opportunity to warn them once again not to assume that those "who suffered death, in tortures of consuming flames, 'were sinners above' thousands in this gay metropolis whose days 'are given to pleasures'; whose nights are devoted to theatrical amusements" and extends them the small "comfort" that "spirits, sent forth to minister, soothed to the last, momentary pangs of expiring virtue: that angels breathed the requiem of celestial peace around the bitterness of agonistic death; as death approached infantile forms enrobed in living flames" (27).

These last images, of course, recall those that we saw in Alexander's sermon, and, as in that address, the suffering bodies of virtuous women once again become the vanishing point through which the dictates of piety are articulated. This becomes all the more clear when, in turning to the female counterparts of those "young men" in the assembly, he strikes a very different

chord. Appalled by reports that some women may have attended a pantomime performance at the very same time that the men were marching in
procession through the streets of Philadelphia, he directs toward them the full
force of the gothic horrors that await them for such egregious displays of
impiety:

> Daughters of Pennsylvania! A theatre exists in your smile; a theatre
> expires at your frowns. Forgive the speaker for the thought; it pains
> him at the very heart, to think, that delicate woman, has shown less
> sensibility, than sterner man. Is it possible? can it be true? that our
> young men repaired in solemn procession, to the temple of their
> God, and wept with those that wept, the living, and the dead? and
> that any of our young women, tripped in frolic mood, to yon
> Olympian dome, and smiled at pantomimic folly, laughing in the
> sober face of death himself? . . . And can there be a female in exis-
> tence, who did not consecrate one mournful night, to weep for kin-
> dred female forms, enwrapt in living fires, and shrieking, crisping,
> shrivelling, dying in surrounding flames? Boast not, my thoughtless
> friends, of past security. The peaceful calm, is but the herald of the
> coming storm. Those spacious stairs, and wide unfolding doors,
> which promise to redeem from death, may fail of power, to snatch
> you from an instant grave. (28–29)

As a class, women in this representation become both the origin and scapegoat of immorality and profaneness. Wanting in the requisite sympathy for
"kindred female forms" that had been displayed so duly by their male betters,
these shameful "Daughters of Pennsylvania" are treated precisely to the kind
of harrowing spectacle of bodies—"enwrapt in living fires, and shrieking,
crisping, shrivelling, dying in surrounding flames"—that through the shock
of emotional force were thought instrumental in moving the masses toward
acts of conversion.[114] As if prognosticating their deaths, otherwise, in the Philadelphia theater, Richards directs their attention to one last "instructive
scene": "Ah! see that gay assemblage, beauty, elegance and taste, who crowd
the theatre at Venice! The whirlwind sweeps; the tempest roars; the storm descends; the thunders roll; the lightnings blast; the dead, the dying lay in heaps
around the floor; the groanings of the wounded fair, are horrible indeed. Electric fluid sears the loveliest face, where smiles and dimples played. The scorching fire has withered beauty's fading rose. . . . O! think upon the terrors of this

awful night; and tremble at the words of everlasting truth, thus ye may perish" (29). For Richards, then, "the temporal happiness of the United States, and the never-ending felicity of all its inhabitants" depend upon the acts of contrition that his sermon strives to elicit. His own prayer is that "every individual may listen with serious, and with solemn attention, to the awakening language of the Lord Jesus Christ himself" (30). Awakening and repentance are thus cast in his sermon as collective acts that the nation is enjoined to perform not simply as a body politic under the jurisdiction of human law but rather as a Christian body public regulated by the transcendent spirit of divine law. Binding the sins and the sinners of the nation together throughout his sermon, he thus affirms, in Universalist terms, that only by embracing such a performative mode of Christian religiosity might Americans "improve this awful dispensation of divine providence, in such profitable mode, as best becometh rational, accountable, and immortal beings" (4).

As oratorical performances dedicated to the work of revival and awakening, the sermons preached on the occasion of the Richmond Theater fire illustrate the deep inroads made by the new evangelical forces into urban centers.[115] In focusing on the well-being of the national body, moreover, they drew on lingering resentments in the post-Revolutionary era that still associated the theater with British influence and tapped into the desire to distinguish the new nation from its former colonial ruler.[116] Indeed, as Heather Nathans has argued, "At the heart of the pro- and anti-theater debates of the post-war era lay complex questions about the formation of American nationalism, and about who should most properly guide the fledgling nation in its cultural, political, and economic progress."[117] Over and over again in these sermons, then, we are treated to an explication of the conditions for entry into the evangelical Christian community, a growing body public in nineteenth-century America that would have a lasting impact on the texture of public, private, and political life in the nation.[118] Transposing the vernacular argot of gothic, sentimental, and melodramatic spectacles to an eschatological framework in which they could adeptly play the dilations of sympathy against the constrictions of repentance, the clergymen who preached on this occasion aimed not simply at closing the theaters but rather more expansively at transforming the American public into a Christian body public. In this manner, the tragedy of the fire at the Richmond Theater was rewritten and enacted as a comedy upon the divine stage of Providence in which the sacrifices of a few would lead to the redemption of the many. With dramatic exhortations the order of the day, preachers directed communities of the faithful to take up their parts in this divine comedy and perform them for the good of the nation.

In their efforts at reform and renewal, these clergymen were joined by a moralizing cadre of antitheatrical pamphleteers who used many of the same rhetorical strategies.[119] Yet, while some patrons may have been put off temporarily from going to the playhouse for fear of a similar calamity befalling them, theaters were not wanting in audiences for long. Even in Richmond, the turn toward more sober pursuits failed to prove long lasting. While the Executive Council prohibited the "exhibit of any public shew or spectacle, or . . . any public dancing assembly" for a period of four months, the town soon returned to many of its former pleasures.[120] Thus despite heartfelt predictions by some that "for years [Richmond will] hear nothing but the cries of sorrow," Samuel Mordecai wrote to his sister Rachel as early as 12 February 1812 that "the Sensations of distress, piety and charity, which the dreadful disaster here in December, caused to be so strongly felt (but of which still more was said) appear to have subsided, even in those who had greatest cause for affliction. Except in a few instances we see the same undivided attention paid to the accumulation of overflowing wealth, while the inferior passions of envy resume their stations."[121] On the second anniversary of the fire, moreover, Ellen Mordecai was so distressed by the lack of solemnities that she wrote to her brother Solomon:

The more I see of the world the more I see to condemn and the more *I* even *I*, wonder at its thoughtlessness. To day is the *twenty-sixth*, but it is remembered by few, and observed by only here and there a pious individual. Yesterday there were several dinner parties in town, and today Carriages are continually passing. . . . Louisa also spoke of the cottillian [sic] parties which are every Thursday night I expressed some surprise when she said there would be one next evening. Lord she said why that happened *two* years ago, and on new years day, *last year* we had a party! The less excusable I replied. I dare say she thought me affected and I am sure I thought her unfeeling.[122]

Clearly, the events of the fire, and even the turn to religiosity in Richmond, did not prevent its citizens from recovering their sense of sociability and play. Indeed, even in the weeks leading up to and following the dedication of Monumental Church, Samuel Mordecai reports that Richmond audiences avidly took part not just in events at the church but also in any number of delightful and urbane distractions.[123] Not a few persons, moreover, both in and beyond Richmond, were offended by what they construed as kind of "blasphemy" in the sermonic claims that those who had perished in the fire that night had been punished for their sinful attendance at the playhouse, and many of those who took offense also offered strong defenses of the stage.[124] By 1816, plans were made to build a new theater in Richmond, and, with the support of many of Richmond's most prominent citizens, the new theater opened in 1819 on the corner of Seventh and Broad Streets, not very far from Monumental Church, returning Richmond to its status as a major theatrical center on whose stage all of the great actors of the period made an appearance.[125]

This is not to say that there was no resistance to the return to sociability or to the building of a new theater. In 1816, for instance, the *Enquirer* reported that "the ethics and wisdom of playgoing on the part of church people had been one of the questions discussed in the Episcopal Convention held in Richmond on May 21st."[126] It is to say, however, that a heightened commitment to religiosity and churchgoing was not mutually exclusive with theatergoing and that theatrical affinities remained alive and well amid an increasingly religious body public. In short, while the Richmond Theater fire may have inspired, and provided the leverage for, ministers and preachers up and down the East Coast to impel their congregations toward Christian awakening and conversion, the theatrical impulse still persevered. Like a phoenix rising from the ashes, it would continue to play a central role both on the stages of American culture and on the broader platform of American cultural politics for many years to come. So too, however, as we shall see in the final chapter, would the peculiar legacy of American antitheatricalism with its political roots in evangelical religiosity.

Chapter 5

Adjudicating Bodies Public
in *NEA v. Finley*

In June 1990, at the height of the Culture Wars of the late 1980s and early 1990s, the chairperson of the National Endowment for the Arts (NEA), John Frohnmayer, took the highly unusual step of overruling the agency's peer-review process and denied the grants of four queer performance artists—Karen Finley, John Fleck, Holly Hughes, and Tim Miller.[1] Under heightened congressional scrutiny, Frohnmayer had first singled out the applications of Fleck, Hughes, and Miller for reconsideration by the Peer Review Panel, but his initial strategy of interference was rebuffed when the panel again returned a unanimous recommendation in support of the three artists.[2] In the case of Finley, Frohnmayer stated on record that at first he thought "reconsideration of Finley's application was unnecessary because two of his close friends had attended a Finley show and had reported to him that it was not obscene."[3] He appeared to have second thoughts on the matter, however, when a syndicated column in the *Washington Post* counseled that only the judicious exercise of his veto powers could prevent that "nude, chocolate-smeared young woman" from becoming the "Mapplethorpe case of 1990."[4]

Having been singled out in this very public way, the artists responded by filing suit against the NEA, charging the agency with breaching confidentiality and with improperly denying their grants. Several months later, amid the sustained firestorm of controversy, Congress moved to extend its influence over the agency by passing an amendment to NEA statutes requiring that "in establishing . . . regulations and procedures the Chairperson shall ensure" not only that "artistic excellence and artistic merit are the criteria by which applications are judged" but that "general standards of decency and respect for the

diverse beliefs and values of the American public" be "tak[en] into consideration" in rendering those judgments.[5] Alarmed by these developments and by
the potentially chilling effect that the new "decency and respect" clause might
have on the arts, the National Association of Artists' Organizations (NAAO)
joined the performers' suit, and together they lodged an amended complaint
against the NEA that mounted a facial challenge to the statute on both First
and Fifth Amendment grounds.[6] While the NEA Four, as the artists became
known, would prevail at both the district (1992) and appeals court (1996) levels and would receive their grants through an out-of-court settlement in 1993,
they ultimately lost their constitutional challenge in an eight-to-one decision
handed down by the Supreme Court in June 1998.

For all the attention that the performance artists and their case garnered
in the immediate aftermath of Frohnmayer's funding veto, by the time the
Supreme Court actually handed down its decision eight years later, interest in
the case had waned and the Culture Wars of the 1990s had moved on to other
battlefronts. Aside, then, from a law review article here and there, few scholars
have attended in any sustained fashion either to the particularities of the decision or to the rhetorical and legal implications of its language. While there is
much left to be said, then, and that will be offered in this chapter, about the
artists, their performance work, and the Culture Wars in which they found
themselves both celebrated and excoriated, I will steer the discussion and analysis in this chapter toward unpacking the cultural logic that could allow Justice
Sandra Day O'Connor to punctuate her decision for the majority with the
pronouncement that "when the Government is acting as patron rather than as
sovereign, the consequences of imprecision are not constitutionally severe."[7]

Setting aside, at least initially, the obviously troubling question of what
degree of constitutional "severity" would have to be experienced, or what legal
test would have to be applied before the vagueness or "imprecision" of the
statute in question—§954(d)(1)—could be understood to violate certain constitutionally guaranteed rights and freedoms, this final chapter will turn first
to a consideration of what it meant *in this instance*, both as a historic principle
of law and as a matter of pragmatic and rhetorical understanding, to describe
the government as acting in the capacity of "patron" rather than as "sovereign."[8] Only then, I argue, can we fully understand what was ultimately at
stake both in defining "general standards of decency" and its potentially contradictory companion phrase, "respect for the diverse beliefs and values of the
American public," and in determining what degree of "severity" was to be
visited upon which bodies public.

The first part of this chapter will explore both how the controversy over the NEA played out across the news media and within the halls of Congress and how the Culture Wars were used, in particular by Christian conservatives, to galvanize, cultivate, and consolidate constituencies on the right. Situating the irruption of the Culture Wars as a response to the AIDS crisis, I will then turn to an examination of works by two of the artists in the case—Tim Miller and Karen Finley—in order to illustrate how, through an aesthetic of what I term the "hyper-real real," they sought to make visible bodies public that challenged the normative ideologies of gender and sexuality that were sustained not only on the right but in the mainstream as well. By exercising great care to detail the performative rhetorics at play on all sides of the NEA controversy, we will be far better prepared both to engage O'Connor's decision and to understand how her abstract pronouncements merely mark the culmination of a normative cultural logic that was and still is deeply influential both in American law and in the conception of the American body politic.

The Culture Wars

The Culture Wars were already well under way by the time the NEA Four were caught in its crosshairs.[9] The first major shots across the bow had been fired in April 1989 when Christian conservatives publicized NEA funding of an exhibition and catalog featuring Andres Serrano's *Piss Christ* and followed up with an attack on the *Perfect Moment*, a retrospective of the works of Robert Mapplethorpe, which was partially funded by the NEA.[10] Leading the charge was the director of the American Family Association, Reverend Donald Wildmon, who sent a letter to over a million people in which he decried Serrano's large-scale photograph of a crucifix submerged in urine as an outrageous example of rampant "bias and bigotry against Christians" in American culture.[11] Members of Congress, led by Senators Alphonse D'Amato (R-NY) and Jesse Helms (R-NC), followed suit and took to the floor to declaim against the use of "taxpayers money" to support such "trash." In an impressive fit of histrionic pique, D'Amato tore to shreds the *Visual Arts* exhibition catalog in which Serrano's photograph was published and avowed, "This is not a question of free speech. This is a question of abuse of taxpayer's money . . . to defame us and to use our money. . . . If people want to be perverse, in terms of what they recognize as art or culture, so be it, but not with my money, not with the taxpayers' dollars, and certainly not under the mantle of this great

Nation." Never one to be outdone on such occasions, Helms called Serrano a "jerk" and accused the artist and the NEA of "insulting the very fundamental basis of this country," that is, of "taunting the American people" by engaging in "blasphemy and insensitivity toward the religious community." "Do not dishonor our Lord," he exclaimed on the floor of the Senate. "I resent it and I think the vast majority of the American people do."[12]

Two strategies that would be played out repeatedly in the NEA controversy are immediately evident in these remarks. First, D'Amato insists that freedom of speech is not at issue, that this was simply a commonsensical question of how government resources ought to be allocated. But this "commonsensical" utterance also begs the more pertinent question of who precisely is figured in this invocation of the "taxpayers" and hence to whom, as a consequence, do the protections of the "mantle of this great Nation" extend. Who, in other words, what constituencies, what bodies public compose the taxpaying "us" that has purportedly been defamed, and what bodies public, in contradistinction, fall under the canopy of the implied "them"?

We are not left in suspense very long, as Helms's remarks point strategically to one of the dominant modes for forming such identifications and drawing such distinctions in American politics. With his strong reference to "*the* religious community," his claims to represent the "vast majority of *the* American people," and his invocation of "*our* Lord" (emphases mine), Helms sent a clear signal not only that he considered America one nation under a Christian God but also that the Christian community in America was unified in its views, constituting a "vast" body public with considerable political power and influence.[13] Thus, following a pattern observed by Ann Pelligrini and Janet Jakobsen whereby "Christian theological pronouncements have become so institutionalized in the official life of the nation that they can be taken for just good old American values," Helms articulates an exclusionary rather than an inclusionary idea of "the American people."[14] In the intensifying furor over Mapplethorpe's *The Perfect Moment*, it would become increasingly clear that the "American people" whom Helms was summoning to mind and for whom he envisioned himself as protector and defender were to be understood not simply as Christian but also as heterosexual.

Of the 175 photographs that were included in the Mapplethorpe retrospective, the 13 prints that composed his X Portfolio attracted the most attention. These images featured explicit depictions of homoerotic, sadomasochistic activities, including Mapplethorpe's 1978 self-portrait with a bullwhip inserted into his rectum; and they were meant to be juxtaposed on display with the 13 complementary images each that composed his Y and Z Portfolios of flowers and black male nudes, respectively. As Wendy Steiner has observed, "Mapplethorpe apparently saw them as parallel, the composition and sensuousness of the different subjects linking them in an overall artistic system."[15] Such formal considerations were not of great interest to Christian conservatives, and, as the controversy continued to build, resulting in the show's cancellation at the Corcoran Gallery and obscenity and child pornography charges against the curators at the Contemporary Art Center in Cincinnati, it dramatized ever more sharply the ways in which the conservatives sought to use the moment both to cultivate their constituency and to police what I term the "normative real," that is, the set of social, cultural, and aesthetic conventions that regulate conduct and confer visibility within the state.

Though the Cincinnati curators would ultimately be acquitted, the legal proceedings and the ongoing controversy kept Mapplethorpe and his works in the news as bywords for immorality, degeneracy, and perversion and helped propel the 1989 passage of Helms's notorious obscenity amendment enjoining the use of NEA funds for materials "which may be considered obscene, including but not limited to, depictions of sadomasochism, homoeroticism, the sexual exploitation of children, or individuals engaged in sex acts."[16] Strategically, again, Helms cast the amendment as one that "simply provide[d] for some *common sense* restrictions on what is and is not an appropriate use of Federal funding for the arts" (italics mine), arguing "no artist has a preemptive claim on the tax dollars of the American people," especially one whose art is as "sick" and "depraved" as Mapplethorpe's. "Federal funding for sadomasochism, homoeroticism, and child pornography is," he contended, "an insult to taxpayers."[17]

Though the 1989 Helms amendment would be struck down in short order by a federal district court, the discursive damage had been done: homoerotic representations had been cast as obscene, and homosexuality had been equated with criminal activities beyond the pale of the normative, such as pedophilia.[18] The bodies with which the delineated categories were associated were pathologized, moreover, both as perverse agents of disease and as threats to the health of the national body politic. Further, as Carol Vance has observed, in taking up the cause of "the taxpayer," Helms's speech had a dual effect: not only did he install "the fiction of a singular public with universally shared taste," but in doing so, he effected "the displacement of a diverse public composed of many constituencies of different tastes."[19] The rhetorical strategies at work on the conservative side thus shaped the discourse and in effect mobilized a prejudicial set of associations for stigmatizing queer bodies and homosexual persons.

The conservative tactic of inciting the NEA debates and then exploiting them as an opportunity to police the normative real through discursive and legislative means was coupled with a second set of tactics that leveraged the controversies in order to build a constituency. No better example of this pattern can be found than in what has famously come to be known as the "red envelope" campaign, a direct mailing signed by the Reverend Pat Robertson as part of an effort to kick off a fundraising drive on behalf of his newly formed Christian Coalition. The "red envelope" in question was enclosed within a separate white envelope, which also contained a letter that immediately warned its recipients, "The enclosed red envelope contains graphic descriptions of homosexual erotic photographs that were funded by your tax dollars."[20] Demurring in reference to the Mapplethorpe works that "I'd never send you the photos, but I did want you to know about the vile contents of your tax funded material," Robertson goes on to situate himself as the outspoken champion of those who might otherwise be cowed by what he strategically characterizes as the liberal censors in Congress and the American Civil Liberties Union.[21] "I *won't* be silent," he heroically avows, and he "pray[s] you won't either." Then comes the extended pitch in which he encourages the addressees to send in their membership forms immediately in exchange for which they will receive an "official membership card and lapel pin" to wear to "civic and political meetings as a way of identifying others who are concerned about the moral decadence that has invaded the heart of America." Vowing to "organize chapters in every state, every Congressional District, and God willing, every precinct in America," he envisions a day when "God-fearing Americans" can "insist that candidates for every office tell us their views on religious freedom, abortion, prayers in schools, sex education, pornography, and other issues important to the moral fiber of *our nation*" and "force America to face the moral issues that threaten to destroy us."[22] Having made his case, Robertson concludes the letter with a final exhortation that indeed appears to be the entire point of the exercise: "Return your membership form today. Together we can begin to turn back the tide of pornography, filth and moral decay that is attacking every level of *our society*."[23]

Robertson's letter is carefully crafted to construct and to cultivate an "us" that could be opposed to a "them." He speaks repeatedly to a discursive collective, the "our" in "our society" and "our nation;" and he seeks, moreover, to engender a visible "body public" that is united not simply by the shared address of discursive texts but also, as signaled through the display of those "lapel pins," by the experience of physical presence and mutual recognition in public spaces designed for civic and political meetings. Drawing on the long American tradition of voluntarism that, as demonstrated in the previous chapter, played such a significant role in the rhetoric surrounding the gathering of a Christian body public in early nineteenth-century America, Robertson's appeal allows for competing forms of affiliation and identification and intimates the tension that abides between the bodies public that compose the body politic and the body politic itself.[24]

Once we look inside the red envelope, we can begin to cobble together a clearer picture of the "them" to whom Robertson's "us" must be opposed. On a single sheet of paper, we find two headings that are seemingly at odds with one another. The first reads, "I encourage you to exercise your freedom immediately by destroying the vulgar information about the photographs." The second provides the formal heading for the enumeration to follow:

TAX-PAYER FUNDED
Photographs Too Vulgar to Print[25]

Ought one to destroy the "vulgar information" even before perusing it, that is to say, immediately? Or ought one to destroy that information only *after* one has taken a moment to read down the page for the nine itemized descriptions of photographs that were purportedly too "vulgar" to print? Either way the rhetorical situation generated by the tensions between the interdiction, the warning, and the enumeration provided a performative occasion for the addressee to demonstrate his or her affinity with the Christian Coalition, even before sending in a membership card. By destroying the list, the reader could enact not only his or her distaste for the "vulgar" but also his or her embrace of Robertson's "us."

Dated 25 October 1989, just two days after the passage of Helms's obscenity amendment, Robertson's letter is careful to cultivate many of the same discursive associations, especially that statute's alignment of homosexuality and pedophilia. Indeed, as Richard Meyer has pointed out, not only did Robertson, by virtue of his direct-mail campaign, put Mapplethorpe's name into circulation as a household word, he also did so by manufacturing some of the supposed "evidence" against the artist.[26] Among the nine descriptions that compose the complete list, eight reference images from the Mapplethorpe exhibit, including "a photo of a man urinating in another man's mouth" and "a

photo of a man's arm (up to the forearm) in another man's rectum." Yet there
is also one description, as Meyer documents, that fails to reference any "photograph by Robert Mapplethorpe—or by any other federally funded artist": "a
photo of naked children in bed with a naked man."[27] Meyer reads both Robertson's and Helms's pursuit of Mapplethorpe as of a piece with their determination to associate homosexuality with pedophilia, sickness, and disease.[28]
Mapplethorpe's death from AIDS in March 1989 provided further fuel for
their fire, and the vitriol spewed on the occasion vividly illustrates the extent
to which conservative attacks on the NEA were not simply coincident but
also deeply imbricated with the AIDS crisis in America.

The Culture Wars and the AIDS Crisis

At a distance of so many years and counting, when the news is filled not only
with announcements about promising advances in the search for a cure for
HIV infections but also with reports about daily advances in the struggle for
gay rights and marriage equality, it is difficult to convey to those who did not
live through those initial years of crisis just how deadly AIDS was when it first
appeared in the early 1980s and just how fearful and hateful the responses
were to those who were suffering and dying from the wide range of opportu-
nistic, infectious diseases that made up the syndrome. The struggles of the
mid-1980s to the early 1990s marked a period when massive amounts of mis-
and disinformation were circulating about the syndrome and the risks of infection. Activist groups like ACT-UP breached protocols of politeness to
respond angrily and publicly to government indifference to the deaths of so
many, and protested the ways that "AIDS [was] effectively being used as a
pretext throughout the West to justify calls for increasing legislation and regulation of those who [were] considered to be socially unacceptable."[29] Indeed,
as any number of observers at the time noted, the deadliness of AIDS itself
was matched only by the virulence of the attacks on those populations that
were among the first to be affected by HIV in the United States, especially
homosexual and bisexual men.[30] Perhaps even more pertinent for our purposes here, the emergence of AIDS, as historian Jennifer Brier has pointed
out, forced discussions of sexuality and sexual practices into the public
sphere.[31] In particular, as Priscilla Wald has observed, "HIV ma[de] sex visible; it show[ed] that people's desires [were] not bound by either the social
sanction of marriage or the social classifications of race, gender, and sexuality,

and it demonstrate[d] the indifference of those desires . . . to national boundaries as well."[32] The anxieties and fears thus raised by the specter of AIDS were
manifold, and, as activists and moralists alike struggled to shape the narrative
of the disease, it gave rise discursively to what cultural critics such as Paula
Treichler and Simon Watney have variously described as "an epidemic of signification" or a "crisis of representation."[33] Because of the historical accident,
moreover, that consigned AIDS, at least initially in the United States, almost
exclusively to homosexual populations, this "discursive explosion" was concentrated in particular on what Thomas Yingling has termed the "question of
homosexuality."[34] Thus, as governmental and cultural authorities struggled to
restore and defend social, sexual, and national distinctions and to cordon off
what they construed as the encroaching threat of homosexual contagion, "debates about sexuality and representation" moved to the forefront of American
politics and, indeed, as Watney has demonstrated, to the center of "the political imagination of [the] times."[35] In that context, attacks upon and defenses of
cultural institutions not only took on new significance but also became a politically expedient way to express, either directly or indirectly, a variety of responses to the AIDS crisis and all that it represented.

In the language and rhetorics that came to characterize the debates over
the NEA, we find a perfect illustration of this broader discursive effort to mobilize the public imaginary against the purportedly pathological dangers presented by homosexuality and homosexual bodies.[36] As the debate raged in the
House and Senate over the 1989 Helms obscenity amendment, for instance,
pundits on the right, such as Patrick Buchanan, took the opportunity to shape
public discourse not simply by calling for the defunding of "the poisoners of
culture" but also by deriding artists like "poor, pathetic Robert Mapplethorpe
for having photographed . . . the degraded acts by which he killed himself."[37]
Buchanan's hostile references to "degraded acts" and the "poisoners of culture"
evince the general sense of disturbance that characterized the American discourse on AIDS, a discourse suffused with irrational fear that received perhaps
its most notorious articulation on the op-ed pages of the *New York Times*,
when William F. Buckley warned, "*Our society* is generally threatened," and
recommended that "everyone with AIDS should be tattooed in the upper-
forearm to protect common-needle users, and on the buttocks, to prevent the
victimization of other homosexuals."[38]

In just these two examples of the kind of vitriol that splashed across edi-
torial pages, we can see how persons with AIDS were routinely resituated as
perpetrators of the disease and as threats not only to their own lives but also to

the lives of those around them.[39] Further, just as many critics have noted the first major article about AIDS in the *New York Times* speculated as to whether the disease posed a potential threat to the "general public," so too does Buckley's invocation of "our society" intimate the ways in which homosexuals and persons with AIDS were not to be considered part of either.[40] Instead, the "general public" and "our society" are imagined as bodies public composed exclusively of heterosexual bodies and positioned as Michel Foucault's essays on biopolitics help us to see, as that which "must be defended" against the homosexual "poisoners of culture."[41]

These remarks, then, were not merely symptomatic but rather performative enactments of what Foucault has termed a biopolitics in which "life as a political object . . . more than the law . . . became the issue of political struggle" and in which cultural warfare could serve as the technology through which power could speak "*of* sexuality and *to* sexuality" and the "action of the norm" could be instituted.[42] Accordingly, Helms echoed Buchanan's alignment of homosexuality with depravity and disease to argue that it was no more or less than "an issue of soaking the taxpayer to fund the homosexual pornography of Robert Mapplethorpe, who died of AIDS while spending the last years of his life promoting homosexuality."[43] "The general public," represented here by the implicitly heterosexual "taxpayer," was thus deployed, as Leo Bersani might note, as "at once an ideological construct and a moral prescription," and the attacks on the NEA were used as an effective screen to mount a defense of the supposedly threatened (heterosexual) body politic.[44]

In short, if AIDS drove questions of sexual identity and homosexual practices into the foreground of public consciousness and challenged conservative efforts to suppress knowledge about bodies and the things that people do with their bodies, then the passage of the 1989 Helms obscenity amendment was of a piece with what Lauren Berlant and Michael Warner have termed the practice of "sex in public," that is, with the elision of queer bodies and queer practices from the public horizon of visibility and the simultaneous consolidation and instantiation of heteronormativity and heteronormative practices under the cover of law.[45] The emergence of HIV/AIDS threatened the spread of ideas, concepts, and art that so many had worked so long to keep from the public eye, and, as Peggy Phelan has observed, "Not only d[id] this art make homosexuality, death, and anger visible, it admit[ted] that these experiences can be beautiful and worthy of artistic meditation."[46] In many respects, as we have seen, the fear of the spread of this knowledge was considered more of a threat than the actual spread of AIDS itself, and the desire to

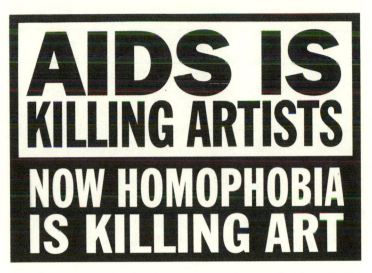

Figure 20. "AIDS Is Killing Artists / Now Homophobia Is Killing Art" (1989).
Art+Positive Archives.
Private Collection of Dr. Daniel S. Berger, Chicago.

keep homosexual and queer bodies outside the frame of the "general public" became the priority of many (Figure 20). Hence, when Congress responded to the 1990 controversy over the NEA Four by passing the new amendment that imposed the "decency and respect" clause, there was little mystery as to its intent.[47] Rather, it was proof yet again, as Jill Dolan has pointed out in the Mapplethorpe case, that in the late 1980s and early 1990s, "speaking of homo or lesbian sex, as opposed to identity, in public forums [was] still transgressive enough to activate the machinery of state power."[48] Resonating with other seemingly innocuous terms, such as "our society" and the "general public," the imposition of "general standards of decency and respect" articulated a stipulation that consolidated the claims of a heteronormative body public and defended against the forms of knowledge conveyed by queer bodies and queer art. Even more important, it demonstrated once again the lengths to which conservative forces would go to keep queer bodies out of the frame of intelligibility, outside the frame of the normative real, beyond the ken of "our society."

Interrogating Decency and Respect:
The Hyper-Real Real of the NEA Four

If conservatives used the occasion of the NEA debates to try to exorcise the specter of AIDS and to reify and promote a heteronormative real, all four of the defunded artists in the NEA case not only responded to the AIDS crisis with works that explored the virulent effects of homophobia but also insisted in their performances on bringing into the field of public vision both the pleasures of queer bodies and the exacting pains of heteronormative regulation.[49] Adamantly refusing the conventions of withdrawal behind a theatrical fourth wall, these artists developed what I term an aesthetic of the "hyper-real real," an aesthetic that both refuses and unravels the abstract and disembodied illusions of "realism" and instead forces audiences to confront lived bodily experience, beneath the veneer of the real, in all of its messiness—its desires, its excretions, its pleasures, and its pains. While these operations are apparent in the work of all four artists, for the sake of illustration, I will discuss Tim Miller's *My Queer Body*, a piece he completed in 1992 when the case of the NEA Four was in the early stages of wending its way through the court systems, and Karen Finley's "The Black Sheep," which formed a part of *We Keep Our Victims Ready* and was first published in her collection *Shock Treatment* in 1990.

Tim Miller's My Queer Body

Miller describes his performance practice as dedicated to telling stories that "chart the emotional, spiritual, sexual, and political topography of [his] identity as a gay man."[50] Autobiographical in nature, his performance pieces are as engaged with those metaphorical topographies as they are with how those topographies map literally onto the body—his body, my body, your body. All of his work endeavors, moreover, not only to assemble a body public in the space of performance but also to make that gathering visible and concrete, an operation that begins in *My Queer Body* with an entrance in which he announces that he "needs to gather a few things" and then proceeds to grasp various body parts of individual audience members, from fingers to toes to buttocks, bringing his body into contact with their bodies and making it clear that there will be no fourth wall dividing his body from theirs. From touch he moves on to voice, calling upon audience members to name their favorite places on the body—either theirs or someone else's—and eliciting shouts of thighs, breasts, and lips, until, with a bit of coaxing from Miller, a few bold audience members find their way to what he terms the "*naughty stuff,*" to "*Dicks!!! Pussies!!! [and] Butthole[s]*" (86). In this manner, Miller deliberately initiates his performance with a "collaborative ritual" (xviii) that licenses a collective loss of inhibition and gathers together, quite literally, not just a "few things" but rather a fleshly and queer body public that acknowledges all of its parts and that, however fragmented, will enter as one with him into what he fondly refers to as the "sweaty reality of live performing" (xvi). "Good!" he exclaims at the end of this prologue, "We have summoned the body! The body is here!" (85–86).

Throughout the performance, Miller will take great care to maintain this tactile and intimate relationship with his audience, asking one member to rub his heart (88) and touching another member's hair (107) (Figure 21). Each glancing touch, each moment in which he meets the audience's gaze with his own, is meant to affirm, as he does setting himself down naked in someone's lap, "I AM here with you" (107). Miller's practice is thus dedicated not simply to assembling the individual body but rather to gathering the collective of bodies in an intimate yet still public space to produce what Robert Wallace has termed, in his own discussion of Miller, the performance of a "queer sociality."[51]

My Queer Body traces an arc that begins with the climactic moment of Miller's own conception and then passes through a series of anticlimaxes that confound conventional dramaturgy. Through a series of linked vignettes, Miller repeatedly conjures the queer body both as it comes into being and as it discovers its own pleasures. But this is not simply a piece about gay sexual liberation; it is also a profound meditation on the soul- and bone-crushing struggles of both the queer body personal and the queer body public in the age of AIDS.[52] The triple threats of hatred, violence, and death all play a significant role in this linked series of monologues, sometimes hovering at the edges, sometimes front and center, but always haunting the text with an inexorable grief and a bottomless anger. For Miller, the cumulative effect of this grief and anger is a potentially debilitating aloneness, precisely the kind of isolation that society has dictated ought to be the fate of the queer: alone in fear, alone in suffering, alone in death—a life lived on the margins beyond the frame of everyday intelligibility.

To stanch the flow of this aloneness, Miller initially embarks upon a dramatic flight into the magical real, stripping his body naked, as he follows a bear, which has peeled away from the state flag of California to lead him away from an ACT-UP protest at a museum, where the same fingers, hands, and

Figure 21. Tim Miller,
My Queer Body.
Courtesy of Tim Miller and
Dona Ann McAdams.
© Dona Ann McAdams.

wrists that he had conjured earlier are getting crushed and maimed, on a journey that eventually brings him to the edge of the rim and then into the crater
of a volcano. In that crater, Miller, now bathed in a theatrical red light, performs the time-honored, primordial ritual of man alone on stage, confronting
his shame, passions, and fears, a ritual that usually requires that the audience
watch and wait for that moment of catharsis, or in this case for that volcanic
eruption that will transform the topography of this man, exorcising his fear
and restoring the body that has been shamed and broken, as he tells us, "here
where Reagan and Bush smile their do-nothing holocaust grins while [his]
friends died," "here and here where [his] own embarrassment twisted [his]
spine" and "here and here dick and balls smashed off by the hammers of
Helms and Buchanan, and Sheldon and Wildmon" (106). Invoking the names

of those whose rancorous crusades against homosexuality and the NEA Four had only forced the question of sexuality and its ties to the AIDS epidemic all the more sharply into the public light, Miller raises our expectations to a feverish pitch and then suddenly, abruptly, in an anticlimactic moment that thwarts what we thought was our desire, he stops: "I'm gonna stop there. If it's okay with you," he says. "Actually, even if it's not I'm gonna stop there" (107). Calling for a simple white spot, Miller then confesses, "I made all that up. All that about the volcano and the beast. I lied to you. . . . The only thing I really know is that I'm here naked in front of all of you right now." Wandering through the audience, still naked, he takes that seat in someone's lap and rehearses that key phrase noted earlier: "I AM here with you" (107).

For Miller in this moment, the typical rituals and conventions of theater are not only insufficient for his purposes, but they also veil the truths he wants to tell. The mythopoetic dreamscape that forms the theatrical real detaches him, cuts him off from his audience, from those he loves and especially, as he explains, from all of life that is "a lot wetter and messier and more human and complicated than when I stand up there naked in the red theatrical light and pretend I'm going into the volcano" (108). This is no mere show of the kind of antitheatrical theatricalism that has historically been used by playwrights and performers to claim greater authority or truthfulness for their art.[53] Rather, for Miller, there is no catharsis to be had amid this moment of crisis precisely because we have been led by his artistic measures, that is, by the aesthetic conventions of the theatrical real, to mistake our own desires. What Elin Diamond has identified as the "shudder of catharsis" might be what the neat arc of tragedy conventionally requires, but to submit to that dramaturgical demand would be to foist to the margins what both Miller in his practice and Diamond in her criticism know to be the "messiness" and materiality that was AIDS in that moment and to forget that his "queer friends [were still] getting beat up back at the museum" and that the true volcano lay, as he tells us now, not in his individual journey through living memory but in the "outlines of [the] hundreds and thousands of people who had died" (108).[54] Beginning then with an incantatory series of exhortations to his flaccid penis to "get hard" and ending with an anatomically graphic narration of sexual encounter, Miller searches for a new kind of ritual shudder, one that rejects aloneness in favor of collectivity, one that seeks not so much to expiate as to incorporate, and one that is grounded in the body rather than in the abstracted forms of theatrical embodiment.

Not insignificantly, the "Get Hard" sequence in *My Queer Body* has attracted a great deal of critique from the political right and left. For performance theorist and critic Peggy Phelan, for instance, Miller's performance concentrates too narrowly on the "white male penis" as a locus of queer history, queer subjectivity, and queer identification.[55] Not only does she submit that "a mantra to induce the swelling erection of a penis is less than a revolutionary political desire," but she also contends that "there must . . . be something other than the penis, flaccid or erect, that is crucial to the nomination of queer bodies."[56] For Phelan, in short, Miller's performance materializes the "real" of the queer in "bodily practices" that are too specific and that leave little room for the multifarious and mobile modes of identification and affective being that theorists have come to privilege as the province of the queer.[57]

Such a doctrinaire appraisal fails to account, however, for much that is salient in Miller's performance. First, Phelan's assessment elides the modes of fantasy and play that Miller mobilizes against the "real" and misses the extent to which he seeks here not so much to produce a new "real" as to engage the spectator's help in "creat[ing] a little alternative reality" (112). "We have to project," he tells his audience, "a bit into the future," a bit, that is, into what David Román has termed Miller's "not *yet* real," where an "imaginative retelling of an event . . . can possibly be rendered as 'real' only from the perspective of the future."[58]

Second, Phelan's position ignores two substantive facts: first, as Román has observed, "the narrative that accompanies Miller's nakedness disturbs this objectification of the gay male body";[59] and second, and perhaps more tellingly and obviously, the penis never does "get hard." Indeed, Miller not only points up this failure but also uses it to leverage the performance from a focus on an individual body part/person—what Phelan presumably objects to—to the collective body public before him. The climax of the piece lies, then, not in the pleasures of individual ejaculation but in a scene of collective transport into the "not *yet* real" future where Miller imagines that he has been appointed "performance art laureate" by the nation's first black lesbian president and commissioned to create for the inaugural gala at the Kennedy Center a "symphonic homoerotic performance art cantata that will exorcise homophobia and bigotry from our land" (112). Mobilizing a queer imaginary, Miller claims a space on the national stage in the not too distant future when the spectacle of "two men inside of each other without a knife, a gun, or a stock portfolio . . . fucking . . . [and] being fucked" and "feel[ing] the blessing of being closer than they told us was possible" might take center stage. "THE CURTAIN RISES," he exclaims, "AND THERE WE ARE" (118–20).

In this sequence, Miller insists both on the adamant presence of queer bodies in the national body politic and on representing that queer body and the actions it performs in graphic terms, that is, on placing before the spectator's eyes that which usually is either veiled in euphemism or simply not rendered within the normative horizon of the visible. By engaging the audience in a participatory call and response—"LET ME HEAR YA SAY *YEAH*/ PUT IT IN"—Miller ensures that the climactic experience of this moment lies not simply in his body but rather in the extent to which he can rouse and arouse the audience as a collective—gay, straight, queer, or other—to embrace sexual pleasure as an act of political defiance, to hear themselves call out in their own mind's eye, "I AM IN MY BODY/ I AM IN MY LIFE" (118–19).

Third, and finally then, Phelan's assessment fails to account for the contexts of Miller's work as he sought both to reclaim the space of performance for a queer body public in the wake of the NEA controversy and to respond to the abject "spectacle of AIDS" that had come to dominate the national imaginary.[60] To be sure, Miller hardly begins to exhaust all sexual practices that could be deemed queer, but to argue that Miller is not representative enough based on whether or not spectators can identify with his specific sexual predilections relies perhaps too narrowly on a strictly identificatory mechanism for the generation of theatrical effects and fails to take into account the extent to which insisting on the visibility of nonheteronormative sexual practices in this moment constituted a queer act in itself. By making the body and the things queer bodies do visible, palpable, and substantial in the paradoxically intimate space of public performance, Miller leverages the lineaments of the hyper-real real to bring into being and to celebrate, even if only for the duration of his show, a recognizably queer body public whose relationship to the social and political topographies of the day was still very much a contestatory work in progress.

Karen Finley's We Keep Our Victims Ready

Miller's practice of taking his concerns directly to the public draws, of course, on the long tradition in performance art of challenging social, cultural, and aesthetic orthodoxies. In this respect, performance, as art historian RoseLee Goldberg points out, has become a vehicle both for "bringing to life the many formal and conceptual ideas on which the making of art is based" and for "shocking the audience into reassessing their own notions of art and its relation to culture."[61] The performance artists who compose the NEA Four follow in this tradition not only by making visible the complex web of binaries through which the normative real is constituted but also by betraying its figural impulse in representation either to displace or to suppress altogether the embodiedness of the body. If realist drama, as so many theorists have suggested, erects the proscenium as a framing device for that which is stipulated as "real" and deploys the technology of the fourth wall both as the screen for all that is marked as normative and natural and as the vanishing point for all that is marked as aberrant and unnatural, then the aesthetic of the hyper-real real that is employed by the NEA Four reveals, first, that no proscenium is required for the performative force of that normative real to be felt in the space of everyday life, and, second, that what lies behind the fourth wall, the depths through which its surface is articulated, are the gendered and sexed bodies whose explicit operations have been subjected to violent distortion.[62] To the extent that each of these artists makes that invisible fourth wall visible and steps out from behind its insulating and regulatory machinery, they also force their audiences to join them outside the usual frames of intelligibility to enter instead into a space of semiotic play that is freed in particular from the restraints of what performance theorist Sue-Ellen Case terms the "normative teleologies" of gender and sexuality.[63]

Indeed, as a number of critics have pointed out, Finley's particular notoriety and the animosity that is so often hurled in her direction stem from her insistence on estranging the processes of mimesis through which "woman" as a normative category is conventionally signified and engaging instead in what Elin Diamond has postulated as a feminist praxis that makes mimesis so palpably "excessive to itself" that it "spill[s] into a mimicry that undermines the referent's authority . . . referring to yet refusing to symbolize its meaning."[64] In performance pieces that feature a series of linked monologues delivered in a riveting trance-like state through a trilling, keening, and at times almost unbearable voice and that often focus on rape, incest, sexual abuse, and molestation, Finley consistently works on two levels to expose the dysfunction, violence, and pain that undergirds the normative real, first, by making the body fully, palpably, and insistently present, and second, by turning the symbolic order that gives shape to the normative real inside out and making its operations visible for all to see.[65] Thus, on the one level, as C. Carr writes, Finley "goes straight to the real dirt beneath the banal," and on the other, as Rebecca Schneider demonstrates, the "symbolic" in Finley's monologues "is translated with a ferocious and unsettling literality of over-satiation."[66]

This is the hyper-real real, then, that Finley insistently renders when, for instance, she rails in *The Constant State of Desire* (1986) against the systemic commodification, consumption, and subjection of women and art, even as she mimics, mocks, and undermines those operations by displaying and then transforming her own naked body, that is, a body that in its excessive woman-liness is usually rendered invisible, into a visibly grotesque and defiantly artic-ulate female nude, lacquered in egg yolk, sprinkled with glitter, and offering a gaping "Mr. Yuppie" quite a bit more than the "artistic experience" he bar-gained for in the form of a threat to cut off his testicles and market them as chocolate-covered balls for the Easter delectation, at "$25 a pound," of all those "Park Avenue, Madison Avenue know-it-alls."[67] Similarly, in the "Why Can't This Veal Calf Walk?" segment of *We Keep Our Victims Ready* (1987), Finley covers her body with a chocolate substitute for the abasement of excrement—hence the epithet the "chocolate-smeared woman"—as she per-forms, in graphic terms, the immobilizing pain, confusion, and self-loathing of a young girl who has been raped and betrayed by a series of male authority figures, an uncle, a doctor, and a police officer, all of whom were supposed to protect her (Figure 22). Each of these authority figures violently reduces the young girl to a sexual property, a simple "hole" for sexual pleasure, a sacrificial victim, who has no credibility because, as Finley makes clear, men control the currency of social truth and credit. The young girl, then, can only exchange her story with her analogue, a penned-in veal calf, standing in the stink of its own excrement, fatted, and awaiting its slaughter.[68]

At issue for Finley, as she performs these acts of ventriloquy in the voices of both the victims and the victimizers, are the forms of violence that are rou-tinely naturalized.[69] Working through the figures of metonymy, or the contig-uous series of substitutions that sustain the continuous ideological systems of patriarchy and heteronormativity, Finley thus explores not only what kinds of pain and violence are inflicted in the name of the "family" but also how our shared cultural narratives of gender and sexuality produce a logic of just des-erts, that is, of who deserves to be punished, who deserves to suffer violence, and who must be sacrificed in order to ensure that the culture of patriarchy can reproduce itself in the next generation.

This logic of just deserts is felt most poignantly in one of Finley's lesser noted, perhaps because not so easily sensationalized, works, "The Black Sheep," a poetic tribute at once utopian and mournful that attempts to con-jure and then gather together a body public composed of outcasts—persons who have been persecuted and tormented precisely because they see and expe-rience the world differently.[70] "The Black Sheep" was not only performed as

Figure 22. Karen Finley,
*We Keep Our
Victims Ready*.
Courtesy of Karen Finley
and Dona Ann McAdams.
© Dona Ann McAdams.

part of *We Keep Our Victims Ready*, but it was also transposed into a public monument when it was cast in bronze, mounted on a concrete pedestal that looked much like a rough-hewn gravestone, and set for one month on First Avenue between First and Houston Streets in New York (Figure 23).[71] Addressed in particular to those who had died from AIDS or were dying from AIDS, Finley's work provided a spontaneous occasion for crowds to pause in the heterogeneously public space of the street and to reflect on the devastating impact AIDS was having on the artistic communities of New York. In this manner, she staged a perhaps more muted, subtle, and open-ended contribution to what Susan Leigh Foster has characterized as the emergent "choreographies of protest" that were orchestrated across major cities in the United States by AIDS activists in the late 1980s and early 1990s.[72]

Figure 23. Karen Finley, "The Black Sheep."
Installation in conjunction with Creative Time.
Courtesy of Karen Finley and Dona Ann McAdams. © Dona Ann McAdams.

Finley's poem begins with an encounter between two friends who never see each other anywhere other than at the endless series of funerals for persons with AIDS that had become part of the landscape of everyday life within certain communities in New York.[73] She dubs both those who have died and those who survive and mourn them as "members of the Black Sheep family," a collective of kin of choice for those who have been rejected by their biological families.[74] Summoning what Peggy Phelan has termed an "emotional truth [that] is a kind of furious integrity in the face of massive hypocrisy," Finley goes on not only to articulate a "creed" for "Black Sheep folk"—they believe "in sexual preferences / believe in no racism / no sexism / no religionism" (141)—but also to fashion her audience into a collective body public by cultivating a sense of belonging for those who so often have been made to feel alone.[75] For these "sheep with no shepherd," Finley aspires not so much to be the shepherd as to offer herself as an inspired *rhetor* of "unconditional love," who, through the operations of *pathos*, might move those "sheep who take the dangerous pathway through / the mountain range / to get to the other side of our soul" (141). Over the course of her delivery, Finley not only exposes the hypocrisy of those biological sisters, brothers, mothers, or fathers who might show up to collect their dead or to celebrate the artistic works left behind by gay artists—"You can't take it with you / written by a former black sheep" (141)—but she also opposes that hypocrisy to the fierce devotion of queer kin who not only claim their dead but celebrate and cherish their living, even when those living are suffering, in pain, and dying. Hence, while there may be no biological sisters, brothers, mothers, or fathers who might be willing to claim their "black sheep," Finley testifies, "I have many sisters with me tonight," "I have many brothers with me here tonight!" "I have many mamas with me here tonight!" "I have many many daddies with me here tonight!" (142). Through this performative invocation of the alternative types of kinship that form the affective sinews of the queer body public, Finley affirms, "tonight we love each other / That's why we're here— / to be around others like ourselves" (142). She thus produces what Jill Dolan might term an instance of the "utopian performative," a moment when "in the performer's grace, in the audience's generosity, in the lucid power of intersubjective understanding, however fleeting," it becomes possible to imagine that "the social scourges that currently plague us . . . might be ameliorated, cured, redressed, solved, never to haunt us again."[76]

As with all utopias, however, the melancholic underside that haunts those moments of euphoria and the troubles that one tries to stave off through acts of imagination are never far away. The "Black Sheep" are not only a lost flock in search of a shepherd; they are also the sacrificial victims of a culture that refuses to recognize, acknowledge, love, and embrace them, and Finley takes great pains to make this truth visible, palpable, and clear. "Black Sheep's destinies," as Finley tells us, "are not necessarily in having / families, having prescribed existences— / like the American Dream." Rather they are "chosen to be sick," "chosen to die," in order "to give meaning in life" (143). The "Black Sheep" are designated culturally, then, as bodies that "matter" only insofar as they "give meaning" to the lives of their others, only insofar as they provide the bodily material against which heteronormativity— "the American Dream"—can define itself.[77] By the end of her monologue, then, the cruel silence of a family member that greets a black sheep at the end of the phone is transformed, as she beats her chest in the rhythmic pulses of a heartbeat, into the even more devastating "silence at the end of the phone" of a beloved black sheep who is dying from AIDS. "I wish," she pleads:

I could relieve you of your suffering.
I wish I could relieve you of your pain.
I wish I could relieve you of your destiny.
I wish I could relieve you of your fate.
I wish I could relieve you of your illness.
I wish I could relieve you of your life.
I wish I could relieve you of your death.
But it's always
Silence at the end of the phone
Silence at the end of the phone.
Silence at the end of the phone. (144)

The echoing silence in each instance is a harbinger of death, of the sense of aloneness inflicted upon outcasts in life, and of the deadly effects of the normative real and its logic of just deserts. In taking up the case of the NEA Four, the Supreme Court would have to adjudicate between the normative real for which the conservative right fought so hard and the hyper-real real that the artists so variously performed. They would have to adjudicate, in other words, which bodies "mattered" and which bodies would be situated beyond the "vanishing point" of the normative real that confers visibility within the state.

Supreme Performatives

Just as in J. L. Austin's classic definition of the performative, the utterance of a sentence is the "doing of an action," to utter a ruling from the Supreme Court bench is to enunciate the law itself.[78] The performance of a judicial opinion and its performative effects cannot be distinguished from one another, as the very act of articulation constitutes the law of the land. When justices read their opinions out from the bench in what one observer of the court has dubbed "ceremonial showtime," they thus personate the law itself and perform a singular role in the administration of the legal system (Figure 24).[79] Through their rulings on the constitutionality of particular actions or statutes, moreover, they not only institute what the law is and what the law is not, but also articulate, as a consequence, what forms of conduct ought to be perceived as legal, legitimate, and licit and what forms understood as illegal, illegitimate, and illicit.

In examining the decision in *NEA v. Finley*, we ought to attend, then, not just to the manner in which Justice O'Connor delivered her opinion and thus

Figure 24. "Ceremonial Showtime" at the Supreme Court.
Photographs in the Carol M. Highsmith Archive, Library of Congress, Prints and Photographs Division.

instituted the law but also to the performative effects of her decision. Who is
interpellated into her performance as a legitimate subject by the rhetorical and
semantic provisions of her locution and who, in this case, is set decidedly outside the bounds of legitimacy? Even more to the point, we should ask, when
the government is granted the prerogative to act as patron and not sovereign,
what are the consequences for how the "American people" or the "American
public" are rhetorically constituted and pragmatically understood?

    In determining the constitutional validity of the "decency and respect" clause, 20 U.S.C. §954(d) (1)—that "general standards of decency and respect for the diverse beliefs and values of the American public" be taken into consideration in making funding decisions—the questions before the court were twofold. With respect to the First Amendment, the court was charged with determining whether the statute was "overbroad" and hence violated the right of freedom of speech. More specifically, the court was asked to decide whether NEA grants merely constituted subsidized speech, in which case the government would be construed as a facilitator of private expression and hence *could not engage* in content- and viewpoint-based discrimination, or whether NEA grants constituted government speech, in which case the government acting in the capacity of speaker was exempt from First Amendment scrutiny and *could engage* in content- and viewpoint-based discrimination in the expression of its views. With respect to the Fifth Amendment, the court was asked to decide whether the phrasing of the "decency and respect" clause was impermissibly vague and hence violated the right to due process. More specifically, the court was asked whether a reasonably clear meaning could be ascribed to either "general standards of decency" or to the "diverse beliefs and values of the American public" and, in any case, whether such a determination could be made on a basis that was not itself discriminatory. It is crucial to emphasize, moreover, that the "decency and respect" clause was passed *after* the artists' grants had already been denied and that this was a facial challenge that bore a heavier burden. While issues of standing would nag at the decisions and at times detract from the issues at hand, especially since both Holly Hughes and Tim Miller applied for and received NEA grants in 1991, the case as it came before the Supreme Court was specifically about the permissibility of the statute "on its face" and hence did not require a specific instance of alleged discrimination to be justiciable.[80]

While these are the questions that were put forward in the case, Supreme Court proceedings are, in the event, never solely or even wholly about the immediate issues at hand. Indeed, every case that comes before the court represents an opportunity to buttress, undermine, amend, affirm, or overthrow a set of legal precedents or principles, which not only derive their force from but also contribute to the articulation of a broader vision of the role of government and governmentality in American society. The filings that composed the docket leading up to oral arguments in *NEA v. Finley* are no exception to this general rule, as they provide a clear sense not only of the local stakes in the case but also of the case's larger role as a site of political contestation over which bodies public could and/or should be said to be represented in a democratic society by a democratically elected government. To the extent that all parties to the case looked to shape and influence the law, we can gain a better understanding of these larger stakes and of the antithetical theories of government the various parties and constituencies embraced by examining both their reasoning and the performative repertoire of precedents that they marshaled as evidence to support their positions in advance of oral arguments at the Supreme Court.

Amici for the NEA: Rust v. Sullivan *as Precedent*

The most illuminating place to begin such an examination is with the amici briefs, for by formal convention "friends of the court" are constrained not only to articulate the lineaments of the constituencies that they claim to represent but also to announce the particular assemblage of interests of those groups in the case. Amicus briefs may be submitted to the court either in concert with, or as supplementary to, those of the parties to the case—the petitioner and the respondent. But they may also, as in one telling instance in the NEA case, be submitted, by permission of the court, over and against the objections of the party with which they claim to side.[81] Not insignificantly, moreover, and certainly echoing the findings in previous chapters, the announcement of an interest in a case and the intent to file an amicus brief often provides an occasion for a group to raise its profile, to cultivate and attract new members and affiliates, and to raise funds to support its activities.[82] As each group works to influence the decision of the court by magnifying certain issues while eliding or diminishing the importance of others, they literally stage themselves as "bodies public" and present carefully choreographed performances of contending interests. In the NEA case, the stakes were thus revealed, precisely and ironically so, in the manner in which each amicus brief lay claim to, and styled itself as representative of, the "diverse beliefs and values of the American public."

Paradoxically, most of the organizations that cast themselves as on the side of the NEA, which acted as the petitioner in the case, also represented themselves as, at best, begrudging supporters of federal funding for the arts. Thus, the American Center for Law and Justice (ACLJ), states upfront that "because of its commitment to defending the family, [it] opposes expenditure of federal funds for arts programs in circumstances in which the financial means to provide such aid is a reliance on taxation of individuals and families." Since it would be difficult to imagine circumstances under which a federally funded program would not depend to some extent on taxpayers' dollars, the better alternative in the opinion of the ACLJ would be to abolish federal funding of the arts altogether. "Confronted," however, "by the de facto existence of such continuing programs of federal financing of art," the ACLJ pronounces, "the restrictions on arts funding that are at issue here . . . appropriate and constitutionally permissible."[83]

Setting aside the question of whether the arts should or should not be funded by the federal government, what is significant here and elsewhere in the amici for the NEA is the extent to which taxpayers are presumptively construed as a homogenous majority and in particular as a vast Christian majority. Thus, Morality in Media baldly advocates that if the criteria for funding the arts need to be made less vague, then Congress should simply act as it meant to act in the first place and add a proscription against blasphemy, a transgression which, they are keen to note, is a "common law crime."[84] In their view, the passage of the NEA amendment was clearly aimed at works such as the "Serrano (Piss Christ abomination) and the Mapplethorpe (Bull Whip Homoerotic) production" (at *2). Since Mapplethorpe's works would surely be proscribed, they reasoned, under current obscenity laws—a reasoning that, of course, strategically relegates Mapplethorpe to the realm of the obscene—that would leave Congress to deal only with those works like Serrano's, which "denigrated the dignity of a person believed by a majority of the American Public to be God Almighty" (at *8).

As shocking as it might be to find a blatant assertion of Christian sovereignty in a brief submitted to the Supreme Court, this articulation not only captures the general tenor of the amici submitted on the side of the NEA but also instantiates the body public that those amici claim to represent. Indeed, Morality in Media offers not one but two possible solutions to the "vagueness" problem, each of which privileges a homogenous Christian majority at its center. In the first instance, they not only argue, as above, for the inclusion of a blasphemy stipulation but in elaborating that position they also "urge[d] this Honorable Court to conflate the term 'Respect for the Diverse Beliefs and Values of the American People' to 'taking into consideration whether or not blasphemous'" (at *2). In the second instance, and drawing on the theory that "half-a-loaf is better than none," they remonstrate that if the vagueness of the phrase "respect for the diverse beliefs and values of the American public" is found to be "incurably overly broad," then the court should act to "save the balance of the language of 954(d)(1) simply by severing this believed to be vague language" and leaving the "general standards of decency" clause to stand on its own (at *10). In both instances, Morality in Media seeks to displace the troubling clause, "respect for the diverse beliefs and values of the American public," which lends itself all too easily, as the amici for the other side make clear, to a pluralistic rather than a singular interpretation and indeed could be read as at odds with, and indeed as contradictory to, the very idea of "general standards."[85] In advocating for the "decency" clause, Morality in Media relies, moreover, as do many parties in the case, on the standard dictionary definition of "indecency": "nonconformance with accepted standards of morality," making it clear that to advocate for "decency" was to privilege, without apology, a majoritarian perspective and to place a premium on common conformity against individual nonconformity. Through both arguments, Morality in Media thus seeks to substitute a Christian body public for "the American public" and hence its presumed moral "beliefs and values" in place of the inchoate and threateningly heterodox "diverse beliefs and values of the American public."

The idea of a threat to American morals and values is extended and amplified in the amicus brief submitted by the National Family Legal Foundation (NFLF).[86] The NFLF takes the tactic of impugning the integrity of the Ninth Circuit ruling in favor of the artists by contending that "what dr[ove] the decision [was] not legal scholarship, but opposition to religion and morality in the public sphere," and they accuse the appeals court of brandishing a "sword to remove morality from democratically enacted legislation" (at *2). In this manner, the NFLF not only suggests that the appeals court has usurped the rule of the majority as enacted through legislation, but also strategically leverages the longstanding tradition in American political discourse, as seen in the previous chapter, of situating religiosity both as under threat and as the last and best defense against the moral decay and inevitable devolution of the American nation. Arguing that "morality is the bedrock on which a free society maintains its existence" and lamenting the fact that "many in America have relegated to folklore the notion that morality is necessary or even possible in modern society," the NFLF points to AIDS as the "devastat[ing]" consequence of a "legacy of immorality . . . in our country" (at *5). Citing the latest Centers for Disease Control statistics on the frequency of unprotected sex among young people, they thus contend:

> Morality is not merely an esoteric notion for philosophers to discuss
> at their leisure, but rather it has a real impact on the quality of peo-
> ple's lives . . . and deaths. Artists who view themselves as

self-appointed prophets of a new morality are not the ones cleaning up the mess created by their libertine philosophies. If mainstream Americans protest the spending of public money on art that challenges conventional mores, it is because those same Americans and their children are paying and will continue to pay the long-term costs. If the right of self-determination does not include the right to refuse to allocate money to support speech reasonably associated with suffering and untimely deaths, then such a right is not very significant. (at *6)

Representing itself as arguing on behalf of "mainstream Americans" and "conventional mores," the NFLF deliberately enlists a populist rhetoric that pits itself against the elitist privilege and presumption of philosophers and aesthetes. The "mainstream" is construed here as being "[un]reasonably]" constrained to subsidize the supposedly immoral behaviors of those who do not conform to "conventional mores," as if those persons were not taxpayers and citizens as well. Even more significantly, through the oft-used, because sentimentally effective, metonymy of the "children," the future posterity of America is envisioned as in grave peril and, per the earlier citation of statistics, as at the mercy of those populations most affected by AIDS—homosexuals and intravenous drug users—whose promiscuous activities, they surmise, will set a bad example that will only encourage the youth of America to engage in unprotected sex and deprive future children of the security of a two-parent family. While this chain of logic may not hold up to scrutiny, it enables the NFLF rhetorically to represent itself and its constituencies as a vast and indeed transgenerational body public whose rights (and future rights) to self-determination have not only been trampled upon but who have been forced to act against their conscience both in having their taxpayers' dollars directed toward the funding of indecent and irreligious art and in having to clean up the "mess" of suffering and death, which in their account was the legacy of such immorality.

As Michael Cobb has pointed out, religious rhetoric of this sort is never simply "about religious belief and practice but rather also about nation and state building." In these contests, he observes, the most effective weapon wielded by the religious right to build a "national consensus" is the "potent appeal of the heterosexual family."[87] Accordingly, in the NFLF amicus brief, the intact American family comes to stand in for the American public, and queer art and its "libertine" producers are positioned as both alien to that body public and as a threat to its very well-being. Leveraging what Cobb has characterized as a rhetoric of persecution, the NFLF thus concludes:

> The First Amendment does not condemn American people to the unenviable position of endorsing what they cannot tolerate, for any art funded by the NEA necessarily bears the imprimatur of the American public. Principles of self-autonomy and of democratic government trump any imagined liberty interest at stake. The American people are entitled to exercise their freedom to use public funds in a manner consistent with their standards and values. To those who smear chocolate on their private parts in public, the American taxpayer is entitled to say, "Don't quit your day job, because we're not paying for this anymore."[88]

Imagined as a massive body public, "the American people" are envisioned here as under assault from indecencies that they "cannot tolerate" and that they are thus "entitled" to repel. Further, the interests of that vast public are not only found to "trump" those of any other "imagined liberty interest" but are grounded in and secured by "principles . . . of democratic government," an assertion that is significant not just because it asserts a majoritarian claim on the operations of democratically elected governments but also because in so doing it buttresses the standing of the precedent upon which the amici for the NEA almost uniformly argued the merits in *NEA v. Finley* must be decided: *Rust v. Sullivan* (1991), also known as the abortion "gag rule" case.

That the amici for the NEA almost uniformly cite *Rust* as the precedent to be followed in *NEA v. Finley* points sharply to the ways in which the case was both enmeshed in, and viewed as a potential threat to, the broader agenda of the religious right. In *Rust v. Sullivan*, religious conservatives had triumphed when the Supreme Court upheld regulations that "limit[ed] the ability of Title X fund recipients to engage in abortion-related activities," including providing patients with information about abortion, even if those patients specifically asked their physicians or family-planning counselors to do so.[89] A number of family-planning grantees and clinic doctors challenged those regulations on the grounds that they violated the First Amendment speech rights of both health care providers and their clients as well as the due process rights of those clients under the Fifth Amendment. In upholding these regulations, the Supreme Court found that they "did not impose viewpoint-discriminatory conditions on a government subsidy" and that "to hold that the government

unconstitutionally discriminates on the basis of viewpoint when it chooses to
fund a program dedicated to advance certain permissible goals, because the
program in advancing those goals necessarily discourages alternative goals,
would render numerous government programs constitutionally suspect" (at
*5, 20). In short, under *Rust*, the government was found to have exercised a
legitimate administrative right to engage in speech in funding Title X programs and in regulating the content of those programs. Further, insofar as
those "regulations did not penalize speech funded with non-Title X moneys,"
they were found not to impose unconstitutional conditions, that is, to in-
fringe upon the speech of others (at *5).

Legal scholars have vigorously debated the merits of the decision in *Rust*,
but almost all have identified the case as crucial to the development of governmental speech doctrine. Questions have been raised about the extent to which
the assertion of governmental speech doctrine may mask the promotion of
other government interests and to what extent government-sponsored speech
might distort the marketplace of ideas.[90] Others have argued, however, that
the doctrine of governmental speech simply allows the government to perform many of its necessary functions and, where appropriate, to advance the
interests and carry out the mandates of the electorate.[91] In the broadest reading, and in an interpretation favored, in particular, by the religious right, *Rust*
created an expansive license for the federal government to impose content-
and viewpoint-based restrictions on all programs that it funded, including
programs for AIDS education and, as the government argued in *NEA v. Finley*, NEA-sponsored awards.

Yet as David Cole, who would ultimately represent the NEA Four, has
pointed out, despite the fact that "*Rust* appear[ed] to support the Justice Department's position that government is free to restrict speech whenever it is
footing the bill," the court also acknowledged in its decision that "its reasoning does *not* mean that 'funding by the Government . . . is invariably sufficient to justify government control over the content of expression,'" and it
specifically identified "public forums and public universities" as sites where
"first amendment dictates restrict the government's ability to control expression even where it is subsidizing speech."[92] The decision in *NEA v. Finley* was
expected to hinge, then, on how speech came to be construed in the context
of a government-funded arts program, and, as the anxious and at times almost
ferocious tone of the amici for the NEA indicate, the case was thus perceived
as a potential threat both to the sweeping reach of government prerogative
created by *Rust* and to the decision's particular effects with respect to the

proscription of information about abortion, a threat that the religious right
was all too eager to foreclose.

In promoting *Rust* and the expansive powers it conveyed to the government, the amici for the NEA also had to take some care to discredit the claims
of competing precedents that might constrict the status and reach of governmental speech. Thus the ACLJ enunciates, "The nature of the federal arts
program is such that it is not a fit subject for analysis under this Court's public
forum doctrine. Rather, the grants and aid program administered by the NEA
is akin to, and its restrictions in funding are as sustainable, as the Title X regulations restricting abortion advocacy by recipients of Title X family planning
funds" (at *3). With this pronouncement, the ACLJ not only bolstered the
standing of Title X regulations and positioned *Rust* as the apposite precedent,
but it also swept away with great efficiency the court's competing public
forum doctrine. Public forum doctrine, which requires consideration of a plurality of voices and viewpoints, was thus eliminated by the ACLJ as a basis for
deciding the merits of *NEA v. Finley*, and privilege was granted instead to the
government speaking in one voice. In a series of subsequent statements that
are rhetorically effective not just for making their case but also, as *Rust* would
dictate, for promoting a view of government as a single agent acting in the
broad "public" interest, the ACLJ opines, for instance, "Like any other art
purchaser, the NEA is entitled to decide what it wants to purchase, and to
insist that it receives what it pays for." Further, and referring yet again to the
precedent set in *Rust* to illustrate its argument in *Finley*, the ACLJ confidently
writes, "Despite the fact that the funding (purchasing) decision relied expressly on the viewpoint of the provider's speech (anybody who would use
funds to counsel or refer for abortions was ineligible for funds), this Court
upheld the restriction because Congress was entitled to define the limits of its
family-planning program to ensure that it received (and could therefore provide to the public) what it paid for—family-planning services that did not
promote abortion" (at *4). In this manner, the amici in favor of the government took the occasion of *NEA v. Finley* not only to protect the particular
interests that prevailed in *Rust*, but also to promote a vision of government
not as sovereign of an inclusive and pluralistic body politic but rather as a
"purchaser" entitled to act in the interests of the majority, or bodies public,
that elected it.

Amici for the Artists: Rosenberger v. Rectors *as Precedent*

If the amici for the NEA invested in a vision of government that was beholden only to, and was understood to speak for, the supposed majority among the electorate, the amici for the artists advocated for an inclusive and pluralistic vision of government with a vested interest in promoting free expression. To make their case for the artists, these amici argued not only that the program for NEA funding met the private speech exception that was articulated in *Rust* but also that the more appropriate precedent to look to in determining the merits of the case was *Rosenberger v. Rectors and Visitors of the University of Virginia* (1995).[93] In *Rosenberger*, the University of Virginia was found to have violated the First Amendment speech rights of a Christian student organization when it refused to fund the activities of that group as it did all other student groups on campus. "The Court's point" in the case, as explicated by Robert C. Post, was that "when the state itself speaks, it may adopt a determinate content and viewpoint, even 'when it enlists private entities to convey its own message.' But when the state attempts to restrict independent contributions of citizens to public discourse, even if those contributions are subsidized, First Amendment rules prohibiting content and viewpoint discrimination will apply."[94] In short, in *Rosenberger*, the court upheld the findings of *Rust*—the ability of the state to determine content and viewpoint when it speaks—but also clarified those exceptional conditions under which speech, *even when* subsidized by the government, should be considered as part of a public forum and hence government may play no role in constricting speech. Among its many findings, then, the court ruled not only that the university's guidelines "violated the principles governing speech in limited public forums" but also that while, as dictated by *Rust*, the university could "regulate the content of expression when it is the speaker or when it enlists private entities to convey its own message," it "may not discriminate based on the viewpoint of private persons whose speech it subsidizes."[95]

In arguing their case, the amici for the artists in *NEA v. Finley* were quite adept both at bending these findings to their end and at expanding on the private speech exception and public forum doctrine. This allowed them tactically to avoid such hot-button issues as abortion and to reassure a court that might be concerned about the repercussions of its decision that a finding in favor of the artists would in no way imperil either the principles or the particular effects of *Rust*. Thus, Americans United for Separation of Church and State stated outright that the court could "strike down the [decency and respect] provision without expanding on its holding in Rosenberger v. Rector at the expense of Rust v. Sullivan."⁹⁶ Hedging their bets in their cause, they submit further that the NEA funding program constituted "a private speech exception to the Rust subsidy rule" and reminded the court that, as they had previously recognized in both *Rust* and *Rosenberger*, "Where a program has a significant expressive function or is expressly dedicated to enhancing free expression among private individuals by encouraging a diversity of views, and where that program touches upon a traditional sphere of free expression such as the arts, the government's ability to impose content and viewpoint conditions is severely curtailed" (at *2). In drawing distinctions between government speech and government-subsidized private speech, they thus argued, the court must consider "whether the overriding purpose or goal of the subsidy program is to encourage diverse views and enhance creative inquiry" (at *3).

To make their case for viewing NEA grants as part of a program to encourage free expression, Americans United returns, as do so many others on this side of the case, to the language in the agency's originating statute, the National Foundation on the Arts and the Humanities Act (NFHA, 1965). There, as the amicus is eager to point out, the express purpose cited for the founding of a National Endowment for the Arts was to "create and sustain not only a climate encouraging freedom of thought, imagination, and inquiry but also the material conditions facilitating the release of this creative talent" (at *5). At least rhetorically, then, support for the arts was thought at the moment of the NEA's inception to be not only a benefit to but also an investment in the best interests of the nation. The program, "unlike the one in Rust," the amicus thus expounds, "expressly expends funds 'to encourage a diversity of views from private speakers'" (at *5). Even further, they assert, there was nothing "to indicate that grant recipients somehow act as surrogates for government speech or are creating art for the benefit of the government" (at *5). Given that the NEA had itself acknowledged that "the funding program is not a mechanism for communicating government messages," there was no reason to conclude anything other than that "the NFHA Act has created a subsidy program in a 'traditional sphere of free expression,' such that the government is prohibited from attaching viewpoint controls on its expenditures" (at *5). The government, in other words, was to be viewed not so much as a "purchaser" of art as a facilitator of artistic expression.

By and large, the amici for the artists all follow this strategic tack of working first to map out the ways in which a decision in their favor would not only be entirely commensurate with the private speech exceptions afforded by *Rust* but would also recognize the ways in which creativity in the arts falls within the traditional sphere of free expression as delineated in *Rosenberger*. Having secured these precedents and assuaged any perceived threat to *Rust*, the amici then go on to the second and, in their view, the more important order of business, that is, to demonstrate the ways in which the "decency and respect" clause not only gives rise to an unconstitutional imposition of "viewpoint controls" but also functions as a locution that fails to articulate clear conditions that could be followed. In these portions of their briefs, moreover, the amici for the artists not only give voice to some of their most high-flying rhetorical flourishes but also give the fullest expression to the pluralistic ethos that both motivates their interest in the case and that starkly distinguishes their conception of the relationship sustained between bodies public and the body politic from that which we saw envisioned by the amici for the other side.

For the New School for Social Research and the Brennan Center for Justice at New York University School of Law, the difficulty with the "decency and respect" clause lay in the extent to which its enforcement was "contingent on conformity with the generalized notions of 'decency' and 'respect' imposed by a temporarily-constituted majority."[97] To convince the court that they should come down on the side of the artists, the amicus enlists the persuasive force of history—"from Plato's discourse in the Republic to the totalitarian state in our own times." Citing the persecution of artists in Stalinist Russia and Nazi Germany, for instance, they urge the court to remember that "it is precisely the capacity to remind us, again and again, that the world view of the transient majority is not the only world view that makes a free society's artists among its most important democratic practitioners" (at *4). If, as the amicus submits, "art, no less than philosophy, shapes the perceptions and attitudes that are antecedent to, and, ultimately, formative of, society's political activity," it follows that a vote against the artists would be understood as a political choice in favor of the tyranny of a perhaps not always enlightened majority over and against a pluralistic society (at *4). By framing their arguments thus, within the long arc of history, the amicus effectively offers the court a choice between guaranteeing their own place in history on the side of the judicious and the just or capitulating to the political will of temporarily constituted majorities.

Indeed, through their emphasis on the "transience" and "temporariness" of those majority views, the New School and the Brennan Center not only highlight the complex relationship sustained between bodies public and the body politic but also betray its temporal contingency: the "'prohibited perspective,'" they argue, is always only "whatever is the current viewpoint of the current majority" (at *5). Adverting once again to the proofs of history, they assert an "almost uncanny parallel" between the "criteria of 'decency' and 'respect' imposed on the NEA by Congress" and the "'sense of decency' and 'nothing disrespectful' standards imposed on art by the Council of Trent in the sixteenth century," a strategic demonstration of the ways in which religious orthodoxies not only change over time but have also been wielded against one another to no good end. To the extent that history thus demonstrates that "the very concept of 'indecency' has been a metaphor for majoritarian orthodoxy," they conclude that "Congress's employment of such criteria in the selective allocation of subsidies can be no more than an indirect way of imposing the majority's 'viewpoint' on a creative process dedicated to discovering new ways of seeing the world" (at *8–9). Once again, then, the brief suggests that were the court to ignore the dictates of history and to rule in favor of the NEA, it would at best be perceived as reactionary and at worst be remembered as the unprincipled instrument of an oppressive majority.

Where the New School amicus focuses on the problem of majoritarian rule and the tyrannous enforcement of conformity, other amici for the artists home in on the problem of reconciling the demand for "general standards of decency," with the mandate of "respect for the diverse values and beliefs of the American public." This tack is exemplified in the amicus brief submitted by Claes Oldenburg, Arthur Miller, Jasper Johns . . . Andres Serrano et al.[98] Like the New School's brief, the artists' amicus looks first to history, and in particular to the history of art, for its most persuasive points of reference. Reviewing the charges of blasphemy that were lowered against some of the greatest artists of the Italian Renaissance, the brief asserts, with reference to Jesse Helms's attacks on *Piss Christ*, for instance, that while it might be tempting "to dismiss such attitudes as the unenlightened views of the 16th and 17th centuries, recent history shows that artists are not immune from those who consider blasphemous the use of religious symbols in artistic expressions" (at *5). Later in the brief, the artists offer not only an extensive overview of important works that "have provoked objections to allegedly explicit sexuality or excessive nudity"—Michelangelo's *Last Judgment*, Rodin's *The Kiss*, Manet's *Déjeuner sur l'herbe*—but also a primer on the ways that artists "throughout history" have "traditionally experimented with what is new and unconventional . . . often compel[ling] the viewer to look at the world in new, often troubling, and provocative ways" (at *4, 13). Through these illustrative means the amicus thus

challenges and looks to persuade the court to demonstrate its own intellectu-
ally enlightened powers and to take the longer and more progressive view on
the case before them—to position themselves, in short, on the right rather
than on the wrong side of history.

While the lessons of art history thus provide *Oldenburg et al.* with an
opportunity to pose abstract questions about right and wrong, the brief is also
especially concerned with the problematic particularities of the new statute.
Confuting the many "commonsensical" arguments put forward by the opposition, they ask, "Is the same general standard applied in Kansas City and
New York City? If there are differing standards, who decides which standard
to apply?" (at *4). Their point here is that in a pluralistic society, where standards and values may differ not only from person to person but from city to
city and state to state, it would seem almost impossible, commonsensically, to
ascertain what "general standard" could or should be observed. Further, they
submit, if a "general standard" cannot be discerned, how much more trying
would it be to determine "which particular set of beliefs and values is to serve
as the standard for selection"? Thus, while they applaud the fact that "the statute recognizes that the beliefs and values of the American public are 'diverse,' "
they are compelled to argue nevertheless that "it fails to indicate which values
should prevail if respecting one set of values means offending another" (at *4).
In this manner, the artists' brief takes aim at the all-too-common presumption
of prevalence, that is, the habit of allowing the majority to elide or even suppress alternative viewpoints to impose a singular, majoritarian point of view.

Finally, in perhaps their most effective sally, the amicus brief invites the
court to carry out a thought experiment: "Imagine the results," they submit,
"if Americans were polled on their 'standards of decency' and their 'beliefs and
values' " (at *14). Such an experiment is designed to trouble the conscience of
the court, for it not only opens up a space in which to conjure the multifarious responses that would need to be recorded—as many different responses as
there are different individuals—but it also tricks the court into perceiving
how easy and indeed commonplace it might be to default to what each presumes to be the majority point of view. In effect, as the amicus concludes, if
"such vague statutory language as the 'decency' and 'respect' provisions mean
anything, they imply a standard of that which is accepted, traditional, and
orthodox" (at *14). Ironically, then, the amici for the artists agree with those
for the NEA that the statute as enacted was too vague—that given its practical
effects, it should have said what it meant. Yet, where the amici for the artists
protest that the statute is tantamount, among other things, to a proscription

against blasphemy, Morality in Media simply calls for the addition of a "blasphemy" clause.

In sum, while the amici for both sides lay claim to the interests of the American public, they each engage in distinct lines of advocacy and offer fundamentally different conceptions of government and its relation to the various bodies that compose bodies public and compose the body politic. On the one side, the amici for the artists emphasize the plurality of beliefs, values, opinions, and viewpoints of the American public. As an aggregate of bodies public, moreover, they make a strong argument for taking into consideration the pluralistic nature of a democratic society. In their briefs, the court is urged to imagine a community, an American public, that values difference, that is broad and capacious and inclusive rather than narrow and straitened and exclusive. Drawing, moreover, on the precedent of *Rosenberger*, the briefs ask the court in no uncertain terms to embrace what David Cole has termed a "republican vision of the first amendment," one that "recognizes the importance of protecting freedom of government-funded speech in those institutions that play a central role in the public and private dialogues through which we constitute ourselves as a community."[99] In this conception, all bodies are bodies public within the body politic and every body ought to have equal access to all means and modes of expression.

On the other side, the amici for the NEA envision the body politic as a mass reasonably governed by majority rule. Their interest in emphasizing the rulings in *Rust* is thus driven by a desire both to protect their gains in the fight against abortion and to expand the prerogatives of government speech. In this respect, they promote as a commonsensical truism the argument promulgated by legal scholar Robert C. Post that "it is precisely because *we* wish our government to exemplify and to advance the particular norms of *our* community that *we* relax these [First Amendment] requirements when the state is acting on its own account to support the nation's arts."[100] The presumption of the majoritarian perspective implicit in the use of "we" and "our" pushes to the margins any questions about how the community or body politic might be constituted otherwise as an amalgam rather than as a homogeneous mass. From this perspective, only those bodies that "exemplify and advance the particular norms" are perceived as bodies public worthy of inclusion and recognition in the body politic.

As a whole, the amicus briefs thus provide us with a broad sense of the various bodies public that considered themselves interested parties in the case. Each advocates for its own beliefs and values, even as they make the argument that those beliefs and values represent those of "the public"—singular and at large. The choreographed performances of these bodies public not only leaves open the question of "who" represents the American public but also magnifies the point that the claim to represent "the public" is precisely what is in contention: "the public" *is* the critical site of contestation. In ruling on the merits in *NEA v. Finley*, the Supreme Court would have to decide these larger questions both in a practical and a symbolic sense. Before it could come to that point, however, the petitioners (the NEA) and the respondents (the NEA Four) would have to submit their own briefs and arguments to the court.

Briefs

By the time a case actually arrives before the Supreme Court for oral arguments, almost all of the pertinent principles, precedents, and positions have been rehearsed at length both in the documents at the district and appeals court levels and in the briefs and amicus curiae submitted to the Supreme Court for consideration. In this regard, the performance at the bar almost seems pro forma, a kind of anticlimactic public display in which each side has the opportunity, in strictly observed intervals of just thirty minutes apiece, to reiterate its arguments and highlight the bases upon which it believes the case ought to be decided. By contrast, the freedom of the justices to ask any question that comes to mind often introduces an element of surprise and may even inject a charge of electrifying suspense into the performance. Indeed, as Lawrence Baum notes, the justices "often raise new ideas and arguments in their questions to the lawyers," and they frequently use the occasion to try to "shape their colleagues' perceptions of a case."[101] The performance at the bar is thus secondary in many respects to the performance on the bench. Under the prodding of the justices, oral arguments may result not only in the introduction of new ideas but also in the articulation of new principles of law. In *NEA v. Finley*, this was precisely the outcome, as under questioning, Solicitor General Seth P. Waxman, was guided by the justices to articulate what became known as the "art patrons rule." That rule, implicit to some extent in the NEA's brief but made explicit in oral arguments, would prove the basis, for good and for ill, on which the court would make its decision. To understand how the case and ultimately the decision swerved from some of the more substantive arguments that we saw rehearsed in the amici, we need to turn to the briefs of the petitioners and the respondents and to the oral arguments they presented before the court.

In the *Brief for the Petitioners*, Waxman essentially argues three points. First, he holds that the new statute only required that the "decency and respect" clause "be taken into consideration," that it "does not impose a categorical requirement," and that, as such, it was "non-dispositive."[102] While the assertion that the clause was virtually meaningless was, as Justice Antonin Scalia would point out, perhaps the most disingenuous protestation in the brief, it was not its most cynical. Rather, in his second point, Waxman argues that, if anything, it is the artists and not the NEA who have taken a stand against diversity. Pitting the implied elitism of the artists against a populist appeal, he writes, "Respondents cannot seriously contend that the NEA's efforts to increase advisory panel diversity beyond what was required in 1990, and thereby further broaden the perspectives that are brought to bear in the grant review process, amounts to a facial violation of the First Amendment" (*11). Thus leveraging the populist against the elitist and intimating that the artists objected to the inclusion of laypersons on artistic award panels, Waxman further impugns their character by suggesting that they were pressing their case in bad faith. "Respondents themselves," he opines, "who have received public funds for their artistic activities in the past, have no objection to public funding for the arts so long as its disbursement is based on criteria of artistic excellence and merit from which any consideration of decency and respect for the diverse American values and beliefs has somehow been excised" (*15). In this somewhat snide manner, Waxman suggests that theirs is not truly a principled stand for free expression; rather the artists were acting selfishly in their own interests without regard to "general decency." It is the artists in this rendition, then, and not the NEA who seek to trample upon the fundamental rights of others and to impose their morals and values upon "the public." Most significantly, in this construction, it is no longer a question of whether the art is "decent" or "indecent" but rather whether the artists themselves have even a shred of decency.

That question is implicitly placed on one side of the balance and is weighed against what Waxman situates as his third and most important point: constitutional considerations of the "public interest." Throughout the brief, we are reminded again and again that it is not only Congress's responsibility but also its right to act in the interests of "the public." Studiously avoiding almost all direct references to the congressional debate that preceded the passage of the amendments—perhaps because the language there makes it all too clear exactly whose interests Congress was looking to protect and which viewpoints it intended to prohibit—Waxman takes great care instead to focus attention on the prerogatives granted to Congress both by the Constitution and by the amended statute. Thus, he points out early in the brief that the "decency and respect" clause was only one among a series of amendments to the originating statute that were all passed at the same time. Amid the language that was added to the statute, for instance, there was also the pronouncement that "government must be sensitive to the nature of public sponsorship. Public funding of the arts and humanities is subject to the conditions that traditionally govern the use of public money. Such funding should contribute to public support and confidence in the use of taxpayer funds. Public funds provided by the Federal Government must ultimately serve the public purposes the Congress defines" (*4). While such high-flown rhetoric might easily be passed over as the usual boilerplate palaver, Waxman cites it strategically to enable a shift in focus away from the particularities of the case to more abstract constitutional concerns and principles of law that touch on the role of Congress and its obligations to "the public." The staccato iteration of all things "public" both in the passage above and throughout the brief works effectively, then, to drown out all other considerations and all other interests.

To further this argument, Waxman makes the bold but tactically advantageous decision to eschew both *Rust* and *Rosenberger* as legal precedents. Arguing that the NEA program neither subsidizes government speech nor creates a public forum, he steers the case instead toward a consideration of Congress's prerogative in shaping "public policy." In his account, the NEA program was "designed to provide a highly selective funding mechanism for artistic projects that are, from Congress's public policy perspective, most deserving of the public's financial support" (*14). Insofar, moreover, as "the Constitution vests Congress with the powers to authorize expenditures for 'the general Welfare of the United States,'" he asserts, "Congress has broad discretion to determine what consideration of public interest should govern the expenditure of public funds" (*15).

In these locutions, as we have seen throughout this study, "the public" is construed as needing no definition—it simply stands for the majority without having to say so explicitly—and the "decency and respect" clause is interpreted accordingly as merely providing some "commonsense basis for allowing some measure of public appreciation to play a role in a program for public funding of the arts in a democracy."[103] Avoiding the thorny issue of government speech, Waxman thus construes the case as simply a matter of using taxpayer dollars to provide "the public" with something it can "appreciate." To

this end, he argues even further that Congress is "entitled to considerable latitude in identifying the criteria that may inform the government's own aesthetic judgments under such a program" (*14). Thus personifying the
government as an agent "entitled" in and of itself and capable of rendering
judgments on behalf of "the public interest," he is able to conclude, "The
NEA program should accordingly be evaluated on the basis of the general and
overarching principle that Congress may selectively fund activities based on
criteria that it rationally concludes, within the confines of the First Amendment, take into account the public interest" (*15). While one can only imagine the horror that the great philosopher of judgment, Immanuel Kant, might
experience over these personified claims for rational and aesthetic judgment,
in *NEA v. Finley* they would ultimately provide the crucial conceptual apparatus for O'Connor's decision in the case.

In stark contrast to the pretensions to "the public interest" that riffle
through the solicitor general's brief, the respondent's brief for the NEA Four
studiously avoids any rhetoric about "the public" and, cleaving closely to the
arguments rendered by their amici, focuses instead on the "chilling effects" of
the amendments on free expression in a pluralistic society. Context, intention,
and the particularities of difference matter in this construction. Thus, where
the solicitor general scrupulously avoids the congressional record of debate,
the NEA Four cite it directly, noting especially the author of the amendment,
Representative Paul Henry, who proudly announced that the new language
would provide "a shell, a screen, a viewpoint that must constantly be taken
into account."[104] Underscoring Congress's purpose in this manner, the NEA
Four thus strive to make it patently clear to the court that the amendment was
not intended to be, and could not be interpreted as, merely hortatory. To the
contrary, they argue, the amendment was clearly meant to proscribe expression precisely by triggering the "statute's disadvantageous treatment" whenever a government official found something that, in his or her viewpoint, was
displeasing (*17).

From the perspective of the respondents, Waxman's claims for the "public
interest" were no more or less than disingenuous distractions designed to
force a political calculus in which the vast interests of the public were weighed
against those of just a few individuals. "Characterizing [the amendment] as an
effort to boost 'public confidence' in the NEA," they thus argue, "is simply an
effort to put a positive spin on the illegitimate aim of disfavoring and suppression of dangerous ideas" (*7). The NEA Four thus push back against the majoritarian logic that guides Waxman's arguments and press instead on the

inability of the new statute to provide clear guidelines for a pluralistic society. Accordingly, they write at length:

> One would be hard pressed to find two people in the United States who would agree on what the "diverse beliefs and values of the American public" are, much less on whether a particular work of art respects them. . . . Similarly, what standards of decency are "general standards of decency"? To the extent that they are even ascertainable, such standards of decency probably vary by generation, culture, ethnic identity, and geographical location. "Decency is likely to mean something very different to a septegenarian in Tuscaloosa and a teenager in Las Vegas." (*19)

Echoing their amici, the NEA Four enumerate just a few of the identity categories that might underwrite differing points of view, but even then, they suggest, identity is not always indexical nor is it necessarily indicative of the meaning of a particular artistic work. That is, of course, where the work of trained artistic professionals comes in and where "standards of artistic merit, like standards of academic merit, are informed by a common language and education in the relevant discipline, and are applied by experts trained to make professional judgments" (*20). In contrast, they note, there is no such "common core of meaning, and no profession whose historical task has been to make judgments about" general standards of decency or the diverse beliefs and values of the American public (*21). How is an artist to know, then, whether his or her work might offend a given person's standard of decency or trespass on that person's beliefs and values? The standard, in other words, was both "arbitrary" and "discriminatory" insofar as the default position would always only be a standard of conformity that militated against discordant, challenging, or heterodox ideas (*20). As such, the brief concludes, the amendment created an "unconstitutional condition" that "penalizes speech beyond the government program" (*21).

Oral Arguments

One might have wished that David Cole had had a greater opportunity to expound on these ideas and on the doctrine of unconstitutional conditions in his oral arguments, but a review of the transcript and taped proceedings reveals that he spent most of his time defending himself against court concerns both that he had registered unsupported allegations that the government was misrepresenting how it had applied the amended statute and that the respondents were pursuing a facial challenge despite the fact that, in the interim, a number of them had been awarded NEA grants.[105] Both of these issues cloud any extended hearing of the relevant issues, and the justices' obvious impatience and sheer incredulity seem to throw Cole somewhat off balance.

These distractions notwithstanding, Cole does manage to make a strong argument that *Rosenberger* applied to the case at hand and that the case was essentially about the illegitimate application of viewpoint discrimination in a public forum where the government was "subsidizing private speakers speaking for themselves" (*9). Cole is consistent on this point over the duration of his presentation, quite clearly arguing and then firmly reiterating the position that "it is unconstitutional for the Government to set up the funding program to fund private speech broadly and then to exclude recipients based on their viewpoint" (*15). But he also makes what I take to be a critical and indeed telling misstep and one that betrays and then concedes all of the assumptions about queer subjects that drove the case in the first place. In response to questions from Justice Stephen Breyer as to when the government might be able to exert a viewpoint, he concedes, "You could imagine a situation in which it would be appropriate or not unconstitutional to deny civil rights protections to gays and lesbians, but the breadth of the statute, the application of it across the board . . ." (*15). Though Cole is cut off here before he can expound on this line of thought, it would seem that the damage is done. In arguing a case in which the founding claim was that the artists had been discriminated against precisely because of their investments in queer perspectives on gender and sexuality, he basically stipulates that under certain circumstances it would be perfectly constitutional to discriminate against gays and lesbians. To be sure, we could split hairs and argue that the amendment applies to viewpoints and not persons, or that there is no federal statute in the United States (then or now) that prohibits discrimination on the basis of sexual orientation. At the end of the day, however, the historical record makes it patently clear that the "decency and respect" clause was motivated by anxieties over gay and lesbian sexuality and would never have been passed if it were not already assumed that gays and lesbians could be discriminated against and, as Cole himself concedes, could be denied civil rights protections. At a crucial moment in his argument, then, Cole acceded to the normative real for which his opponents advocated and that his clients contested and in a perverse sense virtually licensed the decision that the court would ultimately make.

If Cole found himself on his heels, Waxman, who argued first, leaned in and, with the aid of a helpful line of questioning from the bench, finished strong. At first, Waxman was keen to follow up on points of argument in his brief to remind the court that "three of the five plaintiffs in this case received grants under the standard that they had concluded was unconstitutional" and to assert that it thus followed that the NEA had addressed the question of diversity sufficiently by augmenting the diversity of NEA panels (*4–5). The justices, however, seemed rather unimpressed by these lines of argument, and indeed a number of them expressed considerable skepticism at his rather audacious claim that Andres Serrano would not be disadvantaged under the terms of the new statute were he to apply for a grant (*6).

All was not lost, however, as the bold claim itself acted as a kind of provocation. Indeed, Justice Scalia found himself so annoyed that he jumped in soon thereafter to express his disappointment that Waxman would level such a sophistic claim rather than just come out and say that "the Government doesn't have to buy Mapplethorpe pictures to hang up itself, and so also when it funds the arts, it doesn't have to fund Mapplethorpe, and it can say we don't like Mapplethorpe" (*7). Pressed by Scalia as to why he would assume that such an action would be unconstitutional, Waxman finally apprehends Scalia's line of questioning and agrees that "in the unique circumstances of public arts funding, unlike the very different context in Rosenberger, viewpoint distinctions may be constitutionally defensible" (*8). At this point, the argument takes an even more interesting turn, as another Justice jumps in to suggest at length:

> So, you in effect are saying, I'm not going to rest my argument on the claim that the Government is hiring anyone to speak here, or that what it's doing bears an analogy to that, or that in fact the Government is buying art, or that it bears an analogy to that.
>
> You're really saying there's a third rule, the Government—the Government as distributor of largesse to the arts, and that, that's a third rule, but you're not saying that the Government is either the speaker or the buyer. (*8)

Picking up on Waxman's rejection in his brief of both *Rust* and *Rosenberger* as precedent, the question shifts the emphasis of the discussion to his arguments for the exercise of Congress's prerogatives in shaping public policy. Accordingly, Waxman proceeds to compare the government to the Medicis, "behaving as Governments and sovereigns as arts patrons *always have*" when they "bought and funded what they liked" (emphasis mine, *8). When he is asked directly whether he is "saying there is an art patrons' rule," he understood that the obvious answer to offer at this point is "yes . . . and for a variety of reasons" (*8–9).

In this manner, Waxman manages through oral arguments to carve out a special category for arts funding that was based in a long history of sovereign patronage with all the connotations that that might carry. Grounded in the "always have" logic of a mythic time immemorial, Waxman's utterance and his invocation of the Medicis at once conjure a kind of nostalgia for an age when, as theorist Michel Foucault explains, sovereigns wielded the "right to *take* life or *let* live," and at the same time lays the groundwork for a subsequent response that situates government in the modern role of what Foucault terms the "calculated management of life."[106] His arguments thus come to rest neither on the majoritarian argument, which requires fealty to "the public interest," nor on the pluralistic argument, which requires attendance to a diversity of views and viewpoints. Rather, the "art patron's rule" extends the nascent line of thought in Waxman's brief, transforming the government into the likeness of a person—a sovereign person not a sovereign government—who may capriciously pick and choose what he or she likes. This was a critical turn in the proceedings, for the "art patrons rule," as I shall demonstrate below, would enable Justice O'Connor in her final disposition of the case both to deploy a heteronormative cultural logic in adjudicating the standing of various bodies public and at the same time to appear, as Justice Scalia's concurrence and Justice Souter's dissent are only too happy to point out, to evade many of the larger political stakes of the conflict.

The Decision

In rendering the first part of her decision, Justice O'Connor casts aside the artists' claim that the "decency and respect" clause would require the rejection of "any artistic speech that either fails to respect mainstream values or offends standards of decency" in favor of the NEA argument that "the provision is merely hortatory and . . . stops well short of an absolute restriction."[107] To arrive at this conclusion, O'Connor not only accepts the premise tendered by the petitioner that the statute aimed only at "reforming procedures rather than precluding speech"—that is, it required only an administrative increase in the diversity of NEA panelists—but also cruelly marshals the respondents' own arguments on diversity to use against them. Thus, she writes, if, as the respondents claim, "one would be hard-pressed to find two people in the United States who could agree on what the 'diverse beliefs and values of the American public' are," then undoubtedly the more diverse panels organized by the NEA would ensure that the statute could not "engender the kind of directed viewpoint discrimination that would prompt this Court to invalidate the statute on its face" (*12). In this light, she rules that the statute imposed "no categorical requirement" and that, as such, it was "unlikely" that viewpoint-based discrimination would occur (*12). As if to prove her own point and to support her pronouncement that the court would be "reluctant . . . to invalidate legislation 'on the basis of its hypothetical application to situations not before the Court,'" O'Connor later notes, following Waxman's arguments closely, that at least "two of the individual respondents received NEA grants" (*12, 14). Following this logic, she thus concludes this section of her decision with the pronouncement that "unless and until §954(d)(1) is applied in a manner that raises concern about the suppression of disfavored viewpoints . . . we uphold the constitutionality of the provision" (*14).

If that were where the decision ended, we might think that even though O'Connor had denied the claim in this case, she had also established a precedent upon which a future challenge might be mounted. Indeed, as legal scholar Barry J. Heyman has pointed out, O'Connor's ruling in *Finley* was the "first time" the court stated that "the First Amendment places limits on the government even when it acts as patron." Further, "in interpreting the Decency Clause, Justice O'Connor said that under the First Amendment, awards to artists whose work might be considered 'indecent or disrespectful' could not be discriminated against."[108] An applied challenge could *in theory* be raised on these bases at some future date.

This theoretical possibility was certainly enough to leave Justice Scalia fulminating in his concurrence over how O'Connor had "gutt[ed]" the statute in order to save it and, in effect, "emasculated" a law that, in his judgment, provided for a perfectly constitutional form of content- and viewpoint-based discrimination (*15, 18). In Scalia's view, any interpretation that displaced the burden of the statute into a mere modification of NEA procedures—increasing the diversity of awards panels, for instance—was nonsensical and indeed a willful abrogation of the text as it was written. Not only did the Congressional Record make it perfectly clear that the amendment was aimed at denying public funding "to offensive productions as Serrano's 'Piss Christ,' the portrayal of a crucifix immersed in urine, and Mapplethorpe's show of lurid

homoerotic photographs" but such an intent, in Scalia's opinion, was "perfectly constitutional" (*15–17). Taking the majoritarian perspective we have
seen put forward in this case, Scalia argued that since there were other (private) sources for funding the arts than the NEA, "the Government [could]
earmark NEA funds for projects it deems to be in the public interest without
thereby abridging speech" (*17–18). Even further to this effect, he asserts at
length:

> It is the very business of government to favor or disfavor points of
> view on (in modern times at least) innumerable subjects—which is
> the main reason we have decided to elect those who run the govern-
> ment, rather than save money by making their posts hereditary. And
> it makes not a bit of difference, insofar as either commonsense or
> the Constitution is concerned, whether these officials further their
> (and, in a democracy, our) favored point of view by achieving it di-
> rectly (having government-employed artists paint pictures, for ex-
> ample, or government-employed doctors perform abortions); or by
> advocating it officially (establishing an Office of Art Appreciation,
> for example, or an Office of Voluntary Population Control); or by
> giving money to others who achieve or advocate it (funding private
> art classes, for example, or Planned Parenthood). None of this has
> anything to do with abridging anyone's speech. (*18)

With his references to abortions and Planned Parenthood, Scalia not only
deliberately bolstered *Rust* but also the theory of government speech embodied in that decision and supported by those amici in favor of the NEA who
understood the case as putting *Rust* at risk. The government, as he earlier put
it, could, as monarchs had done in the past, "deem" what it took to be "the
public interest," as by virtue of election "their" opinions become "our" opinions, and government becomes representative of a collective "we" that elides
dissent and the problem of either inclusive or pluralistic representation. For
Justice David Souter, by contrast, this set of assumptions was precisely what
made the law unconstitutional.

Ironically, Souter's and Scalia's readings of the statute are quite similar. In
essence, they both believe that it calls for viewpoint-based discrimination;
only Scalia thinks it "perfectly constitutional" where Souter thinks it utterly
unconstitutional. Further, where Scalia takes the majoritarian view advocated
by the amici for the NEA, Justice Souter takes the more pluralistic approach

favored by the amici for the artists and critiques the majoritarian thrust of both the amendment's enactment and Scalia's opinion. While in theory, he observes, the amendment "penalizes any view disrespectful to any belief or value espoused by someone in the American populace. Boiled down to its practical essence, the limitation obviously means that art that disrespects the ideology, opinions, or convictions of a significant segment of the American public is to be disfavored, whereas art that reinforces those values is not" (*21). Using the same example as Scalia, Souter writes, "After all, the whole point of the proviso was to make sure that works like Serrano's ostensibly blasphemous portrayal of Jesus would not be funded . . . while a reverent treatment, conventionally respectful of Christian sensibilities, would not run afoul of the law. Nothing," he concludes, "could be more viewpoint based than that" (*21). To make this point clear in his dissent, Souter strategically employs the tactic of substituting what could be considered mainstream values or patently discriminatory language in the phrasing of the statute—"taking into consideration the centrality of Christianity to the American cultural experience" or "'taking into consideration the superiority of the white race"—to illustrate the implicit claims of the statute and in this manner makes it abundantly clear how the statute and O'Connor's decision in support of it ultimately precludes nonconformity and instantiates normative values (*23).

Even more significant for Souter was not just that O'Connor's decision essentially legitimated viewpoint-based discrimination, but that it did so by "liberat[ing] government-as-patron from First Amendment strictures not by placing it squarely within categories of government-as-buyer or government-as-speaker, but by recognizing a new category by analogy to those accepted ones" (*23). In so doing, as Randall Bezanson has pointed out, the decision raised the curious question, "How can we know when government is acting as speaker or as regulator of speech, as patron or as sovereign?"[109] Bezanson calls "the transformation" effected by O'Connor's decision "subtle and obliquely accomplished," as in making its arguments it "transform[ed] government's role from that of regulator of private speech to that of speaker and thus escap[ed] the established First Amendment rules that apply to government regulation of speech, rules that the NEA amendment otherwise could not satisfy."[110] Even more particularly, "As patron, the Court implied, government is acting in a quasi-private capacity in the speech . . . marketplace."[111] This seems to be the larger, critical point that Scalia misses amid his tirade. For while O'Connor's decision may betray the possibility of a future challenge, its rhetorical thrust suggests that the decision has more in common with Scalia's arguments than Scalia would like to admit. Indeed, if the decision raises the possibility of a challenge in the first part, the latter parts in which O'Connor articulates the "patron not sovereign" doctrine make it all too clear that such challenges would not be given weight. In focusing so much of his attention on the earlier part of O'Connor's decision, Scalia failed, in short, to note how O'Connor's distinction between government as patron and government as sovereign in the final part of her opinion not only extended the heteronormative impetus that shaped the statute in the first place but, in doing so, also instituted a far subtler provision for content- and viewpoint-based discrimination.

As students of the earlier periods will almost immediately recognize, to cast the government in the dual role of "patron" and "sovereign" harkens back to what Ernst Kantorowicz has deemed the "mystic fiction" of the "King's Two Bodies."[112] Under this medieval and early modern conception of kingship, the powers of the sovereign were understood to reside both in the material body of the king, that is, in the body personal or natural, and in the abstract or invisible body politic, which exceeds and indeed transcends the mortal coils of any particular king. By reaching back to this medieval model of kingship and providing for a set of conditions under which the government of the United States might be able constitutionally to effect such a division within itself, Justice O'Connor raised the question not only of when the government might perform its functions in the capacity of "patron" and when in the capacity of "sovereign" but also, and more crucially for this discussion, of who or what the government might represent in each capacity.

As I have demonstrated throughout this chapter, distinctions between and the representational status of both the sovereignty of government and the sovereignty of the people lay at the heart of the case and were intensely argued not only by the plaintiffs and respondents but also in the amici briefs submitted on their behalves. Ought the government to be construed at all times as acting in its public capacity as the representative embodiment of an inclusive sovereignty figured in the all-encompassing "We the People" of the body politic, or was it entitled in this instance, and perhaps in others, to exercise prerogatives more akin to those of the body personal of a private patron, in which case a sovereign government may act exclusively in the interests of the majority that elected it? By coming down in favor of this latter conception of sovereignty, that is, of sovereign as "patron," O'Connor's decision not only gave the lie to the abstract, rhetorical ideal of an inclusive body politic, but it also provided for a practice whereby various bodies public might be differently valued according to the whims of a government acting in the capacity of a body personal.

If we return now to the phrase that concludes O'Connor's statement, the performative effects of her pronouncement are that much more clear. For in declaring that "when the Government is acting as patron rather than as sovereign, the consequences of imprecision are not constitutionally severe," O'Connor essentially ruled that since only a small number of persons might be affected by the imprecision of the "decency and respect" clause, government as patron need not concern itself with the issue of content- or viewpoint-based discrimination. In this sense, her rhetoric is akin in spirit if not in kind to the heteronormative cultural logic that held that the government need not be concerned about the impact of AIDS unless and until it became a threat to the "general public." Government in O'Connor's decision was understood not so much as a public entity facilitating private speech as a private entity speaking in public, buying or funding, in the capacity of private patron, anything that it might like and rejecting anything that it did not. The idea of representative government, whether majoritarian or pluralistic in its outlook, was utterly suspended by this act of privatization. In sum, by instituting a distinction between patron and sovereign, Justice O'Connor not only extended a normative cultural logic but in doing so also found a novel way to introduce into American law a principle for distinguishing among various bodies public that at once harkened back nostalgically to what Foucault termed the ancient sovereign power over death and at the same time created a new instrument for modern biopower's management of life. As such, the so-called "art patron's rule" not only sustained a proscription against queer bodies in performance, it also effected a more general proscription against the performative presence of those same bodies in the political and public spaces that constituted the normative real of late twentieth-century America.

Notes

---

1. Barish, *The Antitheatrical Prejudice*, 2.

2. For a useful summary of theoretical and documentary work done at the intersections of anthropology and performance, see Carlson, *Performance: A Critical Introduction*, esp. chapter 1. As Carlson writes, while there may be some disagreement about "what performance accomplishes and how it accomplishes this . . . there has been general agreement that within every culture there can be discovered a certain kind of activity, set apart from other activities by space, time, attitude, or all three, that can be spoken of and analyzed as performance" (13). Especially influential work in this line of scholarship includes Turner, *From Ritual to Theatre: The Human Seriousness of Play* and *The Anthropology of Performance*; Geertz, *The Interpretation of Culture* and *Local Knowledge*; and Schechner, *Between Theater and Anthropology* and *Performance Theory*.

3. Barish, *Antitheatrical Prejudice*, 4. It should be said, however, that throughout his study and despite his overarching claim, Barish himself implicitly acknowledges many of these "local considerations," writing amid one discussion, for instance, "One recurrent feature of the history of theater is the fact that outbursts of antitheatrical sentiment tend to coincide with the flourishing of the theater itself. The stage provokes the most active and sustained hostility when it becomes a vital force in the life of a community. It is then that its own values seem most dangerously to collide with the received values of church and state" (66).

4. Others, of course, have made this claim about antitheatricality's instrumental purpose with respect to particular historical controversies, but no one has essayed to describe it as an essential, rather than merely incidental, characteristic of antitheatrical discourse. For two important studies—the one material and political and the other philosophical and theoretical—that examine antitheatrical discourse and its instrumental aims in their respective periods, see Howard, *The Stage and Social Struggle in Early Modern England*, esp. 22–46; and Puchner, *Stage Fright: Modernism, Anti-Theatricality and Drama*.

5. Prynne, *Histrio-Mastix*, 8.

6. For Augustine's and Tertullian's seminal antitheatrical writings, see respectively *Concerning the City of God Against the Pagans,* and *De Spectaculis.*

7. Tracy C. Davis and Thomas Postlewait, in their introduction to *Theatricality*, have succinctly summarized this antitheatrical tradition: "So, while the theatre reveals an excessive quality that is showy, deceptive, exaggerated, artificial, or affected, it simultaneously conceals or masks an inner emptiness, a deficiency or absence of that to which it refers. Plato, Saint Augustine, Tertullian, Puritan pamphleteers, Rousseau, Nietzsche, and many others have presented a series of indictments against the theatre and theatricality on this basis" (5). But they also advise

us to "keep in mind that a very wide range of positive and negative attitudes towards theatre and performance has existed throughout the cultures and societies of the world" (6).

8. For important discussions that both reflect upon and operate from this latter premise, see Bennett, *Theatre Audiences*; Butsch, *The Citizen Audience*; and Wiles, *Theatre and Citizenship*. This is also one of the premises from which Elizabeth Maddock Dillon proceeds in formulating her notion of the "performative commons," writing that for the revolutionary Atlantic eighteenth century, the theater was a space "at which large numbers of common (and elite) people gathered with regularity, and, thus, a space at which the body of the people was, literally, materialized. . . . The people not only gathered at the theatre, but also performed themselves as a people in the space of the theatre" (*New World Drama*, 4). Dillon's book came out too late for me to engage fully with its many provocative arguments, but suffice it to say that I find a great deal of resonance between her interest in tracing the ways in which playhouses across the eighteenth-century Atlantic world served as a kind of "performative commons" where the conflicts between the ideal, figurative, and representational notions of the populist "commons" and the palpably uneven and inequitable distribution of political rights could be staged, and my efforts over the course of this volume to articulate the series of breaches that are made visible in each antitheatrical incident between the abstract ideal of a transcendent body politic and the multiple and contestatory bodies public that jockey for political authority within and against that formation.

9. For illuminating work on the weighted, yet elusive idea of "the American people," see Frank, *Constituent Moments: Enacting the People in Postrevolutionary America*.

10. See Roman Jakobson's *The Metaphoric and Metonymic Poles*.

11. Jennifer Greiman is also interested in the metonymic force that lies behind invocations of the "public" in America and has located a similar dynamic in the conflicts that motivated and that were then played out through the Astor Place Riots in 1849, writing that "if such contests over the composition of the public were bitter and violent, this is because the public was understood less as a location or a field of action than as the form that grants that action legitimacy. The 'public' was not simply conceived as a common space that preceded the riots and the massacre, nor as a shared stage on which events spectacularly unfolded. Rather, the public became the form of sovereignty to which heterogeneous groups in conflict with one another made claim" (*Democracy's Spectacle*, 25).

12. As Warner writes early on in his study, "To address a public or to think oneself as belonging to a public is to be a certain kind of person, to inhabit a certain kind of social world, to have at one's disposal certain media and genres, to be motivated by a certain normative horizon, and to speak within a certain language ideology" (*Publics and Counterpublics*, 10).

13. Warner, *Publics and Counterpublics*, 16.

14. Warner writes, "The ideal unity of the public sphere is best understood as an imaginary convergence point that is the backdrop of critical discourse in each of these contexts and publics—an implied but abstract point that is often referred to as 'the public' or 'public opinion' and by virtue of that fact endowed with legitimacy and the ability to dissolve power" (*Publics and Counterpublics*, 55).

15. Meyer, *Outlaw Representation*, 28.

16. With these interests in mind, I have chosen deliberately not to focus on the passage of antitheatrical legislation or specific instances of state censorship, preferring to keep the focus instead on the many and multifarious nonregulatory bodies public whose emergence as a cultural and political force both within, and in counterpoise to, the ideal of the body politic have not yet been sufficiently attended to or indeed even recognized. For two well-known studies of

theater censorship and antitheatrical legislation, see, however, Connolly, *The Censorship of English Drama, 1737–1824*, and Thomas et al., *Theatre Censorship: From Walpole to Wilson*.

17. In the ensuing gap between my initial discovery and the publication of this volume, the manuscript has also been identified and written about by historian Mark Kishlansky in "A Whipper Whipped: The Sedition of William Prynne."

CHAPTER 1

1. Whitelocke, *Memorials of the English Affairs*, 19. A written record of "The Manner of the Progression of the Masque" is held in the Folger Shakespeare Library collections, Folger MS Z.e.1 (25), with selections reproduced in its Digital Image Collections at http://luna.folger.edu/luna/servlet/view/search?sort=Call_Number%2CAuthor%2CCD_Title%2CImprint&q=Call_Number%3D%22Z.e.1+%2825%29%22+LIMIT%3AFOLGERCM1-6-6&pgs=250&res=2.

2. Whitelocke, 18.

3. MS Eng 1359, Houghton Library, Harvard University, 202v–203. Unless otherwise noted, all citations of the Prynne trial of February 1633–34 will be from this version of the trial proceedings. Later in this chapter, I will discuss at length the differences among the various extant manuscript accounts of the trial.

4. The only sustained rejoinder to Prynne, Richard Baker's *Theatrum Redivivum, or the Theatre Vindicated*, existed solely in manuscript and was not published until 1662.

5. Kastan, "Performances and Playbooks," 169.

6. The response in printed or performed plays ranged from the circumscribed—Thomas Heywood referred briefly to *Histrio-Mastix* in both his dedication to *The English Traveller* (1633) and his address to the reader for *A Pleasant Comedy, Called A Mayden-Head Well Lost* (1634); James Shirley mocked Prynne in his dedication for *The Bird in a Cage* (1633); and William Strode satirized Prynne in *The Floating Island* (1636; printed 1655)—to the oblique—the seventh antimasque of William Davenant's *Temple of Love* (1634) featured a figure of libelous dissent who has been taken for Prynne; and Milton's *Comus* (acted at Ludlow Castle in 1634, printed in 1637–38) has often been read as a rebuke not just to Prynne and the Puritan forces but also to the aesthetic regime of the court.

7. The now disputed notion that Prynne's work marked the culmination of a Puritan antitheatrical movement first acquired a strong foothold in theater history with the publication of Edmund S. Morgan's "Puritan Hostility to the Theatre," and gained further traction with the influential account found in Barish's *The Antitheatrical Prejudice*, esp. pp. 80–83. More recently, however, theater historians have argued that the closing of the playhouses in 1642 had more to do with concerns about public order than with Puritan concerns over the immorality of playacting. See, for instance, Kastan, "'Publike Sports' and 'Publike Calamities.'"

8. Martin Butler, *Theatre and Crisis*, 96.

9. Annabel Patterson argues similarly that Prynne's case was "paradigmatic" insofar as the "law was forced to take particular cognizance of problems of interpretation" and questions "about how the state functioned as a 'reader' of texts" were brought forward in an extraordinary fashion (*Censorship and Interpretation*, 10).

10. See Gardiner, ed., *Documents Relating to the Proceedings Against William Prynne*; and *A Complete Collection of State-Trials* (1730). The account in *State-Trials* was itself drawn almost entirely from John Rushworth's supposed eyewitness and indubitably skewed account of the trial in his *Historical Collections* (1680).

11. The exception here is Cyndia Clegg's *Press Censorship in Caroline England*. I am indebted to Professor Clegg for her generosity in sharing her work in progress with me while I was a fellow at the Huntington Library in 2005–2006.

12. I discovered this manuscript at the Houghton when I was conducting research there in 2007 and presented many of my findings, detailed at the end of this chapter, at the Newberry Library Fellows Seminar in May 2011. As noted in the introduction, this manuscript has now also been identified and discussed by historian Mark Kishlansky in "A Whipper Whipped: The Sedition of William Prynne."

13. For influential work in this field, see Cust, "News and Politics"; Fox, "Rumour, News and Popular Political Opinion"; Zaret, *Origins of Democratic Culture*; Atherton, "The Press and Popular Political Opinion"; and Lake and Pincus, eds. *Politics of the Public Sphere*.

14. Heinemann, "Drama and Opinion in the 1620s," 261; and Balme, *The Theatrical Public Sphere*, 73.

15. Somerville, *Politics and Ideology in England*, 37.

16. Prest, *Inns of Court Under Elizabeth I and the Early Stuarts*, 211.

17. See Mary Hume Maguire, "Attack of the Common Lawyers on the Oath *Ex Officio*."

18. Prest, *Inns of Court*, 197.

19. For an excellent discussion of the kneeling controversy, see Ferrell, "Kneeling and the Body Politic."

20. Prest, *Inns of Court*, 229.

21. See also Martin Butler's "Politics and the Masque," where he similarly notes, "Normally masques were exclusive affairs and watched by only a narrow social and political élite, but the lawyers saw to it that their statement was addressed to a wider public: *The Triumph of Peace* is that unique object, a Caroline masque that reached both a courtly and a plebeian audience" (127).

22. See also Brent Whitted who observes, "The entire efficacy of the common law as a source of authority . . . depended on the manner in which the carefully choreographed spectacle simultaneously appeased the royal eye and mystified the public one" ("Street Politics," 9).

23. See Geertz, "Centers, Kings, and Charisma"; Bergeron, *English Civic Pageantry*; Mullaney, *The Place of the Stage*; and Knowles, "The Spectacle of the Realm."

24. Knowles, "The Spectacle of the Realm,"182.

25. Geertz, "Centers, Kings, and Charisma," 125.

26. Mullaney, *Place of the Stage,* 18.

27. Howard, *Theater of a City*, 4–5.

28. Judith Richards, " 'His Nowe Majestie' and the English Monarchy," 75.

29. Bergeron, *English Civic Pageantry*, 106.

30. Indeed, as R. Malcom Smuts notes, "It is remarkable how infrequently they employed cultural works to project a flattering image of the king to audiences beyond the court itself. With few exceptions, court theatricals, royal portraits, and panegyrics were created for a restricted society with access to the king's palaces. They would have been singularly ineffective vehicles for arguments aimed at a broad public" (*Court Culture and the Origins of a Royalist*, 5).

31. I borrow the term "scenario" here as theorized in Diana Taylor's *The Archive and the Repertoire*, pp. 28–33. "Scenarios," as Taylor explains, are to be understood in their most basic sense as, "meaning-making paradigms that structure social environments, behaviors, and potential outcomes" (28). The scenario extends both to a sense of physical location and to the embodiment of the social actors, and it forces us to "situate ourselves in relationship to it; as participants, spectators, or witnesses" (32). Moreover, as much as they "are formulaic structures that

predispose certain outcomes," they also "allow for reversal, parody, and change" in their play upon cultural memory (31).

32. Bergeron, *English Civic Pageantry*, 6.

33. Whitelocke, *Memorials of the English Affairs*, 20. For a theorization of the operations of performance memory and surrogation, see Roach, *Cities of the Dead*.

34. In Bentley, *The Jacobean and Caroline Stage*, v.1156.

35. Kevin Sharpe takes a similar view of the event and anticipates some of my comments below, writing, "The whole occasion was more evocative of an Elizabethan progress than a Caroline masque. The mob pressed and jostled to see—and it is clear that they were intended to do so. Consisting of beggars, cripples, birds and Northern pipers, part of the procession comprised a Brechtian visual antimasque which appears to have been staged consciously for an audience outside as well as within court" (*Criticism and Compliment*, 215–16).

36. Orgel and Strong, *Inigo Jones*, I.64. Lawrence Venuti elaborates: "Without a Parliament willing to vote him the subsidies he needed to cover his expenses, the king and his ministers developed independent sources of revenue by exploiting loopholes in the Statute of Monopolies, a parliamentary bill which prohibited patents to individuals in 1624" ("The Politics of Allusion," 197).

37. Carlson, *Places of Performance*, 19.

38. Whitelocke, *Memorials of the English Affairs*, 20.

39. For this description of the basic pattern of the masque form, I am especially indebted to David Lindley's "Introduction" to *The Court Masque*.

40. See, Lindley, *Court Masque*, 1; Orgel and Strong, *Inigo Jones*, I.1; Orgel, *The Illusion of Power*, 39; and Sharpe, *Criticism and Compliment*, 179.

41. Orgel, *Illusion*, 38.

42. Martin Butler, "Politics and the Masque," 122.

43. Orgel and Strong, *Inigo Jones*, I.66.

44. See Bevington and Holbrook, *The Politics of the Stuart Court Masque*, esp. p. 8.

45. Butler, "Courtly Negotiations," 28.

46. Butler, "Politics and the Masque," 121.

47. I have taken my text from James Shirley's *The Triumph of Peace*, in *A Book of Masques*, ed. Clifford Leech. All references to this text will be cited by line number. For information about the music for the masque, see Sabol, "New Documents on Shirley's Masque 'The Triumph of Peace,'" and Lefkowitz, "New Light on Shirley's *Triumph of Peace*."

48. See also Norbrook, "The Reformation of the Masque," 104.

49. Butler, "Politics and the Masque," 133.

50. Sharpe, *Criticism and Compliment*, 219–20. A notable exception to this general view on the artisans' intrusion appears in Barbara Lewalski's "Milton's *Comus* and the Politics of Masquing," where she takes the view that *The Triumph of Peace* "locate[s] the evils of social disorder in the lower classes" (313).

51. For this definition of the Brechtian *gestus* or "gest," see Diamond,"*Gestus* and Signature," 519.

52. Leech, "Introduction" to *The Triumph of Peace*, in *Book of Masques*, 279.

53. Whitelocke, *Memorials of the English Affairs*, 19.

54. Shohet, "Reading Triumphs," 71.

55. See Bentley, *Jacobean and Caroline Stage*, V.1162.

56. Ibid., V.1161.

57. Ibid., V.1154, Letter of Thomas Coke to Sir John Coke, 17 October 1633; V.1161.

58. Parry, "Entertainments at Court," 209.

59. Whitelocke, *Memorials of the English Affairs*, 21.

60. The OED locates the first usage of this term in 1631.

61. All citations are from the Huntington Library's Hoe copy of William Prynne, *Histrio-Mastix: The Players Scourge or the Actors Tragaedie* (London, 1633), and will be cited parenthetically by page number.

62. Postlewait, "Theatricality and Antitheatricality in Renaissance London," 105; Barish, *Antitheatrical Prejudice*, 86; and Orgel and Strong, *Inigo Jones*, I.51.

63. Barish, *Antitheatrical Prejudice*, 85.

64. Lake and Questier, *The Antichrist's Lewd Hat*, 438.

65. Spurr, *English Puritanism*, 87.

66. Lake and Questier, *Antichrist's Lewd Hat*, 345; Prynne, *The Vnlouelinesse, Of Love-Lockes* (London, 1628), 21. See also Prynne's *Healthes: Sickness* (London, 1628), a pamphlet in which he castigates those who apply themselves more avidly to toasting and drinking the king's health than to praying for it.

67. See Oldridge, *Religion and Society*, 1–20. On "Anti-Calvinisim" and "Arminianism," see Tyacke, *Anti-Calvinists*. On "Laudianism," see Lake, "The Laudian Style." For a brief summary of this problem of "nomenclature," see Webster, "Religion in Early Stuart Britain," 259.

68. Oldridge, *Religion and Society*, 33. See also Fincham and Lake, "The Ecclesiastical Policies of James I and Charles I."

69. Fincham, "Introduction," *The Early Stuart Church*, 5.

70. These included *The Perpetuitie of a Regenerate Man's Estate* (1627); *A Briefe Svrvay and Censvre of Mr. Cozens His Couzening Deuotions* (1628); *God No Impostor nor Delvder* (1629); *Anti-Arminianisme. Or the Chvrch of Englands Old Antithesis of New Armianisme* (1629; second edition much enlarged, 1630); and finally *Lame Giles His Havltings* (1630). For more on Prynne's earlier publications, see Kirby, *William Prynne*, 11–17.

71. *Stuart Royal Proclamations*, II.92.

72. See Hill, "Censorship and English Literature"; Siebert, *Freedom of the Press in England*; Milton, "Licensing, Censorship, and Religious Orthodoxy"; Towers, *Control of Religious Printing*; and Clegg, *Press Censorship*.

73. Towers, *Control of Religious Printing*, 9–10.

74. Clegg, *Press Censorship*, 98.

75. Milton, "Licensing, Censorship, and Religious Orthodoxy," 650.

76. Ibid., 634.

77. Ibid., 637.

78. Fincham, "Introduction," *Early Stuart Church*, 20.

79. Prynne was certainly not the first to draw upon the figure of the theater in composing an antitheatrical tract; see, for example, Gosson's *Playes Confuted in Five Actions*. As I will discuss later, Prynne clearly sought to play upon the popular conception of the world as "God's Theatre."

80. Ringler, "The First Phase of the Elizabethan Attack on the Stage." More recently, see Lake and Questier, *Antichrist's Lewd Hat*, 425–520; and Postlewait, "Theatricality and Antitheatricality."

81. For a documentary history and description of the London theaters during the Jacobean and Caroline periods, see Bentley, *Jacobean and Caroline Stage*, vol. vi.

82. Hackel, "'Rowme' of Its Own," 116.

83. It is worth noting that this moment in the epistles dedicatory marks one of the only references to actual playwrights in Prynne's thousand-plus-page tome; and even here they rate only an annotation rather than a direct mention, a fact that suggests Prynne's disinterest in actual plays and playwrights.

84. Farmer and Lesser, "Canons and Classics," 22–23.

85. Ibid., 23.

86. Lake and Questier, *Antichrist's Lewd Hat*, 429.

87. Halasz, *The Marketplace in Print*, 4.

88. Ibid., 184.

89. Taylor, *The Archive and the Repertoire*, 26.

90. Gurr, *Playgoing in Shakespeare's London*, 211. See also Martin Butler, *Theatre and Crisis*, 106.

91. Howard, *Theater of a City*, 4-5; Butler, *Theater and Crisis*, 110.

92. Heinemann, "Drama and Opinion in the 1620s," 261.

93. Butler, *Theater and Crisis*, 1–2. For more on Puritan involvement in theatrical commerce and the Puritan affinities of plays in the Caroline period, see Heinemann, *Puritanism and Theatre*, and Paul Whitefield White, "Theater and Religious Culture."

94. Kastan, "'Publike Sports,'" 216–17.

95. Henrietta Maria's appearances in court entertainments are thought to have prompted one of Prynne's more notorious indexical entries in *Histrio-Mastix*: "*Women-Actors,* notorious whores. p 162, 214, 215, 1002, 1003. Vnlawfull"; and many believed this entry motivated his prosecution. For more on Henrietta Maria's involvement in theatrical entertainments and the response to female actors in the period, see Veevers, *Images of Love and Religion*; Walker, "New Prison"; and Tomlinson, *Women on Stage.*

96. On the history of English Sabbatarianism, see Collinson, *Godly People.*

97. As Leah Marcus explains, "By placing their official stamp of approval on the old pastimes, James and Charles I attempted to extend royal power into an area of ambivalence and instability, to channel the equivocal status of popular festival into what we can perhaps call an official 'paradox of state'—a condition of happy ambiguity in which the license and lawlessness associated with the customs could be interpreted as submission to authority" (*The Politics of Mirth*, 3).

98. *The King's Maiesties Declaration to His Subiects, Concerning lawfull Sports to be vsed*, 7.

99. Marcus, *Politics of Mirth*, 5.

100. See Spurr, *English Puritanism*, 77, 88, and passim.

101. Marcus, *Politics of Mirth*, 14–15.

102. For more on the Puritan naming controversy, see Spurr, *English Puritanism*, 17–27.

103. Here I echo David Norbrook, who writes of *Histrio-Mastix*, "Criticising plays or masques was a way of indirectly indicating a general discontent with the state of the nation under rulers who seemed unaware of the dangers which Protestantism was confronting" ("Reformation of the Masque," 100).

104. For more on Laud's ceremonial policies, see Tyacke, "Archbishop Laud," and Lake, "The Laudian Style."

105. *Stuart Royal Proclamations*, 92.

106. Braun, *Juan de Mariana and Early Modern Spanish Political Thought*, 6.

107. Ibid, 9.

108. Douce MSS 173, flyleaf.

109. For three accounts of this sort, see Shuger, *Censorship and Cultural Sensibility*, chap. 8; Cressy, "The Portraiture of Prynne's Pictures"; and Patterson, *Censorship and Interpretation*, chap. 2.

110. See Clegg, *Press Censorship*, 164–78.

111. Pocock, "Texts as Events."

112. Love, *Scribal Publication in Seventeenth-Century England*, 33.

113. While cases involving royal authority began to increase during the era of Personal Rule, by 1634 the Star Chamber had not yet achieved its now settled reputation as an instrument and emblem of gross tyranny, abuse of power, and spectacular punishment. Indeed, Prynne's 1634 trial, and even more so his trial with Burton and Bastwick in 1637, constitute two of the major cases upon which that notoriety is based. For histories of Star Chamber that describe its less controversial origins, jurisdictions, and procedures, see Cheyney, "The Court of Star Chamber," and Barnes, "Star Chamber Mythology."

114. Discussions of the role of manuscript newsletters in the spread of information and in the cultivation of public opinion in the 1630s can be found in Cust, "News and Politics"; Fox, "Rumour, News and Popular Political Opinion"; Baron, "The Guises of Dissemination"; and Woolf, "News, History and the Construction of the Present."

115. Arber, ed., *A Transcript of the Registers of the Company of Stationers*, IV.207.

116. This account of how the case came about is disputed by some scholars who take Heylyn's and Laud's word that Laud had nothing to do with instigating the prosecution of Prynne. For more on these accounts and the need to revise standard narratives of Laud's vengeance and Prynne's martyrdom, see Kishlansky, "A Whipper Whipped," 608–9. How the prosecution came about does not materially affect my arguments about the circulation of competing accounts of the trial; indeed, the discrepancies in the reports only underline my point that the differing accounts were meant to cultivate differing bodies public.

117. I have collated the information that makes up this account from a number of sources, including Kirby, *William Prynne*; Lamont, *Marginal Prynne*; and Clegg, *Press Censorship*.

118. Rushworth, *Historical Collections*, II.220–41; *A Complete Collection of State-Trials*, I.396–406; Gardiner, ed., *Documents Relating to the Proceedings Against William Prynne*, 1–28.

119. Clegg, *Press Censorship*, 166–67.

120. Love, *Scribal Publication*, 78.

121. Clegg, *Press Censorship*, 167.

122. The full citations for these manuscript accounts are as follows: Tanner MSS 299, fos.123–134v, Bodleian Library; Stowe MSS 159, fos. 45–78, British Library; Eng 835, Houghton Library, Harvard University; HM 80, Huntington Library; and Douce MSS 173, Bodleian Library. According to Kishlansky ("A Whipper Whipped," 606, fn. 19), we can also add British Library Egerton MSS 253 and Cambridge University Library MSS D.d.6.23. I have not had the opportunity to examine these last two myself.

123. The variants in Bodleian Douce MSS 173, however, are remarkably similar to those found in British Library Stowe MSS 159, suggesting that one may have been copied from the other.

124. Clegg, *Press Censorship*, 167. Love writes, "Entrepreneurial publication is to be suspected whenever a text survives in two or more copies in the same non-authorial hand" (*Scribal Publication*, 77).

125. Kishlansky, "A Whipper Whipped," 611. There is little known about the provenance of this miscellany, except that it was delivered by Edward Jones Smith into the hands of Judy Masserene of Antrim Castle in Northern Ireland in June 1824 and was later purchased by the

Harvard College Library Fund in 1983. The mystery of who copied the records into the miscellany and when is compounded by the fact that it was copied in more than one hand. Other more speculative information about the provenance of this manuscript can be found at the Houghton in the unpublished typescript of a talk delivered by Theodore Hoffmann, the rare-book dealer who sold the manuscript to Harvard, to the Bibliographical Society of London in 1968 (typescript call number, 94M-46). My thanks to John Overholt at the Houghton, who facilitated access to this typescript for me.

126. For the comparative reading below, I have selected HM 80 because the Huntington manuscript was the first version of this variant that I had occasion to review and hence the version of this variant to which I compared the others.

127. Kishlansky, "A Whipper Whipped," 610.

128. State Papers (hereafter SP) 16/534, Document 71, f. 123. *The Passages Against the King and State in Histrio Mastix*, British National Archive, Microfilm, SP 16/534 Document 71, pp. 122–134v. A secondary heading, *Such also as occurre against the Churche & Clergie, in ye same Author*, appears both on the title page and again on f. 134v, but the collection of passages that may have followed is missing. It is unclear whether this section of the document was simply never finished or whether it was lost at some point. As Clegg has already noted, each of the seven sections in this document is composed of illustrative passages from *Histrio-Mastix* identified by page number and glossed for their significance in the margins, and followed by a summation of the "inferences" that might be drawn from those passages to construct a case of seditious libel (173–75).

129. SP 16/534, f. 134.

130. SP 16/534, Document 71, f. 123.

131. While I have reviewed the original manuscript, given its wider availability, it seemed appropriate to quote instead from Gardiner's published transcription of BL11764. All subsequent citations will be from this text and will be cited by page number.

132. *Statutes of the Realm*, "An Acte wherby divers offences be made high treason, and takynge waye all Sayntuaries for all maner of high treason," 26 Henry 8, cap. 13.

133. Lemon, *Treason by Words*, 3.

134. Ibid., 5.

135. Patterson, *Censorship and Interpretation*, 10.

136. That Herne's speech had been deliberately cut in HM80 becomes clear once again when Laud later refers to his claim that Prynne's crime was no more than an "omission of his dutie" (HM80, f. 49v).

137. Clegg, *Press Censorship*, 178.

138. As Cheyney explains, "by well established precedent," the Court of Star Chamber "possessed a power of punishment extending to all lengths short of the death penalty" ("The Court of Star Chamber," 741).

139. Sommerville, *Politics and Ideology in England*, 35.

140. This refers to the 1352 treason statute, 25 Edward 3, c. 2.

CHAPTER 2

1. For a cogent discussion of the ways in which the Glorious Revolution of 1688–89 could be considered "revolutionary" in all of these respects, see Pincus, *1688*.

2. See Houston and Pincus, eds., "Introduction," in *A Nation Transformed*, 2.

3. The exemplary revisionist text of this kind is J. C. D. Clark's *English Society 1688–1832*.

4. Houston and Pincus, *A Nation Transformed*, 10, 18.

5. For a useful history of the nonjuring church, see Hawkins, *Allegiance in Church and State*. While Collier and the nonjurors were adamant in calling James II's removal from the throne a "deposition," their political counterparts were careful to characterize his removal as an "abdication." For more on the terms of engagement and their significance in this political struggle, see Kenyon, *Revolution Principles*.

6. Jeremy Collier, *A Perswasive to Consideration*, 3rd ed., corrected (London, 1695), 22, 24. For an exhaustive account of Collier's essays, see Ressler, "Jeremy Collier's Essays."

7. Among Collier's pamphlets in the case were *A Defence of the Absolution Given to Sir William Perkins* (1696) and *A Further Vindication of the Absolution Given to Sir William Perkins* (1696). For just one response to Collier, see the anonymously written *An Answer to Mr. Collier's Defence of His Absolution of Sir William Perkins* (London, 1696).

8. Important work in this vein can be found in Barish, *Antitheatrical Prejudice*, 221–55; Krutch, *Comedy and Conscience After the Restoration*, 89–120; Hume, "Jeremy Collier and the Future of the London Theater in 1698;" and Kinservik, "Theatrical Regulation During the Restoration Period." In *The Emergence of Dramatic Criticism in England*, Paul D. Cannan takes a different approach to Collier, focusing on the author's significance as a literary critic and on the controversy as one that shaped the incipient style and substance of literary criticism as well as its professionalization and popularization as a discipline (83–108).

9. For an exhaustive month-to-month and then year-to-year catalog of the published exchanges in the Collier controversy, see Anthony, *The Jeremy Collier Stage Controversy 1698–1726*.

10. See Krutch, *Comedy and Conscience*, 89.

11. For an overview of these developments, see Lake and Pincus, "Rethinking the Public Sphere."

12. Spurr, "Religion in Restoration England," 433. For others who either note the shifting emphasis to lay religion and reform, or trace the emergence of policies of indulgence and toleration to earlier periods, see, respectively, Worden, "The Question of Secularization," and Mark Knights, "'Meer Religion' and the 'Church-State' of Restoration England."

13. For useful accounts of these developments, see Rose, *England in the 1690s*; and Harris, *Politics Under the Later Stuarts*.

14. See Pincus, "From Holy Cause to Economic Interest."

15. Worden, "Question of Secularization," 31.

16. Ibid., 32, 39.

17. Claydon, *William III and the Godly Revolution*, 3.

18. On Whig and Tory politics and ideology, see Rose, *England in the 1690s*, 64–69; and Harris, *Politics Under the Later Stuarts*, 152–61.

19. Knights, *Representation and Misrepresentation*, 20.

20. See De Krey, *A Fractured Society*, 279. See also Harris, *Politics Under the Later Stuarts*.

21. Knights, *Representation and Misrepresentation*, 6.

22. Ibid., 5.

23. John Brewer, "'The Most Polite Age and the Most Vicious,'" 345. The most influential and far-reaching critique in this vein can be found in Harold Mah's essay "Phantasies of the Public Sphere: Rethinking the Habermas of Historians." In a persuasive account, Mah contends that "the findings of social history suggest that Habermas's universal public sphere, based on an order of abstract individuality, entails a double fiction. Not only has there never been a public sphere that has been genuinely universal, there also has never been the kind of individualism

that it presupposes." He calls, then, for a "reformulation of Habermas's project for historians" that is congruent with the interests of this study in that he obliges historians not "to treat the idea of the public sphere as if it were or ever could be a real institution" but rather to explore what conditions enable "certain groups to make their social or group particularity invisible so that they can then appear as abstract individuals and hence universal" (168).

24. Alexandra Halasz demonstrates, for instance, that from its inception the market in print was never abstract, free, or indifferent but rather was engaged in "promoting certain interests and hostile to others" (*Marketplace in Print,* 163). On the coffeehouses as sites for both the proliferation and the "radical fracturing of the vast information exchange," see Love, *Scribal Publication in Seventeenth-Century England,* 194.

25. De Krey, *A Fractured Society,* 218.

26. The discourse of politeness has most often been associated in critical and historical scholarship with the Whig party, but increasingly scholars are noting that Tories, too, made use of this discourse to stake their claims to public affections. On Whiggish associations with the discourse of politeness, see Klein, *Shaftesbury and the Culture of Politeness,* and "The Political Significance of 'Politeness.'" For a more expansive assessment of its strategic use by both Tories and Whigs, see Knights, *Representation and Misrepresentation,* 53–57, and *passim.*

27. See Weil, "Matthew Smith Versus the 'Great Men,'" for just one account of the intense conflicts over how credibility could be produced during this period. Weil expands on these arguments in *A Plague of Informers.*

28. The phrase "fluid social assemblages" is derived from Bruno Latour's *Reassembling the Social: An Introduction to Actor-Network-Theory.* What I think Latour helps us to do in this case is to resist the interpretive impulse to reduce what are dynamic, complex, and often contradictory representations and to approach them instead as assemblages with multiple vectors, each of which anticipates but does not necessarily consolidate any one position.

29. See Kenyon, in *Revolution Principles,* who argues that both Whig and Tory ideologies were still very much confused and contradictory during this period. For an illuminating account of the types of ideological admixtures that emerged around party in this period, see also Schmidgen, *Exquisite Mixture,* esp. pp. 101–45.

30. Collier, *A Short View,* Preface, A2r–A3. All subsequent references to this text will be cited parenthetically by page number.

31. As Christopher Hill writes, "The Green Ribbon Club, established in London in 1675, may be regarded as the first party headquarters. Its green colours were those of the Levellers. The ghosts of the Interregnum were walking again" (*The Century of Revolution 1603–1714,* 199).

32. Backscheider, *Spectacular Politics,* 65.

33. Kinservik, "Theatrical Regulation," 47.

34. For works exploring these issues, see Canfield, *Heroes and States* and *Tricksters and Estates;* Owen, *Restoration Theatre and Crisis;* Nancy Klein Maguire, *Regicide and Restoration;* and Staves, *Players' Scepters.*

35. Hopes, "Politics and Morality in the Writings of Jeremy Collier," 160.

36. Hume, *The Development of English Drama,* 381.

37. Ibid., 380.

38. Hughes, *English Drama,* 331.

39. On the ludic qualities of theater, see Turner, *From Ritual to Theatre.*

40. See also Julie Stone Peters, in "'Things Govern'd by Words,'" who argues that Collier and other reformers took aim at figurative uses of language and the fragmentation of meaning that resulted from the emphasis on metaphorical play in Restoration comedies.

41. According to *The London Stage*, Parts I and II were first performed in May 1694 and Part III made its debut in November 1695 (Van Lennep et al., eds.). All three parts were first performed at Dorset Garden under Christopher Rich's management, and D'Urfey complained that the third part suffered from the inferior company of actors and singers that remained there after Betterton led a breakaway company to Lincoln's Inn Fields.

42. Hume, *Development*, 385.

43. Hughes, *English Drama*, 340.

44. Thomas D'Urfey, *The Comical History of Don Quixote, Part I* (London, 1694), Part I, I.i, p. 1), Early English Books Online (EEBO). All subsequent references to this text will be cited by part, act, scene, and page number.

45. Thomas D'Urfey, *The Comical History of Don Quixote, Part the Second* (London, 1694), EEBO.

46. See Claydon for the most extensive discussion of the various strategies adopted by William III to cast himself as a "providential ruler who had a divine commission to protect the protestant church in England, and to return the nation to is pristine faith, piety, and virtue" (*William III*, 3).

47. Illustrating his general interest in defending traditional hierarchies, Collier's other main preoccupation was with the treatment of persons of "Quality." In the conclusion to the chapter that immediately precedes Collier's attack on the four works under discussion, he harangues, for instance, "Must all Men be handled alike? Must their Roughness be needs play'd upon Title? And can't they lash the Vice without pointing upon *Quality*? . . . What necessity is there to kick the *Coronets* about the *Stage*, and to make a Man a Lord, only in order to make him a Coxcomb. I hope the *Poets* don't intend to revive the old Project of Levelling, and *Vote* down the House of *Peers*" (175–76). On Collier's interest in "elite society," see Dawson, *Gentility and the Comic Theatre of Late Stuart London*, 205–16.

48. See "Upon the Office of a Chaplain," in Collier's *Essays Upon Several Moral Subjects*.

49. Rose, *England in the 1690s*, 173.

50. Thomas D'Urfey, "Preface," *The Campaigners*, 2.

51. I have not included a discussion of Dryden's *King Arthur* (1691) in this chapter. The dramatic opera is no less politically engaged than Dryden's *Amphitryon*, but the musical aspects of the representation complicate matters significantly in ways that I thought would detract from the flow of discussion. Characteristically, Collier was most troubled by the blending of both truth and fiction and heathenism and Christianity that ran through the piece and attacked these admixtures as perilous forms of levelling. For two discussions of *King Arthur*, see Dugaw, "'The Rationall Spirituall Part,'" and Winn, "Dryden's Songs."

52. I have taken many of the basic biographical details here from the entry for "John Dryden" in the *Oxford Dictionary of National Biography*. DOI: 10.1093/ref: odnb/8108.

53. Winn, 414.

54. On his unanticipated and not wholly happy return to the stage, see Dryden's "Preface" to *Don Sebastian* (1690) in volume 15 of *The Works of John Dryden*, pp. 65–72, esp. 65–66.

55. The phrase "Petticoat Affair" is offered up derisively by Mercury to refer to Jupiter's frequent wanderings from Juno's bed (I.i.12). All references to *Amphitryon* have been taken from volume 15 of *The Works of John Dryden* and will be cited parenthetically by act, scene, and line number.

56. For a detailed discussion of Dryden's use of sources for his *Amphitryon*, see Allen, *The Sources of John Dryden's Comedies*, esp. pp. 225–39; and appendices E and F.

57. Garrison, "Dryden and the Birth of Hercules," 194–195, 184.

58. Bywaters, *Dryden in Revolutionary England*, 34–74. For readings that take a similar view, see Hume, *Development*, 382–84; Hughes, *English Drama*, 342–43; Laura Brown, *English Dramatic Form, 1660–1760*, 34–36; and Canfield, "Poetical Injustice," 23–45. By contrast, in *Producible Interpretations*, Judith Milhous and Robert D. Hume resist specific political interpretations of *Amphitryon*. Casting the reading of Jupiter-Alcmena-Amphitryon as William-England-James as "farfetched" (220), they read the comedy into a history of theatrical inheritance as a stalwart holdout in a dwindling line of rakish Carolean sex comedies.

59. Bywaters, *Dryden in Revolutionary England*, 66.

60. In Brian Corman's *Genre and Generic Change in English Comedy*, Alcmena is practically an afterthought when he writes, "It is Amphitryon, not Jupiter who is deserving of the sympathies of the audience, as, of course, is his wife Alcmena" (64).

61. Allen, *Sources of John Dryden's Comedies*, 229–30.

62. Markley and Dalporto, *Amphitryon*, 1,735.

63. Bowers, *Force or Fraud*, 5.

64. For more on rape law and rape cases in the late seventeenth century, see Rudolph, "Rape and Resistance."

65. Bowers, *Force or Fraud*, 50.

66. Schille, "Self-Assessment in Dryden's *Amphitryon*," 557–58.

67. See also Canfield in *Tricksters and Estates*, who similarly observes of *Amphitryon*, "If the only Absolute is Desire and even God subverts the law by doubling, by a supplementation that is at once a repetition and a supplanting, then integrity and identity are radically threatened" (245).

68. David Gelineau reads Dryden's derangement of those relations as a satire of the arbitrary principles that sustained the Whig discourse on identity, property, and authenticity. See Gelineau, "Identity in Dryden's *Amphitryon*."

69. Sherman, "Dryden and the Theatrical Imagination," 28.

70. Tories rationalized their collusion in the events of 1688 by maintaining that they had not violated their principles of passive obedience and nonresistance, but rather that James II had vacated the throne, that William had thus gained the crown by force, and that his claim of legitimacy could be recognized de facto while reserving de jure recognition for James II (see Harris, *Politics Under the Late Stuarts*, 137–38, as well as Kenyon, *Revolution Principles*, 21–34).

71. Sir John Vanbrugh, *The Relapse or Virtue in Danger Being the Sequel of The Fool in Fashion* (1696–97), Regents Restoration Drama Series, I.ii.28. All subsequent references to this text will be cited parenthetically by act, scene, and line number.

72. On Collier's indifference with respect to Coupler and the status of homosexuality in the late seventeenth century, see Orvis, "'Old Sodom' and 'Dear Dad.'"

73. Laura Brown, *English Dramatic Form*, 118.

74. Cordner, *Sir John Vanbrugh: Four Comedies*, 14.

75. Gómez, "Kicking Conscience Downstairs," 105.

76. Zimbardo, *A Mirror to Nature*, 178.

77. See Claydon, *William III*, esp. 28–52.

78. Vanbrugh's deliberate (though common) analogy between state politics and the politics of marriage is vividly articulated in Amanda's extended exchange with Berinthia in Act 2. There, Amanda not only avouches that her husband "sits triumphant in [her] heart, and nothing can dethrone him" but that she would "preserve the vacant throne" even if he were to "abdicate

again" for "ten tedious winters more" (II.545–56). For more on the intersection of politics and gender politics in Vanbrugh's plays, see Gómez, "Courtship, Marriage Vows, and Political Metaphor in Vanbrugh's *The Relapse* and *The Provoked Wife*."

79. For an extended discussion of stage fops and their social and political significance, see Dawson, *Gentility and the Comic Theatre of Late Stuart London*, chaps. 7–9.

80. Staves, "A Few Kind Words for the Fop," 428.

81. Freeman, *Character's Theater*, 197.

82. Faller, "Between Jest and Earnest," 18.

83. See editor's note in Regents Restoration Drama Series edition used here, p. 22.

84. See Hughes, "Vanbrugh and Cibber," 66.

85. Colley Cibber would revive the character of Lord Foppington once more in his *The Careless Husband* (1705), and there we discover that Foppington has indeed secured a wife whose large fortune could easily "pay [his] debts at play" even as any offspring she produced would provide him the means to "disinherit [his] younger brother," II.ii.125–26.

86. For brief comments on the shifts in comedy especially with respect to the trickster figure, see Canfield, *Tricksters and Estates*, 250.

87. Gollapudi, *Moral Reform in Comedy and Culture, 1696–1747*, 19–38.

88. See Derrida, "The Law of Genre."

89. Collier, "The Office of a Chaplain," in *Essays on Moral Subjects* , 211–12.

90. Charles Hinnant has tied Collier's arguments here to his adherence to the theory of patriarchalism promoted by Sir Robert Filmer in *Patriarcha* (1680); see Hinnant, "Collier, Congreve, and the Patriarchalist Debate."

91. Collier, *A Perswasive to Consideration*, 22.

92. Ibid., 29, 25.

93. Ibid., 8.

94. Collier, *A Defence of the Short View*, 70.

95. Ibid.

96. Ibid., 76.

97. Ibid., 72.

98. In "The Artist and the Clergyman," Novak thus reads the Collier controversy as a fight not over whether the stage would be reformed but over who would reform it.

99. Collier, *A Perswasive to Consideration*, 8.

100. Hopes, "Politics and Morality in the Writings of Jeremy Collier," 161.

101. Congreve, *Amendments of Mr. Collier's False and Imperfect Citations*, 10. All subsequent references to this text will be cited parenthetically by page number.

102. Vanbrugh, *A Short Vindication*, 40.

103. Dennis, *The Usefulness of the Stage*, 64.

104. Ibid., 65, 117–18.

105. See also Aubrey Williams, who observes, "the remarkable sophistication of critical insight exhibited by Congreve and others on his side, as well as the grossness of critical and moral sensibility exhibited by Collier and his supporters" ("No Cloistered Virtue," 235). It should be conceded here, however, that a number of Congreve's contemporaries thought he had missed his mark. Colley Cibber commented, for instance, that Congreve "seem'd too much hurt, to be able to defend himself," and Samuel Johnson suggested that he had brandished "the sword without the arm of Scanderberg" (Cibber, *An Apology for the Life of Colley Cibber*, 151; Samuel Johnson, "William Congreve," in *Lives of the Poets*, 229).

106. See, for instance, Peters, " 'Things Govern'd By Words.' "

107. Marshall, *The Figure of Theater*.

108. Pocock, "Modes of Political and Historical Time," 91, 92. For more on the writing of history as a partisan activity in the late seventeenth century and early eighteenth centuries, see Knights, "The Tory Interpretation of History in the Rage of Parties."

109. As cited in Ressler, "Jeremy Collier's Essays," 241.

110. As Krutch has noted, "It cannot but have been a thorn in [Collier's] side that opposition to the stage in England had been most closely connected with the Puritans" (*Comedy and Conscience*, 140). In fact, Collier was mocked in any number of pamphlets for taking a position on the stage that aligned him with his Puritan enemies. The anonymous author of *The Stage Acquitted* asserts sardonically, for instance, that Collier has indeed found himself a "fit yoke-mate" in Ridpath (*The Stage Condemned*, 48).

111. [George Ridpath], *The Stage Condemned*, 4. All subsequent references to this text will be cited parenthetically by page number.

112. Claydon, *William III*, 110–21.

113. Ibid., 120.

114. Among other urbane precedents, *The Stage Acquitted* follows in particular *A Letter to A. H. Esq.; Concerning the Stage* (1698), in which the anonymous author admonished his readers that "Men of Probity and Learning . . . are not to be mov'd by the Opinions of others no longer than those Opinions are agreeable to Reason" (3). Like Congreve, too, *A Letter* suggests that comedy, civility, and civil discourse could act as a bulwark against the kinds of "Civil Broils, intestine Wars, and unnatural Murthers" encouraged by seditious clergy in the pulpit (11).

115. Anon., *The Stage Acquitted*, (London, 1699), 3. All subsequent references to this text will be cited parenthetically by page number.

116. This position also echoes *A Vindication of the Stage* (1698) in which the anonymous author focuses on Collier's nonjuring status and writes, "Nay, Mr. *Collier* himself, and all others of their Principles, are more bitter and sharp Invectives against the Order, by their Refractory and Obstinate Separation from the Greatest and most Pious Part of their Brethren, than any can be writ by the most Atheistical Pen; and wound it more severely" (18–19). In the same spirit, *A Defence of Dramatick Poetry* (1698) sardonically refers to Collier as a "sometimes Minister of the English Church" and explicitly casts Collier's attack on the stage as a "second *Perswasive*" (48, 98).

117. Knights, *Representation and Misrepresentation*, 56. On the discourse of politeness, see again Klein, *Shaftesbury and the Culture of Politeness*.

CHAPTER 3

1. I have taken the details for this account of Home's journey to London and of his efforts to get his play mounted from Alexander Carlyle's *Autobiography*, pp. 316–25.

2. Ibid., 320, 324, 327.

3. See Emslie, "Home's *Douglas* and Wully Shakspeare," 128–29.

4. Mackenzie, *Life and Writings of John Home*, 39.

5. An excellent summation of the events surrounding the *Douglas* controversy, along with the reprinted text of many of the significant documents in the case can be found in Gipson, *John Home*, chaps. 4–5. For more immediate documentation of these events, I have consulted the *Scots Magazine*. For the "Admonition and Exhortation by the Rev. Presbytery of Edinburgh to all within their bounds," 5 January 1757, see *Scots Magazine*, 19 (January 1757): 18–19. For the Glasgow notice, see *Scots Magazine* 19 (January 1757): 47–48.

6. For the Synod's judgment, see *Scots Magazine* 19 (April 1757): 217–18; for the vote in the General Assembly upholding this ruling, see *Scots Magazine* 19 (May 1757): 263.

7. For more on Home's relationship with Bute, see Sher, "'The Favourite of the Favourite.'"

8. The March 1757 issue of the *Scots Magazine* noted, for instance, that "Several domestic articles are deferred" to make room for items about the *Douglas* controversy, 160.

9. Gipson, *John Home*, 71.

10. As David Daiches explains, "There was no general agreement among those who considered themselves Moderates on detailed theological matters—they left these things to the High Flyers or committed Calvinists—and they tended to emphasize benevolence and morality rather than discuss election and predestination and other Calvinist doctrines" (*The Scottish Enlightenment*, 15). See also Richard B. Sher, who emphasizes the importance of the emergent discourse of politeness throughout his seminal account of the rise of moderatism: *Church and University in the Scottish Enlightenment*. For more on the rise of the moderates, see also Sefton, "'Neu-lights and Preachers Legall.'"

11. Carlyle, *Autobiography*, 312. See "*Sensus Communis*: An Essay on the Freedom of *Wit* and *Humour*" (1709), where Shaftesbury writes, "All Politeness is owing to Liberty. We polish one another, and rub off our Corners and rough Sides by a sort of *amicable collision*" (I.42). For a useful history of these clubs and societies, see McElroy, *Scotland's Age of Improvement*.

12. Carlyle, *Autobiography*, 159, 266–67.

13. Callum Brown, *Social History of Religion in Scotland*, 16.

14. Jones, "The Scottish Professoriate and the Polite Academy," 90.

15. "An Account of the Select Society of Edinburgh," *Scots Magazine* 17 (March 1755): 126.

16. In an indication of the kind of public attention devoted to these groups, the account noted above begins by observing, "As the meetings and transactions of the Select Society have for some time engaged the attention of the public, our readers will probably desire some account of its institution and intention" (126).

17. R. Wodrow, 9 May 1728, *Analecta; or, Materials for a History of Remarkable Providences; Mostly Relating to Scotch Ministers and Christians*, as documented in Rendall, *Origins of the Scottish Enlightenment*, 68.

18. For an informative historical study of these patronage disputes, including statistics on their frequency, see Sher and Murdoch, "Patronage and Party in the Church of Scotland."

19. Callum Brown, *Social History of Religion in Scotland*, 29. I have taken other basic historical details in my account of patronage from Brown.

20. Sher and Murdoch, "Patronage," 213–14.

21. As a number of historians have demonstrated, patronage disputes became one of the main causes of secessions from the Established Church of Scotland. In the Jedburgh case, dissenters would come to account for more than 70 percent of the adult population (Brown, *Social History of Religion in Scotland*, 31).

22. "Reasons of dissent from the sentence of the general assembly, May 15, 1751," *Scots Magazine* 13 (May 1751): 220.

23. In addition to acting as the leader of the Moderates, William Robertson was a founding member of the Select Society and in 1762 would be appointed principal of Edinburgh University. Under his leadership until 1793, the university would attain unrivaled status (see Rendall, *Origins of the Scottish Enlightenment*, 35–36, 210).

24. "Reasons of dissent, entered on the 15th of May 1751, from the sentence of the general

assembly, censuring the Rev. members of the presbytery of Linlithgow," *Scots Magazine* 13 (May 1751): 220–21.

25. *Scots Magazine* 14 (1752): 154–55. A committee was appointed by the commission to respond to that dissent. "An abstract of the Answers to the Reasons of Dissent from the sentence of the commission, March 11, 1752" can be found in *Scots Magazine* 14 (May, 1752): 229–38.

26. "Reasons of dissent from the judgment and resolution of the commission, March 11, 1752," *Scots Magazine* 14 (April, 1752): 191.

27. Ibid., 191–92, 193.

28. *Scots Magazine* 14 (May 1752): 261.

29. Ibid., 262.

30. Wodrow, *Analecta*, in Rendall, *Origins of the Scottish Enlightenment*, 68.

31. The orthodox faction explicitly articulates these principles of governance in their dissent, writing, "We have always, from our first entrance into this church, conceived, that Presbyterian government, as distinguished from all other forms of church-government, consisted in the parity of pastors and subordination of church-judicatures; as it is described, both in the form of our subscription, and in the laws of our establishment; without implying that even the supreme judicature was vested with absolute authority" (*Scots Magazine* 13 (May 1751): 221. For basic background on the structure of the Presbyterian Church, see Cross, *The Oxford Dictionary of the Christian Church*, 1,322.

32. For a similar argument, see also Daiches, *Scottish Enlightenment*, 17.

33. See, for instance, Rendall, *Origins of the Scottish Enlightenment*, 207; Sher, *Church and University*, 53–54.

34. Jones, "Scottish Professoriate," 174–75.

35. *Scots Magazine* 14 (April 1752): 192.

36. Such an understanding of these events becomes all the more compelling when we consider, first, a parallel case making its way through the Scottish court system in which patronage was treated not as a matter of faith or ecclesiastical law but rather as a matter of property rights and civil law and, second, the growing parliamentary efforts to enforce patronage rights by threatening to withhold stipends from those who were considered in breach of the law. See *Scots Magazine* 13 (June 1751): 277–80, for the patronage case of Culross; and *Scots Magazine* 13 (May 1751): 217–19, and (July 1751): 329, for items related to the enforcement of patronage laws by Parliament.

37. This statute can be found in Kames's own *Statute Law of Scotland Abridged* (1757); see Ross, *Lord Kames and the Scotland of His Day*, 153.

38. For a more extensive account of these events, see Ross, *Lord Kames*, 152–60.

39. Anderson's first foray into this field can be found in *An Estimate of the Profit and Loss of Religion* (Edinburgh, 1753). Other pamphlets on the orthodox side include [Reverend John Bonar of Cockpen], *An Analysis of the Moral and Religious Sentiments Contained in the Writings of SOPHO, and David Hume* (Edinburgh, 1755); "Sopho's doctrine of necessity explained and exposed," *Scots Magazine* 17 (September 1755): 417–25; and Anon., *Infidelity: A Proper Object of Censure* (Glasgow, 1756). On the Moderate side, Hugh Blair sought to defend Kames with his *Observations upon a Pamphlet Intitled an Analysis of the Moral and Religious Sentiments in the Writings of Sopho and David Hume* (Edinburgh, 1755).

40. I will offer only the briefest of overviews to highlight my particular interests in Kames's *Essays*. For more extensive explications of the *Essays*, see McGuinness, *Henry Home, Lord Kames*, 28–57; and Ross, *Lord Kames*, 98–110.

41. Price, *Collected Works of Henry Home, Lord Kames*, ix.

42. Henry Home, Lord Kames, *Essays on the Principles of Morality and Natural Religion*, 63–64. All subsequent references to this work will be cited parenthetically by page number.

43. Kames's first biographer, Alexander Fraser Tytler, captured this shock, writing, "The author certainly could not have foreseen, that a work, professing to place the principles of morals on an immutable basis, to enforce the proofs of the existence and attributes of the Deity, and to combat the doctrines of the sceptical philosophy, and expose its pernicious tendency, was destined to draw upon him the reproach of scepticism and impiety" (*Memoirs of the Life*, I.138).

44. Anderson, *An Estimate*, 78.

45. In perhaps the most succinct summation of the charges against the *Essays*, for instance, the author of "A Letter on Sopho's Doctrine of NECESSITY" wrote, "He is accused of maintaining a *necessity* which destroys the accountableness of men" (421). See also Anon., *Infidelity: A Proper Object of Censure*, 3. For an account of the striking fact that the orthodox faction appears to place greater emphasis here on the power of "reason" where Kames relies on the "moral sense," see Ahnert, *The Moral Culture of the Scottish Enlightenment*, 96–105.

46. Blair's *Observations*, extracts in *Scots Magazine* 17 (May 1755): 233.

47. It is worth noting at this juncture that a number of pamphlets, including *Infidelity: A Proper Object of Censure*, 32–33, explicitly connected the patronage battles and the infidelity cases. Others such as the anonymously written *Letter to the Reverend the Moderator, and Members of the Presbytery of Haddington*, 4–5, would go on to link the patronage and infidelity battles to the *Douglas* controversy.

48. "Admonition and Exhortation by the Rev. Presbytery of Edinburgh to all within their bounds," *Scots Magazine* 19 (January 1757): 18.

49. Ibid.

50. Ibid., 19.

51. [Adam Ferguson], *The Morality of Stage-Plays Seriously Considered*, 19.

52. Anon., *The Immorality of Stage-Plays*, 4.

53. Thorne Compton makes a similar argument for such a philosophical divide in "Adam Ferguson and John Witherspoon in 'Satan's Seminary.'"

54. The Revd. John Witherspoon, *The Moderator*, ii, 1757, as cited in Ross, *Lord Kames*, 154.

55. David Hume, "Dedication," *Four Dissertations*, ii–iii.

56. Brougham, *Life and Times of Henry, Lord Brougham*, I.541–42.

57. Oliver Goldsmith, "Douglas, A Tragedy: As It Is Acted at the Theatre-Royal in Covent-Garden," in *Collected Works of Oliver Goldsmith*, I.13.

58. Since my interest lies in the controversy as it arose in Scotland rather than in the London production, I have taken my text, cited by act and page number, from John Home's *Douglas* in *Eighteenth Century Tragedy*, ed. and intro. Michael R. Booth. Booth's text is drawn from the first Edinburgh edition (E1) rather than the first London edition (L1). For an extensive discussion of the differences among the early editions of *Douglas*, see McGinley, "The First Edinburgh and London Editions." For other work on the editions of *Douglas*, see Macmillan, "First Editions of *Douglas*."

59. See Lee, "Giants in the North," and Megan Morgan, "Speaking with a Double Voice." For readings that examine *Douglas* not just in the wake of the Union but also in the aftermath of the rebellion of 1745, see Simpson, "Rationalism and Romanticism," and Sorenson "Varieties of Public Performance." For a fascinating reading of the ways in which Home's adaptation of the character names in *Douglas* reflected his dual interest in elevating Scottish cultural claims and in achieving a post-1745 rapprochement with England, see McGinley, "'My Name Is Norval?'"

60. See, for instance, Anon., *The Tragedy of* Douglas *Analysed*, which works "methodically" to provide "proofs" of the tragedy's excellence (7).

61. Gentleman, *The Dramatic Censor*, 132, 134.

62. See, for instance, Anon., *Douglas, a Tragedy, Weighed in the Balances, and Found Wanting*, which found "in each character through the whole drama, more than enough to disgust every Christian mind," and in Lady Randolph in particular, "such a number and variety of the most unscriptural principles and practices, such a composition of errors and wickedness, that instead of becoming the favourite of unwary spectators, it is beyond measure amazing she does not fill them with horror and contempt" (20, 23). For a useful review of the many attacks on Home for portraying a suicide, see Lonsdale, "Thomas Gray, David Hume and John Home's *Douglas*."

63. Anon., *The Immorality of Stage-Plays*, 4.

64. On Witherspoon's rejection of the passions as the ground of moral action, see Ahnert, *The Moral Culture of the Scottish Enlightenment*, 114.

65. Goldsmith, "*Douglas*, A Tragedy," I.11; Elizabeth Inchbald, "Remarks" on *Douglas*. Inchbald's remarks were especially motivated by her experience watching Sarah Siddons perform the part of Lady Randolph, a performance that was famous and famously praised for directing almost all attention to the expression of the maternal passions. Susan Staves notes that this focus was relatively new when *Douglas* was first produced and argues that "Douglas's creation of such spectacles of maternal feeling appealed to the eighteenth-century bourgeois taste for exemplary character, for pathos, and for generality" ("Douglas's Mother," 61). For others who view *Douglas* as part of an emergent discourse of sensibility, see Wheeler, "The Pathetic and the Sublime," and Backscheider, "John Home's *Douglas*."

66. Worthen, *Idea of an Actor*, 97.

67. Donohue, *Dramatic Character in the English Romantic Age*, 65.

68. Anon., *Tragedy of Douglas Analysed*, 12.

69. Inchbald, "Remarks"; Gentleman, *Dramatic Censor*, 2.135.

70. Gentleman, *Dramatic Censor*, 2.136.

71. John MacLaurin, *The Philosopher's Opera* in *Scottish Ballad Operas III*. All subsequent references will be to this text and will be cited by act and page number. MacLaurin is also credited with a second burlesque of the success of *Douglas* in the form of a puppet show, *The Deposition, or Fatal Miscarriage*, as well as a pamphlet contribution to the *Douglas* controversy, *Apology for the Writers Against the Tragedy of Douglas*. For more on Scottish productions that touched on *Douglas*, see Tobin, *Plays by Scots*, 36, as well as Ian Brown, who holds that the success of *Douglas* provided the necessary momentum for the establishment of a patent theater in Edinburgh ("Public and Private Performance," 35).

72. Lee, "Giants of the North," 114.

73. For reasons that will become clear below, I will be taking my text here from John Witherspoon, *A Serious Inquiry into the Nature and Effects of the Stage: And a Letter Respecting Play Actors*.

74. For a review of Witherspoon's philosophical and theological objections to theater and its influence on society, see Ahnert, "Clergymen as Polite Philosophers."

75. Indeed, the Moderates in Scotland had almost succeeded in denying Witherspoon's calling by the parish at Paisley as revenge for his satirical pamphlet, *Ecclesiastical Characteristics* (1753), which named and took aim at the Moderate faction.

76. Collins, *President Witherspoon*, 1.98.

77. Noll, "The Irony of the Enlightenment for Presbyterians in the Early Republic."

78. Noll, "The Irony," 155–56. For an exhaustive discussion of the dual and often contradictory legacy of Witherspoon and his enormous influence on American Presbyterianism of both the enlightened and evangelical kind, see Noll, *Princeton and the Republic*.

79. Morrison, "John Witherspoon," 553.

80. For this and other information about theater in the early American republic, see Hewitt, *Theatre U.S.A. 1665–1957*.

81. Collins, *President Witherspoon*, 174.

82. For more on Witherspoon's mixed legacy and its influence on figures like Miller as well as for Miller's role in the founding of Princeton Theological Seminary, see Noll, *Princeton and the Republic*, 283–88, 258–66.

83. See Samuel Miller, D. D., *A Sermon, Delivered January 18, 1812*.

84. Prefatory Address to Witherspoon, *Serious Inquiry*, 5.

85. Ibid., 20.

86. Ibid., 19.

87. Fleischacker, "The Impact on America," 333.

CHAPTER 4

1. In some of the first reports of the fire, as many as 160 were said to have died. The official list of the dead included only 72 individuals and can be found in *A Full Account of the Burning of the Richmond Theatre*. An appended table in George Richards's *Spirit of an Evening Lecture* records a total of 75 dead, annotated in pencil in a Virginia Historical Society copy as follows: "19 Gentlemen, 18 Ladies Married, 32 Young Ladies, 4 Children, and 2 Colored Women." Another somewhat discrepant list of the dead can be found in *A Collection of Facts and Statements, Relative to the Fatal Event*.

2. See Muir, "Signs of the Times," and "Repentance, or Richmond in Tears," in *Ten Sermons*; Hill, *A Sermon Delivered in the Presbyterian Meeting-House in Winchester*; and Dana, *Tribute of Sympathy*.

3. Indeed, insofar as "the people" constitutes the foundational abstraction of American democracy, the struggle over that question has never ended. See Frank, *Constituent Moments*.

4. I am using the term "narrativize" in the sense theorized by Hayden White in "The Value of Narrativity in the Representation of Reality."

5. Heading quoted from "A Letter from a Gentleman in Richmond, to the Hon. M. Clay, a Representative of Virginia, December 27, 1811," in *Distressing Calamity*. For my account of the fire and the scene at the theater that night, I draw on the following: *An Account of the Awful Calamity*; *Calamity at Richmond*; *A Collection of Facts and Statements, Relative to the Fatal Event*; *Distressing Calamity*; *A Concise Statement of the Awful Conflagration of the Theatre*; *A Full Account of the Burning of the Richmond Theatre*; *Narrative and Report of the Causes and Circumstances of the Deplorable Conflagration*; and *Particular Account of the Dreadful Fire at Richmond*. A more recent and detailed account of the fire, drawing on many of the same archival sources, can be found in Baker, *The Richmond Theater Fire*.

6. For an account of Jews in Richmond in the early nineteenth century, see Berman, *Richmond's Jewry*, esp. 64–132.

7. For my description of Richmond in 1811, I have drawn upon the following sources: Bondurant, *Poe's Richmond*; Chadwick, *I Am Murdered*; Christian, *Richmond, Her Past and*

Present; Dabney, *Richmond, The Story of a City*; Little, *History of Richmond*; Mordecai, *Richmond in By-Gone Days*; *Richmond, Capital of Virginia*; Sanford, ed., *Richmond: Her Triumphs, Tragedies, and Growth*; and Tyler-McGraw, *At the Falls*.

8. Click, *Spirit of the Times*, 4.

9. Shockley, *The Richmond Stage*, 3. Not insignificantly, given the discussions in the previous chapter, Ryan selected for his first night a performance of John Home's *Douglas*, complemented by a presentation of Isaac Bickerstaffe's musical entertainment *The Padlock* (Shockley, 10).

10. Susanne Sherman, *Comedies Useful*, 45.

11. Click, *Spirit of the Times*, 49. For detailed descriptions of the seasons and the plays offered by each resident company, see Shockley, *The Richmond Stage*, and Sherman, *Comedies Useful*.

12. For a classic study of the popularity of melodrama in the United States during this period, see Grimstead, *Melodrama Unveiled*.

13. Shockley, *The Richmond Stage*, 214. As Dabney writes, "The city's standing in the theatrical world in those years may be partially grasped from the fact that in the late eighteenth and early nineteenth centuries twenty-four English plays were presented in Richmond for the first time in America" (*Richmond*, 87).

14. For many of these details, see "Report of the Committee of Investigation," in *Full Account*, 23–31.

15. For narratives of such escapes, see the "Statements of Eye-Witnesses," collected by Thomas Ritchie of the *Richmond Enquirer* and reprinted in multiple publications, including *Full Account*, pp. 42–60. All of these accounts were submitted by men, and many of them provide vivid descriptions of the panic and pandemonium in the playhouse, as people scrambled to survive and, pressed by the crowd, literally climbed over one another to get to the windows. As M. W. Hancock put it, "All ceremony was forgotten in conforming to the first law of nature" (45).

16. Thomas Brown, *Recollections of the Events of My Life*. Accession 36108, Personal Papers Collection, Library of Virginia, Richmond, VA, p. 102–3. In 1828, Brown moved from Virginia to Florida, where he would go on not only to serve in the Florida Legislature (1845) but also to become the governor of the state (1849–53).

17. "Overwhelming Calamity," *Enquirer*, 28 December 1811, reprinted in *Particular Account*, 6.

18. The concept of sublime terror was, of course, eloquently theorized by Edmund Burke in his *A Philosophical Enquiry into the Origin of Our Ideas of the Sublime and the Beautiful* (1756). For a discussion of the central role played by Burke's treatise in conceptualizing the gothic linkage between sublimity and terror, see Punter, *The Literature of Terror*, 39–40.

19. "Most Dreadful Calamity," *American Standard*, 27 December 1811, reprinted in *Particular Account*, 11. For expansive accounts of the theory and mechanisms of sentiment and sensibility, see Todd, *Sensibility*; and Barker-Benfield, *The Culture of Sensibility*.

20. T. Brown, "Recollections," 103.

21. *Narrative and Report*, 6; also reprinted in *Particular Account*, 17.

22. Such expressions of consternation were not restricted to Richmond. In Philadelphia, the author of the "Preface" to *Calamity at Richmond* reflects in his final paragraph, "It is not less worthy of observation, that there should have been so great a disproportion in the sexes of the sufferers. Alas! how fatal to the softer and weaker sex! Of the 70 lost, 50 were females! 46 of which were whites: only 18 were men!" (xi). Perhaps an even greater and telling irony, as Robert Gamble reported, is that "perhaps 1/4 of all the men, believe[d] each—that they were the very

last person that escaped." See Robert Gamble to General James Breckinridge, Member of Congress, Richmond, 5 January 1812, Breckinridge Family Papers, 1740–1902, Virginia Historical Society.

23. *A Collection of Facts and Statements*, 38.

24. For just three examples of how this phrase is used in both public and private commentary, see "Committee of Investigation" in *Full Account*, 31; Mordecai, *A Discourse Delivered at the Synagogue in Richmond*, mss. p. 3; and John Campbell to David Campbell, Richmond, 27 December 1811, Campbell Family Papers, Duke University.

25. I take my cue here from Teresa Goddu, who has demonstrated in the context of a slightly later period in American literature that "if the gothic is informed by its historical context, the horrors of history are also articulated through gothic discourse" (*Gothic America*, 2).

26. The performance as described scene by scene on the playbill for that evening corresponds to *Airs, Glees, and Choruses in a New Grand Ballet Pantomime of Action, Called Raymond and Agnes; Or the Castle of Lindenbergh*, composed by Charles Farley (London, 1797). See *The London Stage*, part 5, vol. 3 (1776–1800). *Raymond and Agnes* proved quite popular, with twenty-one additional performances in its first season and numerous performances in the years that followed. This adaptation is often wrongly attributed to Lewis himself, who in 1809 would produce his own two-act adaptation with dialogue and music for presentation on the stage at Norwich, England. See Ranger, *"Terror and Pity Reign in Every Breast,"* 75–77; and Evans, *Gothic Drama*, 145, 159–60.

27. See Shockley, *The Richmond Stage*, 359; and Sherman, *Comedies Useful*, 234.

28. Other plays by Matthew Lewis that had been performed on the Richmond stage include *Adelgitha; or The Fruits of a Single Error, The True Patriot; or, Alphonso, King of Castile, The Castle Spectre, Rivers; or, The East-Indian*, and *The Wood Demon, or The Clock Has Struck*; see Shockley, *The Richmond Stage*.

29. Richard Beale Davis, *Intellectual Life in Jefferson's Virginia*, 78.

30. Matthew Lewis, *The Monk*.

31. Ibid., 8, 16.

32. Ibid., 19.

33. Sherman, *Comedies Useful*, 240; Baker, *Richmond Theater Fire*, 53.

34. "Burning of the Richmond Theatre," in *Ladies Garland* I.16 (May 1838): 299–301.

35. See, for instance, "Lines Sacred to the Memory of Miss Maria Nelson," "Tribute to Lucy Gwathmey," and "Miss Margaret Copland."

36. Reprinted in *Particular Account*, 19.

37. Reprinted in *Full Account*, 35–36.

38. For more on the Barbary Wars, see Lambert, *The Barbary Wars*, and London, *Victory in Tripoli*. For a tumultuous account of the cruelties suffered by those from the *Philadelphia* who were imprisoned in Tripoli, see William Ray, *Horrors of Slavery*.

39. Baker, *Richmond Theater Fire*, 58.

40. "For the Argus," *Virginia Argus*, 23 January 1812.

41. I have taken the phrase above from Lewis's *The Monk*, where it is used to describe the ill-fated Antonia as well as the astonishing attractions of Matilda's breast (9, 65).

42. Thomas R. Joynes to Levin S. Joynes, Richmond, 27 December 1811, Joynes Family Papers, 1776–1898, section 3, Virginia Historical Society. As a note appended to a printed version of this letter indicates, Joynes was a member of the Virginia House of Delegates at the time of the fire and hence was one of the many members of the legislature who escaped that night ("The

Burning of the Richmond Theatre, 1811," *Virginia Historical Magazine of History and Biography* 51.3 [July 1943]: 297–99).

43. It is not insignificant, then, that the tale of Gilbert Hunt, a slave who helped to rescue many from the fire, emerged only much later. His role in rescue efforts is not mentioned in any of the initial reports; rather it became publicized only in 1859 when a small pamphlet recounting his heroic feats was issued as part of an effort to solicit donations for the support of this now free but old man. In almost every twentieth-century account of the fire, a recapitulation of the tale of Gilbert Hunt now takes pride of place alongside that of Sally Conyers and Lieutenant Gibbon. See Philip Barrett, *Gilbert Hunt*. It is also important to note that there were rumors in circulation that some slaves may have taken advantage of the pandemonium at the scene to slip quietly away (Baker, *Richmond Theater Fire*, 72).

44. A letter by then Secretary of State James Monroe provides an interesting footnote to this discussion of reproductive anxieties, as after expressing relief that his daughter had not been at the theater that night, he went on to explain: "Our daughter's situation, being advanc'd in her pregnancy, xxxx exposed ^her^ to much danger, from meer simpathy & participation in the affliction of others, & there was much to [be] feard for her on that account." James Monroe to Paul Bentalou, Washington, 1 January 1812, Mrs. Edmund Waller Collection, 1780–1825, Accession 22068, Personal Papers Collection, Library of Virginia, Richmond.

45. For Milton's rendition of these lines, see John Milton, *Paradise Lost*, VIII.488–89.

46. "For the Argus," *Virginia Argus*, 23 January 1812.

47. This is, in fact, the premise, theme, and central problematic of any number of popular eighteenth- and early nineteenth-century novels. For just two well-known instances, see Frances Burney's *Evelina, or, The History of a Young Lady's Entrance into the World* (1778) and Jane Austen's *Emma* (1816).

48. In all of the accounts that I have come across, only *The Port Folio*, a political and literary magazine published in Philadelphia, saw fit to correct the widespread reports of a romantic relationship between Gibbon and Conyers. Having included in an earlier issue an extraordinarily vivid account of the Richmond fire, featuring a profile of Lieutenant Gibbon's unusual valor—not simply his forbearance in captivity under a "barbarous and mercenary foe" but also his perseverance when it seemed his way to the "bower of felicity" might be blocked by powers beyond his control, they took the occasion in a subsequent issue to correct their unintentional mistake. See "A Retrospect of the Year 1811," *Port Folio*, VII.2 (February 1812): 148–66, 163–65; and "Mortuary," *Port Folio*, VII.3 (March 1812): 303–5.

49. Reverend Dr. E. S. Ely, "Richmond's Lament." I have not been able to identify the poem's original date of composition or publication.

50. Samuel Gilman, *Monody on the Victims and Sufferers*.

51. Ibid., "Advertisement" and pp. 11–12.

52. Almost every magazine or newspaper article commemorating the Richmond Theater fire recounts the romantic tale of Miss Sally Conyers and Lieutenant Gibbon. For just two relatively recent examples, see Jeffers, "Richmond Theatre's Tragic Fire," and "December 26, 1811: Two Lovers Perished Together."

53. Tales of a mother's grief or the death of more than one family member also circulated, but none as widely and as consistently as that of Sally Conyers and James Gibbon.

54. There are now innumerable accounts of the cultural work performed in this period by genres such as the sentimental, the gothic, and the melodramatic. For two influential examples, see, for instance, Tompkins, *Sensational Designs*, and Stern, *The Plight of Feeling*.

55. "An Ordinance to Amend the Ordinance, Entitled 'An Ordinance concerning the conflagration of the Theatre, in the City of Richmond,'" 28 December 1811, *Particular Account*, 27.

56. "Interment of the Dead," *Particular Account*, 28–29.

57. See *Distressing Calamity*, 7.

58. Mordecai, "A Discourse Delivered at the Synagogue."

59. Blair, *A Sermon Occasioned by the Dreadful Calamity*, mss. pp. 2, 5, 6. The original is held in the Robert Alonzo Brock Collection at the Huntington Library. A cover page in another hand suggests a date of 29 December, but in his address, Blair notes the occasion of his sermon as the official day set aside for humiliation and prayer, which was 1 January 1812.

60. *Particular Account*, 27.

61. Fisher, *History and Reminiscences of the Monumental Church*, 35.

62. *Richmond, Capital of Virginia*, 94–95. James Waddel Alexander, *Life of Archibald Alexander*, 196. Rice became so devoted to the cause of Presbyterianism in Virginia that he would later turn down the presidency of Princeton.

63. For an in-depth account of the growth of religion in Richmond following the fire, see Baker, *Richmond Theater Fire*, 176–214. See also Murrell, *"Calamity at Richmond": Fire and Faith in a Young Virginia City.*

64. For an account of these developments, see Matthews, *Toward a New Society*.

65. For a compelling account of church membership in decline and its subsequent ascent during the Second Great Awakening, see Jon Butler, *Awash in a Sea of Faith*. Carroll Smith Rosenberg tells us that while only one of every fifteen Americans were members of a church in 1800, the Second Great Awakening increased that number to one in every eight (*Religion and the Rise of the American City*, 46).

66. Boles, *The Great Revival*, 12. For similar assessment and an account of how New England clergy led by Lyman Beecher responded to this despair with a renewed vision of religiosity, see Abzug, *Cosmos Crumbling*, esp. 30–56.

67. See Wilson, "Religion, Government, and Power in the New American Republic," 83–85; and Lambert, *Religion in American Politics*, 1, 14–40.

68. Wood, *Empire of Liberty*, 588. For more on the influential role played by evangelical interests in the ratification of the Constitution and the passage of the First Amendment, see Grenda, "Revealing Liberalism in Early America."

69. Lambert, *Religion in American Politics*, 17.

70. See Abzug, *Cosmos Crumbling*, 30–56; and Boles, *The Great Revival*, 29–31.

71. Hatch, "Democratization of Christianity," 104, 98.

72. Hatch, *Democratization of American Christianity*.

73. Gaustad, *Neither King nor Prelate*, 110.

74. Hatch, "The Christian Movement and the Demand for a Theology of the People," 554.

75. See Hatch, *Democratization*, 170–79.

76. Wood, *Empire of Liberty*, 609. See also Boles, who writes, "As a matter of record, Presbyterians caught up in the revival tended either to avoid their traditional denominational doctrines or dilute them almost past recognition" (*The Great Revival*, 136–37). For a study of the transformation in theological doctrine and its relation to religiosity across this period, see Holifield, *Theology in America*.

77. For more on the abolition of all state establishments, see Jon Butler, *Awash in a Sea of Faith*, 260–68.

78. Smith-Rosenberg, *Religion and the Rise of the American City*, 49.

79. Ibid., 47–48; Jon Butler, *Awash in a Sea of Faith*, 278.

80. Lambert, *Religion in American Politics*, 5.

81. *Autobiography of Caroline Hommasel*, 1, 23. Hommasel's diaries are also on file at the Virginia Historical Society and reveal her to be a woman of devout faith (see MSS1 G8368 a10-19, Section 4). Hommasel was lowered out of a window of the burning playhouse by the man who would become her husband, Dr. Phillip Thornton.

82. Robert Mills to Miss Sarah Jane, Richmond, VA, 13 December 1812. Mills is best known for his design of the Washington Monument later in his career.

83. As reproduced in *Particular Account*, 31–32. The third chaplain from the Methodist denomination to be appointed to that post in the house, Snethen had only assumed office on 4 November 1811. In 1803, Snethen had led one of the most successful revivals of the Methodist Episcopal Baltimore Annual Conference. He was known for his very close ties to one of the most prominent Methodist leaders of the era, Bishop Francis Asbury, who was instrumental in the 1828 schism that gave birth to the Methodist Protestant denomination. For more on Asbury and Snethen, see Bilhartz, *Urban Religion and the Second Great Awakening*, 87–88.

84. See Stevenson, *Sensational Devotion*, esp. pp. 24–49. Though Stevenson focuses her discussion on twenty-first-century American evangelicism, she traces the emergence of evangelical techniques to the late eighteenth and early nineteenth centuries and links the effects of those techniques transhistorically to medieval devotional practices. Stevenson describes evangelical dramaturgy as a "system of strategies aimed at situating users/readers/spectators within kinaesthetically constructed encounters that will promote specific embodied beliefs" (26). The principal tactic she identifies in these endeavors, and the focus of the discussion below, is the "reappropriat[ion of] 'secular,' familiar, and often popular cultural forms . . . for sacred purposes" (30).

85. For extensive discussions of this theological tradition as well as its ties to a theatrical dramaturgy, see Stout, *The New England Soul* and *The Divine Dramatist*; as well as Richards, *Theater Enough*, esp. part II, pp. 99–173. For Winthrop's invocation of the "City on a Hill," see his sermon "A Model of Christian Charity."

86. Snethen, in *A Particular Account*, 30–31.

87. For an interesting reflection on the ways in which the twinned motifs of fire and renewal have shaped the ever-fleeting history of theater and nation, see MacKay, "Theatre as a Self-Consuming Art."

88. For the classic exposition of the American Jeremiad, see Bercovitch, *American Jeremiad*.

89. Alexander, *A Discourse Occasioned by the Burning of the Theatre*. All subsequent references to this text will be cited parenthetically by page number.

90. James Waddel Alexander, *The Life of Archibald Alexander*, 193. For the central role played by Hampden-Sydney College in the Presbyterian evangelical movement, see Boles, *The Great Revival*, 8 and passim.

91. Noll, *Princeton and the Republic*, 265. See Miller, *A Sermon, Delivered January 19, 1812*.

92. Noll, *Princeton and the Republic*, 260.

93. *A Collection of Facts and Statements*, 32.

94. For more on the intersections of stoicism, sentiment, and masculinity, see Ellison, *Cato's Tears*.

95. For a provocative meditation on the visual, sonic, and performed aspects of punctuation, a great deal of which can also be applied to typographic variation, see Brody, *Punctuation*.

96. Jackson, "America's First Mass Media."

97. Stout, *The New England Soul*, 23.

98. See Gustafson, *Eloquence Is Power*.

99. Henderson, "The Imperfect Dead," 488.

100. Elliot, "The Development of the Puritan Funeral Sermon," 156.

101. Van Engen, "Puritanism and the Power of Sympathy," 540.

102. Jackson, "America's First Mass Media," 412.

103. Ibid., 411.

104. Halttunen, "Humanitarianism," 304.

105. See Adam Smith, *The Theory of Moral Sentiments*.

106. Hendler, *Public Sentiments*, 22.

107. For more on this dynamic in sentimental fiction, see Burgett, *Sentimental Bodies*.

108. Dashiell, *A Sermon, Occasioned by the Burning of the Theatre*; Sabin, *A Discourse, Preached*; and Richards, *The Spirit of an Evening Lecture*.

109. Sabin, *A Discourse, Preached*, 7.

110. For more on Dow, see Hatch, *Democratization*, 36–40, 130–33.

111. Dashiell, *A Sermon*, 8.

112. Bilhartz, *Urban Religion*, 47. On Dashiell and his controversial role in Episcopal Church politics in Maryland, see Bilhartz, pp. 40, 47–49, 55–56, 126–28.

113. For a recent account of the Universalist movement in the United States, see Bressler, *Universalist Movement in America*.

114. Here Richards also echoes a passage from a local preface to an account of the fire, *Calamity at Richmond* (Philadelphia, 1812): "Ah! how little thought the fair one whose curls were adjusted—whose garments, costly and elegant, were disposed, so as to produce on the spectator, the most impressive effect, that those curls were, that same night, to be crisped with devouring flame; and those garments to be denied the service of a winding-sheet!" (ii).

115. On the impact of the Second Great Awakening on urban centers, see Rosenberg, *Religion and the Rise of the American City*, and Bilhartz, *Urban Religion*.

116. For detailed discussions of the cultural politics motivating antitheatrical legislation in the pre-Revolutionary period, see Nathans, *Early American Theatre*, esp. chaps. 1–2; Withington, *Toward a More Perfect Union*, esp. chaps. 2–4; and Peter A. Davis, "Puritan Mercantilism." All three illustrate how the theater came to be politicized as an emblem of imported British commodities and argue that the Continental Congress's 1774 ban against theatrical entertainments was grounded more deeply in political concerns than in religious ones. As Nathans writes, war with Britain, "fundamentally changed the nature of anti-theatricalism in American, transforming it from a simple matter of religious preference to one of patriotic duty" (37).

117. Nathans, *Early American Theatre*, 12.

118. While they may not have been working in concert, James Muir's references in his *Ten Sermons* to sermons preached by Hill in Winchester, Virginia; Alexander in Philadelphia; Miller in New York; and Dashiell in Baltimore suggest that they were all clearly aware of one another's efforts and that collectively they held the view that the event offered the potential to tip the scales toward conversion. See Muir, *Ten Sermons*, Appendix, 67.

119. For examples of antitheatrical pamphleteering on the occasion of the Richmond Theater fire, see Ann Alexander of York, England, *Remarks on the Theatre*; Edwards, *An Address, To All Play-Actors, Play-Hunters*; *Five Important Questions*; Lloyd, *The Richmond Alarm*; and May, *A Voice from Richmond*.

120. "Ordinance," 27 December 1811, in *Distressing Calamity*, 6–7.

121. John Campbell to David Campbell, Richmond, 27 December 1811, Campbell Family

Papers; Samuel Mordecai to Rachel Mordecai, Richmond, 12 February 1812, Jacob Mordecai Papers, Duke University.

122. Ellen Mordecai to Solomon Mordecai, Richmond, 26 December 1813, Jacob Mordecai Papers.

123. Samuel Mordecai to Rachel Mordecai, Richmond, 20 May 1814, Jacob Mordecai Papers. In a letter from the same collection dated 5 May 1814, he wrote, "The Monumental Church was opened a few days since. . . . Today it is to be dedicated and I shall go to hear the celebrated Mr. Meade—The other amusements of this past week were the Races, the learned Pig, Wests Comic songs, and the Circus. The last was the only one I partook of. . . . Good morning my dear, I must go to church, where I will pray for you all."

124. See "Lines on the Folly of Ascribing to Divine Vengeance, the Accidents Which Result from Human Indiscretion" and "Crumbs of Comfort for the Mourners of Richmond."

125. See Shockley, "The Proprietors of Richmond's New Theatre of 1819." Among the prominent actors who appeared at the Richmond Theater in this period were Junius Brutus Booth, father of Edwin and John Wilkes Booth; Thomas Abthorpe Cooper; Edwin Forrest; Charles Kean; and Clara Fisher (see Bondurant, *Poe's Richmond*, 148; Dabney, *Richmond*, 102).

126. Richmond *Enquirer*, 25 May 1816, as cited in Bondurant, *Poe's Richmond*, 144–45.

CHAPTER 5

1. For reasons that will become clear over the course of this chapter, I use the term "queer" rather than gay or lesbian or feminist to describe the multiple forms of resistance to normativity embraced and embodied by these artists. For a strong account of the "multiplicity of homophobias" that circulated around their performances, see Hart, "Karen Finley's Dirty Work."

2. I have taken many of the details for this summary from the district court case decision: *Karen Finley, John Fleck, Holly Hughes, Tim Miller and National Association of Artists' Organizations, Plaintiffs, v. National Endowment for the Arts; and John E. Frohnmayer, in his official capacity as Chairperson National Endowment for the Arts.*

3. District Court, at *5.

4. Rowland Evans and Robert Novak, "The NEA's Suicide Charge," *Washington Post,* 11 May 1990, reproduced in Bolton, *Culture Wars*, 208–9.

5. The statute in question and from which I am quoting here is 20 U.S.C. §954(d)(1).

6. A number of scholarly accounts mistakenly claim that this law was in effect when the artists' grants were denied; such a claim confuses a facial challenge to the statute with an applied challenge, or an actual claim of discrimination, in the case.

7. *National Endowment for the Arts, et al., Petitioners v. Karen Finley*, at *14.

8. The question of "severity" is a legal term of art used either to distinguish between criminal and civil consequences, or to describe the significance of the constitutional harm imposed. Taking up the latter meaning, I am interested here, as I have been throughout this book, in exploring the discursive reach of language in delineating and distinguishing among bodies public.

9. In producing this brief history of the events, I am relying in large part upon the chronology compiled by Debra Singer and Philip Brookman in Bolton, *Culture Wars*, 331–63.

10. In 1988, Serrano's visually stunning, large-scale photograph of a crucifix submerged in his own urine had been jury selected for inclusion in the Southeastern Center for Contemporary Art (SECCA) Awards in the Visual Arts program, an annual traveling exhibition of contemporary works partially supported by a $15,000 grant from the NEA. The Institute for

Contemporary Art in Philadelphia had received a grant of $30,000 to help produce the Mapplethorpe retrospective.

11. Rev. Donald Wildmon, letter concerning Serrano's *Piss Christ*, 5 April 1989, reproduced in Bolton, *Culture Wars*, 27. For more on the activities of Wildmon, see Bolton, 8–10, and the *New York Times* profile by Selcraig, "Reverend Wildmon's War on the Arts."

12. "Debate in Senate over NEA . . . May 19, 1989," in Bolton, *Culture Wars*, 28–31.

13. For a study of how the concept of "community" circulates through the NEA controversy, see Joseph, *Against the Romance of Community*, esp. 25–29, 119–45. Where my interest in publics leads to a broader investigation of both discursive influence and material effects, Joseph is specifically concerned with how, despite their differences, each of the emergent "communities" in the NEA controversy lends itself, via a discourse of "rights," to subsumption under the rubrics of global capital. For a study that touches more closely on my interest in publics and definitions of the public sphere but which, like Joseph, also construes the controversy over the NEA as part of a broader neoliberal agenda, see Schlossman, *Actors and Activists*, esp. 252–57.

14. Pelligrini and Jakobsen, *Love the Sin*, 3. Pelligrini and Jakobsen's project is similar to my own in that they are interested in the ways that "public debates about any number of morally contentious issues—homosexuality and gay rights among them—become part of a process of constituting 'the public'" (15). Pelligrini and Jakobsen's call for exploration of how the dominant cultural logic of Christian morality functions to marginalize and exclude draws upon and extends many of the arguments to disestablish heterosexuality in Lisa Duggan's "Queering the State."

15. Steiner, *The Scandal of Pleasure*, 19. For other accounts of the Culture Wars, see Bolton, *Culture Wars*, and Wallis, Weems, and Yenawine, eds., *Art Matters*. For a subtle discussion of these images and Mapplethorpe's development as artist, see Meyer, *Outlaw Representation*, 158–223.

16. 101st Congress, Public Law 101-121, 23 October 1989, excerpted in Bolton, *Culture Wars*, 121–23. The 1989 Helms Amendment marked the first time that content-based restrictions on NEA funding policies had been imposed and as such violated the principles of viewpoint neutrality that had been the hallmark of the agency's operations since its inception in 1965. For accounts of some of the convoluted maneuvers taken to ensure passage of this amendment, see Honan, "Helms Amendment Is Facing a Major Test in Congress," and Dowd, "Unruffled Helms Basks in Eye of Arts Storm." For histories of the NEA, see Binkiewicz, *Federalizing the Muse*, and Brenson, *Visionaries and Outcasts*.

17. Taken from the Senate debate, 26 July 1989, over the 1989 Helms Amendment, as excerpted in Bolton, *Culture Wars*, 73–86.

18. The Helms Amendment was struck down on both First and Fifth Amendment grounds in federal district court in 1991 in *Bella Lewitzky Dance Foundation v. John E. Frohnmayer*.

19. Vance, "War on Culture," 228.

20. All citations from Robertson are taken from the excerpt of his "red envelope" letter published in Bolton, *Culture Wars*, 123–25.

21. A more pragmatic reason for why Robertson might not have sent the photos can be gleaned from the slighter later case of the artist David Wojnarowicz against Donald Wildmon. In an outraged flyer sent to a 200,000-person mailing list, Wildmon reproduced images taken from Wojnarowicz's *Sex Series* (1988–89), decrying the use of NEA funds in the production of the exhibit's catalog. Wojnarowicz sued Wildmon for libel and copyright infringement and won in federal district court (*Wojnarowicz v. American Family Association*, 745 F Supp. 130 [S.D.N.Y

1990]). For an extended account of this incident and the ironic ways in which it actually expanded the scope of circulation for images that Wildmon found offensive, see Meyer, *Outlaw Representation*, 255–64.

22. Robertson in Bolton, *Culture Wars*, 124, italics mine.

23. Ibid., italics again mine.

24. In "The Children of John Adams: A Historical View of the Fight over Arts Funding" (in *Art Matters*, 253–75), Lewis Hyde argues that the strong theme of voluntarism that came out of the Awakenings of the eighteenth and nineteenth centuries was transmogrified via a "crablike logic" into ideas about the actions of individual taxpayers.

25. Robertson in Bolton, *Culture Wars*, 124.

26. Meyer, *Outlaw Representation*, 3–5. Using a tactic that anticipated Robertson's red envelope mailing, Jesse Helms circulated four Mapplethorpe images that he labeled "indecent" to conference committee members. Sent in envelopes marked "personal and confidential" and "for member's eyes only," Helms opined, "It's your call as to whether the taxpayers' money should be used to fund this sort of thing." See Swisher, "Helms's 'Indecent' Sampler."

27. Meyer, *Outlaw Representation*, 3–4.

28. Ibid., 218–23.

29. Watney, *Policing Desire*, 3. For an insightful discussion about the kinds of mis- and disinformation that circulated, see Treichler, *How to Have Theory in an Epidemic*, esp. 11–41. For a useful history of the formation and activities of ACT-UP and of the failure of the government to respond adequately to the crisis, see Brier, *Infectious Ideas*, esp. 78–121, 156–89.

30. Among the other demographic groups initially affected by the AIDS virus were intravenous drug users and hemophiliacs. Homosexual men, however, became the lightning rods for attacks on those infected by HIV, and those attacks are the focus of my concerns here. For a few of the earliest and most influential attempts to document and report on both the initially feeble governmental response to AIDS and the often fraught responses to the disease by and within the gay community, see Patton, *Inventing AIDS*; Crimp, ed., *AIDS: Cultural Analysis/Cultural Activism*; and Altman, *AIDS in the Mind of America*. More recent histories, memoirs, and analyses of the AIDS epidemic can be found in, Brier, *Infectious Ideas*; Bordowitz, *The AIDS Crisis Is Ridiculous*; and the documentary film *How to Survive a Plague* (2012), dir. David France.

31. Brier, *Infectious Ideas*, 1.

32. Wald, *Contagious*, 240.

33. Treichler, *How to Have Theory in an Epidemic*, 1; and Watney, *Policing Desire*, 9.

34. Yingling, *AIDS and the National Body*, 22.

35. Watney, *Policing Desire*, 143.

36. In the discussion below, I am going somewhat beyond the ideas advanced by Peggy Phelan, who wrote that "it would be disingenuous not to consider the huge specter of AIDS, with all its contaminating popular lies, with all its grief, with all its expense, as the largest ghost which haunts these debates," to argue that AIDS as specter in the NEA debates was often much more than ghostly; it was, in fact, made fully present in the flesh (Phelan, "Money Talks Again," 131). For Phelan, visibility itself constitutes a kind of trap, and while I am sympathetic to this argument in certain theoretical aspects, I am more compelled at least in the instance of the NEA Four artists by the political, which is to say, the life-and-death necessity of making certain bodies public visible as constitutive parts of the body politic (see Phelan, *Unmarked*).

37. Buchanan, "Pursued by Baying Yahoos," in Bolton, *Culture Wars*, 86–88.

38. Buckley, "Identify All the Carriers," italics mine.

39. See also Wald, *Contagious*, 225–26, and Watney, *Policing Desire*, 23.

40. Watney, *Policing Desire*, 9; Wald, *Contagious*, 219, 222. See Lawrence K. Altman, "New Homosexual Disorder Worries Health Officials," *New York Times*, 11 May 1982, C1, C6.

41. See Foucault, *The History of Sexuality* and *"Society Must Be Defended."* For a fascinating study of how seemingly innocuous terms such as "general population" came to signify in shaping public consciousness about AIDS, see Grove, "AIDS: Keywords."

42. Foucault, *The History of Sexuality*, 144–47.

43. Congressional Record, 28 September 1989, cited in Meyer, *Outlaw Representation*, 207.

44. Bersani, "Is the Rectum a Grave?" 203.

45. See Berlant and Warner, "Sex in Public."

46. Phelan, "Serrano, Mapplethorpe, the NEA, and You," 13.

47. See also Meyer, *Outlaw Representation*, 278–79.

48. Dolan, "Practicing Cultural Disruption," 344.

49. See also Phelan, who wrote, "One of the things at stake in this debate is the possibility of different communities, communities of people whose bonds and bodies are not familial or familiar. Helms and friends want to keep those bonds and bodies invisible, unacknowledged, unfunded" ("Money Talks Again," 139).

50. Miller, "Introduction," *Body Blows*, xvi. All subsequent references to this text and to *My Queer Body* will be cited parenthetically by page number. In June 1991, I saw Miller perform an early rendition of *My Queer Body* at the Painted Bride in Philadelphia.

51. Wallace, "Performance Anxiety," 110.

52. For a history of AIDS performance that takes a similar view of Miller's work, see Román, *Acts of Intervention*, esp. 142–44, and "Performing All Our Lives: AIDS, Performance, Community."

53. For discussions of how this dynamic has played out historically in the theater, see my own *Character's Theater*, esp. chap. 2, and Puchner, *Stage Fright*.

54. Diamond, "The Shudder of Catharsis."

55. Phelan, "Tim Miller's *My Queer Body*," 34.

56. Ibid., 32–33.

57. For an important work in this vein, see Cvetkovich, *An Archive of Feelings*.

58. Román, *Acts of Intervention*, 143.

59. Ibid., 143.

60. Ibid., 37.

61. Goldberg, *Performance Art*, 7–8.

62. For an expansive theorization of these dynamics in the context of feminist performance art, see Schneider, *The Explicit Body in Performance*, esp. chap. 2. For the classic essay on this topic, see Diamond's brilliant "Mimesis, Mimicry, and the 'True-Real,'" where she asserts, "Realism is more than an interpretation of reality passing as reality; it produces *reality* by positioning its spectator to recognize and verify its truths" (366).

63. See Case's groundbreaking essay "Toward a Butch-Femme Aesthetic."

64. Diamond, "Mimesis, Mimicry, and the 'True-Real,'" 368, 379. For criticism on Finley that takes this position as its point of departure, see Prammagiore, "Resisting/Performing/Femininity"; Hart, "Motherhood According to Finley"; and Forte, "Focus on the Body." This view of Finley's performances is also taken in Forte, "Women's Performance Art," and Goldstein, "Raging in Tongues," but they also express concerns that, especially in the wake of the NEA controversy, Finley's performances could be recuperated and contained through their commercial circulation and consumption.

65. It is important to note here that Finley became notorious as much for what she actually did on stage as for what she was purported to have done. See, for instance, Fuchs, "Staging the Obscene Body," in which Finley is reported to have "actually put yams up her ass on stage" (48) and the response to this representation in a letter to the editor by Michael Overn, manager for Karen Finley, in which he writes, "Once and for all: *SHE HAS NEVER DONE THIS!!!* She smeared tinned (whipped) yams on her buttocks but she has never, repeat, never put a yam up anywhere. It may seem like a petty mistake but you wouldn't believe the problems this mistake has caused Karen over the years" (9). For more on this controversy, see *A Different Kind of Intimacy* in which Finley documents this widespread misrepresentation, the notoriety it generated, and the damage it inflicted on her career. Characteristically, however, she defends her right to do whatever she might like with her own body: "But what if I had? SO WHAT?" (Finley, *A Different Kind of Intimacy*, 28).

66. Carr, "Unspeakable Practices, Unnatural Acts," 148; Schneider, *The Explicit Body in Performance*, 103.

67. *The Constant State of Desire* was first performed at the Kitchen in New York City in December 1986. No two of Finley's performances are the same, but she has published texts for many of her performance pieces. *The Constant State of Desire* was first published in *TDR* 32.1 (Spring 1988): 139–51 (http://www.jstor.org/stable/1145875) and can also be found in Karen Finley, *Shock Treatment* (San Francisco: City Lights, 1990), 1–26. I have taken my citations above from the *TDR* text, 140–42.

68. "Why Can't This Veal Calf Walk?" from *We Keep Our Victims Ready*, published in Karen Finley, *Shock Treatment*, 128–33.

69. See Hart, "Karen Finley's Dirty Work," 9.

70. See Goldstein, "Raging in Tongues," and Forte, "Women's Performance Art," as well as Erickson, "Appropriation and Transgression," for discussions of how easily some of Finley's more notorious works could be construed and contained as sensational.

71. This project was sponsored by Creative Time and was on display from May 1990 to April 1991. See http://www.creativetime.org/programs/archive/1990/TheBlackSheep.

72. Foster, "Choreographies of Protest."

73. For a useful discussion of this constant wave of memorials and vigils as social performance in the public sphere, see Román, *Acts of Intervention*, esp. 10–40.

74. I have taken my text for "The Black Sheep" from Karen Finley, *Shock Treatment* (San Francisco: City Lights, 1990), 139–44. All subsequent citations will appear parenthetically by page number.

75. Phelan, "Radical Democracy and the Woman Question," 757–58.

76. Dolan, "Performance, Utopia, and the 'Utopian Performative,'" 456–57, 479.

77. In using the term "matter" here, I am deliberately echoing some of the ideas and concepts laid down by Judith Butler in *Bodies That Matter*.

78. See Austin, *How to Do Things with Words*, 5.

79. Walter Dellinger of *Slate* magazine, 28 June 2004, as cited in Baum, *The Supreme Court*, 113. It should be noted that an actual reading from the bench is a rarity; Supreme Court justices may choose but are not required to read their opinions from the bench. In the absence of a reading, the text itself constitutes the performance.

80. The question of how Miller's and Hughes's 1991 NEA applications affected their case is an important one. On the one hand, insofar as the "decency" clause "circumscribe[d] their artistic freedom, because they fear[ed] stepping across an invisible line of 'decency,'" they were able to claim potential injury in the case and hence gain standing for the NEA Four at the district

court level. On the other hand, despite the fact that the Supreme Court case was to be decided on the face of the statute, O'Connor and the other justices were certainly aware that at least two of the NEA Four had received NEA grants before the "decency" clause was enjoined and hence had reason to believe that even if the clause was more than hortatory, it had not resulted in any actual case of injury. This position presumes, of course, that all queer artists only ever produce "queer" art and elides the possibility, as Miller and Hughes suggest, that out of fear for "stepping across an invisible line of 'decency,'" they felt compelled to censor themselves and shape their new proposals to conform to the standards of the new law (District Court, at *12).

81. The NEA Four denied permission to the Family Research Institute of Wisconsin (FRI) to file an amicus brief in their favor, arguing that their "interests [were] not aligned," but the FRI filed nevertheless: *Motion for Leave to File Brief Amicus Curiae* and *Brief Amicus Curiae of the Family Research Institute of Wisconsin in Support of Respondents.*

82. Baum, *The Supreme Court*, 76–82.

83. *Brief Amicus Curiae of the American Center for Law and Justice Supporting Petitioners*, at *1.

84. *Brief of Morality in Media, Inc. as Amicus Curiae in Support of Petitioner*, at *1, *10.

85. Not insignificantly, this view was clearly stated as well in both the district and appeals court decisions in favor of the artists. For the U.S. Court of Appeals for the Ninth Circuit, Judge James R. Browning wrote, "The individual members of a pluralistic society, and particularly our own, have a great variety of beliefs and values, largely unascertainable" (*United States Court of Appeals for the Ninth Circuit*, at *15). For the district court, Judge A. Wallace Tashima, submitted that for all practical purposes "such words as 'decency' and 'respect' are contentless in the context of American society: the very nature of our pluralistic society is that there are an inherent number of values and beliefs, and correlatively, there may be no national 'general standards of decency'" (District Court, at *15).

86. *Brief of Amicus Curiae National Family Legal Foundation in Support of the United States.*

87. Cobb, *God Hates Fags*, 26–27, 4.

88. See ibid., 5. *National Family Legal Foundation*, at *7.

89. *Irving Rust, et al., Petitioners v. Sullivan, Louis W., Secretary of Health and Human Services*, at *1.

90. See, respectively, Corbin, "Mixed Speech," and Cole, "Beyond Unconstitutional Conditions."

91. See, for instance, Post, "Subsidized Speech."

92. Cole, "Beyond Constitutional Conditions," at *2, citing *Rust.*

93. *Rosenberger, et al., Petitioners v. Rector and Visitors of the University of Virginia.*

94. Post, "Subsidized Speech," *3.

95. *Rosenberger v. Rector*, at *12.

96. *Brief Amicus Curiae of Americans United for Separation of Church and State in Support of Respondents*, at *1, 2.

97. *Brief Amici Curiae of the New School for Social Research and the Brennan Center for Justice in Support of Affirmance*, at *1, 3.

98. *Brief for Claes Oldenburg, et al. Amici Curiae, Supporting Respondents.*

99. Cole, "Beyond Constitutional Conditions," *13.

100. Post, "Subsidized Speech," *18, italics mine. In a similar vein, Post also writes, "Decency is not a matter of partisan politics. It is a shared value, not a preference" (*16).

101. Baum, *The Supreme Court*, 109.

102. *Brief for the Petitioners*, *8–11.

103. Ibid., *15–16. Drawing on the majoritarian rationale laid out by legal scholar Robert

C. Post (see above), Waxman made the political case for his arguments even more explicit in his *Reply Brief for the Petitioner*, *6.

104. *Respondents Brief*, *4

105. See 1998 U.S. Trans. LEXIS 57. A recording of the Supreme Court oral arguments in *NEA v. Finley* can be downloaded from the website of the Oyez Project, sponsored and produced by the Chicago-Kent College of Law at Illinois Institute for Technology: *http://www.oyez.org/cases/1990-1999/1997/1997_97_371*.

106. Foucault, *History of Sexuality*, 136, 140.

107. *NEA v. Finley*, at *11.

108. Heyman, "The National Endowment for the Arts v. Finley," *11.

109. Bezanson, "The Government Speech Forum," *7.

110. Ibid., *9.

111. Ibid., *10.

112. Kantorowicz, *The King's Two Bodies*, 3.

Works Cited

MANUSCRIPTS

Histrio-Mastix

Additional MSS 11,1764, fols. 8b-29. British Library, London.

Douce. MSS 173. Bodleian Library. Oxford University, Oxford, UK.

HM 80. Huntington Library, San Marino, CA.

MS Eng 835. Houghton Library, Harvard University, Cambridge, MA.

MS Eng 1359, fols. 180–318. Houghton Library. Harvard University, Cambridge, MA.

State Papers 16/534. *The Passages Against the King and State in* Histrio Mastix. Microfilm, SP 16/534 Document 71, fols. 122–134v. British National Archive, London.

Stowe MSS 159, fols. 45–78. British Library, London.

Tanner MSS 299, fols. 123–134v. Bodleian Library, Oxford University, Oxford, UK.

Richmond Theater Fire

"Autobiography of Caroline Homassel, Wife of Dr. Phillip Thornton." MSS 5:1 T3945:1. Typescript. Virginia Historical Society, Richmond, VA.

Breckinridge Family Papers, 1740–1902. Virginia Historical Society, Richmond, VA.

Brown, Thomas. "Recollections of the Events of My Life." Accession 36108, Personal Papers Collection, Library of Virginia, Richmond, VA.

Campbell Family Papers. Duke University, Durham, NC.

Joynes Family Papers, 1776–1898, Section 3. Virginia Historical Society, Richmond, VA.

Robert Mills to Miss Sarah Jane, Richmond, VA, 13 December 1812. MSS 2 M6283a2. Virginia Historical Society, Richmond, VA.

Mordecai Family Papers. Collection Number 847, Southern Historical Collection. Wilson Library. University of North Carolina, Chapel Hill.

Jacob Mordecai Papers. Duke University, Durham, NC.

Mrs. Edmund Waller Collection, 1780–1825. Accession 22068. Personal Papers Collection. Library of Virginia, Richmond, VA.

PRIMARY WORKS

Histrio-Mastix

Arber, Edward, ed. *A Transcript of the Registers of the Company of Stationers of London 1559–1640 AD.* 5 volumes. London, 1877.

Baker, Richard. *Theatrum Redivivum, or The Theatre Vindicated.* London, 1662.

A Complete Collection of State-Trials, and Proceedings for High-Treason, and Other Crimes and Misdemeanours; From the Reign of King Richard II, to the End of the Reign of King George I. Second edition. 6 volumes. London, 1730.

Davenant, William. *The Temple of Love.* London, 1634.

Gardiner, Samuel Rawson, ed. *Documents Relating to the Proceedings Against William Prynne, in 1634 and 1637.* London: Camden Society, 1877. Reprint, New York: Johnson Reprint, 1965.

Gosson, Stephen. *Playes Confuted in Five Actions.* London, 1582.

———. *The School of Abuse.* London, 1579.

Heywood, Thomas. *The English Traveller.* London, 1633.

———. *A Pleasant Comedy, Called a Mayden-Head Well Lost.* London, 1634.

The King's Maiesties Declaration to His Subjects, Concerning Lawfull Sports to Be Vsed. London, 1618.

Milton, John. [*Comus.*]*A Maske Presented at Ludlow Castle, 1634 on Michaelmasse Night, Before the Right Honorable, Iohn Earle of Bridgewater, Vicount Brackly, Lord Praesident of Wales, and One of His Maiesties Most Honorable Privie Counsell.* London, 1637.

———. *Paradise Lost.* Edited by Scott Elledge. New York: W. W. Norton, 1975.

Munday, Arthur. *A Second and Third Blast of Retrait from Plaies and Theaters.* London, 1580.

Prynne, William. *Anti-Arminianisme. Or the Chvrch of Englands Old Antithesis of New Arminianisme.* Second edition. London, 1630.

———. *A Briefe Svrvay and Censvre of Mr. Cozens His Couzening Deuotions.* London, 1628.

———. *God No Impostor nor Delvder.* London, 1629.

———. *Healthes: Sickness.* London, 1628.

———. *Histrio-Mastix: The Players Scourge or the Actors Tragaedie.* London, 1633.

———. *Lame Giles His Havltings.* London, 1630.

———. *The Perpetuitie of a Regenerate Man's Estate.* London, 1627.

———. *The Vnlouelinesse, of Love-Lockes.* London, 1628.

Rushworth, John. *Historical Collections: The Second Part.* London, 1680.

Shirley, James. *The Bird in a Cage.* London, 1633.

———. *The Triumph of Peace.* 1634. In *A Book of Masques: In Honour of Allardyce Nicoll*, edited by Clifford Leech. Cambridge: Cambridge University Press, 1980.

Statutes of the Realm: Printed by Command of His Majesty King George the Third, In Pursuance of an Address of the House of Commons of Great Britain. London: Printed by George Eyre and Andrew Strahan, 1810–1822.

Strode, William. *The Floating Island.* 1636. London, 1655.

Stuart Royal Proclamations. Volume 2: Royal Proclamations of King Charles I 1625–1646. Edited by James F. Larkin. Oxford: Clarendon, 1983.

Stubbes, Phillip. *The Anatomie of Abuses.* London, 1583.

Whitelocke, Bulstrode. *Memorials of the English Affairs: Or, An Historical Account of What Passed from the Beginning of the Reign of King Charles the First, to King Charles the Second His Happy Restauration.* London, 1682.

The Collier Controversy

Anon. *An Answer to Mr. Collier's Defence of His Absolution of Sir William Perkins.* London, 1696.

———. *A Defence of Dramatick Poetry.* London, 1698.

———. *A Letter to A. H. Esq.; Concerning the Stage.* 1698. Introduction by H. T. Swedenberg, Jr. Augustan Reprint Series; Series Three: *Essays on the Stage.* London, 1946.

———. *The Stage Acquitted. Being a Full Answer to Mr. Collier, and the Other Enemies of the Drama.* London, 1699.

———. *A Vindication of the Stage.* London, 1698.

Cibber, Colley. *An Apology for the Life of Colley Cibber.* Edited by B. R. S. Fone. Ann Arbor: University of Michigan Press, 1968.

———. *The Careless Husband.* 1705. Edited by William W. Appleton. Regents Restoration Drama Series. Lincoln: University of Nebraska Press, 1966.

Collier, Jeremy. *A Defence of the Absolution Given to Sir William Perkins.* London, 1696.

———. *A Defence of the Short View of the Profaneness and Immorality of the English Stage.* 1699. Preface by Arthur Freeman. New York: Garland, 1972.

———. *Essays upon Several Moral Subjects. In Two Parts.* 1697. Sixth edition, corrected. London, 1709.

———. *A Further Vindication of the Absolution Given to Sir William Perkins.* London, 1696.

———. *A Perswasive to Consideration.* London, 1695.

———. *A Short View of the Immorality and Profaneness of the English Stage.* London, 1698. Preface by Arthur Freeman. New York: Garland, 1972.

Congreve, William. *Amendments of Mr. Collier's False and Imperfect Citations.* London, 1698. Preface by Arthur Freeman. New York: Garland, 1972.

Dennis, John. *The Usefulness of the Stage.* 1698. Preface by Arthur Freeman. New York: Garland, 1972.

Dryden, John. *Amphitryon; or, the Two Sosias.* 1690. In *The Works of John Dryden*, volume 15, edited by Edward Niles Hooker and H. T. Swedenberg, Jr. Berkeley: University of California Press, 1976.

———. *Don Sebastian.* 1690. In *The Works of John Dryden*, volume 15, edited by Edward Niles Hooker and H. T. Swedenberg, Jr. Berkeley: University of California Press, 1976.

———. *King Arthur.* London, 1691.

D'Urfey, Thomas. *The Campaigners: Or, the Pleasant Adventures at Brussels. A Comedy. With a Familiar Preface upon a Late Reformer of the Stage.* London, 1698. EEBO.

———. *The Comical History of Don Quixote, Part I.* London, 1694. EEBO.

———. *The Comical History of Don Quixote, Part the Second.* London, 1694. EEBO.

———. *The Comical History of Don Quixote, The Third Part.* London, 1696. EEBO.

Johnson, Samuel. *Lives of the Poets.* Edited and introduction by Edmund Fuller. New York: Avon, 1965.

[Ridpath, George]. *The Stage Condemned.* London, 1698.

Vanbrugh, John. *The Relapse or Virtue in Danger. Being the Sequel of* The Fool in Fashion. 1696. Edited by Curt Zimansky. Regents Restoration Drama Series. Lincoln: University of Nebraska Press, 1970.

———. *A Short Vindication of the* Relapse *and the* Provok'd Wife *from Immorality and Prophaneness*. 1698. Preface by Arthur Freeman. London: Garland, 1972.

The Douglas Controversy

"Admonition and Exhortation by the Rev. Presbytery of Edinburgh to All Within Their Bounds." *The Scots Magazine* 19 (January 1757): 18–19.

Anderson, Rev. George. *An Estimate of the Profit and Loss of Religion, Personally, and Publicly Stated: Illuminated with References to Essay on Morality and Natural Religion*. Edinburgh, 1753.

Anon. *Douglas, A Tragedy, Weighed in the Balances, and Found Wanting*. Edinburgh, 1757.

———. *The Immorality of Stage-Plays in General and of the Tragedy of* Douglas, *In Particular, Briefly Illustrated; In a Letter from Athelstaneford to the Moderator of the Presbytery of Haddington*. Edinburgh, 1757.

———. *Infidelity: A Proper Object of Censure*. Glasgow, 1756.

———. *A Letter to the Reverend the Moderator, and Members of the Presbytery of Haddington*. Edinburgh, 1757.

———. *The Tragedy of Douglas Analysed*. London, 1757.

Blair, Hugh. *Observations upon a Pamphlet Intitled* An Analysis of the Moral and Religious Sentiments in the Writings of Sopho and David Hume, Esq. Edinburgh, 1755.

Bonar, Reverend John of Cockpen. *An Analysis of the Moral and Religious Sentiments Contained in the Writings of SOPHO, and David Hume, Esq; Addressed to the Consideration of the Reverend and Honourable Members of the General Assembly of the Church of Scotland*. Edinburgh, 1755.

Carlyle, Alexander. *Autobiography of Alexander Carlyle of Inveresk 1722–1805*. London: T. N. Foulis, 1910.

Ferguson, Adam. *The Morality of Stage-Plays Seriously Considered*. Edinburgh, 1757.

Gentleman, Francis. *The Dramatic Censor; or Critical Companion*. Two volumes. London, 1770.

Goldsmith, Oliver. "*Douglas*, A Tragedy. As It Is Acted at the Theatre-Royal in Covent-Garden." In volume 1, *Collected Works of Oliver Goldsmith*, edited by Arthur Friedman. Oxford: Clarendon, 1966.

Home, Henry, Lord Kames. 1751. *Essays on the Principles of Morality and Natural Religion*. New York: Garland, 1983.

Home, John. *Douglas*. In *Eighteenth-Century Tragedy*, edited and introduction by Michael R. Booth. London: Oxford University Press, 1965.

Hume, David. *Four Dissertations*. London, 1757.

Inchbald, Elizabeth. "Remarks" on *Douglas; A Tragedy, In Five Acts; By Mr. Home as Performed at the Theatre Royal, Covent Garden*. London, 1810.

Maclaurin, John. *Apology for the Writers Against the Tragedy of* Douglas. *With Some Remarks on That Play*. Edinburgh, 1757.

———. *The Deposition, or Fatal Miscarriage: A Tragedy*. London, 1757.

———. *The Philosopher's Opera*. 1757. In *Scottish Ballad Operas III*, selected by Walter H. Rubsamen. New York: Garland, 1974.

The Scots Magazine. Volumes 13–19. 1751–1757. Edinburgh.

Tytler, Alexander Fraser, Lord Woodhouselee. *Memoirs of the Life and Writings of the Honourable*

Henry Home of Kames. 1807. In Volume 1, *The Collected Works of Henry Home, Lord Kames*. London: Routledge/Thoemmes, 1993.

Witherspoon, John. *A Serious Inquiry into the Nature and Effects of the Stage: And a Letter Respecting Play Actors*. 1757. New York, 1812.

Richmond Theater Fire

An Account of the Awful Calamity Occasioned by the Conflagration of the Theatre, at Richmond, Virginia. London, 1812.

Alexander, Ann. *Remarks on the Theatre, and on the Late Fire at Richmond, in Virginia*. York, England, 1812.

Alexander, Archibald. *A Discourse Occasioned by the Burning of the Theatre in the City of Richmond, Virginia. By Which Awful Calamity a Large Number of Lives Were Lost. Delivered in the Third Presbyterian Church, Philadelphia, on the Eighth Day of January, 1812, at the Request of the Virginia Students Attached to the Medical Class, in the University of Pennsylvania*. Philadelphia, 1812.

Blair, John D. *A Sermon Occasioned by the Dreadful Calamity with Which the City of Richm[on]d Was Visited on the Night of the 26th of Dec[embe]r 1811*. Library of Virginia Microfilm Reel 41008.

"Burning of the Richmond Theatre." In *The Ladies Garland*. 1 no. 16 (May 1838): 299–301.

"The Burning of the Richmond Theatre, 1811." *Virginia Historical Magazine History and Biography* 51 no. 3 (July 1943): 297–99.

Calamity at Richmond, Being a Narrative of the Affecting Circumstances Attending the Awful Conflagration of the Theatre, in the City of Richmond. Philadelphia, 1812.

A Collection of Facts and Statements, Relative to the Fatal Event, Which Occurred at the Theatre, In Richmond, On the 26th December, 1811. Principally Extracted from the Enquirer. Richmond, 1812.

A Concise Statement of the Awful Conflagration of the Theatre, in the City of Richmond. Philadelphia, 1812.

"Crumbs of Comfort." In *Virginia Argus*, 13 February 1812.

Dana, Joseph. *Tribute of Sympathy: A Sermon Delivered at Ipswich (Mass.) January 12, 1812, on the Late Overwhelming Calamity at Richmond in Virginia*. Newburyport, MA, 1812.

Dashiell, George. *A Sermon, Occasioned by the Burning of the Theatre in the City of Richmond, Virginia on the Twenty-Six of December 1811. Delivered in St. Peter's Church, Baltimore; on the Twelfth of January, 1812*. Early American Imprints, series 2, no. 25218. Baltimore, 1812.

Distressing Calamity. A Brief Account of the Late Fire at Richmond, (Virg.) In which the Theatre Was Burnt, and Upwards of One Hundred and Sixty Persons, Perished in the Flames. Boston, 1812.

Edwards, John. *An Address, to All Play-Actors, Play-Hunters, Legislators, Governors, Magistrates, Clergy, Churchmen, Deists, and the World at Large*. Early American Imprints, series 2, no. 25321. New York, 1812.

Ely, Reverend Dr. E. S. "Richmond's Lament." In *The Orator's Guide; Selections, Elegant Extracts in Poetry and Prose*, 59–61. Philadelphia, 1822.

Farley, Charles. *Airs, Glees, and Choruses in a New Grand Ballet Pantomime of Action, Called Raymond and Agnes: Or the Castle of Lindenbergh*. London, 1797.

Fisher, George D. *History and Reminiscences of the Monumental Church, Richmond, VA, from 1814 to 1878*. Richmond, 1880.

Five Important Questions, on the Subject of the Divine Government of the World, Occasioned by Serious Reflections on the Alarming and Awfully Severe Visitation of the Theatre in Richmond, December 1811, Stated and Answered, in a Letter to an Honourable Young Gentleman in Office. 1812.

"For the Argus." In *Virginia Argus*, 23 January 1812.

A Full Account of the Burning of the Richmond Theatre. Richmond, 1858.

Gilman, Samuel. *Monody on the Victims and Sufferers by the Late Conflagration in the City of Richmond, Virginia.* Boston, 1812.

Hill, William. *A Sermon Delivered in the Presbyterian Meeting-House in Winchester, on Thursday the 23d of Jan. 1812; Being a Day of Fasting and Humiliation, Appointed by the Citizens of Winchester on Account of the Late Calamitous Fire at the Richmond Theatre.* Winchester, VA, 1812.

Lewis, Matthew. *The Monk.* 1796. Edited by Howard Anderson. Introduction by Emma McEvoy. Oxford World Classics. Oxford: Oxford University Press, 2008.

"Lines on the Folly of Ascribing to Divine Vengeance, the Accidents Which Result from Human Indiscretion." In *Virginia Argus*, 26 January 1812.

"Lines Sacred to the Memory of Miss Maria Nelson." In *Virginia Argus*, 30 January 1812.

Lloyd, Rees. *The Richmond Alarm: A Plain and Familiar Discourse in the Form of a Dialogue Between a Father and His Son in Three Parts.* Early American Imprints, series 2, no. 31946. Philadelphia, 1814.

May, Reverend Robert. *A Voice from Richmond, and Other Addresses to Children and Youth.* Philadelphia, 1842.

Miller, Samuel, D. D. *A Sermon, Delivered January 18, 1812, at the Request of Young Gentlemen in the city of New York Who Had Assembled to Express Their Condolence with the Inhabitants of Richmond, on the Late Mournful Dispensation of Providence in That City.* New York, 1812.

"Miss Margaret Copland." In *Richmond Enquirer*, 7 January 1812.

Mordecai, Samuel. *A Discourse Delivered at the Synagogue at Richmond, of the First Day of January 1812. A Day Devoted to Humiliation and Prayer, in Consequence of the Loss of Lives Caused by the Burning of the Theatre on the 26 Day of December 1811.* Mordecai Family Papers, Collection Number 847. Series 3.2, Box 8, File 112. Southern Historical Collection. University of North Carolina, Chapel Hill.

———. *Richmond in By-Gone Days.* Second edition, 1860. Richmond, VA: Dietz, 1946.

"Mortuary." *The Port Folio* VII.3 (March 1812): 303–5.

Muir, James. *Ten Sermons.* Alexandria, 1812.

Narrative and Report of the Causes and Circumstances of the Deplorable Conflagration at Richmond. Richmond, 1812.

Particular Account of the Dreadful Fire at Richmond, Virginia . . . to Which Is Added, Some Observations on Theatrical Performances. Baltimore, 1812.

"A Retrospect of the Year 1811." *The Port Folio* VII.2 (February 1812): 148–66.

Richards, George. *The Spirit of an Evening Lecture, February 12, 1812; On the Late Calamity at Richmond, Virginia. Most Respectively Inscribed to the Universalist Church.* Philadelphia, 1812.

Sabin, Elijah. *A Discourse, Preached on Tuesday, February 11, 1812, in the Presence of the Supreme Executive of Massachusetts, by Request of the Young Men of Boston, Commemorative of the Late Calamitous Fire at Richmond.* Boston, 1812.

"Tribute to Lucy Gwathmey." In *Virginia Argus*, 17 February 1812.

NEA v. Finley

20 U. S. C. §954(d)(1).

101st Congress, Public Law 101-121, §304(a).

1998 U. S. Trans. NEA v. Finley. LEXIS 57.

Bella Lewitzky Dance Foundation v. John E. Frohnmayer; Newport Harbor Art Museum v. National Endowment for the Arts, 754 F. Supp. 774, U. S. District Central California 1991. LEXIS 332.

Bolton, Richard, ed. *Culture Wars: Documents from the Recent Controversies in the Arts.* New York: New Press, 1992.

Brief Amicus Curiae of the American Center for Law and Justice Supporting Petitioners. 1998 U.S. S. Ct. Briefs. LEXIS 93.

Brief Amicus Curiae of Americans United for Separation of Church and State in Support of Respondents. 1998 U.S. S. Ct. Briefs. LEXIS 102.

Brief Amicus Curiae National Family Legal Foundation in Support of the United States, 1998 U.S. S. Ct. Briefs. LEXIS 95.

Brief Amicus Curiae of the New School for Social Research and the Brennan Center for Justice in Support of Affirmance. 1998 U.S. S. Ct. Briefs. LEXIS 113.

Brief for Claes Oldenburg, Arthur Miller, Jasper Johns, Hans Haacke, Coosje Van Bruggen, E. L. Doctorow, Nancy Spero, Leon Golub, Andres Serrano, Robert Colescott, Tony Kushner, Luis Cruz Azaceta, Terrence McNally, Barbara Kruger, David Hammons, Adrian Piper, Susan Rothenberg, Bruce Nauman, Erica Jong, and Richard Serra, Amici Curiae, Supporting Respondents. 1998 U.S. S. Ct. Briefs. LEXIS 1387.

Brief for the Petitioners, 1998 U.S. S. Ct. Briefs. LEXIS 15.

Brief of Morality in Media, Inc., as Amicus Curiae in Support of Petitioner. 1998 U.S. S. Ct. Briefs. LEXIS 6.

Buckley, William F. "Identify All the Carriers." *New York Times,* 18 March 1986, A27. ProQuest.

Creative Time, http://www.creativetime.org/programs/archive/1990/TheBlackSheep.

Finley, Karen. "The Black Sheep." In *Shock Treatment,* 139–44. San Francisco: City Lights, 1990.

——. *The Constant State of Desire.* In *TDR: The Drama Review* 32 no. 1 (Spring 1988): 139–51. JSTOR.

——. *A Different Kind of Intimacy: The Collected Writings of Karen Finley, A Memoir.* New York: Thunder's Mouth, 2000.

——. *Shock Treatment.* San Francisco: City Lights, 1990.

——. *We Keep Our Victims Ready.* In *Shock Treatment,* 128–33. San Francisco: City Light, 2000.

Karen Finley, John Fleck, Holly Hughes, Tim Miller and National Association of Artists' Organizations, Plaintiffs, v. National Endowment for the Arts; and John E. Frohnmayer, in His Official Capacity as Chairperson National Endowment for the Arts, Defendants. 795 F. Supp 1457, U.S. District Central California (9 June 1992). LEXIS 8070.

Miller, Tim. *My Queer Body.* In *Body Blows: Six Performances,* 79–121. Madison: University of Wisconsin Press, 2002.

Motion for Leave to File Brief Amicus Curiae and *Brief Amicus Curiae of the Family Research Institute of Wisconsin in Support of Respondents. National Endowment for the Arts v. Finley,* 524 U. S. 569. 1998 U.S. S. Ct. Briefs. LEXIS 99.

National Endowment for the Arts, et al., Petitioners v. Karen Finley, et al. 524 U. S. 569 (1998). 1998 LEXIS 4211.

The Oyez Project: NEA v. Finley. http://www.oyez.org/cases/1990-1999/1997/1997_97_371.

Reply Brief for the Petitioner, 1998 U.S. S. Ct. Briefs. LEXIS 181.

Respondents Brief, 1998 U.S. S. Ct. Briefs. LEXIS 110.

Rosenberger v. Rector and Visitors of the University of Virginia. 515 U. S. 819 (1995). 1995 U.S. LEXIS 4461.

Rust v. Sullivan 500 U.S. 173 (1991). 1991 U.S. LEXIS 2908.

United States Court of Appeals for the Ninth Circuit, 100F.3d.671. 1996. LEXIS 28837.

SECONDARY SOURCES

Abzug, Robert H. *Cosmos Crumbling: American Reform and the Religious Imagination.* New York: Oxford University Press, 1994.

Ahnert, Thomas. "Clergymen as Polite Philosophers. *Douglas* and the Conflict Between Moderate and Orthodox in the Scottish Enlightenment." *Intellectual History Review* 18 no. 3 (2008): 375–83. doi. 10.1080/17496970802319276.

———. *The Moral Culture of the Scottish Enlightenment, 1690–1805.* New Haven: Yale University Press, 2014.

Alexander, James Waddel. *The Life of Archibald Alexander, D. D.* New York, 1854.

Allen, Ned Bliss. *The Sources of John Dryden's Comedies.* New York: Gordian, 1967.

Altman, Dennis. *AIDS in the Mind of America: The Social, Political, and Psychological Impact of a New Epidemic.* New York: Anchor, 1987.

Altman, Lawrence K. "New Homosexual Disorder Worries Health Officials." *New York Times* 11 May 1982, C1, C6.

Anthony, Sister Rose. *The Jeremy Collier Stage Controversy, 1698–1726.* 1937. New York: Benjamin Blom, 1966.

Atherton, Ian. "The Press and Popular Political Opinion." In *A Companion to Stuart Britain,* edited by Barry Coward, 88–110. Oxford: Blackwell, 2003.

Augustine, Saint. *Concerning the City of God Against the Pagans.* New York: Penguin, 1984.

Austin, J. L. *How to Do Things With Words.* Second edition. Cambridge, MA: Harvard University Press, 1975.

Backscheider, Paula. "John Home's *Douglas* and the Theme of the Unfulfilled Life." *Studies in Scottish Literature* 14 (1979): 90–97.

———. *Spectacular Politics: Theatrical Power and Mass Culture in Early Modern England.* Baltimore: Johns Hopkins University Press, 1993.

Baker, Meredith Henne. *The Richmond Theater Fire: Early America's First Great Disaster.* Baton Rouge: Louisiana State University Press, 2012.

Balme, Christopher. *The Theatrical Public Sphere.* Cambridge: Cambridge University Press, 2014.

Barish, Jonas. *The Antitheatrical Prejudice.* Berkeley: University of California Press, 1981.

Barker-Benfield, J. G. *The Culture of Sensibility: Sex and Society in Eighteenth-Century Britain.* Chicago: University of Chicago Press, 1992.

Barnes, Thomas G. "Star Chamber Mythology." *American Journal of Legal History* 5 no. 1 (January 1961): 1–11.

Baron, Sabrina A. "The Guises of Dissemination in Early Seventeenth-Century England: News in Manuscript and Print." In *The Politics of Information in Early Modern Europe,* edited by Brendan Dooley and Sabrina A. Baron, 41–56. London: Routledge, 2001.

Barrett, Philip. *Gilbert Hunt, The City Blacksmith*. Richmond, 1859.

Baum, Lawrence. *The Supreme Court*. Tenth edition. Washington, DC: CQ Press, 2010.

Bennett, Susan. *Theatre Audiences: A Theory of Production and Reception*. London: Routledge, 1990.

Bentley, Gerald Eades. *The Jacobean and Caroline Stage*. 7 volumes. Oxford: Clarendon, 1941–1968.

Bercovitch, Sacvan. *The American Jeremiad*. Madison: University of Wisconsin Press, 1978.

Bergeron, David. *English Civic Pageantry, 1558–1642*. Columbia: University of South Carolina Press, 1971.

Berlant, Lauren, and Michael Warner. "Sex in Public." *Critical Inquiry*, 24 no. 2 (Winter 1989): 547–66. JSTOR.

Berman, Myron. *Richmond's Jewry, 1769–1976: Shabbat in Schockoe*. Charlottesville: University Press of Virginia, 1979.

Bersani, Leo. "Is the Rectum a Grave?" *October* 43 (Winter 1997): 197–222. JSTOR.

Bevington, David, and Peter Holbrook, eds. *The Politics of the Stuart Court Masque*. Cambridge: Cambridge University Press, 1998.

Bezanson, Randall P. "'The Government Speech Forum': Forbes and Finley and Government Speech Selection Judgments," *Iowa Law Review* 83 (August 1998). Iowa L. Rev. 953, Lexis/Nexis Academic.

Bilhartz, Terry D. *Urban Religion and the Second Great Awakening: Church and Society in Early National Baltimore*. Teaneck, NJ: Fairleigh Dickinson University Press, 1986.

Binkiewicz, Donna M. *Federalizing the Muse: United States Arts Policy and the National Endowment for the Arts, 1965–1980*. Chapel Hill: University of North Carolina Press, 2004.

Boles, John. *The Great Revival, 1787–1805*. Lexington: University Press of Kentucky, 1972.

Bondurant, Agnes M. *Poe's Richmond*. Richmond, VA: Garrett and Massie, 1942.

Bordowitz, Gregg. *The AIDS Crisis Is Ridiculous and Other Writings, 1986–2003*. Edited by James Meyer. Cambridge, MA: MIT Press, 2004.

Bowers, Toni. *Force or Fraud: British Seduction Stories and the Problem of Resistance, 1660–1760*. Oxford: Oxford University Press, 2011.

Braun, Harald Ernst. *Juan de Mariana and Early Modern Spanish Political Thought*. Aldershot, UK: Ashgate, 2007.

Brenson, Michael. *Visionaries and Outcasts: The NEA, Congress, and the Place of the Visual Artist in America*. New York: New Press, 2001.

Bressler, Ann Lee. *The Universalist Movement in America, 1770–1880*. Oxford: Oxford University Press, 2001.

Brewer, John. "'The Most Polite Age and the Most Vicious': Attitudes Towards Culture as a Commodity, 1660–1800." In *The Consumption of Culture, 1600–1900: Image, Object, Text*, edited by Ann Bermingham and John Brewer, 341–61. London: Routledge, 1995.

Brier, Jennifer. *Infectious Ideas: U.S. Political Responses to the AIDS Crisis*. Chapel Hill: University of North Carolina Press, 2009.

Brody, Jennifer DeVere. *Punctuation: Art, Politics, Play*. Durham: Duke University Press, 2008.

Brougham, Henry, Lord. *The Life and Times of Henry, Lord Brougham, Written by Himself*. 3 volumes. Edinburgh, 1871.

Brown, Callum G. *The Social History of Religion in Scotland Since 1730*. London: Methuen, 1987.

Brown, Ian. "Public and Private Performance: 1650–1800." In *The Edinburgh Companion to Scottish Drama*, edited by Ian Brown, 22–40. Edinburgh: Edinburgh University Press, 2011.

Brown, Laura. *English Dramatic Form, 1660–1760*. New Haven: Yale University Press, 1981.

Burgett, Bruce. *Sentimental Bodies: Sex, Gender, and Citizenship in the Early Republic*. Princeton: Princeton University Press, 1998.

Burke, Edmund. *A Philosophical Inquiry into the Origins of Our Ideas of the Sublime and the Beautiful*. (1757). Oxford: Oxford University Press, 1990.

Butler, Jon. *Awash in a Sea of Faith: Christianizing the American People*. Cambridge, MA: Harvard University Press, 1990.

Butler, Judith. *Bodies That Matter: On the Discursive Limits of "Sex."* New York: Routledge, 1993.

Butler, Martin. "Courtly Negotiations." In *The Politics of the Stuart Court Masque*, edited by David Bevington and Peter Holbrook, 20–40. Cambridge: Cambridge University Press, 1998.

———. "Politics and the Masque: *The Triumph of Peace*." *Seventeenth Century* 2 (1987): 117–41.

———. *Theatre and Crisis, 1632–1642*. Cambridge: Cambridge University Press, 1984.

Butsch, Richard. *The Citizen Audience: Crowds, Publics, and Individuals*. New York: Routledge, 2008.

Bywaters, David. *Dryden in Revolutionary England*. Berkeley: University of California Press, 1991.

Canfield, J. Douglas. *Heroes and States: On the Ideology of Restoration Tragedy*. Lexington: University of Kentucky Press, 1997.

———. "Poetical Injustice in Some Neglected Masterpieces of Restoration Drama." In *Rhetorics of Ordering/Ordering of Rhetorics in English Neoclassical Literature*, edited by J. Douglas Canfield and J. Paul Hunter, 23–45. Newark: University of Delaware Press, 1989.

———. *Tricksters and Estates: On the Ideology of Restoration Comedy*. Lexington: University of Kentucky Press, 1997.

Cannan, Paul D. *The Emergence of Dramatic Criticism in England: From Jonson to Pope*. Basingstoke, UK: Palgrave Macmillan, 2006.

Carlson, Marvin. *Performance: A Critical Introduction*. Second edition. New York: Routledge, 2004.

———. *Places of Performance: The Semiotics of Theatre Architecture*. Ithaca, NY: Cornell University Press, 1989.

Carr, C. "Unspeakable Practices, Unnatural Acts: The Taboo Art of Karen Finley." In *Acting Out: Feminist Performance*, edited by Lynda Hart and Peggy Phelan, 141–51. Ann Arbor: University of Michigan Press, 1993.

Case, Sue-Ellen. "Toward a Butch-Femme Aesthetic." In *Making a Spectacle*, edited by Lynda Hart, 282–99. Ann Arbor: University of Michigan Press, 1989.

Chadwick, Bruce. *I Am Murdered: George Wythe, Thomas Jefferson, and the Killing That Shocked a New Nation*. Hoboken, NJ: John Wiley, 2009.

Cheyney, Edward P. "The Court of Star Chamber." *American Historical Review* 18 no. 4 (July 1913): 727–50.

Christian, W. Asbury. *Richmond, Her Past and Present*. Richmond, VA: L. H. Jenkins, 1912.

Clark, J. C. D. *English Society, 1688–1832: Ideology, Social Structure and Political Practice During the Ancien Regime*. Cambridge: Cambridge University Press, 1985.

Claydon, Tony. *William III and the Godly Revolution*. Cambridge: Cambridge University Press, 1996.

Clegg, Cyndia. *Press Censorship in Caroline England*. Cambridge: Cambridge University Press, 2008.

Click, Patricia. *The Spirit of the Times: Amusements in Nineteenth-Century Baltimore, Norfolk, and Richmond*. Charlottesville: University Press of Virginia, 1989.

Cobb, Michael. *God Hates Fags: The Rhetorics of Religious Violence*. New York: New York University Press, 2006.

Cole, David. "Beyond Unconstitutional Conditions: Charting Spheres of Neutrality in Government-Funded Speech." *New York University Law Review* 67 (October 1992). N.Y.U.L Rev. 675. Lexis/Nexis Academic.

Collins, Varnum Lansing. *President Witherspoon: A Biography*. 2 volumes. Princeton: Princeton University Press, 1925.

Collinson, Patrick. *Godly People: Essays on English Protestantism and Puritanism*. London: Hambledon, 1983.

Compton, Thorne. "Adam Ferguson and John Witherspoon in 'Satan's Seminary': *Douglas*, the Critics, and Moral Philosophy." *Studies in Scottish Literature* 18 (1983): 166–76.

Connolly, L.W. *The Censorship of English Drama, 1737–1824*. San Marino, CA: Huntington Library, 1976.

Corbin, Caroline Mala. "Mixed Speech: When Speech Is Both Private and Governmental." *New York University Law Review* 83 (June 2008). N.Y.U.L. Rev 605 Lexis/Nexis Academic.

Cordner, Michael, ed. and intro. *Sir John Vanbrugh: Four Comedies*. London: Penguin, 1989.

Corman, Brian. *Genre and Generic Change in English Comedy, 1660–1710*. Toronto: University of Toronto Press, 1993.

Cressy, David. "The Portraiture of Prynne's Pictures: Performance on the Public Stage." In *Travesties and Transgression in Tudor and Stuart England: Tales of Discord and Dissension*, 213–233. Oxford: Oxford University Press, 2000.

Crimp, Douglas, ed. *AIDS: Cultural Analysis/Cultural Activism*. Cambridge, MA: MIT Press, 1988.

Cross, F. L. *The Oxford Dictionary of the Christian Church*. Third edition. Edited by E. A. Livingstone. Oxford: Oxford University Press, 1997.

Cust, Richard. "News and Politics in Early Seventeenth-Century England." *Past and Present* 112 (August 1986): 60–90. JSTOR.

Cvetkovich, Ann. *An Archive of Feelings: Trauma, Sexuality, and Lesbian Public Cultures*. Durham: Duke University Press, 2003.

Dabney, Virginius. *Richmond, The Story of a City*. Garden City, NY: Doubleday, 1976.

Daiches, David. *The Scottish Enlightenment: An Introduction*. Edinburgh: Saltire Society, 1986.

Davis, Peter A. "Puritan Mercantilism and the Politics of Anti-Theatrical Legislation in Colonial America." In *The American Stage: Social and Economic Issues from the Colonial Period to the Present*, edited by Ron Engle and Tice L. Miller, 18–29. Cambridge: Cambridge University Press, 1993.

Davis, Richard Beale. *Intellectual Life in Jefferson's Virginia, 1790–1830*. Chapel Hill: University of North Carolina Press, 1964.

Davis, Tracy C., and Thomas Postlewait. "Theatricality: An Introduction." In *Theatricality*, edited by Tracy C. Davis and Thomas Postlewait, 1–39. Cambridge: Cambridge University Press, 2003.

Dawson, Mark S. *Gentility and the Comic Theatre of Late Stuart London*. Cambridge: Cambridge University Press, 2005.

"December 26, 1811: Two Lovers Perished Together in the Burning Richmond Theatre." Miscellaneous Clippings File, Virginia Historical Society.

De Krey, Gary Stuart. *A Fractured Society: The Politics of London in the First Age of Party, 1688–1715*. Oxford: Clarendon, 1985.

Derrida, Jacques. "The Law of Genre." Translated by Avital Ronell. *Critical Inquiry* 7 (1980): 55–81.

Diamond, Elin. "*Gestus* and Signature in Aphra Behn's *The Rover*." *ELH* 56 no. 3 (Fall 1989): 519–41.

———. "Mimesis, Mimicry and the 'True-Real.'" In *Acting Out: Feminist Performances*, edited by Lynda Hart and Peggy Phelan, 363–82. Ann Arbor: University of Michigan Press, 1993.

———. "The Shudder of Catharsis in Twentieth-Century Performance." In *Performativity and Performance*, edited by Andrew Parker and Eve Kosofsky Sedgwick, 152–72. New York: Routledge, 1995.

Dillon, Elizabeth Maddock. *New World Drama: The Performative Commons in the Atlantic World, 1649–1849*. Durham: Duke University Press, 2014.

Dolan, Jill. "Performance, Utopia, and the 'Utopian Performative.'" *Theatre Journal* 53 no. 3 (October 2001): 455–79. JSTOR.

———. "Practicing Cultural Disruption: Gay and Lesbian Representation and Sexuality." In *Critical Theory and Performance*, edited by Janelle G. Reinelt and Joseph R. Roach, 334–54. Revised and enlarged edition. Ann Arbor: University of Michigan Press, 2007.

Donohue, Joseph W. Jr. *Dramatic Character in the English Romantic Age*. Princeton: Princeton University Press, 1970.

Dowd, Maureen. "Unruffled Helms Basks in Eye of Arts Storm." *New York Times*, 28 July 1989, A1. LexisNexis Academic.

Dugaw, Dianne. "'The Rationall Spirituall Part': Dryden and Purcell's Baroque *King Arthur*." In *Enchanted Ground: Reimagining John Dryden*, edited by Jayne Lewis and Maximillian E. Novak, 273–89. Toronto: University of Toronto Press, 2004.

Duggan, Lisa. "Queering the State." *Social Text* 39 (Summer 1994): 1–14.

Elliot, Emory. "The Development of the Puritan Funeral Sermon and Elegy: 1660–1750." *Early American Literature* 15 (1980): 151–64.

Ellison, Julie. *Cato's Tears and the Making of Anglo-American Emotion*. Chicago: University of Chicago Press, 1999.

Emslie, MacDonald. "Home's *Douglas* and Wully Shakspeare." *Studies in Scottish Literature* 2 no. 2 (October 1964): 128–29.

Erickson, Jon. "Appropriation and Transgression in Contemporary American Performance: The Wooster Group, Holly Hughes, and Karen Finley." *Theatre Journal* 42 no. 2 (May 1990): 225–36. JSTOR.

Evans, Bertrand. *Gothic Drama from Walpole to Shelley*. Berkeley: University of California Press, 1947.

Faller, Lincoln. "Between Jest and Earnest: The Comedy of John Vanbrugh." *Modern Philology* 72 no. 1 (August 1974): 17–29. JSTOR.

Farmer, Alan B., and Zachary Lesser. "Canons and Classics: Publishing Drama in Caroline England." In *Localizing Caroline Drama: Politics and Economics of the Early Modern English Stage, 1625–1642,* edited by Adam Zucker and Alan B. Farmer, 17–41. New York: Palgrave Macmillan, 2006.

Ferrell, Lori Anne. "Kneeling and the Body Politic." In *Religion, Literature, and Politics in Post-Reformation England, 1540–1688*, edited by Donna B. Hamilton and Richard Strier, 70–92. Cambridge: Cambridge University Press, 1996.

Fincham, Kenneth, ed. "Introduction." In *The Early Stuart Church, 1603–1642*, 1–22. Stanford, CA: Stanford University Press, 1993.

Fincham, Kenneth, and Peter Lake. "The Ecclesiastical Policies of James I and Charles I." In *The Early Stuart Church, 1603–1642*, edited by Kenneth Fincham, 23–49. Stanford, CA: Stanford University Press, 1993.

Fleischacker, Samuel. "The Impact on America: Scottish Philosophy and the American Founding." In *The Cambridge Companion to the Scottish Enlightenment*, edited by Alexander Broadie, 316–37. Cambridge: Cambridge University Press, 2003.

Forte, Jeanie. "Focus on the Body: Pain, Praxis, and Pleasure In Feminist Performance." In *Critical Theory and Performance*, edited by Janelle G. Reinelt and Joseph R. Roach, 248–62. Ann Arbor: University of Michigan Press, 1992.

———. "Women's Performance Art: Feminism and Postmodernism." *Theatre Journal* 40 no. 2 (May 1988): 217–35. JSTOR.

Foster, Susan Leigh. "Choreographies of Protest." *Theatre Journal* 55 no. 3 (October 2003): 395–412. JSTOR.

Foucault, Michel. *The History of Sexuality, Volume I: An Introduction*. New York: Vintage, 1980.

———. *"Society Must Be Defended": Lectures at the Collège de France, 1975–1976*. Translated by David Macey. New York: Picador, 2003.

Fox, Adam. "Rumour, News and Popular Political Opinion in Elizabethan and Early Stuart England." *Historical Journal* 40 no. 3 (September 1997): 597–620. JSTOR.

France, David, dir. *How to Survive a Plague*. 2012.

Frank, Jason. *Constituent Moments: Enacting the People in Postrevolutionary America*. Durham: Duke University Press, 2010.

Freeman, Lisa A. *Character's Theater: Genre and Identity on the Eighteenth-Century English Stage*. Philadelphia: University of Pennsylvania Press, 2002.

Fuchs, Elinor. "Staging the Obscene Body." *TDR: The Drama Review* 33 no. 1 (Spring 1989): 33–58. JSTOR.

Garrison, James D. "Dryden and the Birth of Hercules." *Studies in Philology* 77 no. 2 (Spring 1980): 180–201.

Gaustad, Edwin S. *Neither King Nor Prelate: Religion and the New Nation, 1776–1826*. Grand Rapids, MI: William B. Eerdmans, 1993.

Geertz, Clifford. "Centers, Kings, and Charisma: Reflections on the Symbolics of Power." In *Local Knowledge: Further Essays in Interpretive Anthropology*. Third edition, 121–46. New York: Basic, 2000.

———. *The Interpretation of Cultures: Selected Essays*. New York: Basic, 1973.

———. *Local Knowledges: Further Essays in Interpretive Anthropology*. New York: Basic, 1983.

Gelineau, David. "Identity in Dryden's *Amphitryon*: Cuckolds of Order." *SEL: Studies in English Literature* 38 (1998): 427–45. EBSCO.

Gipson, Alice Edna. *John Home: A Study of His Life and Works, with Special Reference to the Tragedy of Douglas and the Controversies which Followed Its First Representations*. Ph.D. dissertation, Yale University, 1916.

Goddu, Teresa. *Gothic America: Narrative, History, and Nation*. New York: Columbia University Press, 1997.

Goldberg, RoseLee. *Performance Art: From Futurism to the Present*. Revised and expanded edition. London: Thames and Hudson, 2001.

Goldstein, Lynda. "Raging in Tongues: Confession and Performance Art." In *Confessional Politics: Women's Sexual Self-Representations in Life Writing and Popular Media*, edited by Irene Gammel, 99–116. Carbondale: Southern Illinois University Press, 1999.

Gollapudi, Aparna. *Moral Reform in Comedy and Culture, 1696–1747*. Burlington, VT: Ashgate, 2011.

Gómez, Carlos J. "Courtship, Marriage Vows, and Political Metaphor in Vanbrugh's *The Relapse* and *The Provoked Wife.*" *Journal for Early Modern Cultural Studies* 1 no. 2 (Fall/Winter 2001): 93–123. Project Muse.

———. "Kicking Conscience Downstairs: Tom Fashion's Rebellion in Vanbrugh's *The Relapse.*" *Restoration: Studies in English Literary Culture, 1660–1700,* 24 no. 2 (Fall 2000): 98–119.

Greiman, Jennifer. *Democracy's Spectacle: Sovereignty and Public Life in Antebellum American Writing.* New York: Fordham University Press, 2010.

Grenda, Christopher S. "Revealing Liberalism in Early America: Rethinking Religious Liberty and Liberal Values." *Journal of Church and State* 45 no. 1 (2003): 131–63.

Grimstead, David. *Melodrama Unveiled: American Theater and Culture, 1800–1850.* Foreword by Lawrence W. Levine. Berkeley: University of California Press, 1968.

Grove, Jan Zita. "AIDS: Keywords." In *AIDS: Cultural Analysis/Cultural Activism,* edited by Douglas Crimp, 17–30. Cambridge, MA: MIT Press, 1988.

Gurr, Andrew. *Playgoing in Shakespeare's London.* Third edition. Cambridge: Cambridge University Press, 2004.

Gustafson, Sandra. *Eloquence Is Power: Oratory and Performance in Early America.* Chapel Hill: University of North Carolina Press, 2000.

Habermas, Jürgen. *The Structural Transformation of the Public Sphere.* Translated by Thomas Burger with Frederick Lawrence. Cambridge, MA: MIT Press, 1989.

Hackel, Heidi Brayman. "'Rowme' of Its Own: Printed Drama in Early Libraries." In *A New History of Early English Drama,* edited by John D. Cox and David Scott Kastan, 113–30. New York: Columbia University Press, 1997.

Halasz, Alexandra. *The Marketplace in Print: Pamphlets and the Public Sphere in Early Modern England.* Cambridge: Cambridge University Press, 1997.

Halttunen, Karen. "Humanitarianism and the Pornography of Pain in Anglo-American Culture." *American Historical Review* 100 no. 2 (April 1995): 303–34. JSTOR.

Harris, Tim. *Politics Under the Late Stuarts: Party Conflict in a Divided Society, 1660–1715.* London: Longman, 1993.

Hart, Lynda. "Karen Finley's Dirty Work: Censorship, Homophobia and the NEA." *Genders* 14 (Fall 1992): 1–15.

———. "Motherhood According to Finley: 'The Theory of Total Blame,'" *TDR: The Drama Review* 36 no. 1 (Spring 1992): 124–34. JSTOR.

Hatch, Nathan O. "The Christian Movement and the Demand for a Theology of the People." *Journal of American History* 67 no. 3 (December 1980): 545–67. JSTOR.

———. *The Democratization of American Christianity.* New Haven: Yale University Press, 1989.

———. "The Democratization of Christianity and the Character of American Politics." In *Religion and American Politics: From the Colonial Period to the Present,* edited by Mark A. Noll and Luke E. Harlow, 93–119. Second edition. Oxford: Oxford University Press, 2007.

Hawkins, L. M. *Allegiance in Church and State: The Problem of the Nonjurors in the English Revolution.* London: George Routledge, 1928.

Heinemann, Margot. "Drama and Opinion in the 1620s: Middleton and Massinger." In *Theatre and Government Under the Early Stuarts,* edited by J. R. Mulryne and Margaret Shewring, 237–65. Cambridge: Cambridge University Press, 1993.

———. *Puritanism and Theatre: Thomas Middleton and Opposition Drama Under the Early Stuarts.* Cambridge: Cambridge University Press, 1980.

Henderson, Desirée. "The Imperfect Dead: Mourning Women in Eighteenth-Century Oratory and Fiction." *Early American Literature* 39 no. 3 (December 2004): 487–509.

Hendler, Glenn. *Public Sentiments: Structures of Feeling in Nineteenth-Century American Literature*. Chapel Hill: University of North Carolina Press, 2001.

Hewitt, Barnard. *Theatre U.S.A., 1665–1957*. New York: McGraw-Hill, 1959.

Heyman, Barry J. "The National Endowment for the Arts v. Finley: The Supreme Court's Artful Yet Indecent Proposal." *New York Law School Journal of Human Rights* 16 (1999). N.Y.L. Sch. J. Hum. Rts 439. Lexis/Nexis Academic.

Hill, Christopher. "Censorship and English Literature." In *The Collected Essays of Christopher Hill*, vol. 1, 32–71. Amherst: University of Massachusetts Press, 1985.

——. *The Century of Revolution, 1603–1714*. New York: W. W. Norton, 1982.

Hinnant, Charles. "Collier, Congreve, and Patriarchalist Debate." *Eighteenth-Century Life* 44 no. 4 (1978): 83–86.

Holifield, E. Brooks. *Theology in America: Christian Thought from the Age of the Puritans to the Civil War*. New Haven: Yale University Press, 2003.

Honan, William H. "Helms Amendment Is Facing a Major Test in Congress." *New York Times*, 13 September 1989, C17. ProQuest.

Hopes, J. "Politics and Morality in the Writings of Jeremy Collier." *Literature and History* 8 (1978): 159–74.

Houston, Alan, and Steven Pincus, eds. *A Nation Transformed: England After the Restoration*. Cambridge: Cambridge University Press, 2001.

Howard, Jean. *The Stage and Social Struggle in Early Modern England*. London: Routledge, 1994.

——. *Theater of a City: The Places of London Comedy, 1598–1642*. Philadelphia: University of Pennsylvania Press, 2007.

Hughes, Derek. *English Drama 1660–1700*. Oxford: Clarendon, 1996.

——. "Vanbrugh and Cibber: Language, Place, and Social Order in *The Relapse*." *Comparative Drama* 21 no. 1 (Spring 1987): 62–83.

Hume, Robert D. *The Development of English Drama in the Late Seventeenth Century*. Oxford: Clarendon, 1976.

——. "Jeremy Collier and the Future of the London Theater in 1698." *Studies in Philology* 96 no. 4 (Fall 1999): 480–511.

Hyde, Lewis. "The Children of John Adams: A Historical View of the Fight over Arts Funding." In *Art Matters: How the Culture Wars Changed America*, edited by Brian Wallis, Marianne Weems, and Philip Yenawine, 253–75. New York: New York University Press, 1999.

Jackson, Gregory S. "America's First Mass Media: Preaching and the Protestant Sermon Tradition." In *A Companion to the Literatures of Colonial America*, edited by Susan Castillo and Ivy Schweitzer, 402–25. Malden, MA: Blackwell, 2005.

Jakobson, Roman. "The Metaphoric and Metonymic Poles." In Roman Jakobson and Morris Halle, *Fundamentals of Language*, chap. 5. The Hague: Mouton, 1956.

Jeffers, Harl LaPlace. "Richmond Theatre's Tragic Fire: Out of the Ashes to Monumental Church." *Old Times* 2.6 (Winter 1987/8): 2–11.

Jones, Peter. "The Scottish Professoriate and the Polite Academy, 1720–1746." In *Wealth and Virtue: The Shaping of Political Economy in the Scottish Enlightenment*, edited by Istvan Hont and Michael Ignatieff, 89–117. Cambridge: Cambridge University Press, 1983.

Joseph, Miranda. *Against the Romance of Community*. Minneapolis: University of Minnesota Press, 2002.

Kantorowicz, Ernst H. *The King's Two Bodies: A Study in Mediæval Political Theology*. 1957. Princeton: Princeton University Press, 1997.

Kastan, David Scott. "Performances and Playbooks: The Closing of the Theatres and the Politics of Drama." In *Reading, Society and Politics in Early Modern England*, edited by Kevin Sharpe and Steven N. Zwicker, 167–84. Cambridge: Cambridge University Press, 2003.

———. "'Publike Sports' and 'Publike Calamities': Plays, Playing, and Politics." In *Shakespeare After Theory*, 201–20. New York: Routledge, 1999.

Kenyon, J. P. *Revolution Principles: The Politics of Party, 1689–1720*. Cambridge: Cambridge University Press, 1977.

Kinservik, Matthew. "Theatrical Regulation During the Restoration Period." In *A Companion to Restoration Drama*, edited by Susan J. Owen, 36–52. Oxford: Blackwell, 2001.

Kirby, Ethyn Williams. *William Prynne: A Study in Puritanism*. 1931. New York: Russell and Russell, 1972.

Kishlansky, Mark. "A Whipper Whipped: The Sedition of William Prynne." *Historical Journal* 56 no. 3 (September 2013): 603–27. doi: 10.1017/S0018246X13000149.

Klein, Lawrence E. "The Political Significance of 'Politeness' in Early Eighteenth Century Britain." In *Politics, Politeness and Patriotism*, vol. 5, edited by Gordon Schochet. Washington, DC: Folger Institute for the History of Political Thought Proceedings, 1993.

———. *Shaftesbury and the Culture of Politeness*. Cambridge: Cambridge University Press, 1994.

Knights, Mark. "'Meer Religion' and the 'Church-State' of Restoration England." In *A Nation Transformed: England After the Restoration*, edited by Alan Houston and Steven Pincus, 41–70. Cambridge: Cambridge University Press, 2001.

———. *Representation and Misrepresentation in Later Stuart Britain: Partisanship and Political Culture*. Oxford: Oxford University Press, 2005.

———. "The Tory Interpretation of History in the Rage of Parties." *Huntington Library Quarterly* 68 nos. 1–2 (March 2005): 353–73. JSTOR.

Knowles, James. "The Spectacle of the Realm: Civic Consciousness, Rhetoric and Ritual in Early Modern London." In *Theatre and Government Under the Early Stuarts*, edited by J. R. Mulryne and Margaret Shewring, 157–89. Cambridge: Cambridge University Press, 1993.

Krutch, Joseph Wood. *Comedy and Conscience After the Restoration*. New York: Columbia University Press, 1924.

Lake, Peter. "The Laudian Style: Order, Uniformity and the Pursuit of the Beauty of Holiness in the 1630s." In *The Early Stuart Church, 1603–1642*, edited by Kenneth Fincham, 161–85. Stanford, CA: Stanford University Press, 1993.

Lake, Peter, and Steven Pincus, eds. *The Politics of the Public Sphere in Early Modern England*. Manchester, UK: Manchester University Press, 2007.

———. "Rethinking the Public Sphere in Early Modern England." In *The Politics of the Public Sphere in Early Modern England*, 1–30. Manchester, UK: Manchester University Press, 2007.

Lake, Peter, and Michael Questier. *The Antichrist's Lewd Hat: Protestants, Papists, and Players in Post-Reformation England*. New Haven: Yale University Press, 2002.

Lambert, Frank. *The Barbary Wars: American Independence in the Atlantic World*. New York: Hill and Wang, 2005.

———. *Religion in American Politics: A Short History*. Princeton: Princeton University Press, 2008.

Lamont, Willliam M. *Marginal Prynne 1600–1669*. London: Routledge & Kegan Paul, 1963.

Latour, Bruno. *Reassembling the Social: An Introduction to Actor-Network-Theory*. Oxford: Oxford University Press, 2005.

Lee, Yoon Sun. "Giants of the North: *Douglas*, the Scottish Enlightenment, and Scott's *Redgauntlet*." *Studies in Romanticism* 40 (Spring 2001): 109–21. Wilson Web.

Lefkowitz, Murray. "New Light on Shirley's *Triumph of Peace*." *Journal of American Musicological Society* 17 (1965): 42–60.

Lemon, Rebecca. *Treason by Words: Literature, Law, and Rebellion in Shakespeare's England.* Ithaca, NY: Cornell University Press, 2006.

Lewalski, Barbara. "Milton's *Comus* and the Politics of Masquing." In *The Politics of the Stuart Court Masque*, edited by David Bevington and Peter Holbrook, 296–320. Cambridge: Cambridge University Press, 1998.

Lindley, David, ed. *The Court Masque.* Manchester, UK: Manchester University Press, 1984.

Little, John P. *History of Richmond.* Introduction by Rev. A. A. Little. Richmond, VA: Dietz, 1933.

London, Joshua E. *Victory in Tripoli: How America's War with the Barbary Pirates Established the U.S. Navy and Built a Nation.* Hoboken, NJ: John Wiley, 2005.

Lonsdale, Roger. "Thomas Gray, David Hume and John Home's *Douglas*." In *Re-constructing the Book: Literary Texts in Transmission*, edited by Maureen Bell, Shirley Chew, Simon Eliot, Lynette Hunter, and James L. W. West III, 57–70. Burlingon, VT: Ashgate, 2001.

Love, Harold. *Scribal Publication in Seventeenth-Century England.* Oxford: Clarendon, 1993.

MacKay, Ellen. "The Theatre as a Self-Consuming Art." *Theatre Survey* 49 no. 1 (May 2008): 91–107. Cambridge Journals.

Mackenzie, Henry. *An Account of the Life and Writings of John Home, Esq.* Edinburgh, 1822.

Macmillan, Dougald. "The First Editions of *Douglas*." *Studies in Philology* 26 no. 3 (July 1929): 401–9. JSTOR.

Maguire, Mary Hume. "Attack of the Common Lawyers on the Oath *Ex Officio* as Administered in the Ecclesiastical Courts in England." In *Essays in History and Political Theory in Honor of Charles Howard McIlwain*, edited by Carl Wittke, 199–229. New York: Russell and Russell, 1936.

Maguire, Nancy Klein. *Regicide and Restoration: English Tragicomedy, 1660–1671.* Cambridge: Cambridge University Press, 1992.

Mah, Harold. "Phantasies of the Public Sphere: Rethinking the Habermas of Historians." *Journal of Modern History* 72 no. 1 (March 2000): 153–82. JSTOR.

Marcus, Leah. *The Politics of Mirth: Jonson, Herrick, Milton, Marvell, and the Defense of Old Holiday Pastimes.* Chicago: University of Chicago Press, 1986.

Markley, Robert, and Jeannie Dalporto, eds. *Amphitryon.* In *The Broadview Anthology of Restoration and Eighteenth-Century Drama*, general editor, J. Douglas Canfield. Ontario: Broadview, 2001.

Marshall, David. *The Figure of Theater: Shaftesbury, Defoe, Adam Smith, and George Eliot.* New York: Columbia University Press, 1986.

Matthews, Jean V. *Toward a New Society: American Thought and Culture, 1800–1830.* Boston: Twayne, 1991.

McElroy, Davis D. *Scotland's Age of Improvement: A Survey of Eighteenth-Century Literary Clubs and Societies.* Pullman: Washington State University Press, 1969.

McGinley, Kevin J. "The First Edinburgh Editions of John Home's *Douglas* and the Play's Early Stage History." *Theatre Notebook* 60 no. 3 (2006): 134–45.

———. "My Name Is Norval?: The Revision of Character Names in John Home's *Douglas*." *Journal of Eighteenth-Century Studies* 35 no. 1 (2012): 67–83.

McGuinness, Arthur E. *Henry Home, Lord Kames.* New York: Twayne, 1970.

Meyer, Richard. *Outlaw Representation: Censorship and Homosexuality in Twentieth-Century American Art.* Boston: Beacon, 2002.

Milhous, Judith, and Robert D. Hume. *Producible Interpretations*. Carbondale: Southern Illinois University Press, 1985.

Milton, Anthony. "Licensing, Censorship, and Religious Orthodoxy in Early Stuart England." *Historical Journal* 41 no. 3 (September 1998): 625–51. JSTOR.

Morgan, Edmund S. "Puritan Hostility to the Theatre." *Proceedings of the American Philosophical Society* 110 no. 5 (October 1966): 340–47.

Morgan, Megan Stoner. "Speaking with a Double Voice: John Home's *Douglas* and the Idea of Scotland." *Scottish Literary Review* 4 no. 1 (2012): 35–56.

Morrison, Jeffry Hays. "John Witherspoon and 'The Public Interest of Religion.'" *Journal of Church and State* 41 no. 3 (1999): 551–73.

Mullaney, Steven. *The Place of the Stage: License, Play and Power in Renaissance England*. Ann Arbor: University of Michigan Press, 1988.

Murrell, Amy E. *"Calamity at Richmond": Fire and Faith in a Young Virginia City*. M.A. thesis, University of Virginia, December 1995.

Nathans, Heather S. *Early American Theatre from the Revolution to Thomas Jefferson: Into the Hands of the People*. Cambridge: Cambridge University Press, 2003.

Noll, Mark A. "The Irony of the Enlightenment for Presbyterians in the Early Republic." *Journal of the Early Republic* 5 (Summer 1985): 149–75.

———. *Princeton and the Republic, 1768–1822: The Search for a Christian Enlightenment in the Era of Samuel Stanhope Smith*. Princeton: Princeton University Press, 1989.

Norbrook, David. "The Reformation of the Masque." In *The Court Masque*, edited by David Lindley, 94–110. Manchester, UK: Manchester University Press, 1984.

Novak, Maximillian. "The Artist and the Clergyman: Congreve, Collier and the World of Play." *College English* 30 no. 7 (April 1969): 555–61.

Oldridge, Darren. *Religion and Society in Early Stuart England*. Aldershot, UK: Ashgate, 1998.

Orgel, Stephen. *The Illusion of Power: Political Theater in the English Renaissance*. Berkeley: University of California Press, 1975.

Orgel, Stephen, and Roy Strong. *Inigo Jones: The Theatre of the Stuart Court*. 2 volumes. Berkeley: University of California Press, 1973.

Orvis, David L. "'Old Sodom' and 'Dear Dad': Vanbrugh's Celebration of the Sodomitical Subject in *The Relapse*." *Journal of Homosexuality* 57 (2010): 140–62. Taylor and Francis Group Online.

Overn, Michael, and Elinor Fuchs. "Finley Facts or Fictions?" *TDR: The Drama Review* 33 no. 4 (Winter 1989): 8–10. JSTOR.

Owen, Susan J. *Restoration Theatre and Crisis*. Oxford: Clarendon, 1996.

Oxford Dictionary of National Biography. Online.

Parry, Graham. "Entertainments at Court." In *A New History of Early English Drama*, edited by John D. Cox and David Scott Kastan, 195–211. New York: Columbia University Press, 1997.

Patterson, Annabel. *Censorship and Interpretation: The Conditions of Writing and Reading in Early Modern England*. Madison: University of Wisconsin Press, 1984.

Patton, Cindy. *Inventing AIDS*. New York: Routledge, 1990.

Pelligrini, Ann, and Janet R. Jakobsen. *Love the Sin: Sexual Regulation and the Limits of Religious Tolerance*. Boston: Beacon, 2004.

Peters, Julie Stone. "'Things Govern'd By Words': Late 17th-Century Comedy and the Reformers." *English Studies* 2 (1987): 142–53.

Phelan, Peggy. "Money Talks Again," *TDR: The Drama Review* 35 no. 3 (Autumn 1991): 131–41. JSTOR.

———. "Radical Democracy and the Woman Question." *American Literary History* 5 no. 4 (Winter 1993): 750–63. JSTOR.

———. "Serrano, Mapplethorpe, the NEA, and You: 'Money Talks': October 1989." *TDR: The Drama Review* 34 no. 1 (Spring 1990): 4–15. JSTOR.

———. "Tim Miller's *My Queer Body*: An Anatomy in Six Sections." *Theater* 24 no. 2 (1993): 30–34.

———. *Unmarked: The Politics of Performance*. London: Routledge, 1993.

Pincus, Steven. *1688: The First Modern Revolution*. New Haven: Yale University Press, 2009.

———. "From Holy Cause to Economic Interest: The Study of Population and the Invention of the State." In *A Nation Transformed: England After the Restoration*, edited by Alan Houston and Steven Pincus, 272–98. Cambridge: Cambridge University Press, 2001.

Pocock, J. G. A. "Modes of Political and Historical Time in Early Eighteenth Century England." In *Virtue, Commerce, and History*, 91–102. Cambridge: Cambridge University Press, 1985.

———. "Texts as Events: Reflections on the History of Political Thought." In *The Politics of Discourse*, edited by Kevin Sharpe and Steven N. Zwicker, 21–34. Berkeley: University of California Press, 1987.

Post, Robert C. "Subsidized Speech," *Yale Law Journal* 106 (October 1996). Yale L.J. 151, Lexis/Nexis Academic.

Postlewait, Thomas. "Theatricality and Antitheatricality in Renaissance London." In *Theatricality*, edited by Tracy C. Davis and Thomas Postlewait, 90–126. Cambridge: Cambridge University Press, 2003.

Prammagiore, Maria T. "Resisting/Performing/Femininity: Words, Flesh, and Feminism in Karen Finley's *The Constant State of Desire*." *Theatre Journal* 44 no. 3 (October 1992): 269–90. JSTOR.

Prest, Wilfred R. *The Inns of Court Under Elizabeth I and the Early Stuarts, 1590–1640*. Totowa, NJ: Rowman and Littlefield, 1972.

Price, John Vladimir, intro. *The Collected Works of Henry Home, Lord Kames*. London: Routledge/Thoemmes, 1993.

Puchner, Martin. *Stage Fright: Modernism, Antitheatricality, and Drama*. Baltimore: Johns Hopkins University Press, 2002.

Punter, David. *The Literature of Terror: A History of Gothic Fictions from 1765 to the Present Day*. Volume 1: The Gothic Tradition. Second edition. London: Longman, 1996.

Ranger, Paul. *"Terror and Pity Reign in Every Breast": Gothic Drama in the London Patent Theatres, 1750–1820*. London: Society for Theatre Research, 1991.

Ray, William. *Horrors of Slavery or, the American Tars in Tripoli*. 1808. Edited and introduction by Hester Blum. New Brunswick, NJ: Rutgers University Press, 2008.

Rendall, Jane. *The Origins of the Scottish Enlightenment*. New York: St. Martin's, 1978.

Ressler, Kathleen. "Jeremy Collier's Essays." In *Seventeenth Century Studies*, second series, edited by Robert Shafer 179–285. Princeton: Princeton University Press, 1933.

Richards, Jeffrey H. *Theater Enough: American Culture and the Metaphor of the World Stage, 1607–1789*. Durham: Duke University Press, 1991.

Richards, Judith. "'His Nowe Majestic' and the English Monarchy: The Kingship of Charles I Before 1640." *Past and Present* 113 (November 1986): 70–96. JSTOR.

Richmond, Capital of Virginia: Approaches to Its History. Richmond, VA: Whitter and Shepperson, 1938.

Ringler, William. "The First Phase of the Elizabethan Attack on the Stage, 1558–1579," *Huntington Library Quarterly* 4 (July 1942): 391–418.

Roach, Joseph. *Cities of the Dead: Circum-Atlantic Performance.* New York: Columbia University Press, 1996.

Román, David. *Acts of Intervention: Performance, Gay Culture, and AIDS.* Bloomington: Indiana University Press, 1998.

———. "Performing All Our Lives: AIDS, Performance, Community." In *Critical Theory and Performance,* edited by Janelle G. Reinelt and Joseph R. Roach, 208–21. Ann Arbor: University of Michigan Press, 1992.

Rose, Craig. *England in the 1690s: Revolution, Religion and War.* Oxford: Blackwell, 1999.

Ross, Ian Simpson. *Lord Kames and the Scotland of His Day.* Oxford: Oxford University Press, 1972.

Rudolph, Julia. "Rape and Resistance: Women and Consent in 17th Century English Legal and Political Thought." *Journal of British Studies* 39 no. 2 (April 2000): 157–84.

Sabol, Andrew J. "New Documents in Shirley's Masque 'The Triumph of Peace.'" *Music and Letters* 47 no. 1 (January 1966): 10–26.

Sanford, James K., ed. *Richmond: Her Triumphs, Tragedies, and Growth.* Richmond, VA: Metropolitan Richmond Chamber of Commerce, 1975.

Schechner, Richard. *Between Theater and Anthropology.* Philadelphia: University of Pennsylvania Press, 1985.

———. *Performance Theory.* Revised and expanded edition. New York: Routledge, 1988.

Schille, Candy B. K. "Self-Assessment in Dryden's *Amphitryon.*" *SEL: Studies in English Literature* 36 (1996): 545–60. EBSCO.

Schlossman, David A. *Actors and Activists: Politics, Performance, and Exchange Among Social Worlds.* New York: Routledge, 2002.

Schmidgen, Wolfram. *Exquisite Mixture: The Virtues of Impurity in Early Modern England.* Philadelphia: University of Pennsylvania Press, 2013.

Schneider, Rebecca. *The Explicit Body in Performance.* London: Routledge, 1997.

Sefton, Henry. "'Neu-lights and Preachers Legall': Some Observations on the Beginnings of Moderatism in the Church of Scotland." In *Church, Politics, and Society: Scotland, 1408–1929,* edited by Norman Macdougall, 186–96. Edinburgh: John Donald, 1983.

Selcraig, Bruce. "Reverend Wildmon's War on the Arts." *New York Times,* 2 September 1990. ProQuest.

Sharpe, Kevin. *Criticism and Compliment: The Politics of Literature in the England of Charles I.* Cambridge: Cambridge University Press, 1987.

Sher, Richard. *Church and University in the Scottish Enlightenment: The Moderate Literati of Edinburgh.* Princeton: Princeton University Press, 1985.

———. "'The Favourite of the Favourite': John Home, Bute, and the Politics of Patriotic Poetry." In *Lord Bute: Essays in Re-Interpretation,* edited by Karl W. Schweizer, 181–208. Leicester, UK: Leicester University Press, 1988.

Sher, Richard, and Alexander Murdoch. "Patronage and Party in the Church of Scotland, 1750–1800." In *Church, Politics, and Society: Scotland, 1408–1929,* edited by Norman Macdougall, 197–220. Edinburgh: John Donald, 1983.

Sherman, Stuart. "Dryden and the Theatrical Imagination." In *The Cambridge Companion to John Dryden,* edited by Steven N. Zwicker, 15–36. Cambridge: Cambridge University Press, 2004.

Sherman, Susanne Ketchum. *Comedies Useful: A History of the American Theatre in the South, 1775–1812.* Williamsburg, VA: Celest, 1998.

Shockley, Martin Staples. "The Proprietors of Richmond's New Theatre of 1819." *William and Mary Quarterly* (second series) 19 no. 3 (July 1939): 302–8.

———. *The Richmond Stage, 1784–1812*. Charlottesville: University Press of Virginia, 1977.

Shohet, Lauren. "Reading Triumphs: Localizing Caroline Masques." In *Localizing Caroline Drama: Politics and Economics of the Early Modern Stage, 1625–1642*, edited by Adam Zucker and Alan B. Farmer, 69–96. New York: Palgrave Macmillan, 2006.

Shuger, Debora. *Censorship and Cultural Sensibility: The Regulation of Language in Tudor-Stuart England*. Philadelphia: University of Pennsylvania Press, 2006.

Siebert, Fredrick Seaton. *Freedom of the Press in England, 1476–1776*. Urbana: University of Illinois Press, 1952.

Simpson, K. G. "Rationalism and Romanticism: The Case of Home's *Douglas*." *Scottish Literary Journal* 19 no. 1 (May 1982): 21–47.

Smith, Adam. *The Theory of Moral Sentiments*. 1759. Edited by D. D. Raphael and A. L. Macfie. Indianapolis: Liberty Fund, 1984.

Smith-Rosenberg, Carroll. *Religion and the Rise of the American City: The New York City Mission Movement, 1812–1870*. Ithaca, NY: Cornell University Press, 1971.

Smuts, R. Malcolm. *Court Culture and the Origins of a Royalist Tradition in Early Stuart England*. Philadelphia: University of Pennsylvania Press, 1987.

Sommerville, J. P. *Politics and Ideology in England, 1603–1640*. London: Longman, 1986.

Sorenson, Janet. "Varieties of Public Performance: Folk Songs, Ballads, Popular Drama and Sermons." In *The Edinburgh History of Scottish Literature*, volume 2, edited by Susan Manning, 133–42. Edinburgh: Edinburgh University Press, 2007.

Spurr, John. *English Puritanism, 1603–1689*. London: Macmillan, 1998.

———. "Religion in Restoration England." In *Blackwell Companion to Stuart Britain*, edited by Barry Coward, 416–35. Malden, MA: Blackwell, 2003.

Staves, Susan. "Douglas's Mother." In *Brandeis Essays in Literature*, edited by John Hazel Smith, 51–67. Waltham, MA: Brandeis University Press, 1983.

———. "A Few Kind Words for the Fop." *SEL: Studies in English Literature* 22 no. 3 (Summer 1982): 413–28.

———. *Players' Scepters: Fictions of Authority in the Restoration*. Lincoln: University of Nebraska Press, 1979.

Steiner, Wendy. *The Scandal of Pleasure: Art in an Age of Fundamentalism*. Chicago: University of Chicago Press, 1995.

Stern, Julia. *The Plight of Feeling: Sympathy and Dissent in the Early American Novel*. Chicago: University of Chicago Press, 1997.

Stevenson, Jill. *Sensational Devotion: Evangelical Performance in Twenty-First Century America*. Ann Arbor: University of Michigan Press, 2013.

Stout, Harry S. *The Divine Dramatist: George Whitefield and the Rise of Modern Evangelicism*. Grand Rapids, MI: William B. Eerdmans, 1991.

———. *The New England Soul: Preaching and Religious Culture in Colonial New England*. New York: Oxford University Press, 1986.

Swisher, Kara. "Helms's 'Indecent' Sampler; Senator Sends Photos to Sway Conferees." *Washington Post*, 8 August 1989, B1. LexisNexis Academic.

Taylor, Diana. *The Archive and the Repertoire: Performing Cultural Memory in the Americas*. Durham: Duke University Press, 2003.

Tertullian. *De Spectaculis*. Cambridge, MA: Harvard University Press, 1977.

Thomas, David; David Carlton; and Anne Etienne. *Theatre Censorship: From Walpole to Wilson*. Oxford: Oxford University Press, 2007.

Tobin, Terrence. *Plays by Scots, 1660–1800*. Iowa City: University of Iowa Press, 1974.

Todd, Janet. *Sensibility: An Introduction.* London: Methuen, 1986.

Tomlinson, Sophie. *Women on Stage in Stuart Drama.* Cambridge: Cambridge University Press, 2005.

Tompkins, Jane. *Sensational Designs: The Cultural Work of American Fiction 1790–1860.* New York: Oxford University Press, 1985.

Towers, S. Mutchow. *Control of Religious Printing in Early Stuart England.* Woodbridge, UK: Boydell, 2003.

Treichler, Paula. *How to Have Theory in an Epidemic: Cultural Chronicles of AIDS.* Durham: Duke University Press, 1999.

Turner, Victor. *The Anthropology of Performance.* New York: PAJ, 1987.

———. *From Ritual to Theatre: The Human Seriousness of Play.* New York: PAJ, 1982.

Tyacke, Nicholas. *Anti-Calvinists: The Rise of English Arminianism, c. 1590–1649.* Oxford: Clarendon, 1987.

———. "Archbishop Laud." In *The Early Stuart Church, 1603–1642*, edited by Kenneth Fincham, 51–70. Stanford, CA: Stanford University Press, 1993.

Tyler-McGraw, Marie. *At the Falls: Richmond, Virginia, and Its People.* Chapel Hill: University of North Carolina Press, 1994.

Van Engen, Abram. "Puritanism and the Power of Sympathy." *Early American Literature* 45 no. 3 (2010): 533–64. Project Muse.

Van Lennep, William; Emmett L. Avery; Arthur H. Scouten; and George Winchester Stone, Jr., eds. *The London Stage, 1660–1800; a Calendar of Plays, Entertainments and Afterpieces, Together with Casts, Box-Receipts and Contemporary Comment.* 5 volumes. Carbondale: Southern Illinois University Press, 1960–1968.

Vance, Carol S. "The War on Culture." In *Art Matters: How the Culture Wars Changed America*, edited by Brian Wallis, Marianne Weems, and Philip Yenawine, 221–31. New York: New York University Press, 1999.

Veevers, Erica. *Images of Love and Religion: Queen Henrietta Maria and Court Entertainments.* Cambridge: Cambridge University Press, 1989.

Venuti, Lawrence. "The Politics of Allusion: The Gentry and Shirley's *The Triumph of Peace*." *ELR* 16 (1986): 182–205.

Wald, Priscilla. *Contagious: Cultures, Carriers, and the Outbreak Narrative.* Durham: Duke University Press, 2008.

Walker, Kim. "New Prison: Representing the Female Actor in Shirley's *The Bird in a Cage* (1633)." *ELR* 21 (1991): 385–400.

Wallace, Robert. "Performance Anxiety: 'Identity,' 'Community,' and Tim Miller's *My Queer Body*." *Modern Drama* 39 (1996): 97–116.

Wallis, Brian; Marianne Weems; and Philip Yenawine, eds. *Art Matters: How the Culture Wars Changed America.* New York: New York University Press, 1999.

Warner, Michael. *Publics and Counterpublics.* New York: Zone, 2002.

Watney, Simon. *Policing Desire: Pornography, AIDS and the Media.* Third edition. Minneapolis: University of Minnesota Press, 1996.

Webster, Tom. "Religion in Early Stuart Britain, 1603–1642." In *A Companion to Stuart Britain*, edited by Barry Coward, 253–70. Oxford: Blackwell, 2003.

Weil, Rachel. "Matthew Smith Versus the 'Great Men': Plot Talk, the Public Sphere and the Problem of Credibility in the 1690s." In *The Politics of the Public Sphere in Early Modern England*, edited by Peter Lake and Steven Pincus, 232–51. Manchester, UK: Manchester University Press, 2007.

———. *A Plague of Informers: Conspiracy and Political Trust in William III's England.* New Haven: Yale University Press, 2013.

Wheeler, David. "The Pathetic and the Sublime: The Tragic Formula of John Home's *Douglas.*" In *Man, God, and Nature in the Enlightenment*, edited by Donald C. Mell, Jr., Theodore E. D. Braun, and Lucia M. Palmer, 173–82. East Lansing, MI: Colleagues Press, 1988.

White, Hayden. "The Value of Narrativity in the Representation of Reality." In *The Content of the Form: Narrative Discourse and Historical Representation*, 1–25. Baltimore: Johns Hopkins University Press, 1987.

White, Paul Whitefield. "Theater and Religious Culture. In *A New History of Early English Drama*, edited by John D. Cox and David Scott Kastan, 133–51. New York: Columbia University Press, 1997.

Whitted, Brent. "Street Politics: Charles I and the Inns of Court's *Triumph of Peace.*" *Seventeenth Century* 24 no. 1 (Spring 2009): 1–25. EBSCO.

Wiles, David. *Theatre and Citizenship: The History of a Practice.* Cambridge: Cambridge University Press, 2011.

Williams, Aubrey. "No Cloistered Virtue: Or, Playwright Versus Priest in 1698." *PMLA* 90 (1975): 234–46.

Wilson, John F. "Religion, Government, and Power in the New American Republic." In *Religion and American Politics: From the Colonial Period to the Present*, edited by Mark A. Noll and Luke E. Harlow, 79–92. Second edition. Oxford: Oxford University Press, 2007.

Winn, James A. "Dryden's Songs." In *Enchanted Ground: Reimagining John Dryden*, edited by Jayne Lewis and Maximillian E. Novak, 290–317. Toronto: University of Toronto Press, 2004.

———. *John Dryden and His World.* New Haven: Yale University Press, 1987.

Winthrop, John. "A Model of Christian Charity." In *Winthrop Papers* Volume 2. 282–295. Boston: Massachusetts Historical Society, 1929.

Withington, Ann Fairfax. *Toward a More Perfect Union: Virtue and the Formation of American Republics.* Oxford: Oxford University Press, 1991.

Wojnarowicz v. American Family Association, 745 F. Supp. 130 (S.D.N.Y, 1990).

Wood, Gordon S. *Empire of Liberty: A History of the Early Republic, 1789–1815.* Oxford: Oxford University Press, 2009.

Woolf, Daniel. "News, History and the Construction of the Present in Early Modern England." In *The Politics of Information in Early Modern Europe*, edited by Brendan Dooley and Sabrina A. Baron, 80–118. London: Routledge, 2001.

Worden, Blair. "The Question of Secularization." In *A Nation Transformed: England After the Restoration*, edited by Alan Houston and Steven Pincus, 20–40. Cambridge: Cambridge University Press, 2001.

Worthen, W. B. *The Idea of the Actor: Drama and the Ethics of Performance.* Princeton: Princeton University Press, 1984.

Yingling, Thomas E. *AIDS and the National Body.* Edited and introduction by Robyn Wiegman. Durham: Duke University Press, 1997.

Zaret, David. *Origins of Democratic Culture: Printing, Petitions, and the Public Sphere in Early-Modern England.* Princeton: Princeton University Press, 2000.

Zimbardo, Rose. *A Mirror to Nature: Transformations in Drama and Aesthetics, 1660–1732.* Lexington: University of Kentucky Press, 1986.

Index

§954(d)(1) ("decency and respect" clause), 241–42, 251, 264–65, 267–68, 273–78, 280–84, 286–89

ACT-UP, 248, 253

affect, aesthetics of, 7, 177–78, 180, 219, 222–33, 238, 256–57, 261–62

AIDS, 8, 243, 268–69, 271, 291; and performance, 252–63; and public culture, 248–51, 251 (fig. 20)

Alexander, Archibald, 221, 232, 236, 233, 236; *A Discourse Occasioned by the Burning of the Theatre in Richmond, Virginia*, 221, 222, 223–31

American Christianity: and conversion, 215, 217, 218, 220–21, 223–24, 233–34, 237, 240; and "divine drama," 191, 220–21, 223, 230–33, 238–39; and American exceptionalism, 191, 216, 220–21, 234; and the rise of evangelism, 214–18, 238. *See also* Second Great Awakening

American Family Association, 243

American public, the: as a Christian body public, 8, 191–92, 212, 214–18, 219–24, 228–31, 233–34, 238–39, 244, 246–47, 267–70, 277–78, 288–89; as a national body public, 4, 8, 234–36, 244, 250–51, 263–66, 270, 277–83, 289, 291

American taxpayer, 243–47, 250, 267, 269–70, 281

Anderson, George, 163; *Estimate of the Profit and Loss of Religion*, 165–69

Anglicanism. See Church of England

antitheatricality, 1–3, 6, 14, 16–17, 34, 39, 98–99, 136–39, 151, 170, 174, 181–82, 188, 191, 219, 234, 238, 240, 268–69, 293 n. 4, 295 n. 7

antitheatrical precedents, 2, 8, 9, 34, 46, 55, 92, 134, 172–73, 228, 234, 255, 275–76

Arminianism, 36, 37, 49, 91–93, 217. *See also* Laudianism

arts patron rule. *See* "government as patron"

Arundel, Earl of, 90

Austin, J. L., 263

Backscheider, Paula, 106

Balme, Christopher, 16

Barish, Jonas, 1–2, 32, 293 n.3

Baum, Lawrence, 279

Bentley, Gerald, 29–30

Bergeron, David, 20, 21

Berlant, Lauren, 250

Bersani, Leo, 250

Bezanson, Randall, 289

Blair, Hugh, 154, 158, 166, 176

Blair, John D., 213, 214

bodies public, 3–6, 95, 103–4, 120, 141–42, 145, 151, 173, 179, 188, 260, 266, 278, 291; and American Christianity, 8, 191–92, 212, 214–18, 219–24, 228–29, 230–31, 233–34, 238–39, 244, 246–47, 267–70, 277–78, 288–89; and American national identity, 4, 8, 234–36, 244, 250–51, 263–66, 266, 270, 277–83, 289, 291; and the body politic, 4–5, 15, 30, 32, 95, 103–5, 131, 134, 145–46, 217–18, 247, 272, 275–79, 288, 294 n. 8; and the cultivation of a godly body public, 31–32, 34, 39, 44–46, 48–50, 53–55, 57–59, 68, 76; and the Inns of Court, 16–17, 19, 22, 24, 28–30, 44–45; and Moderatism, 158, 161, 173; and nonjurancy, 99, 105–7; and public opinion, 60–61, 80, 85, 87, 95, 105; and the public sphere, 103–4, 138–39, 145–46, 151, 168–69, 173, 175; and the Richmond Theater Fire, 191–92, 212, 219–20, 230–31, 234, 240; and the queer community, 243, 253, 256–57, 259, 261–63

Bodleian Library Douce MSS 173, 59–60, 62

body politic, 2–5, 8, 15, 30–32, 52, 68, 72, 86, 95, 103–5, 131, 134, 145–46, 294 n. 8; and the body personal, 89, 133, 290–91; in the

Acknowledgments

A dean at my university once asked me what I needed to do my best work. The answer to that question lies in these acknowledgments: sustained periods of time to read, think, and write; access to excellent research libraries and archival collections; the intellectual inspiration and generosity of brilliant colleagues; and the love and support of friends and family. In all of these, I have been fortunate; and my gratitude and debts are immense.

Research for this project has been supported by a Mellon Postdoctoral Fellowship at the Huntington Library and a National Endowment for the Humanities Fellowship at the Newberry Library, as well as by fellowships and grants from the British Academy/Newberry Library exchange program, the American Society for Theatre Research, and the Virginia Historical Society. With financial support from the College of Liberal Arts and Sciences at the University of Illinois at Chicago (UIC), additional research for this book was conducted at the Bodleian Library at Oxford University, the British Library, the British National Archives, the Houghton Library at Harvard University, the Library of Virginia, the Rare Book Collection at the University of North Carolina, Chapel Hill, and the Rubenstein Rare Book and Manuscript Library at Duke University. I am greatly indebted to the staff at each of these institutions as well as to the many hosts and fellow scholars who helped make my time at each place so productive, especially Jennifer Brody, Cyndia Clegg, Lois Cucullu, Anna Currence, Diane Dillon, Barbara Donegan, Jacob Dorman, Lori Ann Ferrell, Leon Fink, Jill Gage, Paul Gehl, Elliot Gorn, Danny Green, Barbara Hanawalt, Sue Hodson, Sharon Holland, Rachel Howarth, Aida Kahn, Nergis Mavalvala, Susan McDonough, Liesl Olson, John Overholt, Sarah Pearsall, Frances Pollard, Roy Ritchie, Sarah Rivett, Mary Robertson, Susan Sleeper-Smith, Scott Stevens, and Helen Thompson.

Over the years, I have presented parts of this work at venues including Carnegie Mellon University; Duke University; the Huntington Library Redefining British Theatre series; the Newberry Library Scholl Center for

American History and Culture; the Southern California Eighteenth-Century Seminar; the UIC Forum for Research on Law, Politics, and the Humanities; the University of Pennsylvania; the University of Tennessee; Washington University in St. Louis; and Yale University. At Yale, I am particularly indebted to the brilliant Joseph Roach, who invited me to present some of my first work for this study at a tercentenary conference and who encouraged me with his enduring faith and unwavering support to pursue this project to the end. Joe, as it turns out was also one of the readers for the press, and he along with my second reader, the superlatively thoughtful and generous Daniel O'Quinn, have made this an infinitely better book. My gratitude extends to Jerry Singerman at the University of Pennsylvania Press, who selected these excellent readers and who has shepherded this project through with such great care, patience, and good humor. I am grateful to the UIC Institute for the Humanities and the LAS Award for Faculty Research in the Humanities for a subvention to support the publication of this book.

None of this work would have been possible without the enduring support as well of Jean Howard, Felicity Nussbaum, and Kristina Straub: I am forever in their debt. Any number of academic colleagues and friends have either read pieces of this book or offered insights and support at critical junctures along the way. I am indebted to the generosity of Emily Anderson, Misty Anderson, Robin Bernstein, Toni Bowers, Pannill Camp, Tita Chico, Tracy Davis, Elizabeth Dillon, Michael Dobson, Peggy Elliot, Jody Enders, Dan Gustafson, George Haggerty, Brian Herrera, Peter Holland, Suvir Kaul, David Lazarus, Kim Marra, Paige McGinley, Sean Metzger, Heather Nathans, Phyllis Rackin, Laura Rosenthal, Laura Runge, Nigel Smith, Priscilla Wald, and David Worrall. I am also continually grateful for and astonished by the tremendous intellectual company and camaraderie of my colleagues in the English department at UIC, including Sunil Agnani, Jennifer Ashton, Mark Canuel, Peter Coviello, Lennard Davis, Judith Kegan Gardiner, Robin Grey, Christopher Grimes, Rachel Havrelock, Anna Kornbluh, Nasser Mufti, Mary Beth Rose, Jessica Williams, and especially Walter Benn Michaels.

Friends dearest to me, whose constant encouragement and support over the years has meant the world to me and whose love and friendship has enriched my life, include Debra Bernard, Jennie Brier, Jennifer Brody, Mark Canuel, Anne Cubilié, Tracy Davis, Karen Girard, Jackie Goldsby, Jay Grossman, Katharine Hathaway, Sharon Holland, E. Patrick Johnson, Stephen Lewis, Lisa Litt, Jeffrey Masten, Nergis Mavalvala, Ramón Rivera-Servera, Jon Rosner, Robin Schachtel, Joel Valentín-Martinez, Lynn Watson, and Joy Whitman.

In a class all their own are three amazing women: Rene Lederman, Jackie Loewe, and Jill Pollack. I do not know where I would be without all of you—the very best friends not only through every high and every low but also through the very mundane yet precious details of each and every day that makes up our lived lives. I cherish each of you and consider our friendship as beyond all measure.

The constant and unstinting love and support of my family informs everything I do and everything that I am. My only sorrow, as you all know, is that I live so far from you. My parents, Jack and Ellen Freeman, are two of the most inspiring and fiercely loving people I know, and I think only my father was happier than me when I finally finished the manuscript for this book. My siblings, their spouses, and my niece and many nephews bring unconditional love into my life, and I am grateful to them all: Laurie, Yoji, Evan, and Ken Shimizu; Jodie, Howard, Emma, Ben, and Sam Adler; Robert, Philippa, Luke, Jeremy, and Thomas Freeman. And for my sister Jodie especially, whose illness while I was working on this book was both a shock and a revelation—we have been through the wars together and come out on the other side better and stronger.

Finally, I need to thank my wife, Heather Schmucker, to whom this book is dedicated. You have brought immeasurable joy and happiness into my life and, along with Petunia, have made our house a home filled with love, laughter, and warmth. You were right; two is better than one.

The Practical Approach in Chemistry Series

SERIES EDITORS

L. M. Harwood
Department of Chemistry
University of Reading

C. J. Moody
Department of Chemistry
University of Exeter

The Practical Approach in Chemistry Series

Organocopper reagents
Edited by Richard J. K. Taylor

Macrocycle synthesis
Edited by David Parker

High-pressure techniques in chemistry and physics
Edited by Wilfried B. Holzapfel and Neil S. Isaacs

Preparation of alkenes
Edited by Jonathan M. J. Williams

Transition metals in organic synthesis
Edited by Susan E. Gibson (née Thomas)

Transition Metals in Organic Synthesis

A Practical Approach

Edited by

SUSAN E. GIBSON (née Thomas)

Department of Chemistry,
Imperial College of Science, Technology and Medicine,
London, UK

OXFORD   NEW YORK   TOKYO
OXFORD   UNIVERSITY   PRESS
1997

Oxford University Press, Great Clarendon Street, Oxford OX2 6DP

Oxford   New York
Athens   Auckland   Bangkok   Bogota   Bombay   Buenos Aires
Calcutta   Cape Town   Dar es Salaam   Delhi   Florence   Hong Kong
Istanbul   Karachi   Kuala Lumpur   Madras   Madrid   Melbourne
Mexico City   Nairobi   Paris   Singapore   Taipei   Tokyo   Toronto   Warsaw
and associated companies in
Berlin   Ibadan

Oxford is a trade mark of Oxford University Press

Published in the United States
by Oxford University Press Inc., New York

A catalogue record for this book is available from the British Library

Library of Congress Cataloging in Publication Data
Transition metals in organic synthesis: a practical approach/edited
by Susan E. Gibson.
Includes bibliographical references and index.
1. Organic compounds–Synthesis.   2. Transition metal compounds.
I. Gibson, Susan E.
QD262.T727   1997   547'.056–dc21   96–52085
ISBN 0 19 855846 5 (Hbk)
ISBN 0 19 855845 7 (Pbk)

Typeset by Footnote Graphics, Warminster, Wilts
Printed in Great Britain by
Bookcraft (Bath) Ltd
Midsomer Norton, Avon

Preface

The use of transition metals in organic synthesis has increased so dramatically in recent years that the importance and value of this area of chemistry is now beyond question. The teaching of the practical aspects of this topic, however, has lagged behind developments in the research laboratories, perhaps because some of the techniques associated with this area of chemistry have not traditionally been dealt with in organic chemistry undergraduate laboratories. It was with this omission in mind that this volume in the Practical Approach in Chemistry Series was compiled. Many of the protocols are suitable for advanced undergraduate experiments or short projects, whilst others are designed to provide guidance to more experienced research workers interested in applying a specific area of transition metal chemistry to their own particular research problem.

The coverage of the use of transition metals in organic synthesis in this volume is necessarily highly selective. The areas included, however, have been chosen to provide insight into the practical techniques associated with both catalytic and stoichiometric applications of transition metal complexes. Each chapter contains many valuable practical 'tips' on specific reagents, reactions, and techniques.

The chapters in this volume have been written by scientists with considerable expertise and experience in both laboratory practice and University teaching. I am indebted to all of them not only for their enthusiasm at the start of the project but also for their subsequent dedication to what at times seemed like a rather distant goal. The chapter authors and I are very grateful to the following people, all of whom provided invaluable advice and comments on the protocols described: Waldemar Adam, Howard Alper, Angela Brickwood, Ann Cotterill, Timothy N. Danks, Stephen G. Davies, Vittorio Farina, Alan Ford, Mike Harris, Laurence M. Harwood, Mark E. Howells, Eric N. Jacobsen, Richard F. W. Jackson, Russell James, Suresh Kapadia, Tsutomu Katsuki, Steven V. Ley, Robin Lord, Tim Luker, Jason Macro, David J. Miller, Norio Miyaura, Christopher J. Moody, Andy Mulvaney, Gareth Probert, Greg P. Roth, K. Barry Sharpless, Kenkichi Sonogashira, Lee Spence, Elizabeth Swann, Julie S. Torode, Barry M. Trost, Simon Tyler, Motokazu Uemura, Edwin Vedejs and Tohru Yamada. Finally, we also thank Domenico Albanese, Stephen A. Benyunes, Stefano C. G. Biagini, Miguel Gama Goicochea, Siân L. Griffiths, Nathalie Guillo, Gary R. Jefferson, Liang K. Ke, Stephen P. Keen, Patrick Metzner, Mark A. Peplow, Ellian Rahimian and Adam T. Wierzchleyski for proofreading the manuscript at various stages of production.

Imperial College, London   S. E. G.
September 1996

Contents

Contents

3. Organoiron chemistry 1: ferrocene and dienyl iron tricarbonyl cation chemistry   65

Christopher J. Richards

4. Organoiron chemistry 2: iron acyl and π-allyltricarbonyliron lactone chemistry   99

Martin Wills

5. Titanocene and zirconocene η^2-π complexes   133

Richard J. Whitby

6. Arene chromium tricarbonyl chemistry   167

Stéphane Perrio

Contents

Contributors

ANDREW F. BROWNING
Department of Chemistry, The Donnan and Robert Robinson Laboratories, PO Box 147, Liverpool L69 3BX, UK.

NICHOLAS GREEVES
Department of Chemistry, The Donnan and Robert Robinson Laboratories, PO Box 147, Liverpool L69 3BX, UK.

NATHALIE GUILLO
Department of Chemistry, Imperial College of Science, Technology and Medicine, South Kensington, London SW7 2AY, UK.

STÉPHANE PERRIO
Laboratoire des Composés Thio-organiques, ISMRA, 6 Boulevard Du Maréchal Juin, 14050 Caen, France.

CHRISTOPHER J. RICHARDS
Department of Chemistry, University of Wales, Cardiff, PO Box 912, Cardiff CF1 3TB, UK.

RICHARD J. WHITBY
Department of Chemistry, The University, Southampton SO17 1BJ, UK.

MARTIN WILLS
Department of Chemistry, University of Warwick, Coventry CV4 7AL, UK.

SIMON WOODWARD
School of Chemistry, University of Hull, Cottingham Road, Kingston upon Hull HU6 7RX, UK.

Protocol checkers

ANGELA BRICKWOOD
Department of Chemistry, University of Reading, Whiteknights, Reading RG6 6AD, UK.

ANN COTTERILL
Department of Chemistry, Loughborough University, Loughborough, Leicestershire LE11 3TU, UK.

Protocol checkers

TIMOTHY N. DANKS
Department of Chemistry, University of Surrey, Guildford, Surrey GU2 5XH, UK.

ALAN FORD
School of Chemistry, University of Hull, Cottingham Road, Kingston upon Hull HU6 7RX, UK.

NICHOLAS GREEVES
Department of Chemistry, The Donnan and Robert Robinson Laboratories, University of Liverpool, PO Box 147, Liverpool L69 3BX, UK.

LAURENCE M. HARWOOD
Department of Chemistry, University of Reading, Whiteknights, Reading RG6 6AD, UK.

MARK E. HOWELLS
Department of Chemistry, University of Surrey, Guildford, Surrey GU2 5XH, UK.

RICHARD F. W. JACKSON
Department of Chemistry, Bedson Building, University of Newcastle, Newcastle upon Type NE1 7RU, UK.

RUSSELL JAMES
Dyson Perrins Laboratory, University of Oxford, South Parks Road, Oxford OX1 3QY, UK.

ROBIN LORD
School of Chemistry, University of Hull, Cottingham Road, Kingston upon Hull HU6 7RX, UK.

JASON MACRO
Dyson Perrins Laboratory, University of Oxford, South Parks Road, Oxford OX1 3QY, UK.

DAVID J. MILLER
Department of Chemistry, Loughborough University, Loughborough, Leicestershire LE11 3TU, UK.

CHRISTOPHER J. MOODY
Department of Chemistry, University of Exeter, Stocker Road, Exeter EX4 4QD, UK.

ANDY MULVANEY
Department of Chemistry, University of Wales, Cardiff, PO Box 912, Cardiff CF1 3TB, UK.

STÉPHANE PERRIO
Laboratoire des Composés Thio-organiques, ISMRA, 6 Boulevard Du Maréchal Juin, 14050 Caen, France.

Protocol checkers

CHRISTOPHER J. RICHARDS
Department of Chemistry, University of Wales, Cardiff, PO Box 912, Cardiff CF1 3TB, UK.

LEE SPENCE
Department of Chemistry, The Donnan and Robert Robinson Laboratories, University of Liverpool, PO Box 147, Liverpool L69 3BX, UK.

ELIZABETH SWANN
Department of Chemistry, Loughborough University, Loughborough, Leicestershire LE11 3TU, UK.

SIMON TYLER
Department of Chemistry, University of Reading, Whiteknights, Reading RG6 6AD, UK.

SIMON WOODWARD
School of Chemistry, University of Hull, Cottingham Road, Kingston upon Hull HU6 7RX, UK.

Abbreviations

acac	acetylacetonate
AD	asymmetric dihydroxylation
AE	asymmetric epoxidation
Binap	2,2'-bis(diphenylphosphino)-1,1'-binaphthyl
Bn	benzyl
BOC	*t*-butyloxycarbonyl
Bz	benzoyl
CAN	ceric ammonium nitrate
Cp	cyclopentadienyl
dba	dibenzylideneacetone
de	diastereomeric excess
DET	diethyl tartrate
DIBAL-H	diisobutylaluminium hydride
DMAP	*p*-dimethylaminopyridine
DMPU	1,3-dimethyl-3,4,5,6-tetrahydro-2(1*H*)-pyrimidinone
dppe	1,2-bis(diphenylphosphino)ethane
ee	enantiomeric excess
Fc	ferrocenyl
hex	hexyl
HLADH	horse liver alcohol dehydrogenase
HMPA	hexamethylphosphoramide
HPLC	high performance liquid chromatography
LDA	lithium diisopropylamide
macH	3-methyl-2,4-pentanedione
NADH	reduced nicotinamide adenine dinucleotide
NBS	*N*-bromosuccinimide
NMP	*N*-methylpyrrolidine
PCC	pyridinium chlorochromate
PDC	pyridinium dichromate
p.s.i.	pounds per square inch
py	pyridine
R_f	retention factor
salen	*N,N'*-disalicylidene-ethylenediaminato
SAMP	[(*S*)-1-amino-2-(methoxymethyl)pyrrolidine]
TBS	*t*-butyldimethylsilyl
Tf	trifluoromethanesulfonyl
TFA	trifluoroacetic acid
THF	tetrahydrofuran
TLC	thin layer chromatography

Abbreviations

TMEDA	*N*,*N*,*N*′,*N*′-tetramethylethylenediamine
TMM	trimethylenemethane
TMS	trimethylsilyl

1

Transition metal-promoted oxidations

SIMON WOODWARD

1. Introduction

Few other areas of modern synthetic organic chemistry offer the diversity shown by homogeneous catalytic oxidation reactions. Practically all the transition metals have complexes showing oxidation activity; widely disparate mechanisms of action are standard.

It is the aim of this chapter to present in detail a few selected examples of useful organic transformations promoted by Group 4–11 (Ti–Cu) metals rather than to give a comprehensive listing of all possible transformations, as this information is available in several other excellent books.[1,2] The protocols are selected to demonstrate the most common oxygenation (addition of O atoms) or oxidation (removal of H atoms) pathways encountered in transition metal-promoted reactions of organic substrates.

> **Caution!** As all oxidation reactions represent controlled highly exothermic reactions, and most involve the handling of toxic materials, all of the protocols in this chapter should be carried out in an efficient hood with explosion resistant sashes. Eye protection and disposable gloves must be worn. Clean reaction flasks are essential to avoid the accidental inclusion of materials known to bring about the rapid decomposition of high energy oxidants.

2. Group 4 metal-promoted oxidations: Sharpless–Katsuki asymmetric epoxidation

The generalised stereoselective epoxidation of allylic alcohols **1** by *t*-butyl hydroperoxide in the presence of titanium(IV) isopropoxide and tartrate esters to the epoxides **2** (Scheme 1.1) constitutes a seminal landmark in metal-mediated asymmetric oxidations. The catalytic version of this reaction is often the most effective procedure and is especially useful for the kinetic resolution of 1-substituted allylic alcohols, as in the transformation of **3** to **4**. The epoxidation of (*E*)-2-hexen-1-ol is demonstrated here to allow comparison with a stoichiometric protocol described in *Organic Synthesis*.[3]

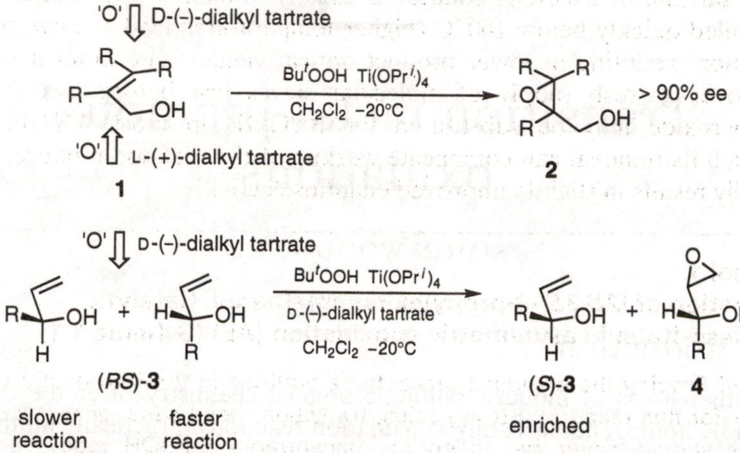
'O'
D-(–)-dialkyl tartrate
'O'
L-(+)-dialkyl tartrate
Bu^tOOH $Ti(OPr^i)_4$
CH_2Cl_2 –20°C
> 90% ee
1
2
D-(–)-dialkyl tartrate
(*RS*)-3
slower reaction
faster reaction
(*S*)-3
enriched
4

Scheme 1.1

Full mechanistic details of asymmetric epoxidation (AE) reactions can be found in a comprehensive review.[4] The features of the transition state which leads to high enantioselectivities over such a wide range of allyl functions have been intensively studied,[5,6] but it is arguably more instructive from a practical point of view to indicate the behaviour of some commonly encountered substrates with this catalyst. Tri- and tetra-substituted allylic alcohols with their electron-rich double bonds react rapidly, even at −35 °C. 3-(*E*)-Monosubstituted allylic alcohols also react rapidly (1–4 h, as in Protocol 1) while other mono-substitution patterns dramatically slow down the reaction (10–50 h), necessitating the use of cryostatic cooling units. These reactivity patterns are summarised in Scheme 1.2.

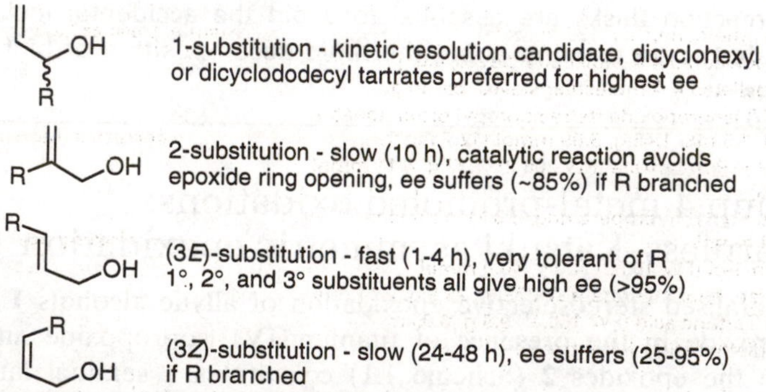
1-substitution - kinetic resolution candidate, dicyclohexyl or dicyclododecyl tartrates preferred for highest ee
2-substitution - slow (10 h), catalytic reaction avoids epoxide ring opening, ee suffers (~85%) if R branched
(3*E*)-substitution - fast (1-4 h), very tolerant of R 1°, 2°, and 3° substituents all give high ee (>95%)
(3*Z*)-substitution - slow (24-48 h), ee suffers (25-95%) if R branched

Scheme 1.2

Although the AE reaction tolerates many functional groups, it is incompatible with RCO_2H, RSH, ArOH, PR_3, and most amines. If the substrate is free of these functions and the procedure fails, moisture contamination of the dialkyl tartrate or Bu^tOOH solution is usually to blame. The former should be distilled quickly below 100°C (higher temperatures lead to tartrate polymerisation, resulting in lower product optical yields). The latter should be dried over a fresh supply of molecular sieves just before use. Cumene hydroperoxide may be substituted for Bu^tOOH in most AE reactions. Although its removal can complicate workup of the reaction mixture, its use normally results in slightly improved enantioselectivities.

Protocol 1.
Preparation of (2S,3S)-3-propyloxiranemethanol. Catalytic Sharpless–Katsuki asymmetric epoxidation (AE) (Scheme 1.1)

Caution! Employ the standard precautions outlined in the introduction to this chapter for this reaction. Strong acids, transition metal salts, or metal syringe needles should **never** be added to concentrated Bu^tOOH stock solutions. Aliquots of Bu^tOOH remaining after use in reactions should **not** be returned to the stock solutions. 1,2-Dichloroethane should **not** be used as a solvent with Bu^tOOH, despite early recommendations.[7]

Equipment

- Three-necked, round-bottomed flask (250 mL)
- Teflon-bladed overhead mechanical stirrer and ⸸ 24/40 sleeve adapter
- Low temperature thermometer and ⸸ 19/22 cone/screw thread adapter
- ⸸ 19/22 socket/cone adapter with T connection
- Well-insulated low-temperature bath
- Septa
- All-glass Luer syringes (2 mL and 20 mL)

- Needles (10 cm, 20 or 22 gauge)
- Pressure-equalising addition funnel (50 mL)
- Glass funnel
- Beaker (50 mL)
- Erlenmeyer flasks (3 × 50 mL)
- Source of dry inert gas (nitrogen or argon)
- Separating funnel (1 L)

Materials

- Dry dichloromethane,[a] *ca.* 120 mL total — volatile, toxic at high concentrations
- Activated powdered 4 Å molecular sieves, 4.0 g — hydroscopic
- Activated pelleted 4 Å molecular sieves, *ca.* 10 g — hydroscopic
- Titanium(IV) isopropoxide (tetraisopropyl orthotitanate) (FW 284.3), 1.5 mL, 1.45 g, 5.09 mmol (12.7 mol%) — corrosive, moisture sensitive
- Diethyl L-(+)-(R,R)-tartrate (FW 206.2), 1.27 g, 6.11 mmol (15.3 mol%) — harmful
- Anhydrous *t*-butyl hydroperoxide, 5.5 M in nonane,[b] 25 mL, 138 mmol — oxidising agent, flammable
- (E)-2-Hexen-1-ol (FW 100.2), 4.0 g, 40.0 mmol — harmful
- Iron(II) sulfate heptahydrate (FW 278.0), 29.9 g, 0.11 mol
- L-(+)-(R,R)-Tartaric acid (FW 150.1), 9.9 g, 0.05 mol
- Technical diethyl ether for extraction — flammable

1. Clean all glassware, syringes, and needles sequentially in soap solution, water, and acetone. Allow the acetone to evaporate[c] and then dry every-

Protocol 1. *Continued*

 thing in an electric oven (105°C) for at least 1 h. **Caution!** – Thoroughly dry
 the thermometer with paper tissues and a hair dryer just before use; do
 not over-heat it.

2. Rapidly assemble the glassware as in Fig. 1.1 and start the inert gas flow.
 Apply one drop of liquid paraffin to the sleeve adapter of the paddle stirrer,
 to ensure an air-tight fit. Rapidly weigh activated powdered 4 Å molecular
 sieves (4.0 g) into a small glass beaker. Add the molecular sieves to the
 flask using a funnel (lift it slightly to avoid air locks). Rinse in the residual
 amounts of molecular sieves left in the beaker with three 25 mL portions of
 dichloromethane.

3. Cap the remaining ⏀ 19/22 joint with a septum and cool the reaction mixture
 to about −20°C using an acetone/dry ice bath (the bath temperature will be
 about −23 to −25°C). If necessary increase the inert gas flow to avoid 'suck
 back' of the bubbler. From now on monitor the reaction periodically to
 ensure it is stirring at about −15 to −20°C, adding more dry ice if necessary.

4. Add 25 mL of stock 5.5 M *t*-butyl hydroperoxide to a 50 mL Erlenmeyer flask
 and add *ca.* 5 g of pelleted 4 Å molecular sieves to the solution. Cap the flask
 loosely with a septum or bung and set it aside to pre-dry the Bu^{t}OOH.

5. Using a Pasteur pipette, put diethyl L-(+)-(*R,R*)-tartrate (0.62 g, 3.01 mmol)
 into a 50 mL Erlenmeyer flask. Dilute it with 5 mL of dichloromethane and
 cap the flask with an air-tight stopper or bung.

6. Draw up 1.5 mL of titanium(IV) isopropoxide into a 2 mL syringe as shown
 in Fig. 1.2. Inject this into the reaction flask through the septum.

7. Using the 20 mL syringe transfer the L-(+)-(*R,R*)-tartrate solution to the
 reaction flask (keep the reaction temperature below −15°C). Wash any
 residual tartrate into the reaction mixture with a further 5 mL of
 dichloromethane using the syringe.

8. Using the 20 mL syringe, slowly add 20 mL of the pre-dried Bu^{t}OOH solution
 carefully keeping the reaction temperature in the range −20 ± 3°C. Allow
 the mixture to stir for 30 min at −20°C.^{d} During this period weigh (*E*)-2-
 hexen-1-ol (4.0 g, 40.0 mmol) into a 50 mL Erlenmeyer flask. Add
 dichloromethane (20 mL) and some pelleted 4 Å molecular sieves to pre-
 dry the substrate. Cap the flask.

9. Change the septum for a 50 mL pressure-equalising dropping funnel (tap
 shut) and, using a Pasteur pipette, charge it with the (*E*)-2-hexen-1-ol solution. Rinse the Erlenmeyer flask with a further 5 mL of dichloromethane
 and pipette this into the dropping funnel.

10. Add the (*E*)-2-hexene-1-ol solution to the reaction mixture dropwise over a
 period of 20 min ensuring that the reaction mixture remains in the range
 −15 to −20°C.

11. Let the reaction stir at −15 to −20°C for 2 h, adding dry ice as required.

4

Completion of the reaction may be confirmed by TLC analysis if appropriate [Merck Kieselgel 60 F_{254} plates, 7:3 hexane:ethyl acetate eluent, visualisation by $KMnO_4$ spray].

12. Let the mixture come to $-10\,°C$. Meanwhile prepare a solution of 29.9 g of iron(II) sulfate heptahydrate and 9.9 g L-(+)-(*R,R*)-tartaric acid in water (90 mL) and chill this solution using an ice bath.

13. Add the chilled iron(II) solution to the reaction mixture once its temperature has reached $-10\,°C$ (**care!**).[e] Stir for 5 min at $-10\,°C$ and then continue stirring at room temperature until two layers are formed.

14. Transfer the mixture to a 1 L separating funnel, run off the lower dichloromethane layer, and retain it.[f] Extract the aqueous layer with two 50 mL portions of diethyl ether and combine these with the dichloromethane fraction. Remove the solvents with a rotary evaporator to give the crude wet product. This may be stored overnight in a freezer if necessary.

15. Wash out the reaction flask (it may be left wet) and add to it sodium chloride (5 g), sodium hydroxide (15 g), and water (50 mL). Set up the flask as in Fig. 1.1 but neglecting the low temperature thermometer and inert gas supply. Replace the acetone in the cooling bath with ice and some water. Stopper the remaining open joints.

16. Once the sodium hydroxide solution has cooled, add the crude epoxide dissolved in 50 mL of diethyl ether to the hydrolysis mixture and rinse any remaining epoxide left in the flask in with two 30 mL portions of diethyl ether. Let the reaction stir vigorously for 1 h.

17. Transfer the mixture to a 1 L separatory funnel and add water (50 mL). Separate the phases[f] (retaining both), and extract the aqueous phase with two 50 mL portions of diethyl ether. Combine the organic fractions and dry them with sodium sulfate.

18. Filtration and rotary evaporation of the filtrate yields (2*S*,3*S*)-3-propyloxiranemethanol as a pale oil contaminated with nonane (about 8.5 g). The nonane is removed by careful Kugelröhr distillation ($25-60\,°C$, 8 mmHg), followed by the product as a colourless oil (b.p. $100-110\,°C$, 8 mmHg). About 3.5 g (75%) $\{[\alpha]_D^{25}\ -46.6°\ (c\ 1.0,\ CHCl_3)\}$ is obtained. A procedure is available for determining the optical purity of the product via its α-methoxy-α-(trifluoromethyl)phenylacetic acid ester (Mosher's ester).[3]

[a] Distilled from calcium hydride; each portion should be collected just before use.
[b] If the Aldrich product (41,806-4) is not available, this reagent may be prepared from aqueous 70% Bu^{t}OOH by known procedures;[8] toluene solutions can also be used. Commercial solutions of 3.0 M Bu^{t}OOH are available but can lead to inferior results[9] and therefore should be avoided. Similarly, Bu^{t}OOH solutions in decane may lead to a problematic distillation in the final step. Methods for determining the purity of *t*-butyl hydroperoxide are outlined in Protocol 2.
[c] Evaporation may be promoted by careful use of a hair dryer.
[d] This ageing of the catalyst is vital for high enantioselectivities and cannot be eliminated.
[e] **Caution!** For larger scale reactions the reaction mixture should be added to the stirred cold iron(II) sulfate solution to avoid the possibility of violent catalytic decomposition of the Bu^{t}OOH.
[f] If an emulsion forms, phase separation is promoted by filtration through Celite.

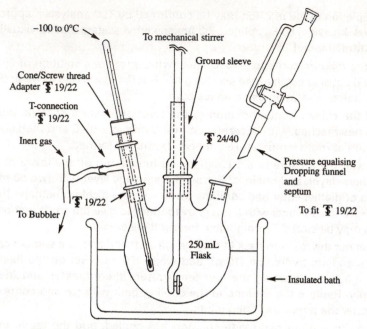

Fig. 1.1 Assembled reaction apparatus for Protocols 1 and 3.

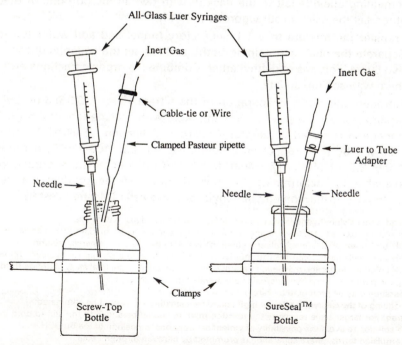

Fig. 1.2 Collecting air- and moisture-sensitive liquids.

6

Protocol 2.
Determination of the molarity of *t*-butyl hydroperoxide samples[a][7]

Caution! Employ the standard precautions outlined in the introduction to this chapter for this reaction.

Equipment
- Erlenmeyer flasks (1 × 250 mL and 2 × 100 mL)
- Glass funnel
- Measuring cylinders (1 × 5 mL, 1 × 10 mL, and 1 × 100 mL)
- Electric hot air gun (paint stripper)

- An appropriate sized analytical pipette (0.25 mL for *ca.* 5 M Bu^{t}OOH)
- Appropriate sized volumetric flasks
- Graduated burette for titration

Materials
- Sodium iodide, 11 g .... toxic
- Isopropanol, *ca.* 300 mL .... toxic
- Glacial acetic acid .... corrosive, malodorous
- 0.1 M sodium thiosulfate .... toxic
- Starch solution

1. Clean all glassware sequentially in soap solution, water, and acetone. Totally evaporate the acetone using a commercial hot air gun.

2. Dissolve 11 g of sodium iodide in 50 mL of isopropanol in a 100 mL Erlenmeyer flask by swirling the mixture and heating with the hot air gun.[b] Filter the solution into a fresh 100 mL Erlenmeyer flask. Put 10 mL of this solution in a 250 mL Erlenmeyer flask, and add glacial acetic acid (2 mL), and isopropanol (25 mL).

3. Accurately measure out a sample of *tert*-butyl hydroperoxide, containing no more than 2.5 mmol of active oxygen, using an analytical pipette and add this to the sodium iodide/acetic acid mixture. Bring the dark solution to reflux using the hot air gun until a constant colouration is attained (*ca* 30 sec).

4. Dilute the sample with 100 mL of distilled water and immediately titrate the liberated iodine with 0.1 M sodium thiosulfate. The endpoint is most easily visualised by addition of starch indicator (~ 1 mL) once a pale yellow colour is obtained. The blue colour disappears at the end point.

5. The concentration is calculated according to the equation: $[S \times M]/[2 \times (\text{mL of the sample})]$ = molarity of the Bu^{t}OOH solution, where S = mL of thiosulfate for the titration and M = molarity of the thiosulfate solution.

[a] For *t*-butyl hydroperoxide solutions in toluene, an approximate molarity may be obtained from the ^{1}H NMR spectrum of the neat solution using the equation:

$$X/(0.1X + 0.32Y) = \text{molarity of the Bu}^t\text{OOH solution}$$

where X = integration of *t*-butyl resonance and Y = integration of toluene methyl resonance. However, this method is not as accurate as titration assays.
[b] Improved rates of dissolution may be attained by addition of small amounts of water; this does not affect the subsequent analysis.

3. Group 4 metal-promoted oxidations: asymmetric oxidation of sulfides

The original Katsuki–Sharpless system, with a titanium:tartrate ratio of ~1:1, is rather poor at the asymmetric conversion of sulfides to sulfoxides (enantiodifferential oxidation of one of the sulfur lone pairs in R_2S). Modification of the reaction procedure by addition of 1 equiv. of water and addition of extra tartrate ligands leads to an effective reagent for the stoichiometric oxidation of ArSMe species, although the structure of the active reagent is not known.[10,11] The sulfide 4-MeC_6H_4SMe **5** is a popular test substrate as its oxidation to (*R*)-**6** (Scheme 1.3) proceeds with high optical induction using natural tartrates; this is described in Protocol 3.[12] The strong binding of the product sulfoxides to the titanium oxidant precludes the development of catalytic protocols for these tartrate-mediated sulfide oxidations. However, switching to binaphthol-based ligands may offer a solution to this problem.[13,14]

Protocol 3.

Preparation of (*R*)-methyl 4-tolyl sulfoxide (Structure 6). The modified Sharpless–Katsuki oxidation reagent (Scheme 1.3)

Caution! Employ the standard precautions outlined in the introduction to this chapter for this reaction. Strong acids, transition metal salts, or metal syringe needles should **never** be added to concentrated Bu^{t}OOH stock solutions. Aliquots of Bu^{t}OOH remaining after use in reactions should **not** be returned to stock solutions. 1,2-Dichloroethane should **not** be used as a solvent for Bu^{t}OOH, despite early recommendations.[7]

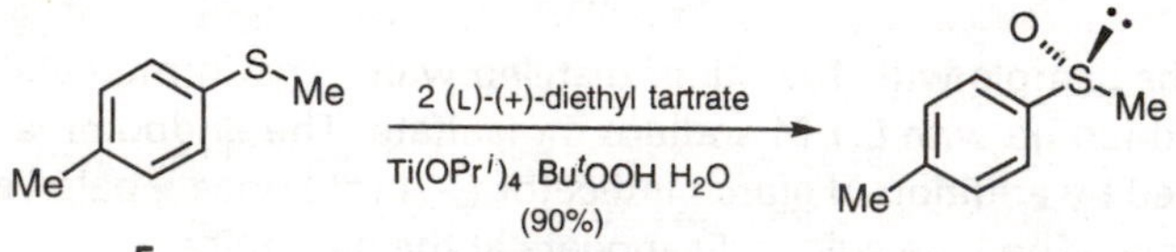

Scheme 1.3

Equipment

- Three-necked, round-bottomed flask (250 mL)
- Teflon-bladed overhead mechanical stirrer and ⌷ 24/40 sleeve adapter
- Low-temperature thermometer and ⌷ 19/22 cone/screw thread adapter
- ⌷ 19/22 socket/cone adapter with T connection
- Well-insulated low-temperature bath
- Septa

- All-glass Luer syringes (5 mL and 10 mL)
- Needles (10 cm, 20 or 22 gauge)
- Syringe (250 µL)
- Glass funnel
- Erlenmeyer flask (50 mL)
- Separating funnel (500 mL)
- Source of dry inert gas (nitrogen or argon)

Materials

- Dry dichloromethane,[a] *ca.* 100 mL total   **volatile, toxic at high concentrations**
- Titanium(IV) isopropoxide (tetraisopropyl orthotitanate)
  (FW 284.3), 1.8 mL, 1.7 g, 6.0 mmol   **corrosive, moisture sensitive**
- Diethyl L-(+)-(*R,R*)-tartrate (FW 206.2), 2.5 g, 12.1 mmol   **harmful**
- Anhydrous *t*-butyl hydroperoxide, 3.0 M in isooctane,[b]
  2.2 mL, 6.6 mmol   **oxidising agent, flammable**
- Methyl 4-tolyl sulfide **5** (FW 138.2), 0.84 g, 6.00 mmol   **toxic, malodorous**
- Technical diethyl ether, for extraction   **flammable**

1. Clean all glassware, syringes, and needles sequentially in soap solution, water, and acetone. Allow the acetone to evaporate[c] and then dry everything in an electric oven (105 °C) for at least 1 h. **Caution!** Thoroughly dry the thermometer with paper tissues and a hair dryer just before use; do not over-heat it. Do not oven dry microlitre syringes as they are easily damaged by excessive heating.

2. Promptly assemble the glassware as in Fig. 1.1 and start the inert gas flow. Apply one drop of liquid paraffin to the sleeve adapter of the paddle stirrer to ensure an air-tight fit. Weigh diethyl L-(+)-(*R,R*)-tartrate (2.5 g, 12.1 mmol) into the 50 mL Erlenmeyer flask, dissolve it in 30 mL of dichloromethane and pour this solution into the reaction flask using the funnel (lift it slightly to avoid air locks). Rinse the Erlenmeyer flask with a further 50 mL of dichloromethane and add this to the reaction flask as well.

3. Cap the remaining ∓ 19/22 joint with a septum and commence stirring. Draw up 1.8 mL of titanium(IV) isopropoxide into a 5 mL syringe as shown in Fig. 1.2. Inject this into the reaction flask through the septum.

4. Measure 180 μL of water into the 250 μL syringe and add this to the reaction mixture through the septum (guide the fine needle with your thumb and forefinger to avoid bending it). Stir the very pale yellow solution for 20 min at room temperature.

5. Dissolve methyl 4-tolyl sulfide **5** (0.84 g, 6.00 mmol) in dichloromethane (5 mL) and add it to the reaction mixture by syringe.

6. Cool the reaction mixture to about −20 °C using the acetone/dry ice bath. If necessary increase the inert gas flow to avoid bubbler 'suck back'. From now on periodically monitor the reaction to ensure it is stirring close to −20 °C, adding more dry ice if necessary.

7. Add 2.2 mL of *t*-butyl hydroperoxide dropwise to the solution using a clean dry 5 mL syringe over 5 min. Stir the reaction for 4 h keeping the temperature close to −20 °C.[d]

8. Using a syringe, add water (1 mL) to the reaction mixture and remove the flask from the low-temperature bath. Stir the reaction at room temperature for 1.5 h.

9. Filter the white gel produced through a pad of Celite and wash the pad with three 10 mL portions of dichloromethane. The slow filtration can be

Protocol 3. *Continued*

    promoted by gentle scratching of the Celite surface with a spatula. Retain the filtrate.

10. Wash out the reaction flask and add to it sodium chloride (5 g), sodium hydroxide (15 g), and water (50 mL). Set up the flask as in Fig. 1.1 but omitting the low-temperature thermometer and nitrogen supply. Replace the acetone in the cooling bath with ice and some water.

11. Once the sodium hydroxide solution has cooled, add the dichloromethane solution from step 9 to the hydrolysis mixture. Rinse in any remaining crude sulfoxide left in the flask with small additional amounts of dichloromethane. Allow the hydrolysis reaction to stir vigorously for 1 h.

12. Transfer the mixture to a 500 mL separatory funnel. Separate the phases (retaining both) and extract the aqueous phase with two 20 mL portions of dichloromethane. Combine the organic fractions and dry them over sodium sulfate.

13. Filtration and removal of the solvent from the filtrate by rotary evaporation yields crude (*R*)-methyl 4-tolyl sulfoxide **6** (about 0.8 g, 85%) which may be purified by chromatography on silica gel with 1:9 hexane:ethyl acetate. This produces a colourless solid (m.p. 76–77 °C). Optically pure **6** shows $[\alpha]_D$ + 146 ±1 (c 1.0, acetone), while that produced by this protocol has an optical purity of *ca.* 90%.[12,e]

[a] Distilled from calcium hydride; each portion should be collected just before use.
[b] If the Fluka product (19998) is not available, this reagent may be prepared from aqueous 70% Bu^{t}OOH by known procedures;[8] toluene solutions can also be used (Fluka 20 000). Methods for assessing the purity of *t*-butyl hydroperoxide are outlined in Protocol 2.
[c] Evaporation may be promoted by careful use of a hair dryer.
[d] Alternatively, the reaction mixture can be sealed under nitrogen or argon [using lightly greased stoppers and KECK clips (Aldrich Z15,043-6 and Z15,044-4)] and stored at −23 °C overnight in a domestic freezer to complete conversion to the sulfoxide.
[e] The enantioselectivity depends strongly on the reaction temperature and is greatest in the range −25 to −20 °C. Both higher and lower temperatures lead to lower optical yields.

---

4. Group 5 metal-promoted oxidations: epoxidations using vanadyl acetylacetonate

The complex $V(=O)(acac)_2$ is another highly useful catalyst for epoxidation of allylic alcohols using Bu^{t}OOH. Only double bonds proximal to the alcohol are epoxidised under high rate acceleration. For example, the less reactive double bond in geraniol **7** is epoxidised to generate the 2,3-epoxide **8** rather than the 6,7-epoxide **9** (Scheme 1.4),[15] suggesting that both the substrate and the Bu^{t}OOH are bound to vanadium in the catalytic cycle. Supporting this notion, $V(=O)(acac)_2$-catalysed reactions often proceed with high levels of diastereoselectivity, as illustrated by the epoxidation of cyclohexenol **10** to the *syn* product **11** rather than the *anti* compound **12** (Scheme 1.4). The stereoselectivity in V(=O)(acac)$_2$-catalysed oxidations can be correlated to relief of strain between the 1,2- and 1,3-disposed substituents either within the substrate or between the substrate and catalyst, thus allowing the identity of the major stereoisomer to be predicted. These ideas are summarised in two excellent reviews.[7,16] The regioselective 2,3-epoxidation of geraniol **7** is presented in detail.

Although it is added to the reaction mixture, V(=O)(acac)$_2$ is not the actual catalyst in these reactions. The acetylacetone ligands are degraded to formic and acetic acid and V(=O)(OR)$_3$ species quickly form. The acidic by-products can cause problems in reactions leading to acid-sensitive epoxides. In these cases it is better to use isolated trialkyl vanadates as catalysts. The species V(=O)(OR)$_3$ (R = Et, Pr, Pr^i) work best.

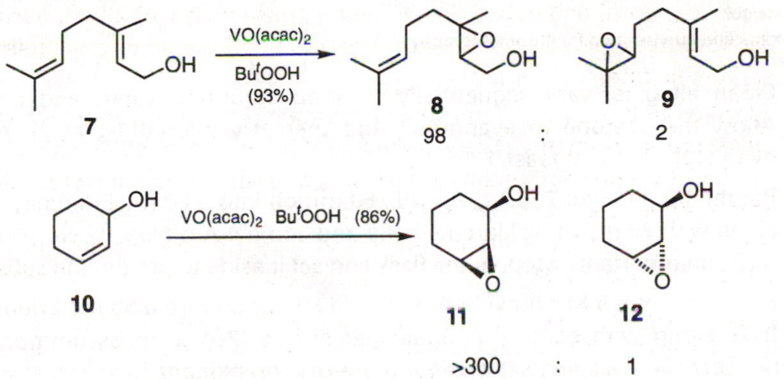

Scheme 1.4

Protocol 4.
Preparation of 2,3-epoxygeraniol. Regioselective epoxidation by V(=O)(acac)$_2$ (Scheme 1.4)

Caution! Employ the standard precautions outlined in the introduction to this chapter for this reaction. Strong acids, transition metal salts, or metal syringe needles should **never** be added to concentrated Bu^{t}OOH stock solutions. Aliquots of Bu^{t}OOH remaining after use in reactions should **not** be returned to stock solutions. 1,2-Dichloroethane should **not** be used as a solvent with Bu^{t}OOH despite early recommendations.[7]

Equipment
- Three-necked, round-bottomed flask (250 mL)
- Stirrer hot plates (× 2)
- Teflon-covered magnetic stirring bars, *ca.* 4 × 0.8 cm (× 2)
- Pressure-equalising dropping funnel (50 mL)
- Beaker (500 mL)

- Glass funnel
- Separating funnel (1 L)
- Sinter funnel
- Büchner flask (500 mL)
- ⚥ 19/22 cone to tube adapter
- Reduction adapter (⚥ 24/40 to ⚥ 19/22)

Protocol 4. *Continued*

- Septa
- Erlenmeyer flasks (50 mL) with stoppers (× 2)
- Source of dry inert gas (nitrogen or argon)
- Cooling bath

Materials

- Dry dichloromethane,[a] *ca.* 120 mL total   **volatile, toxic at high concentrations**
- Activated pelleted 4 Å molecular sieves   **hydroscopic**
- Vanadyl acetylacetonate, V(=O)(acac)$_2$ (FW 265.2), 0.66 g, 2.4 mmol, 4.8 mol%   **toxic**
- Anhydrous *t*-butyl hydroperoxide, 5.5 M in nonane,[b] 20 mL, 110 mmol   **oxidising agent, flammable**
- (*E*)-Geraniol **7** (FW 154.3), 8.2 g, 9.2 mL, 53 mmol   **toxic**
- Iron(II) sulfate heptahydrate (FW 278.0), 16.5 g, 0.06 mol
- L-(+)-(*R,R*)-Tartaric acid (FW 150.1), 6.6 g, 0.04 mol
- Technical diethyl ether, for extraction   **flammable**
- Silica gel
- Hexane and ethylacetate for chromatography   **flammable**

1. Clean all glassware sequentially in soap solution, water, and acetone. Allow the acetone to evaporate[c] and then dry everything in an electric oven (105 °C) for at least 1 h.

2. Put the (*E*)-geraniol **7** (8.2 g, 9.2 mL, 53 mmol) into a 50 mL Erlenmeyer flask along with 25 mL of dichloromethane and some 4 Å molecular sieves (2–4 g, mass unimportant). Stopper the flask and set it aside to pre-dry the substrate.

3. Put 20 mL of 5.5 M *t*-butyl hydroperoxide solution into a 50 mL Erlenmeyer flask along with some 4 Å molecular sieves (2–4 g, mass unimportant). Stopper the flask and set it aside to pre-dry the oxidant.

4. Set up the equipment as shown in Fig. 1.3 (with a stirrer hot plate under the apparatus) and fill the cooling bath with a mixture of ice and water. Using a glass funnel, add the solid vanadyl acetylacetonate (0.66 g) to the reaction flask. Wash any remaining catalyst adhered to the funnel into the reaction flask using the (*E*)-geraniol **7** solution prepared in step 2 (lift the funnel slightly to avoid any air locks). Be careful **not** to add the molecular sieves left in the Erlenmeyer flask to the reaction mixture as well. Rinse the geraniol flask with three 25 mL portions of dichloromethane, adding these to the reaction flask as well. Remove the funnel and insert the septum.

5. Ensure the stopcock on the dropping funnel is shut. Charge the dropping funnel with 5.5 M *t*-butyl hydroperoxide solution (15 mL).

6. Add the Bu^{t}OOH solution to the reaction dropwise over about 10 min with stirring. The colour of the reaction mixture will change from blue to green to dark red.

7. Stir the reaction at room temperature for 1 h 45 min; completion of the reaction is best indicated by TLC (Merck Kieselgel 60 F$_{254}$ plates; 7:3 hexane:ethyl acetate eluent, visualisation by KMnO$_4$ spray).

8. Prepare a solution of 16.5 g of iron(II) sulfate heptahydrate and 6.6 g L-(+)-

12

(*R,R*)-tartaric acid in water (90 mL) in a 500 mL beaker. Stir and chill this solution to 0°C using an ice bath on a stirrer hot plate.

9. Add the reaction mixture to the chilled iron(II) solution. Stir the mixture for 5 min at 0°C and then continue stirring at room temperature until two layers are formed.

10. Transfer the mixture to a 1 L separating funnel, add 100 mL of water, and run off the lower pink dichloromethane layer and retain it. Extract the aqueous layer with two 50 mL portions of diethyl ether and combine these with the dichloromethane fraction. Dry the organic fractions (Na_2SO_4), filter the pale yellow solution, and remove the solvents with a rotary evaporator to give the crude product.

11. The product is purified by filtration chromatography. Place a 7 cm diameter by 5 cm high porosity 3 sinter funnel on a 500 mL Büchner flask (not connected to an aspirator). Fill the sinter with 40 g of chromatographic silica gel. Prepare 250 mL of a 10:1 mixture of hexane:ethyl acetate. Add 80 mL of this solution to the silica and stir the resulting slurry. Promptly dissolve the crude geraniol epoxide in 30 mL of eluent and carefully pour it onto the silica pad. Allow the solution to filter through the silica under gravity and then add another 30 mL of eluent. After this has filtered through under gravity apply suction to the Büchner flask and elute with the remaining 10:1 solution. Prepare 100 mL of a 4:1 mixture hexane:ethyl acetate and suck this through the silica pad as well.

12. Removal of the solvent on a rotory evaporator (water bath temperature 60°C) yields 2,3-epoxygeraniol as a slightly coloured oil (about 7.9 g, 87%). The product may be further purified by formation of its acetate followed by vacuum distillation (0.025 mmHg, 104–106°C) to yield 2,3-epoxygeranyl acetate as a colourless liquid containing only traces of its 6,7-isomer.[15]

---

[a] Distilled from calcium hydride.
[b] If the Aldrich product (41,806-4) is not available this reagent may be prepared from aqueous 70% Bu^{t}OOH by known procedures;[8] toluene solutions can also be used. Methods for assessing the purity of *t*-butyl hydroperoxide are outlined in Protocol 2.
[c] Evaporation may be promoted by careful use of a hair dryer.

---

5. Group 6 metal-promoted oxidations: enolate oxygenation with MoOPH

Although molybdenum complexes are also potent activators of Bu^{t}OOH,[7] it seems appropriate here to consider instead the rather different behaviour of $[MoO_5(py)\{OP(NMe_2)_3\}]$ (MoOPH). This complex is one of the few reagents capable of direct oxygenation of enolate anions, leading to hydroxy ketones in moderate to good yields.[17] The behaviour of camphor **13** is exemplary,[18] resulting in the hydroxy ketone **14** (Scheme 1.5).

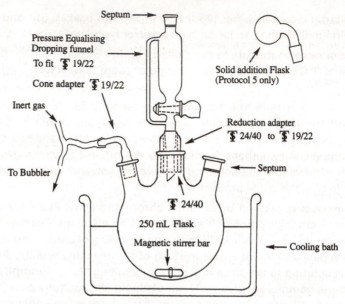

Septum ⟶

Pressure Equalising
Dropping funnel
To fit ℸ 19/22

Cone adapter ℸ 19/22

Inert gas

Solid addition Flask
(Protocol 5 only)

Reduction adapter
ℸ 24/40 to ℸ 19/22

To Bubbler

Septum

ℸ 24/40

250 mL Flask

Magnetic stirrer bar

Cooling bath

Fig. 1.3 Assembled reaction apparatus for Protocols 4 and 5.

Protocol 5.
Preparation of 1,7,7-trimethyl-3-hydroxybicyclo[2.2.1]heptan-2-one (Structure 14). Hydroxylation of camphor (Structure 13) by [MoO$_5$(py){OP(Nme$_3$)$_3$}] (MoOPH) (Scheme 1.5)

Caution! Employ the standard precautions outlined in the introduction to this chapter for this reaction. The MoOPH reagent should be treated as **potentially explosive**; a safety screen should be used. Complexes containing OP(NMe$_2$)$_3$ (HMPA) and other sources of this material should be treated with respect as HMPA is classed as a potent carcinogen. All operations should be conducted in an efficient hood using gloves. All residues should be bottled for appropriate disposable.

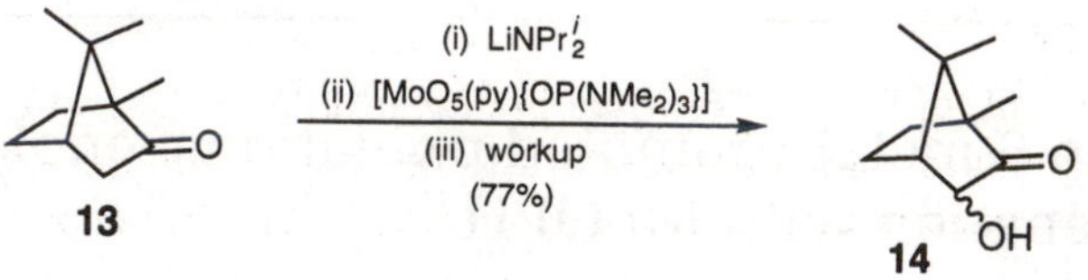

$$
\text{13} \quad \xrightarrow[\substack{\text{(iii)\ workup} \\ \text{(77\%)}}]{\substack{\text{(i)\ LiNPr}_2^i \\ \text{(ii)\ [MoO}_5\text{(py)\{OP(NMe}_2)_3\}]}} \quad \text{14}
$$

Scheme 1.5

Equipment

- Three-necked, round-bottomed flask (250 mL)
- Electric heat gun (paint stripper)
- Magnetic stirrer

- Teflon-covered magnetic stirrer bar, *ca.* 4 × 0.8 cm
- Well-insulated low-temperature bath

- Low-temperature thermometer to monitor cooling bath temperatures
- All-glass Luer syringe with 10 cm needles (5 and 20 mL, gauge no: 20 or 22)
- Separating funnel (500 mL)
- Glass filtration frit
- Büchner flask
- ⏆ 19/22 cone to tube adapter
- Reduction adapter (⏆ 24/40 to ⏆ 19/22)
- Pressure-equalising dropping funnel (200 mL)
- Septa
- Inert atmosphere solid addition flask[a]
- Source of dry inert gas (nitrogen or argon)

Materials

• Dry THF,[b] 125 mL total	**flammable, hydroscopic**
• Dry diisopropylamine[c] (FW 101.2), 2.45 mL, 1.75 g, 17.5 mmol	**toxic, malodorous**
• 1.6 M Bu^{n}Li in hexane, 11.0 mL, 17.6 mmol	**air sensitive**
• [MoO$_5$(py){OP(NMe$_3$)$_3$}] (MoOPH),[d] 10.45 g, 17.65 mmol	**toxic**
• Camphor **13** (FW 152.2), 2.44 g, 16.05 mmol	**toxic**
• Technical diethyl ether, for extraction	**flammable**
• Silica gel for filtration chromatography, 40 g	**irritant dust**
• 1:1 hexane:diethyl ether, 900 mL for chromatography	**flammable**

1. Clean all glassware sequentially in soap solution, water, and acetone. Allow the acetone to evaporate[e] and then dry the glassware in an electric oven (105°C) for at least 1 h.

2. Set up the apparatus as in Fig. 1.3, but without the cooling bath in place, and with a stirrer hot plate under the apparatus. Start the inert gas flow. Heat the apparatus with an electric heat gun (>100°C), but avoid scorching the rubber septa. Leave the apparatus to cool.

3. Remove one septum and add to the flask diisopropylamine (2.45 mL, 17.5 mmol) and 50 mL of THF (collected from the still just before use). Replace the septum.

4. Cool the mixture to *ca.* −78°C using an acetone/dry ice cooling bath. Do **not** add excess dry ice to the bath as this will make raising the bath temperature later very difficult.

5. Rapidly assemble an oven-dried all-glass 20 mL syringe. Pierce the septum of the reaction flask and with the tip of the needle in the head-space, draw up about 15 mL of inert gas; pull out the syringe needle and expel the gas from the syringe. Repeat this twice more to remove traces of oxygen from the syringe.

6. Collect 11 mL of Bu^{n}Li (1.6 M) as indicated in Fig. 1.2 and add this to the reaction mixture. Allow the mixture to stir for 15 min generating the LDA *in situ*. The yield of LDA is near quantitative under these conditions.

7. Charge the dropping funnel (tap shut) with camphor **13** (2.44 g, 16.05 mmol) and 100 mL of freshly distilled THF. Ensure that the camphor has dissolved completely.

8. Add the camphor to the LDA solution dropwise over 30 min keeping the bath temperature at *ca.* −78°C. Allow the mixture to stir at this temperature for a further 10 min.

Protocol 5. *Continued*

9. Warm the bath temperature to -25 to $-20\,°C$ by adding more acetone to the cooling bath.

10. Increase the inert gas flow to the reaction. Fill the solid addition flask with 10.45 g, 24.05 mmol of $[MoO_5(py)\{OP(NMe_3)_3\}]$ (MoOPH). Replace the septum with the solid addition flask and secure it in place with a KECK clip (Aldrich Z15,043-6). Reduce the gas flow to the reaction flask.

11. Add the MoOPH over 1–2 min by rotating the solid addition flask slowly and tapping it gently. After the addition, continue to stir the reaction mixture for a further 20 min at -25 to $-20\,°C$.

12. Add 50 mL of saturated sodium sulfite (Na_2SO_3) solution to the reaction mixture. Allow the solution to come to room temperature and then continue to stir it for a further 10 min.

13. Transfer the mixture to a 500 mL separating funnel and shake it with saturated brine (50 mL). Extract the mixture with two 50 mL portions of diethyl ether, combine the organic extracts and wash them once with a mixture of 10% aqueous hydrochloric acid (25 mL) and saturated brine (25 mL). Re-extract the acidic brine with more diethyl ether (50 mL) to ensure all the product is obtained.

14. Combine the diethyl ether fractions and dry them over magnesium sulfate, filter the solution and remove the solvent by rotary evaporation.

15. Suspend 40 g of silica gel in 100 mL of 1:1 hexane:diethyl ether and place the suspension in a 7 cm diameter 5 cm high glass filtration frit, mounted on a Büchner flask. Dissolve the blue-green oil in the minimum amount of the same solvent and apply the solution to the silica pad. Elute the product with 750 mL of the same solvent system using suction.

16. Remove the solvent by rotary evaporation and recrystallise the residue by dissolution in the minimum quantity of hexane (*ca*. 10 mL) followed by cooling to $-20\,°C$ to give the pure material. The mother liquors contain appreciable amounts of product and should be evaporated and the crystallisation repeated with smaller volumes of hexane until an acceptable yield (*ca*. 1.9 g, 70%, m.p. 170–183 °C) is obtained. The product **14** is obtained as a mixture of two stereoisomers whose ratio may be determined by ^1H NMR spectroscopy.[18]

[a] Shown in Fig. 1.3. The bulb has a volume of *ca*. 50 mL, the L bend should suit the reaction flask and end in a ⊺ 19/22 joint.
[b] Distilled from sodium benzophenone ketyl under an inert atmosphere immediately prior to use.
[c] Dried over 4 Å molecular sieves for at least 24 h prior to use.
[d] Prepared as described in *Organic Synthesis*.[18] **Caution!** In the two hundred or so uses of this reagent reported in the literature no explosions are noted. Prof. Vedejs has informed us, however, of two exothermic decompositions which lead to cracked glassware. Appropriate safety screens should be used. Although the DMPU analogue of MoOPH, [MoO_5(py)(DMPU)], is undoubtedly less toxic than MoOPH and readily prepared[19] it **is** explosive under some conditions.[20]
[e] Evaporation may be promoted by careful use of a hair dryer.

6. Group 7 metal-promoted oxidations: epoxidation by salen manganese complexes

The ability of manganese(III) salen complexes to catalyse alkene epoxidation using appropriate oxygen atom sources was first systematically studied by Kochi.[21] Jacobsen and Katsuki have developed these reactions into highly efficient asymmetric processes for the epoxidation of *cis*-disubstituted alkenes such as the epoxidation of dihydronaphthalene **15** (Scheme 1.6).[22–24] The pyridine *N*-oxides added to these reactions do not act as terminal oxidants; rather they serve to ligate the active [Mn(=O)(salen)] intermediates formed in the reaction, thus improving their stability and enantioselectivity.[24] The most effective pre-catalysts are based on structures (*S,S*)-**17** and (*S,S,R,R*)-**18** (Scheme 1.6); the former is particularly attractive as it is readily prepared from commercial materials in two simple highly reproducible preparations.[25] One particularly useful oxygen atom source for these reactions is a buffered solution of bleach (NaOCl, Clorox) and this is used here in the epoxidation of dihydronaphthalene.

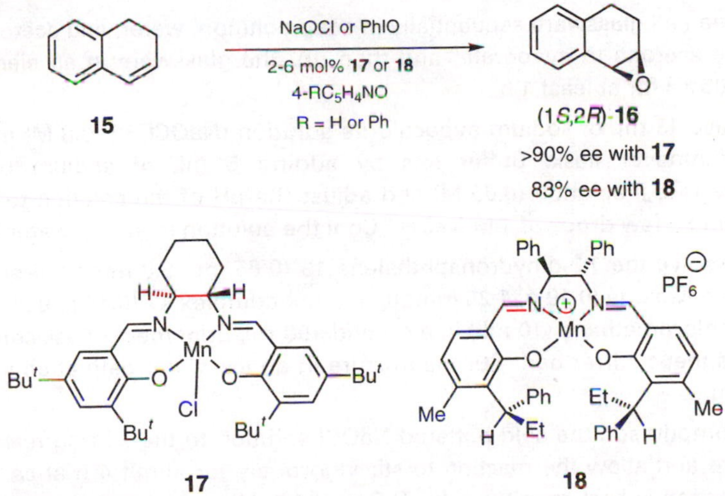

Scheme 1.6

Protocol 6.
Preparation of (1*S*,2*R*)-1,2-epoxy-1,2,3,4-tetrahydronaphthalene (Structure 16). Asymmetric epoxidation using NaOCl catalysed by Jacobsen's chiral manganese salen complex (Structure 17), (Scheme 1.6)

Caution! Employ the standard precautions outlined in the introduction to this chapter for this reaction.

Protocol 6. *Continued*

Equipment

- Erlenmeyer flasks (2 × 50 mL)
- Magnetic stirrer
- All-glass Luer syringe (1 mL)
- Needle (5 cm, 20 or 22 gauge)
- Thermometer
- Teflon-covered magnetic stirrer bar (*ca.* 2.5 × 0.5 cm)
- Measuring cylinder (20 mL)
- Chromatography column (1.5 cm OD)
- Separating funnel (100 mL)

Materials

- Commercial undiluted household bleach (NaOCl, Clorox, *ca.* 0.8 M) 13 mL, *ca.* 10 mmol — **oxidising agent, strongly basic, toxic**
- 0.05 M sodium phosphate (Na_2HPO_4) solution 10 mL — **toxic**
- Dichloromethane, *ca.* 30 mL — **volatile, toxic at high concentrations**
- 1,2-Dihydronaphthalene **15** (FW 130.2), 0.65 mL, 0.65 g, 5.0 mmol — **toxic**
- 4-Phenylpyridine *N*-oxide (FW 171.2), 0.19 g, 1.25 mmol, 25 mol% — **toxic**
- Complex **17**[*a*] (FW 546.8), 0.19 g, 0.25 mmol, 5 mol% — **toxic**
- Silica gel for chromatography 25 g — **irritant dust**
- Sand for chromatography
- 30:1 hexane:diethyl ether for flash chromatography — **flammable, toxic**

1. Clean all glassware sequentially in soap solution, water, and acetone. Allow the acetone to evaporate[*b*] and then dry the glassware in an electric oven (105 °C) for at least 1 h.

2. Place 13 mL of sodium hypochlorite solution (NaOCl, *ca.* 0.8 M) in a 50 mL Erlenmeyer flask. Buffer this by adding 5 mL of sodium phosphate (Na_2HPO_4) solution (0.05 M) and adjust the pH of the solution to about 11 using a few drops of 1 M NaOH.[*c*] Cool the solution in an ice–water bath.

3. Dissolve the 1,2-dihydronaphthalene **15** (0.65 mL, 5.0 mmol), 4-phenylpyridine *N*-oxide (0.19 g, 1.25 mmol), and the complex **17** (0.16 g, 0.25 mmol) in dichloromethane (10 mL) in a second 100 mL Erlenmeyer flask containing a magnetic stirrer bar. Stir the mixture in an ice–water bath at about 4 °C for 5 min.

4. Promptly add the cold buffered NaOCl solution to the stirring reaction mixture and allow the reaction to stir vigorously for about 4 h at *ca.* 4 °C. The reaction is best monitored by TLC analysis (4:1 hexane:diethyl ether) of the organic layer (visualisation is best achieved by $KMnO_4$ staining and heating).

5. Transfer the reaction mixture to a 100 mL separating funnel and rinse the reaction flask with two 10 mL portions of dichloromethane adding these to the funnel. Separate the phases and wash the organic layer once with 40 mL of saturated brine. Dry the organic layer (Na_2SO_4), filter, and evaporate the filtrate to yield a crude oil.

6. Slurry silica gel (25 g) in 50 mL of 30:1 hexane:diethyl ether. Pour the slurry in to a 2 cm diameter chromatography column half filled with the same eluent and containing a 1 cm high plug of sand at its base. Allow the solvent to

flow out of the column while firmly tapping with a short (10 cm) piece of thick rubber tube. Once the silica has compacted, protect the column top with more fine sand (*ca.* 1 cm). Run the eluent down until it is just level with the sand and then stop the solvent flow.

7. Dissolve most of the crude oil in a small amount of eluent and apply this to the top of the column using a Pasteur pipette. Open the column tap and allow the surface of the solvent to just come level with the sand again. Repeat this operation twice more.

8. Carefully load the top of the column with uncontaminated eluent, open the column stopcock, and start collecting fractions in test tubes. The presence of the epoxide (1*S*,2*R*)-**16** may be ascertained by TLC analysis of the fractions. The order of elution is: **15**, naphthalene (an impurity in commercial dihydronaphthalene), followed by (1*S*,2*R*)-**16**. If the epoxide does not elute pure, diethyl ether should be applied to the column.

9. Evaporation of the (1*S*,2*R*)-1,2-epoxy-1,2,3,4-tetrahydronaphthalene **16** fractions yields about 0.6 g (82%) of a low melting point solid. The optical purity is determined to be *ca.* 90% ee by ^{1}H NMR analysis in the presence of the chiral shift reagent Eu(hfc)$_3$.

[a] Aldrich (40,443-8), or Fluka (14717); alternatively reliable preparations of complex **17** are available.[25,26]
[b] Evaporation may be promoted by careful use of a hair dryer.
[c] The exact quantities of sodium phosphate (Na$_2$HPO$_4$) and sodium hydroxide used depend somewhat on the source of bleach used; adjustment of these volumes may be necessary.

---

7. Group 8 metal-promoted oxidations: alkene cleavage and asymmetric dihydroxylation

In the presence of relatively strong oxidising agents, most ruthenium and osmium salts are smoothly converted to their highest oxidation state; solutions of the tetraoxides MO$_4$ (M = Ru, Os) are therefore rather easily prepared.[27] Both complexes react with alkenes to generate new organic products and the metals in lower oxidation states. Only catalytic amounts of metal are needed in these reactions providing that a sacrificial oxidant is available to provide a continuous supply of MO$_4$. Ruthenium tetraoxide and its osmium counterpart react with alkenes rather differently. Although both are known to yield a common cyclic diester intermediate **19**,[28,29] ruthenium leads to the C–C bond cleavage product **20**, while OsO$_4$ generates the dihydroxylated product **21** on workup. If the initial C-C cleavage product **20** is an aldehyde, rapid further oxidation to the carboxylic acid takes place (Scheme 1.7).

Ligation of the metal centres can have profound effects on the chemistry of MO$_4$ oxidations. For example, while the use of acetonitrile/water/CCl$_4$ solvents dramatically improves the efficiency of RuO$_4$-catalysed C-C cleavage,

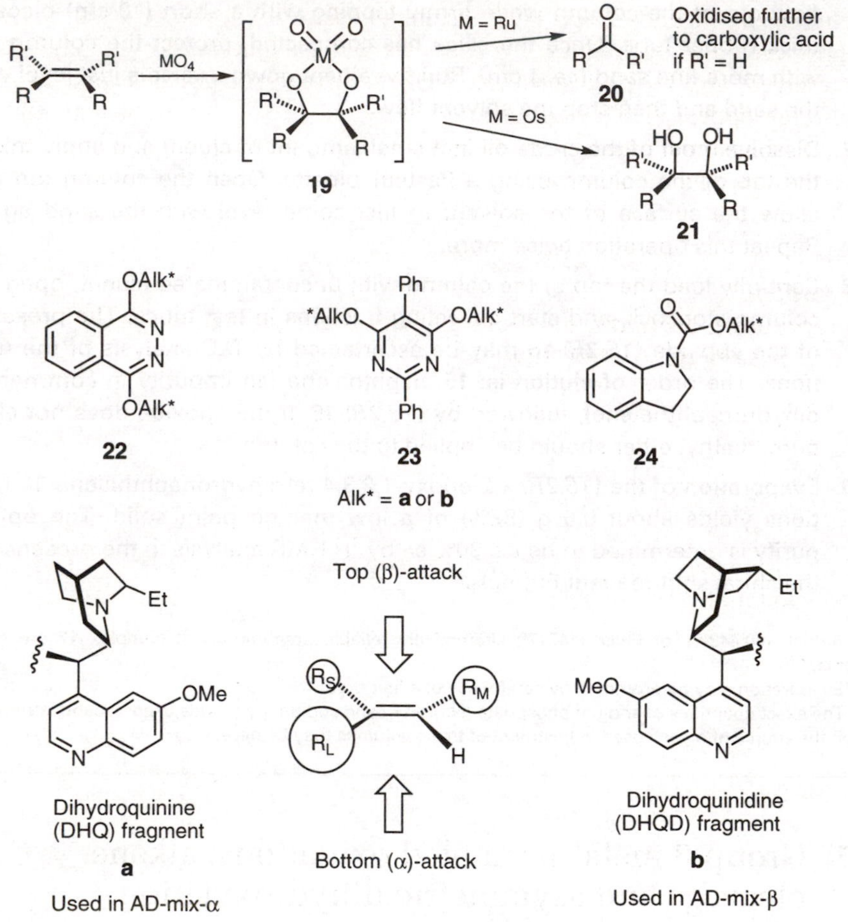
MO4
M = Ru
M = Os
19
Oxidised further
to carboxylic acid
if R' = H
20
21
22
23
24
Alk* = a or b
Top (β)-attack
Bottom (α)-attack
Dihydroquinine
(DHQ) fragment
a
Used in AD-mix-α
Dihydroquinidine
(DHQD) fragment
b
Used in AD-mix-β

Scheme 1.7

as demonstrated in Protocol 7,[30] the addition of other ligands, particularly bipyridyl or phenanthroline derivatives, changes the reaction pathway to epoxidation.[31] The origin of this change in chemoselectivity is the instability of [RuO_4L] adducts, leading to decomposition to catalysts of lower oxidation state and different behaviour.[27] In contrast, the species [OsO_4L] are stable, well-behaved, and generally result in faster dihydroxylation reactions than OsO_4 alone. In the cases where L is a phthalazine **22**,[32] pyrimidine **23**,[33] or indoline **24**[34] derivative, quite remarkable degrees of asymmetric induction are observed if pendant dihydroquinine (DHQ) **a** or dihydroquinidine (DHQD) **b** alkaloids are used. Although DHQD and DHQ are diastereoisomers, they differ only in the chirality of the 4- and 5-stereocentres and behave as enantiomeric ligands in asymmetric dihydroxylation (AD). These AD reactions are very simple to carry out as demonstrated in Protocol 8. The phthalazine ligands **22a/b** give excellent results (typically 80–99% ee) with most substrates. However, for most terminal alkenes the pyrimidine **23** is preferred, and for *cis*-disubstituted alkenes even specially designed **24** gives inferior optical yields. Suggestions on ligand choice for particular alkenes have been summarised.[35] The asymmetric dihydroxylation reaction is demonstrated here for styrene, which has the advantage of reacting quite quickly in the presence of **22** and 1 mol% OsO_4.

Protocol 7.
Preparation of pentanoic (valeric) acid. C=C bond cleavage by catalytically generated RuO_4

Caution! Employ the standard precautions outlined in the introduction to this chapter for this reaction. Ruthenium tetraoxide is volatile and toxic so an efficient hood **must** be used. Carbon tetrachloride and sodium periodate residues are environmentally unacceptable and so every attempt should be made to recover these materials. Carbon tetrachloride should be redistilled and stored for reuse while aqueous sodium periodate residues (mostly $NaIO_3$) should be bottled for appropriate disposal.

Equipment
- Erlenmeyer flask (25 mL)
- Magnetic stirrer
- Teflon-covered magnetic stirring bar (*ca.* 1 × 0.5 cm)
- Measuring cylinder (5 mL)
- Syringe (250 μL)
- Separating funnel (50 mL)
- Glass filtration frit
- Single-necked, round-bottomed flasks (2 × 100 mL)

Materials
- Carbon tetrachloride (tetrachloromethane), 2 mL — highly toxic
- Acetonitrile, 2 mL — flammable, toxic
- (*E*)-5-Decene (FW 140.3), 189 μL, 140 mg, 1 mmol — flammable, toxic
- Sodium periodate[a] (FW 213.9), 875 mg, 4.1 mmol — toxic, oxidising agent
- Ruthenium trichloride hydrate[b] (FW 207.4), 13 mg, 0.04 mmol, 5 mol% — highly staining, toxic
- Dichloromethane for extraction — volatile, toxic at high concentrations
- Diethyl ether for extraction — flammable
- Celite

1. Clean all glassware sequentially in soap solution, water, and acetone. Allow the acetone to evaporate[c] and then dry everything in an electric oven (105 °C) for at least 1 h.

2. Introduce into the Erlenmeyer flask carbon tetrachloride (2 mL), acetonitrile (2 mL), (*E*)-5-decene (189 μL, 140 mg, 1 mmol), a solution of sodium metaperiodate (875 mg, 4.1 mmol) in distilled water (8 mL), and the magnetic stirrer bar.

3. Add 13 mg of ruthenium trichloride hydrate to the reaction mixture, stopper the flask, and stir the two-phase reaction vigorously for 2 h at room temperature.

Protocol 7. *Continued*

4. Transfer the reaction mixture to a 50 mL separating funnel, rinse the Erlenmeyer flask with 5 mL of dichloromethane and add the washings to the separating funnel as well. Repeat this operation with a further 5 mL of dichloromethane.

5. Separate the lower organic phase and then re-extract the aqueous layer three times with 10 mL of dichloromethane. Combine all the organic extracts and dry them with Na_2SO_4. Filter the dried solution into a 100 mL round-bottomed flask, washing the Na_2SO_4 twice with small portions of dichloromethane.

6. Remove nearly all of the solvent by rotary evaporation and treat the oily residue with 20 mL of diethyl ether. Filter the resulting suspension through about 1 cm of Celite packed on a small glass filtration frit into a fresh weighed round-bottomed flask. Wash the Celite through with two *ca.* 7 mL portions of diethyl ether.

7. Evaporation of the diethyl ether yields about 180 mg (88%) of pentanoic acid (valeric acid), which may be further purified by microdistillation at reduced pressure (23 mmHg, 96°C) to yield a colourless oil with expected spectroscopic properties.

[a]The protocol may also be carried out using H_5IO_6 instead of $NaIO_4$; in many cases its use results in faster and cleaner reactions.
[b]Ruthenium trichloride hydrate is an ill-defined mixture of ruthenium(III) and (IV) compounds which may be approximated to the formula $[RuCl_3 \cdot H_2O]$. The compound should be a free flowing dark solid which becomes 'sticky' with increased water contamination.
[c]Evaporation may be promoted by careful use of a hair dryer.

Protocol 8.
Preparation of (1*R*)-1,2-dihydroxy-1-phenylethane. Catalytic asymmetric dihydroxylation (AD)

Caution! Employ the standard precautions outlined in the introduction to this chapter for this reaction. Osmium tetraoxide, formed *in situ* in this reaction, is volatile and highly toxic and so an efficient hood **must** be used.

Equipment
- Single-necked, round-bottomed flask (25 mL and 100 mL)
- Magnetic stirrer
- Teflon-covered magnetic stirrer bar, *ca.* 1 × 0.5 cm
- Separating funnel (50 mL)
- Glass filtration frit
- Büchner flask
- Cooling bath
- Syringe (250 μL)

Materials
- Modified[a] AD-mix-β 1.4 g, enough for 1 mmol of alkene — **highly toxic**
- Styrene (FW 104.2), 114 μL, 104 mg, 1 mmol — **malodorous, toxic**

22

- *t*-Butyl alcohol 5 mL
- Sodium metabisulfite, 1.5 g, 7.9 mmol
- Dichloromethane for extraction
- Silica gel for chromatography 10 g
- 7:3 ethyl acetate:hexane for chromatography, 100 mL

toxic
moisture sensitive
volatile, toxic at high concentration
irritant dust
flammable, toxic

1. Clean all glassware sequentially in soap solution, water, and acetone. Allow the acetone to evaporate[b] and then dry the glassware in an electric oven (105°C) for at least 1 h. **Caution!** Do not oven-dry microlitre syringes as they are easily damaged by overheating.

2. Load the 25 mL round-bottomed flask with modified[a] AD-mix-β (1.4 g) and the magnetic stirrer bar. Add 5 mL of *t*-butyl alcohol and 5 mL of distilled water.

3. Stir the mixture at room temperature until two clear phases are formed; the lower aqueous layer should be bright yellow.

4. Cool the reaction to 0°C using an ice–water bath and ensure that the solution is still stirring. Add styrene (114 μL, 104 mg, 1 mmol) using a microlitre syringe and allow the heterogeneous slurry to stir vigorously at 0°C for 3.5 h.

5. Slowly add 1.5 g of sodium metabisulfite ($Na_2S_2O_5$) to the reaction mixture, remove the flask from the ice bath, and allow the suspension to stir at room temperature for 30 min.

6. Transfer the reaction mixture to a 50 mL separating funnel, rinse the round-bottomed flask with 5 mL of dichloromethane and add this to the separating funnel as well. Repeat the rinsing operation with a further 5 mL of dichloromethane.

7. Separate the lower organic phase and then re-extract the aqueous layer three times with 10 mL of dichloromethane. Combine all the organic extracts and dry them with Na_2SO_4. Filter the drying mixture into a 100 mL round-bottomed flask, washing the Na_2SO_4 twice with small portions of dichloromethane. Evaporate the dichloromethane solution under reduced pressure to a yellow oil. Dissolve the oil in 7:3 ethyl acetate:hexane (5 mL).

8. Slurry silica gel (10 g) in 7:3 ethyl acetate:hexane (50 mL) and pour the slurry onto a suitable glass sintered filtration frit with a diameter of about 2 cm on top of a Büchner flask. When the solvent falls to the level of the silica gel, pipette on the crude yellow diol (already dissolved in ethyl acetate–hexane). Wash any residual diol in the flask onto the silica plug using fresh 7:3 ethyl acetate:hexane eluent until the added solution is clear. Elute the diol by passing 75 mL of 7:3 ethyl acetate:hexane through the plug of silica gel using suction.

9. Evaporation of the solvent mixture leads to about 110 mg (80%) of (1*R*)-1,2-dihydroxy-1-phenylethane with the expected spectroscopic properties.[33]

Protocol 8. Continued

The optical purity is determined to be at least 90% ee by preparation of the bis-α-methoxy-α-(trifluoromethyl)phenylacetic acid ester (Mosher's bis-ester).[33]

[a]Asymmetric dihydroxylation reactions using the commercial materials (AD-mix-α, Aldrich 39,275-8; AD-mix-β, Aldrich 39,276-6) result in typical reaction times of 16–24 h for most alkenes at 0 °C. For 1,2-disubstituted, trisubstituted, and tetrasubstituted alkenes further promotion by addition of methanesulfonamide is also required. The dihydroxylation rate is considerably improved by increasing the osmium concentration in the commercial product from 0.2 mol% to 1 mol% by adding 3.68 mg of finely ground $K_2[Os(=O)_2(OH)_4]$ per 1.4 g of AD-mix-α (or AD-mix-β) and mixing well.
[b]Evaporation may be promoted by careful use of a hair dryer.

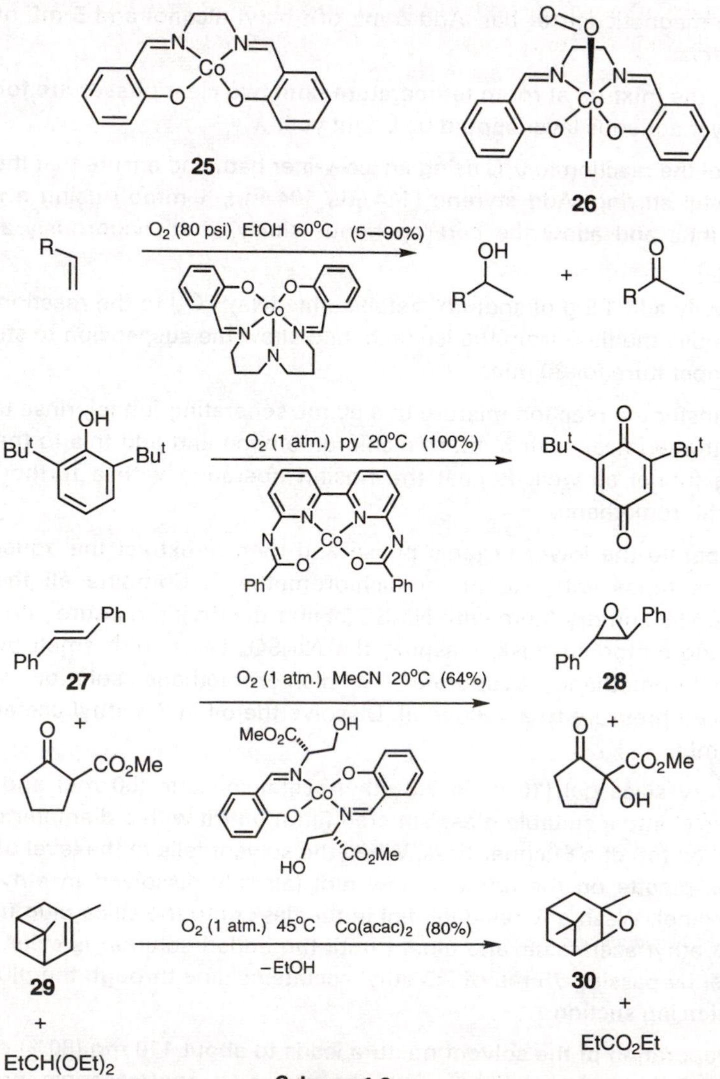

Scheme 1.8

24

8. Group 9 metal-promoted oxidations: aerobic epoxidation of alkenes

Molecular oxygen is rather unreactive towards organic molecules under mild conditions as it has a triplet (paramagnetic) ground state which has the wrong symmetry for reaction with singlet ground state organics. These problems may be overcome by coordination of the molecular oxygen to transition metal centres. For example, in the presence of added amine ligands, the Co(salen) complex **25** reacts with O_2 to yield the adduct **26** (Scheme 1.8).[36,37] This behaviour has important consequences in that the bonding of the bound oxygen is modified, allowing reaction with singlet (diamagnetic) organic molecules. Many cobalt complexes other than **25** bind molecular oxygen and generally cobalt complexes are preferred for transition metal-catalysed reactions using this oxidant.

Cobalt species can be employed in oxidations of saturated hydrocarbons,[38] alkenes,[39-42] and phenols;[43,44] typical examples are shown in Scheme 1.8. These examples employ one of two reaction pathways; either H• abstraction from RH followed by trapping of the R• radical with a second molecule of L_nCo-O_2, or direct reaction of alkenes with L_nCoOOH. These radical reactions both result in the formation of hydroperoxide radicals (ROO•) which are stabilised by coordination to the cobalt centre. Under certain conditions these species may be isolated.[38,44] Developments in this area have involved the use of organic species that form stabilised hydroperoxides rather easily; these can be used *in situ* for the epoxidation of alkenes, as in the transformation of **27** to **28**[39] and α-pinene **29** to its epoxide **30** (Scheme 1.8).[40] The latter reaction is described in detail.

Protocol 9.

Preparation of α-pinene oxide (Structure 30). Mukaiyama's catalytic aerobic epoxidation using propionaldehyde diethyl acetal and Co(mac)$_2$[a] (Scheme 1.8)

Caution! Employ the standard precautions outlined in the introduction to this chapter for this reaction.

Equipment

- Schlenk tube (40 mL capacity, internal diameter *ca.* 4 cm)
- ℥ 24/40 stopcock
- Magnetic stirrer
- Teflon-covered magnetic stirrer bars (2 × *ca.* 2 × 0.5 cm)
- All-glass Luer syringe (1 mL)
- Needle (5 cm, 20 or 22 gauge)
- Thermometer
- Single-necked, round-bottomed flask (100 mL)
- Oil bath
- Oxygen supply

Materials

- (1*R*)-(+)-α-Pinene (FW 136.2), 0.5 mL, 0.43 g, 3.15 mmol — flammable
- Propionaldehyde diethyl acetal (FW 132.2), 20 mL, 16.3 g, 0.12 mol — flammable, toxic

25

Protocol 9. *Continued*

- Co(mac)$_2$[a] (FW 287.2), 65 mg, 0.22 mmol, 7.2 mol%   **toxic**
- Activated powdered 4 Å molecular sieves 1.0 g   **hydroscopic**
- Silica gel, 20 g   **irritant dust**
- Diethyl ether for chromatography   **flammable**
- Hexane for chromatography   **flammable**

1. Clean all glassware sequentially in soap solution, water, and acetone. Allow the acetone to evaporate[b] and then dry the glassware in an electric oven (105°C) for at least 1 h. **Caution!** Do not oven dry the thermometer.

2. Allow the oil bath to equilibrate at 50°C for at least 0.5 h on the stirrer hot plate. Place the molecular sieves (1.0 g) in the Schlenk tube and stopper the flask with a greased stopper. Heat the molecular sieves vigorously with an electric heat gun while placing the Schlenk tube under high vacuum (<0.2 mmHg). Allow the apparatus to cool under vacuum. Set up the equipment as shown in Fig 1.4, but with the oxygen supply turned off. In the Schlenk tube place the magnetic stirrer bar, propionaldehyde diethyl acetal (20 mL), and (using a 1 mL syringe), α-pinene (0.5 mL, 3.15 mmol).

3. Promptly weigh out the Co(mac)$_2$ (65 mg, 0.22 mmol) into a small glass vial. Remove the stopcock from the Schlenk tube neck and add the catalyst to the reaction. Remove the stopcock and start the oxygen flow.

4. Stir the green reaction mixture at 50°C for 10–17 h.

5. Transfer the reaction mixture to a 100 mL round-bottomed flask and then rinse the Schlenk tube with small amounts of diethyl ether to ensure complete transfer of the reaction mixture.

6. Remove most of the propionaldehyde diethyl acetal by rotary evaporation (keep the water bath at room temperature to avoid product loss).

7. Prepare a 10 cm high by 2 cm diameter chromatography column with 20 g of silica suspended in hexane (100 mL). Dissolve the crude reaction product in the minimal amount of hexane and apply it to the column. Residual α-pinene is eluted first followed by the epoxide on slowly changing over the eluent to a 4:1 mixture of hexane:diethyl ether (about 0.24 g, 50% is isolated).

[a]The complex Co(mac)$_2$ (macH = 3-methyl-2,4-pentanedione) is the best catalyst for this reaction but is not available commercially. It is prepared by treating a mixture of macH (2.40 g) and CoCl$_2$·6H$_2$O (2.50 g) in methanol (15 mL) and water (40 mL) with aqueous ammonia (*ca.* 2 M, 15 mL) under an inert atmosphere. The resulting orange solid must be filtered under an inert atmosphere and dried under high vacuum at 90°C.
[b]Evaporation may be promoted by careful use of a hair dryer.

---

9. Group 10 metal-promoted oxidations: catalytic oxidative carbonylation

Perhaps the best-known example of oxidation by the Group 10 metals is the Wacker oxidation of ethene **31** (R = H) to ethanal **32** (R = H) (Scheme 1.9).

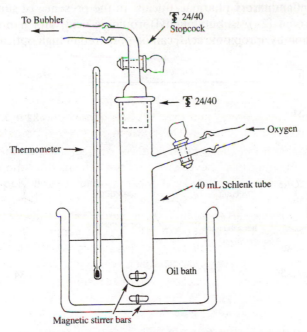

Fig. 1.4 Assembled reaction apparatus for Protocol 9.

In this process palladium(II) is reduced to palladium(0) and a copper(II) promoter is added to allow oxidative recycling of the palladium to the active +2 state *via* aerial oxidation. While the reaction is highly successful for ethene, there are often selectivity problems when higher alkenes are used in the reaction (**31**, R ≠ H); isomeric ketones and partially halogenated products are normally formed. Given these problems, few organic workers have applied such approaches in their synthetic strategies. However, if appropriate conditions are employed these difficulties can be partially or fully overcome.[45,46] Also of note here are palladium-catalysed 1,3-diene oxidations developed by Bäckvall.[47,48] These reactions, in which benzoquinone is used as a reoxidant rather than oxygen, result in 1,4-diacetate structures. It is possible to control the relative stereochemistry to a high degree by modifying the reaction conditions: for example in the absence of chloride ions the diene **33** is converted to *trans*-**34** (>90%), but if $Li_2[PdCl_4]$ is used as the oxidant then *cis*-**34** is isolated (Scheme 1.9). The chloride plays a blocking role at the metal centre only allow *exo* delivery of the acetate groups. Another approach to oxidation with palladium is to carry out reactions under a mixed oxygen/carbon monoxide atmospheres, following chemistry developed by Alper.[49] Under these conditions α-substituted alkenes are selectively functionalised to secondary carboxylic acids. The oxidative carbonylation of 1-decene **35** is demonstrated here (Scheme 1.9). This reaction is of considerable interest for the preparation of anti-inflammatory pharmaceuticals. In the presence of suitable chiral ligands ibuprofen [2-(*p*-isobutylphenyl)propionic acid] and naproxen [2-(6-methoxy-2-naphthyl)propionic acid] can be prepared in high optical purities.[50]

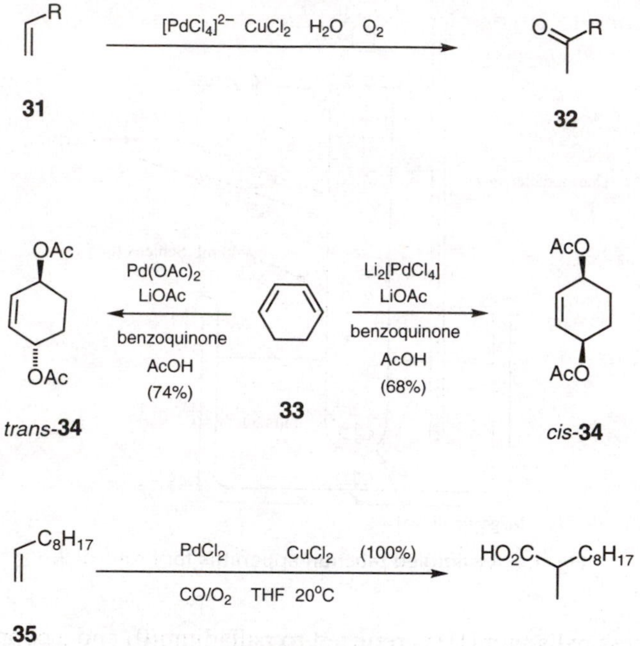

Scheme 1.9

Protocol 10.
Preparation of 2-methyldecanoic acid. Alper's oxidative carbonylation of terminal alkenes (Scheme 1.9)

Caution! Employ the standard precautions outlined in the introduction of this chapter for this reaction. Carbon monoxide is odourless and **highly toxic** even at low concentration; it **must** only be used in an efficient fume hood.

Equipment
- Three-necked, round-bottomed flask (100 mL)
- Separating funnel (200 mL)
- Single-necked, round-bottomed flask
- Magnetic stirrer
- Teflon-covered magnetic stirrer bar (*ca.* 1 × 0.5 cm)
- ‡ 19/22 cone adapter
- Septa
- Needle-tubing connectors (Aldrich, Z10,116-8)
- All-glass Luer syringe (2 mL)
- Needles (5 cm and 10 cm, 20 or 22 gauge)
- Oxygen supply
- Carbon monoxide supply

Materials
- Tetrahydrofuran, 30 mL[a]   **flammable, peroxide risk**
- 1-Decene (FW 140.3), 1.45 mL, 1.07 g, 7.65 mmol   **toxic**

28

- Palladium(II) chloride (FW 177.3), 0.14 g, 0.78 mmol, 10 mol% **toxic**
- Copper(II) chloride (FW 134.5), 0.20 g, 1.50 mmol **toxic**
- Hydrochloric acid (37% w/v), 1 mL **corrosive, toxic**

1. Clean all glassware sequentially in soap solution, water, and acetone. Allow the acetone to evaporate[b] and then dry the apparatus in an electric oven (105°C) for at least 1 h.

2. Set up the apparatus as shown in Fig. 1.5. Put 30 mL of tetrahydrofuran, 1 mL of water, a magnetic stirrer bar, palladium(II) chloride (0.14 g, 0.78 mmol), copper(II) chloride (0.20 g, 1.50 mmol), and 1 mL of concentrated hydrochloric acid into the flask by temporarily removing the ᵀ 19/22 cone adapter.

3. Stir the mixture and adjust the carbon monoxide gas regulator so that the exit bubbler shows a flow of about two bubbles per second. Start the oxygen flow and adjust its rate until it is about half that of the carbon monoxide. The combined gas flow as measured by the exit bubbler should be about 2–3 bubbles per second. The flow rate of the carbon monoxide must be significantly greater than that of the oxygen or the regioselectivity of the reaction suffers.

4. Using a syringe measure out 1.45 mL of 1-decene (7.65 mmol) and inject this into the reaction mixture. Let the reaction stir for at least 4 h; the progress of the reaction may be monitored by the disappearance of the 1-decene as judged by TLC or GC.

5. Turn off both the oxygen and carbon monoxide gas flows and disassemble the apparatus ensuring any excess carbon monoxide has been vented into the hood. Transfer the reaction mixture to a 200 mL separating funnel. Rinse out the reaction flask with 50 mL of water and transfer these washings to the separatory funnel.

6. Extract the aqueous mixture with hexane (40 mL) and separate the layers (retaining both). Repeat the hexane extraction twice more. Combine the organic fractions and dry these with sodium sulfate. Filter the drying mixture into an appropriate round-bottomed flask and remove the hexane by rotary evaporation to give the crude product in essentially quantitative yield.

7. To purify the 2-methyldecanoic acid treat the crude product with 1 M NaOH (75 mL) and diethyl ether (75 mL) and transfer the mixture to a 200 mL separating funnel. Extract the acid into the aqueous layer as its sodium salt, discarding the diethyl ether layer. Reacidify the aqueous fraction to about pH 0–2 using concentrated HCl and extract the purified acid into 75 mL of fresh diethyl ether. After drying with sodium sulfate, removal of the diethyl ether, and drying under high vacuum, the 2-methyldecanoic acid, a clear oil (b.p. 137–139°C, 14 mmHg), shows the expected spectroscopic properties.

[a] Distilled from sodium benzophenone ketyl under an inert atmosphere.
[b] Evaporation may be promoted by careful use of a hair dryer.

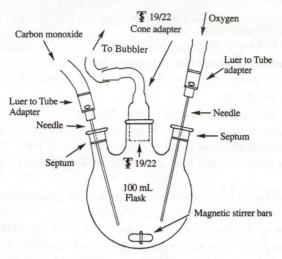

Fig. 1.5 Assembled reaction apparatus for Protocol 10

10. Group 11 metal-promoted oxidations: oxidative biaryl coupling

The ready accessibility of $Cu(II) \rightarrow Cu(I) \rightarrow Cu(0)$ redox pathways together with the high insolubility of many copper(I) compounds causes simple copper(II) salts to be potent oxidants under appropriate conditions. One practical outcome is that copper(II) salts show facile C-H activation behaviour towards aromatic alcohols. Of particular interest is the ready formation of $(\pm)$-1,1'-bi-2-naphthol **36** from 2-naphthol (Scheme 1.10),[51] as enantiomerically enriched **36** is a popular ligand for many asymmetric transformations. The mechanism of this reaction is believed to involve oxidation of intermediate $[L_nCu_2(OC_{10}H_7)_2]$ complexes by internal and/or external redox processes. A number of attempts have been made to carry out this reaction in an asymmetric fashion, with varying degrees of success.[52–54] Nevertheless, the racemic version has its merits as a number of effective low cost resolutions of **36** have appeared.[55,56]

Protocol 11.
Preparation of (±)-1,1'-bi-2-naphthol (Structure 36). Oxidative dehydrogenation by copper(II) (Scheme 1.10)

Caution! Employ the standard precautions outlined in the introduction to this chapter for this reaction.

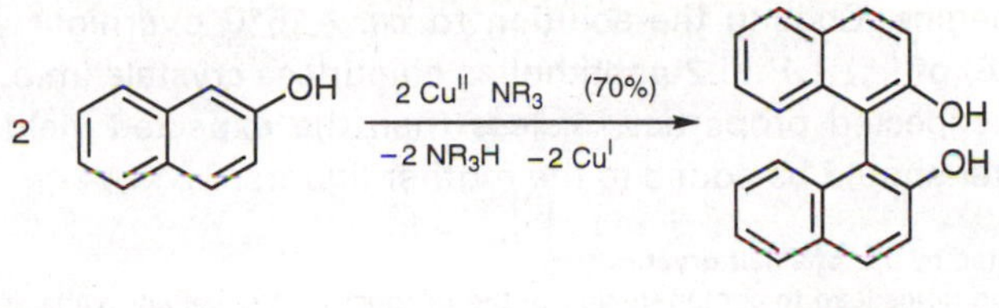

36

Scheme 1.10

Equipment

- Single-necked, round-bottomed flask with a ⊺ 24/40 joint (500 mL)
- Magnetic stirrer
- Teflon-covered magnetic stirrer bar approximately 4 cm × 0.8 cm
- All-glass Luer syringe
- Ground-glass ⊺ 24/40 stopper
- Measuring cylinders (25 mL and 250 mL)
- Erlenmeyer flask (500 mL)
- Reflux condenser
- Glass funnel

Materials

- Technical methanol, 220 mL   toxic
- Copper(II) nitrate (FW 187.6), 9.4 g, 0.05 mol   toxic
- Benzylamine (FW 107.2), 13 mL, 12.75 g, 0.12 mol   toxic
- 2-Naphthol (FW 144.2), 5.66 g, 0.04 mol   toxic

1. Clean all glassware, syringes, and needles sequentially in soap solution, water, and acetone. Allow the acetone to evaporate[a] and then dry everything in an electric oven (105°C) for at least 1 h.

2. Put the copper(II) nitrate (9.4 g, 0.05 mol), and the magnetic stirrer bar into the round-bottomed flask and add methanol (120 mL). Stir the mixture until all of the solid has dissolved to give a bright blue solution.

3. Add 13 mL of benzylamine by syringe over a period of about 10 min.

4. Dissolve 2-naphthol (5.66 g, 0.04 mol) in methanol (100 mL). Add this solution to the reaction mixture to give a dark green solution. Stopper the flask sealing it with one or two wraps of Nesco film or Parafilm. Allow the reaction to stir at room temperature for 1 week.[b]

5. After 1 week a dark brown suspension should have formed. Acidify the mixture with 40 mL of concentrated hydrochloric acid (37% w/v) dissolved in 500 mL of distilled water. Filter the crude off-white product, wash it with copious quantities of water, and allow it to dry with suction.

Protocol 11. *Continued*

6. The crude product is dissolved in boiling methanol (about 100 mL is required) in a 500 mL Erlenmeyer flask equipped with a reflux condenser and magnetic stirring bar. Add three spatulas full of decolourising charcoal to the mixture and heat it under reflux (30 min). Filter the hot solution through fluted filter paper and allow it to cool to room temperature. Water (about 17 mL) is added slowly with occasional gentle swirling until crystallisation begins. Cooling the solution to *ca.* −15°C overnight yields about 3.9 g (70%) of (±)-1,1'-bi-2-naphthol as colourless crystals (m.p. 214–217°C) with the expected properties.[c] If less than the expected yield is realised, more water should be added to the mother liquors.

[a] May be promoted by use of a hair dryer.
[b] Shorter reaction times lead to contamination of the product with small and variable amounts of 2-naphthol.
[c] At scales much above the one presented in this protocol use of a mechanical stirrer is preferred over magnetic stirring. Under these conditions this protocol may be scaled up by at least a factor of ten (0.4–0.5 mol).

References

1. Hudlický, M. *Oxidations in Organic Chemistry*; American Chemical Society: Washington DC, **1990**, Vol. 186.
2. Sheldon, R. A.; Kochi, J. A. *Metal-Catalysed Oxidation of Organic Compounds*; Academic: New York, **1981**.
3. Hill, J. G.; Sharpless, K. B.; Exon, C. M.; Regenye, R. *Org. Synth.* **1985**, *63*, 66–78.
4. Johnson, R. A.; Sharpless, K. B. in *Comprehensive Organic Synthesis*; Trost, B. M.; Fleming, I. eds, Pergamon: Oxford, **1991**, Vol. 7, Chap. 3.2, pp. 389–436.
5. Woodward, S. S.; Finn, M. G.; Sharpless, K. B. *J. Am. Chem. Soc.* **1991**, *113*, 106–113.
6. Finn, M. G.; Sharpless, K. B. *J. Am. Chem. Soc.*, **1991**, *113*, 113–126.
7. Sharpless, K. B.; Verhoeven, T. R. *Aldrichimica Acta* **1979**, *12*, 63–74.
8. Gao, Y.; Hanson, R. M.; Klunder, J. M.; Ko, S. Y.; Masamune, H.; Sharpless, K. B. *J. Am. Chem. Soc.*, **1987**, *109*, 5765–5780.
9. Sharpless, K. B. Comment in *Aldrichimica Acta* **1992**, *25*, 2.
10. Di Furia, F.; Modena, G.; Seraglia, R. *Synthesis* **1984**, 325–326.
11. Pitchen, P.; Duñach, E.; Deshmukh, M. N.; Kagan, H. B. *J. Am. Chem. Soc.* **1984**, *106*, 8188–8193.
12. Zhao, S. H.; Samuel, O.; Kagan, H. B. *Org. Synth.* **1990**, *68*, 49–55.
13. Komatsu, N.; Hashizume, M.; Sugita, T.; Uemura, S. *J. Org. Chem.* **1993**, *58*, 4529–4533.
14. Komatsu, N.; Hashizume, M.; Sugita, T.; Uemura, S. *J. Org. Chem.* **1993**, *58*, 7624–7626.
15. Sharpless, K. B.; Michaelson, R. C. *J. Am. Chem. Soc.* **1973**, *95*, 6136–6137; Hoh, T.; Kaneda, K.; Teranishi, S. *J. Chem. Soc., Chem. Commun.* **1976**, 421–422; Rossiter, B. E.; Verhoeven, T. R.; Sharpless, K. B. *Tetrahedron Lett.* **1979**, 4733–4736.

16. Hoveyda, A. H.; Evans, D. A.; Fu, G. C. *Chem. Rev.* **1993**, *93*, 1307–1370.
17. Vedejs, E.; Engler, D. A.; Telschow, J. E. *J. Org. Chem.* **1978**, *43*, 188–196.
18. Vedejs, E.; Larsen, S. *Org. Synth.* **1986**, *64*, 127–137.
19. Anderson, J. C.; Smith, S. C. *Synlett* **1990**, 107–108.
20. Paquette, L. A.; Koh, D. *Chem. Eng. News* **1992**, *70* (37), 2.
21. Srinivasan, K.; Michaud, P.; Kochi, J. K. *J. Am. Chem. Soc.* **1986**, *108*, 2309–2320.
22. Jacobsen, E. N.; Zhang, W.; Muci, A. R.; Ecker, J. R.; Deng, L. *J. Am. Chem. Soc.* **1991**, *113*, 7063–7064.
23. Hosoya, N.; Hataayama, A.; Yanai, K.; Fujii, H.; Irie, R.; Katsuki, T. *Synlett* **1993**, 641–645.
24. Irie, R.; Ito, Y.; Katsuki, T. *Synlett* **1991**, 265–266.
25. Deng, L.; Jacobsen, E. N. *J. Org. Chem.* **1992**, *57*, 4320–4323.
26. Larrow, J. F.; Jacobsen, E. N.; Gao, Y.; Hong, Y.; Nie, X.; Zepp, C. M. *J. Org. Chem.* **1994**, *59*, 1939–1942.
27. Griffith, W. P. *Chem. Soc. Rev.* **1992**, *21*, 179–185.
28. Lee, D. G.; Chang, V. S.; Helliwell, S. *J. Org. Chem.* **1976**, *41*, 3644–3646.
29. Göbel, T.; Sharpless, K. B. *Angew. Chem., Int. Ed. Engl.* **1993**, *32*, 1329–1330.
30. Carlsen, P. H. J.; Katsuki, T.; Martin, V. S.; Sharpless, K. B. *J. Org. Chem.* **1981**, *46*, 3936–3938.
31. Bevaloine, G.; Eskernazi, C.; Meunier, F.; Rivière, H. *Tetrahedron Lett.* **1984**, *25*, 3187–3190; Eskénazi, C.; Bevaloine, G.; Meunier, F.; Rivière, H. *J. Chem. Soc., Chem. Commun.* **1985**, 1111–1113.
32. Sharpless, K. B.; Amberg, W.; Bennani, Y. L.; Crispino, G. A.; Hartung, J.; Jeong, K.-S.; Kwong, H.-L.; Morikawa, K.; Wang, Z.-M.; Xu, D.; Zhang, X.-L. *J. Org. Chem.* **1992**, *57*, 2768–2771.
33. Crispino, G. A.; Jeong, K.-S.; Kolb, H. C.; Wang, Z.-M.; Xu, D.; Sharpless, K. B. *J. Org. Chem.* **1993**, *58*, 3785–3786.
34. Wang, L.; Sharpless, K. B. *J. Am. Chem. Soc.* **1992**, *114*, 7568–7570.
35. Morikawa, K.; Park, J.; Andersson, P. G.; Hashiyama, T.; Sharpless, K. B. *J. Am. Chem. Soc.* **1993**, *115*, 8463–8464.
36. Bailey, C. L.; Drago, R. S. *Coord. Chem. Rev.* **1987**, *79*, 321–332.
37. Nishinaga, A.; Tomita, H. *J. Mol. Catal.* **1980**, *7*, 179–199.
38. Saussine, L.; Brazi, E.; Robine, A.; Minoun, H.; Fischer, J.; Weiss, R. *J. Am. Chem. Soc.* **1985**, *107*, 3534–3540.
39. Punniyamurthy, T.; Bhatia, B.; Iqbal, J. *Tetrahedron Lett.* **1993**, *34*, 4657–4658.
40. Mukaiyama, T.; Yorozu, K.; Takai, T.; Yamada, T. *Chem. Lett.* **1993**, 439–442.
41. Hamilton, D. E.; Drago, R. S.; Zombeck, A. *J. Am. Chem. Soc.* **1987**, *109*, 374–379.
42. Kato, K.; Yamada, T.; Takai, T.; Inoki, S.; Isayama, S. *Bull. Chem. Soc. Jpn.* **1990**, *63*, 179–186.
43. Araki, K.; Kuboki, T.; Otohata, M.; Kishimoto, N.; Yamada, M.; Shiraishi, S. *J. Chem. Soc., Dalton Trans.* **1993**, 3647–3651.
44. Nishinaga, A.; Tomita, H.; Nishizawa, K.; Matsuura, T.; Ooi, S.; Hirotsu, K. *J. Chem. Soc., Dalton Trans.* **1981**, 1504–1514.
45. Tsuji, J. *Synthesis* **1984**, 369–384.
46. Alper, H.; Januszkiewicz, K.; Smith, D. J. H. *Tetrahedron Lett.* **1985**, *26*, 2263–2264.
47. Bäckvall, J.-E. *Acc. Chem. Res.* **1983**, *16*, 335–342.

48. Bäckvall, J.-E.; Granberg, K. L.; Andersson, P. G.; Gatti, R.; Gogoll, A. *J. Org. Chem.* **1993**, *58*, 5445–5451.
49. Alper, H.; Woell, J. B.; Despeyroux, B.; Smith, D. J. H. *J. Chem. Soc., Chem. Commun.* **1983**, 1270–1271.
50. Alper, H.; Hamel, N. *J. Am. Chem. Soc.* **1990**, *112*, 2803–2804.
51. Smrčina, M.; Lorenc, M.; Hanuš, V.; Kočovský, P. *Synlett* **1991**, 231–232.
52. Smrčina, M.; Lorenc, M.; Hanuš, V.; Sedmera, P.; Kočovský, P. *J. Org. Chem.* **1992**, *57*, 1917–1920.
53. Smrčina, M.; Poláková, J.; Vyskočil, S.; Kočovský, P. *J. Org. Chem.* **1993**, *58*, 4534–4538.
54. Brussee, J.; Groenendijk, J. L. G.; te Koppele, J. M.; Jansen, A. C. A. *Tetrahedron* **1985**, *41*, 3313–3319.
55. Brunel, J.-M.; Bruno, G. *J. Org. Chem.* **1993**, *58*, 7313–7314.
56. Kawashima, M.; Hirata, R. *Bull. Chem. Soc. Jpn.* **1993**, *66*, 2002–2005.

2

Palladium-catalysed carbon–carbon bond formation

ANDREW F. BROWNING and NICHOLAS GREEVES

1. Introduction

The use of palladium complexes as catalysts for a range of reactions has been one of the most remarkable developments in synthetic organic chemistry over the last 25 years.[1] The variety of reactions that can be catalysed, together with the range of functional groups tolerated and usually excellent chemo- and regioselectivity, has meant that an increasing amount of research has gone into this area of chemistry and that there are several important industrial applications.[2] Indeed, such is the widespread use of these compounds, there is seldom a total synthesis project that does not involve palladium chemistry in one or more key steps. For example, compounds containing an ene-diyne function, a class of molecules which has been under considerable scrutiny in recent years, have been targeted for total synthesis by a number of research groups. Frequently, the ene-diyne unit of these molecules is constructed using a Sonogashira coupling in excellent yield.

Palladium chemistry is dominated by two oxidation states. The lowest, palladium(0), present in tetrakis(triphenylphosphine)palladium, for example, is nominally electron rich, and will undergo oxidative addition with suitable substrates such as halides and triflates, resulting in a palladium(II) complex. Oxidative addition is thought to occur on the coordinatively unsaturated 14-electron species **1** present as a result of the ligands dissociating in solution.

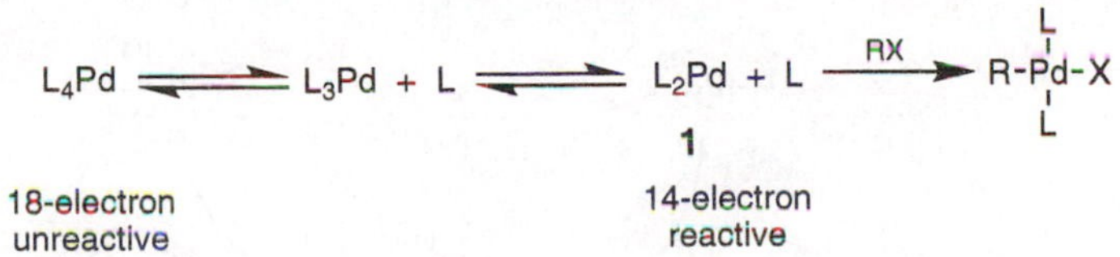

$$L_4Pd \rightleftharpoons L_3Pd + L \rightleftharpoons L_2Pd + L \xrightarrow{RX} R\text{-}\underset{L}{\overset{L}{Pd}}\text{-}X$$

1

18-electron	14-electron
unreactive	reactive

The resulting σ-alkyl bond in such complexes is very reactive, especially towards carbon–carbon π-bonds. Thus the presence of an alkene in the reacting system will lead to coordination followed by insertion into the palladium–

carbon σ-bond to give **2**. Theoretically, it is possible for the process of alkene coordination and insertion to continue. However, more frequently, palladium is expelled from the system by a β-hydride elimination reaction.

The rate of this intramolecular β-hydride elimination is such that no polymeric species are ever observed. Indeed, this possible pathway means that the original substrate for the oxidative addition reaction must be chosen with care – the presence of a hydrogen at a sp³ carbon in the β position must be avoided. Thus, substrates for oxidative addition reactions in palladium chemistry are frequently vinylic, allylic, or aromatic.

For the process described to be catalytic, a palladium(0) complex must be regenerated from the palladium(II) product of β-hydride elimination. This may be achieved by the presence of base in the system, which removes HX from the palladium species.

All the individual steps outlined above combine to make up the catalytic pathway in the Heck reaction (Fig 2.1).

Other than β-hydride elimination, another important pathway for palladium(II) intermediates is reductive elimination. This is the reverse of oxidative addition, and forms the basis of the mechanism for the Stille, Suzuki and other coupling reactions (Fig 2.2).[3] Once again, substrates must be chosen with care, as β-hydride elimination leads to undesired products and termination of the catalytic cycle.

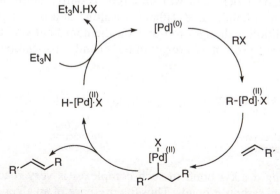

Fig. 2.1 Catalytic cycle for the Heck reaction (ligands omitted for clarity).

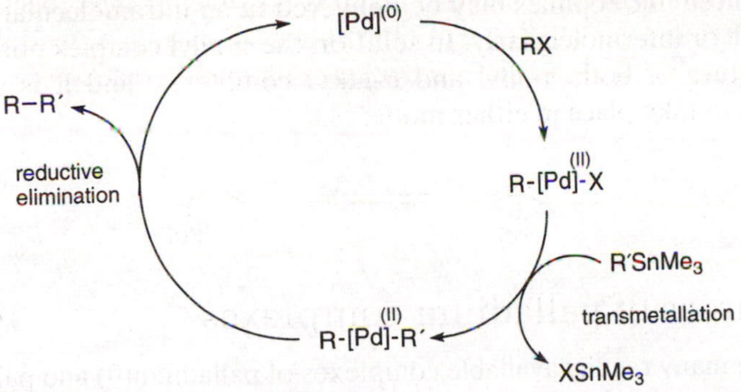

Fig. 2.2 Catalytic cycle for the Stille coupling, showing the reductive elimination step (ligands omitted for clarity).

Another important class of palladium(II) complexes is that in which an η^3-π-allyl ligand is coordinated to the metal, as in **3**. It is possible to synthesise these types of complexes from both palladium(0) and palladium(II) starting materials. The most widely used method is the formation of an allyl complex from an allylic acetate, carbonate, sulfonate, or other suitable leaving group (X), and palladium(0).

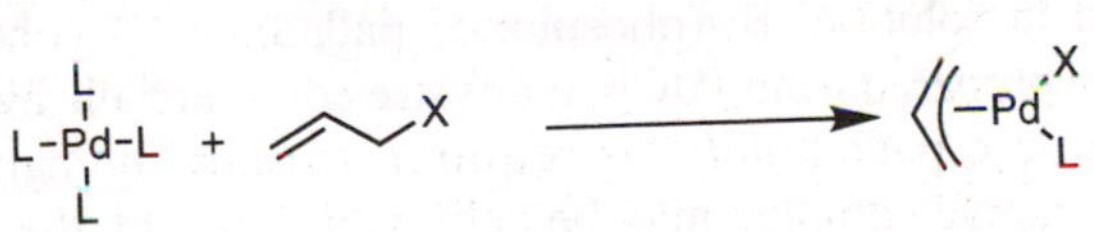

The synthesis of η^3-π-allyl complexes from palladium(II) may be achieved by transmetalation with an allylic Grignard such as **4** or directly from alkenes such as **5**.

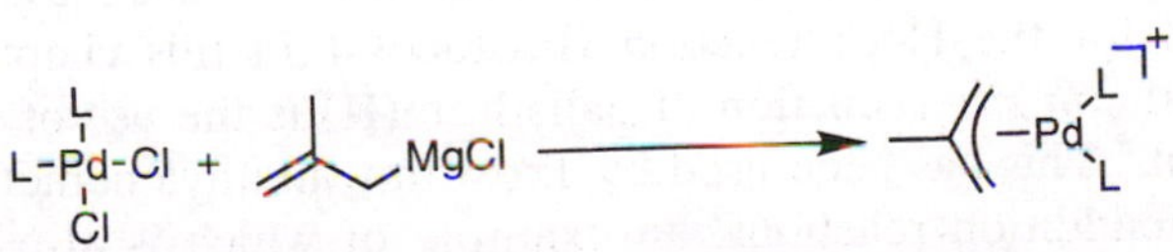

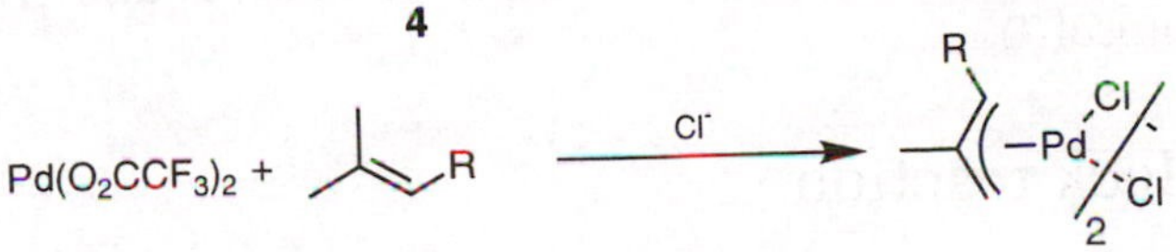

π-Allyl complexes are generally more stable than σ-bonded ones due to the bidentate nature of the ligand, and because of the delocalised π system. The complexes are prone to nucleophilic attack by a wide range of nucleophiles. These nucleophiles may be delivered in an intramolecular fashion *via* the metal, or intermolecularly. In solution the π-allyl complex normally exists as a mixture of both π-allyl and σ-alkyl complexes, and it is possible for reactions to take place in either mode.

2. Sources of palladium complexes

There are many readily available complexes of palladium(0) and palladium(II). Tetrakis(triphenylphosphine)palladium(0), $Pd(PPh_3)_4$, and tris(dibenzylidene-acetone)dipalladium(0), $Pd_2(dba)_3$, or the chloroform complex, $Pd_2(dba)_3 \cdot CHCl_3$, which is air stable, are the most common sources of palladium(0). $Pd(PPh_3)_4$ is bright yellow in colour when freshly synthesised, but is mildly air sensitive and is best stored under an inert atmosphere. The commercially obtained material is of variable quality, but generally good enough for most reactions.

Palladium(II) complexes are generally more stable than their palladium(0) counterparts. $PdCl_2$ exists as a polymer and is relatively insoluble in most organic solvents. However, $(PhCN)_2PdCl_2$ and $(MeCN)_2PdCl_2$ (both easily prepared from $PdCl_2$) can be thought of as soluble forms of $PdCl_2$, as the nitrile ligands are readily displaced in solution. Bis(phosphine) palladium(II) complexes are air stable and readily prepared from $PdCl_2$; many are commercially available.

In reactions where palladium(0) is required to start the catalytic process, formation of the active complex may be achieved *in situ* by the reduction of a suitable palladium(II) complex, e.g. $Pd(OAc)_2$. This process also has the advantage that any phosphine may be used in the reaction, without the need to synthesise and isolate the corresponding palladium(0) phosphine complex. Using this method, only 2–3 equiv of phosphine may be used, rendering the resulting palladium(0) complex coordinatively unsaturated and therefore very reactive. A good example of this is the use of $Pd(OAc)_2/P(o\text{-tolyl})_3$ in the protocol for the Heck reaction (Protocol 1 in this chapter). Another method for the *in situ* reduction of palladium(II) is the use of DIBAL-H as the reductant.[4] This has been used by Trost in trimethylenemethane (TMM) [3 + 2] cycloaddition reactions, an example of which is also given in this chapter (Protocol 7).

3. The Heck reaction

The palladium-catalysed addition of vinyl or substituted vinyl groups to organic halides or triflates, the Heck reaction, is one of the most synthetically useful palladium-catalysed reactions. The method is very efficient, and carries out a transformation on alkenes **6** that frequently cannot be accomplished in 'one pot' by more traditional techniques.

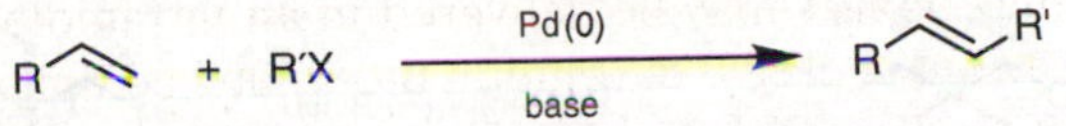

6

As outlined in the introduction to this chapter, the choice of substrates R'X is limited to aryl, heteroaryl, vinylic and benzylic halides, as the presence of a sp^3-carbon in the β-position carrying a hydrogen rapidly results in β-hydride elimination. The reaction tolerates a variety of functional groups, and works well with both electron withdrawing and electron donating groups on either substrate. The mechanism, as outlined in detail in the introduction (Fig. 2.1), involves the oxidative addition of the halide, insertion of the alkene, and elimination of the product by a β-hydride elimination process. The palladium(0) catalyst is then regenerated by a base. With alkenic substrates that are unsymmetrical, the alkyl group of the alkyl-palladium intermediate acts as the largest group, and therefore adds at the less hindered end of the double bond, providing there are no over-riding electronic factors. In the β-hydride elimination step, the palladium and hydride must be co-planar for reaction to take place, as this is a *syn*-elimination process. As a result of steric interactions, the R group will tend to eclipse the smallest group on the adjacent carbon as elimination occurs, leading predominantly to a *trans* double bond in the product.

The reaction has also been extended to alkynyl halides, although this is less well documented. For example, the reaction of 1-iodoalkynes **7** with α,β-unsaturated substrates may be carried out under very mild phase-transfer conditions, with moderate yields.[5]

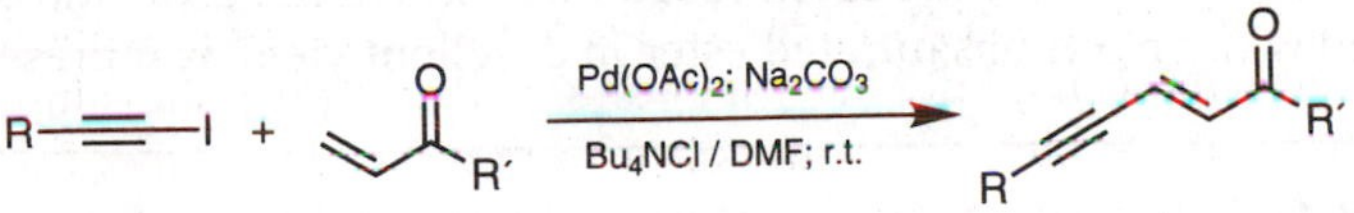

7

The reaction of allylic substrates frequently leads to a rearranged product resulting from double bond migration, as shown by the reaction of the allylic alcohol **8**.

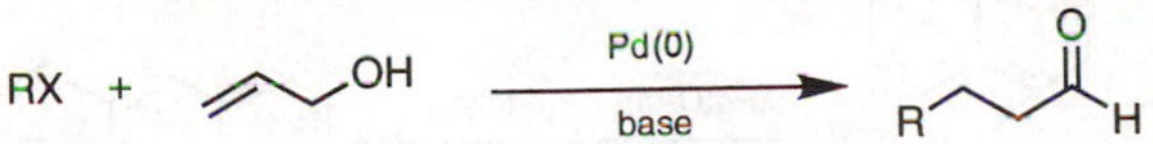

8

More recently, the Heck reaction has been used in cascade cyclisations, and under enantioselective conditions.[6] For example, the intramolecular synthesis of decalin derivative **9** has been achieved in good enantiomeric excess, using an optically pure phosphine (Binap) as part of the palladium catalyst.[7]

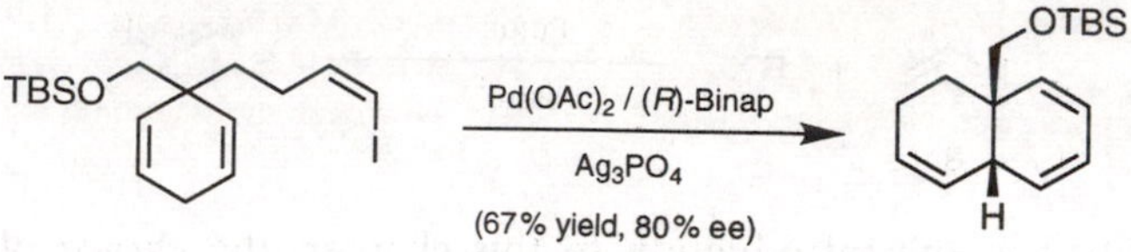

9

The presence of silver ions accelerates the reaction as well as preventing double bond isomerisation in the original substrate. The use of a non-coordinating counterion base was found to be essential, and it is thought that this prevents disruption of the ideal square planar transition state.

The use of palladium catalysts in the construction of complex ring systems, using the Heck reaction, has also generated widespread interest.[8] Grigg has shown that spiroindoles may be synthesised using this methodology, creating two or more new rings in one step.[9] Overman has also used an intramolecular Heck reaction to construct the ring system of scopadulcic acid B **10** as part of a total synthesis project.[10]

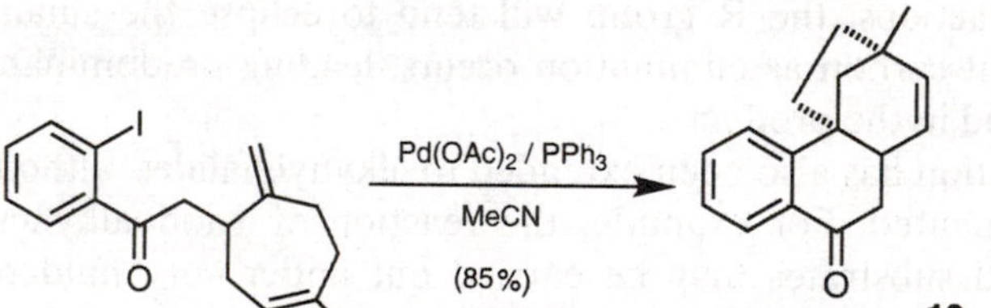

10

The protocol given for the Heck reaction, in which the aromatic bromide **11** is coupled with an α,β-unsaturated ester in excellent yield, is representative.

Protocol 1.
Heck reaction of 2-bromonaphthalene (Structure 11) and ethyl acrylate

Caution! All procedures should be carried out in a fume hood. Disposable vinyl or latex gloves and safety glasses should be worn.

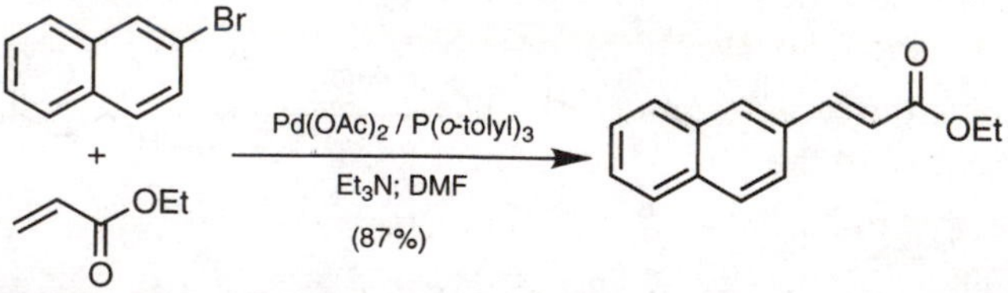

Equipment
- Stirrer hot plate
- Two-necked, round-bottomed flask (250 mL)
- Single-necked, round-bottomed flask (250 mL)
- Septum
- Needles (medium gauge)
- Source of dry argon

40

- Teflon-covered magnetic stirrer bar (2.5 cm long)
- All-glass syringes with needle-lock Luers (2 × 2 mL)
- Water-jacketed condenser
- Oil bath
- Chromatography column (45 cm × 4 cm)
- Source of vacuum (1 mmHg)

Material

• Dry DMF,[a] 70 mL	irritant
• Palladium acetate (FW 224.5), 104 mg, 0.48 mmol	
• Tri(*o*-tolyl)phosphine (FW 304.4), 588 mg, 1.96 mmol	irritant
• Ethyl acrylate (FW 100.1), 1.2 mL, 11.1 mmol	flammable liquid, cancer-suspect agent
• Triethylamine[b] (FW 101.2), 1.6 mL, 11.5 mmol	flammable liquid, corrosive
• 2-Bromonaphthalene **11** (FW 207.1), 2.0 g, 9.64 mmol	
• Ethyl acetate technical grade	flammable liquid, irritant
• Petroleum ether (40-60)	flammable liquid, toxic
• Dichloromethane	toxic, irritant
• Silica gel (80 g)	irritant

1. Clean all glassware, the stirrer bar and syringes and dry overnight in a hot oven before use.

2. Clamp the two-necked flask (containing the stirrer bar) fitted with the condenser, in the oil bath above the stirrer hot plate. Fit the argon source to the top of the condenser. Flush the assembly with argon by allowing the gas to flow through the flask for a few seconds before sealing the apparatus by fitting the septum.

3. Remove the septum and put palladium acetate (108 mg, 0.48 mmol), tri(*o*-tolyl)phosphine (588 mg, 1.96 mmol), and 2-bromonaphthalene (2 g, 9.64 mmol) into the flask. (Moderate the argon flow to facilitate this operation.)

4. Charge the flask with dry DMF (70 mL), flush the apparatus again with argon, and replace the septum.

5. Add triethylamine (1.6 mL, 11.5 mmol) and ethyl acrylate (1.2 mL, 11.1 mmol) through the septum using the 2 mL syringes.

6. Heat the mixture to reflux for 3 h, using the oil bath at *ca.* 160°C.

7. After cooling, transfer the mixture to a single-necked round-bottomed flask (250 mL) and remove the solvent and excess volatile reagents on a rotary evaporator, using a vacuum pump (1 mmHg).

8. Suspend 80 g of silica gel in a 9:1 mixture of petroleum ether (40-60)/ethyl acetate, and load into the chromatography column.[c]

9. Dissolve the crude product of the reaction in *ca.* 4 mL of dichloromethane and load onto the top of the column.

10. Elute the material with a 9:1 mixture of petroleum ether (40-60)/ethyl acetate.

11. Pool the appropriate fractions, remove the solvent under reduced pressure, and dry the product under high vacuum. The product is isolated as a white solid (1.9 g, 87%).

Data

M.p. 62–63°C. δ_H(200 MHz, solvent CDCl$_3$, reference SiMe$_4$): 1.36 (3H, t, J = 7.2 Hz), 4.29 (2H, q, J = 7.2 Hz), 6.55 (1H, d, J = 16.0 Hz), 7.47–7.96 (8H, m). δ_C(63 MHz, CDCl$_3$, SiMe$_4$): δ 14.3, 60.4, 118.4, 123.4, 126.6, 127.1, 127.7, 128.5, 128.6, 129.8, 114.5, 131.9, 133.2, 134.1, 166.9.

[a] DMF was dried by distillation from CaSO$_4$ under reduced pressure and stored over molecular sieves.
[b] Triethylamine was dried by distillation from CaH$_2$.
[c] Solvents for chromatography were distilled before use.

---

4. The Stille coupling

Since the first reported use in the late 1970s, the Stille coupling has been widely used for the coupling of both aromatic and vinylic systems.[3,11]

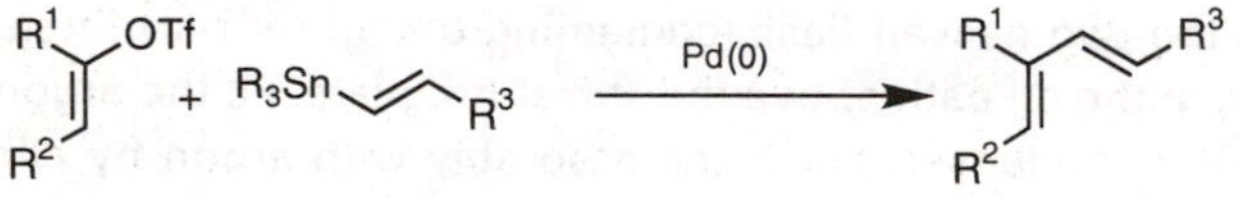

The mechanism (see Fig. 2.2) involves the oxidative addition of the vinyl or aromatic triflate or halide **12** to give a palladium intermediate. This then undergoes a transmetalation reaction with the organostannane **13**, giving an organopalladium intermediate in which both components are σ-bound. This complex then undergoes a reductive elimination step, releasing the product and thereby regenerating the palladium(0) catalyst. The reaction will also occur if a vinyl or aryl halide is used in place of the analogous triflate. However, the triflates have been more widely used as they are readily prepared from phenols or enolisable aldehydes or ketones. In these reactions, the presence of a source of halide (typically LiCl) is generally (but not always) required. It is thought that this is because the triflate merely acts as a counterion to the palladium rather than a ligand, and that a ligand is required, giving the desired square planar geometry, for the transmetalation to occur.

The phosphine or other ligand that is used to stabilise the palladium(0) catalyst can have a dramatic effect on the rate of the reaction. Both tri(2-furyl)phosphine and triphenylarsine can be used in place of the more normal triphenylphosphine in reactions where this ligand gives poor yields.[12] Indeed, the protocol for the Stille reaction between vinyl triflate **14** and organostannane **15** contained in this chapter (Protocol 2) is an excellent example of this. The reaction was originally reported not to proceed.[13] However, with triphenylarsine, Roth and co-workers have obtained excellent yields under mild conditions, without the need for added LiCl.[14]

The Stille reaction, which represents over 50% of all 1992 cross-coupling reactions[14] has been used in total synthesis with excellent results. Nicolaou's synthesis of rapamycin,[15] for example, uses the reaction in the macrocyclisation step, and the synthesis of indanomycin is also a good example of the Stille reaction at work.[16] The reaction may also be carried out intramolecularly and with alkynyl stannanes such as **16** instead of the more normal aryl or vinyl stannanes.[17]

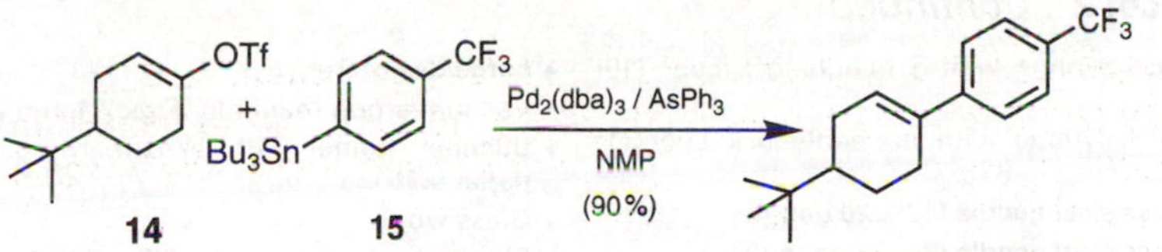

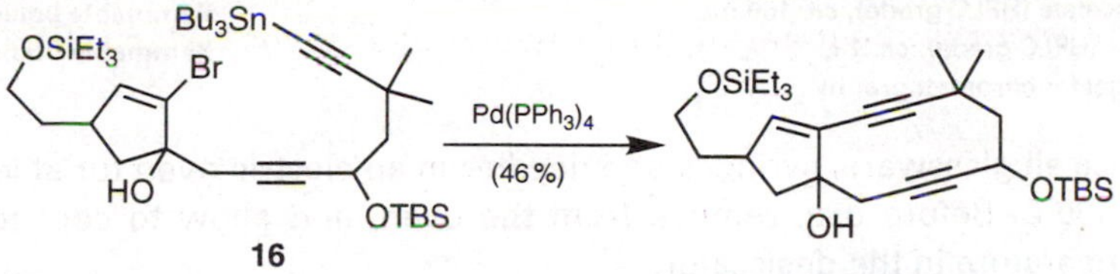

Acid chlorides may also be used as substrates for the reaction leading to carbonylated products.[18] However, an atmosphere of carbon monoxide is frequently required to prevent decarbonylation after the oxidative addition step.[19] More recently, it has been shown that carbonylated products may also be accessed by performing the normal Stille reaction in the presence of carbon monoxide. Initially these reactions were performed under high pressures,[20] but recent developments have shown that the reaction can take place in a carbon monoxide saturated solution, under one atmosphere of pressure.[21] Using these conditions, excellent yields of the carbonylated product can be obtained, without any of the normal coupling product being present. An example of a carbonylative Stille coupling, which generates the unsaturated ketone **17**, is also given in this chapter (Protocol 3).

Protocol 2
Stille Coupling of 4-*t*-butyl-cyclohexen-1-yloxytriflate (Structure 14) with *p*-(trifluoromethyl)phenyltributyltin (Structure 15)

Caution! Triphenylarsine is very toxic. All procedures should be carried out in an efficient fume hood. Disposable vinyl or latex gloves and safety glasses should be worn.

Equipment
- Stirrer hotplate
- Oil bath
- Thermometer
- Two-necked, round-bottomed flask (25 mL)
- Pear-shaped flask (25 mL)
- Septa

Protocol 2   *Continued*

- All-glass syringe with a needle-lock Luer (10 mL)
- All-glass syringe with a needle-lock Luer (1 mL)
- Stainless steel needle (12″, 20 gauge)
- Stainless steel needle (3″, 22 gauge)
- Teflon-covered magnetic stirrer bar
- Large desiccator
- Vacuum/argon manifold (Figs 7.1 and 7.2)
- Büchner funnel with Whatman no. 1 filter paper 4.25 cm
- Glass wool
- Chromatography column (55 cm × 4 cm)
- Separating funnel (250 mL)

Material

- Triphenylarsine (FW 306.2), 92 mg, 0.3 mmol   **highly toxic**
- Tris(dibenzylideneacetone)dipalladium(0) (FW 915.7), 33.2 mg, 0.036 mmol
- 4-*t*-Butyl-cyclohexen-1-yloxytriflate[a] (FW 435.1), 1.15 g, 4.0 mmol
- *p*-(Trifluoromethyl)phenyltributyltin[a] (FW 435.1), 1.9 g, 4.4 mmol   **highly toxic**
- Anhydrous *N*-methylpyrrolidinone (NMP), *ca.* 10 mL   **irritant, hygroscopic**
- 1 M potassium fluoride solution   **toxic, corrosive**
- Ethyl acetate (HPLC grade), *ca.* 100 mL   **flammable liquid, irritant**
- Hexane (HPLC grade), *ca.* 1 L   **flammable liquid, irritant**
- Silica gel for chromatography   **irritant**

1. Place all glassware, syringes and needles in an electric oven for at least 2 h at 130°C. Before use, remove from the oven, and allow to cool to room temperature in the desiccator.

2. Clamp the two-necked flask over the stirrer hot plate, insert the stirrer bar, and cap with two septa.

3. Remove a septum and quickly put triphenylarsine (92 mg, 0.3 mmol), the triflate (1.15 g, 4.0 mmol), and the palladium catalyst (33.2 mg, 0.072 mmol) into the flask. Replace the septum, add NMP (5 mL) by syringe, and begin stirring.

4. Connect the flask to the vacuum/argon manifold by a flexible tubing connection equipped with a hypodermic needle, and saturate the solution with argon by applying three cycles of vacuum/argon (chapter 7, Protocol 2).

5. In the pear-shaped flask, dissolve the stannane (1.91 g, 4.4 mmol) in NMP (2 mL), and saturate the solution with argon as above.

6. Stir the flask containing the palladium complex until the deep red colour is discharged. When all the solids are dissolved, and the solution is a yellow or pale green colour, add the solution of the stannane using the dry 1 mL syringe. Rinse the flask with fresh aliquots of NMP (2 × 0.5 mL).

7. Heat the reaction mixture to *ca.* 55°C for 21 h. Monitoring of the reaction by TLC (hexane eluent) indicates all the triflate is consumed after this time.

8. Cool the reaction, and add 1 M aqueous potassium fluoride solution (5 mL). Stir for 30 min at room temperature, pour into ethyl acetate (50 mL), and then filter the resulting solution. Rinse the solids with a further portion of ethyl acetate (50 mL).

9. Dry the ethyl acetate solution over sodium sulfate, filter, and remove the solvent on a rotary evaporator.

10. Load the chromatography column with silica gel to reach a height of 19 cm. Pour on hexane and flush under pressure to remove trapped air.

11. Dissolve the crude product in hexane (*ca.* 3 mL), and load onto the top of the column. Elute the product with hexane.

12. Pool the appropriate fractions and remove the solvent under reduced pressure.

13. If necessary, the product may be recrystallised from methanol, giving colourless needles (90%, m.p. 84–85°C) which display the appropriate spectroscopic data.[14]

---

[a] 4-*t*-Butyl-cyclohexen-1-yloxytriflate[22] and *p*-(trifluoromethyl)phenyltributyltin[23] were prepared according to literature methods.

Protocol 3.
Carbonylative Stille coupling of iodobenzene and 1-ethoxy-(1-trimethylstannyl)ethene

Caution! Carbon monoxide is a highly toxic, flammable gas. All procedures should be carried out in an efficient fume hood. Disposable vinyl or latex gloves and safety glasses should be worn at all times.

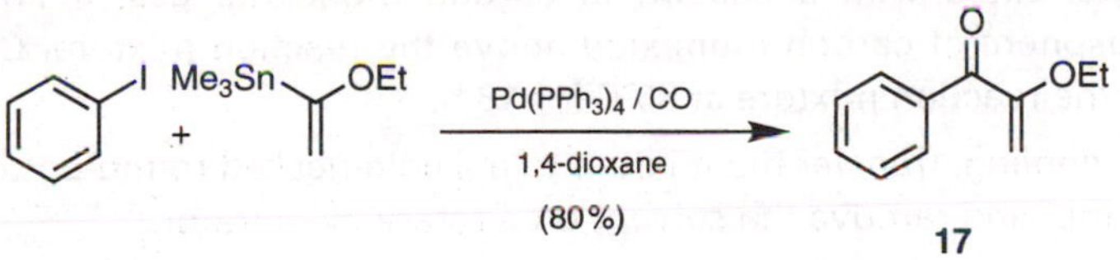

$$\text{PhI} + \text{Me}_3\text{Sn}\!\!-\!\!C(=CH_2)\text{OEt} \xrightarrow[\text{1,4-dioxane}]{\text{Pd(PPh}_3)_4 / CO} \text{product } \mathbf{17} \quad (80\%)$$

Equipment

- Stirrer hotplate
- Two-necked, round-bottomed flask (100 mL)
- Single-necked, round-bottomed flask (100 mL)
- Septum
- Teflon-covered magnetic stirrer bar (2.5 cm long)
- Syringe (500 μL)
- Source of dry argon
- Source of carbon monoxide
- Water-jacketed condenser
- Oil bath
- Chromatography column (35 cm × 3 cm)
- Dreschel bottle
- Needle (wide bore)
- Dry flexible tubing
- Oil bubbler

Material

- Iodobenzene (FW 204.0), 816 mg, 4 mmol — **irritant, light sensitive**
- 1-Ethoxy-(1-trimethylstannyl)ethene (FW 234.9), 940 mg, 4 mmol — **moisture sensitive, irritant**
- Tetrakis(triphenylphosphine)palladium(0) (FW 1155.6), 92 mg, 80 μmol — **air sensitive**
- Carbon monoxide — **highly toxic gas, flammable**
- 1,4-Dioxane,[a] 40 mL — **flammable, cancer-suspect agent**
- Ethyl acetate technical grade — **flammable liquid, irritant**
- Petroleum ether (40–60) — **flammable liquid, toxic**
- Silica gel for chromatography — **irritant**

45

Protocol 3 *Continued*

1. Clean all glassware, the stirrer bar, and syringe and dry overnight in a hot oven before use.

2. Clamp the two-necked flask (containing the stirrer bar) fitted with the condenser, in the oil bath above the stirrer hotplate. Fit the argon source to the top of the condenser. Flush the assembly with argon by allowing the gas to flow through the flask for a few seconds before sealing the apparatus by fitting the septum.

3. Remove the septum and put iodobenzene (816 mg, 4 mmol), 1-ethoxy-1-(trimethylstannyl)ethylene (753 μL, 940 mg, 4 mmol), tetrakis(triphenylphosphine)palladium (92 mg, 80 μmol), and 1,4-dioxane (40 mL) into the flask.

4. Attach the carbon monoxide cylinder, *via* the Dreschel bottle and flexible tubing, to the needle. Ensure the needle is securely attached to prevent the gas leaking.

5. Replace the argon source with an oil bubbler fitted to the top of the condenser. Pierce the septum with the needle and bubble carbon monoxide through the solution for 1 h whilst slowly warming the oil bath to 85°C. Ensure the gas is vented into the top of the fume hood *via* the oil bubbler.

6. Remove the needle from the flask. Replace the oil bubbler with a gas adapter fitted with a balloon of carbon monoxide gas, maintaining an atmosphere of carbon monoxide above the reaction mixture. Continue to heat the reaction mixture at 85°C for 18 h.

7. After cooling, transfer the mixture to a single-necked round-bottomed flask (200 mL) and remove the solvent on a rotary evaporator.

8. Suspend 50 g of silica gel in petroleum ether (40–60) and load into the chromatography column.[b]

9. Load the oily product directly onto the top of the column. Remove the tin residues from the material by eluting with 500 mL of petroleum ether. The product can then be eluted using a 9:1 mixture of petroleum ether (40–60)/ethyl acetate.

10. Remove the solvent under reduced pressure and dry the product under high vacuum. The product is isolated as a yellow oil (560 mg, 80%).

Data

δ_H(250 MHz, solvent $CDCl_3$, reference $SiMe_4$): 1.38 (3H, t, J = 7.0 Hz), 3.89 (2H, q, J = 7.0 Hz), 4.75 (1H, d, J = 2.8 Hz), 4.98 (1H, d, J = 2.8 Hz), 7.35–7.57 (3H, m), 7.80–7.88 (2H, m). δ_C(63 MHz, $CDCl_3$, $SiMe_4$): 14.0, 63.6, 94.5, 127.8, 129.5, 132.3, 136.5, 157.9, 191.2.

[a] 1,4-Dioxane was stored over molecular sieves before use. All other reagents were used as supplied.
[b] Solvents for chromatography were distilled before use.

5. The Suzuki coupling

Since first being reported in 1979,[24] the Suzuki coupling has come to represent an important class of cross-coupling reactions, totalling 25% of all palladium-catalysed cross-coupling reactions in 1992.[14] The original report showed the reaction of an alkyl acetylene with catecholborane **18**, followed by coupling with an aromatic iodide or bromide.

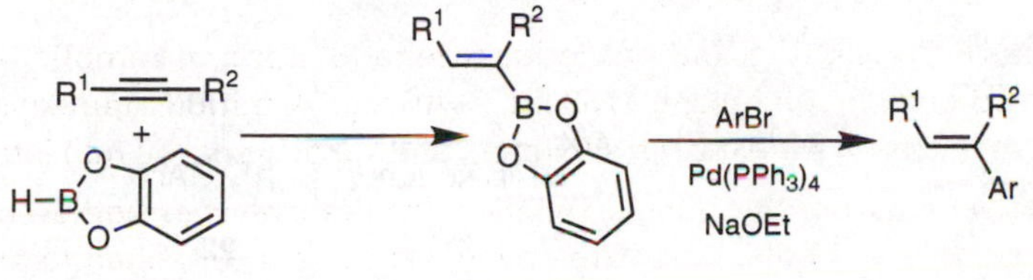

18

The mechanism is very similar to that of the Stille coupling. Oxidative addition of the vinylic or aromatic halide to the palladium(0) complex generates a palladium(II) intermediate. This then undergoes a transmetalation with the alkenylboronate, from which the product is expelled by reductive elimination, regenerating the palladium(0) catalyst.

The importance of the reaction stems from the ability to preserve alkene geometry in both starting materials. A good example of this forms the basis for Protocol 4. Thus, the (*E*)-alkenylboronate **19** synthesised from 1-octyne couples with the (*Z*)-alkenylbromide **20**, leading to (*E*) and (*Z*) double bonds in the product.

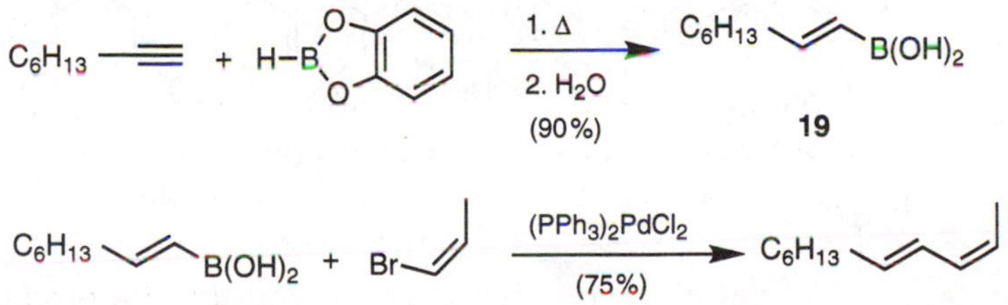

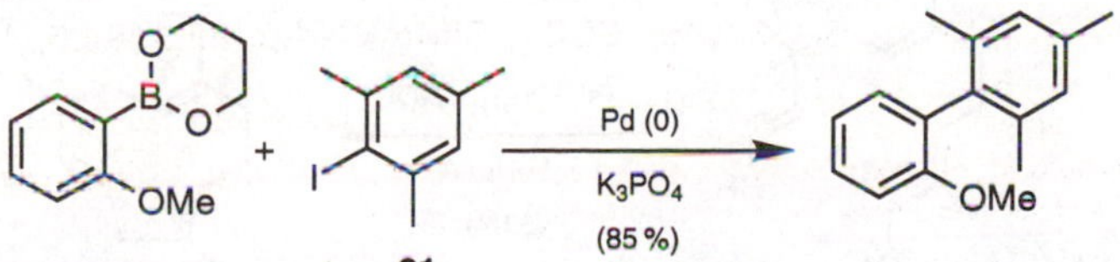

Sterically demanding substrates such as **21** are tolerated well,[25] and the methodology has been used in a wide range of aryl–aryl cross-couplings, including the synthesis of hindered binaphthol derivatives, used as ligands in asymmetric synthesis.[26]

The Suzuki coupling may be used to prepare ketones by two methods. Firstly by performing the usual coupling in the presence of *t*-butylisonitrile, acidic hydrolysis of the resulting ketimine **22** gives the corresponding ketone in good yield.[27] The mechanism of the reaction is thought to involve the insertion of the isonitrile into the original oxidative addition product, forming an iminoacyl intermediate.

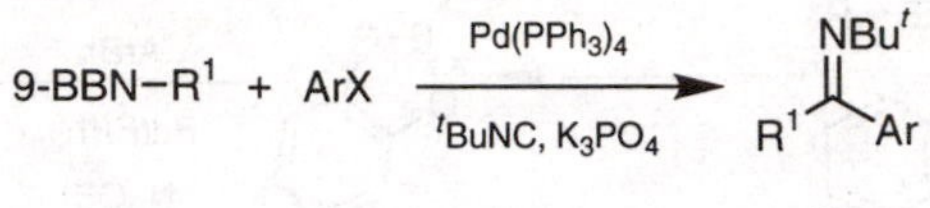

Similarly, the reaction of substrates under normal coupling conditions, but in the presence of an atmosphere of CO, gives excellent yields of the ketones directly, without the need for hydrolysis of an intermediate species.[28]

Due to the excellent stereoselectivity of the Suzuki coupling, the reaction has been used in the synthesis of the unsaturated units of a range of natural products. In an example drawn from the synthesis of trisporol B, a dienylic borane and a vinyl iodide are coupled to give the triene **23**.[29]

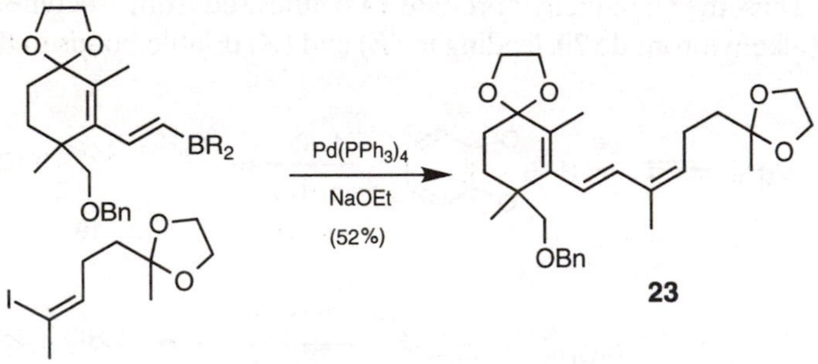

Macrocyclisations have also successfully been carried out using this methodology. The generation of the 11-membered ring of humulene **24** from an *allylic* bromide and vinylic borane in 32% yield is a good example.[30]

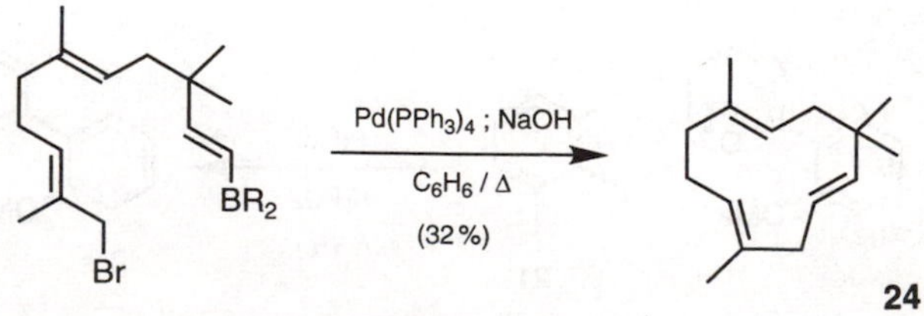

Protocol 4.
Synthesis of (2*Z*, 4*E*)-undecadiene

Caution! All procedures should be carried out in a fume hood. Disposable vinyl or latex gloves and safety glasses should be worn.

Equipment

- Stirrer hotplate
- Two-necked, round-bottomed flask (200 mL)
- Teflon-covered magnetic stirrer bar
- Oil bath
- Reflux condenser
- All-glass syringes with a needle-lock Luer (volume appropriate for quantity of solution to be transferred)
- Needles (6″, medium gauge)
- Source of dry nitrogen

- Büchner flask (100 mL)
- Büchner funnel
- Appropriately sized filter paper
- Water-jacketed semi-micro short-path distillation apparatus
- Septa
- Nitrogen adapter
- Separating funnel (100 mL)
- Beaker (50 mL)

Material

- 1-Octyne[a] (FW 110.2), 5.9 mL, 40 mmol — **flammable, irritant**
- Catecholborane[b] (FW 119.9), 4.9 mL, 44 mmol — **flammable, moisture sensitive**
- Bis(triphenylphosphine)palladium(II) chloride (FW 701.8), 0.42 g, 0.6 mmol — **hygroscopic**
- Dry toluene, 45 mL — **flammable, toxic**
- (*Z*)-1-Bromo-1-propene **20** (FW 120.9), 2.8 mL, 33 mmol — **flammable, irritant**
- Aqueous 3 M KOH solution, 26.7 mL, 80 mmol — **corrosive**
- Hexane for extraction, 40 mL — **flammable, irritant**
- Saturated brine
- Magnesium sulfate

1. Clean all glassware, syringes, needles and the stirrer bar and dry in an oven (*ca.* 120°C) before use.

2. Clamp the two-necked flask (containing the stirrer bar) fitted with the condenser, in the oil bath above the stirrer hotplate. Fit the nitrogen source to the top of the condenser. Flush the assembly with nitrogen by allowing the gas to flow through the flask for a few seconds before sealing the apparatus by fitting the septum.

3. Assemble the syringes and allow to cool to room temperature in a desiccator.

4. Put 1-octyne (5.9 mL, 40 mmol) into the flask through the septum using a syringe. To this, add catecholborane (4.9 mL, 44 mmol) dropwise using a syringe through the septum over a period of 1 min whilst stirring the solution.

5. Stir the mixture for 30 min, and then warm the flask slowly to 70°C. Keep the mixture at this temperature for 2 h.

6. Cool the flask using an ice-water bath. Quench the excess borane by careful addition of water (1–2 mL).

7. After the evolution of hydrogen has ceased, disconnect the nitrogen

49

Protocol 4 *Continued*

source, add a further amount of water (40 mL), stir for 1 h at room temperature, and then heat to 70–80°C for 1 h.

8. Cool the flask to 0°C, stand for 2 h, and then collect the precipitate by Büchner filtration through a filter paper, with suction. Wash the solid three times with ice-cold water (3 × 12 mL). Dry the solid overnight in a beaker. The octenylboronic acid obtained can be used for the coupling reaction without further purification (5.63 g, 90%).

9. Clean and dry the apparatus and assemble the flask and condenser as before in the oil bath placed on the stirrer hot plate.

10. Remove the septum and put bis(triphenylphosphine)palladium(II) chloride (0.42 g, 0.6 mmol) and 1-octenylboronic acid (4.7 g, 30 mmol) into the flask. Flush the apparatus with nitrogen and replace the septum.

11. Add toluene (45 mL), (*Z*)-1-bromo-1-propene (2.8 mL, 33 mmol), and aqueous KOH solution (26.7 mL, 80 mmol), using a syringe, through a septum. Stirring becomes difficult due to the precipitation of a light brown solid.

12. Heat the flask to 70°C for 3 h with stirring. After this time, most of the precipitate dissolves, resulting in a brown solution.

13. Cool the flask to room temperature and add hexane (30 mL) to dilute the reaction mixture.

14. Transfer the mixture to a separating funnel. Discard the basic aqueous layer, and wash the organic fraction with brine (2 × 30 mL). (If visualisation of the two layers proves difficult, add more water.) Dry the organic layer over magnesium sulfate, filter, and remove the solvent under reduced pressure.

15. Transfer the oily residue to the distillation apparatus. Distil the crude product under reduced pressure (84–86°C, 11 mmHg) to obtain (2*Z*,4*E*)-undecadiene (3.4 g, 75%).

Data

δ_H(300 MHz, solvent CDCl$_3$, reference SiMe$_4$): 0.89 (3H, t, *J* = 7.1 Hz), 1.23–1.43 (8H, m), 1.74 (3H, dd, *J* = 7.1, 1.7 Hz), 2.11 (2H, td, *J* = 7.2, 7.0 Hz), 5.37 (1H, dq, *J* = 10.9, 7.1 Hz), 5.66 (1H, dt, *J* = 15.1, 7.0 Hz), 5.97 (1H ddd, *J* = 11.0, 10.9, 1.7 Hz), 6.33 (1H, ddd, *J* = 15.1, 11.0, 1.2 Hz).

[a] 1-Octyne was purified by distillation prior to use.
[b] Catecholborane was distilled under nitrogen (58°C, 52 mmHg) and stored in a fridge under an inert atmosphere.

6. The Sonogashira coupling

The coupling of terminal alkynes **25** with aryl or vinyl halides under palladium catalysis is known as the Sonogashira reaction. The catalytic process requires the use of a palladium(0) complex, is performed in the presence of base, and generally uses copper iodide as a co-catalyst.

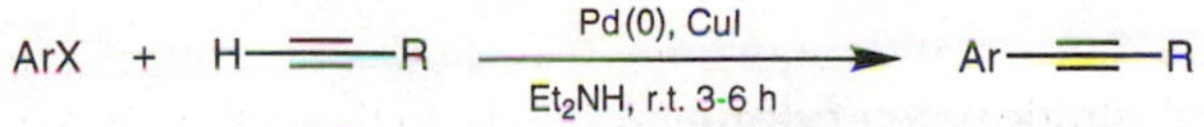

$$ArX \quad + \quad H \!\!=\!\!=\!\! R \quad \xrightarrow[\text{Et}_2\text{NH, r.t. 3-6 h}]{\text{Pd(0), CuI}} \quad Ar \!\!=\!\!=\!\! R$$

25

The reaction tolerates a wide range of substrates, including heteroaromatic halides, aryl and alkyl alkynes. The mild conditions usually employed (frequently room temperature) means that the reaction can be used with thermally sensitive substrates. The mechanism of the reaction is similar to that of the Stille and Suzuki couplings. Oxidative addition of the organic halide gives a palladium(II) intermediate which then undergoes a transmetalation reaction with the alkynylcuprate (generated from the terminal alkyne, base, and copper iodide). The resulting complex then undergoes reductive elimination giving the product and regenerating the palladium(0) catalyst. In many reactions, bis(triphenylphosphine)palladium(II) chloride is used as the source of palladium. This is rapidly reduced *in situ* to give a co-ordinatively unsaturated, catalytically active, palladium(0) species.

The reaction has received widespread current usage as a result of the huge interest generated by the potential of ene-diyne antibiotics. Symmetrical ene-diyne moieties of such molecules may be synthesised in one step from the appropriate alkyne and (*Z*)-dihaloethene **26**. More usually, however, the reaction is performed sequentially, thereby allowing different functionality on each of the alkyne units.

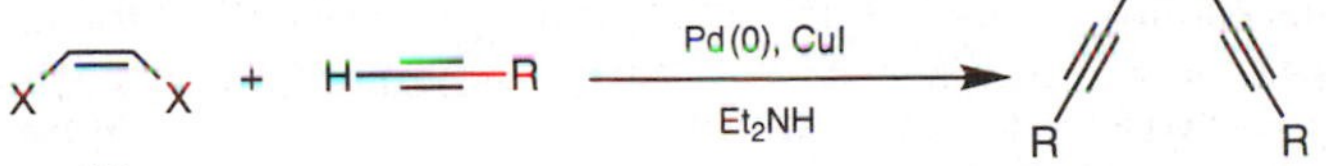

26

As is the case with the Suzuki coupling, the geometry of the alkene is generally preserved.[31] This is illustrated by the couplings of **27** and **28** with 1-heptyne.

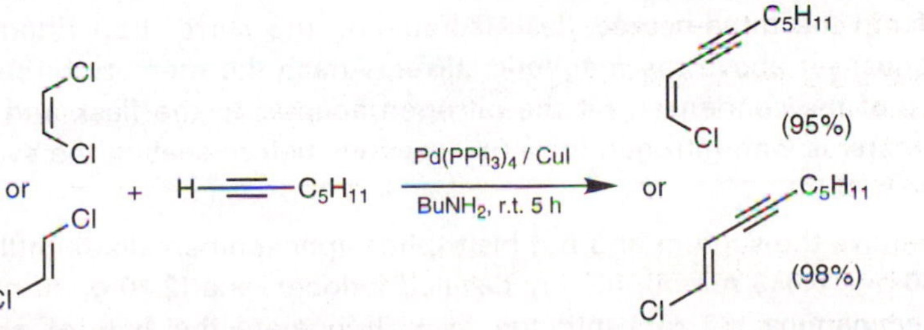

both > 99% isomeric purity

The protocol given for this reaction involves the coupling of acetylene with 2 equiv. of iodobenzene **29** and is representative of the reaction.

Protocol 5.
Synthesis of diphenylacetylene

Caution! All procedures should be carried out in a fume hood. Disposable vinyl or latex gloves and safety glasses should be worn.

$$H\!-\!\!\equiv\!\!-\!H \ + \ 2\,PhI \ \xrightarrow[\text{Et}_2\text{NH, r.t.}]{\text{(PPh}_3)_2\text{PdCl}_2\,/\,\text{CuI}} \ Ph\!-\!\!\equiv\!\!-\!Ph$$

$$\underset{\textbf{29}}{} \qquad \underset{(89\%)}{}$$

Equipment

- Magnetic stirrer
- Three-necked, round-bottomed flask (100 mL)
- Single-necked, round-bottomed flask (100 mL)
- Reflux condenser
- Teflon-covered magnetic stirring bar
- Source of nitrogen
- Nitrogen adapter
- Mercury bubbler
- Septum
- An empty 200 mL Dreschel bottle as a safety trap for acetylene cylinder
- Gas inlet tube
- Separating funnel (200 mL)
- Source of vacuum
- Chromatography column (10 cm × 2.7 cm)

Material

- Diethylamine,[a] 60 mL — flammable, irritant
- Copper(I) iodide (FW 190.4), 20 mg, 0.11 mmol — irritant
- Bis(triphenylphosphine)palladium(II) chloride (FW 701.89), 30 mg, 0.043 mmol — irritant
- Iodobenzene[a] **29** (FW 204.02), 2.40 g, 10 mmol — light sensitive, irritant
- Acetylene gas (cylinder) — flammable
- Toluene, *ca.* 400 mL — flammable
- Anhydrous calcium chloride (or sodium sulfate) — irritant, hygroscopic
- Technical hexane, *ca.* 500 mL — flammable
- Aluminium oxide, activated, neutral, 150 mesh for chromatography — irritant

1. Clean all glassware and the magnetic stirrer bar, and dry in an oven before use.

2. Clamp the three-necked flask (containing the stirrer bar) fitted with the condenser above the magnetic stirrer. Attach the mercury bubbler to the top of the condenser. Fit the nitrogen adapter to the flask and flush the apparatus with nitrogen for a few seconds before sealing the system with the septum.

3. Remove the septum and put bis(triphenylphosphine)palladium(II) chloride (30 mg, 0.043 mmol), freshly distilled iodobenzene (2.40 g, 10 mmol) and diethylamine (60 mL) into the flask. (Moderate the flow of nitrogen to facilitate this.)

4. Flush the equipment with nitrogen, and add copper(I) iodide (20 mg, 0.11 mmol). Flush the equipment again, and replace the septum.

5. Replace the nitrogen adapter with a gas inlet tube linked to the acetylene cylinder *via* a Dreschel bottle. Adjust the gas inlet tube to extend below the surface of the liquid.

6. Pass a slow stream of acetylene through the gas inlet tube (about 1–2 bubbles per second, otherwise appreciable evaporation of the diethylamine will occur). The reaction should begin immediately as indicated by formation of a white precipitate of diethylamine hydroiodide.

7. Bubble acetylene gas through the reaction mixture for 6 h at room temperature.

8. Transfer the mixture to a single-necked round-bottomed flask and remove the solvent under reduced pressure. Transfer the residue to a separating funnel containing water (50 mL). Extract the product with toluene (3 × 50 mL). Wash the combined organic fractions with water (2 × 20 mL), and dry them over calcium chloride or sodium sulfate.

9. Filter, remove the solvent under reduced pressure, and suspend the residue in a small amount of hexane.

10. Pack a chromatography column (10 cm × 2.7 cm) with neutral alumina in hexane. Load the product onto the column and elute with hexane until all the iodobenzene is removed and then elute with a 1:1 mixture of hexane/toluene.

11. Pool the appropriate fractions and remove the solvent under reduced pressure.

12. Recrystallisation from ethanol (*ca.* 10 mL) affords 1.58 g (89%) of white needles (m.p. 60–61°C).

[a] Diethylamine and iodobenzene were freshly distilled before use.

---

7. Allylic alkylations

The use of π-allyl complexes of palladium as intermediates in nucleophilic displacement reactions enables both the stereochemistry and regiochemistry of the reaction to be controlled.

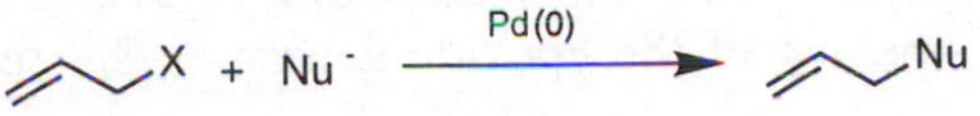

30

Whilst allylic acetates (**30**, X = OAc) are most commonly used, a wide range of other functionality (X = Cl, Br, OPh, OCO_2R) will perform a similar role. For carbon–carbon bond formation, stabilised enolates such as malonates may be used as nucleophiles, but the reaction is frequently equally successful with alkoxides, amines, and thioalkoxides. The reaction usually proceeds with *retention* of configuration at the reacting centre. At first, this might appear puzzling, as one would reasonably expect the oxidative addition/nucleophilic attack sequence to invert the stereocentre. However, the normal pathway of the reaction is coordination of the allylic acetate to give **31**, followed by an oxidative elimination step, which proceeds with inversion. Thereafter, the nucleophile attacks from the less-hindered face of the resulting π-allyl complex **32** (i.e. away from the metal) leading to overall *retention* of configuration.[32]

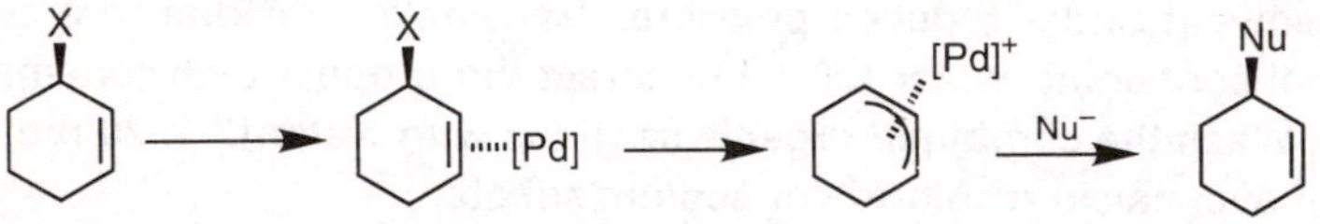

31   **32**

The 'double inversion' process has been used in the synthesis of aristeromycin from epoxycyclopentadiene **33**.[33]

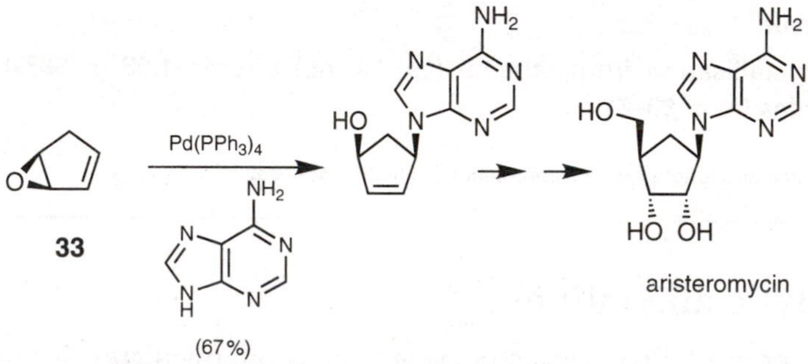

33

(67%)

aristeromycin

It is noteworthy that the 1,4-*syn* stereochemistry of such carbocycles may be produced in one step using this methodology. Base is not required in this reaction, as the opening of the epoxide generates the required alkoxide *in situ*.

π-Allyl intermediates may also be used in cyclisation reactions,[34] including the synthesis of three-membered rings such as **34** using an intramolecular nucleophilic displacement.[35]

More recently, a number of research groups have shown that the use of

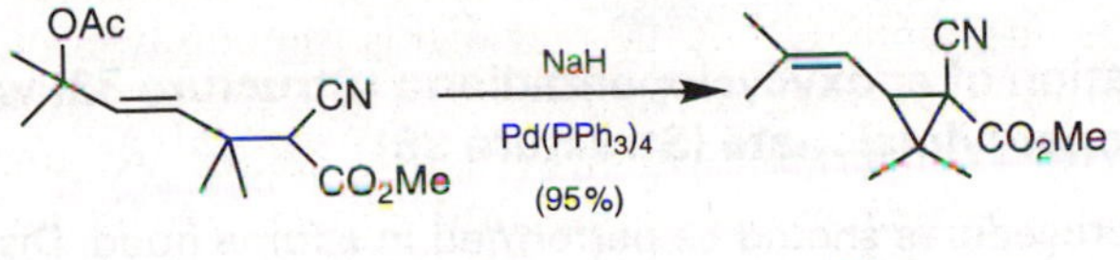

34

optically pure ligands enables the allylic alkylation reaction to be carried out on some substrates with good enantiomeric excess.[36] Initial studies of enantioselective allylic alkylations using readily available chiral phosphines as the ligand gave relatively low values.[37] Since these original studies however, improvements have been made by changing the ligand. Excellent enantioselectivity (up to 88% ee) may be obtained, for example, with optically pure bisoxazolines such as **35**.[38,39]

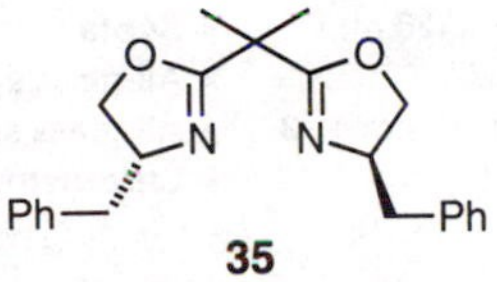

35

It has also been demonstrated that the choice of nucleophile can have a dramatic effect on the enantioselectivity of an allylic alkylation reaction, as indicated for the nucleophiles **36** and **37**.[40]

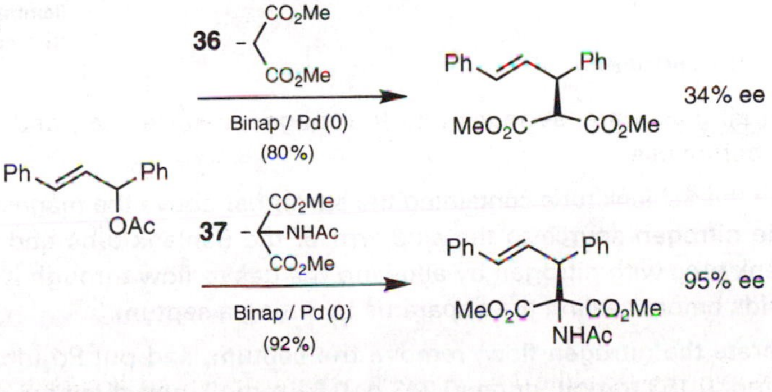

Williams has shown that the use of non C_2-symmetric ligands is equally effective. The regiochemical approach of the nucleophile is influenced by the relative *trans* effect of the two coordinating atoms in the optically pure ligand (i.e. approach *trans* to sulfur and phosphorus is favoured over nitrogen).[41,42] Protocol 6, which involves the reaction of epoxycyclopentadiene **33** with dimethyl propargylmalonate **38**, demonstrates the excellent stereochemical control that can be obtained using this reaction.

Protocol 6.
Allylic alkylation of epoxycyclopentadiene (Structure 33) with dimethyl propargylmalonate (Structure 38)

Caution! All procedures should be performed in a fume hood. Disposable vinyl or latex gloves and safety glasses should be worn.

Equipment

- Schlenk tube (25 mL) (Fig. 7.3)
- Single-necked, round-bottomed flask (25 mL)
- Magnetic stirrer
- Teflon-covered magnetic stirrer bar (1 cm × 3 mm)
- Source of dry nitrogen
- Septa
- All-glass syringe with a needle-lock Luer (10 mL)
- All-glass syringe with a needle-lock Luer (1 mL)
- Chromatography column (*ca.* 25 cm × 2 cm)

Material

• Epoxycyclopentadiene*ᵃ* (FW 82.1), 0.5 g, 6.1 mmol	**flammable**
• Pd$_2$(dba)$_3$·CHCl$_3$ (FW 1035.2), 158 mg 0.153 mmol	**irritant**
• 1,2-Bis(diphenylphosphino)ethane (dppe) (FW 398.4), 243 mg, 0.61 mmol	
• Dimethyl propargyl malonate*ᵃ* (FW 170.2), 1.24 g, 7.32 mmol	**flammable, irritant**
• THF (8 mL)	**flammable, irritant**
• Hexane	**flammable, irritant**
• Diethyl ether	**flammable, irritant**
• Silica gel for chromatography	**irritant**

1. Clean all glassware, syringes and the magnetic stirrer bar, and dry in an oven before use.

2. Clamp the Schlenk tube containing the stirrer bar above the magnetic stirrer. Fit the nitrogen source to the side-arm of the Schlenk tube and flush the Schlenk tube with nitrogen by allowing the gas to flow through it for a few seconds before sealing the apparatus by fitting a septum.

3. Moderate the nitrogen flow, remove the septum, and put Pd$_2$(dba)$_3$·CHCl$_3$ (158 mg, 0.153 mmol), dppe (0.243 g, 0.61 mmol), and dimethyl propargyl malonate (1.24 g, 7.32 mmol) into the Schlenk tube.

4. Flush the Schlenk tube again with dry nitrogen, and replace the septum.

5. Using a syringe, add dry THF (8 mL), cool the Schlenk tube in an ice bath to 0°C and begin stirring.

6. Using a syringe, add epoxycyclopentadiene (0.5 g, 6.1 mmol), over a period of 2 h, maintaining the temperature at 0°C.

7. After addition is complete, maintain the temperature at 0°C for a further 3 h, and then allow the Schlenk tube to warm to room temperature overnight.

8. Transfer the mixture to the 25 mL single-necked round-bottomed flask, and remove the solvent under reduced pressure.

9. Suspend silica gel (*ca.* 40 g) in diethyl ether-hexane (3:2), and load into the chromatography column.

10. Dissolve the product in a little solvent and load onto the top of the column.

11. Elute the product using diethyl ether/hexane (3:2).

12. Pool the appropriate fractions and remove the solvent under reduced pressure, yielding the product as an oil (840 mg, 55%) which displays the appropriate spectroscopic data.[8]

---

[a] Epoxycyclopentadiene[43] and dimethylpropargyl malonate[44] were prepared using literature methods.

8. Trimethylenemethane [3 + 2] cycloaddition reactions

The presence of five-membered rings such as cyclopentanes, cyclopentenes, and dihydrofurans in a wide range of target molecules has led to a variety of methods for their preparation. One of the most successful of these is the use of the trimethylenemethane (TMM) [3 + 2] cycloaddition, catalysed by palladium(0) complexes. The TMM unit in these reactions is derived from 2-[(trimethylsilyl)methyl]-2-propen-1-yl acetate **39**. Formation of the palladium π-allyl complex is followed by removal of the trimethylsilyl group and nucleophilic attack of the resulting acetate ion, thus producing a zwitterionic palladium complex **40**.

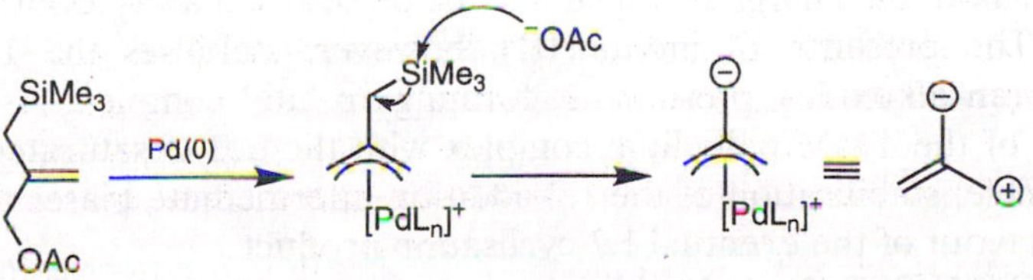

Normally this is reacted with an alkene bearing electron withdrawing substituents, which make the substrate prone to Michael-type 1,4-addition. The resulting cyclisation product, exemplified by **41**, has an *exo* methylene functionality. The mechanism is thought to be stepwise, consisting of nucleophilic attack at carbon followed by attack of the resulting enolate on the π-allyl palladium unit.

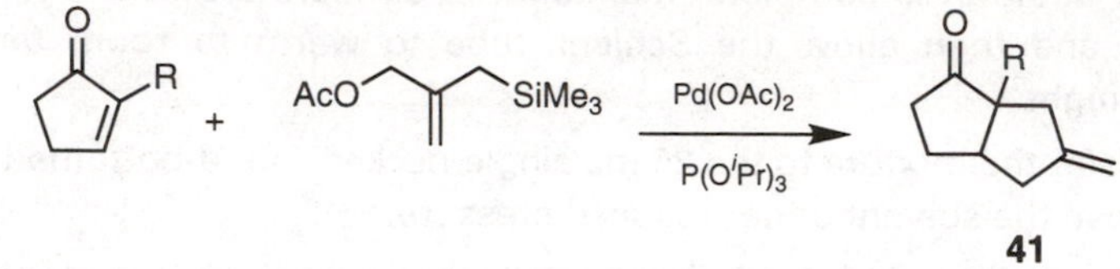

41

The palladium(0) species required for the reaction is sometimes generated *in situ* by the reduction of palladium acetate with DIBAL-H.[4] The resulting palladium(0) intermediate is stabilised by phosphine or phosphite ligands. Whilst palladium(0), in the form of $Pd(PPh_3)_4$ for example, may be directly introduced, the work of Trost suggests that the best catalysts are prepared from $Pd(OAc)_2$ and $P(O^iPr)_3$.[45] Trost has shown that by using a small amount of a co-catalyst [most notably simple complexes of indium(III)], the reaction can be 'switched' to give a 1,2-reaction rather than the more normal 1,4-product, leading to substituted tetrahydrofurans such as **42**.[4]

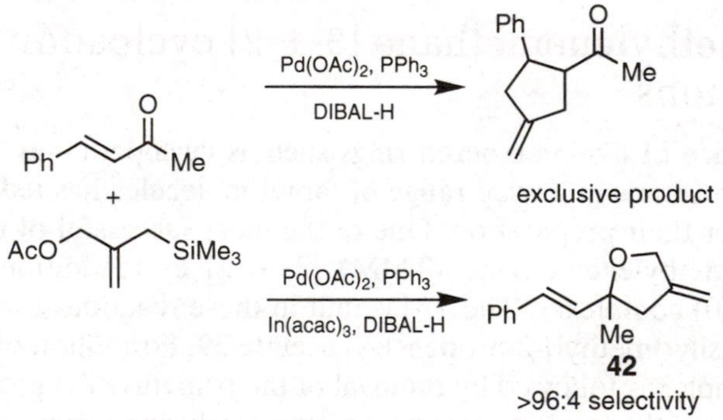

The cause of this remarkable selectivity switch is thought to be due to the relative stability of the two intermediates. Normal 1,4-addition leads to an enolate anion, the charge of which may be delocalised away from the oxygen centre. The presence of indium(III), however, stabilises the 1,2-addition product (an alkoxide), presumably forming an 'ate' complex. As the initial reaction of the TMM palladium complex with the α,β-unsaturated substrate is reversible, stabilisation of the 1,2-addition intermediate biases the equilibrium in favour of the eventual 1,2-cyclisation product.

The TMM [3 + 2] cycloaddition methodology may also be used in the preparation of nitrogen heterocycles by using imines as substrates.[46] The yields of the exomethylene pyrroles produced are generally excellent. Unlike their oxygenated analogues, α,β-unsaturated substrates were found to undergo exclusive 1,2-reaction to give the pyrrole, rather than 1,4-addition, to give the corresponding carbocycle. Interestingly, with the appropriate substrates, [4 + 3] cycloadditions which gave seven-membered ring products such as **43** were observed in preference to the [3 + 2] reaction.

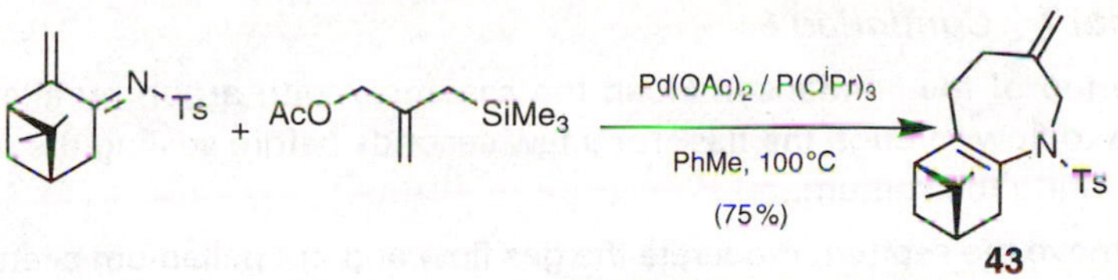

Protocol 7, chosen for this reaction, is representative of the method described. Cycloaddition of the unsaturated diester gives the 1,4-cycloaddition product, with complete *exo* selectivity.

Protocol 7.
Preparation of *endo*-2,6-dimethoxy carbonyl-4-methylenetricyclo [5.2.1.0^{2,6}] decane (Structure 45)

Caution! All procedures should be performed in a fume hood. Disposable vinyl or latex gloves and safety glasses should be worn.

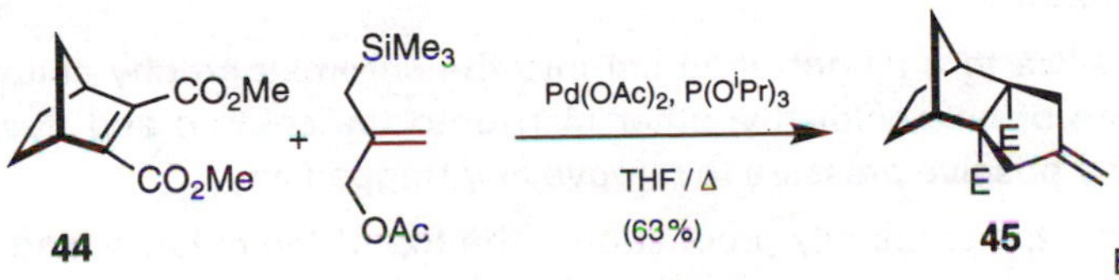

Equipment

- Stirrer hot plate
- Two-necked, round-bottomed flask (100 mL)
- Water-jacketed condenser
- Oil bath
- Septum
- Teflon-covered magnetic stirrer bar
- Needles (medium gauge)

- All-glass syringes with a needle-lock Luer (volume appropriate for quantity of solution to be transferred)
- Bubbler
- Source of dry argon
- Chromatography column (10 cm × 25 cm)

Material

- Palladium acetate (FW 224.5), 0.2 g, 0.89 mmol
- Tri(isopropyl)phosphite (FW 208.2), 1.11 g, 5.34 mmol   **toxic, moisture sensitive**
- Bicyclo[2.2.1]hept-2-ene dicarboxylic acid   **irritant**
  dimethyl ester^a (FW 210.2), 6.27 g, 29.85 mmol
- 2-[(Trimethylsilyl)methyl]-2-propen-1-yl acetate
  (FW 186.3), 5.56 g, 29.85 mmol   **irritant**
- THF, 40 mL   **flammable, irritant**
- Hexane   **flammable, irritant**
- Diethyl ether   **flammable, irritant**
- Silica gel for chromatography   **irritant**

1. Clean all glassware, syringes, needles, and the stirrer bar and dry overnight in an oven before use.
2. Clamp the two-necked flask (containing the stirrer bar) fitted with the condenser, in the oil bath above the stirrer hot plate. Fit the argon source to

59

Protocol 7 *Continued*

the top of the condenser. Flush the assembly with argon by allowing the gas to flow through the flask for a few seconds before sealing the apparatus by fitting the septum.

3. Remove the septum, moderate the gas flow and put palladium acetate (0.2 g, 0.89 mmol) into the flask. Replace the septum and charge the flask with dry THF (20 mL) using a syringe by puncturing the septum on the reaction flask.

4. Put tri(isopropyl)phosphite (1.11 g, 5.34 mmol) into the flask using a syringe by puncturing the septum on the reaction flask. A yellow solution should form.

5. Add 2-[(trimethylsilyl)methyl]-2-propen-1-yl acetate (5.56 g, 29.85 mmol) and bicyclo[2.2.1]hept-2-ene dicarboxylic acid dimethyl ester (6.27 g, 29.85 mmol) in dry THF (20 mL) *via* syringe at room temperature with stirring.

6. Heat the mixture under reflux with stirring for 3.5 h.

7. On cooling, remove the solvent under reduced pressure using a rotary evaporator.

8. Load silica to a height of 16 cm into the chromatography column. Add a mixture of hexane/diethyl ether (4:1) onto the column and flush through under a positive pressure to remove any trapped air.

9. Transfer the crude oily product onto the top of the column, and elute with the above mentioned solvent system.

10. Pool the appropriate fractions, and remove the solvent under reduced pressure. The product is isolated as a colourless crystalline solid (63%, m.p. 52–53°C) which displays the appropriate spectroscopic data.[45]

^aBicyclo[2.2.1]hept-2-ene dicarboxylic acid dimethyl ester[47] was prepared according to literature methods.

---

9. Furan annelation

The furan annelation reaction represents a new method for the preparation of this important class of compounds. Furans are widely found in nature, and highly functionalised furans are desirable targets in total synthesis work, either as products themselves, or as intermediates. Commercially available or readily accessible furans are usually limited to substitution at the more reactive 2- and 5-positions of the ring. The need for the preparation of furans with substitution at other positions on the ring, or with sensitive functional groups present, led to the development in 1987 of a palladium-catalysed method for their preparation.[48]

The original work used β-keto esters and propargyl carbonates as substrates. Under palladium(0) catalysis, these react to give *exo*-methylenefurans

46, which isomerise readily under acidic conditions to give the corresponding furans **47**.

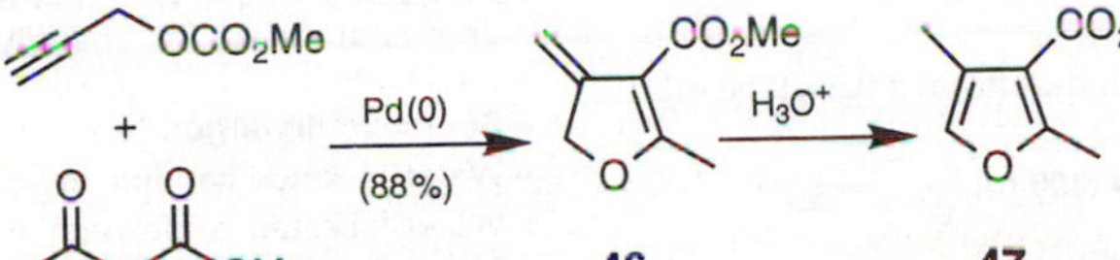

Tsuji found that the β-keto esters could be replaced with acetylacetone derivatives, to give acetyl furans, and with 1,3-cyclohexanedione, to give a ring-fused furan system. A range of alkylated propargyl carbonates could also be used. In all cases the yields of the reaction were excellent.

The key intermediate in the mechanism of the reaction is the formation of a σ-allenylpalladium complex **48** together with methoxide which serves as an *in situ* base to deprotonate the nucleophile.

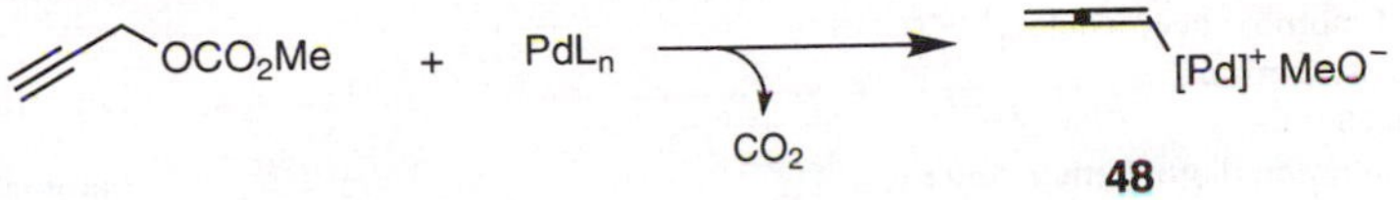

After nucleophilic attack on the central allenyl carbon, the resulting π-allyl intermediate is trapped by an intramolecular nucleophilic reaction, giving the initial 3-alkylidene-2,3-dihydrofuran product, and regenerating the palladium(0) catalyst. A mildly acidic work-up allows aromatisation, giving the final product.

This approach to highly substituted furans was used in the synthesis of a key intermediate in an approach to the synthesis of neoliacine.[49] The method used is described in the Protocol 8. The reaction proceeds very smoothly, giving high yields of furans such as **49** and has been performed on a large scale without complications.

Protocol 8.
Synthesis of methyl 4-methyl 2-(methoxymethyl)-3-furoate
(Structure 49)

Caution! All procedures should be carried out in a fume hood. Disposable vinyl or latex gloves and safety glasses should be worn.

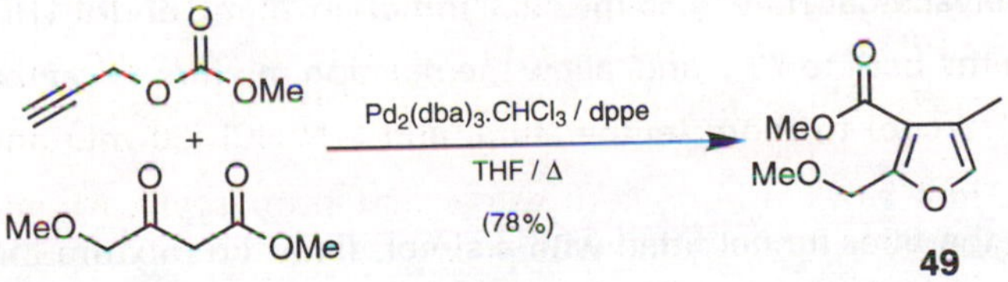

Protocol 8 *Continued*

Equipment

- Magnetic stirrer
- Oil bath
- Two-necked, round-bottomed flask (250 mL)
- Separating funnel
- Erlenmeyer flask (250 mL)
- Thermometer
- Septum
- Teflon-covered magnetic stirrer bar
- Needles (medium gauge)

- All-glass syringes with a needle-lock Luer (volume appropriate for quantity of solution to be transferred)
- Source of dry argon
- Water-jacketed condenser
- Water-jacketed short-path distillation apparatus
- Filter funnel with sinter

Material

- Dry THF, 120 mL — **flammable, irritant**
- Tris(dibenzylideneacetone)dipalladium(0) chloroform (FW 1035), 0.35 g, 0.34 mmol
- 1,2-Bis(diphenylphosphino)ethane (dppe) (FW 398.4), 0.28 g, 0.70 mmol
- Methyl 2-propynyl carbonate[a] (FW 114), 4.02 g, 35.2 mmol — **flammable, irritant**
- Methyl 4-methoxyacetoacetate[b] (FW 146.1), 4.56 mL, 35.2 mmol — **irritant**
- 2 N HCl, 20 mL — **corrosive**
- Technical grade diethyl ether, 150 mL — **flammable, irritant**
- Saturated aqueous sodium hydrogencarbonate solution, 60 mL
- Saturated brine, 30 mL
- Sodium sulfate

1. Clean all glassware, syringes, needles, and the stirrer bar and dry overnight in an oven before use.

2. Clamp the two-necked flask (containing the stirrer bar) fitted with the condenser, in the oil bath above the stirrer hotplate. Fit the argon source to the top of the condenser. Flush the assembly with argon by allowing the gas to flow through the flask for a few seconds before sealing the apparatus by fitting the septum.

3. Remove the septum, moderate the argon flow, and put the palladium catalyst (0.35 g, 0.34 mmol) and dppe (0.28 g, 0.70 mmol) into the flask. Flush with argon for a few seconds before replacing the septum.

4. Charge the flask with dry THF (80 mL) using a syringe by puncturing the septum on the reaction flask. A red solution should form.

5. Add methyl 2-propynyl carbonate (4.02 g, 35.2 mmol) in 20 mL of dry THF *via* a syringe at room temperature with stirring, followed by methyl 4-methoxyacetoacetate (4.56 mL, 35.2 mmol) in 20 mL of dry THF.

6. Warm the bath to 70°C and allow the reaction mixture to reflux for 3 h.

7. Allow to cool to room temperature, add 2 N HCl (20 mL) and stir for 10 min.

8. Using the filter funnel fitted with a sinter, filter the mixture through Celite

with suction to remove any inorganic material, and rinse the flask and filter cake with diethyl ether (3 × 25 mL).

9. Neutralise the filtrate by washing with sodium hydrogencarbonate (3 × 20 mL).

10. Transfer to a separating funnel and separate the two layers. Extract the aqueous layer with diethyl ether (3 × 25 mL). Combine the organic layers and wash with saturated brine (30 mL).

11. Transfer the diethyl ether layer to an Erlenmeyer flask. Dry the layer over anhydrous sodium sulfate and filter through a filter paper. Concentrate the filtrate under reduced pressure using a rotary evaporator.

12. Transfer the residue to a water-jacketed short-path distillation apparatus equipped with a thermometer. Distil the crude product under reduced pressure to obtain methyl 4-methyl-2-(methoxymethyl)-3-furoate (b.p. 165°C/0.8 mmHg) to give a yellow oil which displays appropriate spectroscopic data.[49]

[a] Methyl 2-propynyl carbonate was prepared using a literature method.[49]
[b] Methyl 4-methoxyacetoacetate was distilled prior to use.

References

1. Heck, R. F. *Palladium Reagents in Organic Synthesis*; Academic Press: London, **1985**.
2. Tsuji, J. *Synthesis* **1990**, 739–749.
3. Mitchell, T. N. *Synthesis* **1992**, 803–815.
4. Trost, B. M.; Sharma, S.; Schmidt, T. *J. Am. Chem. Soc.* **1992**, *114*, 7903–7904.
5. Jeffery, T. *Synthesis* **1987**, 70–71.
6. Noyori, R. *Asymmetric Catalysis in Organic Synthesis*; Wiley: New York, **1994**.
7. Sato, Y.; Nukui, S.; Sodeoka, M.; Shibasaki, M. *Tetrahedron* **1994**, *50*, 371–382.
8. Trost, B. M.; Shi, Y. *J. Am. Chem. Soc.* **1993**, *115*, 9421–9438.
9. Grigg, R.; Fretwell, P.; Meerholtz, C.; Siridharan, V. *Tetrahedron* **1994**, *50*, 359–370.
10. Overman, L. E.; Ricca, D. J.; Tran, V. D. *J. Am. Chem. Soc.* **1993**, *115*, 2042–2044.
11. Ritter, K. *Synthesis* **1993**, 735–762.
12. Farina, V.; Krishnan, B. *J. Am. Chem. Soc.* **1991**, *113*, 9585–9595.
13. Houpis, I. N. *Tetrahedron Lett.* **1991**, *32*, 6675–6678.
14. Farina, V.; Krishnan, B.; Marshall, D. R.; Roth, G. P. *J. Org. Chem.* **1993**, *58*, 5434–5444.
15. Nicolaou, K. C.; Chakraborty, T. K.; Piscopio, A. D.; Minowa, N.; Bertinato, P. *J. Am. Chem. Soc.* **1993**, *115*, 4419–4420.
16. Burke, S. D.; Piscopio, A. D.; Kort, M. E.; Matulenko, M. A.; Parker, M. H.; Armistead, D. M.; Shankaran, K. *J. Org. Chem.* **1994**, *59*, 332–347.
17. Hirama, M.; Tokuda, M.; Fujiwara, K. *Synlett* **1991** 651–653.
18. Andersson, C. M.; Hallberg, A. *J. Org. Chem.* **1988**, *53*, 235–239.

19. Renaldo, A. F.; Labadie, J. W.; Stille, J. K. *Org. Synth., Coll. Vol.* **1993**, *8*, 268–274.
20. Stille, J. K. *Angew. Chem., Int. Ed. Eng.* **1986**, *25*, 508–524.
21. Scott, W. J.; Crisp, G. T.; Stille, J. K. *Org. Synth., Coll. Vol.* **1993**, *8*, 97–103.
22. McMurry, J. E.; Scott, W. J. *Tetrahedron Lett.* **1983**, *24*, 979–982.
23. Kozyrod, R. P.; Morgan, J.; Pinhey, J. T. *Aust. J. Chem.* **1985**, *38*, 1147–1153.
24. Miyaura, N.; Suzuki, A. *J. Chem. Soc., Chem. Commun.* **1979**, 866–867.
25. Watanabe, T.; Miyaura, N.; Suzuki, A. *Synlett* **1992**, 207–210.
26. Cox, P. J.; Wang, W.; Snieckus, V. *Tetrahedron Lett.* **1992**, *33*, 2253–2256.
27. Ishiyama, T.; Oh-e, T.; Miyaura, N.; Suzuki, A. *Tetrahedron Lett.* **1992**, *33*, 4465–4468.
28. Ishiyama, T.; Miyaura, N.; Suzuki, A. *Tetrahedron Lett.* **1991**, *32*, 6923–6926.
29. Miyaura, N.; Satoh, Y.; Hara, S.; Suzuki, A. *Bull. Chem. Soc. Jpn.* **1986**, *59*, 2029–2031.
30. Miyaura, N.; Suginome, H.; Suzuki, A. *Tetrahedron Lett.* **1984**, *25*, 761–764.
31. Ratovelomanana, V.; Linstrumelle, G. *Tetrahedron Lett.* **1981**, *22*, 315–318.
32. Stary, I.; Zajicek, J.; Kocovsky, P. *Tetrahedron* **1992**, *48*, 7229–7250.
33. Trost, B. M.; Kuo, G. H.; Benneche, T. *J. Am. Chem. Soc.* **1988**, *110*, 621–622.
34. Trost, B. M. *Angew. Chem., Int. Ed. Engl.* **1989**, *28*, 1173–1192.
35. Genet, J. P.; Piau, F. *J. Org. Chem.* **1981**, *46*, 2414–2417.
36. Frost, C. G.; Howarth, J.; Williams, J. M. J. *Tetrahedron: Asymmetry* **1992**, *3*, 1089–1122.
37. Trost, B. M.; Dietsche, D. J. *J. Am. Chem. Soc.* **1973**, *95*, 8200–8201.
38. Leutenegger, U.; Umbricht, G.; Fahrni, C.; Matt, P. V.; Pfaltz, A. *Tetrahedron* **1992**, *48*, 2143–2156.
39. Pfaltz, A. *Acc. Chem. Res.* **1993**, *26*, 339–345.
40. Yamaguchi, M.; Shima, T.; Yamagishi, T.; Hidi, M. *Tetrahedron Lett.* **1990**, *31*, 5049–5052.
41. Dawson, G. J.; Frost, C. G.; Martin, C. J.; Williams, J. M. J.; Coote, S. J. *Tetrahedron Lett.* **1993**, *34*, 7793–7796.
42. Frost, C. G.; Williams, J. M. J. *Tetrahedron Lett.* **1993**, *34*, 2015–2018.
43. Korach, M.; Nielsen, D. R.; Rideout, W. H. *Org. Synth., Coll. Vol.* **1973**, *5*, 414–418.
44. Trost, B. M.; Lautens, M.; Chan, C.; Jebaratnam, D. J.; Mueller, T. *J. Am. Chem. Soc.* **1991**, *113*, 636–644.
45. Trost, B. M.; Renaut, P. *J. Am. Chem. Soc.* **1982**, *104*, 6668–6672.
46. Trost, B. M.; Marrs, C. M. *J. Am. Chem. Soc.* **1993**, *115*, 6636–6645.
47. Zalkow, L. H.; Hill, R. H. *Tetrahedron* **1975**, *31*, 831–840.
48. Minami, I.; Yuhara, M.; Watanabe, H.; Tsuji, J. *J. Organomet. Chem.* **1987**, *334*, 225–242.
49. Greeves, N.; Torode, J. S. *Synthesis* **1993**, 1109–1112.

3

Organoiron chemistry 1: ferrocene and dienyl iron tricarbonyl cation chemistry

CHRISTOPHER J. RICHARDS

1. Introduction

This chapter deals with two differing applications of organoiron chemistry to organic synthesis. In the first section the chemistry of ferrocene is examined, in particular the reactions required for the construction of ferrocene-based ligands, which have found wide usage in asymmetric catalysis. In contrast, the cationic dienyl iron tricarbonyl complexes studied in the second section have been employed directly in many elegant total syntheses of complex organic structures.

The elucidation of the structure of ferrocene in 1952 was effectively the birth of a new area of research that has led to much of the fascinating chemistry described in this book. Ferrocene was first reported in 1951, isolated accidentally during the attempted synthesis of fulvalene by reaction of cyclopentadienyl magnesium bromide with iron(III) chloride.[1] Initially, the structure of the orange crystalline solid was believed to contain two cyclopentadienyl rings attached to an iron(II) centre by sigma bonds, as represented by **1**. However, there were a number of anomalies arising from this representation which resulted in two groups, led by G. Wilkinson and R. B. Woodward in the United States and E. O Fischer in Germany, independently proposing the novel sandwich structure **2** in which all of the carbon atoms are equidistant from the metal.[2]

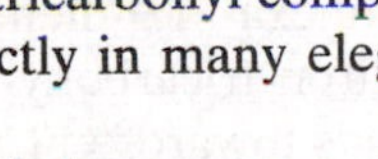

1 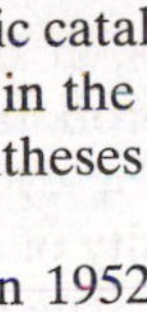   **2**

This type of structure, which arises as a result of the overlap of organic ligand π-orbitals with metal orbitals, had not previously been used to explain experimental observations. Its proposal, and the subsequent synthesis of further complexes containing π-bonded organic ligands, required a leap of imagination for which Fischer and Wilkinson were awarded the Nobel prize for chemistry in 1973. An account of this period of discovery was subsequently written by Wilkinson.[3]

Interestingly, a π-bonded organometallic complex had been synthesised long before ferrocene. In 1930, Reihlen and fellow German co-workers reported that the reaction between $Fe(CO)_5$ and butadiene produced a yellow oil that analysed as $C_4H_6Fe(CO)_3$. Structure **3** was tentatively suggested for this compound.[4] However, it was not until 1958 that the true nature of this material was realised when Pauson and Hallam synthesised an iron tricarbonyl complex of cyclohexa- 1,3-diene and put forward evidence to favour the planar structure **4**, in which the π-orbitals are utilised in the bonding.[5]

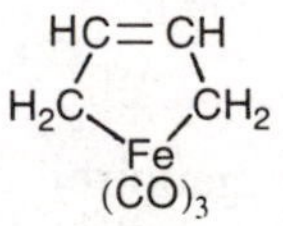

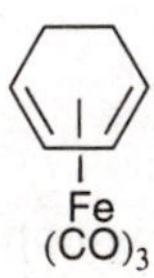

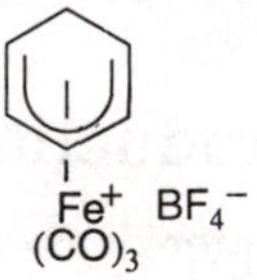

Shortly afterwards, in 1960, Fischer discovered that addition of triphenylcarbenium tetrafluoroborate to η^4-cyclohexa- 1,3-diene iron tricarbonyl **4** produced the novel η^5-cyclohexadienyl iron tricarbonyl cation **5** as a stable salt,[6] and the reactivity of such compounds towards C-C bond formation was soon being explored. The application of organometallic complexes to organic synthesis had begun.

2. Ferrocene chemistry

2.1 Electrophilic substitution

As ferrocene was readily available in large quantities, investigations into its chemistry began almost immediately after its discovery. The name ferrocene was coined as a consequence of the chemistry observed for the cyclopentadienyl rings of the molecule. They were found to undergo electrophilic substitution in the same manner as benzene itself, and thus gave the appearance of having aromatic character. Ferrocene results from the combination of two six-electron cyclopentadienyl anions with Fe^{2+} to give a neutral species in which the aromatic character of the organic ligands is retained. The ligands donate electrons into empty metal orbitals, and back donation of electron density from the metal to the cyclopentadienyl groups results in a strong two-way bonding interaction that accounts for the stability of the system. Detailed molecular orbital calculations accounting for the bonding in ferrocene have been performed.[7]

A range of mild electrophilic reagents give substituted ferrocene derivatives. The reactions most frequently employed are formylation to ferrocenecarbaldehyde **6**, acylation to **7** and **8**, and aminomethylation to **9** and **10**. All of these reactions result in carbon–carbon bond formation and simple derivatives **6–10** have subsequently been employed in the synthesis of numerous ferrocene derivatives. The degree of substitution is readily controlled through the reaction conditions and the stoichiometry of the reagents. The second substituent is always introduced onto the second ring, resulting in a 1,1′-disubstituted product.

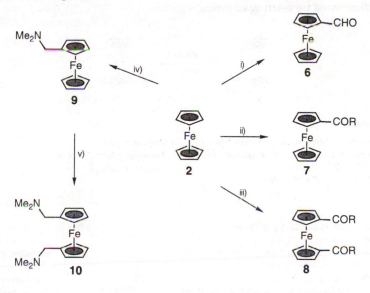

i) PhMeNCHO, $AlCl_3$ ii) 1 eq. RCOCl, 1 eq. $AlCl_3$ iii) 2 eq. RCOCl, 2 eq. $AlCl_3$ iv) $Me_2NCH_2CH_2NMe_2$, AcOH v) $EtNH_2$, Li, $FeCl_2$

The mechanism of Friedel–Crafts acylation is believed to involve rate-determining *exo* attack of the acylating species generating an intermediate **11**, analogous to the Wheland intermediates generated during electrophilic substitution of arenes. Rapid loss of a proton from **11** results in formation of the neutral product **7**.[8]

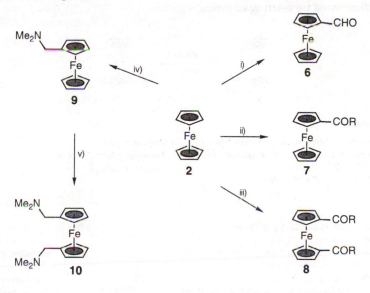

The five-membered cyclopentadienyl rings of ferrocene are relatively electron rich, such that acylation takes place at a rate 10^6 times faster than for benzene, a factor that results in the rapid generation of substituted ferrocenes under mild conditions. Aluminium chloride-promoted Friedel–Crafts acetylation of ferrocene to give acetylferrocene **7a** is representative.

Protocol 1.
Electrophilic substitution. Preparation of acetylferrocene (Structure 7a)

Caution! All procedures should be carried out in an efficient fume hood. Eye protection must be worn at all times.

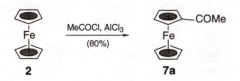

Equipment
- Single-necked, round-bottomed flask (250 mL)
- Teflon-covered egg-shaped magnetic stirrer bar (3 cm length)
- Calcium chloride drying tube
- Magnetic stirrer
- Separating funnel (250 mL)
- Ice-water bath

Materials
- Ferrocene (FW 186.0), 20.0 g, 0.108 mol
- Dry dichloromethane,[a] 90 mL — **toxic, irritant**
- Acetyl chloride (FW 78.5), 9.25 g, 0.118 mol — **corrosive, flammable**
- Anhydrous aluminium chloride (FW 133.3), 14.4 g, 0.108 mol — **corrosive**, **moisture sensitive**
- Technical dichloromethane for work up, *ca.* 70 mL — **toxic, irritant**

1. Ensure that the stirrer bar and glassware are clean, and that they have been dried thoroughly in an oven at 120 °C for 2 h.

2. Add ferrocene (20.0 g, 0.108 mol) to the 250 mL round-bottomed flask and dissolve with stirring in dry dichloromethane[a] (90 mL).

3. To the resultant dark orange/red solution add acetyl chloride (9.25 g, 0.118 mol); attach the drying tube to the flask and immerse the flask in an ice-water bath at 0–5 °C.

4. Weigh out anhydrous aluminium chloride (14.4 g, 0.108 mol) in a glass beaker. Add this in approximately 10 portions to the reaction mixture, allowing approximately 2 min between each addition for heat exchange. Replace the drying tube after each addition. The reaction begins on addition of the first portion of aluminium chloride and the reaction mixture darkens considerably.

5. Stir the reaction for 2 h during which time the ice-water bath is allowed to warm to room temperature.

6. Recool the solution by placing it in a fresh ice-water bath. Remove the drying tube and hydrolyse the reaction mixture by the **slow** addition of 4 × 5 mL portions of cold water. Then add a further 30 mL of cold water more rapidly.

7. Transfer the mixture to a 250 mL separating funnel and separate the organic (lower) phase. As both phases are very dark, take care to ensure a clean separation between the two. The divide between the two phases will become more apparent as it reaches the narrow bottom section of the separating funnel.

8. Extract the aqueous phase with two 25 mL portions of technical dichloromethane. Combine the organic extracts and wash with 25 mL of 5% sodium hydroxide solution followed by 25 mL of saturated aqueous sodium chloride solution. Dry the organic solution over sodium sulfate for 10 min, then filter off the drying agent. Wash the sodium sulfate with 5 mL portions of dichloromethane until it is no longer coloured red from the product. Remove the solvent on a rotary evaporator to give acetylferrocene (19.6 g, 80%) as a red/orange solid showing appropriate spectroscopic data [δ_H (CDCl$_3$), 2.40 (3 H, s, Me), 4.21 (5 H, s, FcH), 4.51 (2 H, brs, FcH), 4.78 (2H, brs, FcH)]. A small portion may be recrystallised from ethyl acetate/ petroleum ether (40-60). Literature m.p. = 85–86°C.[9]

[a] Distil from calcium hydride under an atmosphere of nitrogen.

The range of aromatic substitution reactions that may be performed on ferrocene is limited by the ease with which ferrocene is oxidised to the ferrocenium ion. For example, addition of NO$_2$+ and halogens results in formation of the ferrocenium ion, thus preventing direct formation of nitro- and halogen-substituted ferrocenes. However, such compounds may be generated from other substituted derivatives which are in turn synthesised from metalated ferrocenes.

2.2 Substitution reactions α to ferrocene. Generation of intermediate α-ferrocenylcarbenium ions from α-ferrocenyl alcohols

Much of the chemistry of ferrocene derivatives is concerned with carbon centres directly attached to a cyclopentadienyl ring. The proximity of the metal centre strongly influences both the rate and stereochemical outcome of reactions occurring at this position, which are characterised by the intermediacy of α-ferrocenylcarbenium ions. In order to generate such species, a leaving group must first be introduced at the α-position. This may be readily achieved by reduction of a carbonyl group, introduced during Friedel–Crafts acylation, to the corresponding alcohol.

The relatively high electron density associated with the cyclopentadienyl rings of ferrocene reduces the electrophilicity of an attached carbonyl group. As a result, reduction by sodium borohydride, normally an effective reagent for ketone reduction, is in this instance very sluggish. Instead, reduction may be more effectively achieved with lithium aluminium hydride. The following protocol describing the synthesis of α-ferrocenylethanol **12a** is representative.

Protocol 2.
Lithium aluminium hydride reduction of acetylferrocene (Structure 7a) to α-ferrocenylethanol (Structure 12a)

Caution! All procedures should be carried out in an efficient fume hood. Eye protection must be worn at all times.

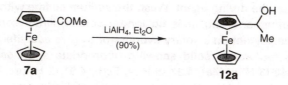

Equipment

- Two-necked, round-bottomed flask (500 mL)
- Teflon-covered egg-shaped magnetic stirrer bar (4 cm length)
- Liebig condenser
- Pressure equalising dropping funnel (250 mL)
- Calcium chloride drying tubes (× 2)

- Erlenmeyer flask (250 mL)
- Glass funnel
- Magnetic stirrer
- Separating funnel (500 mL)
- Büchner funnel
- Büchner flask

Materials

- Acetylferrocene (FW 228.1), 15.0 g, 0.066 mol **harmful**
- Lithium aluminium hydride (FW 38.0), 5 g, 0.132 mol **flammable, caution! lithium aluminium hydride reacts violently with water evolving hydrogen**

- Dry diethyl ether,[a] 250 mL **flammable, irritant**
- Ethyl acetate **flammable, irritant**
- Petroleum ether (40-60) **flammable**

1. Ensure that the glassware is clean and that it has been dried thoroughly in an oven at 120 °C for 2 h.

2. Fit the Liebig condenser and the pressure equalising dropping funnel (250 mL) to the 500 mL two-necked, round-bottomed flask containing the magnetic stirrer bar. Attach calcium chloride drying tubes to the condenser and dropping funnel and allow the apparatus to cool.

3. Add lithium aluminium hydride (5.0 g, 0.132 mol) to the round-bottomed flask followed by dry diethyl ether[a] (100 mL). Add acetylferrocene (15.0 g, 0.066 mol) to the 250 mL Erlenmeyer flask and dissolve in dry diethyl ether (140 mL). Pour this red solution into the dropping funnel and wash the Erlenmeyer flask with an additional 10 mL of dry diethyl ether.

4. Add the acetylferrocene solution to the grey suspension of lithium aluminium hydride at such a rate as to maintain gentle reflux. When the addition is complete stir at room temperature for an additional 10 min. The reaction is complete when the colour of the solution has changed from red to dark yellow.

5. Charge the dropping funnel with ethyl acetate' (10 mL). Add this dropwise to the reaction mixture and stir at room temperature overnight.

6. **Cautiously** add water (10 mL) dropwise (if the ethyl acetate has completely destroyed the excess lithium aluminium hydride no reaction will be observed at this stage). Filter the resultant mixture with a Büchner funnel and flask, washing the collected aluminium salts with diethyl ether (2 × 20 mL). Transfer the filtrate to a separating funnel and wash with water (100 mL). Dry over magnesium sulfate, filter and remove the solvent on a rotary evaporator to give about 13.5 g of a dark yellow crystalline solid. Recrystallise from ethyl acetate/petroleum ether (40-60) to give pure α-ferrocenylethanol displaying the appropriate spectroscopic and microanalytical data [δ_H (CDCl$_3$) 1.44 (3 H, d, J = 6 Hz, Me), 1.84 (1 H, d, J = 5 Hz, OH), 4.16–4.18 (2 H, m, FcH), 4.20 (5 H, s, FcH), 4.21–4.23 (2 H, m, FcH), 4.55 (1 H, quintet, J = 6 Hz, CHMeOH)]. Literature m.p. = 73–75 °C.[10]

---

^{a} Distil from sodium benzophenone ketyl under a nitrogen atmosphere.

The addition of strong acids to α-ferrocenyl alcohols **12** results in rapid formation of α-ferrocenylcarbenium ions **13**, *via* protonation of the alcohol oxygen and loss of water. Unlike the vast majority of purely organic carbenium ions, these species are easily isolated as stable tetrafluoroborate or hexafluorophosphate salts. Their stability stems from the delocalisation of positive charge over the ferrocenyl group, as a consequence of the overlap between the empty p-orbital of the α-sp^2 hybridised carbon and filled metal orbitals. This delocalisation is represented by the two canonical forms **13x** and **13y**, with the actual structure of α-ferrocenylcarbenium ions lying somewhere between the two.

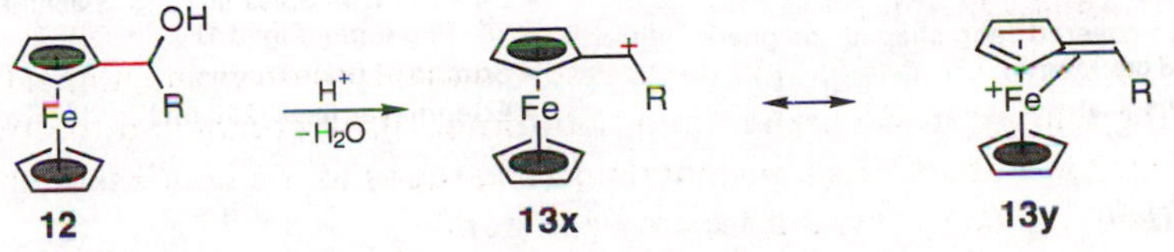

Metal participation in stabilising these species dictates that during their formation, the leaving group departs away (*exo*) from the iron so as to maximise overlap between the metal orbitals and the rehybridising α-carbon (**12** to **13**). Nucleophilic addition to α-ferrocenylcarbenium ions proceeds *via* the reverse mechanism, the nucleophile attacking *exo* to the ferrocenyl group (**13** to **14**). Thus the overall process, **12** to **14**, proceeds with retention of configuration. Rotation about the C_1-C_α bond in **13** is largely prevented by its partial double bond character, but solutions of α-ferrocenylcarbenium ions do racemise very slowly at room temperature.

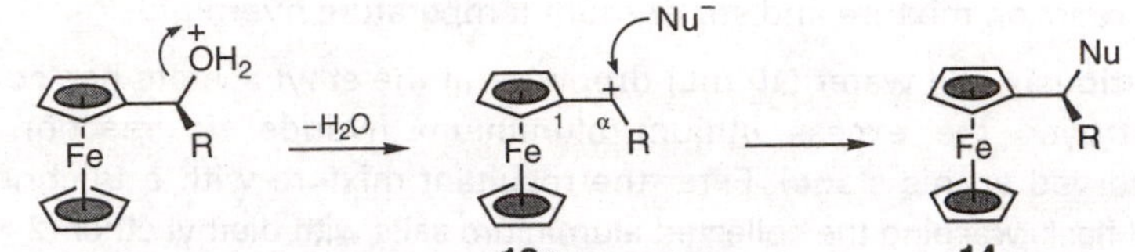

A wide range of heteroatomic nucleophiles such as amines, alcohols and thiols have been shown to add to α-ferrocenylcarbenium ions. Carbon–carbon bond formation can also be achieved by addition of silyl enol ethers.[11] The following protocol involving the generation of α-ferrocenylethylium tetrafluoroborate **13a** and its subsequent reaction with dimethylamine is representative.

Protocol 3.
Synthesis of *N,N*-dimethyl-α-ferrocenylethylamine (Structure 15)

Caution! All procedures should be carried out in an efficient fume hood. Eye protection must be worn at all times.

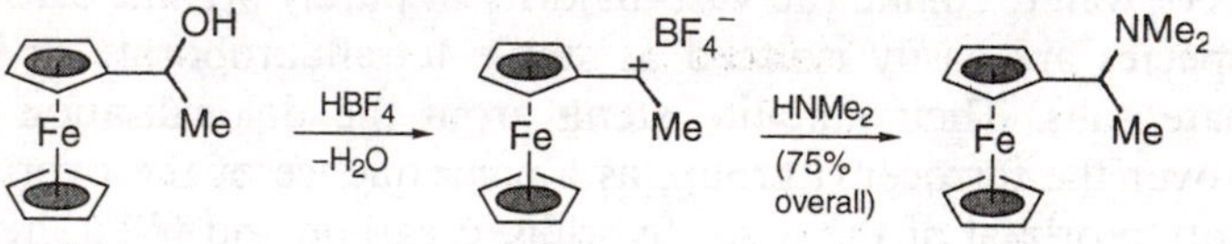

Equipment
- Two-necked, round-bottomed flask (250 mL)
- Cone/flexible tubing adapter
- Septum
- Teflon-covered egg-shaped magnetic stirrer bar (3 cm length)
- Magnetic stirrer
- Glass Luer-lock syringe (3 × 20 mL)
- Needle (3 × 15 cm, 18 gauge)
- Cannula with glass filtering attachment (30 cm, 16–18 gauge) (Fig. 3.1)
- Source of dry nitrogen
- Erlenmeyer flask (250 mL)

Materials
- α-Ferrocenylethanol (FW 230.1), 10.0 g, 0.043 mol
- Dry diethyl ether,[a] 145 mL — **flammable, irritant**
- Tetrafluoroboric acid (FW 87.8) 54% solution in diethyl ether, 7.0 mL, 0.05 mol — **flammable corrosive**
- Dry dichloromethane,[b] 125 mL — **toxic, irritant**
- Dimethylamine (FW 45.1), 40 wt.% solution in water, 50 mL — **irritant**

1. Ensure that the magnetic stirrer bar and all glassware to be used for the reaction is clean and has been in an oven at 120 °C for at least 12 h prior to use.

2. Attach the cone/flexible tubing adapter to the 250 mL two-necked round-bottomed flask containing the magnetic stirrer, connect the nitrogen source and allow the apparatus to cool under a stream of nitrogen.

3. Add α-ferrocenylethanol (10.0 g, 0.043 mol) to the flask and dissolve this with stirring in dry diethyl ether[a] (125 mL). The diethyl ether may be added with a measuring cylinder **provided this is dry**. Attach the septum to the second neck of the two-necked flask.

4. Assemble the 20 mL syringe and needle while hot (**wear gloves!**). With the plunger of the syringe down, put the needle through the septum so that the end of the needle is in the nitrogen atmosphere of the flask. Draw up nitrogen into the syringe, remove the needle from the septum and empty the syringe. Repeat this flushing process once more, refill the syringe with nitrogen and allow to cool.

5. Place the needle into the container containing 54% tetrafluoroboric acid in diethyl ether. Gently draw up the plunger, filling the syringe until it contains 7.0 mL. Place the needle through the septum of the reaction flask. Whilst rapidly stirring the yellow solution of α-ferrocenylethanol in diethyl ether, add the solution of tetrafluoroboric acid at a rate of approximately 2 mL per min. The intermediate α-ferrocenylcarbenium ion will precipitate from the solution as a dark orange solid. If a dark oil is obtained at this stage, continue to rapidly stir the reaction mixture as this should promote formation of crystalline material.

6. After the addition is complete, dismantle the syringe and needle and rinse both thoroughly with water.

7. Attach a 5 cm circle of filter paper over the glass end of the filtering cannula with wire as shown in Fig. 3.1. Briefly remove the septum from the reaction flask and push the metal end of the cannula through the bottom of the septum. Pull the cannula through and replace the septum such that the filter paper-covered glass end of the filtering cannula is now inside the reaction flask.

8. Turn off the stirrer and allow the precipitate to settle. Gently bend the cannula such that the end that is outside the reaction flask lies within a 250 mL Erlenmeyer flask as illustrated in Fig. 3.2. Push the other end into the reaction mixture and provided there is a sufficient positive pressure of nitrogen (20 mbar is normally enough) the supernatant will bleed through the cannula into the Erlenmeyer flask. Remove as much of the solvent as possible to leave the desired α-ferrocenylcarbenium ion.

9. To wash the product, first pull the glass end of the filtering cannula back to

Protocol 3. *Continued*

the top of the flask. Using another 20 mL syringe with needle attached, dried and flushed with nitrogen as before, add 20 mL of dry diethyl ether to the reaction flask. Briefly stir the resulting suspension and filter by pushing the end of the cannula back into the solvent. Again remove as much of the solvent as possible before drying the product under a stream of nitrogen, created by removal of the septum. Remove the cannula from the septum and wash it through with acetone.

10. When the product is dry, replace the septum. Using a fresh syringe and needle, again dried and flushed as before, add dry dichloromethane[b] to the reaction flask. With stirring, dissolve the α-ferrocenylcarbenium ion to give a dark red solution, then place the flask in an ice-water bath. Remove the septum and add 50 mL of dimethylamine (40 wt.% solution in water). After the addition the flask should be disconnected from the nitrogen supply, as there is no further need to protect the reaction from oxygen and water. The reaction is complete when the colour of the reaction mixture has changed from a dark red colour to an orange/yellow colour.

11. Transfer the reaction mixture to a separating funnel. Remove the organic layer and wash the aqueous layer with a further 50 mL of dichloromethane. Combine the organic extracts and dry over sodium sulfate. Filter, washing the sodium sulfate with additional dichloromethane, and remove the solvent on a rotary evaporator. Distil the product under reduced pressure (b.p. 120 °C/2 mmHg) to give a dark red-brown oil (8.4 g, 75%) displaying the appropriate spectroscopic data [δ_H (CDCl$_3$) 1.45 (3 H, d, J = 7 Hz, CH(NMe$_2$)$\underline{\text{Me}}$), 2.08 (6 H, s, CH(N$\underline{\text{Me}}_2$)Me), 3.59 (1 H, q, J = 7 Hz, C$\underline{\text{H}}$(NMe$_2$)Me), 4.10–4.16 (4 H, m, FcH), 4.12 (5 H, s, FcH)]. The distillation should be done as rapidly as possible since prolonged heating of the amine results in a significant level of decomposition.

[a] Distil from sodium benzophenone ketyl under an atmosphere of nitrogen.
[b] Distil from calcium hydride under an atmosphere of nitrogen.

The intermediate α-ferrocenylcarbenium ion need not be isolated in these substitution reactions. Alternatively, introduction of a good leaving group such as acetoxy (OAc) or an ammonium ion at the α-position enables substitution reactions to be carried out directly under mild conditions.

2.3 Routes to optically pure ferrocene derivatives

The presence of four different groups attached to the α-carbon obviously results in a tetrahedral chiral centre. When the compound containing such a centre is *N,N*-dimethyl-α-ferrocenylethylamine **15**, separation of the two enantiomers is readily achieved by a classical resolution with tartaric acid.

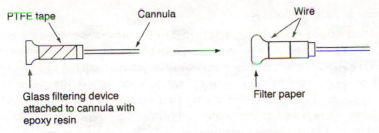

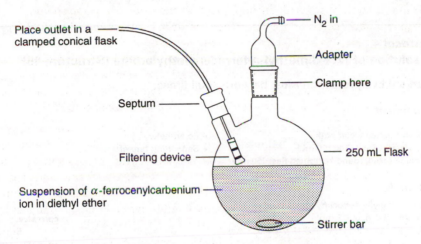

The two diastereomeric tartrate salts of **15** have significantly differing solubilities, enabling them to be easily separated. Subsequent treatment with base releases optically pure (S)-(−)-**15** and (R)-(+)-**15**, $[\alpha]_D$ = −14.1 and +14.1 respectively.[12] Due to the ease of this resolution, N,N-dimethyl-α-ferrocenylethylamine **15** has become the key starting material for the synthesis of many optically active ferrocene derivatives.

The growing importance of **15** has lead to the development of alternative methodologies to obtain this compound enantiomerically pure. One of the most noteworthy uses the lipase from *Pseudomonas fluorescens* to effect a selective esterification of racemic 1-ferrocenylethanol **12a**. At 50% conversion the unreacted alcohol (S)-(+)-**12a** was isolated with an enantiomeric excess of 92% and the acetate **16** had an enantiomeric purity of 96%. Simply stirring this acetate with aqueous dimethylamine resulted in formation of (R)-(+)-N,N-dimethyl-α-ferrocenylethylamine with $[\alpha]_D$ + 12.8, corresponding to an optical purity of 91%.[13]

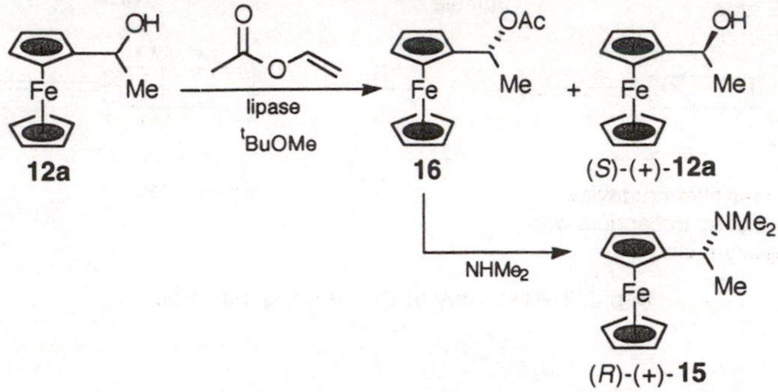

Protocol 4.
Resolution of *N,N*-dimethyl-α-ferrocenylethylamine (Structure 15)

Caution! Eye protection must be worn at all times.

Equipment

- Thermostatted water bath
- Erlenmeyer flask (2 × 100 mL)
- Single-necked, round-bottomed flask (50 mL)

- Polarimeter
- Separating funnel

Materials

- *N,N*-Dimethyl-α-ferrocenylethylamine
  (FW 257.2), 5 g, 0.019 mol   **corrosive, toxic**
- (*R*)-(+)-Tartaric acid (FW 150.1), 5 g, 0.033 mol   **irritant**
- Methanol, 100 mL   **flammable, toxic**
- 20% aqueous sodium hydroxide, 50 mL   **corrosive, toxic**
- Diethyl ether, 20 mL   **flammable, irritant**
- Acetone, 10 mL   **flammable, irritant**

1. Place racemic *N,N*-dimethyl-α-ferrocenylethylamine (5 g, 0.019 mol) and (*R*)-(+)-tartaric acid (2.92 g, 0.019 mol) in separate Erlenmeyer flasks and dissolve each in 10 mL of methanol. Clamp both Erlenmeyer flasks into a thermostatted water bath, pre-set at a temperature of 55 °C.

2. When the solutions in both flasks have reached 55 °C, pour the tartaric acid solution into the amine solution with stirring. Turn off the waterbath and allow this to cool slowly overnight. The ideal rate of cooling is in the order of 2–5 °C per hour.

3. In the next laboratory session, collect the resultant amine tartrate salt by suction filtration and wash with a few mL of cold methanol. Retain and label the mother liquor from the filtration and keep for later use (see step 6).

4. Add the tartrate amine salt to 10 mL of 20% aqueous sodium hydroxide in a separating funnel, and extract the resulting free amine with 3 × 10 mL portions of dichloromethane. Combine the organic extracts, dry over

sodium sulfate, filter (washing the sodium sulfate with additional dichloro-methane) and remove the solvent on a rotary evaporator.

5. Repeat steps 1 to 4 on all of the amine obtained at the end of step 4. The following ratio of materials is employed; 1 g amine, 0.58 g of (*R*)-(+)-tartaric acid, 2 × 2.6 mL of methanol. On converting back to the free amine, remove residual solvent by placing the material under vacuum (< 1 mmHg) at room temperature for a minimum of 1 h. If a Kugelrohr bulb-to-bulb distillation apparatus is available, quickly distil the amine (b.p. 120°C/2 mmHg). Optically pure material should be obtained with $[\alpha]_D^{25} = -14.1$ (*c* 1.6, EtOH). If the optical rotation of the amine is lower, steps 1–4 must be repeated once more.

6. Transfer the mother liquor from the first crystallisation into a 50 mL round-bottomed flask and using a rotary evaporator reduce the volume of this material to *ca.* 5 mL. Slowly add diethyl ether until material just begins to precipitate from solution and stand the flask in a refrigerator overnight.

7. In the next laboratory session, filter off the resultant crystals, washing with a few mL of cold diethyl ether/methanol (1:1). Recrystallise from acetone/water (10:1), allowing 16 mL of solvent for every gram of salt. Wash the product with a few mL of cold acetone/water (10:1) and recrystallise once more from this same solvent mixture.

8. Release the amine from the amine tartrate salt as before. Dry under vacuum (< 1 mmHg) for a minimum of 1 h, or preferably Kugelrohr distil. This material should now be optically pure with $[\alpha]_D^{25} = +14.1$

In addition to being a component of tetrahedral chiral centres, ferrocene compounds with two different substituents on the same cyclopentadienyl ring display planar chirality. For example, the generalised structure **17** where X and Y represent two different substituents is non-superimposible upon its mirror image **ent-17** such that compounds of this sort may be separated into, or synthesised as, their constituent enantiomers. Separation may be achieved through classical resolution where X or Y is a suitable functionality, typically a carboxylic acid.

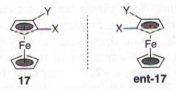

17   **ent-17**

Generally though, planar chirality is introduced by means of an attached tetrahedral chiral centre in reactions that display high diastereoselectivity. The most frequently used examples proceed *via* tne *ortho*-lithiation of optically pure **15**, leading to the diastereoisomers **18** and **19** in a ratio of 96:4.[12]

Subsequent treatment with an electrophile and removal of the minor diastereoisomer by chromatography or recrystallisation has led to the synthesis of numerous optically pure ferrocene derivatives, displaying both planar and tetrahedral chirality. The only major disadvantage of this methodology is that all of the products contain a methyl substituent which cannot be easily removed or exchanged.

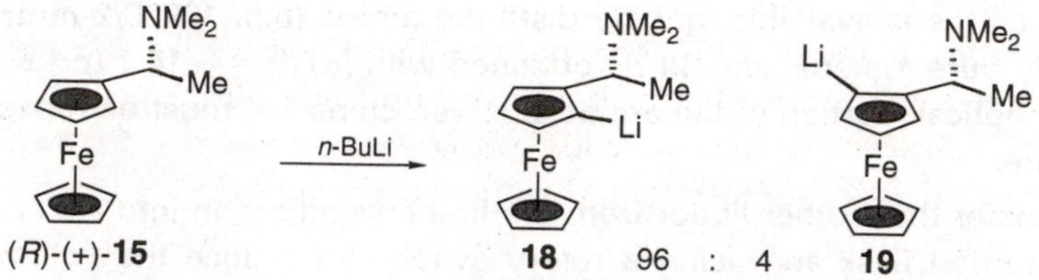

To overcome this problem the ferrocenyl acetal **20** was developed, in which the acetal functionality directs the formation of a single diastereoisomer during the lithiation and electrophile quench sequence. Subsequent addition of aqueous acid then releases enantiomerically pure 2-substituted ferrocenealdehyes **21a–d**.[14] A further advantage of this method is that **20** and its corresponding enantiomer are synthesised from commercially available (*S*)- or (*R*)-1,2,4-butanetriol respectively, thus avoiding the need to perform a classical resolution.

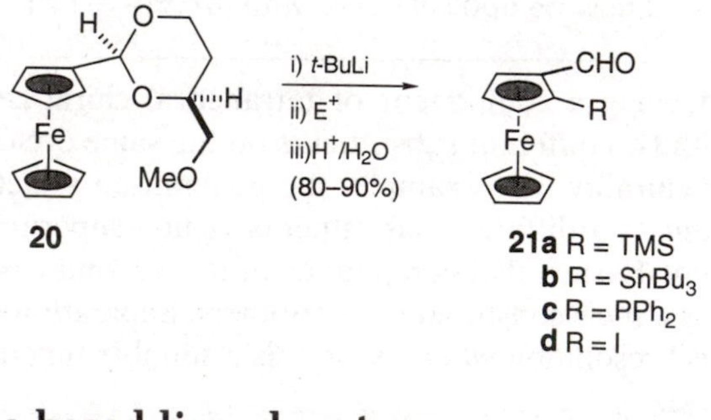

2.4 Ferrocene-based ligand systems

In addition to displaying both planar and tetrahedral chirality, ferrocene derivatives display a substituent geometry that is not available with conventional organic scaffolds. As a consequence, they have found widespread application as novel ligands in a number of transition metal-catalysed asymmetric reactions. For example, **22**, generated by addition of chlorodiphenylphosphine to **18** and **19** followed by recrystallisation, is a highly effective ligand for the palladium-catalysed Grignard cross-coupling of phenyl(trimethylsilyl)methylmagnesium bromide with vinyl bromide.[15]

More widely used are ferrocene derivatives in which both cyclopentadienyl rings are functionalised by diphenylphosphine. The parent to this series of compounds is the 1′,2-bis(diphenylphosphino) derivative **23** and its enantiomer, which are also synthesised from optically pure (*S*)-(−)-**15** and (*R*)-(+)-**15**, respectively. The reaction with *n*-butyllithium is performed in the presence of *N,N,N′,N′*-tetramethylethylenediamine (TMEDA) which promotes additional lithiation of the unsubstituted ring, addition of chlorodiphenylphosphine then yielding the bidentate ligand **23**.[16]

Protocol 5.
Synthesis of (*S*)-*N,N*-dimethyl-1-[(*R*)-1′,2-bis(diphenylphosphino)ferrocenyl]ethylamine (Structure 23)

Caution! All procedures should be carried out in an efficient fume hood. Eye protection must be worn at all times.

Equipment
- Two-necked, round-bottomed flask (100 mL)
- Cone/flexible tubing adapter
- Septum
- Teflon-covered egg-shaped magnetic stirrer bar (1.5 cm length)
- Needles (5 × 10 cm, 20 gauge)
- Glass syringes with needle-luer lock (10 mL, 3 × 5 mL, 1 mL)
- Magnetic stirrer
- Source of dry nitrogen
- Separating funnel (100 mL)

Materials
- (*S*)-(−)-*N,N*-Dimethyl-1-ferrocenylethylamine[a] (FW 257.2), 1.0 g, 3.9 mmol — **irritant**
- Dry diethyl ether,[b] 6 mL — **flammable, irritant**
- *n*-Butyllithium, 1.4 M solution in hexanes,[c] 6.9 mL, 9.7 mmol — **flammable, moisture sensitive**
- *N,N,N′,N′*-Tetramethylethylenediamine[d] (TMEDA) (FW 116.2), 0.53 g, 0.69 mL, 4.6 mmol — **flammable, irritant**
- Chlorodiphenylphosphine (FW 220.6, d 1.23), 2.1 mL, 11.7 mmol — **lachrymator**

Protocol 5. *Continued*

1. Ensure that all the glassware, syringes, needles and the magnetic stirrer bar required for the reaction are clean, and dry them in an oven at 120°C for at least 12 h prior to use.

2. Place the cone/flexible tubing adapter in the two-necked round-bottomed flask containing the magnetic stirrer bar, attach the nitrogen supply and allow the apparatus to cool under a stream of nitrogen.

3. Add (S)-(−)-N,N-dimethyl-1-ferrocenylethylamine (1.0 g, 3.9 mmol) to the flask and place a septum in the remaining neck.

4. Flush a 10 mL syringe and needle with nitrogen as described in Protocol 3, step 4. Use this to transfer dry diethyl ether[b] (6 mL) to the reaction flask by pushing the needle through the septum. Wash down any of the starting amine that may be on the sides of the reaction vessel.

5. Securely clamp the bottle of 1.4 M n-butyllithium in hexanes with the bottom of the bottle placed on the retort stand. Attach a needle to a source of nitrogen and push this through the seal of the bottle containing the butyllithium. This is to ensure that the bottle is maintained under a positive pressure of nitrogen. Assemble a 5 mL syringe and needle, flush with nitrogen and allow to cool. Push the end of this needle through the seal, and into the solution of butyllithium. Gently draw-up the plunger, filling the syringe to the 3.3 mL graduation mark. Withdraw the end of the needle from the butyllithium, then pull up the syringe plunger a little further to draw nitrogen into the needle. Carefully remove from the bottle, push through the septum of the reaction flask and add 3.3 mL of butyllithium over a period of *ca*. 1 min to the stirred solution. Immediately after the addition, rinse the syringe and needle with water.

6. Stir the reaction mixture at room temperature for 1 h. With a dry, nitrogen-flushed 1 mL syringe and 10 cm needle assemblage, add 0.69 mL of TMEDA.[d] Follow this with the addition of a further 3.6 mL of n-butyllithium according to the procedure described in step 5, employing a thoroughly dried 5 mL syringe and needle. Stir the reaction mixture at room temperature for 5 h.

7. Cool the reaction mixture in an ice-water bath. With a 5 mL syringe and needle, once again dried and flushed with nitrogen as before, add chlorodiphenylphosphine (2.1 mL, 11.7 mmol) dropwise to the stirred solution. Wash the needle and syringe thoroughly with acetone after the addition. Leave the reaction mixture stirring overnight with the ice-water bath warming to room temperature.

8. Add 20 mL of saturated aqueous sodium hydrogencarbonate solution and stir for 5 min. Transfer to a separating funnel, and rinse the reaction flask with a further 10 mL of diethyl ether. Separate the organic (upper) layer and wash the aqueous layer with a further 20 mL of diethyl ether. Combine the

organic layers, dry over magnesium sulfate, filter and remove the solvent on a rotary evaporator.

9. Purify the product by flash chromatography on silica gel using a mixed solvent system of 30% ethyl acetate/petroleum ether (40-60). The product is the first major yellow/orange band to be eluted and has an R_f of approximately 0.38. Combine those fractions containing only the desired product and evaporate the solvent to yield 1.16 g of an oil that crystallises on standing. Recrystallise from ethanol to yield pure (*S*)-*N*,*N*-dimethyl-1-[(*R*)-1',2-bis(diphenylphosphino)ferrocenyl]ethylamine **23** displaying the appropriate spectroscopic and rotational data.[16] Literature m.p. = 139–140 °C.[16]

[a] Alternatively start with (*R*)-(+)-*N*,*N*-dimethyl-1-ferrocenylethylamine.
[b] Distil from sodium benzophenone ketyl under a nitrogen atmosphere and use immediately.
[c] Titrate against diphenylacetic acid in dry THF[17] and adjust the quantity of butyllithium employed as appropriate.
[d] Reflux with potassium hydroxide and distil under a nitrogen atmosphere. Store over 4 Å molecular sieves under nitrogen.

Further tuning of the ligand is achieved by stereospecific replacement of the dimethylamino group with other functionalised amines. This is readily carried out by heating, for example, **ent-23** with acetic anhydride, isolation of the acetate **24**, and addition of the appropriate amine in methanol.[16]

ent-23   **24**   **25a** X = NMeCH(CH$_2$OH)$_2$

25b X = NMeCH$_2$CH$_2$—N⟨ ⟩

The exact nature of the replacing amine has been optimised for a number of metal-catalysed reactions. For example, **25a** directs palladium-catalysed allylic amination with up to 97% ee,[18] and **25b** is a very effective ligand for rhodium(I)-catalysed asymmetric hydrogenation (up to 97% ee).[19] In addition, **25b** is the controlling component of gold(I)-catalysed aldol reactions between isocyanoacetate and aldehydes, which generates oxazoline derivatives of general structure **26** with enantiomeric excesses typically greater than 95%.[20]

26

3. Dienyl iron tricarbonyl cation chemistry

3.1 Synthesis of η^4-cyclohexadiene iron tricarbonyl complexes

Fundamental to the development of dienyl iron tricarbonyl chemistry has been the availability of substituted cyclohexadiene precursors arising from the Birch reduction. In this process, a wide range of aromatic compounds are readily reduced to their corresponding unconjugated cyclohexa-1,4-dienes without further reduction to a cyclohexane.[21] The reaction is typically performed by adding sodium to a liquid ammonia solution of the substrate in the presence of an added alcohol.

For aromatic compounds containing electron-donating alkoxy or alkyl groups, the substituent is found in a non-reduced position in the product. Thus, reduction of anisole results in the formation of 1-methoxycyclohexa-1,4-diene and not 3-methoxycyclohexa-1,4-diene. The following protocol for the synthesis of 1-methoxy-4-methylcyclohexa-1,4-diene **28** by Birch reduction of 4-methylanisole **27** is representative.

Protocol 6.
Birch reduction of 4-methylanisole (Structure 27)

Caution! All procedures should be carried out in an efficient fume hood. Eye protection must be worn at all times.

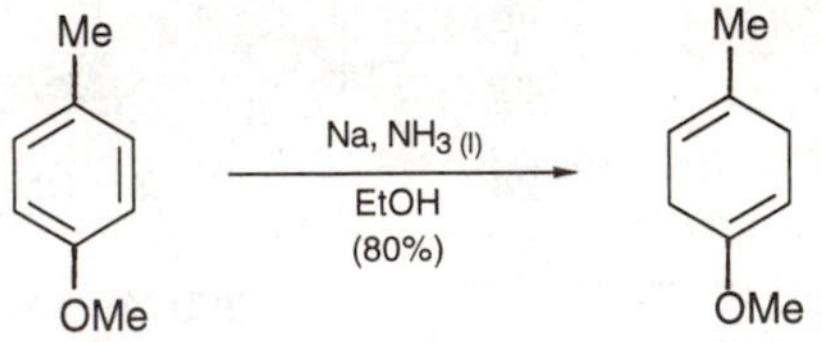

$$\text{27} \xrightarrow[\substack{\text{EtOH} \\ (80\%)}]{\text{Na, NH}_3 \text{ (l)}} \text{28}$$

Equipment
- Three-necked, round-bottomed flask (500 mL)
- Teflon-covered egg-shaped magnetic stirrer bar (4 cm length)
- Dry ice/acetone condenser
- Cone/flexible tubing adapter
- Stopper
- Source of dry nitrogen
- Magnetic stirrer
- Vermiculite insulation
- Drechsel bottle
- Beaker (200 mL)
- Separating funnel (1000 mL)

Materials
- 4-Methylanisole[a] (FW 122.2), 24.4 g, 0.2 mol — flammable, irritant
- Absolute ethanol (FW 46.1), 46.1 g, 1.0 mol — flammable, toxic
- Sodium (FW 23.0), 11.5 g, 0.5 mol — flammable
- Liquid ammonia, *ca.* 200 mL — corrosive, irritant
- Dry hexane,[b] 50 mL — flammable

- Sodium benzoate **irritant**
- Technical petroleum ether (40-60) 200 mL **flammable**

1. Ensure that all the glassware and the stirrer bar are clean, and dry them in an oven at 120°C for at least 12 h prior to use. Place the acetone–dry ice condenser in the central neck of the clamped three-necked flask containing the magnetic stirrer bar, attach the cone/flexible tubing adapter and stopper to the remaining necks of the flask, and allow the apparatus to cool under a stream of nitrogen.

2. Charge the round-bottomed flask with 4-methylanisole (24.4 g, 0.2 mol) followed by ethanol (46.1 g, 1 mol), ensuring that all of the 4-methylanisole is washed into the reaction vessel. Insulate the flask by placing it in a bowl containing vermiculite.

3. Pour acetone into the condenser until it is approximately one-quarter full.

4. To a thoroughly dry 200 mL beaker add 50 mL of dry hexane,[b] place on a top pan balance and tare. Ensure that the bench at which you are working is thoroughly dry. Wearing gloves, remove a stick of sodium from the oil in which it is stored. Cut into small portions (approximately 0.5 g) using a scalpel, wipe off excess oil with a tissue and add to the beaker of hexane. Continue until a total of 11.5 g of sodium has been transferred. Return the remaining stick of sodium to its container as quickly as possible.

5. Disconnect the nitrogen supply and connect the flask to an ammonia cylinder *via* a Drechsel bottle to protect against suck-back. Carefully open the valve of the ammonia cylinder and pass a slow stream of ammonia gas through the apparatus. Slowly add dry ice to the acetone in the condenser, waiting for the frothing to subside between each addition. Continue until the condenser is approximately two-thirds full of the acetone–dry ice mixture. When the condenser is sufficiently cold, ammonia liquid (b.p. −33°C) will begin to drop into the reaction vessel. When this is half full, that is when *ca*. 200 mL of ammonia liquid has condensed, close the valve of the cylinder and reconnect the nitrogen supply.

6. Stir the ammonia solution. Using tweezers, add the sodium in portions to the reaction vessel such that the slight frothing that occurs is given sufficient time to subside. Replace the stopper of the flask between each addition.

7. Stir the blue reaction mixture for a further 10 min after completion of the addition. Destroy the excess sodium by adding powdered sodium benzoate in small portions until the blue colour is discharged.

8. Remove the acetone–dry ice condenser and allow the ammonia solution to evaporate to approximately half the volume. Add water (200 mL) and transfer the resulting solution to a 1000 mL separating funnel. Extract the aqueous phase with petroleum ether (40-60) (2 × 100 mL), combine the organic phases, dry over magnesium sulfate and filter. Remove the solvent on a rotary evaporator to give the crude product. Distil under reduced pressure

Protocol 6. *Continued*

(b.p. 170–172°C at atmospheric pressure) to give 1-methoxy-4-methylcyclo-hexa-1,4-diene (80%) as a colourless oil displaying the appropriate spectro-scopic data [δ_H (CDCl$_3$) 1.69 (3 H, s, Me), 2.70 (4 H, brs, 2 × CH$_2$), 3.55 (3 H, s, OMe), 4.62 (1 H, brs, CH=), 5.36 (1 H, brs CH=)].

[a] Commercial 4-methylanisole may be used without further purification.
[b] A fresh bottle of hexanes (boiling fraction 68–69°C) is sufficiently dry for this purpose.

Iron tricarbonyl complexes of diene ligands nearly always have their double bonds in conjugation with one another. Exceptions are only found with ligands such as norbornadiene where formation of a 1,3-diene would violate Bredt's rule by placing a double bond at a bridgehead position. The 1,4-unconjugated dienes from Birch reductions are often used directly in complexation reactions as iron carbonyl species promote double bond iso-merisation prior to complexation. However, in some instances the yields obtained by this procedure are rather low and it pays to independently iso-merise the diene prior to the addition of the iron carbonyl species. The fol-lowing protocol describes how to isomerise the 1,4-diene **28** to an equilibrium mixture containing predominantly the 1,3-diene **29**.

Protocol 7.
Double bond isomerisation. Generation of equilibrium mixture of Structure 28 and Structure 29[22]

Caution! All procedures should be carried out in an efficient fume hood. Eye protection must be worn at all times.

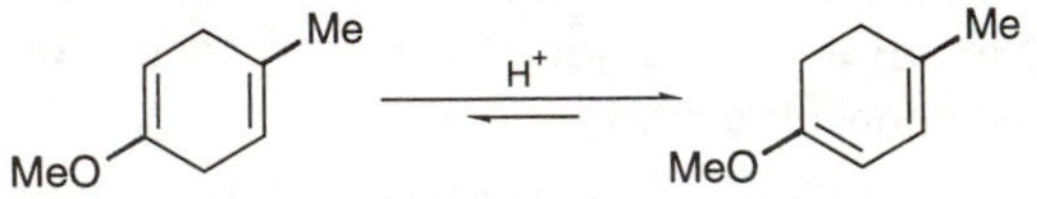

28   29

Equipment

- Stirrer hotplate
- Oil bath
- Two-necked, round-bottomed flask (50 mL)
- Cone/flexible tubing adapter

- Teflon-covered egg-shaped magnetic stirrer bar (length 1.2 cm)
- Source of dry nitrogen
- Vacuum distillation apparatus

Materials

- 1-Methoxy-4-methylcyclohex-1,4-diene
  (FW 124.2), 15.0 g, 0.121 mol
- *p*-Toluenesulfonic acid monohydrate, 0.02 g

flammable
corrosive, toxic

84

1. Using the stirrer hot plate, heat an oil bath until a constant temperature of 80 °C is maintained.

2. To the dry 50 mL two-necked round-bottomed flask containing the magnetic stirrer bar, add 1-methoxy-4-methylcyclohexa-1,4-diene (15.0 g, 0.121 mol) and *p*-toluenesulfonic acid monohydrate (0.02 g). Flush the system with nitrogen *via* the cone/flexible tubing adapter for 2 min and then place a stopper in the remaining neck of the flask.

3. Using the pre-equilibrated oil bath, heat the mixture with stirring at 80 °C for 2 h under a nitrogen atmosphere.

4. After cooling, vacuum distill (b.p. 78 °C, 30 mmHg) the resulting oil from the 50 mL flask to separate the 1:3 equilibrium mixture of unconjugated and conjugated dienes from *p*-toluenesulfonic acid. The product should be obtained in approximately 90% yield and confirmation that the isomerisation process has been successful may be obtained from its ^{1}H NMR spectrum [δ_H (CDCl$_3$) 1.75 (3 H, s, Me), 2.29 (4 H, s, 2 × CH$_2$), 3.56 (3 H, s, OMe), 4.87 (1 H, d, J = 6 Hz, CH=), 5.57 (1 H, d, J = 6 Hz, CH=)].

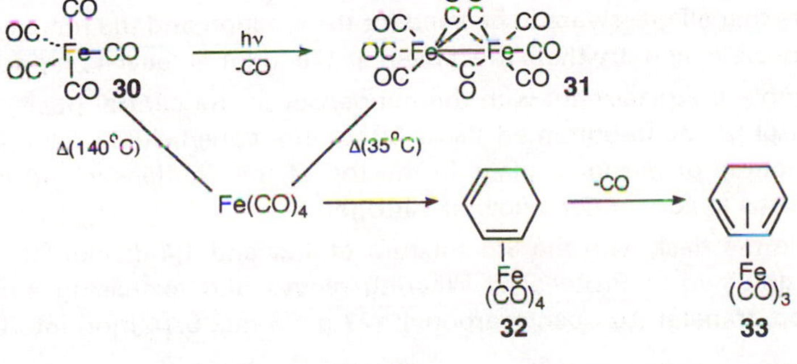

Both iron pentacarbonyl **30** and diiron nonacarbonyl **31**, which are commercially available, are used as sources of iron tricarbonyl during complexation reactions. The former requires considerable thermal energy to bring about rate determining dissociation of a carbon monoxide ligand to form iron tetracarbonyl. This contains a vacant coordination site and adds to one of the double bonds of a diene generating an 18-electron η^2-adduct **32**. Further loss of a carbon monoxide ligand and coordination of the second double bond gives the η^4-diene iron tricarbonyl complex **33**. In contrast, diiron nonacarbonyl dissociates at much lower temperatures into iron pentacarbonyl and iron tetracarbonyl, and the 16-electron tetracarbonyl species then reacts in exactly the same way. The advantages of using iron pentacarbonyl are that it is considerably cheaper than diiron nonacarbonyl and that the relatively high temperatures required will additionally result in double bond isomerisations, as discussed above. Diiron nonacarbonyl is preferred for sensitive substrates, due to the much milder conditions used for complexation, and reactions are typically carried out in diethyl ether heated at reflux. Although relatively expensive to buy, diiron nonacarbonyl is easily synthesised by photolysis of the pentacarbonyl in glacial acetic acid.[23]

The following complexation protocol leading to the isolation of tricarbonyl(1-methoxy-4-methylcyclohexa-1,3-diene)iron **34** is representative.

Protocol 8.
Synthesis of tricarbonyl(1-methoxy-4-methylcyclohexa-1,3-diene)iron (Structure 34)[22]

Caution! All procedures must be carried out in an efficient fume hood. Eye protection must be worn at all times. Chemical resistant gloves must be worn when handling iron pentacarbonyl, tricarbonyl iron complexes and their solutions.

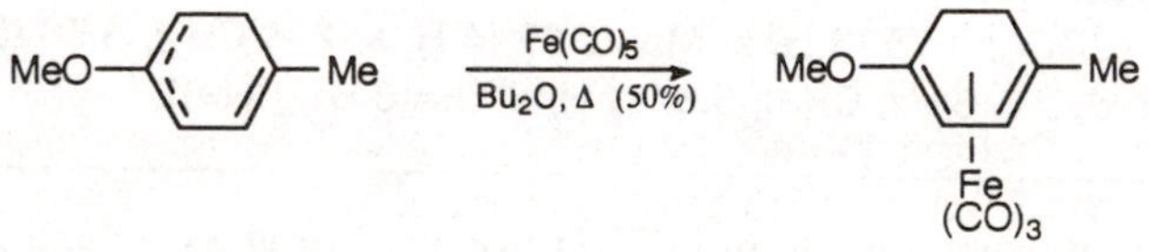

28 + 29   34

Equipment

- Two-necked, round-bottomed flask (250 mL)
- Liebig condenser
- Cone/flexible tubing adapter
- Stopper
- Teflon-covered egg-shaped magnetic stirrer bar (length 3 cm)
- Source of dry nitrogen
- Stirrer hot plate
- Measuring cylinder (50 mL)
- Glass funnel
- Single-necked round-bottomed flask (250 mL)
- 6.5 cm diameter glass sinter Büchner funnel with hose connection

Materials

- 3:1 mixture of 1-methoxy-4-methylcyclohexa-1,3-diene and 1-methoxy-4-methylcyclohexa-1,4-diene (FW 124.2), 10.0 g, 0.08 mol
- Iron pentacarbonyl[a] (FW 195.9), 27 g, 18 mL, 0.14 mol
- Dry di-n-butyl ether,[b] 85 mL
- Celite, ca. 25 g

flammable
highly toxic
flammable, irritant

1. Ensure that all glassware to be used for the reaction and the magnetic stirrer bar are clean and dry them in an oven at 120°C for at least 12 h prior to use.

2. Assemble the glassware with the condenser in the central position of the two-necked round-bottomed flask. Attach the cone/flexible tubing adapter to a source of nitrogen, place in the top of the condenser and allow the apparatus to cool under a flow of nitrogen.

3. Charge the flask with the 3:1 mixture of 1,3- and 1,4-dienes (10.0 g, 0.08 mol) obtained in Protocol 7. **Wearing gloves** and exercising appropriate caution, transfer iron pentacarbonyl[a] (27 g, 18 mL, 0.14 mol) into the flask.

This is done with the aid of a 50 mL measuring cylinder and funnel containing a cotton wool plug, to remove any iron oxide residues that may be present in the iron pentacarbonyl. Use the funnel when pouring the iron pentacarbonyl into the measuring cylinder and again for transfer into the round-bottomed flask. Finally, add freshly distilled di-*n*-butyl ether[b] (75 mL) using the same measuring cylinder and funnel, so as to wash into the flask remaining traces of iron pentacarbonyl. Place the stopper into the neck of the flask and secure with a joint clip.

4. Using the stirrer hot plate and oil bath, heat the reaction mixture at reflux under a nitrogen atmosphere for 48 h. It is essential to ensure that the reaction mixture is efficiently stirred in order to ensure satisfactory yields. On completion of the reaction, allow the resultant very dark reaction mixture to cool to room temperature.

5. Attach the glass sintered Büchner funnel to a clamped, clean and dry 250 mL single-necked round-bottomed flask. Using a spoon, transfer celite into the sinter funnel to a depth of about 3–4 cm. Connect the side-arm of the sinter funnel to a water vacuum pump and carefully decant the reaction mixture onto the celite such that the mixture is filtered through the celite filtering aid. This should ensure an efficient filtration of the reaction mixture which contains pyrophoric particulate iron. It is important to ensure that the celite pad does not run dry, otherwise the iron may ignite.[c] Wash out the flask with an additional 10 mL of di-*n*-butyl ether.

6. Remove the solvent and excess iron pentacarbonyl on a rotary evaporator placed in a fume cupboard.[d] Remove traces of solvent by attaching the flask to a high vacuum pump for an hour, to give the crude tricarbonyl(1-methoxy-4-methylcyclohexa-1,3-diene)iron complex in approximately 50% yield, as a yellow oil displaying appropriate ^{1}H NMR[e] and IR spectroscopic data.[24] This material is sufficiently pure for use in Protocol 9.

[a] Excess iron pentacarbonyl is readily destroyed on treatment with bromine water. This is prepared by shaking bromine (**care!**) (3 g) with water (100 mL) until a homogeneous solution is obtained. All glassware with which iron pentacarbonyl has been in contact should stand in a bromine water solution for an hour, prior to rinsing with water and removal from the fume cupboard.
[b] Distil from sodium benzophenone ketyl under a nitrogen atmosphere immediately prior to use.
[c] Destroy the particulate iron residues with dilute hydrochloric acid.
[d] The iron pentacarbonyl and di-*n*-butyl ether distillate should be treated with bromine prior to disposal. After use, the rotary evaporator should be cleaned. This is best achieved by rotary evaporating a flask containing ethanol and then treating the distillate with bromine prior to disposal.
[e] The signals in the NMR spectrum of this compound may be significantly broadened due to the presence of paramagnetic iron salts. These can be removed by passing the $CDCl_3$ solution of the complex through a small plug of deactivated neutral alumina immediately before the recording of the spectrum. Deactivated neutral alumina is prepared by thoroughly shaking a 10:1 w/w ratio of Grade 1 neutral alumina and water.

Diols resulting from the microbal oxidation of arenes, such as toluene **35**, by *Pseudamonas putida* have recently been used as ligands for the iron tricarbonyl unit. These compounds, which are optically pure and of known absolute configuration, contain the cyclohexa-1,3-diene moiety, the two faces of which are diastereotopic as a consequence of the neighbouring tetrahedral chiral centres. After conversion of diol **36** to its corresponding dimethyl ether, complexation with diiron nonacarbonyl was found to give a single diastereoisomer **37**. The ether groups direct the iron carbonyl moiety to the same side of the cyclohexadiene ring.[25]

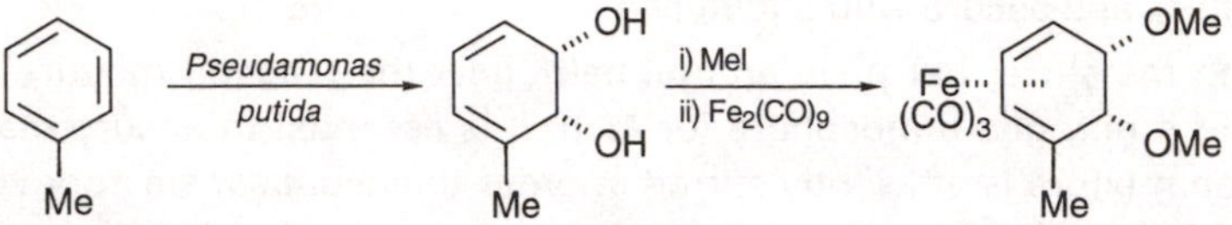

The attraction of this methodology is the rapid access it provides to optically pure diene complexes which have subsequently been converted to dienyl iron complexes. Using Birch substrates as starting materials for diene iron carbonyl synthesis requires a resolution step in order to obtain optically pure material, and to date no efficient method for performing this resolution has been devised.

3.2 Synthesis of η^5-cyclohexadienyl iron tricarbonyl complexes

Triphenylcarbenium salts (Ph_3C^+) readily abstract a hydride from η^4-cyclohexadiene iron tricarbonyl complexes to form cationic η^5-cyclohexadienyl salts, the hydride being removed from one of the methylene groups adjacent to the η^4-diene unit. When the cyclohexadiene ligand is monosubstituted, or has two or more different functionalities attached, a mixture of regioisomers may potentially result. For example, hydride abstraction from **38** results in a 1.5:1 ratio of the two possible regioisomers **39** and **40**.

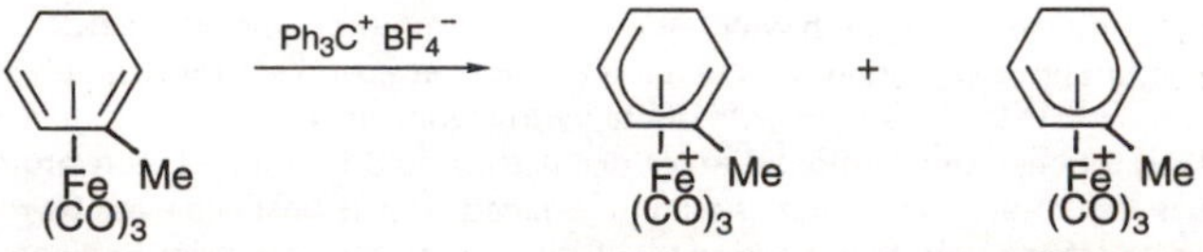

The regioselectivity may be accounted for by the relative HOMO and LUMO energies of the two dienyl cations, the preferred isomer having a stronger synergic two-way interaction with the iron tricarbonyl moiety. If the 2-methyl substituent is changed to a 2-methoxy group, the latter has a stronger pertubation on the relative HOMO and LUMO energies of the two possible dienyl cations. As a result, hydride abstraction from **41** yields almost exclusively the 2-methoxycyclohexadienyl complex **42**. Similarly, hydride abstraction from 1-methoxy-substituted cyclohexadiene ligands gives almost exclusively a single regioisomer.[24]

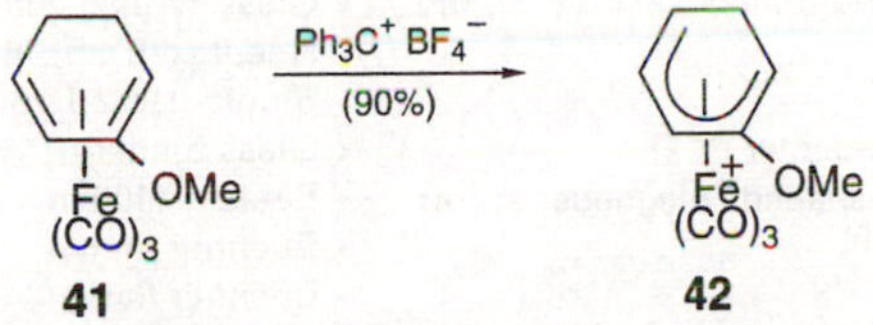

In addition to hydride, other groups may be abstracted from neutral η^4-cyclohexadiene complexes. The reaction between the homochiral complex **37** and the triphenylcarbenium ion resulted in removal of a methoxide anion and formation of a 5:1 mixture of the two possible isomers **43** and **44**.[25] Trifluoro-acetic acid (TFA) may also be used. For **37** this resulted in a lowering of the selectivity, but there are examples where regioisomers do not arise and TFA is the reagent of choice for the removal of methoxide.[26]

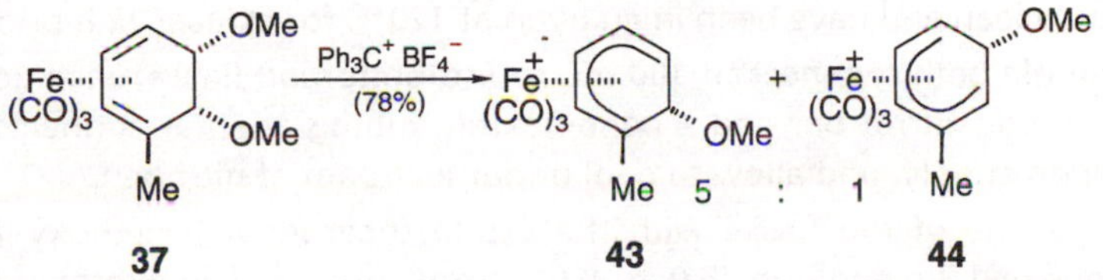

Cyclohexadienyl iron tricarbonyl cations are best isolated as their relatively stable hexafluorophosphate salts. These are easily formed by addition of a saturated aqueous solution of ammonium hexafluorophosphate to an aqueous solution containing the cationic complex arising from either hydride or methoxide abstraction. The following protocol for the hydride abstraction from tricarbonyl(1-methoxy-4-methylcyclohexa-1,3-diene)iron **34** is representative.

Protocol 9.
Synthesis of tricarbonyl(4-methoxy-1-methylcyclohexadienylium)iron hexafluorophosphate (Structure 45)[22]

Caution! All procedures should be carried out in an efficient fume hood. Eye protection must be worn at all times. Chemical resistant gloves must be worn when handling tricarbonyl iron complexes and their solutions.

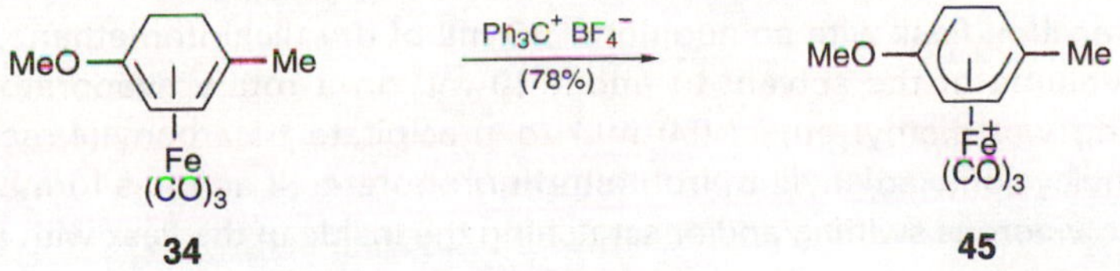

Protocol 9. *Continued*

Equipment

- Two-necked, round-bottomed flask (2 × 100 mL)
- Septum (× 2)
- Cone/flexible tubing adapter (× 2)
- Teflon-covered egg-shaped magnetic stirrer bar (2 × 1.5 cm length)
- Magnetic stirrer
- Glass syringe with needle-luer lock (20 mL)
- Needle (15 cm, 16–18 gauge)
- Single-necked, round-bottomed flask (250 mL)
- Glass funnel
- Beakers (100 mL, 250 mL)
- Büchner funnel
- Büchner flask

Materials

- Tricarbonyl(1-methoxy-4-methylcyclohexa-1,3-diene)iron (FW 264.1), 5.0 g, 0.019 mol   **toxic**
- Triphenylmethylium tetrafluoroborate (FW 330.1), 6.80 g, 0.021 mol   **hygroscopic, toxic**
- Dry dichloromethane,[a] 75 mL   **toxic, irritant**
- Wet diethyl ether,[b] 70 mL   **flammable, irritant**
- Ammonium hexafluorophosphate (FW 163.0), *ca.* 2.5 g, 0.015 mol   **hygroscopic, harmful**

1. Ensure that all glassware to be used for the reaction and the magnetic stirrer bar are clean and have been in an oven at 120 °C for at least 12 h prior to use.

2. Assemble both two-necked 100 mL round-bottomed flasks, each containing a magnetic stirrer bar and a cone/flexible tubing adapter connected to the nitrogen supply, and allow to cool under a stream of nitrogen.

3. Charge one of the flasks with the crude tricarbonyl(1-methoxy-4-methyl-cyclohexa-1,3-diene)iron (5.0 g, 0.019 mol) prepared in Protocol 8, add a septum to the open neck and label as flask A.

4. Disconnect the remaining two-necked round-bottomed flask from the nitrogen supply and weigh into this, as quickly as possible, triphenylmethylium tetrafluoroborate (6.80 g, 0.021 mol). Reconnect to the nitrogen supply, flush the flask through with nitrogen for a couple of minutes, then place a septum into the open neck. Label as flask B.

5. Assemble the 20 mL syringe and needle while hot and flush with nitrogen as described in Protocol 3, step 4. When cool, use the syringe to add dry dichloromethane[a] to flask A (15 mL) and flask B (40 mL). Stir the resulting mixtures to ensure the formation of homogeneous solutions.

6. Using the same syringe, transfer the solution of tricarbonyl(1-methoxy-4-methylcyclohexa-1,3-diene)iron from flask A to flask B, and stir the resulting mixture at room temperature for 1 h.

7. Disconnect the nitrogen supply and transfer the mixture to a clean single-necked round-bottomed flask (250 mL) with the aid of a funnel. Wash out the reaction flask with an additional 10 mL of dry dichloromethane. Reduce the volume of the solvent to about 10 mL on a rotary evaporator before adding wet diethyl ether[b] (50 mL) to precipitate tricarbonyl(4-methoxy-1-methylcyclohexadienylium)iron tetrafluoroborate. (If an oil is formed at this point, vigorous swirling and/or scratching the inside of the flask with a spatula

90

should produce the required solid.) Filter off this yellow solid with a Büchner funnel, wash with an additional 20 mL of wet diethyl ether and proceed immediately with step 8.

8. Transfer the tetrafluoroborate salt to a pre-weighed 250 mL beaker. Reweigh the beaker to determine the mass of the tetrafluoroborate salt (FW 349.9) before dissolving this salt in the minimum quantity of water to obtain a saturated aqueous solution. (Occasionally, a small amount of insoluble scum may form; if this is the case, it should be removed by gravity filtration.) In a 100 mL beaker, add 1.2 equiv. of ammonium hexafluorophosphate (FW 163.0), calculated with respect to the tetrafluoroborate salt, and dissolve in the minimum volume of water.

9. Add the solution of ammonium hexafluorophosphate to the saturated tetrafluoroborate solution, and leave standing at room temperature for 30 min. Filter the resultant precipitate, wash with water (2 × 5 mL) and dry under vacuum to give in the order of 6 g of tricarbonyl(4-methoxy-1-methylcyclohexadienylium)iron hexafluorophosphate as a yellow solid, displaying appropriate spectroscopic data.[24]

[a] Distil from calcium hydride under a nitrogen atmosphere.
[b] Saturate the diethyl ether by shaking with water in a separatory funnel and partitioning the layers.

3.3 Nucleophilic addition to cyclohexadienyl iron tricarbonyl complexes. Applications to natural product synthesis

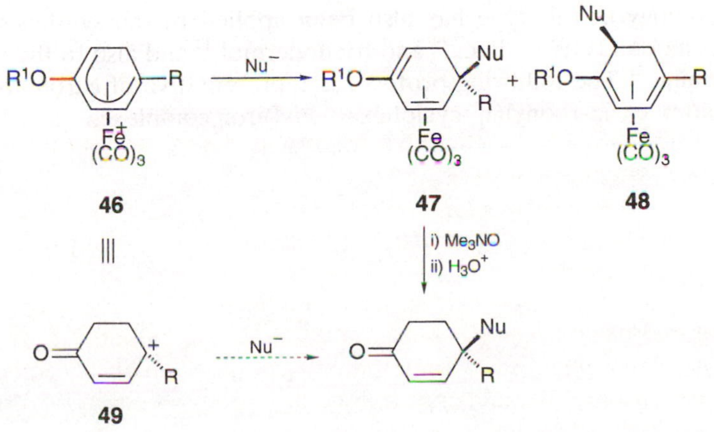

As detailed in the sections above, cyclohexadienyl iron complexes of general formula **46** are readily obtained by Birch reduction, complexation and highly regioselective hydride abstraction. Nucleophilic addition to these complexes occurs only at the terminal positions of the η^5-cyclohexadienyl unit such that two products **47** and **48** may be produced. In the vast majority of cases **47** is the preferred product, the nucleophile attacking *exo* to the bulky iron carbonyl group to produce a single diastereoisomer.[27] The alternative product, which is also formed as a single diastereoisomer, is only produced in significant quantities for certain R^1 substituents (*e.g.* -CH$_2$CH$_2$OAc).[28]

Removal of the organic ligand of **47** followed by hydrolysis of the enol ether yields the 4,4-disubstituted cyclohexenone system and so **46** may be formally regarded as a synthetic equivalent of the cyclohexenone cation **49**. This methodology has been exploited in the synthesis of a number of natural products. For example, addition of the potassium enolate **50** to cyclohexadienyl complex **45** resulted in formation of a neutral complex **51** containing the two contiguous quaternary centres required for the synthesis of 12,13-epoxy-14-methoxytrichothecene **52**.[22]

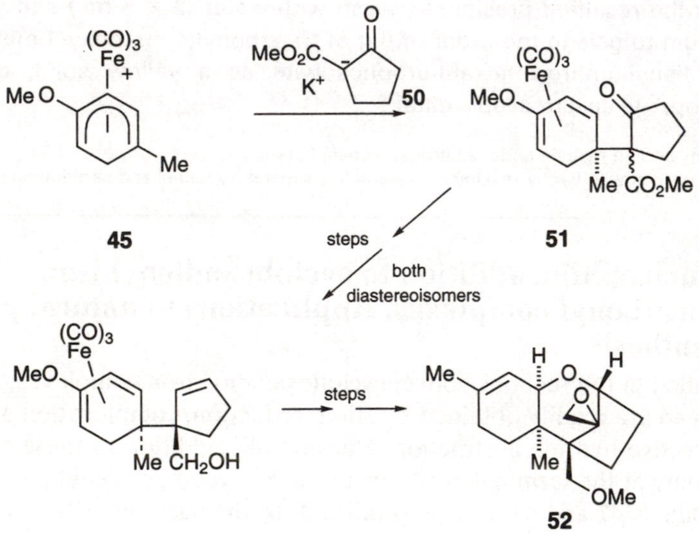

Methodology of this type has also been applied to the synthesis of the related compounds trichodiene[29] and trichodermol,[30] and also to the alkaloid limaspermine.[31] The following protocol is representative of carbanion addition to cationic tricarbonyl(η^5-cyclohexadienyl)iron complexes.

Protocol 10.

Synthesis of tricarbonyl(diethyl 4-methoxy-1-methylcyclohexa-2,4-dienylmalonate)iron (Structure 53)[27]

Caution! All procedures should be carried out in an efficient fume hood. Eye protection must be worn at all times. Chemical resistant gloves must be worn when handling tricarbonyl iron complexes and their solutions.

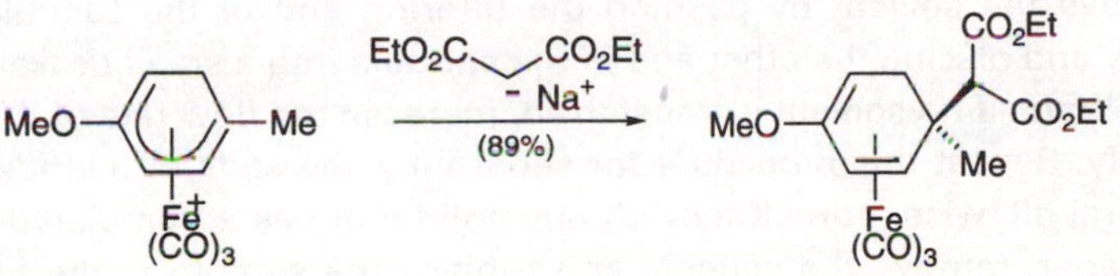

45   **53**

Equipment

- Three-necked, round-bottomed flask (2 × 100 mL)
- Septum (× 2)
- Cone/flexible tubing adapter (× 2)
- Teflon-covered egg-shaped magnetic stirrer bar (2 × 1.5 cm length)

- Stopper (× 2)
- Magnetic stirrer
- Cannula with glass filtering attachment (30 cm, 16–18 gauge) (Fig. 3.1)
- Glass syringe with needle-luer lock (3 × 10 mL)
- Needle (3 × 15 cm, 16–18 gauge)

Materials

- 60% dispersion of sodium hyride in mineral oil (FW 24.0), 0.12 g, 3 mmol — flammable, moisture sensitive
- Dry 40-60 petroleum ether,[a] 15 mL — flammable
- Dry tetrahydrofuran,[b] 25 mL — flammable, irritant
- Diethyl malonate (FW 160.2), 0.48 g, 3 mmol — flammable
- Tricarbonyl(4-methoxy-1-methylcyclohexadienylium)iron hexafluorophosphate (FW 408.0), 0.50 g, 1.22 mmol — toxic
- Petroleum ether 40–60 for extraction and flash chromatography — flammable
- Silica gel for flash chromatography (Merck 9385) — irritant dust
- Ethyl acetate for flash chromatography — flammable, irritant

1. Ensure that all glassware to be used in the reaction and the magnetic stirrer bars are clean and have been in an oven at 120°C for at least 12 h prior to use.

2. Assemble a 100 mL three-necked round-bottomed flask, containing a magnetic stirrer bar, with a septum and a cone/flexible tubing adapter connected to the nitrogen supply, and allow to cool under a stream of nitrogen. Charge the flask with a 60% dispersion of sodium hydride in mineral oil (0.12 g, 3 mmol) and place a stopper in the remaining neck of the flask.

3. Attach a filter paper to the cannula filtering device as described in Protocol 3, step 7. Remove the septum from the flask, push the needle end of the

Protocol 10. *Continued*

filtering cannula through the bottom of the septum and slide the septum down the cannula until it reaches the filtering end. Replace the septum in the neck of the flask such that the resulting apparatus is essentially as shown in Fig. 3.2.

4. Assemble a 10 mL syringe and needle while hot and flush with nitrogen as described in Protocol 3, step 4. Use to transfer 5 mL of dry petroleum ether (40-60)[a] into the flask. Stir the slurry briefly then allow the solid to settle. Remove the solvent by pushing the filtering end of the cannula into the slurry and placing the other end of the cannula into a small beaker to collect the filtrate. If no solvent is transferred, increase the flow rate of the nitrogen supply. Repeat this procedure for separating the sodium hydride from the mineral oil twice more. Knock off any solid that has accumulated on the filter paper, remove the cannula and replace the septum in the neck of the flask.

5. Use a fresh 10 mL syringe and needle, flushed with nitrogen as before, to transfer dry tetrahydrofuran[b] (10 mL) into the flask. Make a solution of diethyl malonate (0.48 g, 3 mmol) in tetrahydrofuran (5 mL) by weighing out the diethyl malonate into a clean, dry glass vial and adding the tetrahydrofuran from a syringe. Immediately draw the resulting solution back into the syringe, then add it dropwise to the sodium hydride/tetrahydrofuran mixture and stir for a further 15 min at room temperature to generate a clear solution of the diethyl malonate anion.

6. Assemble the remaining 100 mL three-necked round-bottomed flask, magnetic stirrer bar, septum and adapter, and cool under nitrogen as described in step 2. Charge this flask with tricarbonyl(4-methoxy-1-methylcyclohexadienylium)iron hexafluorophosphate (0.50 g, 1.22 mmol) and place a stopper into the remaining neck. Using a third 10 mL syringe and needle assembly, add dry tetrahydrofuran[b] (10 mL) and cool the resulting suspension to 0 °C with stirring. Use this same syringe to transfer dropwise 7.5 mL of the diethyl malonate anion solution to the suspension of the hexafluorophosphate salt. The reaction is complete when a homogeneous solution is obtained. If this does not occur, add further 1 mL portions of the diethyl malonate anion solution until homogeneity occurs.

7. Pour the reaction mixture into water (20 mL) and extract with petroleum ether (40-60) (2 × 20 mL). Combine and dry the organic phase over magnesium sulfate, filter and remove the solvent on a rotary evaporator. Purify the product by flash column chromatography on silica gel using 10% ethyl acetate/petroleum ether (40-60) as eluent. Isolate the product as a yellow oil, 0.5 g (89%), displaying appropriate spectroscopic data.[27]

[a] Dry over magnesium sulfate and distil, discarding the first 10% which may contain water.
[b] Distil from sodium benzophenone ketyl under a nitrogen atmosphere and use immediately.

The product of addition to cyclohexadienyl complexes is a neutral η^4-cyclo-hexadiene species. If this contains a suitable leaving group, it may be used to synthesise a second cyclohexadienyl complex to which a second nucleophilic species may be added. In this way the iron carbonyl moiety may be employed to control the formation of two new C-C bonds. For example, addition of 4-lithioanisole to the dimethoxycyclohexadienyl complex **54** proceeds with high regioselectivity to give the neutral species **55**. Removal of the methoxide group with trifluoroacetic acid, precipitation of the hexafluorophosphate salt, followed by addition of a second nucleophilic species gives the product **56**. Further manipulation, removal of the iron and hydrolysis of the enol ether gives the 4,4-disubstituted cyclohexenone **57** such that the starting complex may be regarded as a synthetic equivalent for the cyclohexenone dication synthon **58**.[32]

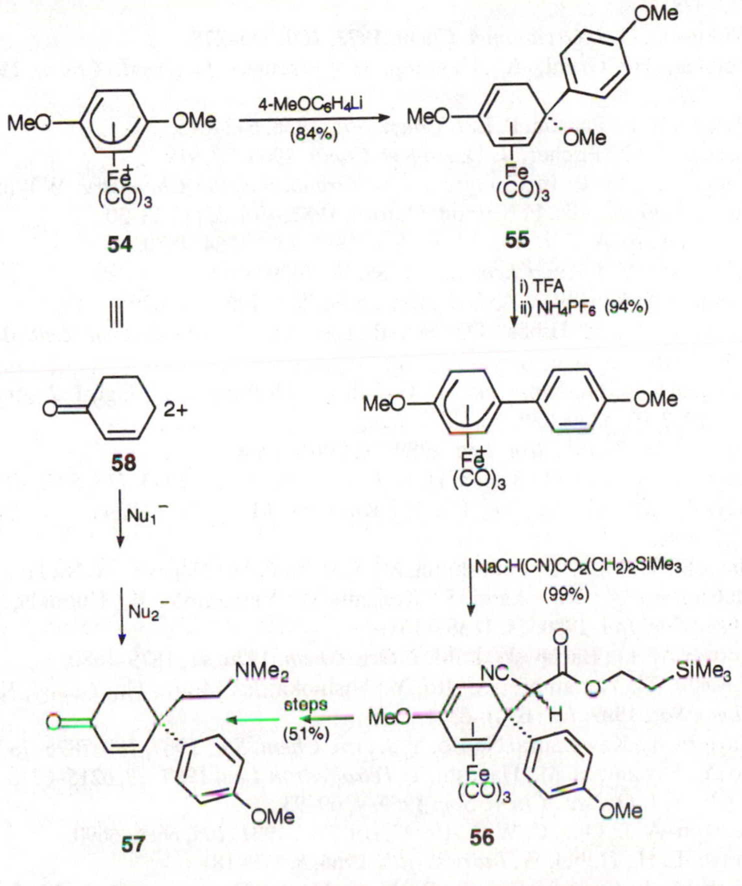

This example illustrates an important extension of the use of iron cyclo-hexadienyl complexes in organic synthesis through multiple use of the metal.

The attraction of organometallic systems for the organic chemist is that they offer reactivity patterns that are not otherwise observed. However, as introduction of the metal centre does require some effort, it must be used to maximum effect, preferably to control two or more reactions with complete regio- and stereocontrol. This type of approach will continue to find use in organic synthesis, especially when utilising complexes that are readily generated in optically pure form.

References

1. Kealy, T. J.; Pauson, P. L. *Nature* **1951**, *168*, 1039–1040. See also Miller, S. A.; Tebboth, J. A.; Tremaine, J. F. *J. Chem. Soc.* **1952**, 632–635.
2. Wilkinson, G.; Rosenblum, M.; Whiting, M. C.; Woodward, R. B. *J. Am. Chem. Soc.* **1952**, *74*, 2125–2126. Fischer, E. O.; Pfab, W. *Z. Naturforsch., Teil B.* **1952**, *7*, 377–378.
3. Wilkinson, G. *J. Organomet. Chem.* **1975**, *100*, 273–278.
4. Reihlen, H.; Gruhl, A.; Hessling, G.; Pfrengle, O. *Anal. Chem.* **1930**, *482*, 161–182.
5. Hallam, B. F.; Pauson, P. L. *J. Chem. Soc.* **1958**, 642–645.
6. Fischer, E. O.; Fischer, R. D. *Angew. Chem.* **1960**, *72*, 919.
7. Mingos, D. M. P. In *Comprehensive Organometallic Chemistry*; Wilkinson, G.; Stone, F. G. A., eds. Pergamon: Oxford, **1982**; Vol. 3, pp. 28–30.
8. Cunningham, A. F. *J. Am. Chem. Soc.* **1991**, *113*, 4864–4870.
9. Weinmayr, V. *J. Am. Chem. Soc.* **1955**, *77*, 3009–3011.
10. Arimoto, F. S.; Haven, A. C. *J. Am. Chem. Soc.* **1955**, *77*, 6295–6297.
11. Richards, C. J.; Hibbs, D.; Hursthouse, M. B. *Tetrahedron Lett.* **1994**, *35*, 4215–4218.
12. Marquarding, D.; Klusacek, H.; Gokel, G.; Hoffmann, P.; Ugi, I. *J. Am. Chem. Soc.* **1970**, *92*, 5389–5393.
13. Boaz, N. W. *Tetrahedron Lett.* **1989**, *30*, 2061–2064.
14. Riant, O.; Samuel, O.; Kagan, H. B. *J. Am. Chem. Soc.* **1993**, *115*, 5835–5836.
15. Hayashi, M.; Konishi, M.; Ito, H.; Kumada, M. *J. Am. Chem. Soc.* **1982**, *104*, 4962–4963.
16. Hayashi, T.; Mise, T.; Fukushima, M.; Kagotani, M.; Nagashima, N.; Hamada, Y.; Matsumoto, A.; Kawakami, S.; Konishi, M.; Yamamoto, K.; Kumada, M. *Bull. Chem. Soc. Jpn.* **1980**, *53*, 1138–1151.
17. Kofron, W. G.; Baclawski, L. M. *J. Org. Chem.* **1976**, *41*, 1879–1880.
18. Hayashi, T.; Yamamoto, A.; Ito, Y.; Nishioka, E.; Miura, H.; Yanagi, K. *J. Am. Chem. Soc.* **1989**, *111*, 6301–6311.
19. Hayashi, T.; Kawamura, N.; Ito, Y. *J. Am. Chem. Soc.* **1987**, *109*, 7876–7878.
20. Ito, Y.; Sawamura, M.; Hayashi, T. *Tetrahedron Lett.* **1987**, *28*, 6215–6218.
21. Birch, A. J. *Q. Rev., Chem. Soc.* **1950**, *4*, 69–93.
22. Pearson, A. J.; Ong, C. W. *J. Am. Chem. Soc.* **1981**, *103*, 6686–6690.
23. Braye, E. H.; Hubel, W. *Inorg. Synth.* **1966**, *8*, 178–181.
24. Birch, A. J.; Chamberlain, K. B.; Hass, M. A.; Thompson, D. J. *J. Chem. Soc., Perkin Trans. 1* **1973**, 1882–1891.
25. Howard, P. W.; Stephenson, G. R.; Taylor, S. C. *J. Chem. Soc., Chem. Commun.*

1988, 1603–1604.

26. Howard, P. W.; Stephenson, G. R.; Taylor, S. C. *J. Organomet. Chem.* **1988**, *339*, C5–8.
27. Pearson, A. J. *J. Chem. Soc., Perkin Trans. 1* **1977**, 2069–2074.
28. Pearson, A. J.; Chandler, M. *J. Chem. Soc., Perkin Trans. 1* **1980**, 2238–2243.
29. Pearson, A. J.; O'Brien, M. K. *J. Chem. Soc., Chem. Commun.* **1987**, 1445–1447.
30. O'Brien, M. K.; Pearson, A. J.; Pinkerton, A. A.; Schmidt, W.; Willman, K. *J. Am. Chem. Soc.* **1989**, *111*, 1499–1501.
31. Pearson, A. J.; Rees, D. C. *J. Am. Chem. Soc.* **1982**, *104*, 1118–1119.
32. Stephenson, G. R.; Owen, D. A. *Tetrahedron Lett.* **1991**, *32*, 1291–1294.

Organoiron chemistry 2: iron acyl and π-allyltricarbonyliron lactone chemistry

MARTIN WILLS

1. Introduction

Two classes of organoiron chemistry will be described in this chapter. The first part concerns the synthesis and applications of acyl derivatives of the enantiomerically pure chiral auxiliary $[(C_5H_5)Fe(CO)(PPh_3)]$. Such complexes may be elaborated through a variety of synthetic transformations with invariably high diastereoselectivity. Removal of the acyl group furnishes enantiomerically enriched or pure products. The second class of organoiron reagents featured in this chapter are iron tricarbonyl π-allyl complexes. These have been employed as intermediates in general methods for the synthesis of lactones and lactams and have been applied to a number of total syntheses of complex natural products.

2. Iron acyl chemistry[1]

2.1 Introduction

The chiral iron acyl complex $[(C_5H_5)Fe(CO)(PPh_3)COCH_3]$ **1** has an octahedral structure in which the acyl, triphenylphosphine and carbon monoxide ligands occupy three coordination sites and lie mutually at right angles to each other.[2] The remaining three sites are occupied by the cyclopentadienyl ligand. The preferred conformation of the acyl group is that in which the acetyl oxygen is *anti* to the carbon monoxide ligand, and this has been observed in all X-ray crystal structures of this class of iron acyl complex solved to date. Deprotonation of **1** with *n*-butyllithium generates the corresponding enolate **2** which may be alkylated cleanly on the carbon atom using a variety of electrophiles.[3] Complex **1** and its derivatives are generally air-stable crystalline solids, although they are prone to oxidation by air when kept in solution. Hence all manipulations of these compounds are routinely carried out under an inert atmosphere. Reactions are carried out in Schlenk tubes or round-bottomed flasks fitted with gas inlets and all manipulations are performed using the vacuum/inert manifold techniques described in Chapter 7 and elsewhere.[4] All solvents should be saturated with nitrogen or argon immediately prior to use and transferred by cannula tubing.

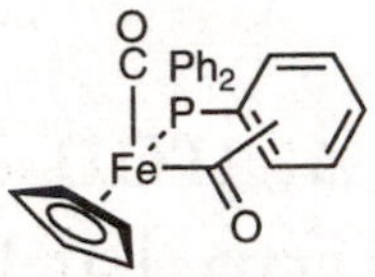

R-(–)-**1** 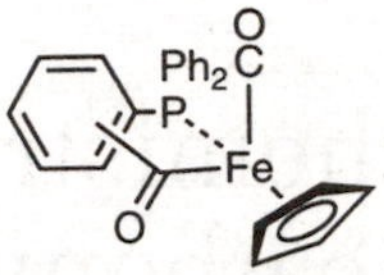   *S*-(+)-**1** 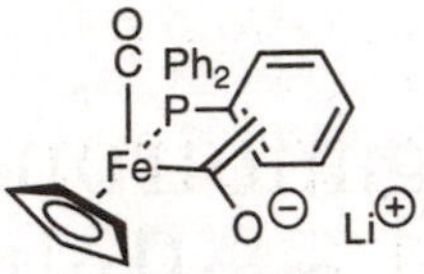   **2**

2.2 Preparation of iron acyl complex 1

Racemic **1** may be prepared in three steps from [(C$_5$H$_5$)Fe(CO)$_2$]$_2$ **3** in a high-yielding large-scale process (Scheme 4.1).[5] This method involves a one-pot reduction of **3** followed by reaction with iodomethane and subsequent treatment with triphenylphosphine. In the last step the methyl group migrates to the carbon monoxide ligand and triphenylphosphine fills the remaining coordination site. Purification of the product at the end of this sequence is achieved by recrystallisation; no chromatography is required.

Protocol 1.
Synthesis of racemic iron acyl complex (Structure 1) (Scheme 4.1)[5,a]

Caution! All procedures should be carried out in a well-ventilated hood, and disposable vinyl or latex gloves and chemical-resistant safety glasses should be worn.

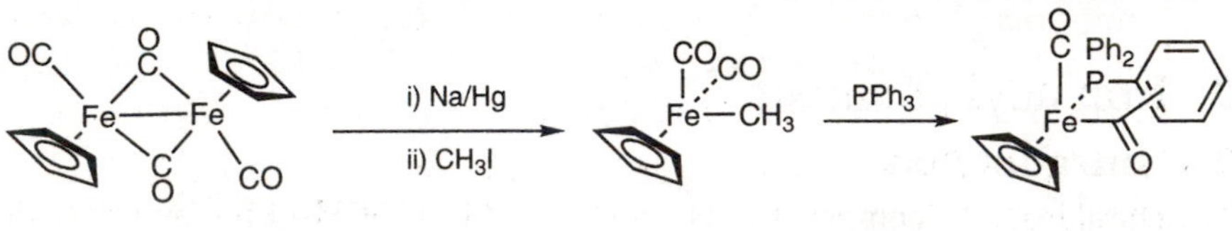

3   racemic-**1**

Scheme 4.1

Equipment
- Three-necked, round-bottomed flasks (2 × 3 L, 2 × 2 L)
- Two-necked, round-bottomed flask (1 L)
- Gas inlets with stopcocks for round-bottomed flasks
- Septa
- Overhead mechanical stirrer apparatus (one motor, two paddles and adapters)
- Pre-trap assembly (see Fig. 4.1) (2 L)
- Pressure-equalising dropping funnel (100 mL)
- All-glass syringes of appropriate volumes with needle-lock luers
- Needles (6″, 20 or 22 gauge)
- Vacuum/nitrogen manifold (Figs 7.1 and 7.2)
- Glass powder funnel
- Large frit (8 cm diameter, 25 cm high), (Fig. 4.2)
- Aluminium foil
- Long spatula (30 cm)
- Cannula or transfer tubing of appropriate size

Materials

- Sodium metal (FW 23.0), 14.5 g, 0.63 mol   **flammable solid, pyrophoric, moisture sensitive**
- Mercury, 56 mL[b]   **highly toxic, irritant**
- [(C₅H₅)Fe(CO)₂]₂ (FW 353.7), 80 g, 0.225 mol   **toxic, irritant**
- Dry THF,[c] 600 mL and 20 mL   **flammable, irritant**
- Iodomethane (FW 141.9), 82.4 g, 36.1 mL, 0.58 mol   **highly toxic, irritant, corrosive**
- Triphenylphosphine (FW 262.3), 119 g, 0.45 mol   **toxic, irritant**
- Dry nitrogen-saturated petroleum ether (30-40), 600 mL   **flammable, irritant**
- Dry nitrogen-saturated acetonitrile, 400 mL   **flammable, lacrymator**
- Dry nitrogen-saturated hexane, 160 mL and 80 mL   **flammable, irritant**
- Dry nitrogen-saturated dichloromethane,[d] 600 mL and 2 × 100 mL   **toxic, irritant**
- Celite   **irritant**
- Alumina (Activated, Grade I)   **irritant**
- Liquid nitrogen for pre-traps   **asphixiant**

1. Clean all glassware, syringes and needles and dry for at least 2 h in a hot oven (>100°C) before use.

2. Attach a 3 L three-necked flask to the overhead stirrer apparatus by the central inlet and insert a gas inlet and a septum into the remaining necks.

3. Support the flask using a clamp and stand with a heavy base.

4. Attach tubing from vacuum/nitrogen manifold to gas inlet.

5. Add the mercury (56 mL) to the flask and adjust the stirrer so that the paddle is just above its surface.

6. Add the sodium (14.5 g) in small pieces (*ca.* 1 g) to the mercury. The sodium should be kept under oil and each piece dried rapidly on a tissue before addition (it is not critical to remove all the oil). Mechanical agitation may be required before the first piece reacts. **CAUTION** – The reaction is highly exothermic and violent. Add the remaining pieces at intervals of *ca.* 5 min during which time the amalgam should remain hot and liquid. Fumes may be taken off at intervals by adjusting the vacuum/nitrogen manifold tap first to vacuum and then to nitrogen (Chapter 7, Protocol 1).

7. Allow the amalgam to cool to room temperature and solidify. This will usually take at least 1 h.

8. With the aid of a glass powder funnel, add the solid [(C₅H₅)Fe(CO)₂]₂ (80 g, 0.45 mol) against a steady stream of nitrogen after removal of the septum, which should be replaced immediately.

9. Assemble a syringe (50 mL) and needle and flush with nitrogen following the procedure given in Chapter 3, Protocol 3, step 4.

10. Add anhydrous THF (600 mL) by syringe (12 portions), taken directly from the still, and start the stirrer.

11. Place the system under vacuum carefully until the solvent just begins to boil, then carefully reintroduce nitrogen (Chapter 7, Protocol 2). Repeat the cycle three times.

Protocol 1. *Continued*

12. Stir the deep purple solution for 16 h at room temperature. After 10 min the amalgam may be a mobile liquid phase, although this may take longer in some cases. After 16 h the solution should be dark orange in colour.

13. Attach a 3 L three-necked flask to an overhead mechanical stirrer apparatus by the central inlet, and connect a gas inlet and a septum to the remaining necks.

14. Support the flask using a clamp and stand with a heavy base.

15. Attach a flexible tubing connection from the vacuum/nitrogen manifold to the gas inlet.

16. Carefully place the flask under vacuum, then slowly reintroduce nitrogen. Repeat two times.

17. Stop the stirrer on the first flask and decant the orange solution to the second flask using a cannula and the method described in Chapter 7, Protocol 4. All experimental details will now refer to the second flask.

18. Start the overhead stirrer.

19. Against a steady stream of nitrogen, replace the septum with the pressure-equalising dropping funnel fitted with a septum.

20. Place the system under vacuum carefully until the solvent just begins to boil and then carefully reintroduce nitrogen. Repeat the cycle three times.

21. Assemble a syringe and needle and flush the syringe with nitrogen.

22. Charge the pressure-equalising dropping funnel with iodomethane (82.4 g, 0.58 mol) and THF (20 mL) taken directly from a still.

23. Add the solution of iodomethane to the stirred orange solution slowly at room temperature. The addition should take around 40 min on this scale. The reaction is exothermic.

24. Stir at room temperature for 16 h. At the end of this time the solution should be an olive-green colour.

25. Replace the dropping funnel and overhead mechanical stirrer with septa and remove the solvent under reduced pressure to give a red-brown solid product. It will be necessary to use a 2 L pre-trap cooled in liquid nitrogen (Fig. 4.1).

26. Add dry nitrogen-saturated light petroleum ether (600 mL) and mechanically agitate the mixture so that a deep red solution over a white solid is formed.

27. Attach a large frit (8 cm diameter, 25 cm high) fitted with a septum and packed with a 10 cm depth of celite to a 2 L three-necked flask. A gas inlet and septum should also be fitted to the flask.

28. Support the flask using a clamp and stand with a heavy base.

29. Attach tubing from the vacuum/nitrogen manifold to the gas inlet.

30. With the use of a cannula, pass the deep red liquid through the frit and into the 2 L round-bottomed flask. Care should be taken not to transfer too much of the solid. The frit may become blocked by a build-up of sediment in which case mechanical clearance using a long spatula will be required. All experimental details will now refer to the second flask.

31. Use two further portions of nitrogen-saturated light petroleum ether (100 mL) to complete the transfer of product to the 2 L flask *via* the frit.

32. Remove the light petroleum ether under vacuum to give a red solid. It will be necessary to use a 2 L pre-trap cooled in liquid nitrogen.

33. Add dry nitrogen-saturated acetonitrile (400 mL) to the red solid.

34. Prepare a 1 L two-necked flask fitted with a condenser/gas inlet on one neck and a septum on the other. Dry the apparatus with an electric heat gun or a small Bunsen burner at reduced pressure (0.5–1 mmHg), allow to cool and refill with nitrogen.

35. Add triphenylphosphine (119 g, 0.45 mol) to the 1 L flask against a steady stream of nitrogen after removal of the septum, which should be replaced immediately.

36. Add the red acetonitrile solution to the 1 L flask by cannula.

37. Surround the flask with aluminium foil.

38. Place the system under vacuum carefully until the solvent just begins to boil, then carefully reintroduce nitrogen. Repeat the cycle three times.

39. Using an oil bath, heat the solution under reflux for *ca.* 55 h under nitrogen. The reaction may be followed by IR spectroscopy since the product and starting materials have characteristic carbonyl absorption bands (starting material at 2000 and 1945 cm^{-1}, product at 1900, 1600 cm^{-1}). During this time the solution changes to an orange colour.

40. Allow the solution to cool to room temperature and remove the acetonitrile under reduced pressure. It will be necessary to use a large pre-trap cooled in liquid nitrogen.

41. Add dry nitrogen-saturated dichloromethane (600 mL) to the solid mass and agitate the orange solution vigorously for 30 min.

42. Attach a large frit (8 cm diameter, 25 cm high) fitted with a septum and packed with a 10 cm depth of alumina to a 2 L three-necked flask. A gas inlet and septum should also be fitted to the flask.

43. Support the flask using a clamp and stand with a heavy base.

44. Attach tubing from the vacuum/nitrogen manifold to gas inlet.

45. With the aid of a cannula, pass the orange liquid through the frit into the 2 L round-bottomed flask. Care should be taken not to transfer too much

Protocol 1. *Continued*

of the solid. The frit may become blocked by a build-up of sediment in which case mechanical clearance using a long spatula will be required.

46. Add further portions of dry nitrogen-saturated dichloromethane (2 × 100 mL) to the first flask and transfer to the 2 L flask *via* the frit as described in step 45.

47. Reduce the volume of the dichloromethane solution to *ca.* 400 mL under vacuum. It will be necessary to use a large pre-trap cooled in liquid nitrogen.

48. Add dry degassed hexane (160 mL). A quantity of crystalline solid may appear by this time.

49. Reduce the volume of the solution to *ca.* 300 mL under vacuum.

50. Stand the solution overnight in a fridge. A large amount of orange crystalline solid should have formed by this stage.

51. Filter the solvent from the crystalline product using a filter cannula (Chapter 7, Protocol 4).

52. Wash the crystals of **1** with cold, dry nitrogen-saturated hexane (2 × 40 mL) injected by syringe, remove using a filter cannula, and dry under vacuum for 2 h. The yield of **1** is typically 120–140 g, 60–70% for the three steps and the material displays the appropriate spectroscopic data.[5] The dry solid is stable indefinitely in air. A further portion (5–10%) may be obtained by concentration of the filtrate.

[a] A three-step procedure without isolation and characterisation of intermediates.
[b] Triple distilled (99.99%) grade.
[c] Freshly distilled from sodium benzophenone ketyl under an inert atmosphere.
[d] Freshly distilled from calcium hydride.

Although a number of methods for the preparation of enantiomerically pure **1** have been published,[6,7] resolution *via* the intermediacy of aldol adduct **4** has emerged as the most efficient (Scheme 4.2).[7] In this procedure racemic enolate **2** is treated with enantiomerically pure (+)-camphor **5** to give the aldol adduct. A significant kinetic resolution effect is observed which results in predominant formation of the product **4** (96% de) from addition of (*S*)-**2**

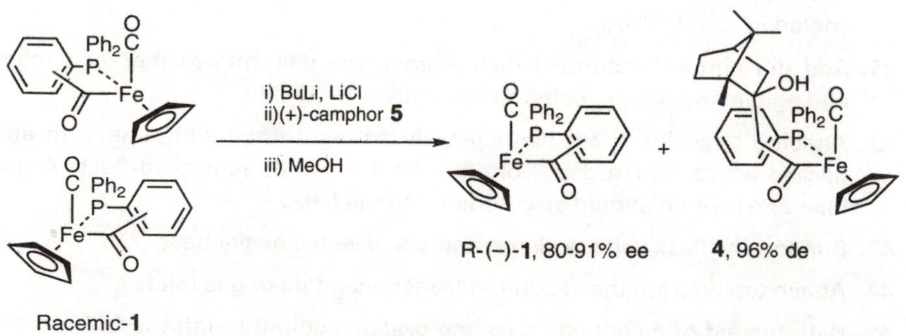

i) BuLi, LiCl
ii)(+)-camphor **5**

iii) MeOH

Racemic-**1**

R-(−)-**1**, 80–91% ee   **4**, 96% de

Scheme 4.2

Dreschel bottle head

From solution →

→ To vacuum

B24

Polystyrene box

Fill box with liquid nitrogen

Fig. 4.1 Pre-trap setup.

to (+)-**5**. Protonation of the reaction mixture reforms starting material which is enriched in (*R*)-**1** (80–91% ee). A single recrystallisation of this material gives enantiomerically pure (*R*)-**1** in 20–35% yield overall. It is essential to carry out this reaction in the presence of lithium chloride (1.5 equiv. is optimal) to achieve the highest levels of selectivity.

Recrystallisation of the aldol product **4** followed by treatment with sodium hydride at reflux results in a retro-aldol reaction to give (*S*)-**1** in 100% ee (Scheme 4.3).[7] Hence both enantiomers of **1** may be prepared in enantiomerically pure form by this method.

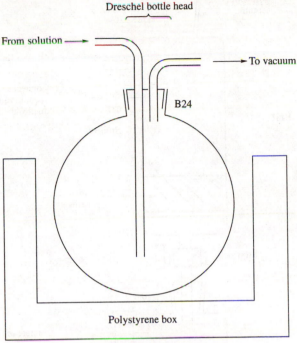

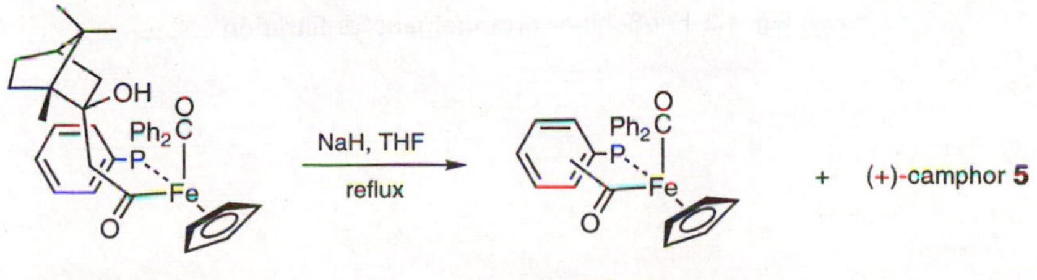

4, 100% de   S-(+)-**1**, 100% ee

NaH, THF
reflux

+   (+)-camphor **5**

Scheme 4.3

105

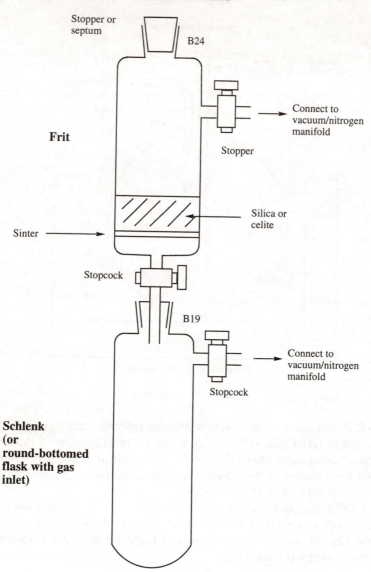

Fig. 4.2 Frit/Schlenk arrangement for filtration.

Protocol 2.
Kinetic resolution of iron acyl complex (Structure 1) *via* aldol reaction with (+)-camphor 5 (Scheme 4.2)[7]

Caution! All procedures should be carried out in a well-ventilated hood, and disposable vinyl or latex gloves and chemical-resistant safety glasses should be worn.

Equipment

- Magnetic stirrer
- Teflon-covered magnetic stirrer bar (5 mm × 5 mm × 15 mm, octagonal or egg-shaped)
- Two-necked, round-bottomed flasks (3 × 50 mL) or Schlenk tubes (3 × 100 mL)[a]
- Gas inlets with stopcocks if round-bottomed flasks are used
- Small frit (2.5 cm diameter, 15 cm high) (Fig. 4.2)

- Septa
- Glass syringes with needle-lock luers of appropriate volumes
- Needles (6″, 20 or 22 gauge)
- Vacuum/nitrogen manifold (Figs 7.1 and 7.2)
- Cannula or transfer tubing of appropriate lengths
- Column for chromatography

Materials

- Racemic iron acyl complex **1** (FW 454.2), 643 mg, 1.42 mmol (Protocol 1)   **toxic**
- *n*-Butyllithium,[b] 1.1 mL of a 1.6 M hexane solution, 1.7 mmol   **flammable, moisture sensitive**
- Lithium chloride (FW 42.4), 90 mg, 2.12 mmol   **toxic**
- (+)-Camphor (FW 152.2), 280 mg, 1.84 mmol[c]   **toxic**
- Dry THF, 15 + 5 mL[d]   **flammable, irritant**
- Dry diethyl ether, 20 mL[d]   **flammable, irritant**
- Methanol, 5 mL   **flammable, irritant**
- Petroleum ether (60-80) for chromatography   **flammable, irritant**
- Ethyl acetate for chromatography   **flammable, irritant**
- Dichloromethane[e] for recrystallisations   **toxic, irritant**
- Technical diethyl ether for extractions   **flammable, irritant**
- Solid carbon dioxide for cooling bath   **asphyxiant**
- Technical grade acetone for cooling bath   **flammable, toxic**
- Silica gel for chromatography (Merck Kieselgel 60)   **irritant**

1. Clean all glassware, syringes, needles and the stirrer bar and dry for at least 2 h in a hot oven (>100 °C) before use. Allow apparatus to cool in a desiccator.

2. Assemble a Schlenk tube or round-bottomed flask/gas inlet, place the stirrer bar in the flask or Schlenk and attach a septum to the remaining neck of the vessel.

3. Support the flask or Schlenk using a clamp and stand with a heavy base.

4. Attach a flexible tubing connection from the vacuum/nitrogen manifold to the gas inlet or side-arm.

5. Dry the apparatus with an electric heat gun or a small Bunsen burner at reduced pressure (0.5 – 1 mmHg), allow to cool and refill with nitrogen.

Protocol 2. *Continued*

6. Add anhydrous lithium chloride (90 mg, 2.12 mmol) and racemic iron acetyl complex **1** (643 mg, 1.42 mmol) to the flask or Schlenk. These compounds should be added rapidly against a gentle stream of nitrogen after removal of the septum, which should be replaced immediately.

7. Assemble a syringe and needle and flush with nitrogen following the procedure given in Chapter 3, Protocol 3, step 4.

8. Add anhydrous THF (15 mL) by syringe, taken directly from the still, and start the stirrer.

9. Place the system under vacuum carefully until the solvent just begins to boil, then carefully reintroduce nitrogen (Chapter 7, Protocol 2). Repeat the cycle three times.

10. Cool the solution to −78°C in a carbon dioxide–acetone bath.

11. Add *n*-butyllithium[b] (1.1 mL of a 1.6 M hexane solution, 1.7 mmol) dropwise over 1 min by syringe. The colour of the solution changes from transparent orange to a deep and opaque red.

12. Stir the solution for 30 min at −78°C.

13. While the solution is stirring, assemble the second Schlenk or flask and attach to the vacuum/nitrogen manifold. Place a septum in the neck of the vessel.

14. Treat the vessel following the procedure given in step 5.

15. Charge the vessel with (+)-camphor (280 mg, 1.80 mmol) by the method given in step 6.

16. Assemble a syringe and needle and flush with nitrogen.

17. Use this syringe to transfer THF (5 mL), taken directly from the still, into the flask or Schlenk containing the (+)-camphor.

18. Transfer the solution of (+)-camphor from this flask to the main reaction flask (still cooled to −78°C) using the same syringe as in step 17. Add the solution dropwise over *ca.* 1 min.

19. Stir the main reaction flask for 90 min at −78°C. The colour of the solution changes from deep red to transparent orange.

20. Assemble a syringe and needle and flush with nitrogen.

21. Add methanol (5 mL) to the reaction mixture dropwise at −78°C. A further lightening of the orange colour may be observed during the addition.

22. Allow the reaction mixture to warm up to room temperature.

23. Remove the THF and methanol under vacuum.

24. Assemble a syringe and needle and flush the syringe with nitrogen.

25. Add dry diethyl ether (20 mL), taken directly from a still, by syringe.

26. Assemble a Schlenk or flask fitted with a gas inlet, and a small frit containing a plug of silica (2 cm depth) and a septum (Fig. 4.2).

27. With the aid of a cannula, filter the reaction solution through a plug of silica in the frit, following the procedure given in Chapter 7.

28. Remove the solvent and purify the products by flash chromatography on silica gel [EtOAc/petroleum ether (60-80), 1:15 → 1:3 v/v] following the procedure given in Chapter 7, Protocol 5. The aldol product **4** is eluted first (>60:1 mixture, 273 mg, 32%), followed by the enantiomerically enriched starting material (303 mg, 47%, 80% ee). Both materials display appropriate spectroscopic data.[7]

---

[a] Due to the design of a Schlenk tube, this must generally be of a larger volume than the corresponding round-bottomed flask for a reaction of a given scale.
[b] Titrate *n*-butyllithium using the Gilman double quench procedure[8] before use (1 mL quenched with 1,2-dibromoethane and 1 mL with water, each titrated with 1 M HCl using methyl orange indicator. Subtraction gives true alkyllithium concentration).
[c] Sublimed immediately prior to use.
[d] Freshly distilled from sodium benzophenone ketyl under an inert atmosphere.
[e] Freshly distilled from calcium hydride.

2.3 Alkylation reactions

As stated above, enolate **2** may be cleanly monoalkylated on the carbon atom by a variety of electrophiles to give adducts such as **6**, in the case of iodomethane addition.[3] Subsequent deprotonation by *n*-butyllithium followed by addition of a second electrophile, such as iodoethane, results in a highly stereoselective alkylation to give **7** (Scheme 4.4), essentially as a single diastereoisomer.[9] Reversal of the order of electrophile addition results in the formation of the opposite diastereoisomer **8**.[9] The high selectivity is the result of the steric 'blocking' of one face of the exclusively (*E*)-enolate, which also exists in the *anti*-conformation of enolate and carbon monoxide C-O bonds,

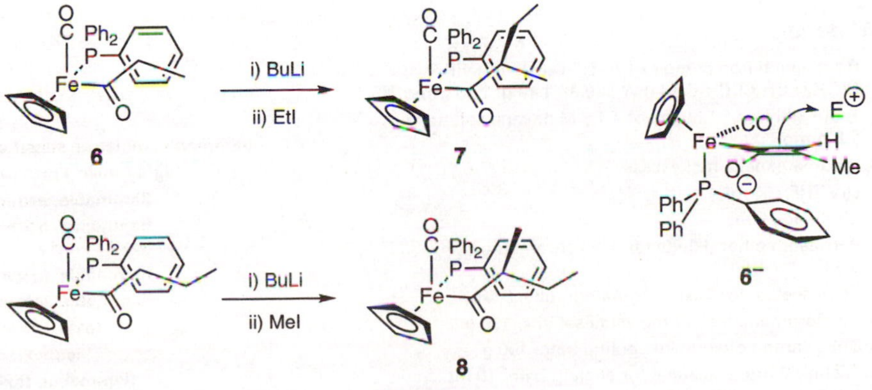

Scheme 4.4

109

by one of the triphenylphosphine phenyl rings.[10] Approach of an electrophile is only possible from the upper face as shown in **6⁻**.[10]

This remarkable alkylation stereocontrol has been exploited in a number of syntheses, including a concise synthesis of homochiral (*S,S*)-captopril and (*S,R*)-*epi*-captopril.[11] The example given in Protocol 3 is for the key step in the synthesis of (*S*)-(+)-2-methylhept-4-ynoate **9** (Scheme 4.5), the sidechain of prostacyclin.[9d]

Protocol 3.
Stereoselective alkylation of an iron acyl complex (Scheme 4.5)[9d]

Caution! All procedures should be carried out in a well-ventilated hood, and disposable vinyl or latex gloves and chemical-resistant safety glasses should be worn.

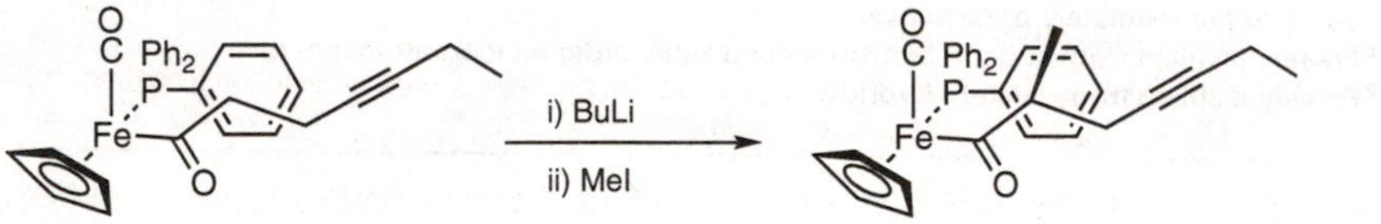

Scheme 4.5

Equipment

- Magnetic stirrer
- Teflon-covered magnetic stirrer bar (5 mm × 5 mm × 25 mm, octagonal or egg-shaped)
- Two-necked, round-bottomed flask (250 mL) or a Schlenk tube (500 mL)[a]
- Gas inlets with stopcocks if round-bottomed flask is used
- Septa

- Glass syringes with needle-lock luers of appropriate volumes
- Needles (6″, 20 or 22 gauge)
- Vacuum/nitrogen manifold (Figs 7.1 and 7.2)
- Cannulae or transfer tubing of appropriate lengths
- Chromatography column

Materials

- Homochiral iron complex [(*R*)-(η⁵-C_5H_5)Fe(CO)(PPh₃)C(O)$CH_2CH_2CCCH_2CH_3$] (FW 520.3), 1.19 g, 2.29 mmol[9d] — toxic
- *n*-Butyllithium,[b] 1.56 mL of a 1.6 M hexane solution, 2.5 mmol — flammable, moisture sensitive
- Iodomethane, 1 mL, excess — highly toxic, corrosive
- Dry THF,[c] 50 mL — flammable, irritant
- Methanol, 5 mL — flammable, irritant
- Petroleum ether (60-80) for flash chromatography, 0.5 L — flammable, irritant
- Ethyl acetate for flash chromatography, 0.5 L — flammable, irritant
- Dichloromethane[d] for recrystallisations, 100 mL — toxic, irritant
- Solid carbon dioxide for cooling bath, 100 g — asphyxiant
- Technical grade acetone for cooling bath, 10 mL — flammable, toxic
- Silica gel for chromatography (Merck Kieselgel 60) — irritant

1. Clean all glassware, syringes, needles and the stirrer bar and dry for at least 2 h in a hot oven (>100 °C) before use. Allow apparatus to cool in a desiccator.

2. Assemble the Schlenk tube or round-bottomed flask/gas inlet, place the stirrer bar in the flask or Schlenk and attach the septum to the remaining neck of the vessel.

3. Support the flask or Schlenk using a clamp and stand with a heavy base.

4. Attach a flexible tubing connection from the vacuum/nitrogen manifold to the gas inlet or side-arm.

5. Dry the apparatus with an electric heat gun or a small Bunsen burner at reduced pressure (0.5–1 mmHg), allow to cool and refill with nitrogen.

6. Add iron complex [(R)-(η^5-C_5H_5)Fe(CO)(PPh$_3$)C(O)CH$_2$CH$_2$CCCH$_2$CH$_3$] (1.19 g, 2.29 mmol) to the flask or Schlenk. This should be added rapidly against a steady stream of nitrogen or argon after removal of the septum, which should be replaced immediately.

7. Assemble a syringe and needle and flush the syringe with nitrogen following the procedure given in Chapter 3, Protocol 3, step 4.

8. Add anhydrous THF (50 mL) by syringe, taken directly from the still, and start the stirrer.

9. Place the system under vacuum carefully until the solvent just begins to boil and then carefully reintroduce nitrogen (Chapter 7, Protocol 2). Repeat the cycle three times.

10. Cool the solution to −78 °C in a carbon dioxide–acetone bath.

11. Add *n*-butyllithium (1.56 mL of a 1.6 M hexane solution, 2.5 mmol) dropwise over 1 min by syringe. The colour of the solution changes from transparent orange to a deep and opaque red.

12. Stir the solution for 60 min at −78 °C.

13. Assemble a syringe and needle and flush the syringe with nitrogen.

14. Add neat iodomethane (1 mL, excess) dropwise by syringe, over 5 min at −78 °C.

15. Stir for 15 min at −78 °C. The colour of the solution changes from deep red to transparent orange.

16. Assemble a syringe and needle and flush the syringe with nitrogen.

17. Add methanol (5 mL) to the reaction mixture dropwise at −78 °C. A further lightening of the orange colour may be observed during the addition.

18. Allow the reaction mixture to warm up to room temperature.

19. Remove the THF and methanol under vacuum (Chapter 7, Protocol 3).

20. Add silica gel (5 g) and dichloromethane (20 mL) to the orange residue. Swirl the flask until a suspension is obtained, and remove the solvent under vacuum to give a free-flowing solid.

Protocol 3. *Continued*

21. Purify the product (978 mg, 80%, m.p. 153–155 °C, 98% de) by flash chromatography on silica gel, eluting with dichloromethane petroleum ether (60-80) (4:1) (Chapter 7, Protocol 5). The product displays the appropriate spectroscopic data.[9d]

---

[a] Due to the design of a Schlenk tube, this must generally be of a larger volume than the corresponding round-bottomed flask for a reaction of a given scale.

[b] Titrate *n*-butyllithium using the Gilman double quench procedure[8] before use (1 mL quenched with 1,2-dibromoethane and 1 mL with water, each titrated with 1 M HCl using methyl orange indicator. Subtraction gives true alkyllithium concentration).

[c] Freshly distilled from sodium benzophenone ketyl under an inert atmosphere.

[d] Freshly distilled from calcium hydride.

2.4 Aldol reactions

Enolates generated from iron acyl compounds such as **1** and **6** add readily to aldehydes.[12] In order to achieve high levels of selectivity in these reactions it is necessary to exchange the lithium for another metal, such as aluminium(III),[12a,b] (which gives diastereoisomer **10**) or tin(II)[12c] (which gives diastereoisomer **11**) prior to addition of the aldehyde (Scheme 4.6).

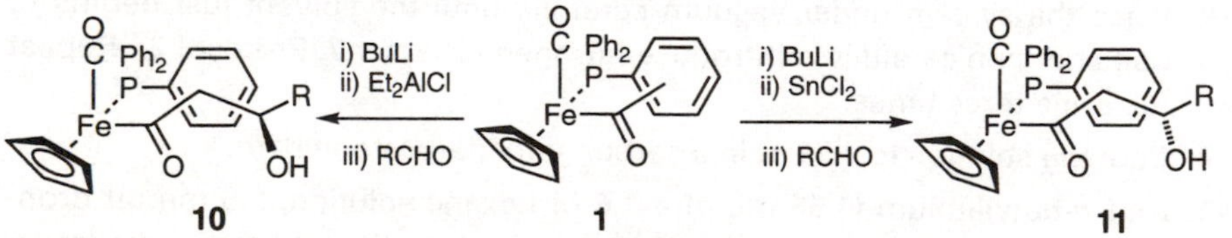

Scheme 4.6

This reaction has been successfully applied to the asymmetric syntheses of bicyclic lactams **12** *via* the intermediate aldol adduct **13** (Scheme 4.7).[13] Although only the reaction with (*R*)-**1** is illustrated, the same sequence using (*S*)-**1** generates the alternative diastereoisomer of pyrrolizidone alkaloid in essentially pure form, demonstrating that the iron acyl stereocontrol overwhelms the inherent stereocontrol of carbonyl addition dictated by the adjacent stereogenic centre in the aldehyde.

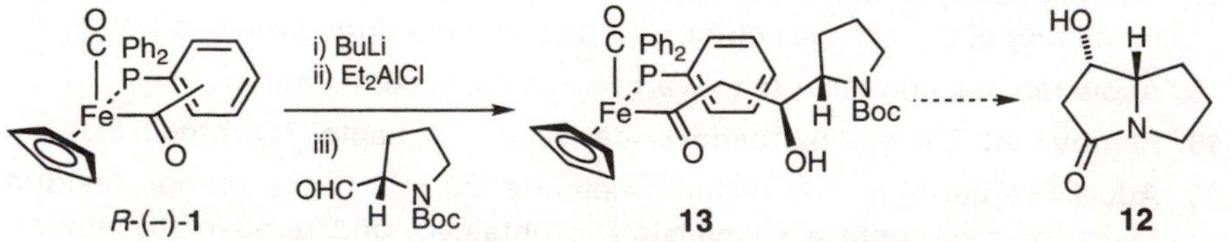

Scheme 4.7

Addition of aldehydes to the lithium enolate derived from propanoyl complex **6** requires prior transmetallation for optimum results.[14] In particular, the use of diethylaluminium chloride has proved to be most valuable when the *anti*-aldol adduct **14** is required, whilst copper cyanide is the transmetallation reagent of choice when the *syn*-aldol adduct **15** is the target (Scheme 4.8).[14] Oxidative cleavage and formation of the *threo* and *erythro* β-hydroxy acids, respectively, is easily achieved by treatment with aqueous bromine solution or CAN.[14] The aluminium(III)-mediated sequence has been employed in the synthesis of an enantiomerically pure degradation product of a marine cyclic peroxide, thereby proving its absolute configuration.[15]

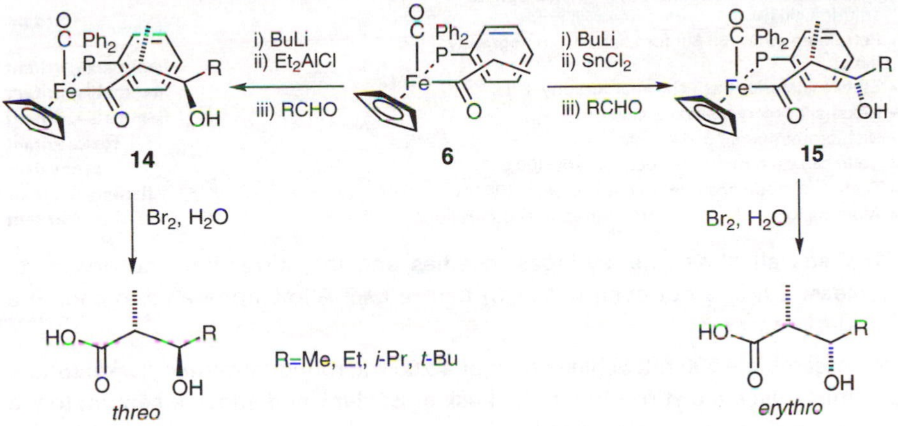

Scheme 4.8

Protocol 4.
Aluminium(III)-mediated aldol reaction of iron acyl complex (Structure 1) with propanal[12b]

Caution! All procedures should be carried out in a well-ventilated hood, and disposable vinyl or latex gloves and chemical-resistant safety glasses should be worn.

Equipment

- Magnetic stirrer
- Teflon-covered magnetic stirrer bar (6 mm × 6 mm × 30 mm, octagonal or egg-shaped)
- Two-necked, round-bottomed flask (250 mL) or Schlenk tube (500 mL)[a]
- Two-necked, round-bottomed flask (50 mL) or Schlenk tube (100 mL)[a]
- Gas inlets with stopcocks if round-bottomed flasks are used
- Septa
- Small frit (2.5 cm diameter, 15 cm high) (Fig. 4.2)
- Glass syringes with needle-lock luers of appropriate volumes
- Needles (6″, 20 or 22 gauge)
- Vacuum/nitrogen manifold (Chapter 7, Figs 7.1 and 7.2)
- Cannulae or transfer tubing of appropriate lengths
- Chromatography column

Protocol 4. *Continued*

Materials

- Iron acetyl complex **1** (FW 454.2), 310 mg, 0.68 mmol (Protocol 1)   **toxic**
- *n*-Butyllithium,[b] 0.9 mL of a 1.5 M hexane solution, 1.35 mmol   **flammable, moisture sensitive**
- Diethylaluminium chloride, 2.0 mL of a 1.8 M solution in toluene, 3.6 mmol   **toxic, moisture sensitive, flammable**
- Propanal (FW 58.1), 0.5 g, 8.62 mmol[c]   **flammable, toxic**
- Dry THF,[d] 80 + 10 mL   **flammable, irritant**
- Methanol, 1 mL   **flammable, irritant**
- Solid sodium hydrogencarbonate, 1.5 g
- Saturated aqueous sodium hydrogencarbonate solution, 50 mL   **irritant**
- Petroleum ether (60-80) for flash chromatography, 0.5 L   **flammable, irritant**
- Ethyl acetate for flash chromatography, 0.5 L   **flammable, irritant**
- Hexane for recrystallisation, 50 mL   **flammable, irritant**
- Dichloromethane,[e] 3 × 40 mL   **toxic, irritant**
- Solid carbon dioxide for cooling bath, 100 g   **asphyxiant**
- Technical grade acetone for cooling bath, 100 mL   **flammable, toxic**
- Alumina (grade 5)[f] for chromatography and filtrations   **irritant**

1. Clean all glassware, syringes, needles and the stirrer bar and dry for at least 2 h in a hot oven (>100°C) before use. Allow apparatus to cool in a desiccator.

2. Assemble a 500 mL Schlenk tube or a 200 mL round-bottomed flask/nitrogen inlet, place the stirrer bar in the flask or Schlenk and attach a septum to the remaining neck of the vessel.

3. Support the flask or Schlenk using a clamp and stand with a heavy base.

4. Attach a flexible tubing connection from the vacuum/nitrogen manifold to the gas inlet.

5. Dry the apparatus with an electric heat gun or a small Bunsen burner at reduced pressure (0.5–1 mmHg), allow to cool and refill with nitrogen.

6. Add iron complex **1** (310 mg, 0.68 mmol) to the flask or Schlenk. This should be added rapidly against a gentle stream of nitrogen after removal of the septum, which should be replaced immediately.

7. Assemble a syringe and needle and flush the syringe with nitrogen following the procedure given in Chapter 3, Protocol 3, step 4.

8. Add anhydrous THF (80 mL) by syringe, taken directly from the still, and start the stirrer.

9. Place the system under vacuum carefully until the solvent just begins to boil and carefully reintroduce nitrogen (Chapter 7, Protocol 2). Repeat the cycle three times.

10. Cool the solution to −78°C in a carbon dioxide–acetone bath.

11. Assemble a syringe and needle and flush the syringe with nitrogen.

12. Add *n*-butyllithium[b] (0.9 mL of a 1.5 M hexane solution, 1.35 mmol) drop-wise over 1 min by syringe. The colour of the solution changes from trans-parent orange to a deep and opaque red.

13. Stir the solution for 30 min at −78°C.

14. Assemble a syringe and needle and flush the syringe with nitrogen.

15. Add diethylaluminium chloride (2.0 mL of a 1.8 M solution in toluene, 3.6 mmol) dropwise over 1 min by syringe.

16. Allow the temperature of the reaction to rise to −40°C and stir for 45 min. The reaction mixture changes to a transparent red colour.

17. Cool the reaction mixture to −100°C (liquid nitrogen in acetone).

18. While the solution is stirring, assemble the second Schlenk or flask and attach to the vacuum/nitrogen manifold. Place septum in the remaining neck of the vessel.

19. Treat the vessel following the procedure given in step 5.

20. Charge the vessel with propanal (0.5 g, 8.62 mmol).

21. Assemble a syringe and needle and flush the syringe with nitrogen.

22. Use this syringe to transfer THF (10 mL), taken directly from the still, into the flask or Schlenk containing the propanal.[c]

23. Transfer the solution of propanal from this flask to the main reaction flask (still cooled to −100°C) using the same syringe as in step 22. Add the solu-tion dropwise over *ca.* 5 min.

24. Stir the main reaction flask for 2.5 h at −100°C. The colour of the solution changes from deep red to transparent orange.

25. Assemble a syringe and needle and flush the syringe with nitrogen.

26. Add methanol (1 mL) to the reaction mixture dropwise at −100°C. A further lightening of the orange colour may be observed during the addition.

27. Allow the reaction mixture to warm up to room temperature.

28. Remove the THF and methanol under vacuum (Chapter 7, Protocol 3).

29. Add nitrogen-saturated aqueous sodium hydrogencarbonate solution (50 mL) to the residue, followed by nitrogen-saturated dichloromethane (40 mL). Agitate well and separate the lower layer. Extract the aqueous layer with further dichloromethane (2 × 40 mL). The extraction should be carried out using a cannula following the method given in Chapter 7, Pro-tocol 4.

30. Place a Schlenk or flask fitted with a gas inlet, under the small frit fitted with a septum containing a plug of alumina (grade 5; 2 cm depth) (Fig. 4.2).

31. With the aid of a cannula, filter the reaction solution through the plug of alumina in the frit into the Schlenk tube.

32. Reduce the solvent to *ca.* 10 mL under vacuum.

Protocol 4. *Continued*

33. Purify the product **10** (R = CH_2CH_3) (295 mg, 85%, >100:1 mixture of diastereoisomers) by chromatography on alumina[f] (deactivated, grade 5) following the procedure given in Chapter 7, Protocol 5. Further chromatography and recrystallisation from dichloromethane hexane gives pure (*R,R*[(*S,S*)]-**10** (R = CH_2CH_3) as an orange crystalline solid.[12b] The product displays the appropriate spectroscopic data.[12b]

---

[a] Due to the design of a Schlenk tube, this must generally be of a larger volume than the corresponding round-bottomed flask for a reaction of a given scale.
[b] Titrate *n*-butyllithium using the Gilman double quench procedure[8] before use (1 mL quenched with 1,2-dibromoethane and 1 mL with water, each titrated with 1 M HCl using methyl orange indicator. Subtraction gives true alkyllithium concentration).
[c] Freshly distilled.
[d] Freshly distilled from sodium benzophenone ketyl under an inert atmosphere.
[e] Freshly distilled from calcium hydride.
[f] Prepared by the combination of grade 1 (activated) alumina and water (4% v/w).

2.5 Preparation of α,β-unsaturated iron acyl complexes

Several methods have been developed for the preparation of α,β-unsaturated iron acyl complexes, a class of complex which is synthetically valuable because its members may be stereoselectively elaborated at two positions.[16] Methylation of the hydroxy group of an aldol reaction product to give **16** followed by sodium hydride-promoted elimination generates the (*E*)-unsaturated iron acyl complex **17**, in many cases exclusively (Scheme 4.9).[16] Since this selectivity is irrespective of the hydroxy group configuration, it is not

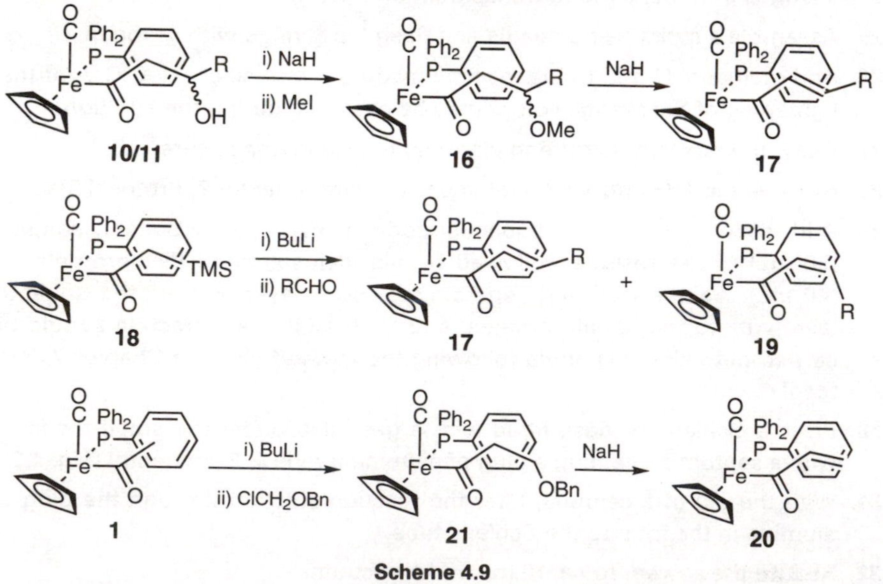

Scheme 4.9

116

necessary to employ a transmetalation strategy in the preparation of the precursor. Peterson elimination of the adduct formed from the enolate of α-trimethylsilyl acyl complex **18** and aldehydes furnishes a mixture of (*E*) and (*Z*) products, **17** and **19** (Scheme 4.9), which may be readily separated by chromatography.[16] The unsubstituted α,β-unsaturated acyl complex **20** may be prepared by sodium hydride-promoted elimination of the adduct **21** formed between the enolate of **1** and benzyl chloromethyl ether (Scheme 4.9).[16]

Protocol 5.
Preparation of (*E*)- (Structure 17) (R = Et) by elimination from the aldol precursor (Scheme 4.9)[16]

Caution! All procedures should be carried out in a well-ventilated hood, and disposable vinyl or latex gloves and chemical-resistant safety glasses should be worn.

Equipment

- Magnetic stirrer
- Teflon-covered magnetic stirrer bars (6 mm × 6 mm × 30 mm, octagonal or egg-shaped)
- Two-necked, round-bottomed flask (100 mL) or Schlenk tube (250 mL)[a]
- Two-necked, round-bottomed flasks (3 × 50 mL) or Schlenk tubes (3 × 100 mL)[a]
- Gas inlets with stopcocks if round-bottomed flasks are used
- Septa

- Short frit (2.5 cm diameter, 15 cm high) (Fig. 4.2)
- Glass syringes with needle-lock luers of appropriate volumes
- Needles (6", 20 or 22 gauge)
- Vacuum/nitrogen manifold (Figs 7.1 and 7.2)
- Cannulae or transfer tubing of appropriate lengths
- Chromatography column

Materials

- Racemic β-hydroxy, pentanoyl iron complex (FW 512.4), 2.97 g, 5.80 mmol (a 1.5:1 mixture of (*R*,*R*)[(*S*,*S*)]/(*R*,*S*)[(*S*,*R*)] isomers; Protocol 4, *via* Li enolate)[12b]   **toxic**
- Sodium hydride – 2 portions: 800 mg of a 50% suspension in oil, 400 mg, 16.7 mmol; 180 mg of a 50% suspension, 90 mg, 3.7 mmol   **toxic, irritant, pyrophoric solid, corrosive**
- Iodomethane (FW 141.9), 1 mL, 2.28 g, 16.1 mmol   **highly toxic, corrosive**
- Dry THF,[b] 2 × 50 + 15 mL   **flammable, irritant**
- Petroleum ether (60–80) for flash chromatography and washing NaH, 300 mL   **flammable, irritant**
- Ethyl acetate for chromatography, 0.5 L   **flammable, irritant**
- Dichloromethane for extractions,[c] 300 mL   **toxic, irritant**
- Alumina (active, grade 1) for chromatography   **irritant**

1. Clean all glassware, syringes, needles and the stirrer bar and dry for at least 2 h in a hot oven (>100°C) before use. Allow apparatus to cool in a desiccator.

2. Assemble the Schlenk tube (250 mL) or the two-necked round-bottomed flask (100 mL)/nitrogen inlet, place the stirrer bar in the flask or Schlenk and attach a septum to the neck of the vessel.

Protocol 5. *Continued*

3. Support the flask or Schlenk using a clamp and stand with a heavy base.

4. Attach a flexible tubing connection from the vacuum/nitrogen manifold to the gas inlet or side-arm.

5. Dry the apparatus with an electric heat gun or a small Bunsen burner at reduced pressure (0.5–1 mmHg), allow to cool and refill with nitrogen.

6. Add sodium hydride (800 mg of a 50% suspension in oil, 400 mg, 16.7 mmol) to the flask or Schlenk. This should be added rapidly against a gentle stream of nitrogen after removal of the septum, which should be replaced immediately.

7. Assemble a syringe and needle and flush the syringe with nitrogen following the procedure given in Chapter 3, Protocol 3, step 4.

8. Add petroleum ether (20 mL) to the flask. Swirl the contents gently then filter off the solvent using a filter cannula following the procedure in Chapter 7, Protocol 4.

9. Remove the last trace of solvent under vacuum to leave a fine flowing powder. **CAUTION** – this is highly active sodium hydride. Gently reintroduce nitrogen into the flask.

10. Assemble a 100 mL Schlenk tube or 50 mL round-bottomed flask/gas inlet and attach to the vacuum/nitrogen manifold. Place a septum in the neck of the vessel.

11. Treat the flask following the procedure given in step 5.

12. Charge the flask with racemic β-hydroxy, pentanoyl iron complex (2.97 g, 5.80 mmol). This should be added rapidly against a gentle stream of nitrogen after removal of the septum, which should be replaced immediately.

13. Assemble a syringe and needle and flush the syringe with nitrogen.

14. Use this syringe to transfer THF (50 mL), taken directly from the still, into the flask or Schlenk containing the complex.

15. Transfer the solution of iron acyl complex from this flask to the main reaction flask, at room temperature, using the same syringe as in step 14. Add the solution dropwise over *ca.* 10 min.

16. Stir for 30 min at room temperature.

17. Assemble a syringe and needle and flush the syringe with nitrogen.

18. Add neat iodomethane (1 mL, 16.1 mmol) dropwise by syringe (1 min).

19. Stir for 30 min at room temperature.

20. Remove the solvent under vacuum (Chapter 7, Protocol 3).

21. Assemble a syringe and needle and flush the syringe with nitrogen.

22. Assemble a second small Schlenk and fit it with a small frit containing a plug of alumina and a septum. Attach the Schlenk to the vacuum/nitrogen manifold (Fig. 4.2).

23. Add nitrogen-saturated dichloromethane (20 mL) to the residue, agitate

briefly and then filter this solution through the short frit. Repeat this extraction twice.

24. Remove solvent from the dichloromethane extracts to give the crude methylated product which may be purified by flash chromatography (Chapter 7, Protocol 5) to give 2.45 g, 80%, of an orange product. Alternatively this mixture may be taken directly on in the next step.

25. Assemble a syringe and needle and flush the syringe with nitrogen.

26. Assemble a third small Schlenk and add a magnetic stirrer bar. Attach the Schlenk to the vacuum/nitrogen manifold.

27. Treat the flask following the procedure given in step 5.

28. Add sodium hydride (180 mg of a 50% suspension, 90 mg, 3.7 mmol) to the flask or Schlenk. This should be added rapidly against a gentle stream of nitrogen after removal of the septum, which should be replaced immediately.

29. Repeat steps 7–9 above on this Schlenk.

30. Assemble a syringe and needle and flush the syringe with nitrogen.

31. Using the syringe from step 30, add THF (15 mL) to the flask containing the methylated β-hydroxy iron acyl complex.

32. Using the syringe from step 30, transfer the solution from step 31 into the Schlenk containing the sodium hydride.

33. Stir this solution at room temperature for 66 h.

34. Remove the solvent under vacuum.

35. Repeat steps 21–23 using three 10 mL portions of dichloromethane.

36. Reduce the solution to *ca.* 5 mL and purify the product, (*E*)-**17** (R = CH_2CH_3) (90 mg, 95%) by flash chromatography on alumina, following the procedure given in Chapter 7, Protocol 5. All materials in this protocol display the appropriate spectroscopic data.[16]

[a] Due to the design of a Schlenk tube, this must generally be of a larger volume than the corresponding round-bottomed flask for a reaction of a given scale.
[b] Freshly distilled from sodium benzophenone ketyl under an inert atmosphere.
[c] Freshly distilled from calcium hydride.

2.6 Conjugate addition reactions

Conjugate addition[17] of nucleophiles, such as alkyllithiums, to (*E*)-α,β-unsaturated iron acyl complexes takes place on the face opposite the phenyl ring of the triphenylphosphine group when the acryloyl group is in the *cisoid* conformation.[17] The intermediate enolates may be trapped by protonation to give **22** or with an electrophile to give the α,β-disubstituted product **23** in which the configuration of the new α-centre is dictated entirely by the iron complex (Scheme 4.10).[17] Such methodology has been successfully applied to the asymmetric synthesis of β-lactams *via* conjugate addition of a lithiated benzylamine.[17] In contrast (Z)-α,β-unsaturated acyl complexes are deprotonated by alkyllithiums to give dienolates which may be subsequently elaborated stereoselectively.[18]

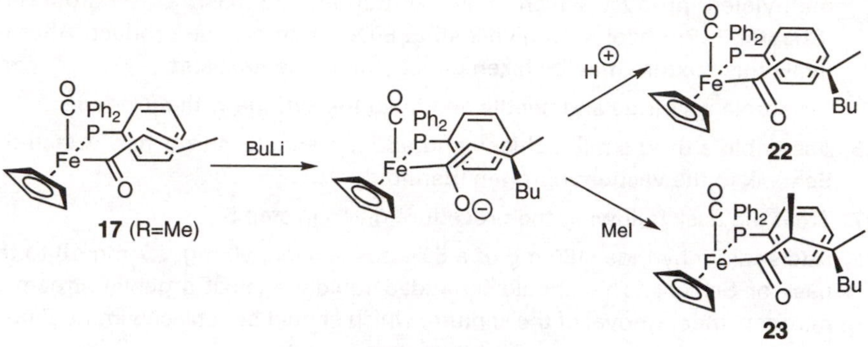

Scheme 4.10

2.7 Other applications

Chiral iron acyl complexes have been applied to the asymmetric synthesis of cyclopropane carboxylic acids,[19] sulfoxides[20] and β-amino acids.[21] Further details and applications may be found in the reviews given in the reference section.[1]

3. π-Allyltricarbonyliron lactone complexes[22]

3.1 Introduction

The reaction of vinyl epoxides with diiron nonacarbonyl in THF solution gives π-allyltricarbonyliron lactone complexes **24** in high yield (Scheme 4.11).[23,24] Alternatively butene-1,4-diols[25] and cyclic sulfites derived from 1,2-diols[26] may be employed as starting materials under appropriate conditions. The π-allyltricarbonyliron lactones may be converted into a number of products including β-lactones and unsaturated γ-lactones upon oxidative extrusion or carbonylation at high pressure, respectively.[22] The corresponding iron lactam complexes **25** may be prepared by treatment of **24** with an amine in the presence of a Lewis acid such as zinc dichloride and these can be converted to β- or γ-lactams in analogous ways (Scheme 4.11).[22]

The iron complexes **24** and **25** are invariably stable crystalline materials which may be purified by chromatography on silica gel, alumina or Florisil without significant decomposition. They are stable to certain oxidising agents including PCC, PDC, ozone, *t*-butyl peroxide, manganese dioxide and iron trichloride. They are unaffected by the reducing agent samarium diiodide and hydrogenation using palladium on a carbon support although they are decomposed by the more vigorous reducing agents sodium borohydride and lithium aluminium hydride. They are stable to water, isonitriles, Lewis acidic organometallics and Wittig reagents. Strongly basic or acidic conditions or

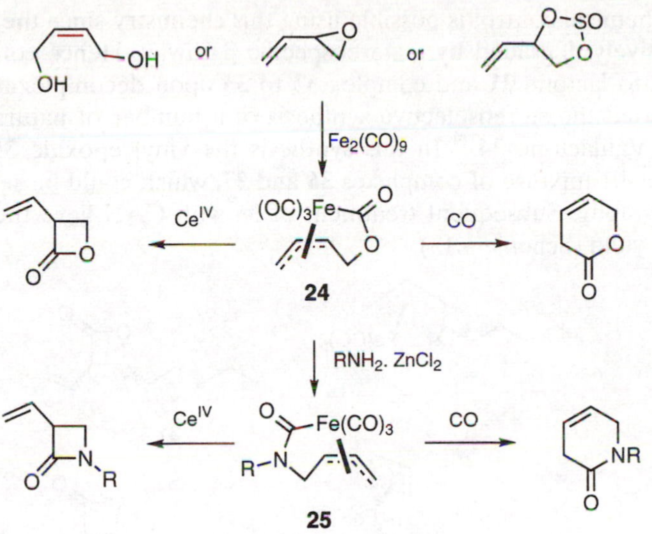

Scheme 4.11

temperatures above 60 °C cause decomposition, although synthetically valuable products may sometimes be formed in the process.[27]

3.2 Synthesis of β-lactones[28]

Oxidative extrusion of β-lactones from the π-allyl complexes is most effect-ively achieved using ceric ammonium nitrate (CAN). It is essential that the structure of the complex does not preclude formation of the four-membered ring. Whilst the β-lactone **26** is readily formed as the major product from the *cis* complex **27**, the larger δ-lactone **28** is formed from the *trans* complex **29** (Scheme 4.12).

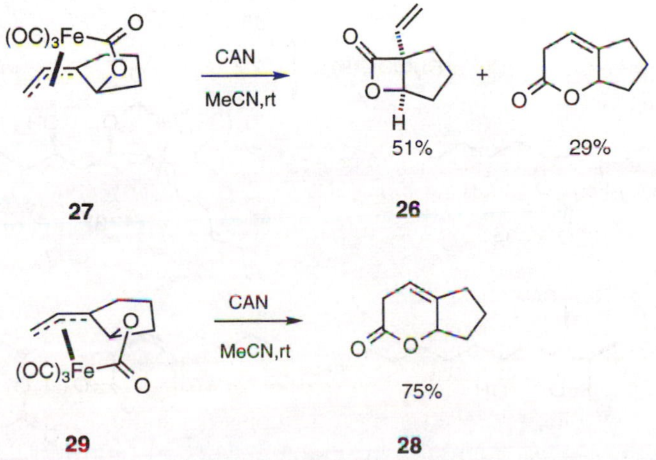

Scheme 4.12

Stereochemical control is possible using this chemistry since the complexes are oxidatively degraded by a stereospecific pathway. Hence complex **30** is converted to lactone **31** and complex **32** to **33** upon decomplexation.[28] This has permitted the stereoselective synthesis of a number of natural products including Valilactone **34**.[29] In this synthesis the vinyl epoxide **35** was converted to a 4:1 mixture of complexes **36** and **37**, which could be separated by chromatography. Subsequent treatment of **36** with CAN gave the β-lactone **38** in 26% yield (Scheme 4.13).

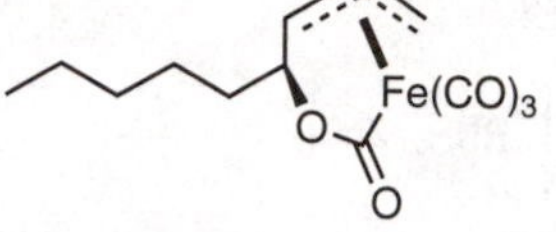

30 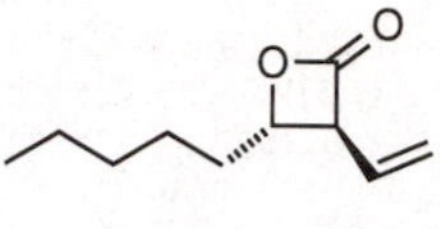　　　　　　　　　　**31**

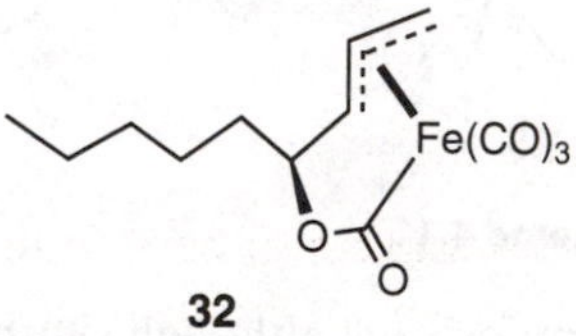

32 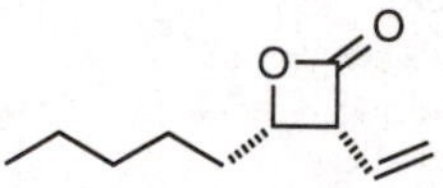　　　　　　　　　　**33**

Protocol 6.

Synthesis of *trans*-β-lactone (Structure 38) from allylic epoxide (Structure 35) *via* intermediate π-allyl iron tricarbonyl complexes (Structures 36 and 37) (Scheme 4.13)[29]

Caution! All procedures should be carried out in a well-ventilated hood, and disposable vinyl or latex gloves and chemical-resistant safety glasses should be worn.

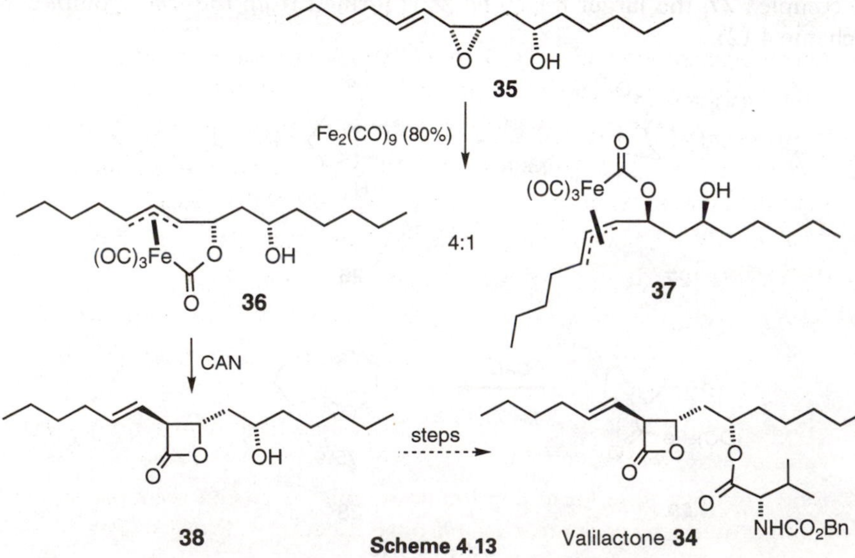

35

Fe₂(CO)₉ (80%)

4:1

36　　　　　　　　　　**37**

CAN

steps

38　　　　**Scheme 4.13**　　　Valilactone **34**　　NHCO₂Bn

122

Equipment

- Magnetic stirrer box
- Teflon-covered magnetic stirrer bars (5 mm × 5 mm × 25 mm, octagonal or egg-shaped)
- Two-necked, round-bottomed flasks (50 mL) or Schlenk tubes (100 mL)[a]
- Gas inlets with stopcocks if round-bottomed flasks are used
- Septa
- Glass syringes with needle-lock luers of appropriate volumes
- Needles (6″, 20 or 22 gauge)
- Vacuum/nitrogen manifold (Figs 7.1 and 7.2)
- Cannulae or transfer tubing of appropriate lengths
- Chromatography column

Materials

- Epoxide **35** (FW 240.1), 115 mg, 0.48 mmol[29]   **toxic**
- Di-iron nonacarbonyl (FW 363.8), 272 mg, 0.75 mmol   **highly toxic, irritant**
- Ceric ammonium nitrate (FW 548.2), 1.29 g, 2.4 mmol   **toxic, irritant**
- Phosphate buffer solution (pH 7), 50 mL   **irritant**
- Dry THF,[b] 5 mL   **flammable, irritant**
- Ethanol, 10 mL   **flammable, irritant**
- Petroleum ether (60-80) for chromatography, 0.5 L   **flammable, irritant**
- Diethyl ether for flash chromatography, 0.5 L   **flammable, irritant**
- Silica gel for chromatography (Merck Kieselgel 60)   **irritant**

1. Clean all glassware, syringes, needles and stirrer bars and dry for at least 2 h in a hot oven (>100°C) before use. Allow apparatus to cool in a desiccator.

2. Assemble a Schlenk tube or round-bottomed flask/nitrogen inlet, place the stirrer bar in the flask or Schlenk and attach a septum to the remaining neck of the vessel.

3. Support the flask or Schlenk using a clamp and stand with a heavy base.

4. Attach a flexible tubing connection from the vacuum/nitrogen manifold to the gas inlet.

5. Dry the apparatus with an electric heat gun or a small Bunsen burner at reduced pressure (0.5–1 mmHg), allow to cool and refill with nitrogen.

6. Assemble a syringe and needle and flush the syringe with nitrogen following the procedure given in Chapter 3, Protocol 3, step 4.

7. Add di-iron nonacarbonyl (272 mg, 0.75 mmol) to the flask or Schlenk.

8. Assemble a second Schlenk or flask and attach to the vacuum/nitrogen manifold. Place a septum in the remaining neck of the vessel.

9. Treat the flask following the procedure given in step 5.

10. Charge the flask with epoxide **35** (115 mg, 0.48 mmol).

11. Assemble a syringe and needle and flush the syringe with nitrogen.

12. Use this syringe to transfer THF (5 mL), taken directly from the still, into the flask or Schlenk containing the complex.

13. Transfer the solution of epoxide **35** from this flask to the main reaction flask, at room temperature, using the same syringe as in step 12.

14. Slowly reduce the pressure in the flask until the stirred solution begins to bubble, then slowly reintroduce nitrogen (Chapter 7, Protocol 2).

Protocol 6. *Continued*

15. Stir for 2 h at room temperature.

16. Remove the solvent under vacuum using a rotary evaporator.

17. Subject the mixture of ferrilactones **36** and **37** to flash chromatography on silica gel using petroleum ether/diethyl ether (1:1) as eluent (Chapter 7, Protocol 5). This gives **36** and **37** as a 4:1 mixture (153 mg, 80%).

18. Assemble a third Schlenk or flask and attach to the vacuum/nitrogen manifold. Place a septum in the remaining neck of the vessel.

19. Treat the flask following the procedure given in step 5.

20. Charge the flask with the 4:1 mixture of ferrilactones **36** and **37** (153 mg, 0.31 mmol) isolated in step 17.

21. Assemble a syringe and needle and flush the syringe with nitrogen.

22. Add ethanol (10 mL) to the flask by syringe.

23. Add solid ceric ammonium nitrate (1.29 g, 2.4 mmol) to the flask. This should be added rapidly against a gentle stream of nitrogen after removal of the septum, which should be replaced immediately.

24. Assemble a syringe and needle and flush the syringe with nitrogen.

25. Add buffer solution (3 drops) to the flask, using the syringe from step 24.

26. Slowly reduce the pressure in the flask until the stirred solution begins to bubble, then slowly reintroduce nitrogen.

27. Stir at room temperature for 2 h.

28. Remove the solvent under vacuum using a rotary evaporator.

29. Purify lactone **38** by flash chromatography on silica gel using petroleum ether/diethyl ether (4:1 to 1:1) as eluent (20 mg, 26% based on recovered starting material). Lactone **38** displays the appropriate spectroscopic data.[29]

[a] Due to the design of a Schlenk tube, this must generally be of a larger volume than the corresponding round-bottomed flask for a reaction of a given scale.
[b] Freshly distilled from sodium benzophenone ketyl under an inert atmosphere.

3.3 Synthesis of δ-lactones

Exhaustive high-pressure carbonylation of π-allyl tricarbonylallyl complexes results in their conversion to unsaturated δ-lactones.[30] The products are usually unsaturated at the γ,δ-position although the double bond can migrate into conjugation with the lactone carbonyl group in some cases. A particularly attractive feature of this chemistry is that certain functional groups, such as hydroxy groups, which would normally require protection can be left unprotected.[30] This chemistry has been applied to numerous synthetic projects including the total synthesis of the antibiotics Malyngolide[30] and Avermectin

Bla.[26b,31] The total synthesis of Routiennocin employed iron tricarbonyl chemistry for the synthesis of the spiroketal unit.[32] In this sequence the allylic epoxide **39** is converted to a mixture of allyl iron complexes **40** and **41** which is not separated but carbonylated together to give lactone **42** as a 9:1 ($\alpha\beta : \beta\gamma$) mixture (Scheme 4.14); this mixture is subsequently reduced to the saturated lactone **43**.[34]

Protocol 7.
Preparation of unsaturated γ-lactones (Structure 42) from epoxide (Structure 39) via intermediate π-allyl irontricarbonyl complexes (Structures 40 and 41) (Scheme 4.14)[32]

Caution! All procedures should be carried out in a well-ventilated hood, and disposable vinyl or latex gloves and chemical-resistant safety glasses should be worn.

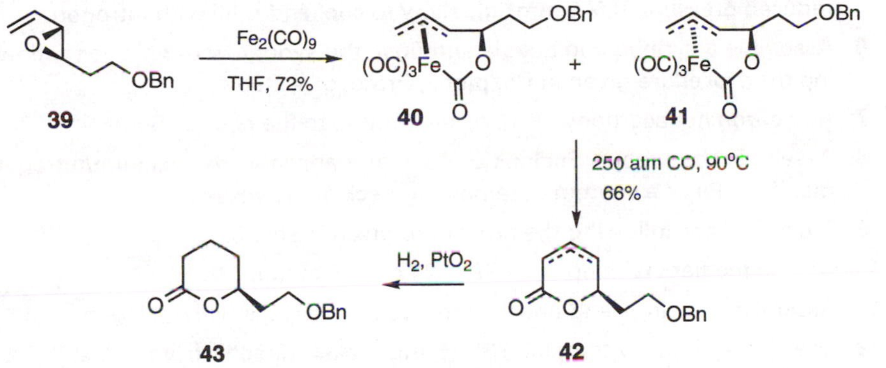

Scheme 4.14

Equipment

- Magnetic stirrer
- Teflon-covered magnetic stirrer bars (6 mm × 6 mm × 30 mm, octagonal or egg-shaped)
- High-pressure (up to 250 atm) steel reaction vessel
- Two-necked, round-bottomed flasks (2 × 100 mL) or Schlenk tubes (2 × 200 mL)[a]
- Gas inlets with stopcocks if round-bottomed flasks are used

- Septa
- Glass syringes with needle-lock luers of appropriate volumes
- Needles (6″, 20 or 22 gauge)
- Vacuum/nitrogen manifold (Figs 7.1 and 7.2)
- Cannulae or transfer tubing of appropriate lengths
- Chromatography column

Materials

- Epoxide **39** (FW 190.1), 2.21 g, 10.8 mmol[32]   toxic
- Diiron nonacarbonyl (FW 363.8), 5.13 g, 14.1 mmol   highly toxic, irritant
- Ceric ammonium nitrate (FW 548.2), 2.96 g, 5.4 mmol   toxic, irritant
- Phosphate buffer solution (pH 7), 100 mL   irritant
- Dry THF,[b] 5 mL   flammable, irritant

Protocol 7. *Continued*

- Dry benzene,[b] 50 mL   **carcinogenic, flammable, irritant**
- A supply of carbon monoxide of 250 atm pressure
- Petroleum ether (60-80) for chromatography, 0.5 L   **flammable, irritant**
- Diethyl ether for flash chromatography, 0.5 L   **flammable, irritant**
- Silica gel for chromatography (Merck Kieselgel 60)   **irritant**

1. Clean all glassware, syringes, needles and stirrer bars and dry for at least 2 h in a hot oven (>100°C) before use. Allow apparatus to cool in a desiccator.
2. Assemble a 200 mL Schlenk tube or 100 mL flask with nitrogen inlet, place the stirrer bar in the flask or Schlenk and attach a septum to the remaining neck of the apparatus.
3. Support the flask or Schlenk using a clamp and stand with a heavy base.
4. Attach a flexible tubing connection from the vacuum/nitrogen manifold to the gas inlet.
5. Dry the apparatus with an electric heat gun or a small Bunsen burner at reduced pressure (0.5–1 mmHg), allow to cool and refill with nitrogen.
6. Assemble a syringe and needle and flush the syringe with nitrogen following the procedure given in Chapter 3, Protocol 3, step 4.
7. Add diiron nonacarbonyl (5.13 g, 14.1 mmol) to the flask or Schlenk.
8. Assemble the second Schlenk or flask and attach to the vacuum/nitrogen manifold. Place a septum in remaining neck of the vessel.
9. Treat the flask following the procedure given in step 5.
10. Charge the flask with epoxide **39** (2.21 g, 10.8 mmol).
11. Assemble a syringe and needle and flush the syringe with nitrogen.
12. Use this syringe to transfer THF (5 mL), taken directly from the still, into the flask or Schlenk containing the complex.
13. Transfer the solution of epoxide **39** from this flask to the main reaction flask, at room temperature, using the same syringe as in step 12.
14. Slowly reduce the pressure in the flask until the stirred solution begins to bubble, then slowly reintroduce nitrogen (Chapter 7, Protocol 2).
15. Stir for 6 h at room temperature.
16. Remove the solvent from the green solution under vacuum (Chapter 7, Protocol 3).
17. Purify the residue by flash chromatography on silica gel using petroleum ether/diethyl ether (7:3) as eluent (Chapter 7, Protocol 5). This gives a mixture of ferrilactones **40** and **41** as a yellow oil (2.7 g, 72%), which displays appropriate spectroscopic data.
18. Charge the high-pressure steel hydrogenation vessel with the purified 4:1 mixture of ferrilactones **40** and **41** (2.7 g, 7.5 mmol).
19. Assemble a syringe and needle and flush the syringe with nitrogen.

20. Add benzene (50 mL) to the high-pressure steel hydrogenation vessel, containing a stirrer bar, by syringe.

21. Seal the high-pressure steel hydrogenation vessel carefully.

22. Pressurise to 250 atm of carbon monoxide.

23. Heat the mixture, under pressure, at 90° C overnight with stirring.

24. Allow the mixture to cool down to room temperature and release the pressure carefully.

25. Remove the solvent under vacuum.

26. Purify the product by flash chromatography on silica gel using petroleum ether/diethyl ether (1:1) as eluent to afford a mixture of unsaturated lactones **42** (1.15 g, 66%, a 9:1 (αβ:βγ) mixture) as a colourless oil. Products **40–42** display appropriate spectroscopic data.[32]

[a] Due to the design of a Schlenk tube, this must generally be of a larger volume than the corresponding round-bottomed flask for a reaction of a given scale.
[b] Freshly distilled from sodium benzophenone ketyl under an inert atmosphere.

3.4 Synthesis of lactams[31–35]

As has been stated above, reaction of π-allyl tricarbonyliron lactone complexes with amines in the presence of Lewis acids such as $ZnCl_2$ results in the formation of the corresponding tricarbonyliron lactam complexes *via* an S_N2' reaction.[24c,d,33] These complexes (e.g. **46**) may be converted by CAN to β-lactams such as **44** (Scheme 4.15) in an exactly analogous way to the method described above.[33] Since β-lactams occur in numerous physiologically important natural products this is a valuable reaction sequence which has been applied to the synthesis of nocardicins[34] and thienamycin.[35] Recently a synthesis of pyrrolizidine alkaloids has been developed using this methodology.[36]

Protocol 8.
Synthesis of π-allyl iron tricarbonyl lactam complex (Structure 46) from a π-allyl iron tricarbonyl lactone complex (Structure 45) (Scheme 4.15)

Caution! All procedures should be carried out in a well-ventilated hood, and disposable vinyl or latex gloves and chemical-resistant safety glasses should be worn.

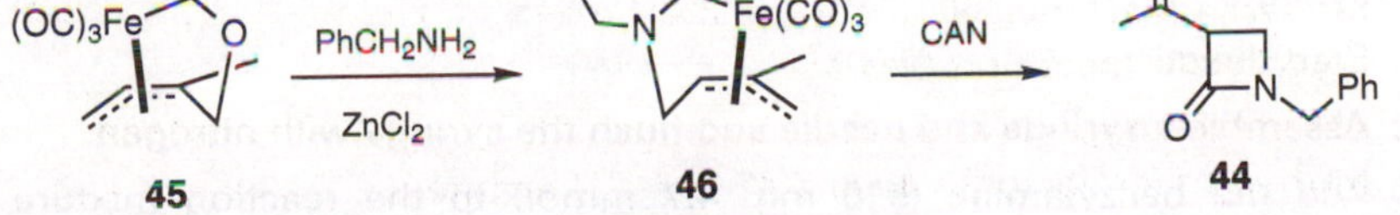

Scheme 4.15

Protocol 8. *Continued*

Equipment

- Magnetic stirrer
- Teflon-covered magnetic stirrer bars (5 mm × 5 mm × 22 mm, octagonal or egg-shaped)
- Two-necked, round-bottomed flask (100 mL) or Schlenk tube (200 mL)[a]
- Gas inlet with stopcock if round-bottomed flask is used

- Septa
- Glass syringes with needle-lock luers of appropriate volumes
- Needles (6", 20 or 22 gauge)
- Vacuum/nitrogen manifold (Figs 7.1 and 7.2)
- Chromatography column

Materials

- Iron lactone complex **45** (FW 252.1), 100 mg, 0.4 mmol[33] **toxic**
- Benzylamine (FW 107.2), 510 mg, 4.7 mmol **toxic**
- Zinc dichloride (FW 136.3), 107 mg, 0.8 mmol **irritant**
- Dry THF,[b] 1.5 mL **flammable, irritant**
- Dry diethyl ether,[b] 3.5 mL **flammable, irritant**
- Petroleum ether (60-80) for chromatography, 0.5 L **flammable, irritant**
- Diethyl ether for chromatography, 0.5 L **flammable, irritant**
- Silica gel for chromatography (Merck Kieselgel 60) **irritant**

1. Clean all glassware, syringes, needles and stirring bars and dry for at least 2 h in a hot oven (>100 °C) before use. Allow apparatus to cool in a desiccator.

2. Assemble a 200 mL Schlenk tube or 100 mL round-bottomed flask and gas inlet, place the stirrer bar in the flask or Schlenk and attach the septum to the remaining neck of the apparatus.

3. Support the flask or Schlenk using a clamp and stand with a heavy base.

4. Attach a flexible tubing connection from the vacuum/nitrogen manifold to the gas inlet.

5. Dry the apparatus with an electric heat gun or a small Bunsen burner at reduced pressure (0.5–1 mmHg), allow to cool and refill with nitrogen.

6. Charge the flask with iron lactone complex **45** (100 mg, 0.4 mmol). This should be added rapidly against a steady stream of nitrogen after removal of the septum, which should be replaced immediately.

7. Assemble a syringe and needle and flush the syringe with nitrogen following the procedure given in Chapter 3, Protocol 3, step 4.

8. Add THF (1.5 mL), taken directly from the still, to the flask by syringe.

9. Assemble a syringe and needle and flush the syringe with nitrogen.

10. Add diethyl ether (3.5 mL), taken directly from the still, to the flask by syringe.

11. Start the stirrer.

12. Assemble a syringe and needle and flush the syringe with nitrogen.

13. Add the benzylamine (510 mg, 4.7 mmol) to the reaction mixture by syringe.

14. Add the zinc dichloride (107 mg, 0.8 mmol). This should be added rapidly against a gentle stream of nitrogen after removal of the septum, which should be replaced immediately.

15. Slowly reduce the pressure in the flask until the stirred solution begins to bubble, then slowly reintroduce nitrogen (Chapter 7, Protocol 2).

16. Stir the reaction mixture at room temperature until no more starting material can be detected by TLC (typically 0.5–3 h).

17. Remove the solvent under vacuum (Chapter 7, Protocol 3).

18. Flash chromatography on silica gel using petroleum ether/diethyl ether (1:2) as eluent (Chapter 7, Protocol 5) serves to purify the lactam complex **46** (128 mg, 95%) as a white crystalline solid. The β-lactam can be prepared from the complex by treatment with CAN following the method in Protocol 7. Complex **46** displays appropriate spectroscopic data.[33]

---

[a] Due to the design of a Schlenk tube, this must generally be of a larger volume than the corresponding round-bottomed flask for a reaction of a given scale.
[b] Freshly distilled from sodium benzophenone ketyl under an inert atmosphere.

References

1. Davies, S. G. *Aldrichemica Acta* **1990**, *23*, 31–52.
2. Davies, S. G.; Seeman, J. I.; Williams, I. H. *Tetrahedron Lett.* **1986**, *27*, 619–622.
3. (a) Aktogu, N.; Davies, S. G.; Felkin, H. *J. Chem. Soc., Chem. Commun.* **1982**, 1303–1304. (b) Aktogu, N.; Davies, S. G.; Felkin, H.; Baird, G. J.; Watts, O. *J. Organomet. Chem.* **1984**, *262*, 49–58.
4. Shriver, D. F.; Dreszdon, M. A. *The Manipulation of Air-Sensitive Compounds* 2nd edn.; Wiley, **1986**.
5. (a) Green, M.; Westlake, D. J. *J. Chem. Soc. (A)* **1971**, 367–371. (b) Bibler, J. P.; Wojcicki, A. *Inorg. Chem.* **1966**, *5*, 889–892.
6. (a) Brunner, H.; Schmidt, E. *J. Organomet. Chem.* **1972**, *36*, C18–22. (b) Brunner, H.; Schmidt, E. *J. Organomet. Chem.* **1973**, *50*, 219–225.
7. Case-Green, S.; Costello, J. F.; Heaton, N.; Heathcock, C. J. R.; Humphries, V. M.; Meltzler, M. M.; Prime, J. C. *J. Chem. Soc., Perkin Trans. 1* **1994**, 933–941.
8. Wakefield, B. J. *Organolithium Methods*, Academic Press: London, **1988**, Chap. 2, p. 18.
9. (a) Baird, G. J.; Davies, S. G. *J. Organomet. Chem.* **1983**, *248*, C1–3. (b) Baird, G. J.; Bandy, J. A.; Davies, S. G.; Prout, K. *J. Chem. Soc., Chem. Commun.* **1983**, 1202–1203. (c) Baker, T. M.; Bodwell, G. J.; Edwards, A. J.; Metzler, M. R. *Tetrahedron* **1993**, *49*, 5635–5647. (d) Bodwell, G. J.; Davies, S. G. *Tetrahedron: Asymmetry* **1991**, *2*, 1075–1082.
10. Brown, S. L.; Davies, S. G.; Foster, D. F.; Seeman, J. I.; Warner, P. *Tetrahedron Lett.* **1986**, *27*, 623–626.
11. Bashiardes, G.; Davies, S. G. *Tetrahedron Lett.* **1987**, *28*, 5563–5564.
12. (a) Davies, S. G.; Dordor, I. M.; Warner, P. *J. Chem. Soc., Chem. Commun.* **1984**, 956–957. (b) Davies, S. G.; Dordor-Hedgecock, I. M.; Jones, R. H.; Prout, K.;

Warner, P. *Organomet. Chem.* **1985**, *285*, 213–223. (c) Liebeskind, L. S.; Welker, M. E.; Fengl, R. W. *J. Am. Chem. soc.* **1986**, *108*, 6328–6343. (d) Cooke, J. W. B.; Davies, S. G.; Naylor, A. *Tetrahedron* **1993**, *49*, 7955–7966.

13. Beckett, R. P.; Davies, S. G.; Mortlock, A. A. *Tetrahedron: Asymmetry* **1992**, *3*, 123–136.

14. (a) Davies, S. G.; Dordor, I. M.; Walker, J. C.; Warner, P. *Tetrahedron Lett.* **1984**, *25*, 2709–2712. (b) Davies, S. G.; Dordor-Hedgecock, I. M.; Warner, P. *Tetrahedron Lett.* **1985**, *26*, 2125–2128. (c) Ambler, P. W.; Davies, S. G. *Tetrahedron Lett.* **1985**, *26*, 2129–2130.

15. Capon, R. J.; Macleod, J. K.; Coote, S. G.; Davies, S. G.; Gravatt, G. L.; Dordor-Hedgecock, I. M.; Whittaker, M. *Tetrahedron* **1988**, *44*, 1637–1650.

16. (a) Davies, S. G.; Dordor-Hedgecock, I. M.; Sutton, K. H.; Walker, J. C.; Bourne, C.; Jones, R. H.; Prout, K. *J. Chem. Soc., Chem. Commun.* **1986**, 607–609. (b) Davies, S. G.; Easton, R. J. C.; Walker, J. C.; Warner, P. *J. Organomet. Chem.* **1985**, *296*, C40–42. (c) Davies, S. G.; Easton, R. J. C.; Walker, J. C.; Warner, P. *Tetrahedron* **1986**, *42*, 175–188.

17. (a) Davies, S. G.; Walker, J. C. *J. Chem. Soc., Chem. Commun.* **1985**, 209–210. (b) Davies, S. G.; Dordor-Hedgecock, I. M.; Sutton, K. H.; Walker, J. C. *Tetrahedron Lett.* **1986**, *27*, 3787–3797. (c) Davies, S. G.; Dordor-Hedgecock, I. M.; Sutton, K. H.; Walker, J. C. *Tetrahedron* **1986**, *42*, 5123–5137.

18. (a) Davies, S. G.; Easton, R. J. C.; Gonzalez, A.; Preston, S. C.; Sutton, K. H.; Walker, J. C. *Tetrahedron* **1986**, *42*, 3987–3997. (b) Davies, S. G.; Easton, R. J. C.; Sutton, K. H.; Walker, J. C.; Jones, R. H. *J. Chem. Soc., Perkin Trans. 1* **1987**, 489–493.

19. Ambler, P. W.; Davies, S. G. *Tetrahedron Lett.* **1988**, *29*, 6979–6982.

20. Davies, S. G.; Gravatt, G. L. *J. Chem. Soc., Chem. Commun.* **1988**, 780–781.

21. Davies, S. G.; Dupont, J.; Easton, R. J. C. *Tetrahedron: Asymmetry* **1990**, *1*, 279–280.

22. Ley, S. V. *Phil. Trans. Roy. Soc. Lond. A* **1988**, 663–640.

23. Horton, A. M.; Hollinshead, D. M.; Ley, S. V. *Tetrahedron* **1984**, *40*, 1737–1742.

24. (a) Auman, R.; Frohlich, K.; Ring, H. *Angew. Chem., Int. Ed. Engl.* **1974**, *13*, 275–276. (b) Chen, K. N.; Moriarty, R. M.; DeBoer, B. G.; Churchill, M. R.; Yeh, H. J. C. *J. Am. Chem. Soc.* **1975**, *97*, 5602–5603. (c) Becker, Y.; Eisenstadt, A.; Shvo, Y. *Tetrahedron* **1976**, *32*, 2123–2126.

25. Bates, R. W.; Diez-Martin, D.; Kerr, W. J.; Knight, J. G.; Ley, S. V.; Sakellaridis, A. *Tetrahedron* **1990**, *46*, 4063–4082.

26. (a) Caruso, M.; Knight, J. G.; Ley, S. V. *Synlett* **1990**, 224–226. (b) Ford, M. J.; Knight, J. G.; Ley, S. V.; Vile, S. *Synlett* **1990**, 331–332.

27. Annis, G. D.; Ley, S. V.; Self, C. R.; Sivaramakrishnan, R. *J. Chem. Soc., Perkin Trans. 1* **1982**, 1355–1361.

28. Annis, G. D.; Ley, S. V.; Self, C. R.; Sivaramakrishnan, R. *J. Chem. Soc., Perkin Trans. 1* **1981**, 270–277.

29. (a) Bates, R. W.; Fernandez-Moro, R.; Ley, S. V. *Tetrahedron Lett.* **1991**, *32*, 2651–2654. (b) Bates, R. W.; Fernandez-Moro, R.; Ley, S. V. *Tetrahedron* **1991**, *47*, 9929–9938.

30. Horton, A. M.; Ley, S. V. *J. Organomet. Chem.* **1985**, *285*, C17–20.

31. (a) Ley, S. L.; Armstrong, A.; Diez-Martin, D.; Ford, M. J.; Grice, P.; Knight, J. G. F.; Kolb, H. C.; Madin, A.; Marby, C. A.; Mukherjee, S.; Shaw, A. N.; Slawin,

A. M. Z.; Vile, S.; White, A. D.; Williams, D. J.; Woods, M. *J. Chem. Soc., Perkin Trans. 1* **1991**, 667–692, and references therein.

32. (a) Kotecha, N. R.; Ley, S. V.; Mantegani, S. *Synlett* **1993**, 395–396. (b) Diez-Martin, D.; Kotecha, N. R.; Ley, S. V.; Menandez, J. C. *Synlett* **1993**, 399–400. (b) Diez-Martin, D.; Kotecha, N. R.; Ley, S. V.; Menandez, J. C. *Tetrahedron* **1992**, *48*, 7899–7938.

33. Annis, G. D.; Hebblethwaite, E. M.; Hodgson, S. T.; Hollinshead, D. M.; Ley, S. V. *J. Chem. Soc., Perkin Trans. 1* **1983**, 2851–2856.

34. Hodgson, S. T.; Hollinshead, D. M.; Ley, S. V.; Low, C. M.; Williams, D. J. *J. Chem. Soc., Perkin Trans. 1* **1985**, 2375–2382.

35. Hodgson, S. T.; Hollinshead, D. M.; Ley, S. V. *Tetrahedron* **1985**, *41*, 5871–5878.

36. Knight, J. G.; Ley, S. V. *Tetrahedron Lett.* **1991**, *32*, 7119–7122.

5

Titanocene and zirconocene η^2-π complexes

RICHARD J. WHITBY

1. Introduction

Titanium and zirconium are Group 4 transition metals. Both are comparatively cheap and non-toxic and as a result stoichiometric applications are practical. The +4 oxidation state is most common, with the +2 oxidation state being important in many reactions. Titanium also has an extensive chemistry in the +3 oxidation state. The high oxidation state makes the +4 complexes strong Lewis acids, a property which has been widely used in synthesis.

Titanium and zirconium chemistry is conveniently divided between 'simple' complexes and those based on the metallocene unit 'Cp$_2$M' (Cp = C$_5$H$_5$ = cyclopentadienyl). Most 'simple' complexes are oligomeric, insoluble, and difficult to characterise, although alkyl titanium complexes such as X$_3$TiR have found some use as 'non-basic' Grignard equivalents.[1] The dicyclopentadienyl metal moiety, Cp$_2$M, renders complexes monomeric, soluble, and easily characterised by NMR spectroscopy, and thus many applications based on these systems have been devised. The most stable electronic configuration of titanocene and zirconocene complexes has only 16 electrons in the valence shell, not the 18 electrons common in most of the rest of the transition metal series. The empty orbital this leaves on the metal is crucial for reactivity.

Organotitanium and -zirconium chemistry already has an established place in organic synthesis and many reactions are covered elsewhere in the *Practical Approach* series. Examples include: reductive coupling of carbonyl compounds with low valent titanium to form 1,2-diols or alkenes;[2] methylenation of ester carbonyl groups with titanocene methylidene (Cp$_2$Ti=CH$_2$);[2] zirconium-catalysed methylalumination of alkynes;[2] and hydrozirconation of alkynes and alkenes with the Schwartz reagent, Cp$_2$ZrHCl.[3]

Described in this chapter is the stoichiometric chemistry of complexes in which a titanocene or zirconocene moiety is η^2-bound to an alkene, alkyne, heteroalkene, or heteroalkyne. These complexes may be viewed as a metallocene [M(II)] species (**1A**) or as the metallacyclopropane/ene [M(IV)] species (**1B**) (Scheme 5.1). Although the complexes have characteristics typical of both structures, the 'extreme back bonding' structure **1B** fits the physical data best and is generally the form drawn. The importance of complexes **1** is based on their ready insertion of unactivated alkenes or alkynes to give metallacyclopentanoids **2** as this makes them excellent carbometallating reagents.

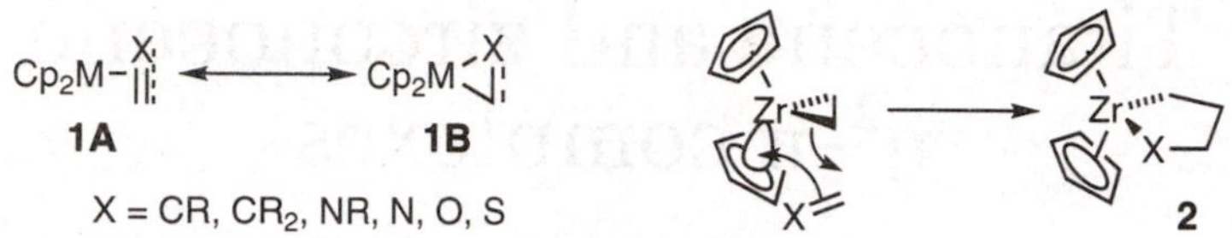

$X = CR, CR_2, NR, N, O, S$

Scheme 5.1

2. Formation of titanocene and zirconocene η^2-π complexes

The two main routes to metallocene η^2-π complexes are (i) direct complexation of the π-component to a metallocene equivalent (ligand exchange), and (ii) oxidation on the metal of the reduced π-component (C-H activation) (Scheme 5.2).

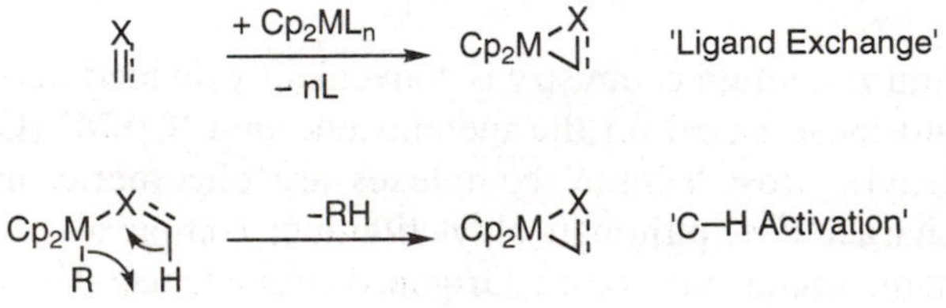

Scheme 5.2

2.1 Direct complexation/ligand exchange

Reaction between a π-component and 'Cp$_2$M' should directly form the required η^2-π complex **1**. The free metallocenes 'Cp$_2$M' are very unstable but they may be generated *in situ* by reduction of Cp$_2$MCl$_2$ with a suitable metal (e.g. Na/Hg or Mg/Hg). Electronically saturated equivalents Cp$_2$M(PMe$_2$R)$_2$ and Cp$_2$Zr(DMAP)$_2$ (DMAP = *p*-dimethylaminopyridine) are relatively stable and are sometimes used as sources of 'Cp$_2$M'. For zirconium it is more convenient to use ligand exchange from zirconocene 1-butene **4** (the 'Negishi reagent'[4]) which is generated *in situ* from dibutyl zirconocene **3**, which in turn is made by the addition of 2 equiv. of *n*-butyllithium to Cp$_2$ZrCl$_2$ (Scheme 5.3). The 1-butene ligand is only weakly bound to the 'Cp$_2$Zr' moiety in **4** and may be readily displaced by other alkenes or alkynes to give **6**. Free zirconocene is probably not an intermediate in such displacements, transfer occurring *via* a di-π complex such as **5**. The rate of co-cyclisation of **5** is much slower than dissociation of 1-butene leaving the more strongly bound alkyne ligand on the metal in **6**. The direct complexation method is not generally useful for the intermolecular cross-coupling of different components since the first formed η^2-π complex **6** reacts rapidly with further uncomplexed component to give homocoupled products such as **7** (Scheme 5.3).

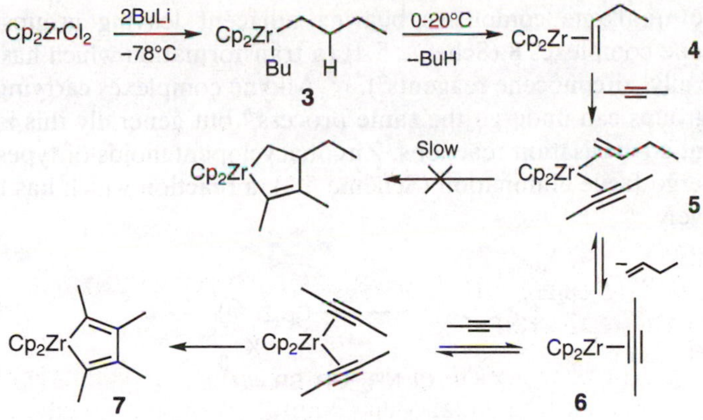

Scheme 5.3

2.2 C–H activation

A valuable route to η^2-π metallocene complexes is through a cyclometalla-tion reaction with removal of a β-proton from the substrate and elimination of an alkane or arene. Typical of this approach is the formation of zir-conocene 1-butene **4** (Scheme 5.3). The C–H activation method avoids the problem of dimerisation of the π-component since there is none of this ini-tially free of the metal. The method also facilitates the formation of η^2-π complexes of components which are unstable in the free state, such as ben-zyne, cycloalkynes, and thioaldehydes. It is normally successful for cross-couplings when the component generated on the metal is strongly bound. If this is not the case, exchange with the second π-component may take place, as described for zirconocene 1-butene (Scheme 5.3), giving the unwanted dimer or mixtures (see Section 5).

3. Practical considerations and known limitations

The main starting materials used in this area of chemistry are Cp_2TiCl_2 and Cp_2ZrCl_2, both of which are commercially available and may be handled in air. All the other metallocene complexes described are moisture and, in most cases, oxygen sensitive, and therefore all reactions must be carried out under anhydrous and oxygen-free conditions. Hydroxyl groups are not tolerated in the substrates but may be protected *in situ* as their lithium salts. Less acidic groups such as terminal alkynes and primary or secondary amines are tolerated in some cases. Ketones, aldehydes, and cyanides react rapidly with η^2-π complexes of the metallocenes so are not compatible with the reactions described below. Esters and amides are sometimes tolerated, particularly by titanocene reagents.

A less obvious limitation is imposed by the facile rearrangement of zirconocene η^2-alkene complexes bearing adjacent leaving groups to allylzirconocene complexes **8** (Scheme 5.4) (a transformation which has provided access to allyl zirconocene reagents[5]). η^2-Alkyne complexes carrying adjacent leaving groups can undergo the same process,[6] but generally this is too slow to prevent co-cyclisation reactions. Zirconacyclopentanoids of types **9** and **10** also undergo facile elimination (Scheme 5.4), a reaction which has been used productively.[7,8]

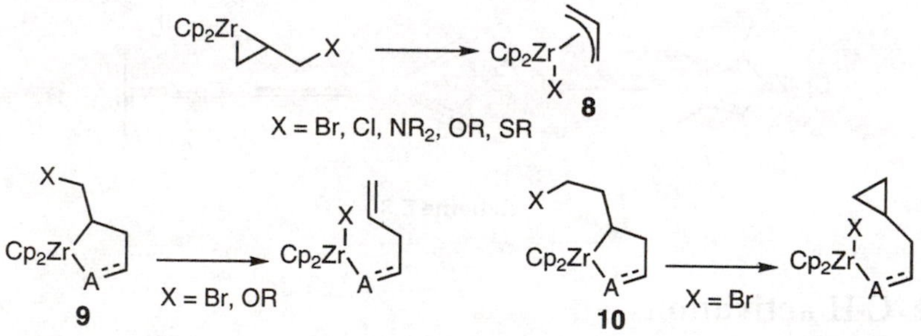

X = Br, Cl, NR$_2$, OR, SR

X = Br, OR

9

X = Br

10

Scheme 5.4

The use of titanocene and zirconocene η^2-π complexes in organic synthesis will now be described in an order which reflects the first formed π-complex. As this is intended to be an illustrative rather than an exhaustive account of the field, the reader is directed towards several excellent reviews which provide access to much more of the primary literature.[9–13]

4. Coupling of η^2-alkyne complexes

4.1 Coupling with alkynes

The intermolecular homocoupling of alkynes to afford metallacyclopentadienes such as **7** (Scheme 5.3) provides, on work-up, a useful synthesis of heavily substituted symmetric dienes.[14] Many sources of the metallocene fragment are used in this chemistry including Cp$_2$TiCl$_2$/Na/Hg/PMe$_2$Ph, Cp$_2$ZrCl$_2$/Mg/Hg, and Cp$_2$ZrCl$_2$/2BuLi. In certain special cases sequential addition of two different alkynes to the zirconocene equivalent Cp$_2$Zr(DMAP)$_2$ gives high yields of the cross-coupled products[15] but there are two more general methods that are commonly used to form the zirconacyclopentadiene.

(i) Hydrozirconation of an alkyne followed by addition of MeMgBr gives the methyl zirconocene complex **11**. Thermal elimination of methane then forms the zirconocene η^2-alkyne complex **6** which may be trapped with a second alkyne to form the mixed zirconacyclopentadiene **14** (Scheme 5.5).[16]

(ii) Reaction of an alkyne with zirconocene ethene **12** (generated *in situ* from diethyl zirconocene in the same fashion as zirconocene 1-butene **4**) forms the zirconoacyclopentene **13**. Thermal elimination of ethene in the presence of a second alkyne then gives the cross-coupled zirconacyclopentadiene **14** (Scheme 5.5).[17]

Both of these processes tolerate terminal alkynes as the first component.

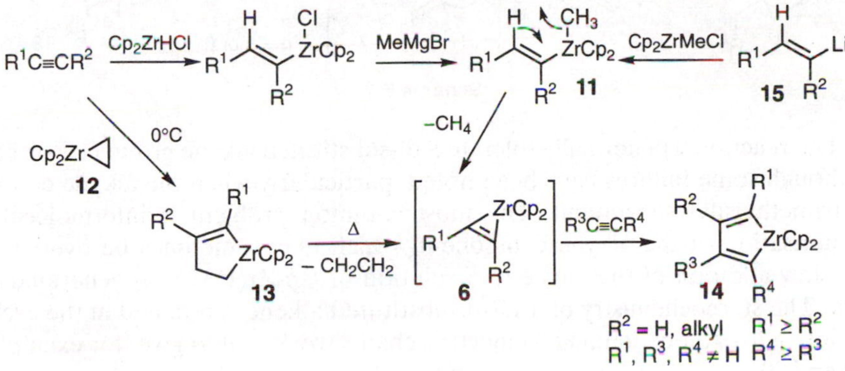

Scheme 5.5

An alternative route to the methyl vinyl zirconocenes **11** is based on the reaction between a vinyllithium **15** and zirconocene methyl chloride. This approach has been used to form several η^2-alkyne complexes.[9,18]

The intramolecular 1,n-diyne coupling with 'MCp$_2$' equivalents is an efficient process which affords exocyclic dienes **16** (Scheme 5.6), valuable substrates for the Diels–Alder reaction. Cp$_2$TiCl$_2$/Na/Hg/PPh$_2$Me and Cp$_2$ZrCl$_2$/Mg reagents have been used but zirconocene 1-butene **4** is more convenient than either and gives excellent yields.[19,20] Using the zirconium reagents, ring sizes from four to seven may be made and very bulky groups on the alkynes are tolerated. Titanocene-induced cyclisations are limited to the formation of five- and six-membered rings, and do not tolerate bulky alkyne substituents. Terminal alkynes are not tolerated, but 1-trimethylsilyl or 1-trimethylstannyl

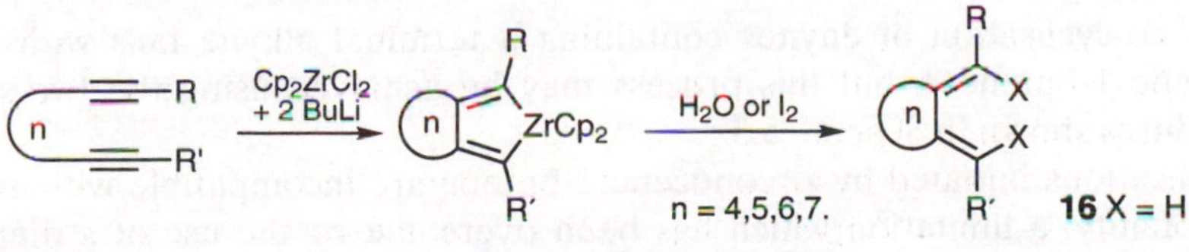

Scheme 5.6

alkynes may be used as masked forms of terminal alkynes. (Note that the stannyl groups are much easier to remove from the organic products.)

4.2 Coupling with alkenes

Intramolecular co-cyclisation of 1,6- and 1,7-enynes using the Negishi reagent **4** gives bicyclic zirconacyclopentenes **18** in excellent yields (Scheme 5.7).[20,21] An η^2-alkyne complex **17** is likely to be the first formed intermediate.

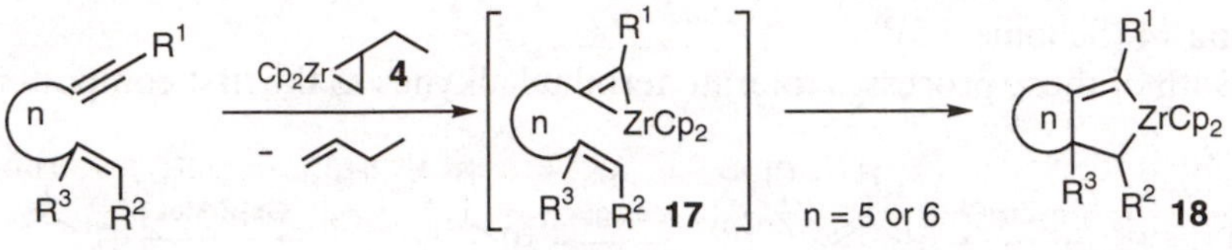

Scheme 5.7

The reaction will normally tolerate a di-substituted alkene group (1,1 or 1,2) although some failures have been noted, particularly when the alkyne carries a trimethylsilyl substituent. The most common problem is intermolecular dimerisation of the alkyne component, which may sometimes be overcome by slow addition of the enyne to a solution of $Cp_2Zr(DMAP)_2$ generated *in situ*. The stereochemistry of a 1,2-disubstituted alkene is retained in the cyclisation. Nitrogen-containing connecting chains work well to give, for example, **19** and **20**.

The co-cyclisation of substituted enynes is often highly diastereoselective. Substituents next to the alkene component exert complete control over the adjacent ring junction stereochemistry: for example, **21** and **22** are formed as single isomers.[22] In some cases the zirconacycles must be given time to equilibrate thermally to the more stable isomer in order to achieve high levels of diastereocontrol (the formation of zirconacyclopentenes is a reversible process).

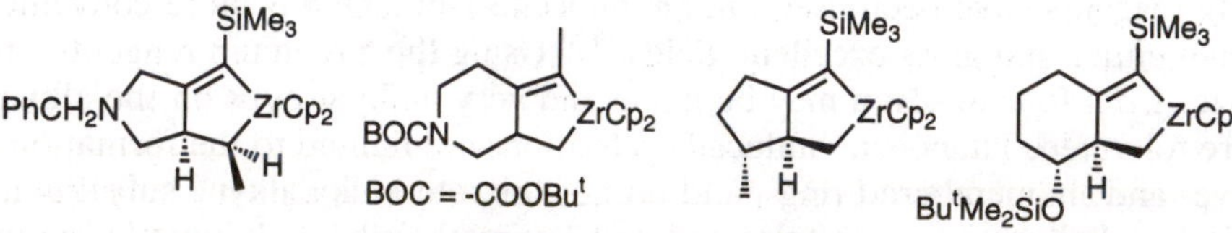

The co-cyclisation of enynes containing a terminal alkyne fails with zirconocene 1-butene **4**, but this process may be achieved using the two-step procedures shown in Scheme 5.5.

Cyclisations initiated by zirconocene 1-butene are incompatible with ester functionality, a limitation which has been overcome by the use of a diethyl titanocene reagent which gives titanocycles exemplified by **23** (Scheme 5.8).

Work-up of the titanacycles with isocyanides gives bicyclic imines **24**, a process which may be made catalytic in titanium since the 'titanocene' liberated from the imine may co-cyclise the enyne.[23,24]

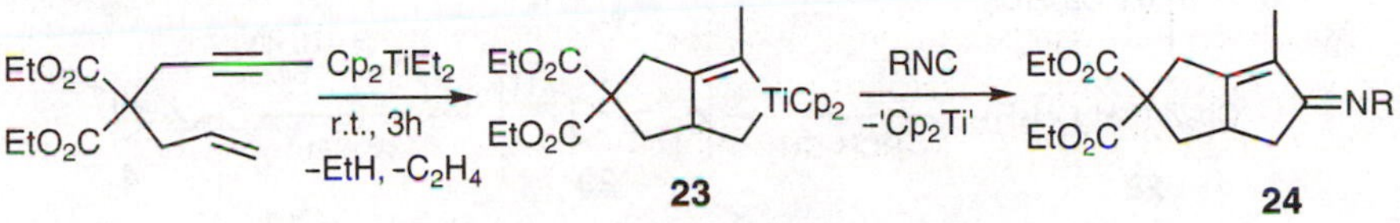

Scheme 5.8

Zirconocene η^2-alkyne complexes generated by the C-H activation method may be trapped intermolecularly with alkenes, but excepting ethene and norbornene the yields are generally low.[9,18]

4.3 Coupling with nitriles and carbonyl compounds

Zirconocene η^2-alkyne complexes generated by elimination of ethene (β–β′ C-C bond activation) or elimination of methane (C-H activation) as illustrated in Scheme 5.5 may be trapped with nitriles and aldehydes to provide enones and allylic alcohols **25** and **26** on hydrolysis (Scheme 5.9).[12,17]

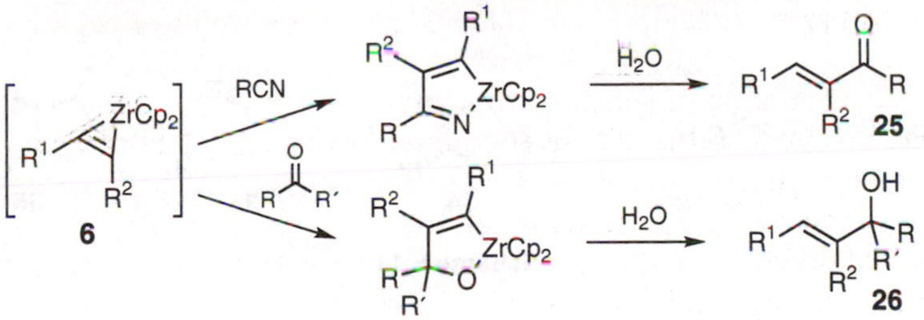

Scheme 5.9

5. Coupling of η^2-alkene complexes

5.1 Coupling with alkenes

Zirconocene alkene complexes **29** are readily prepared by the β-hydride activation route from dialkyl zirconocenes **28** or methyl alkyl zirconocenes **27** (Scheme 5.10). It is also possible to prepare the zirconocene complexes of ethene, styrene, and, to a lesser extent, vinyltrimethylsilane by displacement of the weakly bound 1-butene ligand from **4**.[25]

When zirconocene alkene complexes are formed in the presence of an excess of the same alkene, symmetric dimers **30** are formed with high regio- and stereocontrol.[26] Cross-coupling of different alkenes is not generally successful because the rate of alkene exchange from the first formed η^2-alkene

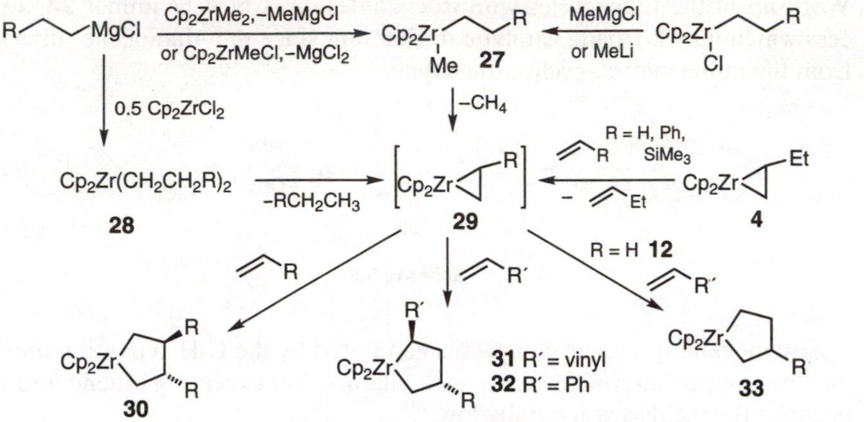

Scheme 5.10

complex is faster than the rate of co-cyclisation to form the required zircona-cyclopentane. The ready reversibility of the alkene addition reaction (i.e. β–β′ carbon–carbon bond cleavage)[27] may also contribute to the lack of selectivity, as illustrated by the reaction of zirconocene 1-butene with 1 equiv. of 1-octene to give a 1:2:1 statistical mixture of the three metallacycles **34–36** (Scheme 5.11).[26]

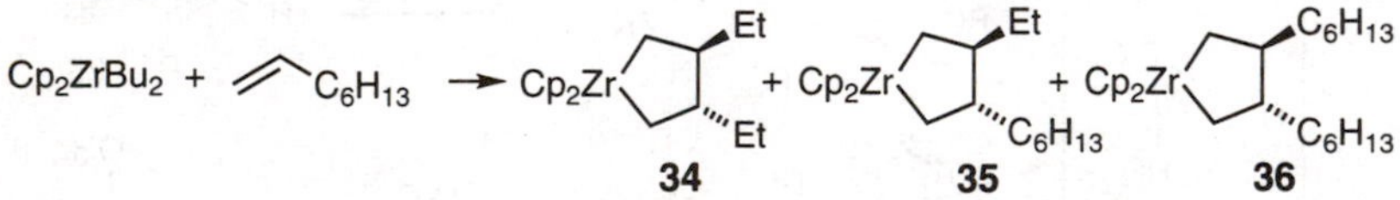

Scheme 5.11

Exceptions are trapping with styrene[26] and conjugated dienes[28] where pair selective products **31** and **32** are obtained (Scheme 5.10). In both these cases the added alkene substituent (phenyl or vinyl) ends up adjacent to the metal – quite different behaviour to other alkenes – and reflects stabilisation of the zirconacycle by phenyl – or vinyl–metal interactions. The most useful class of 'pair selective' couplings is between zirconocene ethene **12** and added alkenes where the ethene remains bound to the metal leading to a single product **33** (Scheme 5.10). The special reactivity of **12** has already been seen in the insertion of alkynes to afford zirconacyclopentenes **13** (Scheme 5.5).[17,29]

The intramolecular co-cyclisation of 1,6- and 1,7-dienes using zirconocene 1-butene **4** affords bicyclic zirconacyclopentanes **37** in high yield (Scheme 5.12). With simple 1,6-dienes the *trans*-fused bicyclo[3.3.0]octane is formed with good selectivity (90–97%). (It is important to leave the zirconacycles at room temperature for 2 h to ensure high stereocontrol.) Inclusion of a nitro-gen atom in the ring gives 67% of the *cis*-fused product, although it has not yet been established whether thermal equilibration will improve the *trans* selectivity in this system. One disubstituted (1,1 or 1,2) double bond is tolerated, but not more,[30] with the exception of styryl systems such as that which leads to the efficient formation of **38**. Sometimes a trisubstituted double bond may be tolerated as in the formation of **39**.[31] A significant limitation to the co-cyclisation, however, is that an ether link in the connecting chain is not tolerated. 1,7-Dienes initially form *cis*-fused zirconacycles **40** (Scheme 5.12) with around 80% selectivity, but heating at 60°C for a few hours isomerises this to the more stable *trans*-fused system **41** (>97%).[32]

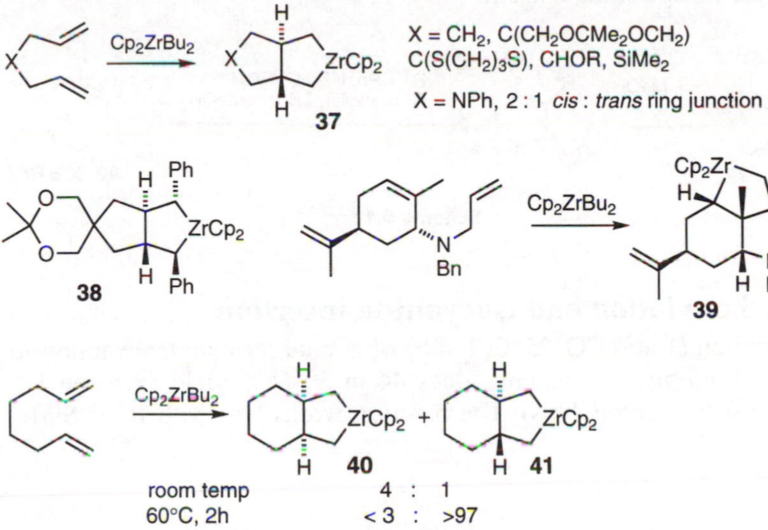

Scheme 5.12

5.2 Other metallocene-mediated couplings

The intramolecular coupling of alkenes (and alkynes) with cyanides or hydrazones induced by zirconocene 1-butene has been reported,[33,34] and the intramolecular coupling between alkenes (and alkynes) and ketones or aldehydes induced by $Cp_2Ti(PMe_3)_2$ is also known.[35]

6. Functionalisation of zirconacyclopentanes and zirconacyclopentenes

Some of the methods available for elaborating zirconacycles are outlined below.

6.1 Halogenolysis

Treatment of zirconacyclopentanes with bromine, iodine, or *N*-bromosuccinimide (NBS) gives the 1,4-dihalide in good yield. Selective monohalogenation is achieved by initial protonolysis followed by halogenolysis.[36] Zirconacy-clopentenes may be diiodinated or dibrominated in a similar way. Selective monohalogenation of the vinyl–zirconium bond to afford for example **42** (Scheme 5.13) is best achieved by protonolysis of the alkyl–zirconium bond followed by addition of iodine (or NBS). When the zirconacyclopentene has a 2-phenyl substituent (R^1), the alkyl halide **43** (Scheme 5.13) may be obtained by iodination or bromination (NBS is best) followed by protonolysis, but with a 2-alkyl substituent this method fails as the halogen attacks the vinyl–zirconium bond first. This problem has been overcome by the use of CBr_4 as the halogenating reagent.[37]

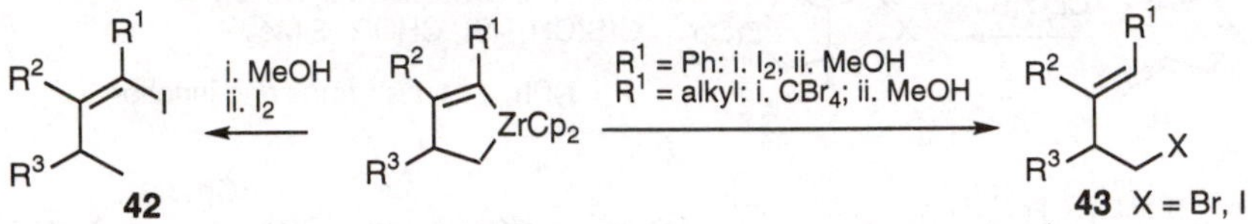

Scheme 5.13

6.2 Carbonylation and isocyanide insertion

Carbonylation (1 atm CO, 25 °C, 1–4 h) of zirconacyclopentenes followed by acidic work-up gives cyclopentenones **44** in 50–65% yield (Scheme 5.14)[20] (*cf.* 80–95% for protonolysis). The reaction works best with $R^1 = SiMe_3$ or $SnMe_3$.

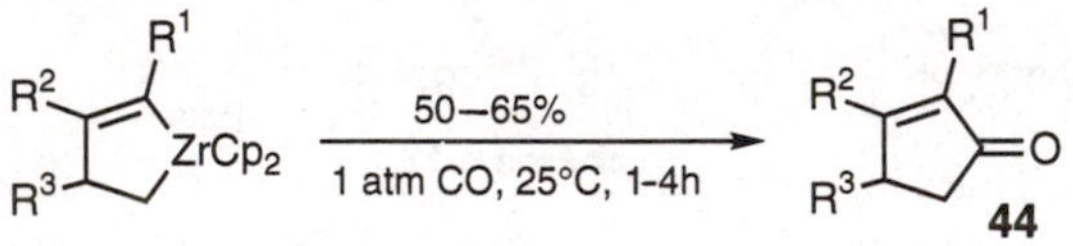

Scheme 5.14

Carbon monoxide insertion into zirconacyclopentanes such as **45** occurs rapidly at −78 °C. Work-up by protonolysis gives the alcohol **49** presumably *via* the η^2-ketone complex **48** (Scheme 5.15).[38] Carbonylation for longer periods at room temperature affords the cyclopentanones **52** but higher yields are obtained by work-up with iodine at low temperature.

Insertion of isocyanides into zirconacyclopentanes and -enes is complete within a few minutes at room temperature to afford iminoacyl complexes such as **47** (Scheme 5.15). With most nitrogen substituents (especially Me_3Si and Ph), these rearrange to the η^2-imine complexes **50** which can be trapped by protonolysis to afford **51**, or by the insertion of alkynes, alkenes, and ketones (see Section 8).[39–41] The rearrangement is induced by the addition of protic solvents, and so quenching the iminoacyl complexes **47** with methanol gives the amines **51** (in around 50% yield).

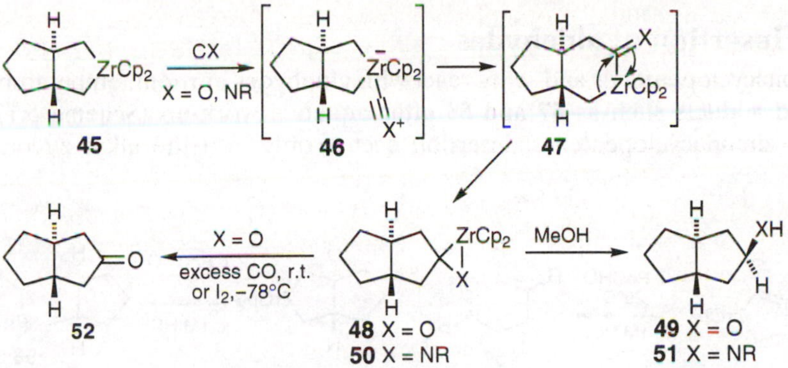

Scheme 5.15

6.3 Insertion of metal carbenoids

The facile insertion of carbenoid species such as carbon monoxide and iso-cyanides into zirconacycles, which contrasts strongly with the low reactivity of conventional electrophiles such as acetone and iodomethane towards these species, is due to their ability to donate a lone pair to the 16-electron zirco-nium centre to give an 18-electron 'ate' complex **46**. Migration of a carbon–zirconium bond returns the metal to the more stable 16-electron con-figuration. This type of reactivity is also shown by metal carbenoids (R^1R^2CMX):[42,43] indeed both lithiated propargyl chloride and lithiated allyl chloride insert extremely rapidly at −78°C into zirconacyclopentanes to afford η³-propargyl and η³-allyl zirconacycles such as **55** and **53**, re-spectively (Scheme 5.16). These may be further elaborated, for example by insertion of RCHO/BF₃ to give **54** and **56**, in very high overall yields.[43] Zirconacyclopentenes may be elaborated in the same way, insertion only occurring into the alkyl–zirconium bond. The overall sequence is a good illustration of the way in which 'zirconocene' may act as a template upon which several carbon–carbon bonds may be formed in tandem processes.

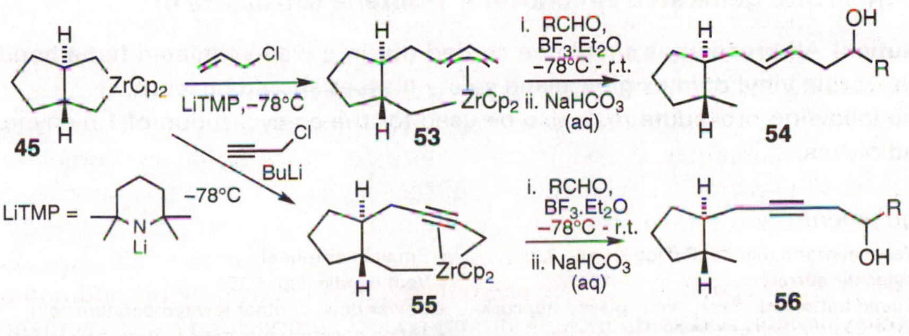

Scheme 5.16

143

6.4 Insertion of aldehydes

Zirconacyclopentanes and -enes react with aldehydes at room temperature to afford adducts such as **57** and **58** after aqueous work-up (Scheme 5.17).[29] With zirconacyclopentenes, insertion occurs only into the alkyl–zirconium bond.

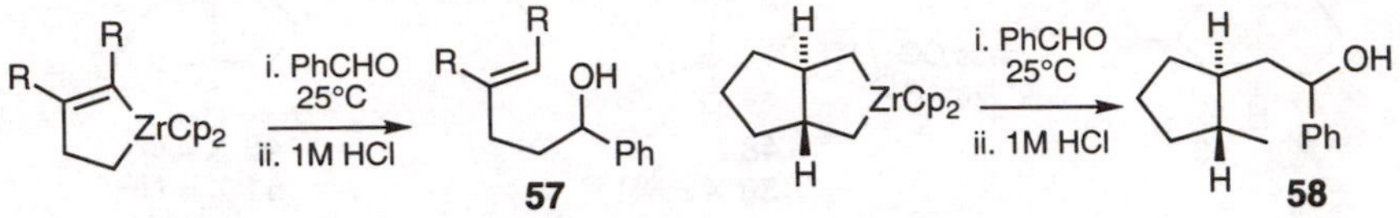

Scheme 5.17

6.5 Metathesis reactions

Reaction of a variety of zirconacyclopentadienes, -enes, and -anes with main group element dihalides (or E_2Cl_2 for E = S, Se) gives the corresponding elementacycles **59–61**.[44]

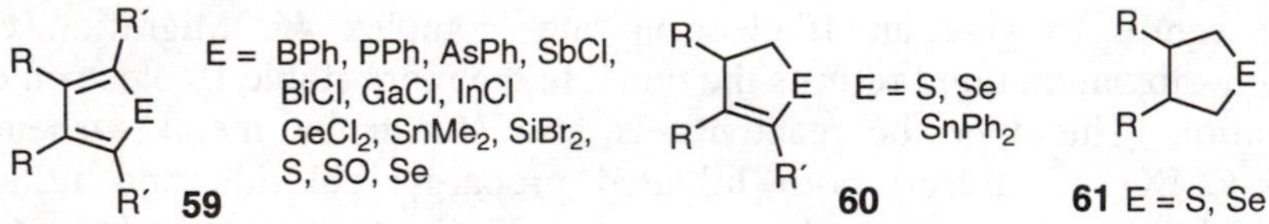

The following protocols describe the synthesis of zirconacycle **45** from 1,6-heptadiene and its characterisation by NMR spectroscopy. Zirconacycle **45** is then elaborated into alcohol **49** by reaction with carbon monoxide, and alcohol **54** (R = Ph) by tandem insertion of lithium chloroallylide and benzaldehyde.

Protocol 1a.

Co-cyclisation of 1,6-heptadiene to give zirconacycle (Structure 45) using *in situ* generated zirconocene 1-butene (Structure 4)

Caution! All procedures should be carried out in a well-ventilated fume hood. Disposable vinyl or latex gloves and safety glasses should be worn.

The following procedure may also be used for the co-cyclisation of 1,*n*-enynes and diynes.

Equipment

- Vacuum/argon manifold[a] (Figs 7.1 and 7.2)
- Magnetic stirrer[b]
- Round-bottomed flask with glass stopcock (B14, 25 mL) (Schlenk flask) (Fig. 5.1A)
- Stopcock unit (B14) (Fig. 5.1B)
- Small filter funnel
- Vent needle (Fig. 5.1C)
- Dewar bowl or other low-temperature bath
- Teflon-covered magnetic stirrer bar (≈1 cm long)

- All-glass tuberculin syringe^c (1 mL)
- All glass syringes (1, 2, and 5 mL)
- Stainless steel needles (4 × 8″, 18 gauge)
- Silicone vacuum grease
- Single-necked, round-bottomed flask (B14, 10 mL)
- Septa^d (3 × B14)

Materials

- 1,6-Heptadiene (FW 96.2), 0.096 g, 1 mmol **flammable, irritant**
- Zirconocene dichloride (FW 292.3), 0.293 g, 1 mmol
- *n*-Butyllithium^e in hexanes, 0.80 mL of a 2.5 M soln, 2 mmol **flammable, moisture sensitive**
- Dry and oxygen free THF, 10 mL^f **flammable, may form explosive peroxides, irritant**

1. All glassware and the stirring bar should be dried overnight in a 150 °C oven and either assembled^g while still warm, or allowed to cool in a desiccator before assembly. Syringes (not assembled) and needles should be dried at 150 °C in an oven overnight, allowed to cool in a desiccator then assembled using Teflon tape to ensure a gas-tight seal between the needle and syringe and to ease removal at the end of the experiment. All syringes should be flushed with argon before use by filling and emptying three times from a suitable source of pure argon.

2. Weigh the zirconocene dichloride into the 25 mL Schlenk flask (Fig. 5.1A), containing the stirrer bar through a small dry funnel, avoiding contamination of the B14 joint which should not be greased. Quickly insert the previously greased stopcock assembly (Fig. 5.1B) into the flask and attach the assembled apparatus to the vacuum/argon manifold as in Fig. 5.2. With stopcock **A** closed, evacuate the system (0.1–1 mmHg). Use an elastic band to ensure that the two parts of the apparatus stay together when a positive argon pressure is applied.

3. Carefully allow argon to enter the apparatus from the manifold, avoiding blowing the zirconocene dichloride around. Repeat the evacuate/refill cycle twice. The apparatus should be left with stopcock **B** open so that the manifold maintains a positive pressure of argon in the flask. Stopcock **A** should be kept closed except when adding reagents.

4. Place a B14 septum over the end of stopcock **A** and flush the space between the septum and the stopcock with argon by inserting a vent needle (Fig. 5.1C) and opening stopcock **A** slightly for a few seconds.

5. Add 5 mL of dry THF to the flask by syringe^h through stopcock **A**. After the zirconocene dichloride has dissolved, cool the flask to −78 °C in an acetone bath cooled with liquid nitrogen or solid carbon dioxide.

6. After 5 min at the low temperature (ignore any precipitation of zirconocene dichloride), add the *n*-butyllithium solution^e (Fig. 5.3) dropwise over 2 min using a 1 mL tuberculin syringe to give a pale yellow solution.

7. Weigh^i the 1,6-heptadiene into a dry 10 mL B14 round-bottomed flask and fit the flask with a septum. Add dry THF (2 mL) and briefly flush the flask

Protocol 1a. *Continued*

with argon using a vent needle and an 'argon needle'[j] from the vacuum/argon manifold. Transfer the solution of 1,6-heptadiene to the reaction flask using the same syringe, and ensure complete transfer by adding and transferring another 1 mL of THF.

8. After at least 20 min at $<-70\,^{\circ}C$, remove the cooling bath, allow the reaction flask to warm to room temperature, and then stir at this temperature ($>20\,^{\circ}C$) for at least 2 h[k] (overnight is all right) to ensure high selectivity for the *trans*-ring junction in the product zirconacycle.

For footnotes, see the end of Protocol 1d.

The above procedure provides a solution of the zirconacycle **45** in 80–100% yield for use in the following protocols.

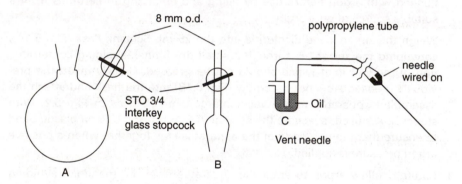

8 mm o.d.

polypropylene tube

needle wired on

STO 3/4 interkey glass stopcock

Oil

Vent needle

A

B

C

Fig. 5.1 Basic apparatus.

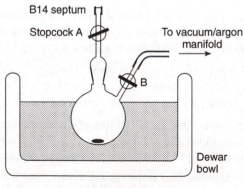

B14 septum

Stopcock A

To vacuum/argon manifold

B

Dewar bowl

Fig. 5.2

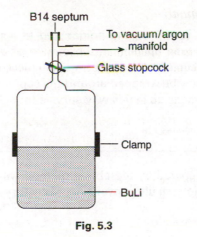

Fig. 5.3

Protocol 1b.
NMR characterisation of the zirconacycle (Structure 45)

Extra equipment required

- All glass syringes (2 × 1 mL and 2 mL)
- Needles (3 × 8″, 18 gauge)
- Single-necked, round-bottomed flask (B14, 10 mL)
- Two-stopcock assembly (Fig. 5.5)
- NMR tube (5 mm) and tight fitting plastic cap
- NMR tube filling apparatus (Fig. 5.4)^l

Extra materials required

- Dry d_6-benzene, 0.7 mL^m

flammable, may cause cancer, toxic – danger of serious damage to health by prolonged exposure

1. Dry the NMR tube for at least 12 h at 100 °C then, while it is still hot, place in the NMR tube filler^l as in Fig. 5.4A and evacuate the system (the septum must be unpunctured). Admit argon and repeat the evacuation/refill cycle twice, leaving the system under argon.

2. Introduce by syringe approx. 2 mL of the zirconacycle solution into the 10 mL round-bottomed flask fitted with the joint carrying two stopcocks (Fig. 5.5) which has been flushed with argon using three evacuate/refill cycles. With stopcock **A** closed, open the vacuum side of the manifold to stopcock **B** and remove the solvent by *carefully* opening the stopcock **B** while swirling the apparatus. A warm water bath ($\approx$40 °C) should be used to help remove the last part of the solvent.

3. When all the solvent has been removed, allow argon back into the apparatus from the manifold. Flush the space above stopcock **A** with argon then add 0.7 mL of dry d_6-benzene by syringe. Allow the lithium chloride precipitate to settle and then take the supernatant back into the 1 mL syringe and transfer to the NMR tube held in the filler (Fig. 5.4A).

Protocol 1b. *Continued*

4. Remove the NMR tube from the holder and fit a tight fitting plastic cap while keeping the tube opening in the stream of argon issuing from the hole previously occupied by the tube. A small piece of 'Labfilm' (2 mm × 5 mm is sufficient) may be wrapped around the cap/tube junction to complete the seal. Samples made up in this way survive for at least 24 h.

For footnotes, see the end of Protocol 1d

The NMR sample prepared by the above method will contain lithium chloride,[n] but this does not usually prevent a satisfactory NMR spectrum being obtained.

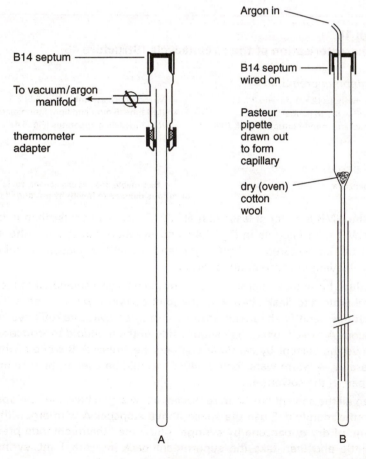

Fig. 5.4

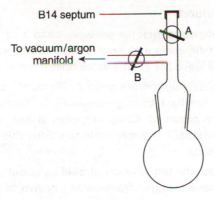

B14 septum

To vacuum/argon manifold ←

A

B

Fig. 5.5

Protocol 1c.
Synthesis of *trans*-bicyclo[3.3.0]octan-3-ol (Structure 49) by insertion of carbon monoxide into 45

N.B. A similar procedure is used for carbonylation of zirconacyclopentenes, except that the reaction is allowed to warm to room temperature under carbon monoxide before quenching, and it produces the ketone rather than the alcohol.

Extra equipment required
- Glass T-piece
- Chromatography column
- Separating funnel

Extra materials required
- Cylinder of carbon monoxide (technical grade is sufficient).

  Caution! This is a very toxic odourless gas. Ensure that the vacuum/argon manifold is vented high in the fume hood flammable, toxic

- Methanol, 3 mL
- Saturated aqueous sodium hydrogencarbonate solution
- Brine
- Anhydrous magnesium sulfate
- Distilled petroleum ether (40-60) for chromatography   **flammable, very toxic**
- Diethyl ether for extraction and chromatography   **flammable, irritant**
- Silica gel (10 g)   **irritant dust**

1. Attach a carbon monoxide cylinder with pressure reduction head and needle valve to the top of stopcock **A** (Fig. 5.2) using a piece of thick-walled flexible tubing containing a T-piece connected to the vacuum/argon manifold. The rubber tubing should be clamped in the fume hood so that if any of the glass connectors breaks the toxic carbon monoxide will be contained. All thick-walled flexible tubing should be of good quality and securely attached using hose connector clamps.

2. With stopcock **A** closed, evacuate the tubing using the vacuum manifold. Close the manifold stopcock and refill the tube with carbon monoxide from

Richard J. Whitby

Protocol 1c. *Continued*

the cylinder. It is important that the pressure head is set to no more than 0.5 p.s.i. Close the needle valve and evacuate the tubing again. Refill with carbon monoxide and leave the needle valve open.

3. Cool the zirconacycle solution prepared in Protocol 1a to −78°C and then evacuate the reaction flask through stopcock **B**. There will be some bubbling as gases are removed. Close stopcock **B** and open stopcock **A** to admit carbon monoxide. For larger scale reactions this evacuate/refill cycle should be repeated.

4. After 1 h (after which the temperature should be about −70°C, and the reaction mixture will have changed from golden brown to orange), close stopcock **A** and the carbon monoxide cylinder. Remove the flexible tubing from tap **A** and replace with a septum. Open stopcock **B** to the argon side of the manifold and then add methanol (3 mL) by syringe through stopcock **A**. Remove the cooling bath and allow the reaction mixture to warm to room temperature.

5. After 40 min (by which time there should be a yellow solution and a white precipitate), pour the reaction mixture into saturated sodium hydrogencarbonate solution and extract into diethyl ether (3 × 25 mL). Wash the combined organic layers with water (2 × 25 mL) and brine (2 × 25 mL) before drying over anhydrous magnesium sulfate.

6. Filter and then remove the solvent by rotary evaporation. Purify the crude product by chromatography on silica gel (10 g, 30% diethyl ether in petroleum ether as eluent) and Kugelrohr distillation (74°C, 1 torr) to afford *trans*-bicyclo[3.3.0]octan-3-ol **49** as a colourless oil (88 mg, 70%). TLC with 25% diethyl ether in petroleum ether as eluent produces a spot at an R_f of about 0.15 which may be visualised by charring the plate with sulfuric acid[o] (it turns red and then dark brown on further heating).

For footnotes see the end of Protocol 1d.

Protocol 1d.
Tandem insertion of lithium chloroallylide and benzaldehyde into the zirconacycle (Structure 45) to give alcohol (Structure 54) (R = Ph)

Extra equipment required
- All glass syringes [5 × 1 mL tuberculin (250 μL gas-tight are better, but expensive), 3 × 2 mL, 5 mL, 20 mL]
- Luer lock needles (10 × 8″, 18 gauge)
- Schlenk flask (B14, 25 mL)
- Schlenk stopcock (B14)
- Small magnetic stirrer bar
- Magnetic stirrer
- Separating funnel (50 or 100 mL)
- Chromatography column

150

Extra materials required

- Allyl chloride (FW 76.5), 0.09 mL, 1.1 mmol — **flammable, very toxic**
- 2,2,6,6-Tetramethylpiperidine[p] (141.3), 0.19 mL, 1.1 mmol
- *n*-Butyllithium in hexanes,[e] 0.44 mL of a 2.5 M soln, 1.1 mmol — **flammable, moisture sensitive**
- Benzaldehyde[q] (FW 106.1), 0.13 mL, 1.3 mmol — **irritant**
- Boron trifluoride etherate[p] (FW 141.9), 0.16 mL, 1.3 mmol — **corrosive, moisture sensitive**
- Dry THF, 2.5 mL — **flammable, may form explosive peroxides, irritant**
- Methanol, 3 mL — **flammable, toxic**
- Diethyl ether for extraction and chromatography — **flammable, irritant**
- Distilled petroleum ether (40–60) for chromatography — **flammable, very toxic**
- Silica gel for chromatography (30 mL) — **irritant dust**
- Saturated aqueous sodium hydrogensulfite solution — **corrosive**
- Saturated aqueous sodium hydrogencarbonate solution
- Brine
- Anhydrous magnesium sulfate

1. Assemble the 25 mL Schlenk flask and stopcock and insert a small stirrer bar. Attach this to the vacuum/argon manifold through the side-arm and fill with argon using three evacuate/refill cycles. Fit a septum to the upper stopcock (so that the apparatus resembles Fig. 5.2) and flush the gap between stopcock **A** and the septum with argon.

2. Through the septum, add tetramethylpiperidine (0.19 mL) *via* a tuberculin syringe and THF (1.5 mL) *via* a 2 mL syringe.

3. Cool the flask to 0 °C and add the *n*-butyllithium solution (0.44 mL) dropwise through the septum using a tuberculin syringe to provide, after stirring for 30 min, a yellow solution of lithium tetramethylpiperidide.

4. Cool the solution of the zirconacycle **45** prepared in Protocol 1a to −85 °C in an acetone/liquid nitrogen bath allowing 10 min for equilibration.

5. Add allyl chloride (0.09 mL) by tuberculin syringe and then add the solution of lithium tetramethylpiperidide prepared above dropwise by a 2 mL syringe. The addition should take ≈10 min. A small additional volume of THF is used to ensure complete transfer of the base.[r] For larger scale reactions an apparatus which allows the reaction mixture temperature to be monitored is required.

6. After 30 min, when the temperature has risen to ≈−60 °C, add benzaldehyde (0.13 mL) followed by boron trifluoride etherate (0.16 mL) using 1 mL tuberculin syringes.

7. Remove the cooling bath and allow the reaction mixture to warm to room temperature over ≈1.5 h during which time the initially clear yellow/orange solution should become yellow and slightly cloudy.

8. Add methanol (3 mL) by syringe (slight effervescence, solution becomes

Protocol 1d. *Continued*

clear golden) followed immediately by saturated aqueous sodium hydrogen-carbonate solution (15 mL). Vigorously stir the white suspension overnight.

9. Pour the reaction mixture into a separating funnel and remove the yellow organic phase. Extract the aqueous layer with diethyl ether (3 × 20 mL). Combine the organic layers and wash with saturated aqueous sodium hydro-gensulfite solution (20 mL), brine (20 mL), and water (20 mL). Dry (MgSO$_4$), filter, and remove the solvent by rotary evaporation to afford a crude product, typically ≈90% pure by NMR spectroscopy. Purify by chromatography on sil-ica gel (30 mL) eluting with 15–25% diethyl ether in petroleum ether to give **54** (R = Ph) as a colourless oil (0.220 g, 90%). The required compound has an R_f of approximately 0.55 on TLC using a diethylether:light petroleum 1:1 as eluent and may be visualised by dipping the plate in a 10% solution of phos-phomolybdic acid in ethanol and then heating.

[a] Dry 'oxygen-free' nitrogen can also be used.

[b] This must have a good enough magnet to stir the flask through the Dewar bowl used for the low-temperature stages.

[c] All glass tuberculin syringes (1 mL) may be difficult to obtain. Hamilton gas-tight syringes (1 mL) will work as well but are expensive. Normal syringes (1 mL) are not accurate enough.

[d] Septa are stored in a desiccator over silica gel containing an indicator.

[e] **Storage and dispensing of *n*-butyllithium**. It is important for this preparation that the *n*-butyllithium used is of good quality – cloudy samples give poor results even if the titre suggests that it is of rea-sonable quality. Aldrich sure-seal bottles do not provide sufficient protection once the septum is pierced by the 18-gauge needles used. We transfer the *n*-butyllithium into storage bottles of the design shown in Fig. 5.3 (similar are available from Aldrich: cat. No. Z10,733-6 for 125 mL capacity).

Dispensing: Use the set-up shown in Fig. 5.3. The space above the stopcock may be flushed with argon using evacuate/refill cycles provided that the septum has never been pierced. Flush the tuber-culin syringe by filling/emptying with argon three times. Open the stopcock, lower the needle into the liquid, and allow the slight positive pressure of argon to force the *n*-butyllithium solution into the syringe. When ≈0.2 mL has entered the syringe it should be inverted and the gas bubble expelled before completing filling. The volume added to the reaction flask is measured between two marks on the syringe. This will leave a residue of *n*-butyllithium solution in the syringe (≈0.2 mL) which may be safely disposed of by squirting into running water in the fume cupboard (not in the open laboratory – the finely divided LiOH produced is very irritating).

[f] The THF is dried and maintained oxygen-free by heating under reflux over sodium benzophenone ketyl from which it is freshly distilled before use (preferably taken directly from the still).

[g] Stopcocks should be lightly greased lengthways, inserted into the socket and rotated. A clear film throughout the joint indicates that sufficient grease has been used. Air channels are easily seen as lighter streaks. After use the silicone vacuum grease should be removed from the stopcock using dichloromethane/tissue and pipe cleaners before the item is dried in the oven. Joints should likewise be greased and when assembled should be checked to ensure that a clear seal has been formed all around the joint. The bottom third of the joint (nearest the reaction flask) is often left ungreased to reduce contamination of the reaction mixture with silicone grease.

[h] It is economical to use the same syringe several times for handling solvent. This may be done, over short timespans, by inserting the needle into a solid rubber bung to protect from moisture between uses.

[i] It is much more convenient to add the appropriate volume of neat 1,6-heptadiene directly to the reaction mixture by syringe, but if reliable yields are required this is not accurate enough.

[j] Fix the Luer lock part from an old syringe into thick wall vacuum tubing from the manifold using a ring clip. Needles can then be fixed to this using teflon tape to ensure a good seal. Before use the tube and needle should be filled with argon using three evacuate/refill cycles after sealing the needle by insertion into a rubber bung. The bung should be used to seal the needle when not in use.

[k]The colour darkens to a golden yellow/brown. If left overnight a brown solution usually forms, but this seems no less pure by NMR spectroscopy than other samples.

[l]This is made from a 'thermometer adaptor' fused to a B14 socket and glass tap side arm. A less satisfactory, but workable, alternative can be made from a drawn out Pasteur pipette as shown in Fig. 5.4B. A constant flow of argon keeps the NMR tube oxygen-free and the solution of the zirconacycle is injected through the septum. The apparatus must be thoroughly flushed with argon before adding the zirconacycle.

[m]The d_6-benzene may be adequately dried by storage over 4 Å molecular sieves or calcium hydride. If the NMR spectrum of smaller quantities of the organometallic is required, the benzene should also be degassed.

[n]If a better NMR spectrum is required, a lithium chloride-free solution of the metallacycle must be prepared by either removing the THF by vacuum transfer (for apparatus and method see Protocol 2, step 7 and Fig. 5.7) and extracting the residue into toluene, or by carrying out the metallacycle preparation in toluene as solvent. In both these cases the lithium chloride is allowed to settle out before removal of the sample for NMR spectroscopy.

[o]Make up a solution of 5% concentrated sulfuric acid in methanol (**Care!** – add the acid very slowly to the methanol with stirring). The TLC plate (aluminium backed!) is then briefly dipped in this and then charred using a hot air gun. All operations should be done in a fume cupboard.

[p]Distilled from calcium hydride.

[q]Purified by washing with aqueous sodium hydroxide solution and then brine, and then drying over anhydrous magnesium sulfate, filtering, and distilling at water pump pressure (≈ 14 mmHg).

[r]The formation of the allyl zirconocene is immediate. To obtain an NMR sample the mixture may be warmed to room temperature and treated as in Protocol 1b.

---

7. η^2-Benzyne zirconocene complexes

Thermolysis of diphenyl zirconocene **62** or an aryl methyl zirconocene **63** forms zirconocene benzyne complexes **64** *via* a C—H activation process (Scheme 5.18).[45,46] The benzyne complexes may be trapped in high yield with

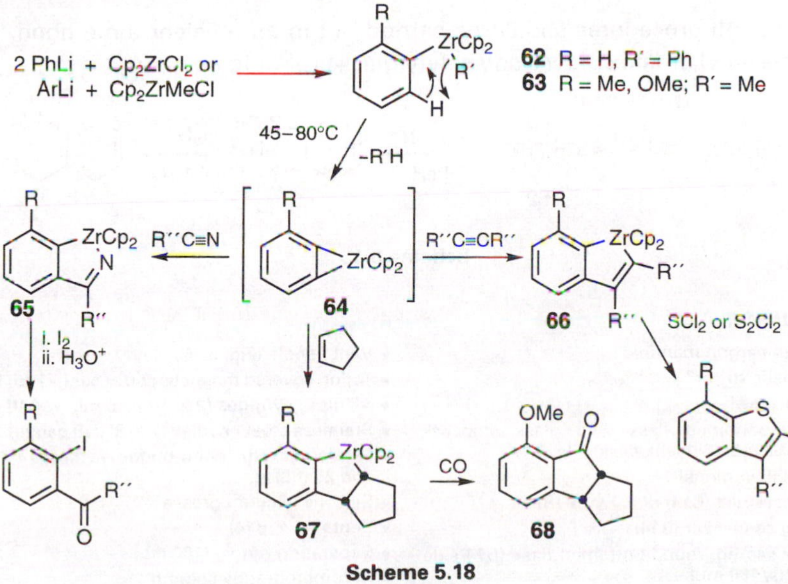

Scheme 5.18

nitriles and alkynes, and in lower yield with alkenes, to form zirconacycles such as **65–67**. When the benzyne complex has an *ortho*-substituent, insertion occurs with good selectivity into the remote carbon–zirconium bond. Terminal alkenes give the 3-substituted zirconaindane whereas unsymmetric alkynes insert with the larger substituent adjacent to zirconium. The insertion of alkenes has not been well explored and only ethene and norbornene have been reported to give good yields. Terminal alkenes, cyclopentene, and cycloheptene do insert but the yields are typically around 50%.

Nitrile adducts **65** undergo hydrolysis or iodinolysis to give *meta*-acylated aromatics thus providing products that are complemenetary to those generated by Friedel–Crafts methods. As well as hydrolysing to give styrenes, zirconaindenes **66** undergo metathesis with S_2Cl_2 or SCl_2 to afford benzothiophenes (Scheme 5.18).[47] Work-up of zirconaindanes by carbonylation gives indanones such as **68**.[48] Work-up with iodine affords 1,4-diiodides which may be cyclised to benzocyclobutanes on treatment with butyllithium.[45]

The need for $Cp_2ZrMeCl$ as a reagent in the above method may be avoided by using *in situ*-generated Cp_2ZrBu^iCl[49] although overall yields are lower.

The synthesis of diphenylzirconocene **62** and its transformation into an η^2-benzyne intermediate is described in Protocol 2 (Scheme 5.19). Subsequent trapping with a nitrile and iodinolysis give 2′-iodopropiophenone.

Protocol 2.
Preparation of diphenylzirconocene (Structure 62), thermolysis in the presence of propionitrile, and iodinolysis

Caution! All procedures should be carried out in an efficient fume hood. Disposable vinyl or latex gloves and safety glasses should be worn.

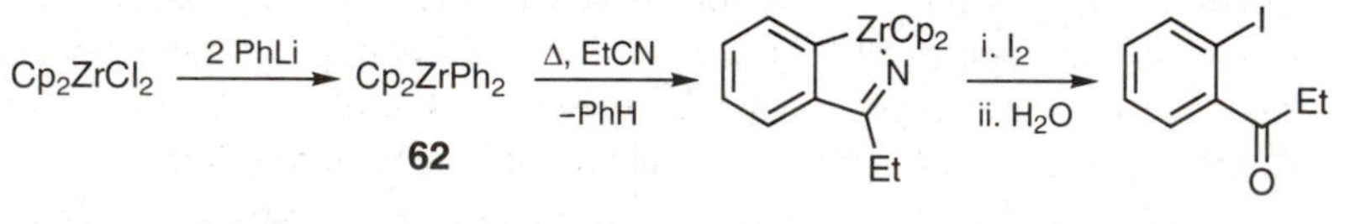

Scheme 5.19

Equipment

- Vacuum/argon manifold[a]
- Magnetic stirrer[b]
- Dewar bowl
- Round-bottomed flask with glass stopcock (B14, 50 mL) (Schlenk flask) (Fig. 5.1A)
- Small filter funnel
- Stopcock unit (B14) (3 × Fig. 5.1B)
- Liebig condenser (B14)
- Three-necked, round-bottomed flask (B14 side sockets, 100 mL)

- Vent needle (Fig. 5.1C)
- Teflon-covered magnetic stirrer bar (≈1 cm long)
- All glass syringes (2 × 1 mL, 5 mL, 4 × 10 mL)
- Stainless steel needles (7 × 8″, 18 gauge)
- Single-necked, round-bottomed flasks (10 mL and 25 mL)
- Silicone vacuum grease
- Septa[c] (4 × B14)
- Separating funnel (100 mL)
- Chromatography column

154

Materials

- Phenyllithium,[d] 2.56 mL of a 1.8 M solution, 4.6 mmol
  - flammable, moisture sensitive
- Zirconocene dichloride (FW 292.3), 0.584 g, 2 mmol
- Dry and oxygen free THF,[e] 11 mL
  - flammable, may form explosive peroxides, irritant
- Dry oxygen-free benzene,[e,f] 25 mL
  - flammable, toxic – danger of serious damage to health by prolonged exposure through inhalation, in contact with skin, and if swallowed, may cause cancer
- Dry trimethylsilyl chloride[e] (FW 108.6), ≈0.13 mL, 1 mmol
  - flammable, causes burns
  - ≈ moisture sensitive, toxic
- Dry propionitrile[e] (FW 55.1), 0.11 g, 0.14 mL, 2 mmol
  - flammable, very toxic
- Iodine (FW 253.8), 0.61 g, 2.4 mmol, 1.2 equiv
  - harmful
- Hydrochloric acid, 4 mL of a 1 M aqueous solution
- Saturated sodium sulfite solution
- Brine
- Anydrous magnesium sulfate
- Diethyl ether for chromatography
  - flammable, irritant
- Petroleum ether (40–60) for chromatography
  - flammable, very toxic
- Silica for chromatography
  - irritant dust

1. All glassware and the stirrer bar should be dried overnight in a 150°C oven and either assembled[g] while still warm, or allowed to cool in a desiccator before assembly. Syringes (not assembled) and needles should be dried at 150°C in an oven overnight, allowed to cool in a desiccator and then assembled using Teflon tape to ensure a gas-tight seal between the needle and syringe and to ease removal at the end of the experiment. All syringes should be flushed with argon before use by filling and emptying three times from a suitable source of pure argon.

2. Weigh the zirconocene dichloride into the 50 mL Schlenk flask containing the stirrer bar through a small dry funnel, avoiding contamination of the B14 joint which should not be greased. Quickly insert the previously greased condenser and stopcock assembly (already attached to the manifold) into the flask (Fig. 5.6) and with stopcock **B** closed evacuate the system (0.1–1 mmHg) through stopcock **A**. Use elastic bands to keep the flasks together when a positive pressure of argon is applied.

3. Carefully allow argon to enter the apparatus from the manifold avoiding blowing the zirconocene dichloride around. Repeat the evacuate/refill cycle twice. The apparatus should be left with stopcock **A** open so that the manifold maintains a positive pressure of argon in the flask. Stopcock **B** should be kept closed except when adding reagents.

4. Place a B14 septum over the end of the side-arm of the 50 mL flask and flush the space between the septum and the stopcock with argon by inserting a vent needle (Fig. 5.1C) and opening stopcock **B** slightly for a few seconds.

5. Add 10 mL of dry THF to the flask by syringe[h] through stopcock **B** and, after the zirconocene dichloride has dissolved, cool the flask to -78°C in an acetone bath cooled with liquid nitrogen or solid carbon dioxide.

Protocol 2. *Continued*

6. After 5 min at the low temperature add the phenyllithium solution by syringe over 2 min to give a dark brown solution. After a further 20 min add trimethylsilyl chloride ($\approx$0.05 mL) and then remove the cooling bath.

7. Once the reaction mixture has reached room temperature, remove the THF by vacuum transfer. Remove the septum on the side-arm and connect to the vacuum/argon manifold. Evacuate/refill the flexible tubing connection three times then open stopcock **B** and close stopcock **A**. Remove the vacuum/argon manifold connection from stopcock **A** and replace with a 0.3–0.5 m length of vacuum tubing connected to a stopcock in the side-arm of a 100 mL three-necked flask. The other side-arm of the flask should contain a stopcock connected to the vacuum/argon manifold so that the whole set-up resembles Fig. 5.7.

8. With stopcocks **C** and **D** open, evacuate the three-necked flask and lower it into the liquid nitrogen. Close stopcocks **B** and **D** and, while stirring or swirling the flask slightly, open stopcock **A**. As the bubbling subsides open the stopcock more. When the bubbling stops, close stopcock **A**, open stopcock **D** and after a few seconds close stopcock **D** and then carefully open stopcock **A** as above. Repeat this process until bubbling persists and a rapid transfer of solvent to the cold trap is occurring (the liquid nitrogen is seen to boil as the vapour gives up its latent heat of vaporisation). This method is better than connecting the flask directly to the vacuum manifold since it ensures that all of the solvent is trapped in the 100 mL flask and it gives a more controllable transfer.

9. When all the solvent has been removed from the reaction flask, close stopcock **C** and open stopcock **B** to allow argon back into the apparatus. Close stopcock **A** and replace the vacuum tubing connecting to the three-necked flask with a connection to the argon manifold. Flush the vacuum tubing with three evacuate/refill cycles and then open stopcock **A**, close stopcock **B**, remove the vacuum tubing from stopcock **B** and replace with a septum (back to Fig. 5.6). The three-necked flask should be removed from the liquid nitrogen, stopcock **D** closed and stopcock **C** opened to prevent a pressure build-up.

10. Add benzene (10 mL) through stopcock **B**.

11. Weigh dry propionitrile[e] into a dry 10 mL round-bottomed flask and fit with a septum. Add benzene (1 mL) and flush the flask with argon. Add this solution to the reaction mixture, followed by another washing of benzene (1 mL) to ensure that all of the propionitrile has been transferred.[i]

12. With stopcock **B** closed and stopcock **A** open to the argon manifold, heat the reaction vessel in an oil bath at 80 °C overnight. The reaction mixture should now be orange with a substantial amount of white precipitate present.

13. Weigh iodine into a dry 25 mL round-bottomed flask, fit a B14 septum and flush the air space with argon using a vent needle and a needle attached to the manifold. Add dry, oxygen-free benzene (10 mL) and swirl the flask to ensure that all the iodine has dissolved (gentle warming helps – if some is found not to have dissolved use more benzene to complete the transfer).

14. Cool the bath to 60°C and then add the iodine solution by syringe to the orange reaction mixture.

15. After stirring at 60°C for 20 min, remove the reaction flask from the oil bath. Once at room temperature remove the top stopcock unit, add hydrochloric acid (4 mL) and stir for 4 h.

16. Pour the reaction mixture into a 100 mL separating funnel and dilute with diethyl ether (30 mL). Wash the organic phase consecutively with saturated sodium sulfite solution (2 × 20 mL), water (2 × 20 mL), and brine (2 × 20 mL), and then dry over anhydrous magnesium sulfate. Filter and then concentrate by rotary evaporation to give a brown oil. Purify by column chromatography on silica gel (40 g, 5% diethyl ether/petroleum ether as eluent) to give 2'-iodopropiophenone as a yellow oil (0.39 g, 75%).

^{a,b}See Protocol 1, footnotes a and b.
^{c}Septa are stored in a desiccator over silica gel.
^{d}Treat as for butyllithium (Protocol 1, footnote e).
^{e}The benzene and THF are taken directly from a still (sodium benzophenone ketyl). Trimethylsilyl chloride and proprionitrile are distilled from calcium hydride under nitrogen.
^{f}Toluene may be used if preferred for safety reasons. A carefully thermostatted oil-bath must be used to maintain the 80°C temperature used in step 11.
^{g,h}See Protocol 1, footnotes g and h.
^{i}It is simpler to just add 0.13 mL of propionitrile to the reaction mixture provided that a good syringe is available and an accurate yield based on the nitrile is not required.

---

8. η^2-Imine zirconocene complexes

Zirconocene η^2-imine complexes **70** (Scheme 5.20) have been made by ligand exchange methods,[33,50] but the C—H activation route from amines provides the best access to these valuable intermediates.[51,52] The rate of the β-hydride activation depends mostly on the nitrogen substituent R^1 (Me$_3$Si > Ar > alkyl) but is also influenced by how activated the hydrogen to be eliminated is (benzylic or not) and by steric constraints for cyclic amines (Table 5.1).[51] The *in situ* generated η^2-imine complexes are trapped in good yield by alkenes (terminal, 1,1- and 1,2-disubstituted), alkynes (including terminal alkynes), allenes and in lower yield by ketones. Good regio- and stereo-control is usually found: alkynes insert with the larger group next to the metal, alkenes with it remote. Terminal alkenes insert into mono-substituted η^2-imine complexes (R^3 = H) with excellent selectivity (90 – >98%) for the *trans*-substituted zirconacycle **71** (Scheme 5.20). The problems of ligand ex-

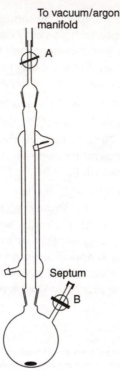

To vacuum/argon
manifold

Septum

Fig. 5.6

change found with η^2-alkene complexes only rarely occur as the imine moiety
is strongly bound to the metal.

The alkyne adducts derived from trimethylsilylamines and alkynes undergo high pressure carbonylation (1500 p.s.i. CO, NH$_4$Cl, r.t. 24 h or 90 p.s.i.
CO, 80 °C, 24 h) to give pyrroles **72** in $\approx$50% overall yield (Scheme 5.20).[53]

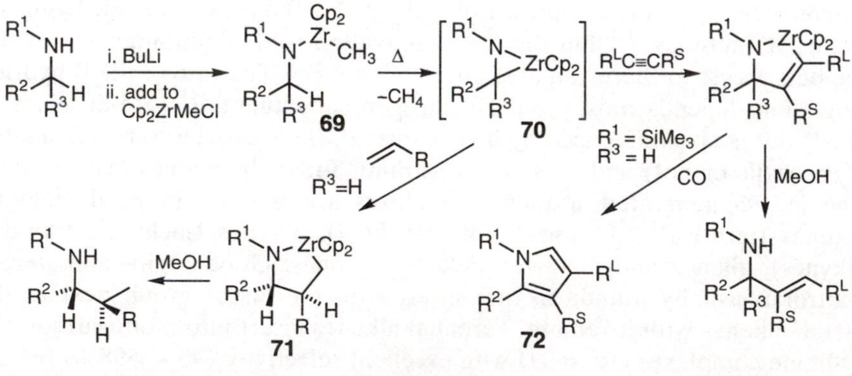

Scheme 5.20

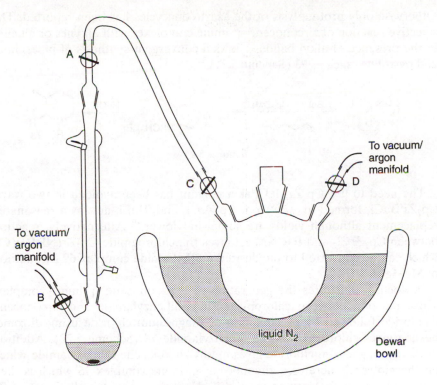

Fig. 5.7

Table 5.1 Formation and trapping of zirconocene η²-imine complexes.

R¹	R²	R³	Conditions (for trapping)	Comments
Me₃Si	Ar	H only	< 20°C (16 h, 20°C)	*a*
Me₃Si	alkyl	H only	20°C, 3 h (16 h, 40°C)	Alkynes only
Ar	Ar	H, (alkyl)	< 20°C (16 h, 20°C)	
Ar	alkyl	H, alkyl	67°C, 5 h	
		H, alkyl	67°C, 16 h	

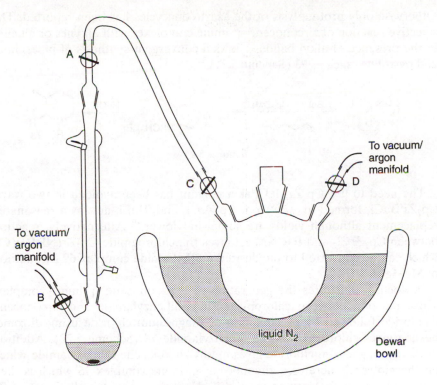

| alkyl | Ar | H only | 67°C, 16 h | |
| alkyl | alkyl | H only | 100°C, 40 h | Alkynes only |

ᵃMust not use THF as the solvent for alkene insertions – use benzene or toluene.

Otherwise only protonolysis of the azazirconacycles has been reported. The selective reaction of zirconocene η^2-imine complexes with alkynes or alkenes in the presence of alkyl halides allows a convergent synthesis of piperidines and pyrrolines such as **73** (Scheme 5.21).[55]

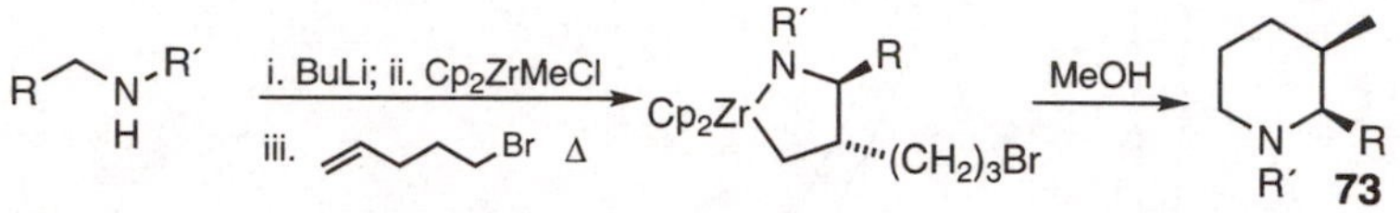

Scheme 5.21

The need to use Cp$_2$ZrMeCl as a reagent has been avoided in two ways. Cp$_2$Zr^{t}BuCl, formed *in situ* from Cp$_2$ZrCl$_2$ and ^{t}BuLi, acts as a reasonable replacement although yields are somewhat lower.[49] Alternatively, reaction between Cp$_2$ZrCl$_2$ and RR'NMgCl gives the chloroamide Cp$_2$Zr(NRR')(Cl) which can be converted to the desired methyl amide complex **69** by addition of MeMgCl.[54]

Protocol 3 illustrates the generation of a zirconocene η^2-imine complex. Thus, reaction between chloromagnesium dibenzylamide and zirconocene dichloride followed by precipitation of magnesium chloride using dioxane/hexane gives chlorozirconocene dibenzylamide **74** (Scheme 5.22). Addition of methylmagnesium chloride gives methylzirconocene dibenzylamide which on thermolysis generates a zirconocene η^2-imine complex **75** which is then trapped *in situ* with 4-octyne to give **76**. Hydrolysis give the allylic amine **77** (Scheme 5.22).

Protocol 3.
Generation and trapping of a zirconocene η^2-imine complex (Scheme 5.22)

Caution! All procedures should be carried out in an efficient fume hood. Disposable vinyl or latex gloves and safety glasses should be worn.

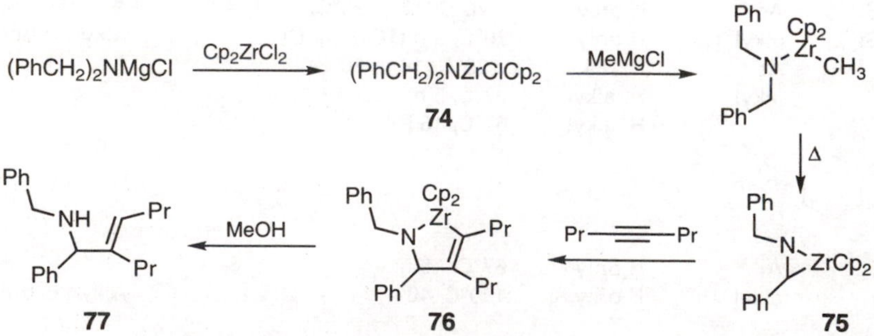

Scheme 5.22

Equipment

- Vacuum/argon manifold[a]
- Magnetic stirrer[b]
- Cooling bath
- Round-bottomed flasks with glass stopcock (B14, 25 and 50 mL) (Schlenk flasks) (Fig. 5.1A)
- Stopcock unit (2 × B14) (Fig. 5.1B)
- Condenser (B14)
- Vent needle (Fig. 5.1C)
- All glass tuberculin syringe[c] (1 mL)

- Teflon-covered magnetic stirrer bars (2 × ≈1 cm long)
- All glass syringes (2 × 10 mL, 2 × 5 mL, 2 × 2 mL and 2 × 1 mL)
- Stainless steel needles (9 × 6'', medium gauge)
- Silicone vacuum grease
- Septa[d] (2 × B14)
- Separating funnel

Materials

- Dibenzylamine[e] (FW 96.2), 1.182 g, 6 mmol   **irritant**
- Zirconocene dichloride (FW 292.32), 1.752 g, 6 mmol
- Methylmagnesium chloride,[f] 4 mL of a 3.0 M soln in THF 12 mmol   **moisture sensitive, flammable, causes burns**
- Dry and oxygen-free THF, 10 mL[e]   **flammable, may form explosive peroxides, irritant**
- Dry hexane,[e] 10 mL   **flammable, harmful**
- Dry dioxane,[e] 0.5 mL, 6 mmol   **flammable, may form explosive peroxides, irritant**
- 4-Octyne[e] (FW 110.2), 0.66 g, 0.88 mL, 6 mmol   **irritant**
- Ethyl acetate for chromatography   **flammable, irritant**
- Distilled petroleum ether (40-60) for chromatography   **flammable, very toxic**
- Diethyl ether for extraction   **flammable, irritant**
- Silica gel for chromatography   **irritant dust**

1. All glassware and stirrer bars should be dried overnight in a 150°C oven and either assembled[g] while still warm, or allowed to cool in a desiccator before assembly. Syringes (not assembled) and needles should be dried at 150°C in an oven overnight, allowed to cool in a desiccator and then assembled using Teflon tape to ensure a gas-tight seal between the needle and syringe and to ease removal at the end of the experiment. All syringes should be flushed with argon before use by filling and emptying three times from a suitable source of pure argon. All liquids should be added by syringe.

2. Weigh the dibenzylamine into the 25 mL Schlenk flask containing the stirrer bar. Insert the greased stopcock assembly to give apparatus as depicted in Fig. 5.2. With stopcock A closed and stopcock B open, flush with argon using three evacuate/refill cycles (the vacuum should only be applied briefly to avoid loss of the amine – lower molecular weight amines should be frozen using a bath containing liquid nitrogen before the evacuate/refill cycles).

3. Place a B14 septum on the stopcock unit and flush the space between it and the stopcock by inserting a vent needle (Fig. 5.1C) and slightly opening stopcock A. Add 5 mL of dry THF by syringe followed by the dropwise addition of 2 mL of the 3.0 M MeMgCl solution. This should give a rapid evolution of methane and the solution should become warm. Allow to stir for 20 min at ambient temperature after addition is complete.

Protocol 3. *Continued*

4. Weigh the zirconocene dichloride into a 50 mL Schlenk flask (Fig. 5.1A), containing a stirrer bar through a small dry funnel, avoiding contamination of the B14 joint which should not be greased. Quickly insert the previously greased B14 condenser and stopcock assembly into the flask and attach the assembled apparatus to the vacuum/argon manifold as in Fig. 5.6. With stopcock **B** closed, evacuate the system (0.1–1 mmHg) through stopcock **A**. Use elastic bands to ensure that the apparatus stays together when a positive argon pressure is applied.

5. Carefully allow argon to enter the apparatus from the manifold avoiding blowing the zirconocene dichloride around. Repeat the evacuate/refill cycle twice. The apparatus should be left with stopcock **A** open so that the manifold maintains a positive pressure of argon in the flask. Stopcock **B** should be kept closed except when adding reagents.

6. Place a B14 septum over the end of the flask side-arm and flush the space between the septum and the stopcock with argon by inserting a vent needle (Fig. 5.1C) and opening stopcock **B** slightly for a few seconds.

7. Add 5 mL of dry THF to the flask by syringe[h] through stopcock **B** and after the zirconocene dichloride has dissolved cool the flask to −30°C in an acetone bath cooled with liquid nitrogen or solid carbon dioxide.

8. After 5 min at the low temperature add the magnesium amide solution prepared in steps 1 and 2 dropwise over 2 min using a 10 mL syringe. Use a further 1 mL of THF to ensure complete transfer. Remove the cooling bath and allow to stir at room temperature for 1 h to give a red solution (dibenzylamine is unusual in this respect – most amines give a yellow solution).

9. Add dry hexane (8 mL) followed by dioxane (0.5 mL, 6 mmol) to give a precipitate of $MgCl_2 \cdot$dioxane.

10. Cool the slurry to −30°C in an acetone/coolant bath and then add MeMgCl (2 mL of 3.0 M soln) dropwise over 2 min. Remove the bath and allow the reaction mixture to stir at room temperature for 4 h.

11. Add 4-octyne using a 1 mL tuberculin syringe and then heat the solution under reflux for 16 h using a thermostatted oil bath.

12. Allow to cool to room temperature and then add methanol (1 mL) and stir for 5 min to give a yellow solution.

13. Pour the reaction mixture into water (60 mL) and diethyl ether (40 mL) in a 250 mL separating funnel. Remove the organic layer and extract the aqueous solution with more diethyl ether (2 × 40 mL). Dry the combined organic layers over anhydrous magnesium sulfate, filter and remove the solvent *in vacuo* to give the crude product.

14. Purify by chromatography on silica gel (4 cm deep by 5 cm diameter col-

umn) using 2% ethyl acetate in petroleum ether (40-60) (450 mL) to give (*E*)-1-*N*-benzylamino-1-phenyl-2-propylhex-2-ene as a colourless or very pale yellow oil (1.43 g, 78%) [**Caution!** Allylic amines are often toxic.] On TLC the product has an R_f of about 0.4 in 3% ethyl acetate/petroleum ether and stains black when charred with sulfuric acid.[i]

[a–d] See Protocol 1, footnotes a–d.
[e] 4-Octyne and dibenzylamine are distilled from calcium hydride. THF, dioxane, and hexane are taken directly from a still in which they are maintained at reflux over sodium benzophenone ketyl. In the last case, dimethyltetraglyme is added to the still to solubilise the blue ketyl radical.
[f] Treat as for *n*-butyllithium (Protocol 1, footnote e).
[g,h] See Protocol 1, footnotes g and h.
[i] See Protocol 1, footnote o.

References

1. Seebach, D.; Weidmann, B.; Widler, L. In *Modern Synthetic Methods*; Scheffold, R., ed.; Wiley: Chichester, **1983**; Vol. 3; pp. 217–353.
2. Williams, J. M. J. (ed.) *Preparation of alkenes: a practical approach*; Oxford University Press, 1996.
3. Taylor, R. J. K. (ed.) *Organocopper reagents: a practical approach*; Oxford University Press, 1995.
4. Negishi, E.; Cedarbaum, F.; Takahashi, T. *Tetrahedron Lett.* **1986**, *27*, 2829–2832.
5. Ito, H.; Taguchi, T.; Hanzawa, Y. *Tetrahedron Lett.* **1992**, *33*, 7873–7876.
6. Ito, H.; Nakamura, T.; Taguchi, T.; Hanzawa, Y. *Tetrahedron Lett.* **1992**, *33*, 3769–3772.
7. Suzuki, N.; Kondakov, D. Y.; Takahashi, T. *J. Am. Chem. Soc.* **1993**, *115*, 8485–8486.
8. Cuny, G. D.; Buchwald, S. L. *Organometallics* **1991**, *10*, 363–365.
9. Broene, R. D.; Buchwald, S. L. *Science* **1993**, *261*, 1696–1701.
10. Negishi, E. I. In *Comprehensive Organic Synthesis*; Paquette, L. A.; ed.; Pergamon: Oxford, 1991; Vol. 5; pp. 1163–1184.
11. Negishi, E.; Takahashi, T. *Synthesis-Stuttgart* **1988**, 1–19.
12. Buchwald, S. L.; Nielsen, R. B. *Chem. Rev.* **1988**, *88*, 1047–1058.
13. Negishi, E.; Takahashi, T. *Acc. Chem. Res.* **1994**, *27*, 124–130.
14. Fagan, P. J.; Nugent, W. A. *Organic Synthesis* **1992**, *70*, 272–277.
15. Vanwagenen, B. C.; Livinghouse, T. *Tetrahedron Lett.* **1989**, *30*, 3495–3498.
16. Buchwald, S. L.; Nielsen, R. B. *J. Am. Chem. Soc.* **1989**, *111*, 2870–2874.
17. Takahashi, T.; Kageyama, M.; Denisov, V.; Hara, R.; Negishi, E. *Tetrahedron Lett.* **1993**, *34*, 687–690.
18. Harris, M. C. J.; Whitby, R. J.; Blagg, J. *Synlett* **1993**, 705–707.
19. Nugent, W. A.; Thorn, D. L.; Harlow, R. L. *J. Am. Chem. Soc.* **1987**, *109*, 2788–2796.
20. Negishi, E.; Holmes, S.; Tour, J.; Miller, J.; Cederbaum, F.; Swanson, D.; Takahashi, T. *J. Am. Chem. Soc.* **1989**, *111*, 3336–3346.
21. Rajanbabu, T. V.; Nugent, W. A.; Taber, D. F.; Fagan, P. J. *J. Am. Chem. Soc.* **1988**, *110*, 7128–7135.
22. Lund, E. C.; Livinghouse, T. *J. Org. Chem.* **1989**, *54*, 4487–4488.

23. Berk, S. C.; Grossman, R. B.; Buchwald, S. L. *J. Am. Chem. Soc.* **1993**, *115*, 4912–4913.
24. Grossman, R. B.; Buchwald, S. L. *J. Org. Chem.* **1992**, *57*, 5803–5805.
25. Takahashi, T.; Xi, Z. F.; Rousset, C. J.; Suzuki, N. *Chem. Lett.* **1993**, 1001–1004.
26. Swanson, D.; Rousset, C.; Negishi, E.; Takahashi, T.; Seki, T.; Saburi, M.; Uchida, Y. *J. Org. Chem.* **1989**, *54*, 3521–3523.
27. Takahashi, T.; Fujimori, T.; Seki, T.; Saburi, M.; Uchida, Y.; Rousset, C.; Negishi, E. *J. Chem. Soc., Chem. Commun.* **1990**, 182–183.
28. Negishi, E.; Miller, S. *J. Org. Chem.* **1989**, *54*, 6014–6016.
29. Coperet, C.; Negishi, E. I.; Xi, Z. F.; Takahashi, T. *Tetrahedron Lett.* **1994**, *35*, 695–698.
30. Maye, J. P.; Negishi, E. *Tetrahedron Lett.* **1993**, *34*, 3359–3362.
31. Mori, M.; Saitoh, F.; Uesaka, N.; Shibasaki, M. *Chem. Lett.* **1993**, 213–216.
32. Taber, D. F.; Louey, J. P.; Lim, J. A. *Tetrahedron Lett.* **1993**, *34*, 2243–2246.
33. Jensen, M.; Livinghouse, T. *J. Am. Chem. Soc.* **1989**, *111*, 4495–4496.
34. Mori, M.; Uesaka, N.; Shibasaki, M. *J. Chem. Soc., Chem. Commun.* **1990**, 1222–1224.
35. Hewlett, D. F.; Whitby, R. J. *J. Chem. Soc., Chem. Commun.* **1990**, 1684–1686.
36. Takahashi, T.; Aoyagi, K.; Hara, R.; Suzuki, N. *Chem. Lett.* **1992**, 1693–1696.
37. Takahashi, T.; Aoyagi, K.; Kondakov, D. Y. *J. Chem. Soc., Chem. Commun.* **1994**, 747–748.
38. Rousset, C.; Swanson, D.; Lamaty, F.; Negishi, E. *Tetrahedron Lett.* **1989**, *30*, 5105–5108.
39. Davis, J. M.; Whitby, R. J.; Jaxa-Chamiec, A. *Synlett* **1994**, 110–112.
40. Davis, J. M.; Whitby, R. J.; Jaxa-Chamiec, A. *Tetrahedron Lett.* **1992**, *33*, 5655–5658.
41. Davis, J. M.; Whitby, R. J.; Jaxa-Chamiec, A. *Tetrahedron Lett.* **1994**, *35*, 1445–1448.
42. Negishi, E.; Akiyoshi, K.; O'Connor, B.; Takagi, K.; Wu, G. *J. Am. Chem. Soc.* **1989**, *111*, 3089–3091.
43. Luker, T.; Whitby, R. J. *Tetrahedron Lett.* **1994**, *35*, 785–788.
44. Fagan, P. J.; Nugent, W. A.; Calabrese, J. C. *J. Am. Chem. Soc.* **1994**, *116*, 1880–1889.
45. Buchwald, S. L.; Watson, B. T.; Lum, R. T.; Nugent, W. A. *J. Am. Chem. Soc.* **1987**, *109*, 7137–7141.
46. Buchwald, S. L.; King, S. M. *J. Am. Chem. Soc.* **1991**, *113*, 258–265.
47. Buchwald, S. L.; Qun, F. *J. Org. Chem.* **1989**, *54*, 2793–2797.
48. Cuny, G. D.; Gutierrez, A.; Buchwald, S. L. *Organometallics* **1991**, *10*, 537–539.
49. Barr, K. J.; Watson, B. T.; Buchwald, S. L. *Tetrahedron Lett.* **1991**, *32*, 5465–5468.
50. Ito, H.; Taguchi, T.; Hanzawa, Y. *Tetrahedron Lett.* **1992**, *33*, 4469–4472.
51. Coles, N.; Harris, M. C. J.; Whitby, R. J.; Blagg, J. *Organometallics* **1994**, *13*, 190–199.
52. Buchwald, S. L.; Watson, B. T.; Wannamaker, M. W.; Dewan, J. C. *J. Am. Chem. Soc.* **1989**, *111*, 4486–4494.
53. Buchwald, S. L.; Wannamaker, M. W.; Watson, B. T. *J. Am. Chem. Soc.* **1989**, *111*, 776–777.
54. Harris, M. C. J.; Whitby, R. J.; Blagg, J. *Tetrahedron Lett.* **1994**, *35*, 2431–2434.
55. Harris, M. C. J.; Whitby, R. J.; Blagg, J. *Tetrahedron Lett.* **1995**, *36*, 4287.

Addendum

Great advances have been made in stoichiometric early transition metal induced reactions since this chapter was written. Chapters in Comprehensive Organometallic Chemistry II,[56] a recent Tetrahedron Symposium-in-Print,[57] and a review of the synthetic applications of acyclic organochlorozirconocene complexes[58] have appeared. The most significant advance is the introduction of Ti(O^{i}Pr)$_4$/2^{i}PrMgBr as a cheap reagent with much of the reactivity of 'Cp$_2$Zr', and better functional group compatibility.[59] Elaboration of zircona-cycles through copper catalysed reaction with acyl chlorides, aryl halides, allyl halides, and enones,[60] as well as development of the tandem allyl carbenoid/electrophile insertion methods[61] continue to enhance the synthetic utility of these intermediates. The range of zirconacycles which can be synthezised, as well as the diastereoselectivity in their formation have been further delineated.[57]

56. Comprehensive Organometallic Chemistry II: A Review of the Literature 1982–1994; Abel, E. W.; Stone, F. E. A.; and Wilkinson, G. Ed.; Pergamon: Oxford, UK, 1995; Broene, R. D. Vol. 12; pp 323–348. Binger, P.; Podubrin, S. Vol; pp 439–464. Buchwald, S. L.; Broene, R. D. Vol. 12; pp 771–784. Guram, A. S.; Jordan, R. F. Vol. 4; pp 589–626.

57. Negishi, E. Ed. *Tetrahedron Symposium-in-Print* **1995**, *51*, 4255–4570.

58. Wipf, P.; Jahn, H. *Tetrahedron* **1996**, *52*, 12853–12910.

59. Gao, Y.; Shirai, M.; Sato, F. *Tetrahedron Lett.* **1996**, *37*, 7787–7790; Urabe, H.; Takeda, T.; Sato, F. *Tetrahedron Lett.* **1996**, *37*, 1253–1256; Urabe, H.; Sato, F. *J. Org. Chem.* **1996**, *61*, 6756–6757; Gao, Y.; Harada, K.; Sato, F. *Chem. Commun.* **1996**, 533–534; Urabe, H.; Hata, T.; Sato, F. *Tetrahedron Lett.* **1995**, *36*, 4261–4264.

60. Lipshutz, B. H.; Segi, M. *Tetrahedron* **1995**, *51*, 4407–4420; Takahashi, T.; Hara, R.; Nishihara, Y.; Kotora, M. *J. Am. Chem. Soc.* **1996**, *118*, 5154–5155; Takahashi, T.; Kotora, M.; Xi, Z. F. *J. Chem. Soc., Chem. Commun.* **1995**, 1503–1504; Taka-hashi, T.; Kotora, M.; Kasai, K.; Suzuki, N.; Nakajima K. *Organometallics* **1994**, *13*, 4183–4185; Takahashi, T.; Xi, Z. F.; Kotora, M.; Xi, C. J.; Nakajima, K. *Tetrahedron Lett.* **1996**, *37*, 7521–7524.

61. Gordon, G. J.; Whitby, R. J. *Synlett* **1995**, 77–78. Luker, T.; Whitby, R. J. *Tetrahedron Lett.* **1996**, *37*, 7661–7664.

Arene chromium tricarbonyl chemistry

STÉPHANE PERRIO

1. Introduction

Although a wide range of η^6-arene transition metal complexes are known,[1] it is only η^6-arene chromium tricarbonyl complexes that have found significant applications in synthetic organic chemistry.[2–10] These complexes have been investigated either as key intermediates in synthesis[6–10] or as efficient catalysts[11] in a variety of processes.

Chromium tricarbonyl complexes range in colour from bright yellow to red. They are air-stable, crystalline solids but are generally air sensitive in solution. The decomposition in solution, leading to chromium oxides, is autocatalytic in nature; as a consequence, when decomposition products are detected, at any stage of a synthesis, a filtration should be carried out. Purification is easily accomplished by chromatography on silica gel and/or recrystallisation from a nonpolar organic solvent.

Characterisation is achieved by normal spectroscopic methods.[4,12] Complexation causes an upfield shift in the ^{1}H NMR spectra of 1–2.5 ppm for the aryl hydrogens relative to the free arene whilst in the ^{13}C NMR spectra, the metal-bound carbons show a 20–40 ppm shift to higher field. Infrared spectra of these complexes display a characteristic pair of carbonyl stretching frequencies in the region of 1940–2000 and 1850–1940 cm^{-1}, respectively. Mass spectrometry is also effective for the identification of such complexes: ions corresponding to the M^+, $(M\text{-}CO)^+$, $(M\text{-}2CO)^+$, $(M\text{-}3CO)^+$ and $(\text{arene})^+$ fragments are typically observed.

Due to the strong electron-withdrawing ability and the steric effect of the chromium tricarbonyl group, η^6-arene chromium tricarbonyl ('benchrotrenic') complexes have some important and characteristic properties.[8–10] The chemical modifications arising from complexation are summarised in Scheme 6.1. η^6-Arene chromium tricarbonyl complexes undergo a variety of efficient bond-forming reactions by both nucleophilic and electrophilic pathways, either at the aromatic nucleus (nucleophilic addition and deprotonation) or in a side-chain position (through the formation and reactivity of benzylic carbocations and carbanions).[8-10] It should be noted that many of these re-actions are impossible to achieve with the corresponding free arene. In addition, most common synthetic transformations, such as acid or base hydrolysis, hydride reduction, carbanion additions to ketones, can be carried out on side chains without disturbing the arene–chromium bond.[8-10]

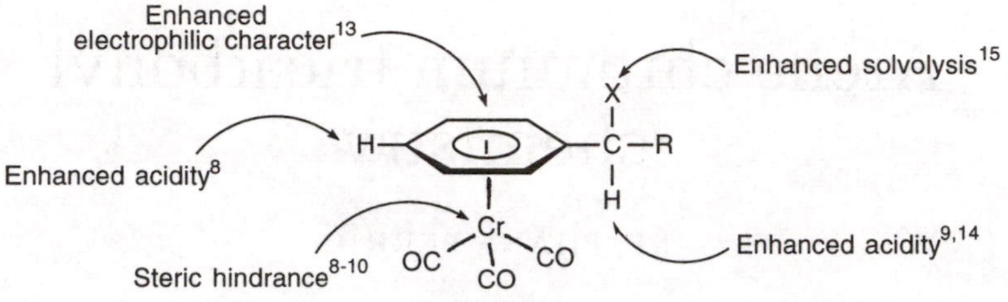

Scheme 6.1

Replacement of one carbonyl ligand by a superior donor ligand, such as a phosphine or phosphite, can be accomplished by photoirradiation (Equation 6.1).[1] This results in a slight modification of the reactivity of the complex, due to an increase in electron density at the metal centre and hence on the ring.

$$(Arene)Cr(CO)_3 + L \xrightarrow{h\nu} (Arene)Cr(CO)_2L + CO \tag{6.1}$$

$$L = PR_3, P(OR)_3$$

Perhaps the most significant property inherent in these complexes is the elimination of the σ plane of the benzene ring.[10] As a result, *ortho-* and *meta-*disubstituted η^6-arene chromium tricarbonyl complexes (with different substituents) become chiral molecules and exist in two enantiomeric forms A and B. This feature, together with the stereofacial selectivity induced by the chromium tricarbonyl group, has led to a rapid development in the use of these species as chiral auxiliaries in synthesis.[10] It should be noted at this point that introduction of an additional stereogenic centre in a side chain leads to diastereoisomers.

A variety of oxidative methods [cerium(IV) ammonium nitrate, I_2, $KMnO_4$, MnO_2, electrochemical oxidation] have been reported for the re-

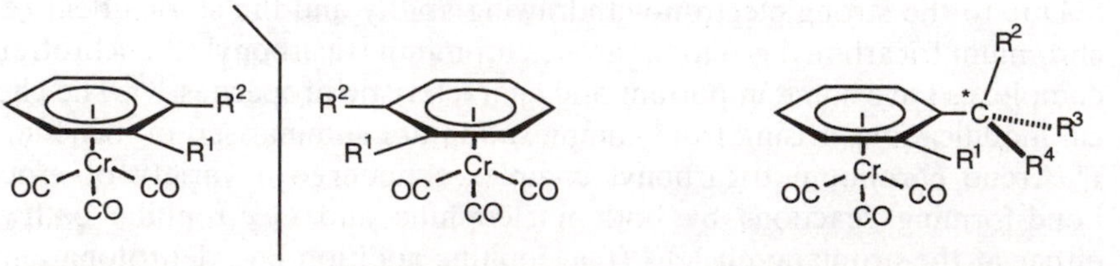

Enantiomer A.   Enantiomer B   One diastereoisomer

168

moval of the chromium tricarbonyl unit.[3] In addition, decomplexation occurs readily upon exposure of an ethereal solution of the complex to atmospheric oxygen and sunlight (Equation 6.2). This is of central importance if the complex is to be used as a stoichiometric reagent for organic synthesis. Alternatively, the thermolysis of η^6-arene chromium tricarbonyl complexes in refluxing pyridine liberates the free arene ligand (Equation 6.3).[3]

$$(\text{Arene})\text{Cr(CO)}_3 \xrightarrow{\text{Oxidant}} \text{Arene} + \text{Cr}_2\text{O}_3 \qquad (6.2)$$

$$(\text{Arene})\text{Cr(CO)}_3 \xrightarrow{\text{Pyridine}} \text{Arene} + (\text{Pyridine})_3\text{Cr(CO)}_3 \qquad (6.3)$$

This chapter will be divided into two distinct parts. Firstly, general methods for making η^6-arene chromium tricarbonyl complexes will be discussed. Particular attention will be paid to complexes bearing sulfinyl substituents[16] and protocols for their synthesis will be given. The second part will deal with enantiopure or enriched complexes. Examples of diastereoselective syntheses of optically pure 1,2-disubstituted complexes with amino and hydroxyl groups at the two benzylic positions[17] will be presented.

2. General methods for the synthesis of η^6-arene chromium tricarbonyl complexes

Arene chromium tricarbonyl complexes may be synthesised in a variety of ways. Two general approaches are available: direct complexation of the corresponding arene ligand or indirect routes involving the formation of an arene or a complex, previously identified as an appropriate precursor.

2.1 Direct complexation of an arene ligand

The simplest and most common procedure for generating η^6-arene chromium tricarbonyl species involves the direct heating of the free arene with chromium hexacarbonyl (Equation 6.4). The thermolysis is usually performed in a suitable solvent such as dioxane,[16] di-*n*-butyl ether[18] or decalin (decahydronaphthalene)[19] under refluxing conditions (the respective refluxing temperatures are 100–101°C, 141°C and 187–189°C). Addition of a small amount of a cosolvent, for example α-picoline,[19] THF[18] or *n*-butyl acetate[19] catalyses the reaction and results in a significant increase in the rate of complexation. The most effective and hence routinely used solvent medium for a wide range of high yielding syntheses is an approximately 10:1 mixture of di-*n*-butyl ether and THF.[18,20] Some practical problems can, however, be encountered with the use of di-*n*-butyl ether: depending on the supplier, it may be contaminated by *para*-xylene, thereby leading to unwanted side-products. Direct heating of the free arene with chromium hexacarbonyl requires special glassware to avoid loss of chromium hexacarbonyl *via*

Stéphane Perrio

sublimation: use of a Strohmeier apparatus,[21] a modified water condenser[19] or an air condenser[16] is necessary in order to wash back into the reaction flask any sublimed chromium hexacarbonyl. Although a wide range of complexes may be formed in moderate to excellent yields with this direct method, the most serious drawbacks comprise long reaction times (up to several days) and relatively high reaction temperatures (in excess of 100°C). Both these problems may be circumvented by using alternative sources of the chromium tricarbonyl group.

$$\text{Arene} + \text{Cr(CO)}_6 \xrightarrow{\text{Heat}} \text{(Arene)Cr(CO)}_3 + 3\,\text{CO} \qquad (6.4)$$

Complexes of structural type $L_3Cr(CO)_3$ undergo ligand exchange under milder conditions (Equations 6.5 and 6.6). The rate and the reaction temperature are dependent on the nature of the ligand L. The L unit can be donor ligands such as acetonitrile,[22] ammonia[23] or pyridine.[24] Use of the tris-pyridine derivative requires, however, the addition of boron trifluoride etherate. η^6-Naphthalene chromium tricarbonyl also undergoes arene exchange under mild conditions with many substituted arenes (Equation 6.7).[25,26] A wider range of reaction temperatures thereby becomes available and in some cases it may be as low as room temperature. As an alternative, photochemical routes may also be used, but these are usually lower yielding than the corresponding thermolytic procedures (Equation 6.8).[7]

$$\text{Arene} + \text{L}_3\text{Cr(CO)}_3 \xrightarrow[\text{L = CH}_3\text{CN, NH}_3]{\text{Heat}} \text{(Arene)Cr(CO)}_3 + 3\,\text{L} \qquad (6.5)$$

$$\text{Arene} + \text{(Pyridine)}_3\text{Cr(CO)}_3 \xrightarrow[25°C]{\text{BF}_3.\text{Et}_2\text{O}} \text{(Arene)Cr(CO)}_3 + 3\,\text{Pyridine} \qquad (6.6)$$

$$\text{Arene} + \text{(Naphthalene)Cr(CO)}_3 \xrightarrow{\text{Heat}} \text{(Arene)Cr(CO)}_3 + \text{Naphthalene} \qquad (6.7)$$

$$\text{Arene} + \text{Cr(CO)}_6 \xrightarrow[25°C]{h\nu} \text{(Arene)Cr(CO)}_3 + 3\,\text{CO} \qquad (6.8)$$

If an *ortho*- or *meta*-disubstituted benzene derivative with a stereogenic centre on one of the side chains is used, complexation may occur with significant diastereoselectivity.[8] This results from delivery of the chromium tricarbonyl group to one of the diastereotopic faces of the arene unit; it is, in general, facilitated by lower temperature conditions for the complexation step. A spectacular example is represented in Scheme 6.2.[17]

Most arenes may, in principle, be coordinated to a chromium tricarbonyl centre. In practice, however, certain types of functional groups are incompatible. For example, arene complexes bearing nitro or nitrile substituents are unknown. π-Electron donating substituents accelerate the rate of complexation, whilst electron withdrawing substituents (e.g. CHO, CO_2H) retard com-

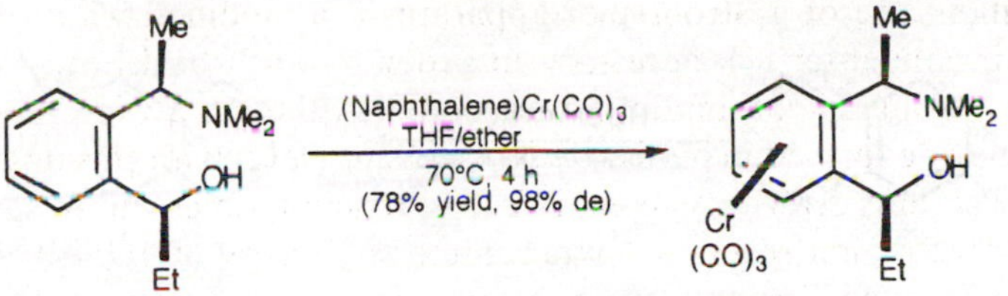

Scheme 6.2

plexation. The complexes are, in this case, best prepared by indirect methods. Table 6.1 indicates the best approach for a range of substituents.

2.2 Indirect routes

In one indirect route to η^6-arene chromium tricarbonyl complexes, an incompatible or reactive functionality is protected in the free arene precursor.[10] Complexation of the protected ligand, followed by deprotection, gives the desired complex. This method is particularly effective, for example, for the synthesis of complexes with ketone or aldehyde functions where the carbonyl group is protected as an acetal. A typical example is represented in Scheme 6.3.[32] By comparison, the direct complexation reaction under standard conditions [$Cr(CO)_6$, n-Bu_2O/THF, reflux, 5 h] afforded the corresponding complex in 4% yield only.[32]

A second indirect method involves derivatisation of a preformed arene complex and is particularly useful with highly functionalised complexes. Included here are a wide range of reactions such as nucleophilic additions on the aromatic nucleus, electrophilic attacks on *in-situ*-generated carbanions (e.g. aldol condensation[34,35]) and the quenching of carbocations with nucleophiles.[8,10]

Table 6.1 General synthetic procedures for the preparation of η^6-arene chromium tricarbonyl complexes.

Direct complexation		Indirect complexation	
Substituent	Reference	Substituent	Reference
NR^1R^2	27	COR	8,10
OR	28	CHO	10
CH_2OH	8	CO_2H	10,19
Alkyl	8	S(O)R	16
F	18	Br	33
Cl	29	I	33
SiR_3	22		
SMe	16		
$S(O_2)R$	30		
OH	31		

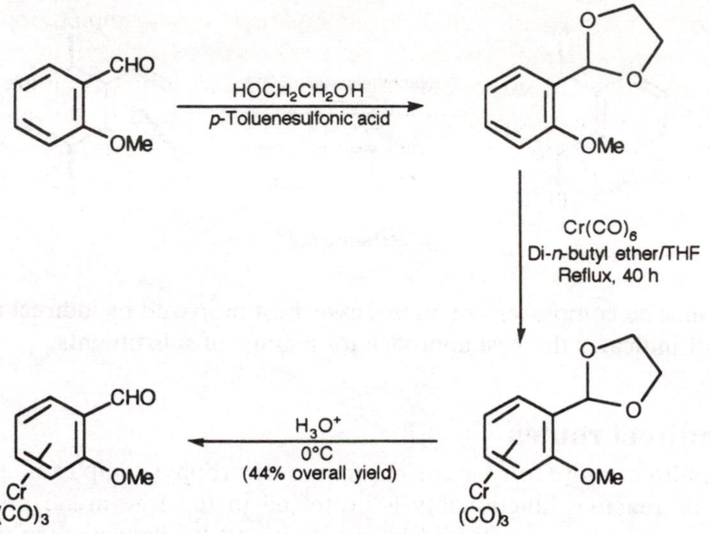

Scheme 6.3

As an example, reaction of a lithiated arene complex with dibromoethane or diiodoethane[33] permits the efficient introduction of bromo and iodo substituents (Scheme 6.4). The direct complexation of the parent free arene would be unsuccessful, giving rise instead to a dehalogenation reaction.[36]

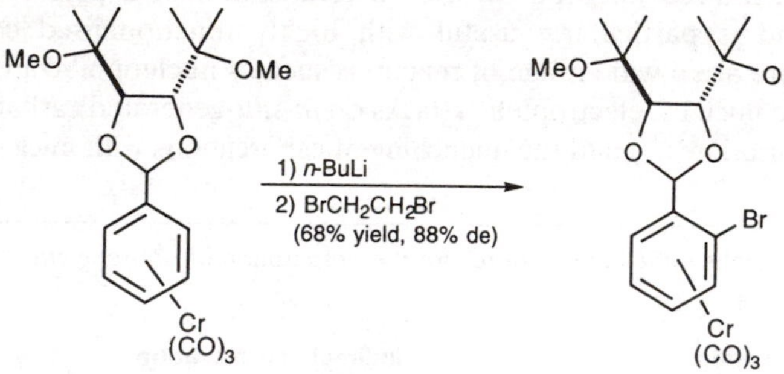

Scheme 6.4

2.3 Synthesis of complexes bearing a sulfinyl substituent

Heating a sulfinyl substituted arene with an appropriate chromium tricarbonyl source does not afford the corresponding η^6-arene chromium tricarbonyl complex. Instead, a complex mixture of products is obtained, arising from an initial reduction of the sulfoxide functional group.[16]

An indirect route to these sulfinyl-substituted derivatives has however been devised. The method consists of a two-step synthesis, involving the formation of a sulfenyl-substituted chromium tricarbonyl complex, followed by oxidation of the sulfenyl substituent. As it has been known for many years that sulfenyl-substituted arenes readily form chromium tricarbonyl complexes,[36] the difficulty was to find an oxidising agent which would oxidise the sulfur centre without disturbing the chromium moiety. It was eventually discovered that dimethyldioxirane could achieve this transformation very efficiently. Protocols 1–4 describe how to synthesise chromium tricarbonyl complexes of sulfinyl substituted arenes using this approach. In applying this method to *ortho*-disubstituted derivatives, high diastereoselectivities were achieved.[16]

Protocol 1 describes the direct complexation of (methylsulfenyl)benzene **1** (Scheme 6.5).

Protocol 1.
Synthesis of tricarbonyl[η⁶-(methylsulfenyl)benzene]chromium(0) (Structure 2). Complexation of (methylsulfenyl)benzene (Structure 1) by thermolysis with chromium hexacarbonyl (Scheme 6.5)

Caution! Due to the potential toxicity of chromium tricarbonyl complexes, all procedures should be carried out in a fume cupboard. Disposable nitrile or latex gloves and safety glasses should be worn. All procedures are performed with the exclusion of air by using standard nitrogen/vacuum line and Schlenk tube techniques. Although η⁶-arene chromium tricarbonyl complexes are generally stable in air in a crystalline state for long periods, many have been found to decompose in solution on exposure to air under laboratory light. Consequently, all glassware used for complexation, filtration and crystallisation should always be protected from exposure to oxygen and light.

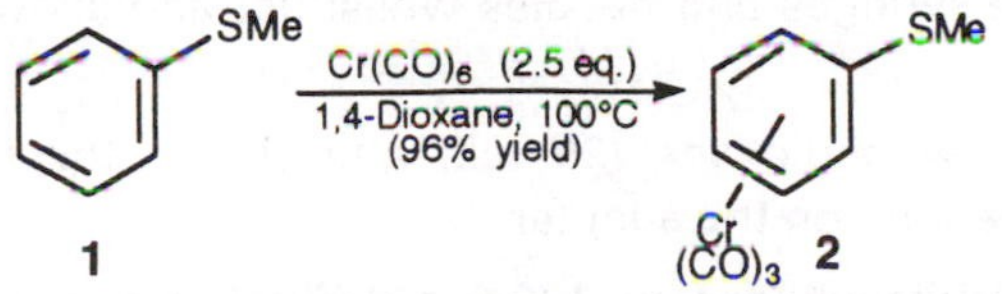

Scheme 6.5

Equipment

- Vacuum/nitrogen manifold (Figs 7.1 and 7.2)
- Stirrer- hot plate
- Single-necked, round-bottomed flask (B24, 50 mL)
- Liebig condenser, used as an air condenser
- Liebig condenser, used as a water condenser
- Side-arm adapter
- Cone/flexible tubing adapter
- Oil bath
- Contact thermometer (up to 200°C)
- Small magnetic stirrer bar (length 1.5 cm)
- Septum

- Aluminium foil
- All glass syringe (volume appropriate for quantity of solution to be transferred)
- Needle (6″, gauge 20 or 22)
- Joint clips (× 3)
- Silicone vacuum grease
- Schlenk tubes for saturating solvents with nitrogen and recrystallisation (× 3)
- Single-necked, round-bottomed flask (B24, 250 mL) for filtration
- Filter column with filter frit (100 mL)

Protocol 1. *Continued*

Materials

- Dry 1,4-dioxane,[a] 20 mL + 2 mL   **flammable, possible carcinogen, may form explosive peroxides**
- Chromium hexacarbonyl[b] (FW 220.1), 2.21 g, 10 mmol   **volatile, highly toxic**
- (Methylsulfenyl)benzene **1**[c] (FW 124.2), 0.5 g, 4 mmol   **harmful, stench**
- Diethyl ether for filtration   **flammable, irritant**
- Kieselguhr[d] for filtration
- Dichloromethane for crystallisation   **harmful, irritant, toxic**
- Petroleum ether (60-80) for crystallisation   **flammable, harmful**

1. Clean all glassware, syringes, needles and stirrer bar and dry for at least 2 h in a 100°C electric oven before use.

2. Prepare an oil bath at 115°C, controlling the temperature by a contact thermometer.

3. Equip the 50 mL round-bottomed flask with the stirrer bar and the side-arm adapter fitted with a septum. Assemble both pieces whilst still hot (Fig. 6.1).

4. Support the assembled flask using a clamp and a stand with a heavy base and connect the apparatus to the vacuum/nitrogen manifold. Apply the vacuum and then the nitrogen supply (Chapter 7, Protocol 1).

5. Remove the septum on the adapter, reduce the nitrogen to a gentle flow and introduce chromium hexacarbonyl (2.21 g, 10 mmol) with the aid of a rolled filter paper. Put the septum back on the adapter.

6. Protect the flask from light using foil.

7. Assemble the syringes and needles whilst hot and allow to cool to room temperature.

8. Fill a syringe with dioxane (20 mL) and charge the flask by injecting through the septum on the adapter.

9. Inject (methylsulfenyl)benzene **1** (0.5 g, 0.47 mL, 4 mmol) into the reaction flask through the septum on the adapter using a syringe.

10. Assemble both condensers and the cone/flexible tubing adapter whilst hot as shown in Fig. 6.2 (grease the joints carefully and use green clips to secure them), connect the cone/flexible tubing adapter to the vacuum/nitrogen manifold and turn on the flow of nitrogen.

11. Remove the side-arm adapter from the flask and replace by the assembled condensers (use a green clip to secure the joint) (Fig. 6.2).

12. Adjust the water condenser (the top one) to give a moderate flow and initiate stirring the suspension.

13. Apply vacuum till vigorous bubbling occurs and refill with nitrogen (Chapter 7, Protocol 2). Repeat a total of 10 times.

14. Immerse the mixture in the oil bath and generously wrap the apparatus with aluminium foil to minimize exposure to light.

15. After a few minutes, reflux will begin. Leave the solution refluxing for 64 h.[e] The solution gradually turns from pale yellow to dark orange.

16. Remove the oil bath and allow the solution to cool down in an ice-water bath (15 min). Unreacted chromium hexacarbonyl will precipitate out of the solution.[f]

17. During this time, pack the filter column with a short pad of Kieselguhr in diethyl ether[g] (Chapter 7, Protocol 5) and position a round-bottomed flask (250 mL), covered with foil, to collect the filtrate.

18. Disconnect the condensers from the water and nitrogen sources and remove the assembled condensers from the flask. Attach instead a side-arm adapter with a septum on top, already connected to the nitrogen source (Fig. 6.1).

19. Transfer the solution onto Kieselguhr *via* a cannula (Chapter 7, Protocol 3). Rinse the residue in the reaction flask with diethyl ether and transfer the resulting pale yellow solution to the filtration column.

20. Run the filtration column using a nitrogen pressure, collecting the yellow solution in the flask (Chapter 7, Protocol 5). Add diethyl ether until the yellow colour is flushed off the column.

21. Concentrate the resulting orange filtrate under reduced pressure (20 mmHg) by means of a rotary evaporator *located in a fume hood* [the use of a hot water bath (60°C) is necessary to remove the dioxane efficiently]. Store the resulting yellow solid, under an inert atmosphere.

22. Saturate dichloromethane and petroleum ether with nitrogen (Chapter 7, Protocol 2). Evacuate the Schlenk tube to be used for the crystallisation and refill with nitrogen (Chapter 7, Protocol 1).

23. Dissolve the crude yellow solid in the minimum amount of nitrogen-saturated dichloromethane.

24. Transfer the resulting yellow solution into the empty Schlenk tube *via* a filter cannula. If any decomposition is seen at this stage, the solution may be filtered through a small bed of Kieselguhr.

25. Rinse the flask with nitrogen-saturated dichloromethane and transfer to the Schlenk tube for crystallisation.

26. Use the vacuum manifold to remove a small portion of the dichloromethane and then add nitrogen-saturated petroleum ether.

27. Concentrate the solution using the vacuum manifold until the first solid appears.

28. In the sealed Schlenk tube, dissolve the crystals using a hot water bath, protect the Schlenk tube with foil and place it in a freezer (−20°C) for 2 days.

Protocol 1. *Continued*

29. Separate the yellow crystals from the mother liquor by filtration using a filtering cannula and collect the mother liquor in a Schlenk tube.

30. Wash the crystals with cold nitrogen-saturated petroleum ether, shake gently, allow the solution to settle and withdraw the supernatant. Dry the yellow crystals at room temperature under reduced pressure and record the ^{1}H NMR spectrum in CDCl$_3$ under nitrogen, as described in Protocol 6 of Chapter 7.

31. Repeat the crystallisation procedure with the mother liquor.

32. Combine both crystallisation crops, which display appropriate spectroscopic data[16] (1.01 g, 3.88 mmol, 96% yield, m.p. 101–102°C), and keep in a vial protected from light with aluminium foil.

---

[a] 1,4-Dioxane is purified by distillation under nitrogen from calcium hydride and then stored under nitrogen over molecular sieves (4Å) in a bottle protected from light.
[b] Chromium hexacarbonyl is purchased from Strem Chemicals and is used as received. It can be weighed in air as it is relatively air stable and non-volatile. The usual precautions appropriate for a potentially toxic metal carbonyl should be employed, but the low volatility makes handling relatively easy.
[c] (Methylsulfenyl)benzene (thioanisole or methyl phenyl sulfide) is used as obtained from Aldrich. The smell of this sulfide is quite unpleasant. In order to destroy any trace of it, all contaminated glassware should be immersed in a bleach bath.
[d] Kieselguhr is supplied by BDH.
[e] During the complexation reaction, carbon monoxide is evolved slowly. Hence, gas evolution should be observed with the bubbler attached to the vacuum/nitrogen manifold.
  If before 64 h of reflux, the reaction mixture develops a green colour, which is indicative of decomposition, stop heating and carry out the work-up. The decomposition is catalytic in nature.
[f] Unreacted chromium hexacarbonyl is destroyed in a well-ventilated hood by oxidation with bleach. If a green residue remains on the inside walls of the glassware, wash with nitric acid.
[g] Diethyl ether is used as obtained for the entire filtration sequence.

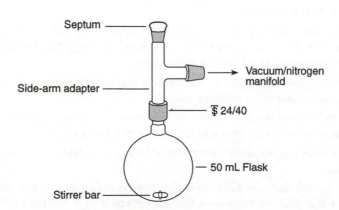

Septum

Side-arm adapter

Vacuum/nitrogen manifold

$ 24/40

50 mL Flask

Stirrer bar

Fig. 6.1 Assembled reaction apparatus.

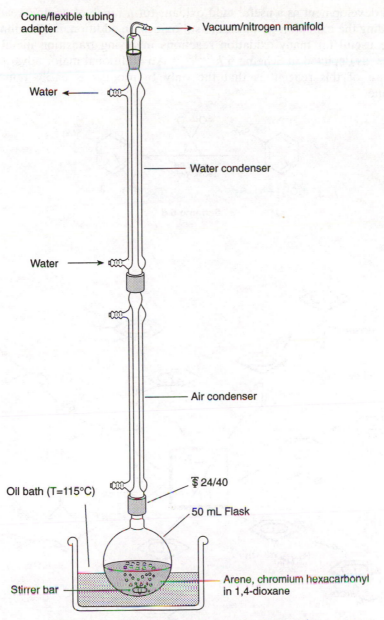

Cone/flexible tubing adapter

Vacuum/nitrogen manifold

Water

Water condenser

Water

Air condenser

Oil bath (T=115°C)

♈ 24/40

50 mL Flask

Stirrer bar

Arene, chromium hexacarbonyl in 1,4-dioxane

Fig. 6.2 Apparatus used for the complexation reactions.

The chromium tricarbonyl complex **2** of (methylsulfenyl)benzene is then oxidised to its sulfinyl derivative **3** using dimethyldioxirane (Scheme 6.6).[37,38]

This cyclic peroxide, formed from potassium peroxymonosulfate and acetone[39] and isolated as a 0.09–0.11 M solution in acetone,[40] has undergone rapid development as a useful mild oxidant for a range of organic reactions, including the oxidation of sulfides to sulfoxides. In addition, it is beginning to prove useful for many oxidation reactions involving transition metal complexes, as depicted in Scheme 6.7.[37,38,41,42] An additional major advantage in the use of this reagent is that the only by-product is easily removable acetone.

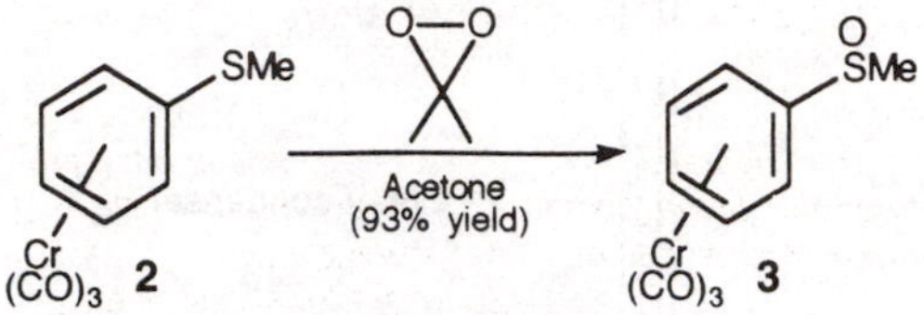

Scheme 6.6

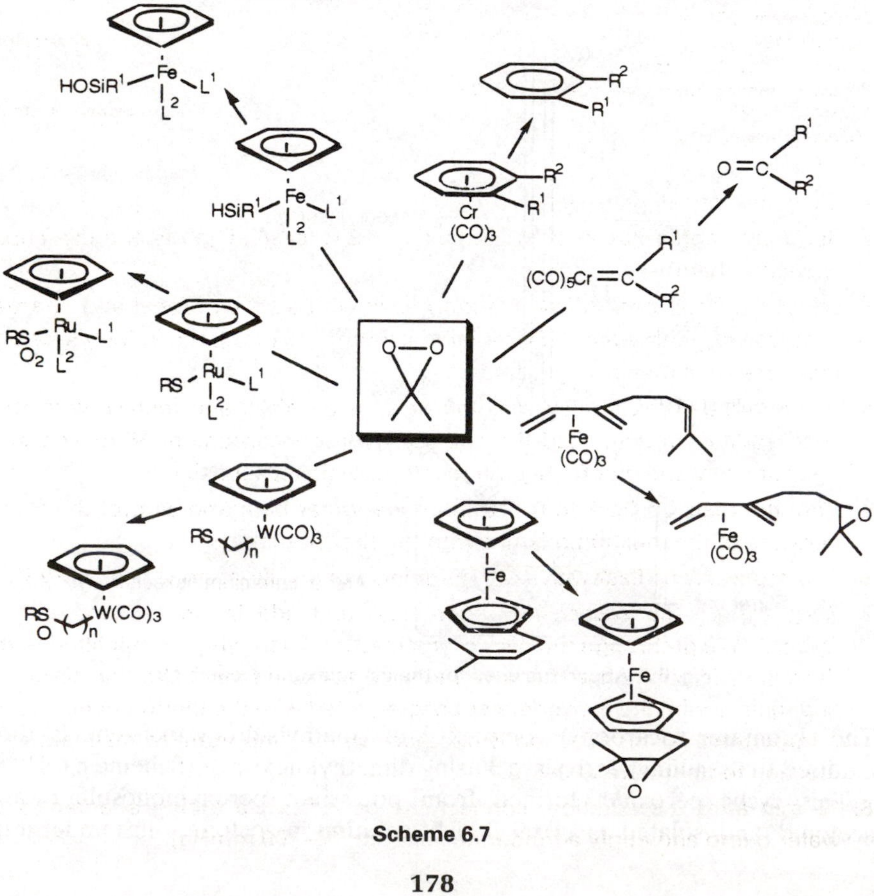

Scheme 6.7

Protocol 2.
Preparation of dimethyldioxirane solution in acetone[39]

Caution! All procedures should be carried out in a fume hood. Disposable vinyl or latex gloves and safety glasses should be worn.

As peroxides may be decomposed when brought in contact with metal utensils (e.g. spatulas), such practice should be avoided.

Equipment

- Overhead mechanical stirrer apparatus
- Three-necked, round-bottomed flask (4000 mL)
- Two-necked, round-bottomed flask (250 mL)
- Pyrex funnel
- Solid addition funnel
- U-Tube (i.d. 25 mm)
- Measuring cylinder (volume appropriate for quantity to be handled)
- Cone/flexible tubing adapter

- Thermometer adapter
- Thermometer (-20 to $110°C$)
- Joint clips
- Silicone vacuum grease
- Source of nitrogen
- Septum
- Glass bottle (200 mL) for storage of the dioxirane solution

Materials

- Distilled water, 254 mL
- Acetone,[a] 192 mL   **flammable**
- Sodium hydrogencarbonate, 58 g
- Potassium monoperoxysulfate (Oxone®)[b] (FW 614.8),
  120 g, 0.195 mol   **oxidant, irritant**
- Molecular sieves[c] (4Å)
- Dry ice

1. Clean and dry all glassware.

2. Set up the apparatus as depicted in Fig. 6.3 (grease all joints and use clips to secure them).

3. Equip the 'free' neck of the reaction flask with a Pyrex funnel and charge successively with water (254 mL) and acetone (192 mL), the volumes being measured in a measuring cylinder.

4. Remove the Pyrex funnel from the neck of the flask and replace with the solid addition funnel. Add the sodium hydrogencarbonate (58 g) and stir mechanically and vigorously the resulting white suspension.[d]

5. Cool the reaction flask to 0–5°C in an ice–water bath and control the temperature of the reaction mixture with the thermometer.

6. Cool the receiving flask with a dry ice–ethanol or dry ice–acetone bath to −78°C.

7. Keep stirring the suspension vigorously[d] and add in one aliquot of the Oxone® (120 g) through the neck of the reaction flask, which is still fitted with the solid addition funnel. Remove the solid addition funnel after the addition and replace with the thermometer adapter, fitted with the thermometer.

   Important! As the reaction is exothermic, it is important to maintain the reaction temperature at 0–5°C.

8. 15 min after the addition, connect the cone/flexible tubing adapter to a water pump and apply a moderate vacuum (80–100 mmHg).

Protocol 2. *Continued*

9. Remove the ice–water bath from the reaction flask and allow the temperature of the reaction mixture to rise to 30 °C by means of a warm water bath.

10. Keep stirring vigorously and collect the effluent pale yellow dimethyldioxirane–acetone solution (150 mL, 0.09–0.11 M, 5% yield) in the cooled receiving flask (−78°C). The distillation takes 2–4 h depending on the vacuum applied.

11. When the distillation is over, disconnect the cone/flexible tubing adapter from the water pump and connect it to the nitrogen source.

12. Remove the U-tube and the reaction flask, add molecular sieves to dry the dimethyldioxirane solution through the 'free' neck of the receiving flask, and stopper with a septum.

13. Pour the dimethyldioxirane solution in a small dry bottle, containing molecular sieves (4Å) and previously cooled in a dry ice–ethanol or dry ice–acetone bath at −20°C. Seal with a septum under a nitrogen atmosphere.

14. Store the bottle in a freezer (−20°C).[e]

[a] Commercial-grade acetone was employed.
[b] Potassium monoperoxysulfate (the triple salt 2 $KHSO_5 \cdot KHSO_4 \cdot K_2SO_4$) was purchased from Aldrich under the trade-name Oxone® and used as supplied. Other commercial sources sell the oxidant under the name Curox® or Caroate®.
[c] The molecular sieves were flame-dried under high vacuum just prior to use.
[d] **Care!** Over-vigorous stirring can cause the reaction mixture to splash up the neck of the flask.
[e] The reagent must be kept cold at all times to avoid decomposition. Once prepared, it can be stored at −20°C under nitrogen for at least 2 months.

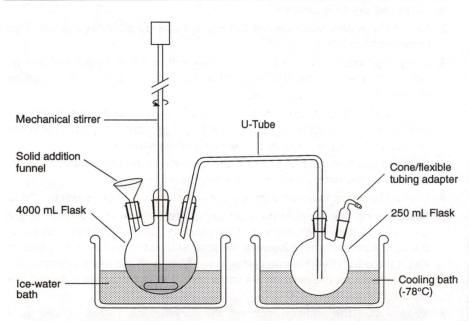

Fig. 6.3 Apparatus used for the preparation of the dimethyldioxirane solution.

Protocol 3.
Iodometric titration of a dimethyldioxirane solution in acetone[40]

Caution! All procedures should be carried out in a well-ventilated hood. Disposable vinyl or latex gloves and safety glasses should be worn.

As peroxides are generally decomposed when brought in contact with metal utensils (e.g. spatulas), such practice should be avoided.

Important! Due to the slight instability of dimethyldioxirane, the concentration of the solution has to be determined before each experiment. The peroxide content is determined by titration with an aqueous sodium thiosulfate solution, *via* iodine.

(1) Dimethyldioxirane is first reacted with potassium iodide in an acidic medium. The oxidation–reduction reaction involved corresponds to the following half-reactions:
(a) Reduction of dimethyldioxirane to acetone:

$$\underset{O}{\overset{O}{\diagdown}}\!\!\diagup + 2e^- + 2H^+ \longrightarrow O=\!\!\diagup + H_2O \qquad (6.9)$$

(b) Oxidation of iodide to iodine:

$$2I^- \longrightarrow I_2 + 2e^- \qquad (6.10)$$

Adding both half-reactions gives the equation:

$$\underset{O}{\overset{O}{\diagdown}}\!\!\diagup + 2H^+ + 2I^- \longrightarrow O=\!\!\diagup + H_2O + I_2 \qquad (6.11)$$
$$\text{(Yellow)}$$

(2) The amount of iodine thereby liberated is subsequently titrated by an aqueous sodium thiosulfate solution according to the half-reactions:
(a) Oxidation of thiosulfate anion into tetrathionate anion:

$$2S_2O_3^{2-} \longrightarrow S_4O_6^{2-} + 2e^- \qquad (6.12)$$

(b) Reduction of iodine into iodide:

$$I_2 + 2e^- \longrightarrow 2I^- \qquad (6.13)$$

Adding both half-reactions gives the equation:

$$2S_2O_3^{2-} + I_2 \longrightarrow S_4O_6^{2-} + 2I^- \qquad (6.14)$$
$$\text{(Yellow)} \qquad\qquad \text{(Colourless)}$$

Protocol 3. *Continued*

The end point is, therefore, indicated by the total disappearance of the characteristic yellow colour of iodine. The formula for calculating the dimethyldioxirane concentration is

$$M_{Dioxirane} = \frac{1}{2} \cdot \frac{M_{Thiosulfate} \cdot V_{Thiosulfate}}{V_{Dioxirane}} \tag{6.15}$$

Equipment

- Erlenmeyer flask (50 mL)
- Measuring cylinder (volume appropriate for quantity to be handled)
- Graduated pipette (1 mL)
- Pipette filler
- Micro-burette (10 mL)
- Aluminium foil
- Dry ice
- Source of nitrogen

Materials

- Dimethyldioxirane solution in acetone, 1 mL, *concentration to be determined*
- Acetic acid/acetone solution 3:2, v/v, 2 mL — **corrosive, flammable irritant, light sensitive**
- Saturated aqueous potassium iodide solution, 2 mL
- Distilled water, 5 mL
- Aqueous $Na_2S_2O_3$ solution (0.01–0.05 M) — **irritant**

1. Ensure that all glassware is thoroughly clean.

2. Charge the Erlenmeyer flask with a 3:2 mixture of acetic acid–acetone (2 mL).

3. Remove the septum of the bottle containing the dimethyldioxirane solution, cooled in a dry ice–ethanol or dry ice–acetone bath at −20°C. Fill the graduated pipette, equipped with the pipette filler, with the dioxirane solution (1 mL) and add it in one aliquot into the Erlenmeyer flask. Put the septum back on the bottle of dimethyldioxirane and fill it with N_2.

4. Add together a saturated aqueous potassium iodide solution (2 mL) and some dry ice to deaerate the mixture. The solution turns immediately dark yellow.

5. Protect the Erlenmeyer flask from light with aluminium foil and store the solution at room temperature for 10 min.

6. During this time, fill the burette with the thiosulfate solution.

7. Add the thiosulfate solution into the Erlenmeyer flask with frequent swirling of the contents of the flask until the yellow colour of iodine disappears. Repeat the same procedure with a second 1 mL aliquot of dimethyldioxirane.

Protocol 4.
Synthesis of tricarbonyl[η^6-(methylsulfinyl)benzene]chromium(0) (Structure 3). Oxidation of tricarbonyl[η^6-(methylsulfenyl)benzene]chromium(0) (Structure 2) with dimethyldioxirane (Scheme 6.6)

Caution! Due to potential toxicity of chromium carbonyl complexes, all procedures should be carried out in a well-ventilated hood. Disposable vinyl or latex gloves and safety glasses should be worn. All procedures are performed anaerobically by using standard vacuum/nitrogen manifold and Schlenk tube techniques. As chromium complexes are unstable in solution when exposed to air and light, the oxidation reaction and subsequent work-up are always carried out under nitrogen in glassware protected with foil.

Equipment

- Vacuum/nitrogen manifold (Figs 7.1 and 7.2)
- Magnetic stirrer
- Schlenk tubes ($\times$ 2)
- Magnetic stirrer bar (length 1.5 cm)
- Septum
- Pipette filler
- Graduated pipette (volume appropriate for quantity of solution to be used)
- Filter funnel with filter frit (100 mL)
- Schlenk tubes for filtration, saturating solvents with nitrogen and recrystallisation
- Aluminium foil

Materials

- Chromium complex **2** (FW 260.2), 89 mg, 0.34 mmol
- Dimethyldioxirane solution in acetone,^{a} 4.3 mL of a 0.095 M solution, 0.41 mmol, 1.2 equiv
- Acetone, 10 mL + 5 mL   **flammable**
- Kieselguhr for filtration
- Dichloromethane for crystallisation   **harmful, irritant, toxic**
- Petroleum ether (60-80) for crystallisation   **flammable, harmful**

1. Clean all glassware and stirrer bars and dry for at least 1 h in a 100°C electric oven before use.

2. Support a Schlenk tube, containing a magnetic stirrer bar, below its side-arm using a clamp and a stand with a heavy base. Attach it to the vacuum/nitrogen manifold *via* its side-arm.

3. Charge the Schlenk tube with sulfide complex **2** (89 mg, 0.34 mmol).

4. Equip the neck of the Schlenk tube with a septum, evacuate and refill with nitrogen (Chapter 7, Protocol 1).

5. Saturate acetone (10 mL) with nitrogen (Chapter 7, Protocol 2) and transfer it into the reaction Schlenk tube *via* a cannula (Chapter 7, Protocol 3).

6. Stir the resulting yellow solution magnetically, cool to −78°C (dry ice–acetone bath temperature) and protect from light using aluminium foil.

7. Saturate some more acetone (5 mL) with nitrogen and cool it in a dry ice–acetone bath at −78°C.

Protocol 4. *Continued*

8. Remove the septum of the bottle containing the dimethyldioxirane solution, cooled in a dry ice–ethanol or dry ice–acetone bath at −20°C. Fill the graduated pipette, equipped with the pipette filler, with the dioxirane solution and introduce the volume into the cooled Schlenk tube containing only acetone. Put the septum back on the bottle of dimethyldioxirane and fill it with nitrogen.

9. Transfer dropwise, *via* a narrow cannula, the diluted dimethyldioxirane solution to the solution of the chromium complex **2** cooled to −78°C as follows:

   (a) Interconnect both Schlenk tubes with the cannula, by insertion through septa. The ends should be above the solutions.

   (b) Hold the end of the cannula inserted in the Schlenk containing the chromium complex with a clamp. It should be placed so that the drops can fall directly into the solution.

   (c) Insert a short needle through the septum of the Schlenk containing the chromium complex to make a nitrogen bleed.

   (d) Dip the tip of the cannula into the dimethyldioxirane solution.

   (e) Slowly close the tap of the Schlenk tube containing the chromium complex until the appearance of the first drops. Regulate until the rate is approximately one drop per second.

   Important! The reaction is sensitive to the addition rate.

10. When the addition is complete, stir the reaction mixture for 15 min at −78°C.

11. Remove the cooling bath, allow the solution to warm up to room temperature and stir for a further hour. The solution will turn slightly green and cloudy.

12. Concentrate the reaction mixture using the vacuum manifold (Chapter 7, Protocol 2).

13. Prepare a filtration funnel packed with Kieselguhr and dichloromethane. Fill a Schlenk tube with nitrogen for collection of the filtrate and cover with foil.

14. Saturate a little dichloromethane with nitrogen.

15. Dissolve the green-yellow solid in the nitrogen-saturated dichloromethane.

16. Transfer the resulting green-yellow solution into the filtration column by cannula. Rinse the reaction Schlenk tube with nitrogen-saturated dichloromethane and transfer.

17. Flush the column with nitrogen-saturated dichloromethane, apply a nitrogen pressure and collect the yellow solution in the Schlenk tube.

18. Concentrate the yellow filtrate using the vacuum manifold. A yellow powder is obtained.

19. Saturate dichloromethane and petroleum ether with nitrogen (Chapter 7, Protocol 2).

20. Transfer the nitrogen-saturated dichloromethane *via* a cannula to dissolve the yellow solid.

21. Evaporate a small portion of dichloromethane using the vacuum manifold (Chapter 7, Protocol 2) and then add nitrogen-saturated petroleum ether *via* a cannula.

22. Concentrate the solution using the vacuum manifold until the appearance of the first crystals.

23. Dissolve the crystals using a warm water bath, protect the Schlenk tube with foil and place it in a freezer for 2 days.
    Caution! Do not use any hot water. The sulfoxide complex is thermally unstable.

24. Separate the yellow crystals from the mother liquor by filtration using a filter cannula and collect the mother liquor in a Schlenk tube under nitrogen (Chapter 7, Protocol 3). Wash the crystals with cooled nitrogen-saturated petroleum ether and remove the supernatant solution.

25. Dry the crystals at room temperature by applying vacuum for 30 min.

26. Repeat the crystallisation with the mother liquor.

27. Combine both crystallisation crops (87.5 mg, 0.32 mmol, 93% yield, m.p. = 82–83°C) and keep in a vial protected from light with foil. The product displays appropriate spectroscopic data.[16] The ^{1}H NMR spectrum should be recorded on a sample prepared in $CDCl_3$ under nitrogen as described in Protocol 6 of Chapter 7.

_____
[a] The concentration is assessed just before doing the reaction.

_____

An enantioselective version of the reaction described in Protocol 4 has been recently investigated.[43] The asymmetric oxidation of the sulfur centre was performed with the Kagan's modified Sharpless system [1.3 equiv of cumene hydroperoxide in the presence of a $Ti(OPr^i)_4$/diethyl tartrate/H_2O catalyst] and afforded the corresponding sulfinyl-substituted complexes with high enantiomeric purity (Scheme 6.8).

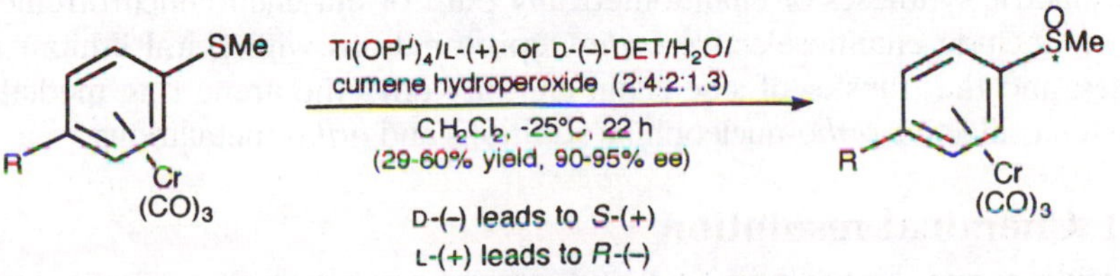

Scheme 6.8

3. Optically pure or enriched η^6-arene chromium tricarbonyl complexes

In the last decade a substantial proportion of research has been focussed on the design and implementation of efficient routes to optically active complexes possessing planar chirality.[10] This fact, in concert with both the ability of the chromium tricarbonyl unit to block effectively one face of the aromatic nucleus and its ease of removal, has led to a rapid increase in the use of chiral complexes as intermediates in asymmetric synthesis.[44]

Enantiomeric excesses of benchrotrenic complexes are generally assayed using classical methods such as NMR spectroscopy[10] in the presence of a chiral solvating or shift reagent or by HPLC with a chiral column.[43] Absolute configurations can only be determined unambiguously using X-ray methods or chemical correlations.[10,45] The (R) or (S) nomenclature used for planar chirality in benchrotrenic complexes derives from an extension of the Cahn–Ingold–Prelog system,[10] which was previously restricted to chiral centres with the classical tetrahedral geometry. The bonds proceeding from the chromium atom to the aromatic ring have to be regarded as single bonds and consequently, the six carbon atoms of the arene can be considered as sp^3 carbons. For example, the enantiomer **4** would be termed $(1S)$ or $(2R)$.

Enantiomer 1·S (or 2R)
4

The preparation of enantiopure or enriched complexes possessing planar chirality has been accomplished either by resolution of racemic mixtures or by asymmetric syntheses. Reported methods for the resolution of planar chirality include both chemical and kinetic resolution procedures, whilst reported asymmetric syntheses of enantiomerically pure or enriched benchrotrenic complexes include enantioselective *ortho*-deprotonations with chiral lithium amide bases, and the transfer of side chain chirality onto the arene ring mediated by diastereoselective *ortho*-nucleophilic additions and *ortho*-metalations.

3.1 Chemical resolution

A wide range of racemic acid and amine complexes have been resolved through the crystallisation of diastereoisomeric ammonium salts obtained with optically pure chiral amines [brucine, quinidine, cinchonidine and $(-)$-α-methylbenzylamine] and optically pure chiral acids [$(+)$-camphorsulfonic acid], respectively.[10] From a practical point of view, this method is, however, rather unattractive, due to the lengthy and tedious nature of the crystallisation techniques involved.

More versatile complexes such as aryl aldehyde complexes have been resolved by the chromatographic separation of diastereoisomeric derivatives such as semioxamazones (**5**) prepared with (S)-$(-)$-5-(α-phenylethyl) semioxamazide,[10] imines (**6**) prepared from L-valinol[32] or aminals (**7**) prepared from chiral diamines.[46] Separation is, in general, easy and efficient because the complexes involved are highly coloured; in addition, the subsequent hydrolysis to release the aldehyde functional group proceeds quantitatively.

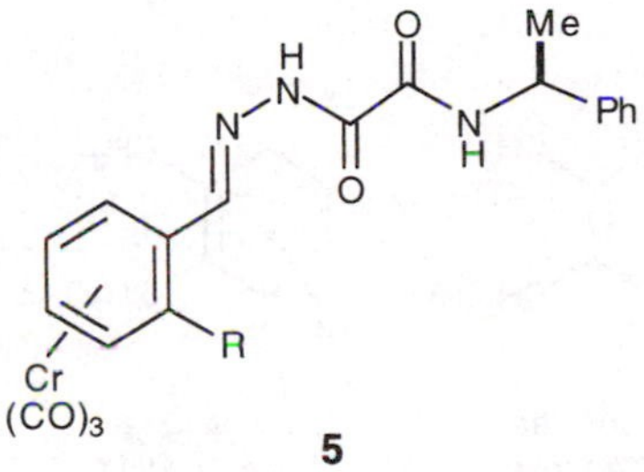

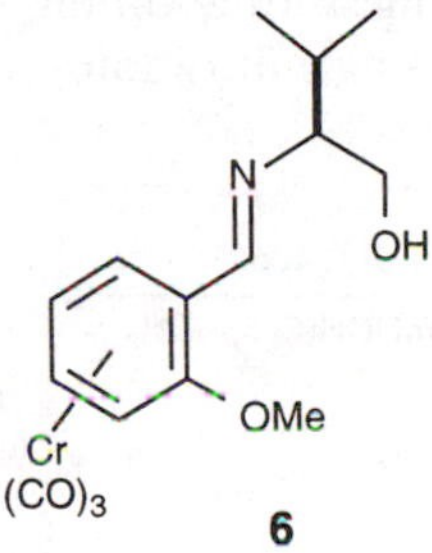

Finally, chromatography using chiral solid supports is showing considerable promise for the separation of racemic mixtures.[47]

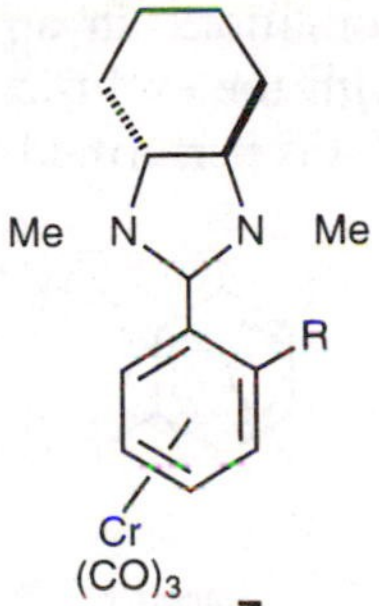

3.2 Kinetic resolution

Since a 1,2- or 1,3-disubstituted arene complex possesses planar chirality and can exist in two enantiomeric forms, kinetic resolution may sometimes be achieved. Both enantiomers react at different rates, thereby allowing a total or partial resolution.[48,49] This technique does, however, require an effective method of monitoring the reaction.

Aromatic aldehyde complexes have been partially resolved by enantioselective reduction using baker's yeast in the presence of D-glucose (Scheme 6.9). The enantiomeric excesses for the alcohol obtained and the 'unchanged' aldehyde enantiomer ranged from moderate to high (52–96% ee).[50] It should be noted, however, that kinetic resolutions using baker's yeast are limited by the low water solubility of the substrates and the necessity for aerobic conditions. Better results were achieved using another reductive resolution procedure, mediated by the horse liver alcohol dehydrogenase (HLADH) and NADH system. Optical purities as good as 100% were obtained.[51]

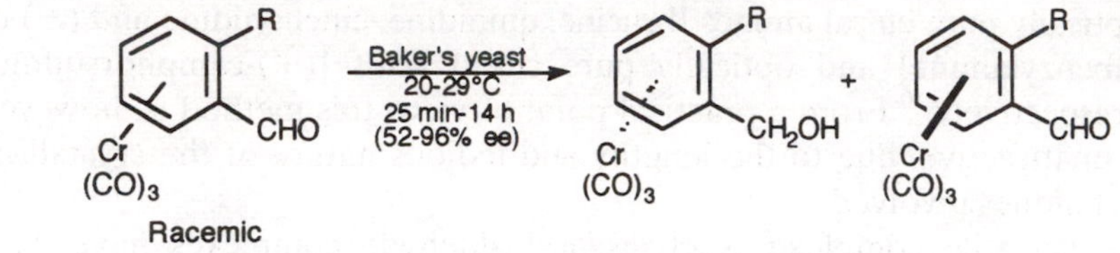

Scheme 6.9

Lipases have been utilised for the resolution of benzyl alcohol derivatives[52,53] and (benzaldehyde oxime) complexes[54] (Scheme 6.10). The reverse reaction (transesterification of the corresponding esters with an alcohol) was also enantioselectively catalysed by these microorganisms.[53,54] These methods, involving lipases, have the advantage of being performed under anaerobic conditions, in an organic solvent (toluene, isopropenyl acetate, *n*-butanol) with the exclusion of light. In addition, the separation of the microbial catalyst is performed by a single filtration.

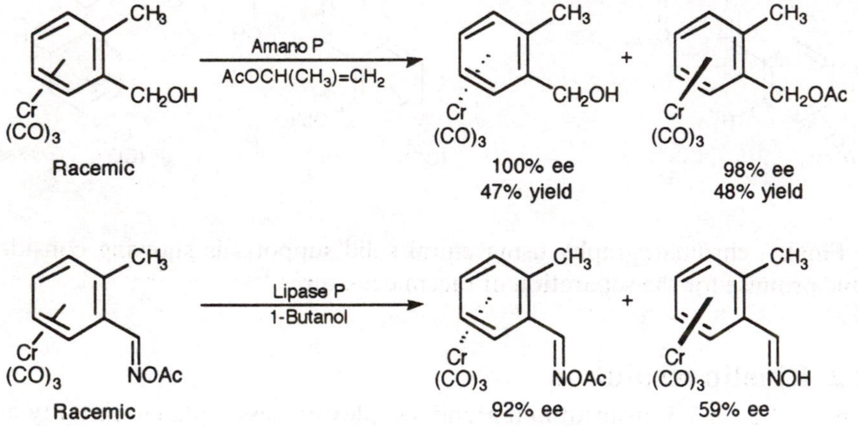

Scheme 6.10

3.3 Desymmetrisation of *meso*-complexes

Starting from *meso*-complexes (achiral species), benchrotrenic planar chirality can be generated. The differentiation of the enantiotopic substituents on the aromatic ring has been achieved using enzymes or a chiral palladium catalyst.

Meso-benzylic diester complexes have been hydrolysed using pig liver esterase to give rise to the corresponding mono-ester analogue with high enantiomeric purity (Scheme 6.11).[55]

The asymmetric cross-coupling of the *meso*-tricarbonyl (*ortho*-dichlorobenzene)chromium complex with a wide range of vinylic metals in the

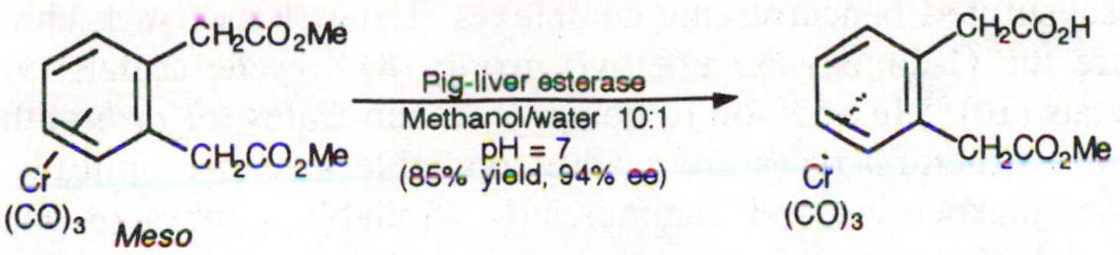

Scheme 6.11

presence of a chiral palladium catalyst gave the corresponding mono-coupling products in up to 44% ee (Scheme 6.12).[56]

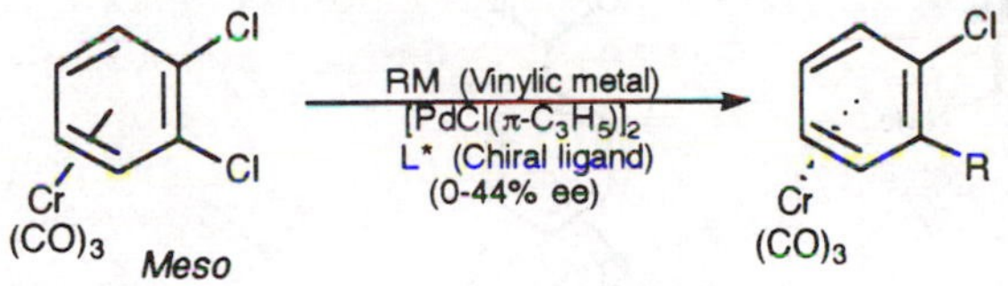

Scheme 6.12

3.4 Diastereoselective nucleophilic addition

Ortho-substituted benzaldehyde complexes have been prepared in high enantiomeric purity (97% ee), and in a one-pot sequence, from an optically pure hydrazone derivative, readily available from η^6-benzaldehyde chromium tricarbonyl and SAMP [(S)-1-amino-2-(methoxymethyl)pyrrolidine].[57] The novelty derives from the combined use of a diastereoselective *ortho*-addition reaction of an organolithium nucleophile and a hydride abstraction with a triphenylmethyl cation. The subsequent acid hydrolysis serves to remove the hydrazone group, thus liberating the aldehyde functionality (Scheme 6.13).

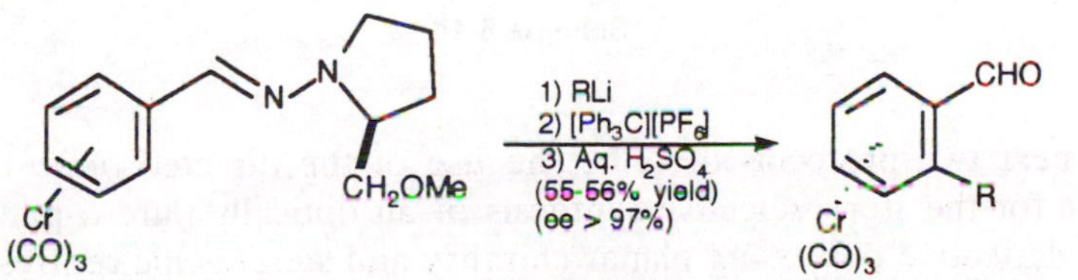

Scheme 6.13

3.5 Diastereo- or enantioselective *ortho*-metalations

The directed *ortho*-lithiation of complexes substituted by an optically pure chiral side chain, followed by quenching with an electrophile, currently provides the best method for the preparation of enantiomerically enriched

189

ortho-disubstituted benchrotrenic complexes. Examples of such chiral side chains are the (1-dimethylaminoethyl) group (**8**),[17] cyclic acetals (**9**)[33] and cyclic ketals (**10**).[58] In addition to being good substrates for *ortho*-lithiation, these chiral structural types are readily available in either optically active form from inexpensive and commercially available sources (α-phenethylamine and diethyl tartrate).

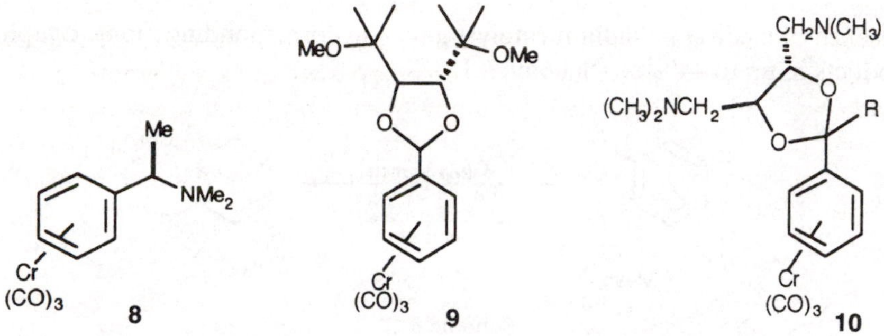

The very first results concerning the enantioselective *ortho*-lithiation of benchrotenic complexes mediated by chiral lithium bases have been reported by the groups of Simpkins[59] and Kündig.[60] Enantiomeric excesses of up to 84% were obtained (Scheme 6.14).

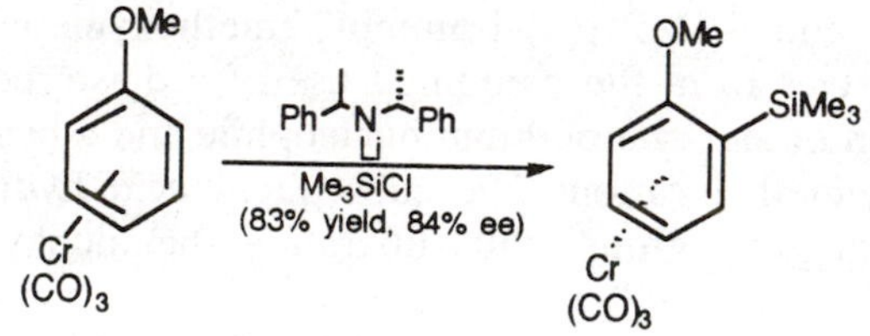

Scheme 6.14

The next two protocols describe the use of the directed *ortho*-lithiation reaction for the stereoselective synthesis of an optically pure α-phenylethylamine derivative possessing planar chirality and stereogenic centres at both benzylic positions.

The conversion[61] of *N,N*-dimethyl-α(*R*)-phenylethylamine **11** into its chromium tricarbonyl derivative **12** was accomplished in 87% yield (Scheme 6.15) by thermolysis under standard conditions [Cr(CO)$_6$/1,4-dioxane/reflux/66 h].

Protocol 5.
Synthesis of tricarbonyl[*N*,*N*-dimethyl-α(*R*)-phenylethylamine] chromium(0) (Structure 12). Complexation of chiral complex 11 by thermolysis with chromium hexacarbonyl

Caution! Due to the potential toxicity of chromium carbonyl complexes, all procedures should be carried out in a fume hood. Disposable nitrile or latex gloves and safety glasses should be worn. All procedures are performed excluding air by using standard vacuum/nitrogen manifold and Schlenk tube techniques. Although chromium arene complexes are generally stable in air in a crystalline state for long periods, many have been found to decompose in solutions on exposure to air under laboratory light. Consequently, all glassware for complexation, filtration and crystallisation should be covered with aluminium foil.

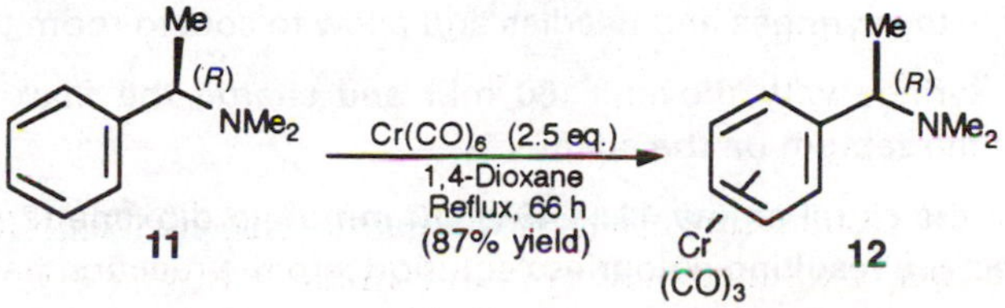

Scheme 6.15

Equipment

- Vacuum/nitrogen manifold (Figs 7.1 and 7.2)
- Stirrer hot plate
- Single-necked, round-bottomed flask (B24, 50 mL)
- Liebig condenser used as an air condenser
- Liebig condenser used as a water condenser
- Side-arm adapter
- Cone/flexible tubing adapter
- Oil bath
- Contact thermometer (up to 200°C)
- Magnetic stirrer bar (length 1.5 cm)
- Septum

- Aluminium foil
- All glass syringe (volume appropriate for quantity of solution to be transferred)
- Needle (6″, 20 or 22 gauge)
- Joint clips (× 3)
- Silicone vacuum grease
- Schlenk tubes for saturating solvents with nitrogen and recrystallisation (× 3)
- Single-necked, round-bottomed flask (B24, 250 mL) for filtration
- Filter column with filter frit (100 mL)

Materials

- Dry 1,4-dioxane,[a] 60 mL + 2 mL

- Chromium hexacarbonyl[b] (FW 220.1), 5.5 g, 25 mmol
- Chiral amine[c] 11 (FW 149.2), 1.49 g, 10 mmol
- Diethyl ether for filtration
- Kieselguhr[d] for filtration
- Diethyl ether for crystallisation
- *n*-Hexane for crystallisation
- CDCl₃ for NMR samples

flammable, toxic, possible carcinogen, may form explosive peroxides
volatile, highly toxic
irritant, air sensitive
flammable, irritant

flammable
flammable, irritant
highly toxic, cancer-suspect agent

191

Protocol 5. *Continued*

1. Clean all glassware, syringes, needles and the stirrer bar and dry for at least 1 h in a 100°C electric oven before use.

2. Prepare an oil bath at 115°C, controlling the temperature using a contact thermometer.

3. Set up apparatus as in Fig. 6.1; whilst the glassware is still hot, evacuate it and refill it with nitrogen (Chapter 7, Protocol 1).

4. Remove the septum on the side-arm adapter, reduce the nitrogen to a gentle flow and introduce chromium hexacarbonyl (5.5 g, 25 mmol) into the flask through the adapter neck with the aid of a rolled filter paper. Put the septum back on the adapter.

5. Evacuate the flask and refill with nitrogen. Protect the flask from light using foil.

6. Assemble the syringes and needles and allow to cool to room temperature.

7. Fill the syringe with dioxane (60 mL) and charge the flask by injecting through the septum on the adapter.

8. Dissolve the chiral amine **11** (1.49 g, 10 mmol) in dioxane (2 mL) in a vial and inject the resulting colourless solution into the reaction flask.

9. Assemble both condensers and the cone/flexible tubing adapter whilst hot as shown in Fig. 6.2 (grease the joints carefully and use the green clips to secure them); then connect the cone/flexible tubing adapter to the vacuum/nitrogen manifold and turn on the flow of nitrogen.

10. Remove the side-arm adapter from the flask and replace with the assembled condensers (use a green clip to secure the joint) (see Fig. 6.2).

11. Pass a moderate flow of water through the top condenser, wire the rubber tubing and begin stirring.

12. Apply vacuum till vigorous bubbling occurs and refill the flask with nitrogen (Chapter 7, Protocol 2). Repeat a total of 10 times.

13. Immerse the mixture in the oil bath and generously wrap the apparatus with aluminium foil to minimise exposure to light.

14. After a few minutes, reflux will begin. Leave the solution refluxing for 66 h.[e] The solution turns gradually from pale yellow to orange.

15. Remove the oil bath and allow the solution to cool down in an ice-water bath (15 min). Unreacted chromium hexacarbonyl will precipitate out of the solution.[f]

16. During this time, pack the filter column with a short pad of Kieselguhr in diethyl ether.[g] Place a round-bottomed flask (250 mL), covered with foil, under the column for collection of the filtrate.

17. Disconnect the condensers from the water and nitrogen sources and replace the assembled condensers with a side-arm adapter with a septum on top, already connected to the nitrogen source (Fig. 6.1).

18. Transfer the solution into the filter column *via* a cannula (Chapter 7, Protocol 4), dissolve the residue in the reaction flask in diethyl ether and transfer.

19. Flush the column with diethyl ether, apply a nitrogen pressure and collect the yellow solution in the flask protected with foil (Chapter 7, Protocol 5).

20. Concentrate the resulting orange filtrate under reduced pressure (20 mmHg) by the means of a rotary evaporator *located in a fume hood* [the use of a hot water bath (60 °C) is necessary to remove efficiently the dioxane]. Store the resulting orange-yellow solid under an inert atmosphere.

21. Saturate some diethyl ether and *n*-hexane with nitrogen (Chapter 7, Protocol 2). Evacuate a Schlenk tube and refill with nitrogen.

22. Dissolve the crude yellow solid in the minimum amount of nitrogen-saturated diethyl ether and transfer the resulting yellow solution into the empty Schlenk tube *via* a filter cannula. If any decomposition is noticed at this stage, the solution may be filtered through a small bed of Kieselguhr.

23. Rinse the flask with nitrogen-saturated diethyl ether and transfer as in the previous step.

24. Use the vacuum manifold to remove a small amount of diethyl ether and add nitrogen-saturated *n*-hexane.

25. Concentrate the solution using the vacuum manifold until the first solid appears.

26. Dissolve the crystals using a hot water bath, protect the Schlenk tube with foil and place it in a freezer (−20 °C) for 2 days.

27. Separate the yellow crystals from the mother liquor by filtration using a filter cannula and collect the mother liquor in a Schlenk tube under nitrogen.

28. Wash the crystals with nitrogen-saturated *n*-hexane, withdraw the supernatant. Dry the yellow crystals under vacuum.

29. Repeat the crystallisation procedure with the mother liquor.

30. Combine both crystallisation crops [2.48 g, 8.7 mmol, 87% yield, m.p. 43 °C, $[\alpha]^{24}_D$ +14.4° (c = 0.78, $CHCl_3$)] and keep in a vial covered with aluminium foil. The crystals display appropriate spectroscopic data.[17] The ^1H NMR spectrum should be recorded on a sample prepared in $CDCl_3$ under nitrogen (Chapter 7, Protocol 6).

---

[a]1,4-Dioxane is purified by distillation under nitrogen from calcium hydride and is then stored under nitrogen over molecular sieves (4Å) in a bottle protected from light.
[b]Chromium hexacarbonyl is purchased from Strem Chemical Company and is used as received. It can be weighed in air as it is relatively air-stable and non-volatile. The usual precautions appropriate for a potentially toxic metal carbonyl should be employed, but the low volatility makes handling relatively easy.
[c]The optically pure amine **11** is purchased from Fluka but is relatively expensive. It can be prepared[59] in a single step from α(R)-phenylethylamine, which is much cheaper.

Protocol 5. *Continued*

[d] Kieselguhr is supplied by BDH.

[e] During the complexation reaction, carbon monoxide is slowly evolved. Hence, gas evolution will be observed with the bubbler attached to the vacuum/nitrogen manifold.

If before 66 h of reflux, the reaction mixture develops a green colour, which signifies decomposition, stop the heating and carry out the work-up. The decomposition is catalytic in nature.

[f] Unreacted chromium hexacarbonyl is destroyed in a well-ventilated hood by oxidation with bleach. If a green residue remains on the inside walls of the glassware, wash with nitric acid.

Important! Do not dispose of these washings in a sink.

[g] Diethyl ether is used as obtained for the entire filtration sequence.

Treatment of complex **12** with *t*-butyllithium in ether at −78°C led to the exclusive deprotonation at one of the two diastereotopic *ortho* positions and hence to the formation of the lithio compound **13** (Scheme 6.16).

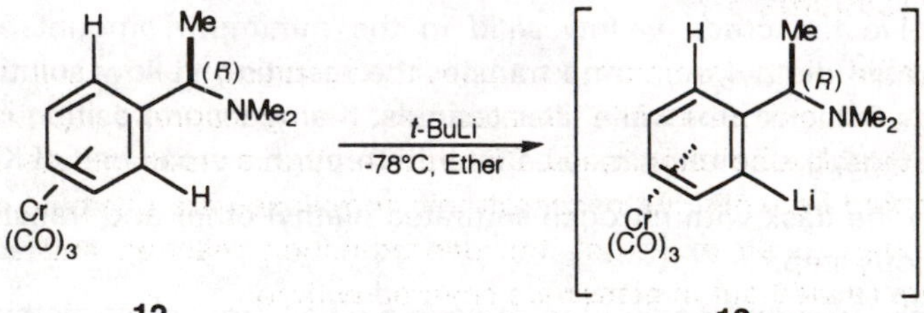

Scheme 6.16

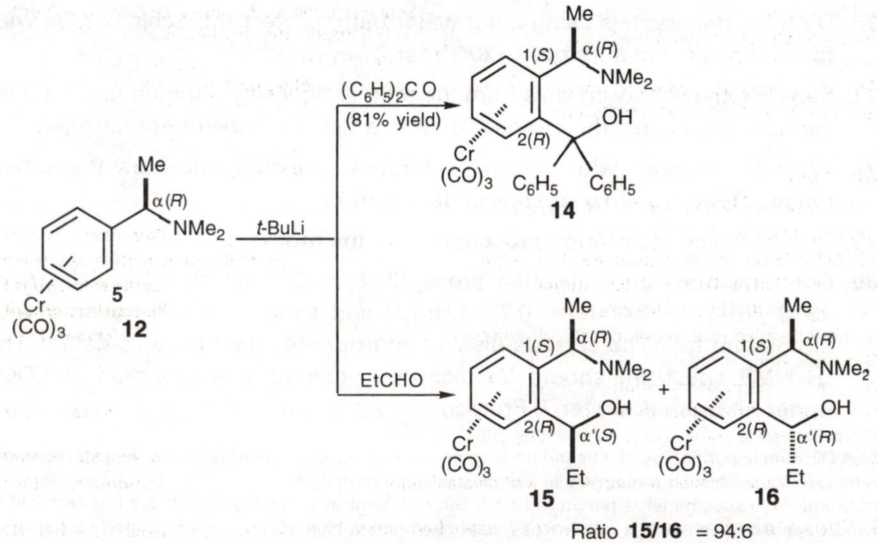

Ratio **15/16** = 94:6
[80% yield (**15**)]

Scheme 6.17

194

Subsequent quenching with benzophenone afforded exclusively the Ar(1S, 2R)-α(R) diastereoisomeric complex **14** in 81% yield. A similar reaction with propanal introduces an additional stereogenic centre (in the α' side-chain position) and thus a mixture of two epimers **15** and **16** was obtained, in a ratio of 94:6 (Scheme 6.17).[17] Their configurations were Ar(1S,2R)-α(R)-α'(S) and Ar(1S,2R)-α(R)-α'(R), respectively. Column chromatography on silica gel, followed by crystallisation led to the isolation of the major diastereoisomer **15** in 80% yield.

Protocol 6.
Synthesis of Ar(1*S*,2*R*)-tricarbonyl{1-[α(*R*)-(*N,N*-dimethylamino)ethyl]-2-[α'(*S*)-hydroxypropyl]benzene}chromium(0) (Structure 15). *Ortho*-lithiation of a chiral complex (Structure 12) followed by quench with propanal (Scheme 6.17)

Caution! When using chromium tricarbonyl complexes and *t*-BuLi, all procedures should be conducted in a well-ventilated hood, using standard vacuum/nitrogen line and Schlenk tube techniques. Disposable vinyl or latex gloves and safety glasses should be worn. As benchrotrenic complexes are unstable in solution when exposed to air and light, the deprotonation reaction and subsequent work-up are carried out in glassware covered with foil.

Equipment
- Vacuum/nitrogen manifold (Figs 7.1 and 7.2)
- Magnetic stirrer
- Schlenk tube
- Magnetic stirrer bar (length 1.5 cm)
- Septum
- All glass syringe (volume appropriate for quantity of solution to be transferred)
- Needle (6", 20 or 22 gauge)
- Filter column with filter frit (100 mL)
- Schlenk tubes for filtration, saturating solvents with nitrogen and recrystallisation
- Aluminium foil
- Dewar or cooling bath

Materials
- Chiral complex **12** (FW 285.2), 100 mg, 0.35 mmol
- Dry diethyl ether,[a] 5 mL + 0.5 mL — flammable, irritant
- *t*-BuLi,[b] 0.18 mL, 2.3 M in pentane, 0.42 mmol — air/moisture sensitive, corrosive
- Propanal[c] (FW 58.1), 31 mg, 0.53 mmol — flammable, irritant
- Technical diethyl ether for extraction — flammable, irritant
- Saturated aqueous ammonium chloride solution — irritant, toxic
- Saturated brine
- Anhydrous magnesium sulfate for drying
- Silica gel for chromatography, 4 g — irritant, dust
- Diethyl ether for column chromatography and crystallisation — flammable, irritant
- *n*-Hexane for column chromatography and crystallisation — flammable, irritant

1. Clean all glassware, syringes, needles and the stirrer bar and dry for at least 4 h in a 100°C electric oven before use.

2. Support a Schlenk tube, containing a magnetic stirrer bar, below its side-

Protocol 6. *Continued*

arm, using a clamp and a stand with a heavy base; attach the Schlenk tube to the vacuum/nitrogen manifold *via* its side-arm.

3. Charge the Schlenk tube with chiral complex **12** (100 mg, 0.35 mmol) and fit the neck of the Schlenk tube with a septum.

4. Evacuate and refill with nitrogen (Chapter 7, Protocol 1).

5. Add nitrogen-saturated dry diethyl ether (5 mL) and begin stirring the resulting yellow solution.

6. Cool the solution in a dry ice–acetone bath at −78°C and protect from light using aluminium foil.

7. Assemble the syringes and needles whilst hot and allow to cool to room temperature in a desiccator.

8. Fill a syringe with *t*-butyllithium in pentane (0.18 mL, 2.3 M in pentane, 0.42 mmol) (Chapter 3, Protocol 5, step 5) and add dropwise to the solution of complex **12** over a period of 5 min, keeping the temperature of the cold bath at −78°C.

9. Allow the bath temperature to warm up to −40°C over 40 min.

10. While maintaining the bath temperature at −40°C, add *via* a syringe propanal (31 mg, 0.53 mmol), previously dissolved in dry diethyl ether (0.5 mL).

11. Allow the mixture to warm to −10°C over 40 min with stirring.

12. Quench with degassed aqueous ammonium chloride solution and add nitrogen-saturated diethyl ether.

13. Remove the aqueous layer *via* a cannula (Chapter 7, Protocol 4).

14. Wash the ethereal layer with nitrogen-saturated brine, removing the resulting aqueous layer *via* a cannula. Dry the organic layer over anhydrous magnesium sulfate.

15. Filter into a Schlenk tube *via* a filtering cannula and concentrate using the vacuum line to give an orange residue.

16. Apply the residue to a silica gel column using a 1:4 mixture of diethyl ether and *n*-hexane. Elute with the combination of solvents (Chapter 7, Protocol 5).

17. Concentrate using the vacuum line.

18. Saturate diethyl ether and *n*-hexane with nitrogen and dissolve the product in the minimum amount of nitrogen-saturated diethyl ether.

19. Add nitrogen-saturated *n*-hexane and concentrate the yellow solution using the vacuum manifold until the first solid appears.

20. Dissolve the crystals using a warm water bath, protect the Schlenk tube with foil and place it in a freezer (−20°C) for 2 days.

21. Separate the yellow crystals from the mother liquor by filtration using a filter cannula and collect the mother liquor in a Schlenk tube under nitrogen.

22. Wash the crystals with cold nitrogen-saturated *n*-hexane and withdraw the supernatant. Dry the yellow crystals under reduced pressure.

23. Repeat the crystallisation procedure with the mother liquor.

24. Combine both crystallisation crops [96 mg, 0.28 mmol, 80% yield, m.p. 62 °C, $[\alpha]^{24}_D$ + 13.5° (c = 0.66, CHCl$_3$)] and keep in a vial protected from light with aluminium foil. The product displays appropriate spectroscopic and chiroptical data.[17] The ^{1}H NMR spectrum should be recorded on a sample prepared in CDCl$_3$ under nitrogen (Chapter 7, Protocol 6).

[a] Distil diethyl ether from lithium aluminium hydride or sodium benzophenone ketyl under an inert atmosphere (nitrogen or argon) and use immediately.
[b] **Be careful!** *t*-BuLi ignites in contact with air. Wash the syringe just after use with dilute hydrochloric acid, water and acetone, respectively.
[c] Propanal was purchased from Aldrich and distilled just prior to use.

The optically pure complex **15** (Scheme 6.17), generated in Protocol 6, may be subjected to additional further transformations.

Photoirradiation of complex **15** in benzene solution with a high-pressure mercury lamp in the presence of triphenylphosphine induces ligand exchange and leads to the formation of the dicarbonyltriphenylphosphine analogue **17** (Scheme 6.18) in 70% yield, as described in Protocol 7.

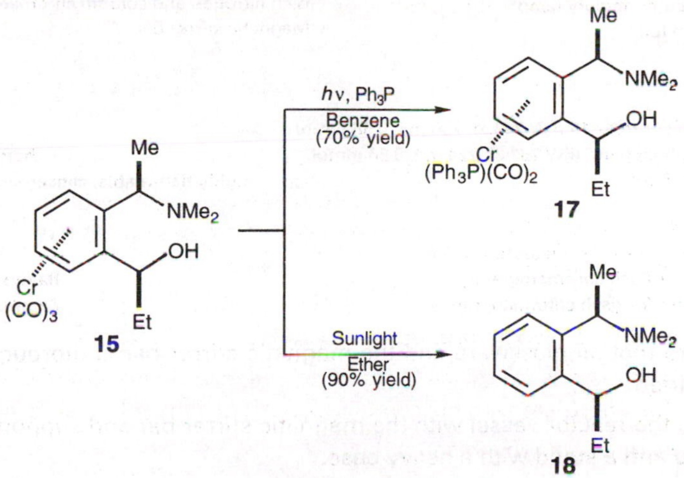

Scheme 6.18

Decomplexation of complex **15** by exposure to sunlight in ethereal solution affords the optically active free amino alcohol **18** in 90% yield, as described in Protocol 8. It is worth noting that recomplexation of this compound **18** by a ligand-transfer reaction with η^6-naphthalene chromium tricarbonyl did not give rise to the precursor **15** but to its diastereoisomeric complex in which the opposite face of the ring is coordinated to the chromium moiety.[17] In this case, the direct complexation reaction and deprotonation/alkylation sequence gave complementary results.

Protocol 7.
Synthesis of Ar(1*S*,2*R*)-dicarbonyltriphenylphosphine{1-[α(*R*)-(*N,N*-dimethylamino)ethyl]-2-[α'(*S*)-hydroxypropyl]}benzene (Structure 17). Photoirradiation of chromium tricarbonyl complex (Structure 15) in the presence of triphenylphosphine (Scheme 6.18)

Caution! Ultraviolet light is extremely dangerous to the eyes and also harmful to the skin. The apparatus should be situated in a fume hood with aluminium foil wrapped around it (this additionally serves as a light reflector). Flexible tubing for cooling water should be wired on and a suitable cut-out device for the lamp incorporated into the circuit. Disposable vinyl or latex gloves and safety glasses should be worn. Benzene is toxic; contact with the liquid should be avoided.

Equipment
- Vacuum/nitrogen manifold (Figs 7.1 and 7.2)
- Quartz vessel [Model UM-103B-B, Ushio electric inc. (Japan)]
- High-pressure mercury lamp[a]
- Aluminium foil
- Filter column with filter frit for filtration and column chromatography
- Schlenk tubes for filtration, saturating solvents with nitrogen and column chromatography
- Magnetic stirrer bar

Materials
- Chromium complex **15** (FW 343.2), 200 mg, 0.58 mmol
- Triphenylphosphine[b] (FW 262.3), 224 mg, 0.86 mmol — **harmful, irritant**
- Benzene,[c] 15 mL — **highly flammable, cancer-suspect agent, highly toxic**
- Kieselguhr[d]
- Silica gel for flash chromatography, 5 g — **irritant, dust**
- *n*-Hexane for flash chromatography — **flammable, irritant**
- Diethyl ether for flash chromatography — **flammable, irritant**

1. Ensure that all glassware and the magnetic stirrer bar is thoroughly clean and dried.

2. Equip the reactor vessel with the magnetic stirrer bar and support it with a clamp and a stand with a heavy base.

3. Connect to water and insert the lamp.

4. Introduce triphenylphosphine (224 mg, 0.86 mmol), complex **15** (200 mg, 0.58 mmol) and benzene (15 mL) successively and surround the whole apparatus with aluminium foil (Fig. 6.4).

5. Remove dissolved oxygen by passing nitrogen through the reaction solution for about 1 h.
   Caution! A nitrogen atmosphere must be maintained throughout the experiment.

6. Switch the lamp on and irradiate for 30 min.

7. Switch the lamp off, remove the lamp from the vessel and disconnect from the water source.

8. Pack the filter column with a short pad of Kieselguhr in diethyl ether,[e] and fill a Schlenk tube, for collection of the filtrate, with nitrogen.

9. Pour the solution onto Kieselguhr and filter by applying a nitrogen pressure and washing through with diethyl ether.

10. Concentrate the resultant filtrate using the vacuum manifold.[c]

11. Apply the residue to a silica gel column using a 1:4 mixture of diethyl ether and n-hexane. Elute with the same combination of solvents (Chapter 7, Protocol 5). After concentration under reduced pressure, complex **17** is obtained as a yellow oil [211 mg, 0.3 mmol, 70% yield, $[\alpha]^{25}_D$ + 5.6° (c = 0.86, CHCl$_3$)] which displays appropriate spectroscopic and chiroptical data.[17] The ^{1}H NMR spectrum should be recorded on a sample prepared in CDCl$_3$ under nitrogen as described in Protocol 6 of Chapter 7.

---

[a] The high-pressure mercury lamp [Model UM-102, Ushio Electric Inc. (Japan)] emits the UV spectrum from about 200 to 1400 nm.
[b] Triphenylphosphine was purchased from Wako Pure Chemical Industries (Osaka) and used as received.
[c] **Caution!** Keep solutions contaminated with benzene in closed bottles.
[d] Kieselguhr is supplied by BDH.
[e] Diethyl ether is used as obtained for the filtration step.

Protocol 8.
Synthesis of 1-[α(*R*)-(*N,N*-dimethylamino)ethyl]-2-[α′(*S*)-hydroxypropyl]benzene (Structure 18). Air-oxidation of complex (Structure 15) (Scheme 6.18)

Caution! All procedures involving chromium complexes should be carried out in a well-ventilated hood. Disposable vinyl or latex gloves and safety glasses should be worn.

Equipment
- Magnetic stirrer
- Single-necked, round-bottomed flask (100 mL)
- Magnetic stirrer bar (length 1.5 cm)
- Condenser
- Chromatography column

Materials
- Chiral complex **15** (FW 343.2), 400 mg, 1.17 mmol
- Diethyl ether, 50 mL — flammable, irritant
- Celite for filtration
- Diethyl ether for filtration
- n-Hexane for flash chromatography — flammable, irritant
- Diethyl ether for flash chromatography — flammable, irritant
- Silica gel for flash chromatography, 4 g — irritant, dust

Protocol 8. *Continued*

1. Ensure that all glassware is clean and dried and support the flask using a clamp and a stand with a heavy base.
2. Charge the flask successively with the stirrer bar, complex **15** (400 mg, 1.17 mmol) and dry diethyl ether (50 mL).
3. Equip the neck of the flask with a water condenser and begin stirring the resulting yellow solution.
4. Stir the solution exposed to light under air for 3 h. The colour of the mixture fades to pale yellow. (Disappearance of the yellow colour signifies decomplexation. This is accompanied by the formation of a green precipitate of chromium oxides.)
5. Disassemble the flask and the condenser.
6. Filter the mixture through Celite under suction to remove the inorganic precipitate and rinse the flask and the filter cake with diethyl ether (3 × 15 mL).
7. Concentrate the filtrate under reduced pressure by means of a rotary evaporator (25°C, 20 mmHg).
8. Load the residual oil onto a flash silica gel column using a 1:4 mixture of diethyl ether and *n*-hexane. Elute the column with the same combination of solvents to obtain pure ligand **18** (186 mg, 1.06 mmol, 90% yield) as a colourless oil, which displays appropriate spectroscopic data.[17]

Several reports of the use of complexes **14**, **15** and **16** or similar substrates as chiral catalysts or auxiliaries have been published. In one example, 5 mol% of the complex **16** catalysed the addition of diethylzinc to benzaldehyde to afford (*S*)-1-phenylpropan-1-ol in 97% yield and 96% ee (Scheme 6.19).[17] Using complexes **14** and **15**, samples of the same enantiomer were produced with an enantioexcess of 93% ee (the isolated yields were 83% and 87%, respectively). By comparison, the corresponding chromium-free derivative **18** resulted in only 24% ee to give the (*S*)-alcohol.

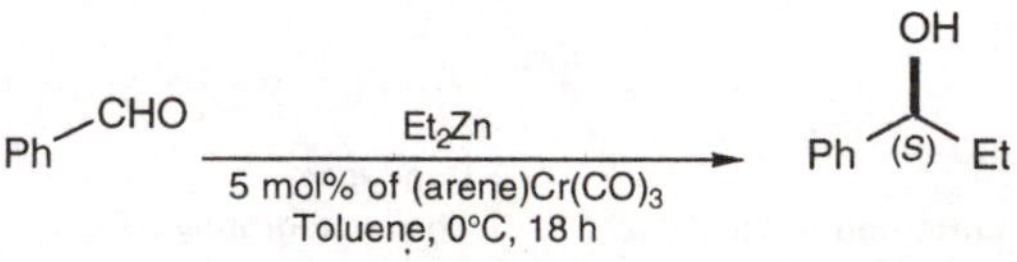

Scheme 6.19

In a second example, the conjugate addition of diethylzinc to chalcone in the presence of a catalyst generated from $Ni(acac)_2$ and a chromium complex was investigated.[62] Using 1 mol% of $Ni(acac)_2$ and 10 mol% of complex **14**, the (*R*)-conjugate addition ketone was obtained in 66% yield and in 36% ee (Scheme 6.20). The asymmetric induction is highly dependent on the amount

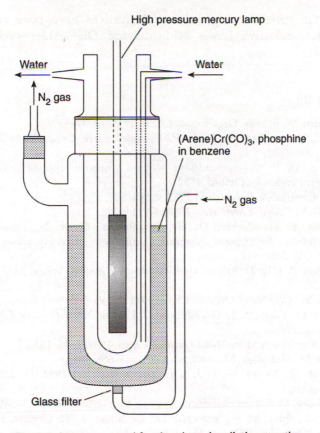

High pressure mercury lamp

Water

N₂ gas

Water

(Arene)Cr(CO)₃, phosphine
in benzene

← N₂ gas

Glass filter

Fig. 6.4 Apparatus used for the photo-irradiation reaction.

of the chiral catalyst used: the enantioselectivity increased to 62% ee with
5 mol% of the catalyst, and to 78% ee under stoichiometric conditions.

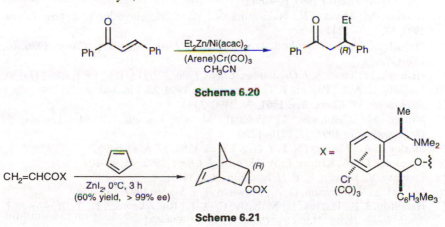

Scheme 6.20

Scheme 6.21

Finally, the corresponding acrylate derivatives have been reported to undergo stereoselective Lewis acid-catalysed Diels-Alder cycloadditions (Scheme 6.21).[63]

References

1. Silverthorn, W. E. *Adv. Organomet. Chem.* **1975**, *13*, 47–137.
2. Davis, R.; Kane-Maguire, L. A. P. *Comprehensive Organometallic Chemistry* **1982**, *3*, 1001–1021.
3. Davies, S. G. In *Organotransition Metal Chemistry: Applications to Organic Chemistry;* Pergamon: Oxford, **1982**.
4. Solladié-Cavallo, A. *Polyhedron* **1985**, *4*, 901–927.
5. Senoff, C. V. *Coord. Chem. Rev.* **1980**, *32*, 111–191.
6. McQuillin, F. G.; Parker, D. G.; Stephenson, G. R. In *Transition Metal Organometallics for Organic Synthesis*; Cambridge University Press: Cambridge, **1991**; pp. 182–208.
7. Harrington, P. J. In *Transition Metals in Total Synthesis*; Wiley: New York, **1990**; pp. 317–345.
8. Uemura, M. *Adv. Metal-Organic Chem.* **1991**, *2*, 195–245.
9. Davies, S. G.; Coote, S. J.; Goodfellow, C. L. *Adv. Metal-Organic Chem.* **1991**, *2*, 1–57.
10. Solladié-Cavallo, A. *Adv. Metal-Organic Chem.* **1989**, *1*, 99–133.
11. Sodeoka, M.; Shibasaki, M. *Synthesis* **1993**, 643–658.
12. Hunter, A. D.; Mozol, V.; Tsai, S. D. *Organometallics* **1992**, *11*, 2251–2262 and references cited.
13. Semmelhack, M. F. *Comprehensive Organic Synthesis* **1991**, *4*, 517–549.
14. Sénéchal-Tocquer, M. C.; Sénéchal, D.; Le Bihan, J. Y.; Gentric, D.; Caro, B. *Bull. Soc. Chim. Fr.* **1992**, *129*, 121–126.
15. Davies, S. G.; Donohoe, T. J. *Synlett* **1993**, 323–332.
16. Pérez-Encabo, A.; Perrio, S.; Slawin, A. M. Z.; Thomas, S. E.; Wierzchleyski, A. T.; Williams, D. J. *J. Chem. Soc., Chem. Commun.* **1993**, 1059–1062; *J. Chem. Soc., Perkin Trans. 1* **1994**, 629–642.
17. Uemura, M.; Miyake, R.; Nakayama, K.; Shiro, M.; Hayashi, Y. *J. Org. Chem.* **1993**, *58*, 1238–1244.
18. Mahaffy, C. A. L.; Hamilton, J. *Synth. React. Inorg. Met.-Org. Chem.* **1986**, *16*, 137–139.
19. Hudecek, M.; Toma, S. *J. Organomet. Chem.* **1990**, *393*, 115–118.; **1991**, *406*, 147–150.
20. Mahaffy, C. A. L.; Pauson, P. L. *Inorg. Synth.* **1990**, *28*, 136–140.
21. Strohmeier, W. *Chem. Ber.* **1961**, *94*, 2490–2493.
22. Morán, M.; Cuadrado, I.; Pascual, M. C.; Casado, C. M.; Losada, J. *Organometallics* **1992**, *11*, 1210–1220.
23. Morley, J. A.; Woolsey, N. F. *J. Org. Chem.* **1992**, *57*, 6487–6495.
24. Holzapfel, C. W.; Kruger, F. W. H. *Aust. J. Chem.* **1992**, *45*, 99–107.
25. Desobry, V.; Kündig, E. P. *Helv. Chim. Acta* **1981**, *64*, 1288–1297.
26. Loft, M. S.; Widdowson, D. A.; Mowlem, T. J. *Synlett* **1992**, 135–136.
27. Hamilton, J. B.; Harvey, L.; Mahaffy, C. A. L.; Radzykewycz, D. T.; Rawlings, J. *Synth. React. Inorg. Met.-Org. Chem.* **1993**, *23*, 629–631.

28. Hamilton, J.; Mahaffy, C. A. L. *Synth. React. Inorg. Met.-Org. Chem.* **1988**, *18*, 243–245.

29. Alemagna, A.; Cremonesi, P.; Del Buttero, P.; Licandro, E.; Maiorana, S. *J. Org. Chem.* **1983**, *48*, 3114–3116.

30. Marcos, C. F.; Perrio, S.; Slawin, A. M. Z.; Thomas, S. E.; Williams, D. J. *J. Chem. Soc., Chem. Commun.* **1994**, 753–754.

31. Heppert, J. A.; Boyle, T. J.; Takusagawa, F. *Organometallics* **1989**, *8*, 461–467.

32. Bromley, L. A.; Davies, S. G.; Goodfellow, C. L. *Tetrahedron: Asymmetry* **1991**, *2*, 139–156.

33. Kondo, Y.; Green, J. R.; Ho, J. *J. Org. Chem.* **1993**, *58*, 6182–6189.

34. Uemura, M.; Minami, T.; Shiro, M.; Hayashi, Y. *J. Org. Chem.* **1992**, *57*, 5590–5596.

35. Mukai, C.; Miyakawa, M.; Mihira, A.; Hanaoka, M. *J. Org. Chem.* **1992**, *57*, 2034–2040.

36. Dickens, M. J.; Gilday, J. P.; Mowlem, T. J.; Widdowson, D. A. *Tetrahedron* **1991**, *47*, 8621–8634 and references cited.

37. Adam, W.; Hadjiarapoglou, L. P.; Curci, R.; Mello, R. In *Organic Peroxides*; Ando, W.; ed.; Wiley: Chichester, **1992**, 195.

38. Adam, W.; Hadjiarapoglou, L. *Top. Curr. Chem.* **1993**, *164*, 45–62.

39. Adam, W.; Bialas, J.; Hadjiarapoglou, L. *Chem. Ber.* **1991**, *124*, 2377.

40. Adam, W.; Chan, Y.-Y.; Cremer, D.; Gauss, J.; Scheutzow, D.; Schindler, M. *J. Org. Chem.* **1987**, *52*, 2800–2803.

41. Lluch, A.-M.; Sánchez-Baeza, F.; Camps, F.; Messeguer, A. *Tetrahedron Lett.* **1991**, *32*, 5629–5630.

42. Lluch, A.-M.; Jordi, L.; Sánchez-Baeza, F.; Ricart, S.; Camps, F.; Messeguer, A.; Moretó, J. M. *Tetrahedron Lett.* **1992**, *33*, 3021–3022.

43. Griffiths, S. L.; Perrio, S.; Thomas, S. E. *Tetrahedron: Asymmetry* **1994**, *5*, 545–548.

44. Mukai, C.; Kim, I. J.; Hanaoka, M. *Tetrahedron: Asymmetry* **1992**, *3*, 1007; *Tetrahedron Lett.* **1993**, *34*, 6081–6082.

45. Dewey, M. A.; Gladysz, J. A. *Organometallics* **1993**, *12*, 2390–2392.

46. Alexakis, A.; Mangeney, P.; Marek, I.; Rose-Munch, F.; Rose, E.; Semra, A.; Robert, F. *J. Am. Chem. Soc.* **1992**, *114*, 8288–8290.

47. Bitterwolf, T. E.; Hubler, T. L.; Todime, R. *J. Macromol. Sci. Chem.* **1990**, *A27*, 1437–1440.

48. Ryabov, A. D. *Angew. Chem., Int. Ed. Engl.* **1991**, *30*, 931–934.

49. Jaouen, G.; Vessières, A.; Butler, I. S. *Acc. Chem. Res.* **1993**, *26*, 361–369.

50. Top, S.; Jaouen, G.; Baldoli, C.; del Buttero, P.; Maiorana, S. *J. Organomet. Chem.* **1991**, *413*, 125–130.

51. Yamazaki, Y.; Hosono, K. *Tetrahedron Lett.* **1989**, *30*, 5313–5314.

52. Nakamura, K.; Ishihara, K.; Ohno, A.; Uemura, M.; Nishimura, H.; Hayashi, Y. *Tetrahedron Lett.* **1990**, *31*, 3603–3604.

53. Yamazaki, Y.; Hosono, K. *Tetrahedron Lett.* **1990**, *31*, 3895–3896.

54. Baldoli, C.; Maiorana, S.; Carrea, G.; Riva, S. *Tetrahedron: Asymmetry* **1993**, *4*, 767–772.

55. Malézieux, B.; Jaouen, G.; Salaün, J.; Howell, J. A. S.; Palin, M. G.; McArdle, P.; O'Gara, M.; Cunningham, D. *Tetrahedron: Asymmetry* **1992**, *3*, 375–376.

56. Uemura, M.; Nishimura, H.; Hayashi, T. *Tetrahedron Lett.* **1993**, *34*, 107–110.

57. Kündig, E. P.; Liu, R.; Ripa, A. *Helv. Chim. Acta* **1992**, *75*, 2657–2660.
58. Aubé, J.; Heppert, J. A.; Milligan, M. L.; Smith, M. J.; Zenk, P. *J. Org. Chem.* **1992**, *57*, 3563–3570.
59. Price, D. A.; Simpkins, N. S.; MacLeod, A. M.; Watt, A. P. *J. Org. Chem.* **1994**, *59*, 1961–1962.
60. Kündig, E. P.; Quattropani, A. *Tetrahedron Lett.* **1994**, *35*, 3497–3500.
61. Blagg, J.; Davies, S. G.; Goodfellow, C. L.; Sutton, K. H. *J. Chem. Soc., Perkin Trans. 1* **1987**, 1805–1811.
62. Uemura, M.; Miyake, R.; Nakayama, K.; Hayashi, Y. *Tetrahedron: Asymmetry* **1992**, *3*, 713–714.
63. Uemura, M.; Hayashi, Y.; Hayashi, Y. *Tetrahedron: Asymmetry* **1993**, *4*, 2291–2294.

General techniques for handling air-sensitive compounds

NATHALIE GUILLO and STÉPHANE PERRIO

The manipulation and purification of many of the compounds described in this *Practical Approach* volume are best performed using a vacuum/inert gas manifold together with Schlenk tubes (or round-bottomed flasks fitted with a gas inlet adapter). The protocols in this chapter describe, in general terms, how a vacuum/inert gas manifold is used to fill Schlenk tubes with an inert gas (nitrogen or argon), how a solvent or solution is saturated with an inert gas using Schlenk techniques, and how solvents are removed from a Schlenk tube. The transfer of liquids from one Schlenk to another, either directly or *via* a filtration device, is also described, as is the column chromatography of air-sensitive materials. Finally, a technique for preparing samples for NMR spectroscopy under an inert atmosphere is detailed.

Protocol 1.
Evacuating and filling a Schlenk tube with an inert gas using a vacuum/inert gas manifold

Caution! All procedures should be performed in a fume hood. Safety glasses should be worn.

Equipment
- Vacuum/inert gas manifold (Figs 7.1 and 7.2)
- Schlenk tube (Fig. 7.3)
- Septum

Materials
- Silicone vacuum grease

1. Ensure that the Schlenk tube is clean and has been dried for at least an hour in a 100°C oven before use.
2. Grease the stopcock[a] and then support the Schlenk tube under its side-arm using a clamp and a stand with a heavy base.

Protocol 1. *Continued*

3. Immediately equip the neck of the Schlenk tube with the septum and attach the side-arm to the vacuum/inert gas manifold *via* one of the flexible tubing connections.

4. Open the Schlenk tube stopcock.

5. Adjust the vacuum/inert gas manifold to vacuum (Fig. 7.2b) and leave for 1 min.

6. Adjust the vacuum/inert gas manifold to gas (Fig. 7.2c) and fill the Schlenk tube with nitrogen/argon.

7. Repeat steps 5 and 6 a total of five times.

[a]Stopcocks should be lightly greased lengthways, inserted into the socket and rotated. A clear film throughout the joint indicates that sufficient grease has been used. Air channels are easily seen as lighter streaks. After use the vacuum grease should be removed from the stopcock using dichloromethane/tissue and pipe cleaners.

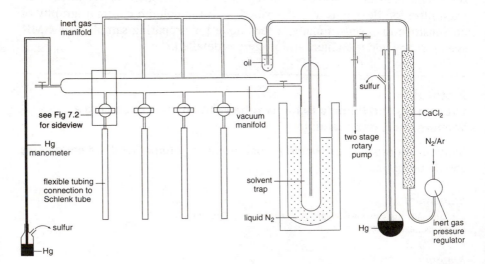

Fig. 7.1 Vacuum/inert gas manifold

7: General techniques for handling air-sensitive compounds

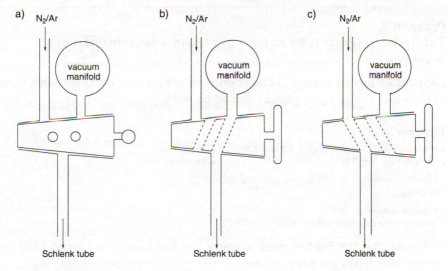

Fig. 7.2 Sideview of manifold stopcock: (a) closed, (b) open to vacuum, (c) open to nitrogen/argon.

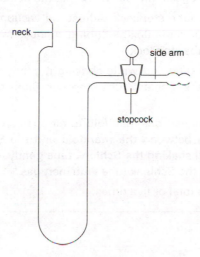

Fig. 7.3 Schlenk tube.

207

Protocol 2.
Saturating solvents with an inert gas using a vacuum/inert gas manifold

Caution! All procedures should be performed in a fume hood. Disposable vinyl or latex gloves and safety glasses should be worn.

Equipment
- Vacuum/inert gas manifold (Figs 7.1 and 7.2)
- Schlenk tube (Fig. 7.3)
- Pyrex funnel
- Septum

Materials
- Silicone vacuum grease
- Solvent to be saturated with inert gas

1. Ensure that the Schlenk tube is clean and has been dried for at least an hour in a 100 °C oven before use.

2. Grease the stopcock, and then support the Schlenk tube under its side-arm using a clamp and a stand with a heavy base.

3. Introduce the solvent into the Schlenk tube through its neck with the aid of a Pyrex funnel.

4. Equip the neck of the Schlenk tube with a septum and attach the side-arm to the vacuum/inert gas manifold *via* one of the flexible tubing connections.

5. Close the Schlenk tube stopcock. Adjust the vacuum/nitrogen manifold to vacuum and evacuate the flexible tubing connection between the manifold and the Schlenk tube stopcock.

6. Hold the Schlenk tube and while shaking it gently, apply the vacuum for 2–3 s by opening the Schlenk tube stopcock. Close the Schlenk tube stopcock.

7. Adjust the vacuum/inert gas manifold to nitrogen/argon and fill the flexible tubing connection between the manifold and the Schlenk tube stopcock with inert gas. Still shaking the Schlenk tube gently, open the Schlenk tube stopcock and refill the Schlenk tube with inert gas.

8. Repeat steps 5–7 a total of five times.

Protocol 3.
Removal of solvents using a vacuum/inert gas manifold

Caution! All procedures should be performed in a fume hood. Disposable vinyl or latex gloves and safety glasses should be worn.

Equipment
- Vacuum/inert gas manifold (Figs 7.1 and 7.2)
- Schlenk tube (Fig. 7.3)
- Septum

Materials
- Silicone vacuum grease
- Solution to be concentrated or evaporated to dryness

1. Attach the Schlenk tube containing the solution to be concentrated to the vacuum/inert gas manifold *via* one of the flexible tubing connections, equip the neck of the Schlenk tube with a septum and close the Schlenk tube stopcock.

2. Adjust the vacuum/inert gas manifold to vacuum and evacuate the flexible tubing connection between the manifold and the Schlenk tube stopcock.

3. Hold the Schlenk tube and while shaking it gently, apply the vacuum for 2–3 s by opening the Schlenk tube stopcock. Close the Schlenk tube stopcock. Repeat this sequence until no vigorous bubbling occurs.

4. Apply the vacuum continuously and while shaking the Schlenk tube gently, let the solvent evaporate. When necessary, use a water bath to avoid formation of ice on the outside of the Schlenk tube.

5. When the desired amount of solvent has been removed, close the Schlenk tube stopcock. Adjust the vacuum/inert gas manifold to nitrogen/argon and fill the flexible tubing connection between the manifold and the Schlenk tube stopcock with inert gas. Still shaking the Schlenk tube gently, open the Schlenk tube stopcock and refill the Schlenk tube with inert gas.

Protocol 4.
Transferring liquids from one Schlenk tube to another *via* a cannula or filtering cannula

Caution! All procedures should be performed in a fume hood. Disposable vinyl or latex gloves and safety glasses should be worn.

Equipment
- Vacuum/inert gas manifold (Figs 7.1 and 7.2)
- Schlenk tube containing the liquid to be transferred (Schlenk tube A)
- Schlenk tube for receiving the liquid (Schlenk tube B)
- Septum
- Stainless steel cannula or filtering cannula (Fig. 3.1)

Protocol 4. *Continued*

Materials

• Solvent, solution or solid/liquid mixture to be transferred or filtered

1. Ensure that Schlenk tube B and the cannula (or filtering cannula) are clean and have been dried for at least an hour in a 100 °C oven before use.

2. Support Schlenk tube B under its side-arm using a clamp and a stand with a heavy base. Fit it with a septum, attach it to the vacuum/inert gas manifold and evacuate it and refill it with inert gas (Protocol 1).

3. Allow the cannula (or filtering cannula) to cool to room temperature. If using a filtering cannula, place and wire a piece of filter paper around the glass filtering device as illustrated in Fig. 3.1.

4. Insert the cannula just through the septum of the Schlenk tube containing the liquid to be transferred (Schlenk tube A). (See Fig. 3.2 for a similar arrangement using a round-bottomed flask rather than a Schlenk. When using a filtering cannula, push the opposite end of the cannula to the filtering device through the bottom of a new septum and replace the septum on Schlenk tube A with this septum.) Purge by allowing inert gas to flow through for one minute.

5. The other end of the cannula (or filtering cannula) is then inserted through the septum of Schlenk tube B.

6. Insert a short needle through the septum of Schlenk tube B to make an inert gas bleed.

7. Lower the tip of the cannula (or filtering cannula) into Schlenk tube A until it is just below the level of the liquid to be transferred.

8. Slowly, close the tap of Schlenk tube B. Control the rate of the transfer of the solution by adjusting the flow of inert gas with the stopcock of Schlenk tube A.

9. Open the stopcock of Schlenk tube B to stop the transfer.

10. Remove the short needle and the end of the cannula.

Protocol 5.
Column chromatography of air-sensitive compounds

Caution! All procedures should be performed in a fume hood. Disposable vinyl or latex gloves and safety glasses should be worn.

Equipment

• Vacuum/inert gas manifold (Figs 7.1 and 7.2)
• Column with side-arm and filter frit (Aldrich Z17, 318-5)
• Septum
• Schlenk tubes for fraction collection
• Aluminium foil

Materials

- Crude sample to be purified
- Silica gel (approximately 5 g for 0.1 g of sample)   **irritant dust**
- Sand (50–100 μm mesh)
- Eluent

1. Find a low viscosity solvent mixture (e.g. *n*-hexane/diethyl ether, petroleum ether/ethyl acetate) which separates the mixture and moves the desired compound on analytical TLC to an R_f of 0.35. If several compounds are to be separated which run very close on TLC, adjust the solvent so that the midpoint between the components is at $R_f = 0.35$. If the compounds are widely separated, adjust the R_f of the less mobile component to 0.35.

2. Clamp the column, prepare the solvent system selected previously, and furnish two or three Schlenk tubes with an inert gas atmosphere (Protocol 1).

3. Weigh out the required amount of silica gel in a fume hood and pour the silica gel into the column in a single portion. Ensure that the column is vertical and tap it gently to pack the gel. Close the stopcock on the side-arm of the column.

4. Carefully pour the solvent system selected above to fill the column completely and fit the top of the column with a septum. Attach the side-arm of the column to the vacuum/inert gas manifold and adjust the vacuum/inert gas manifold to nitrogen/argon. Open the stopcock and compress the gel. Maintain the pressure until all the air is expelled and the lower part of the column is cool. Note that the level of the solvent must always remain above that of the silica gel.

5. When the column is packed, remove the septum from the top of the column and maintain a gentle flow of inert gas over the silica gel using the side-arm stopcock. Place a 3 mm layer of 50–100 μm mesh sand on the flat top of the silica gel bed. Check the column. If there are air bubbles or cracks in the column, start again. Replace the septum on the top of the column.

6. Using Schlenk tube techniques, saturate the eluent with inert gas (Protocol 2), transfer some eluent to the top of the adsorbent bed *via* a cannula (Protocol 4) and allow the inert gas-saturated eluent to run through the column.

7. Place the sample to be purified in a Schlenk tube and dissolve it in the minimum amount of the inert gas-saturated eluent (see Protocol 4 for the transfer of a liquid from Schlenk to Schlenk *via* a cannula). Apply the resulting solution to the top of the sand *via* a cannula.

8. Wash down the walls of the column with a few millilitres of degassed eluent and push the washings into the silica gel as before.

9. Fill the column with inert gas saturated eluent taking care not to disturb the silica bed.

Protocol 5. *Continued*

10. Allow eluent to run through the column until the first compound emerges. Adjust the flow rate with the aid of the side-arm stopcock.

    Important! At no time let the level of the solvent get below the top of the sand. If necessary, stop the flow by removing the septum, add more eluent and start the flow again.

11. Collect fractions in Schlenk tubes with inert gas flowing gently through them and concentrate using the vacuum/inert gas manifold (Protocol 3).

Protocol 6.

Preparation of an NMR sample of an air-sensitive complex under an inert gas

Caution! Due to the potential toxicity of transition metal complexes, prepare the NMR sample in a fume hood and wear disposable vinyl or latex gloves and safety glasses.

NB NMR samples of air-sensitive organometallics should be prepared just before being recorded.

Equipment

- Vacuum/inert gas manifold (Figs 7.1 and 7.2)
- Enlarging adapter (B24 and B19 joints)
- Septum-inlet adapter (B24 and B14 joints)
- Septum
- Parafilm
- High vacuum one-way stopcock

- Vacuum tubing
- NMR tube (5 mm size)
- Septum for 5 mm NMR tube
- Teat pipettes
- Cotton wool
- Aluminium foil

Material

- Complex to be analysed by NMR spectroscopy
- Kieselguhr for filtration
- Appropriate deuterated solvent

1. Prepare the apparatus depicted in Fig. 7.4 as follows: (a) assemble the septum-inlet adapter and the enlarging adapter and secure the joint with Parafilm; (b) carefully pierce a B14 septum in its centre with a hole borer [the NMR tube (5 mm size) must fit exactly into the resulting hole] and equip the bottom joint of the septum inlet adapter with it; (c) connect the septum-inlet adapter to a one-way stopcock using vacuum tubing.

2. Support the apparatus using a clamp and a stand with a heavy base.

3. Introduce the NMR tube into the apparatus through the hole in the septum. The top of the NMR tube should be approximately 5 cm below the top of the apparatus (see Fig. 7.4).

4. Equip the top of the septum-inlet adapter with a septum and attach the

apparatus to the vacuum/inert gas manifold *via* the one-way stopcock. Close the one-way stopcock.

5. Adjust the vacuum/inert gas manifold to vacuum and evacuate the flexible tubing connection between the manifold and the one-way stopcock. Open the one-way stopcock to apply vacuum to the apparatus.

6. Prepare a short Pasteur pipette for filtration of the NMR sample. (This filtration is necessary to remove any paramagnetic material which arises from decomposition. Running the NMR spectrum without filtration would lead to poor resolution and broad signals.) Push a small plug of cotton wool to the bottom of the pipette (use a second pipette), add enough Kieselguhr[a] to form a 2 cm layer over the cotton wool and level the surface by tapping.

7. Close the one-way stopcock. Adjust the vacuum/inert gas manifold to nitrogen/argon and fill the flexible tubing connection between the manifold and the one-way stopcock with inert gas. Open the one-way stopcock and fill the apparatus with inert gas. If necessary, refill the flask or Schlenk tube containing the sample with inert gas.

8. Remove the septum on the apparatus and carefully sit the filtration pipette in the top of the NMR tube.

9. Dissolve the complex ($\approx$10 mg) in a small amount of deuterated solvent (0.3 mL) and transfer the solution *via* a pipette onto the filtration pipette (if highly air-sensitive organometallics are involved, use inert gas-saturated deuterated solvent and transfer any solution *via* a cannula).

10. Equip the filtration pipette with a teat and press the teat. Remove the teat, add deuterated solvent (0.3 mL) and repeat as before.

11. Remove the filtration pipette and put the septum back on the apparatus.

12. Close the stopcock, adjust the vacuum/inert gas manifold to vacuum and evacuate the flexible tubing connection between the manifold and the one-way stopcock. Apply the vacuum momentarily (1–2 s) by opening the stopcock. Adjust the vacuum/inert gas manifold to inert gas and fill the flexible tubing connection between the manifold and the one-way stopcock with inert gas. Open the one-way stopcock and refill the apparatus with inert gas. Repeat this sequence a total of three times.

13. Push the tube up until the top of the tube is $\approx$1.5 cm below the top of the apparatus and insert a septum in the top of the NMR tube under a flow of inert gas. Free the tube from the apparatus.

14. Disconnect the apparatus from the inert gas source and protect the NMR tube with foil if using light-sensitive solutions.

[a] Kieselguhr is introduced dry, without being suspended in any solvent.

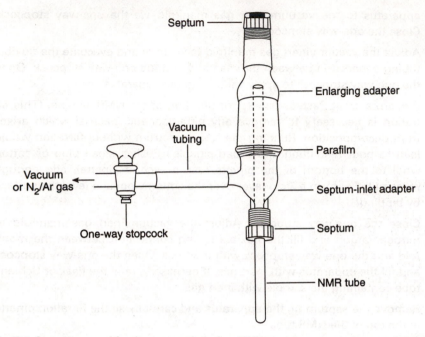

Septum

Enlarging adapter

Vacuum tubing

Parafilm

Vacuum or N₂/Ar gas

Septum-inlet adapter

One-way stopcock

Septum

NMR tube

Fig. 7.4 Apparatus used for the preparation of an NMR sample under an inert atmosphere.

A1

List of suppliers

Aldrich Chemical Co. Ltd
France: BP 701, L'Isle D'Abeau Chesnes, 38297 St. Quentin Fallavier Cedex. Tel. 74822800
Germany: Riedstrasse 2, D-89555 Steinheim. Tel. 7329-9702
Japan: JL Nihonbashi Bldg., 1-10-15 Nihonbashi Horidomecho, Chou-ku, Tokyo 103. Tel. 33258-0155
UK: The Old Brickyard, New Road, Gillingham, Dorset SP8 4JL. Tel. 0800-717181
USA: PO Box 355, Milwaukee, WI 53201. Tel. 414-2733850

A.R. Walker Ltd (inert gas pressure regulators)
UK: Unit 5, Overthorpe Road, Banbury, Oxon OX16 8SX. Tel. 01295-269880

BDH
UK: (Head Office and International Sales) Merck Ltd, Merck House, Poole, Dorset BH15 1TD. Tel. 01202-665599

Fluka Chemika-BioChemika
France: Fluka S.a.r.l., 38297 St. Quentin Fallavier Cedex. Tel. 74822800
Germany: Fluka Feinchemikalien GmbH, D-7910 Neu-Ulm. Tel. 0731-729670
Japan: Fluka Fine Chemical, Chiyoda-Ku, Tokyo. Tel. 03-32554787
UK: Fluka Chemicals Ltd., Gillingham, Dorset SP8 4JL. Tel. 0800-262300

Johnson Matthey Chemical Products
France: Johnson Matthey SA, BP 50240, Rue de la Perdix, ZI Paris Nord LL, 95956 Roissy, Charles de Gaulle Cedex. Tel. 48632299
Germany: Johnson-Matthey GmbH, Zeppelinstrasse 7, D-7500 Karlsruhe-1. Tel. 0721-840070
UK: Catalogue Sales, Materials Technology Division, Orchard Road, Royston, Herts. SG8 5HE. Tel. 01763-253715
USA: Alfa-Johnson Matthey, PO Box 8247, Ward Hill MA 01835-0747. Tel. 0508-5216300

List of suppliers

Lancaster Synthesis
France: Lancaster Synthesis Ltd, 15 Rue de l'Atome, Zone Industrielle, 67800 Bischheim, Strasbourg. Tel. 05035147
Germany: Lancaster Synthesis GmbH, Postfach 15 18, D-63155 Mülheim am Main. Tel. 0130-6562
Japan: Hydrus Chemical Inc., Kurihara Building, 2-12, Uchikanda 3-chome, Chiyoda-ku, Tokyo 101. Tel. 03-32585031
UK: Lancaster Synthesis, Eastgate, White Lund, Morecambe, Lancashire LA3 3DY. Tel. 0800-262336.
USA: Lancaster Synthesis Inc., PO Box 1000, Windham, NH 03087-9977. Tel. 0800-2382324

Orme Scientific Equipment
UK: PO Box 3, Stakehill Industrial Park, Middleton, Manchester M24 2RH. Tel. 0161-6534589

Richardsons of Leicester Ltd. (stainless steel cannulae)
UK: Evington Valley Road, Leicestershire LE5 5LJ. Tel. 01162-736571

Strem
France: Strem Chemicals, Inc., 15 Rue de l'Atome, Zone Industrielle, 67800 Bischheim. Tel. 88625260
Germany: Strem Chemicals GmbH, Postfach 1215, 77672 Kehl. Tel. 07851-75879
UK: Strem Chemicals, 48 High Street, Orwell, Royston, Hertfordshire SG8 5QN. Tel. 01223-207430
USA: Strem Chemicals, Inc., 7 Mulliken Way, Dexter Industrial Park, Newburyport, MA 01950-4098. Tel. 0508-4623191

William Freeman and Co. Ltd. (septa)
UK: Suba Seal Works, Staincross, Barnsley, Yorkshire S75 6DH. Tel. 01226-284081

Wako
Japan: 3-10 Dosho-Machi, Higashi-Ku, Osaka 541. Tel. 06-2033741

Summary of protocols

Chapter 1, Protocol 1, p. 3–5

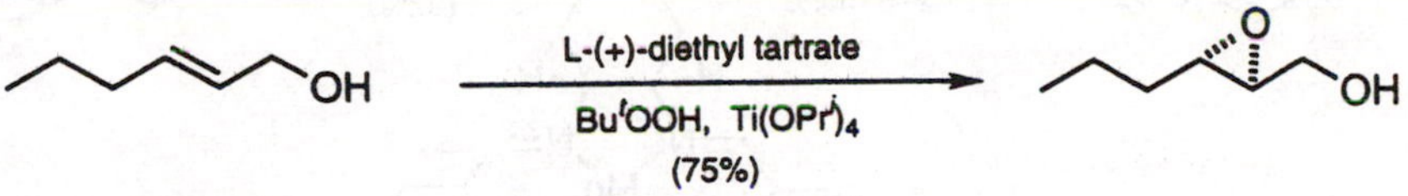

$$\text{(2-hexen-1-ol)} \xrightarrow[\substack{\text{Bu}^t\text{OOH, Ti(OPr}^i)_4 \\ (75\%)}]{\text{L-(+)-diethyl tartrate}} \text{(epoxy alcohol)}$$

Chapter 1, Protocol 2, p. 7

Bu^{t}OOH—molarity determination

Chapter 1, Protocol 3, p. 8–10

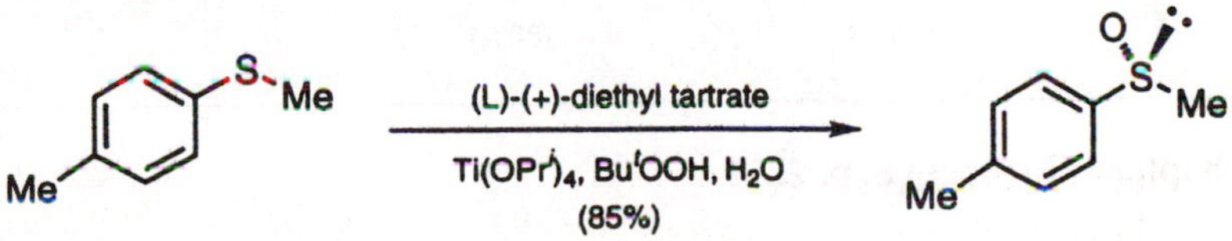

$$\text{(aryl methyl sulfide)} \xrightarrow[\substack{\text{Ti(OPr}^i)_4, \text{Bu}^t\text{OOH, H}_2\text{O} \\ (85\%)}]{\text{(L)-(+)-diethyl tartrate}} \text{(sulfoxide)}$$

Chapter 1, Protocol 4, p. 11–13

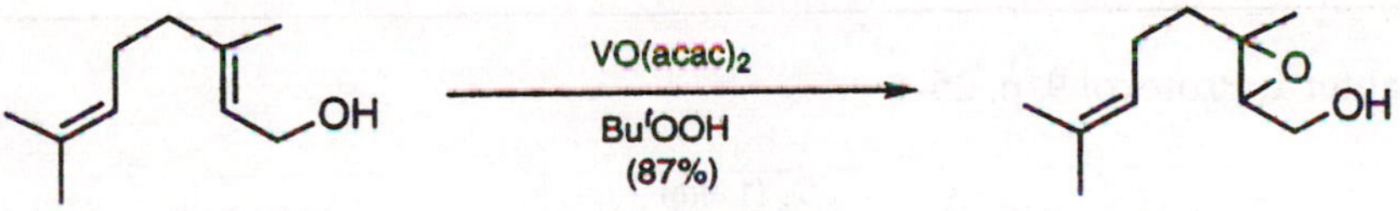

$$\text{(geraniol)} \xrightarrow[\substack{\text{Bu}^t\text{OOH} \\ (87\%)}]{\text{VO(acac)}_2} \text{(epoxide)}$$

Chapter 1, Protocol 5, p. 14–16

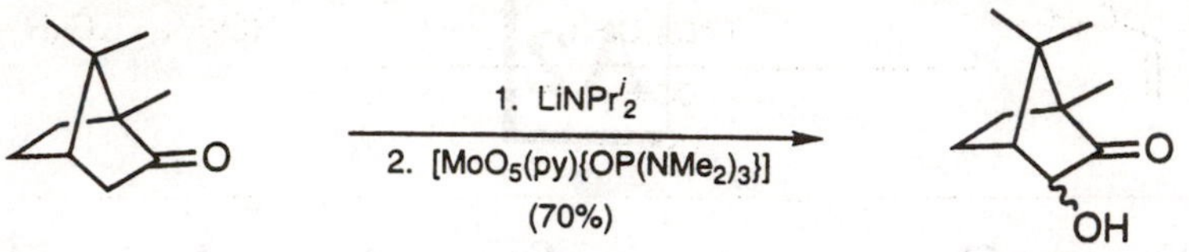

1. LiNPr$^i_2$
2. [MoO$_5$(py){OP(NMe$_2$)$_3$}]
(70%)

Chapter 1, Protocol 6, p. 17–19

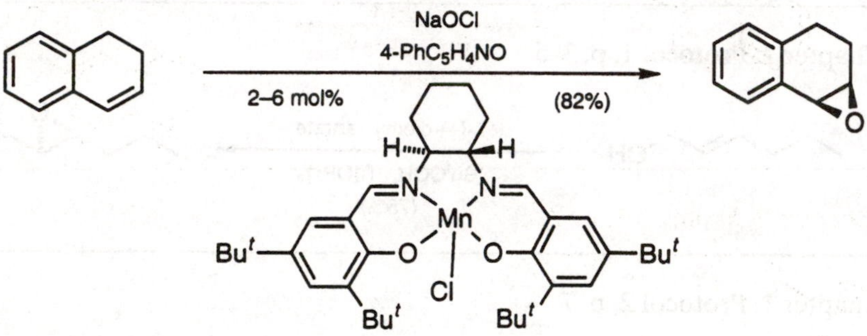

NaOCl
4-PhC$_5$H$_4$NO
2–6 mol%
(82%)

Bu^t

Bu^t

Bu^t

Bu^t

Cl

Chapter 1, Protocol 7, p. 21–2

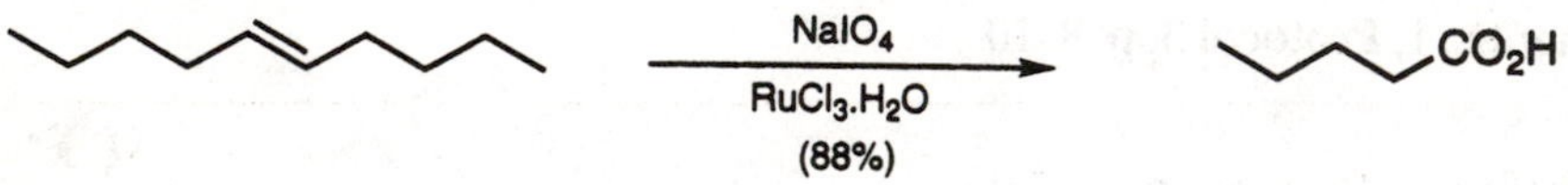

NaIO$_4$
RuCl$_3$.H$_2$O
(88%)

CO$_2$H

Chapter 1, Protocol 8, p. 22–4

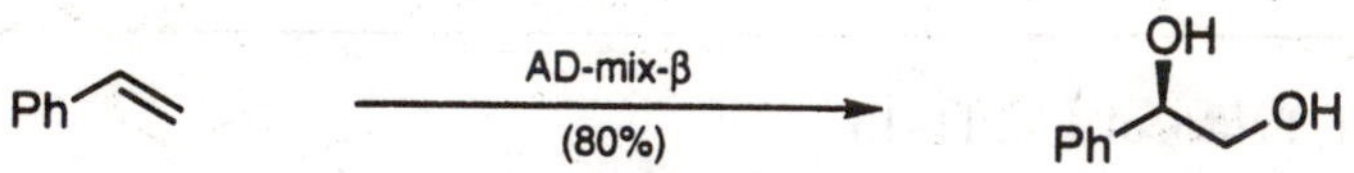

Ph

AD-mix-β
(80%)

OH

OH

Ph

Chapter 1, Protocol 9, p. 25–6

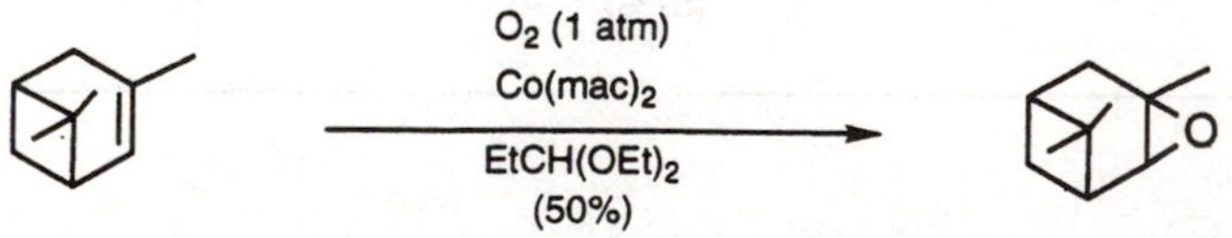

O$_2$ (1 atm)
Co(mac)$_2$
EtCH(OEt)$_2$
(50%)

218

Chapter 1, Protocol 10, p. 28–30

$$CH_2=CH-C_8H_{17} \xrightarrow[\substack{CO/O_2 \\ (100\%)}]{PdCl_2,\ CuCl_2} HO_2C-CH(CH_3)-C_8H_{17}$$

Chapter 1, Protocol 11, p. 31–2

$$\xrightarrow[\substack{PhCH_2NH_2 \\ (70\%)}]{Cu(NO_3)_2}$$

Chapter 2, Protocol 1, p. 40–2

$$\xrightarrow[\substack{Et_3N,\ DMF \\ (87\%)}]{Pd(OAc)_2\ /\ P(o\text{-}tolyl)_3}$$

Chapter 2, Protocol 2, p. 43–5

$$\xrightarrow[\substack{NMP \\ (90\%)}]{Pd_2(dba)_3\ /\ AsPh_3}$$

219

Chapter 2, Protocol 3, p. 45–6

Chapter 2, Protocol 4, p. 49–50

Chapter 2, Protocol 5, p. 52–3

Chapter 2, Protocol 6, p. 56–7

Chapter 2, Protocol 7, p. 59–60

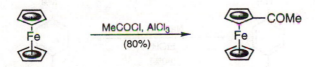

E = CO₂Me

Chapter 2, Protocol 8, p. 61–3

Chapter 3, Protocol 1, p. 68–9

Chapter 3, Protocol 2, p. 70–1

Chapter 3, Protocol 3, p. 72–4

Chapter 3, Protocol 4, p. 76–7

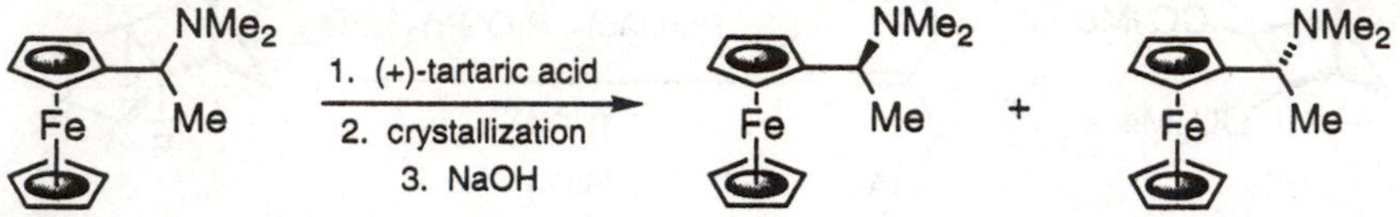
NMe2
Fe
Me
1. (+)-tartaric acid
2. crystallization
3. NaOH
NMe2
Fe
Me
+
NMe2
Fe
Me

Chapter 3, Protocol 5, p. 79–81

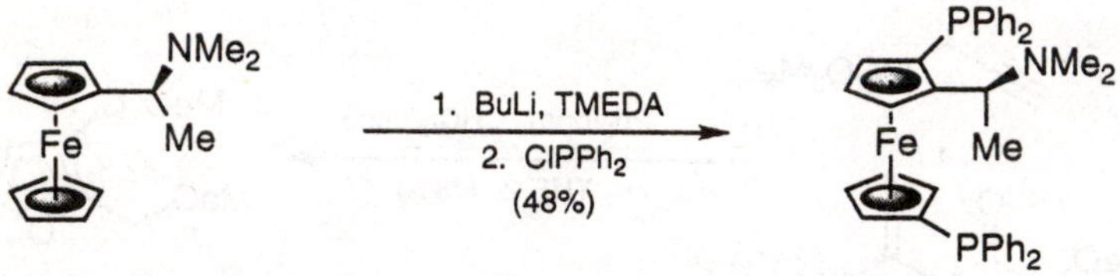
NMe2
Fe
Me
1. BuLi, TMEDA
2. ClPPh2
(48%)
PPh2
NMe2
Fe
Me
PPh2

Chapter 3, Protocol 6, p. 82–4

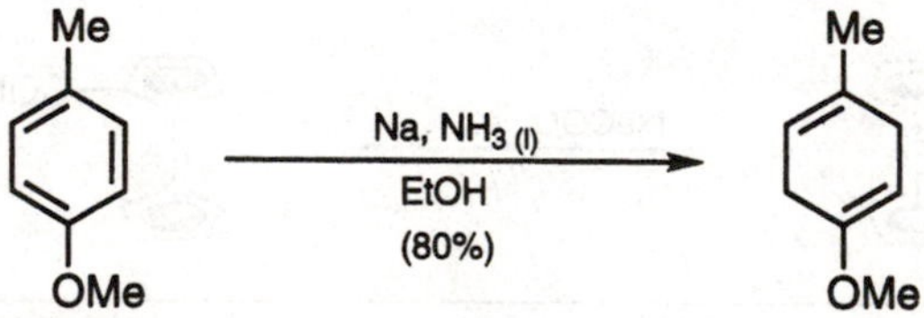
Me
OMe
Na, NH3 (l)
EtOH
(80%)
Me
OMe

Chapter 3, Protocol 7, p. 84–5

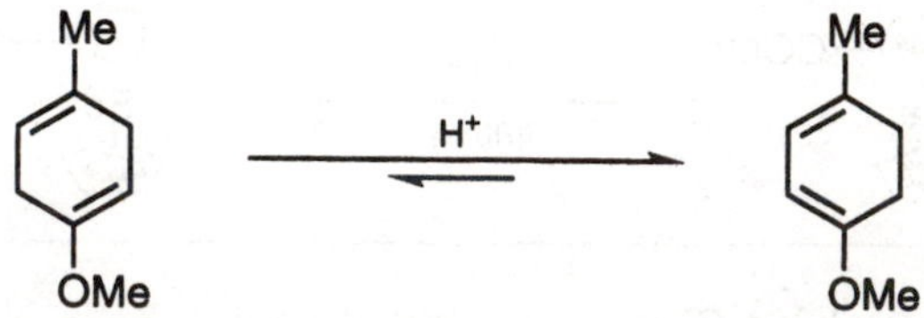
Me
OMe
H+
Me
OMe

Chapter 3, Protocol 8, p. 86–7

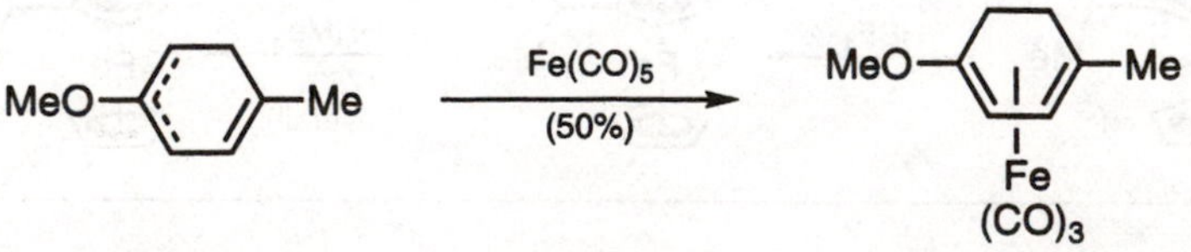
MeO
Me
Fe(CO)5
(50%)
MeO
Me
Fe
(CO)3

Chapter 3, Protocol 9, p. 89–91

Chapter 3, Protocol 10, p. 93–4

Chapter 4, Protocol 1, p. 100–4

Chapter 4, Protocol 2, p. 107–9

Chapter 4, Protocol 3, p. 110–12

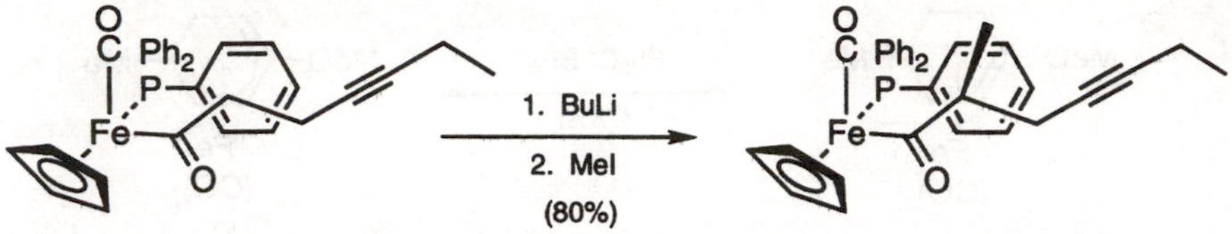

1. BuLi
2. MeI

(80%)

Chapter 4, Protocol 4, p. 113–16

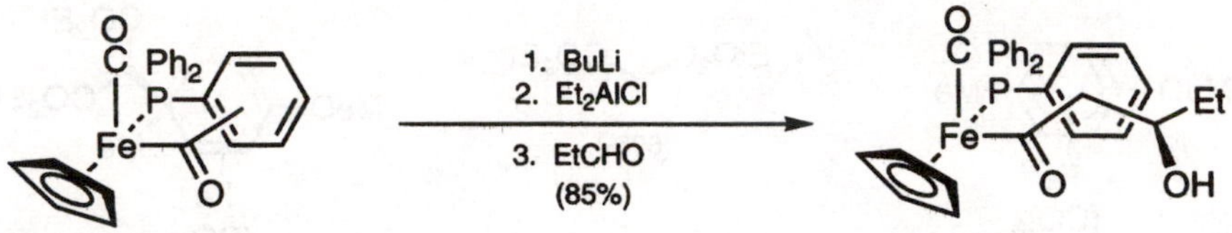

1. BuLi
2. Et₂AlCl
3. EtCHO

(85%)

Chapter 4, Protocol 5, p. 117–19

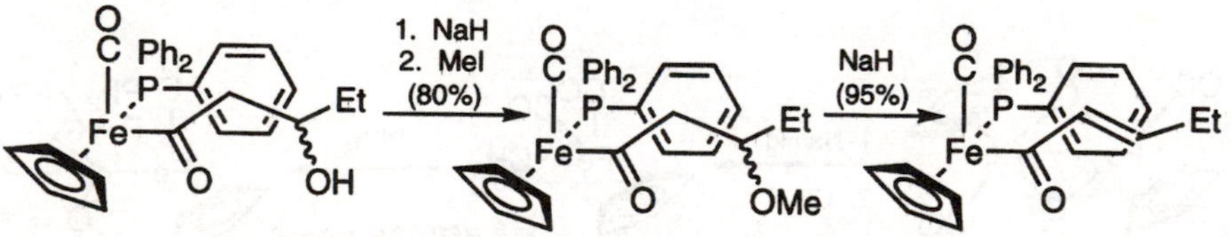

1. NaH
2. MeI
(80%)

NaH
(95%)

Chapter 4, Protocol 6, p. 122–4

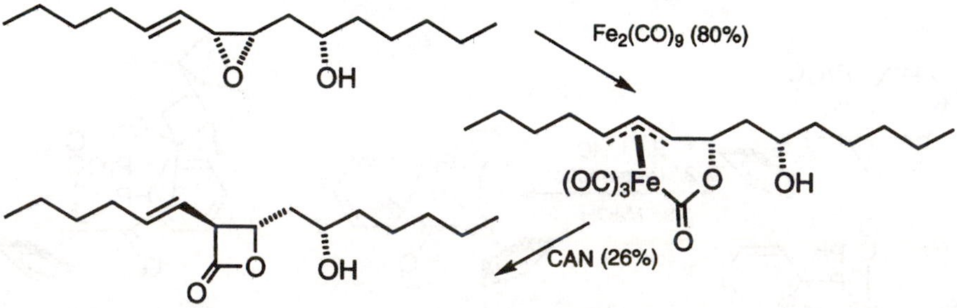

Fe₂(CO)₉ (80%)

CAN (26%)

Chapter 4, Protocol 7, p. 125–7

Chapter 4, Protocol 8, p. 127–9

Chapter 5, Protocol 1a, p. 144–6

Chapter 5, Protocol 1b, p. 147–8

NMR characterization of

Chapter 5, Protocol 1c, p. 149–50

$$\text{(structure with ZrCp}_2) \xrightarrow[\text{(70\%)}]{\text{CO}} \text{(structure with OH)}$$

Chapter 5, Protocol 1d, p. 150–3

$$\xrightarrow[\text{2. PhCHO}]{\substack{\text{1. Allyl chloride / LiTMP} \\ \text{(90\%)}}}$$

Chapter 5, Protocol 2, p. 154–7

$$\text{Cp}_2\text{ZrCl}_2 \xrightarrow{\text{2 PhLi}} \text{Cp}_2\text{ZrPh}_2 \xrightarrow{\text{EtCN}} \text{(structure)} \xrightarrow[\substack{\text{2. H}_2\text{O} \\ \text{(75\% overall)}}]{\text{1. I}_2} \text{(structure)}$$

Chapter 5, Protocol 3, p. 160–3

$$(\text{PhCH}_2)_2\text{NMgCl} \xrightarrow{\text{Cp}_2\text{ZrCl}_2} (\text{PhCH}_2)_2\text{NZrClCp}_2 \xrightarrow{\text{MeMgCl}} \text{(structure)}$$

$$\xrightarrow{\Delta}$$

Summary of protocols

Chapter 6, Protocol 1, p. 173–6

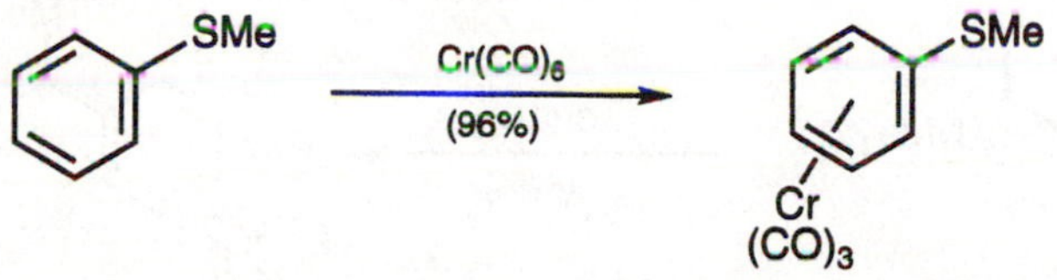

Chapter 6, Protocol 2, p. 179–80

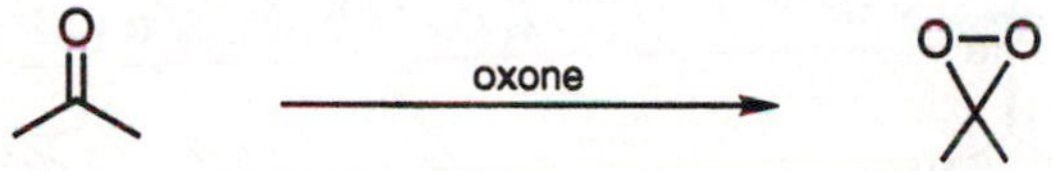

Chapter 6, Protocol 3, p. 181–82

Molarity determination

Chapter 6, Protocol 4, p. 183–5

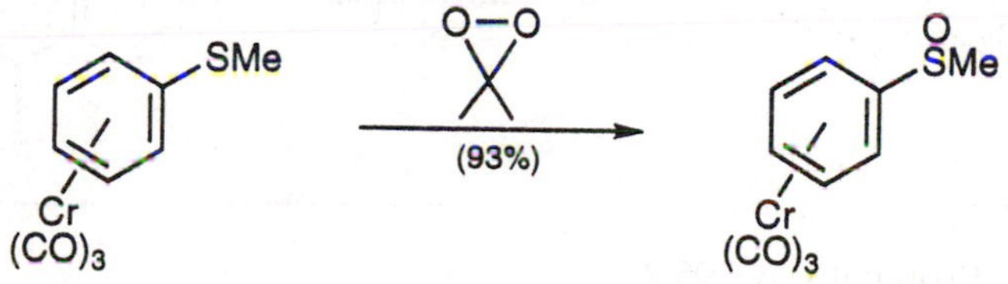

Chapter 6, Protocol 5, p. 191–4

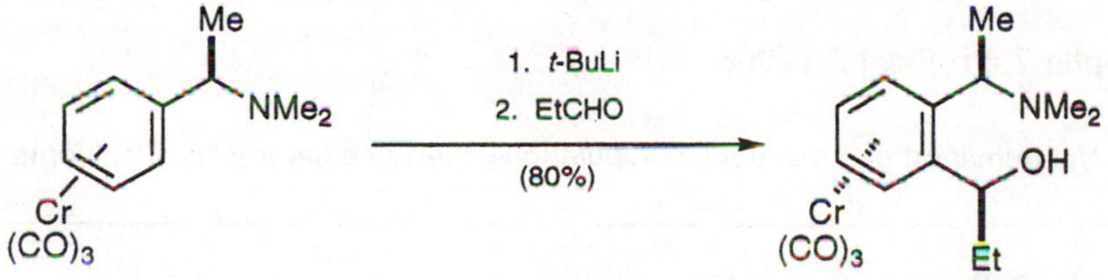

227

Summary of protocols

Chapter 6, Protocol 6, p. 195–7

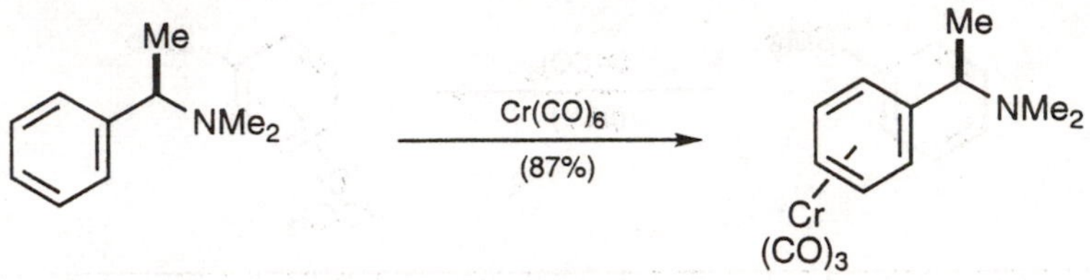

Me, NMe₂ (starting material) → Cr(CO)₆ (87%) → product with Cr(CO)₃

Chapter 6, Protocol 7, p. 198–9

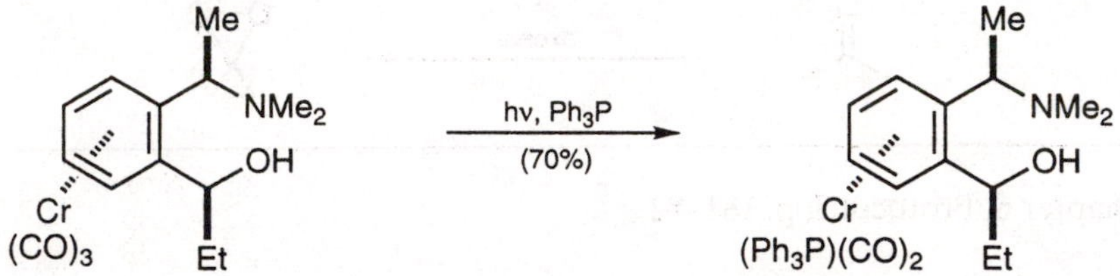

hv, Ph₃P (70%)

Chapter 6, Protocol 8, p. 199–200

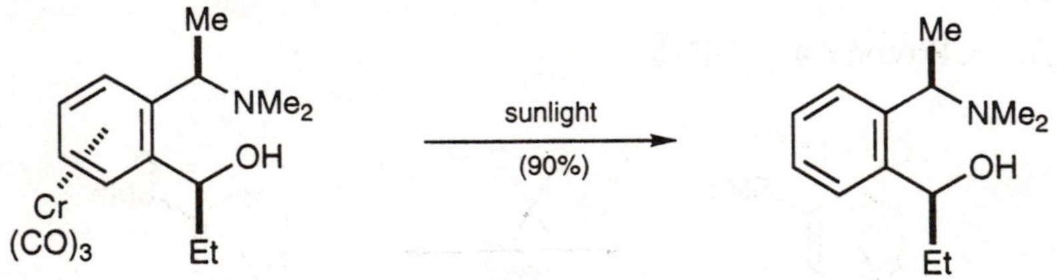

sunlight (90%)

Chapter 7, Protocol 1, p. 205–6

Vacuum/inert gas manifold manipulation—Schlenk tube evacuation/filling

Chapter 7, Protocol 2, p. 208

Vacuum/inert gas manifold manipulation—inert gas saturation of solvents

Chapter 7, Protocol 3, p. 209

Vacuum/inert gas manifold manipulation—removal of solvents

Index

Page entries in italics refer to protocols on those pages